Nicola Gordon Bowe

THE LIFE AND WORK OF HARRY CLARKE

Stained glass, Symbolism, Decadence, Celtic mysticism, National Romanticism, Art Nouveau and the Ballets Russes — all these elements claim a place in the definition of Harry Clarke (1889-1931). This Dublin artist, son of an English father and an Irish mother, worked intensely at his art, as if conscious that death would overtake him at an early age.

He is now recognized internationally as a bizarre genius of his age. He has been called the Irish Beardsley; he was the only Irish artist to introduce what George Moore called 'the poisonous honey of France' during the first dozen years of this century, while also being in the vanguard of the visual manifestation of the much better known literary Celtic Revival. As an Irish Symbolist, his work is analogous with that of his friends, W.B. Yeats and George (Æ) Russell, as well as the early James Joyce, his older contemporary and fellow Belvederian. Æ rightly prophesised the fascination his work would hold for future generations of collectors. Whether in stained glass or in book illustration, his all too rare work has, over the past decade, become increasingly sought after.

This book is the first substantial biography of Clarke and critical survey of his *oeuvre*. As such it provides a chronological and contextual framework of study for his ceaseless and varied output — in Dublin, London, the Aran Islands, Glasgow, Paris and finally America. In Clarke, a fundamentally Arts and Crafts ideology is fused with a Celtic Revivalist spirit seeking expression in a modern idiom, at a fascinating period in Ireland's history.

This is the story of a questing soul whose complex imagination and emotions were sublimated into his life as a prolific artist of outstanding originality. His skill and vision in glass have never been equalled in this century, and provide a bridge with the masterpieces of the medieval cathedrals; his exquisite ability to depict the gruesome and unspeakable is unparalleled.

Nicola Gordon Bowe is a Lecturer in History of Art and Design at the National College of Art and Design, Dublin. She has published and lectured widely on early twentieth-century decorative arts, especially the stained glass and Arts and Crafts revivals early this century; most recently she edited Art and the National Dream *(Dublin, 1994).*

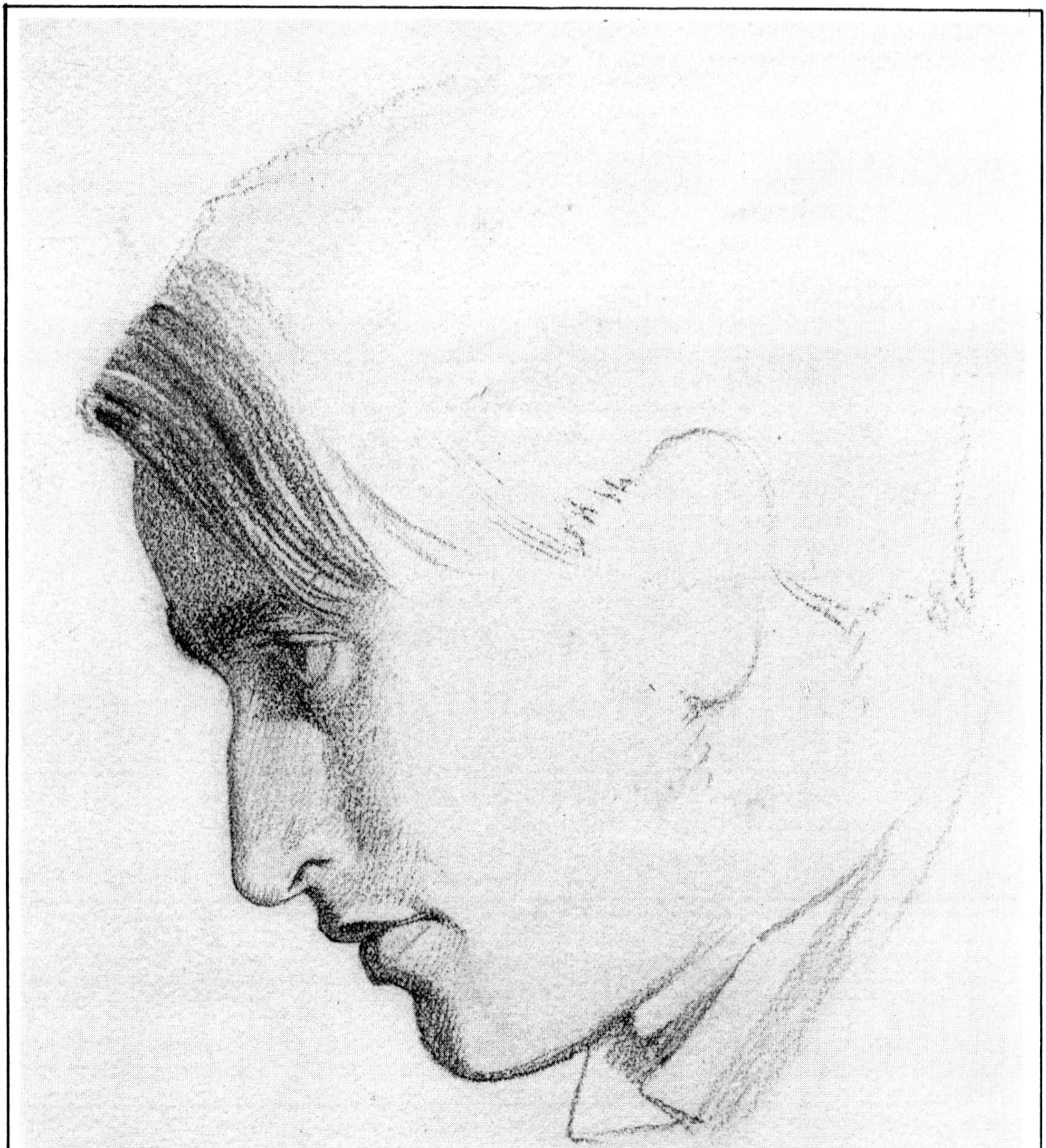

Nicola Gordon Bowe

THE LIFE AND WORK OF

HARRY CLARKE

Prix de la Confédération Internationale
des Négociants en Oeuvres d'Art 1984

IRISH ACADEMIC PRESS

The typesetting for this book was
input by Gilbert Gough Typesetting, Dublin and
output by Type Bureau Ltd, Dublin, for
IRISH ACADEMIC PRESS
Kill Lane, Blackrock, Co. Dublin

and in the United States by
IRISH ACADEMIC PRESS
c/o International Specialized Book Services,
5804 NE Hassalo Street, Portland, OR 97213

A catalogue record for this book is
available from the British Library.

First published in 1989
First paperback edition 1994

ISBN 0-7165-2452-X
ISBN 0-7165-2534-8 pbk

Printed in Ireland by Betaprint.

To my beloved archetype

Forewords

It is tempting to picture Nicola Gordon Bowe's definitive study of Harry Clarke as the revelation of an 'Undiscovered Artist'. The story of the capture of this mythical beast of the art world through the devoted scholarship of a raven-haired damsel would be a subject well suited to Clarke's own style of febrile, fantastical illustration.

In truth, talent is rarely 'undiscovered'. Clarke was recognized by contemporary compatriots as a master of stained glass and an outstanding Symbolist illustrator. His work, however, has been overlooked by historians, as most attention to Ireland's twentieth-century cultural renaissance has focused on its literary exponents.

The very nature of stained glass and the difficulty of photographic reproduction has limited the admirers of Clarke's best work to those who visited the architectural sites for which it was commissioned. Only in his book illustrations was Clarke able to reach a broad audience, notably with two editions of the works of Edgar Allan Poe which were international bestsellers.

There is evidence of a nascent American following for Clarke's work in the 1920s as his drawings were sold by the New York dealer, Byrne Hackett. The artist's thirst for recognition across the Atlantic is witnessed by the importance he accorded his first American commission which came only in the last year of his life. Despite his ailing health he insisted on designing and personally supervising the execution of nine windows for a church in Bayonne, New Jersey. It is poignantly appropriate that the culminating work of Clarke's career, the *Geneva Window* on the theme of Irish literature, commissioned for the League of Nations but rejected by the Irish government, has found a place of honor in the permanent collection of one of America's newest museums, the Wolfsonian Foundation in Miami, Florida.

PENELOPE HUNTER-STIEBEL

Rosenberg & Stiebel Inc., New York
Former Associate Curator
Twentieth Century Art
Metropolitan Museum of Art

Established in 1976 by the Confédération Internationale des Négociants en Oeuvres d'Art, the CINOA prize is an award for outstanding academic studies in the history of art from any of the thirteen countries affiliated to the Confédération and is intended to finance their publication.

Dr Nicola Gordon Bowe's study of Harry Clarke — a Trinity College, Dublin PhD thesis — was the first entry for this competition submitted by Ireland, promoted by the Irish Antique Dealers' Association (IADA) in accordance with the Charter of CINOA; it was awarded the 1984 prize, which was presented to the laureate at its annual congress in Munich that year.

Early arrangements for the publication of the study met unforeseen difficulties; but fortunately a new publisher came forward last year. Additional funds had to be sought and these were provided mainly in the form of a special 1989 CINOA subvention and an IADA grant: Mr Ronald McDonnell, retiring President of the IADA, with great generosity, made a personal contribution matched jointly by the other nine members of its Council.

We are delighted that *The Life and Work of Harry Clarke* is now being published in an edition which does justice to its subject and which appears in the centenary year of the artist's birth. We are confident that this major work will raise the profile not only of Harry Clarke but also of Irish art in general throughout the world.

JOHN O'REILLY

Honorary Secretary,
Irish Antique Dealers' Association

Stained glass — medieval stained glass particularly — has always had an extraordinary fascination for me. Memories of Chartres and Bourges are as evocative as Proust's madeleines. Those rich reds, searing greens and yellows, and blues so deep that the imagination can literally drown in them are the epitome of Ruskin's 'glow of controlled fire' and neither the painted glass of the sixteenth, seventeenth and eighteenth centuries, nor that of my hero, William Morris, can begin to approach it. That extraordinary ability to stimulate and submerge the imagination at one and the same time is like no other worldly experience. I received intimations of the same response the first time I saw Evie Hone's work in the collection of the late Hugo Pitman, and I can remember as a schoolboy travelling to London to visit the exhibition of her work in the Arts Council's beautiful old galleries in St James's Square. Later still I discovered the work of Harry Clarke and realised that Ireland in the twentieth century had revived an art that seemed to have lain dormant for five or six hundred years.

During my earlier years at The Fine Art Society I was lucky enough to be able to handle occasional drawings and watercolours by Harry Clarke, most memorably *Queen Mab*. Then, suddenly, in 1982, I received a letter from New York from Clarke's elder son, Michael, saying that he planned to be in London shortly and would like to make an appointment to see me. Unfortunately illness prevented his coming. For the next two years there was total silence; then came a further letter, a meeting, and an invitation to Dublin.

I remember clearly that first visit with Michael and his younger brother, David. We went into Dublin to the Hugh Lane Municipal Gallery where we looked at the marvellous *Eve of St Agnes* window before unpacking the eight panels of the *Geneva Window* from the box in which they were stored and then, at the Longhouse, at Strawberry Beds, began to unroll cartoon after cartoon for the Honan Chapel windows — St Patrick, St Brigid, St Finn Barr, St Ita and most excitingly, St Gobnait with those miraculous bees. I was by now no longer just an admirer but a fully fledged proselytizer. Slowly the idea for The Fine Art Society's 1988 exhibition *The Stained Glass of Harry Clarke* began to evolve. Apart from the scale of the galleries at 148 New Bond Street, which made them a suitable venue for such an exhibition, it was also historically appropriate as Clarke himself had exhibited there, along with several of his Irish contemporaries, in 1927.

I had already begun to see Harry Clarke very much in the mould of one of the more obscure saints that he so delighted to depict; revered in a small area and virtually unknown in the greater world. Through his book illustrations he had always had a widely scattered international following among bibliophiles and collectors of illustrated books, just as in his native land he had supporters such as Laurence Waldron, Edward Martyn, Thomas Bodkin, James White, Michael Wynne and, most recently, Nicola Gordon Bowe, who have recognized his true worth as a stained glass artist. However, the two audiences seldom overlapped, and a vast number of otherwise well-informed people continued to remain totally unaware of his existence. It became clear to me that although there would be some who, like Thomas MacGreevy in 1923 when Clarke was sending the Dowanhill windows to Glasgow, would decry the export of such native treasures, it was important for the *Geneva Window* to be in a place where it could be seen by the widest possible audience. After all it was never intended that it should remain in Ireland; it was conceived as a celebration of Irish literature: a sort of Cultural Ambassador to the League of Nations. It was only the innate puritanism of the founding fathers of the Irish State that caused the window to be locked away in Dublin instead of trumpeting the glories of Yeats and Synge, Shaw and O'Casey, to an international audience. As Nicola Bowe rightly says, Clarke, himself, had a vision of his glass being sent out to enhance all the corners of the earth.

Shortly after my return to London I told my friend Mitchell Wolfson Jr about the window. He was in the process of setting up a museum in Miami devoted to what he describes as 'Decorative and Propaganda Arts' and I was organising for him an exhibition of the architecture and decorative arts of Britain and the British Empire from 1877 to 1947. Micky Wolfson is interested in all the decorative arts of the late nineteenth and early twentieth centuries, but his special passion is to explore and expose the way in which corporations, states, nations and empires have taken those arts and used them to project their own image, or at least the image which they wished others to have of them. Even the great Sir Christopher Wren once noted that 'architecture has its political uses.' The 1920s and 30s was a particularly fertile period for 'propaganda arts': banks had to look like banks, cinemas like cinemas, theatres like theatres; municipal offices, town halls and parliament buildings all proclaimed their authority. The *Geneva Window* had been created in that same spirit; it was a glorious piece of Propaganda Art. With the blessing of the Clarke brothers we included the window in that exhibition and it looked fantastic against the clear blue Floridian sky. Later, at the time of The Fine Art Society's exhibition, Mr Wolfson acquired the window for his museum.

Miami may not be Geneva, but to listen to Mr Wolfson outlining his vision of the city's role in the twenty-first century it could well become the American continent's equivalent. He sees it as the natural meeting place for all the major conferences between North and South America; it is bilingual, English and Spanish, and geographically it is strategically placed to fulfil such a function. The museum where the *Geneva Window* will be installed is housed in a splendid Spanish Revival-style building of 1926, and once open it will play an important part in the cultural and educational life of the city. The Wolfsonian Foundation, under whose aegis it is being set up, also embraces a twin museum in Genoa, Italy, and publishes the *Journal of Decorative and Propaganda Arts* to which Nicola Gordon Bowe had already contributed an article, 'Wilhelmina Geddes, Harry Clarke, and their Part in the Arts and Crafts Movement in Ireland' (Spring 1988), in which she describes the twenty-one-year-old Clarke as having 'absorbed Burne-Jones, Beardsley, Charles Ricketts, Edmund Dulac, Kay Nielsen, the Glasgow School, Klimt, the Japanese print, the symbolists, and the Russian ballet'. A formidable diet for a young man. The cover of that issue of the Journal was adorned with a glowing colour reproduction of the *Unhappy Judas*, the window which had won the young Clarke a gold medal at South Kensington in 1913.

If even one half of Micky Wolfson's vision comes true, the *Geneva Window* will fully justify the dreams of its curator. It will not only give pleasure to thousands, but it will encourage them to discover or re-read *Juno and the Paycock*, *St Joan*, *The Playboy of the Western World*, and those other works so beautifully illustrated in it. Apart from this it will also be seen in the company of other stained glass by Clarke's European and American peers, including some of E.A. Taylor, a friend from Paris days, who was responsible for the earliest publication of Clarke's work in *The Studio*, and a delightful small panel by the Scottish stained glass artist William Wilson depicting a newspaper seller, very close in spirit to the Joxer panel which, along with the dancing figure displaying her charms to Mr Gilhooley, caused such offence to President Cosgrave and his associates when they viewed the *Geneva Window* in 1930. Ireland should be proud that now, nearly sixty years after his death, her greatest stained glass artist is at last receiving the kind of international recognition that his talents so richly deserve.

PEYTON SKIPWITH

The Fine Art Society

Harry Clarke I never met. I was only seventeen when he died, but I came to know his widow and children and talked with a number of his closest friends, Tom Bodkin, Lennox Robinson, Tom MacGreevy and John Keating. I also interviewed many of his colleagues and associates with a view, eventually, to writing about his work. Finally I decided that I was not mature enough to cope with so fascinating and widespread a range of works and I feared that my affection for his family would prevent me feeling free to interpret them with the kind of detachment necessary in those days of extreme conservatism in Ireland, all the more so since his great *Geneva Window* had been commissioned by the Government and then rejected for what today must surely be regarded as trivial reasons. Now of course I feel justified since Nicola Gordon Bowe has dealt with his biography so skilfully and with such scholarly insight.

My close relationship with Margaret, his widow, has led me to feel an awareness of the kind of boy and man he was. Furthermore, I had attended Belvedere College, where he was a student for some seven years, and I had closely perused the work of three of his contemporaries who were writers and discussed or referred to their experiences there. These were James Joyce and Conall O'Riordain, both novelists, and Austin Clarke the poet. The latter in his biography *Twice Around the Black Church* stated that he found it unnecessary to describe his schooldays in Belvedere College as James Joyce had done it so adequately. He was referring to Joyce's *A Portrait of the Artist as a Young Man*, published in 1916 although it had been written between 1901 and 1906. In this he describes the annual school retreat (a spiritual programme of prayers and lectures) which usually takes place towards the end of the Lenten term. The last event of this is usually a bloodcurdling sermon on hell, wonderfully described by Joyce. Most boys of the time will recall being invited to place a finger for a moment in the flame of a candle so they can feel the pain of fire. They are then asked to contemplate that whereas earthly fire consumes what it burns, the fire of hell, to quote Joyce, 'has this property, that it preserves that which it burns and though it rages with incredible intensity, it rages for ever.' And Joyce builds up the sermon in page after page of descriptive writing which culminates in the threat 'and the damned are so utterly bound and helpless that, as a blessed saint, saint Anselm, writes in his book on similitudes, they are not even able to remove from the eye a worm that gnaws it.' After some twelve pages of this eloquence, the preacher ends by saying, 'O, my little brothers in Christ, ... May it never be our lot, I say! In the last days of terrible reckoning I pray fervently to God that not a single soul of those who are in this chapel today may be found among those miserable beings whom the Great Judge shall command to depart for ever from His sight, that not one of us may ever hear ringing in his ears the awful sentence of rejection: *Depart from me, ye cursed, into everlasting fire which was prepared for the devil and his angels!'*

No doubt the majority of those who experienced Jesuit training and education prior to World War Two would have been able to adjust to the extreme passion of a priest who felt that his vocation was to send out into the world a group of sinless young men. As they matured, the reality of life and an awareness of God's mercy would create a balance for them. But for highly sensitive young men like Harry Clarke and the three writers who shared his schooldays in Belvedere College, their powers of imaginative recall and their emotional natures seem to have set up a religious-sensual conflict which always remained with them and strongly influenced their artistic output. One of Harry's closest friends in school became a Jesuit priest, an alternative to the world of art chosen by many young people who are drawn to a life of a contemplative nature.

Harry confessed to his wife on several occasions that he needed his drawings as an outlet from the religious subject matter with which he was daily involved in his stained glass work. He also admitted that he continued to be haunted by his mother's death and said, 'She died alone, oh so alone. I shall die young and be alone too', as indeed he did. His elder son, Michael, wrote a pen-portrait of his father in the catalogue of Harry's work at The Fine Art Society exhibition in London in May 1988 and referred to this thus:

> During the Belvedere days he was compelled to observe the failing health of his mother whose presence had become a major comfort in his life. With her he conversed, argued, joked, questioned and laughed. With none other had he a sense of being loved. Certainly not Joshua his father, busy, responsible, preoccupied. Not his elder sister who existed only in the orbit of her father. Not his brother or younger sister and above all not the Jesuits. Silently he watched the sole

confidant of his boyhood drift unhappily towards death. He was fourteen years old.

In one respect, however, the priests did make an indelible mark on every sensitive child who listened with care: he would have a grim understanding of the quality of hell and an idealised version of an improbable Paradise. Thus Harry Clarke would carry into the world a comforting picture of the glories of salvation joined inevitably to a fascination with the terror of damnation which had particular bearing on those matters of sensual indulgence which his masters constantly trumpeted as a major road to eternal fire. He would never be a devout Catholic, but would never decry it in others. Much of religion in which he did not believe he found aesthetically pleasing. The peripheral rules he found an irritation. The deeper mysteries filled him with awe.

That Harry always carried the sensual-mystical conflict with him was confirmed for me when I was interviewing his artist-friend John Austen, with whom he shared an exhibition of drawings in London. One night at a party, he told me, a friend asked him suddenly, 'Harry, what would you do if you were told that you would be dead in five minutes?' Back came the reply without any consideration, 'Why, send for a priest, of course.'

Once he settled into work at the Studios and at the Metropolitan College of Art, he came to enjoy a new kind of companionship, particularly when he visited the Aran Islands with his fellow students. One of these, John Doran, still treasured a card he received from Harry some thirty years earlier, encouraging John to join them there in 1914. It read:

> Shawn, they are searching the horizon for you and listening in the wind for the wail of your pipes. You are famous, you are musically two-eyed and therefore King. Hail, Nobly Doran, there isn't a living sinner here can play anything, even a tin whistle, my theory is they don't know any tunes and damn it all they can't play nothing on a concertina, can they?

It was in October 1914 that he married Margaret Crilley, who was teaching at the School of Art where, she told me, she was earning six shillings per week. They had a flat at the top of the house in 33 North Frederick Street and when the Rebellion broke out, because their flat was just a few hundred yards north of the centre of activities, they were not allowed to leave the premises for some days. Their only relief was the nightly visit of John Keating, who used to creep from his room around the corner in Parnell Square during the hours of darkness.

Michael has described how his father loved swimming with them, organizing games of all sorts, and would write them amusing letters enclosing illustrations and altered photographs signed with a melancholy non-de-plume J. Sick; this coincided with the decline in his health and presumably accounts for the light comic touch he was assuming to avoid realities.

All great art is based on conflict. Otherwise it would be always merely a recording of happenings. Few artists have been more concerned with the conflict of religion and sensuality than was Harry Clarke. Though he inherited his stained glass profession, there is no mistaking the fact that he sought the opportunity to work as an illustrator; and he combined it with absolute success in the stained glass field. Finally, one has to come to the conclusion that they were utterly complementary. His domestic stained glass panels as illustrated in this book leave no doubt in the mind that when he applied his minute and precise line to his process of plating and aciding he achieved an art form of extraordinary perfection.

JAMES WHITE

Art historian; former Director,
National Gallery of Ireland

Contents

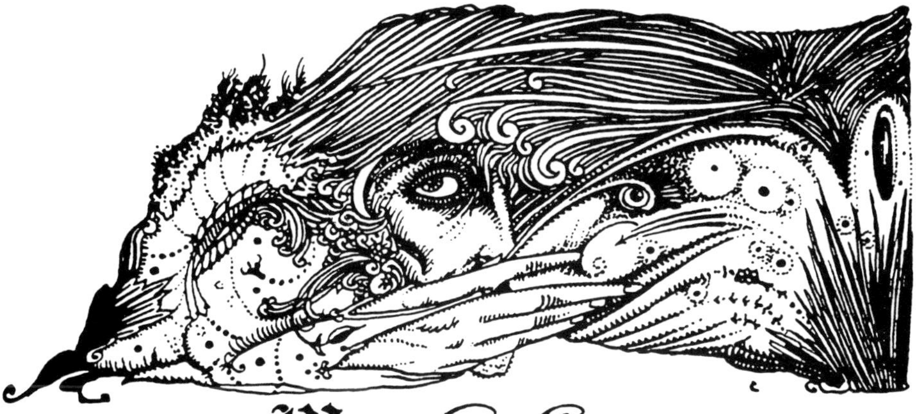

Illustrations

All work is by Harry Clarke unless otherwise stated.

BLACK AND WHITE FIGURES

COLOUR PLATES *following page*

All original work by Harry Clarke illustrated in this book is to be found in private collections unless otherwise stated.

Preface

This book has evolved over the past seventeen years from my initial delight at discovering Harry Clarke's stained glass and book illustrations to a serious study of not only his own life and work but also of the various fields against which these should be seen. These include the last stages of Symbolism and Art Nouveau; the stained glass and Arts and Crafts revivals, born in England but rooted also in Ireland and elsewhere; analogous visual manifestations of National Romanticism and the Celtic Revival, the latter particularly in Dublin; and the optimism of a challenging new age, inspired by a Ruskinian ideology but tempered by war and revolution.

Clarke's work has stood the test of time, even though it was not exhibited between 1931, at his memorial show at the Royal Hibernian Academy, and 1979, at the Rhode Island School of Design Museum's 'Fantastic Illustrations and Design in Britain, 1850-1930' and the much more comprehensive 'Harry Clarke' show at the Douglas Hyde Gallery in Dublin the same year. In America his illustrated books, particularly the two editions of Poe's *Tales of Mystery and Imagination*, have never lost their appeal and his windows have been known to an appreciative few; but his position as a major, if eccentric, figure in the history of twentieth-century, especially Irish, art has never been fully documented. Because his art is in often inaccessible churches and so little of his work appears at auction, it has become all the more sought after, as George Russell prophesied it would.

My quest has taken me to people (many since dead) and unexpected places all over Ireland, England, Scotland, France and America; through some 34,500 letters and documents in the manuscript collection of Trinity College, Dublin, alone; and through the extensive material of the artist's younger son and daughter. None of this had hitherto been studied. My earliest debts are to Jeremy Williams for introducing me to Clarke; to my husband, Paddy, for his patient, unqualified support and tolerance of a protracted *ménage à trois*; and to Professor Anne Crookshank, my mentor and consistently constructive critical source of encouragement; then to the late Ann Bourke, who made her father's material so generously available to me, and to William O'Sullivan, former Keeper of Manuscripts at Trinity College, Dublin. The artist's sister, the late Florence Clarke, the late Dr Henry Lee Willet of Philadelphia, the late Fr Matty Bodkin, SJ, Sean

O'Criádain and Peter Lamb, Dr Michael Wynne, Richard Haughton, the late Victor Wood and Johnny Murphy at the NCAD were in differing ways of key importance in those early years. The most notable of the many others are gratefully listed in the Acknowledgment pages.

In the major hurdle of compiling the 1979 Douglas Hyde Gallery catalogue, my debt was to Anne Crookshank and to my husband; also to Sean McCrum, then the Gallery's curator, to David Davison of Pieterse Davison International photographers, and to David Clarke for making his father's material available to me. In 1978 the discovery and acquisition of the *Eve of St Agnes* window for the Hugh Lane Gallery and the inclusion of the *Judas* panel in the large Royal Exchange *Glass/Light* show in London had, with the inclusion of the *Julian* panel in the important 1979 *Das Bild in Glas* exhibition in Darmstadt, already revived interest in Clarke's extraordinary art and technical skill. This was further acknowledged in 1983 with the publication of *Harry Clarke: His Graphic Art* and in 1984 when the manuscript of my doctoral thesis (1982) was awarded the eighth annual Art History Laureate by CINOA in New York, to enable its publication. A contract to publish the present volume with the Dolmen Press eventually had to be abandoned on the death of Liam Miller in 1987. I am grateful to him for his initial editing and to John O'Reilly for his unmitigating belief in the project. By this time, Peter Cormack, in particular, and Martin Harrison and Martin Steenson had become valued, informed and provocative colleagues. In 1988, the ill-fated Geneva window was finally lost to Ireland after its acclaimed exhibition in London at the Fine Art Society, and Irish Academic Press decided to publish this book before the centenary year of the artist's birth was over. I am inordinately appreciative of the time, trouble and commitment Michael Adams and his staff have since given to producing what I trust will be a definitive work on what Russell termed 'one of the strangest geniuses of his time'.

I am most grateful to Penelope Hunter-Stiebel, John O'Reilly, Peyton Skipwith and James White, who have added a further dimension to the book by each kindly contributing a foreword.

Nicola Gordon Bowe
July 1989

SPECIAL ACKNOWLEDGMENT

The publication of this book
has been made possible by
generous grants in aid from
La Confédération Internationale des Négociants en Oeuvres d'Art
The Irish Antique Dealers' Association
The Abbey Stained Glass Studios
Ken and Muriel Ryan
James Hetley and Company
and
the Very Reverend Thomas Shannon.

Members of CINOA

BUNDESGREMIUM DES HANDELS MIT JUWELEN, GOLD, SILBERWAREN, UHREN, GEMÄLDEN, ANTIQUITÄTEN, KUNSTGEGENSTÄNDEN UND BRIEFMARKEN

KAMER VAN DE ANTIQUAIRES VAN BELGÏE
CHAMBRE DES ANTIQUAIRES DE BELGIQUE

DANISH ANTIQUE DEALERS' ASSOCIATION

SYNDICAT NATIONAL DES ANTIQUAIRES, NEGOCIANTS EN OBJECTS D'ART, TABLEAUX ANCIENS ET MODERNES

CHAMBRE SYNDICALE DE L'ESTAMPE, DU DESSIN ET DU TABLEAU

BUNDESVERBAND DES DEUTSCHEN KUNST-UND ANTIQUITÄTENHANDELS

THE BRITISH ANTIQUE DEALERS' ASSOCIATION

THE SOCIETY OF LONDON ART DEALERS

THE IRISH ANTIQUE DEALERS' ASSOCIATION

FEDERAZIONE ITALIANA MERCANTI D'ARTE

ASSOCIAZIONE ANTIQUARI D'ITALIA

VEREENIGING VAN HANDELAREN IN OUDE KUNST IN NEDERLAND

THE NEW ZEALAND ANTIQUE DEALERS' ASSOCIATION

THE SOUTH AFRICAN ANTIQUE DEALERS' ASSOCIATION

VERBAND SCHWEIZERISCHER ANTIQUARE UND KUNSTHÄNDLER
SYNDICAT SUISSE DES ANTIQUAIRES ET COMMERÇANTS D'ART

KUNSTHANDELSVERBAND DER SCHWEIZ
ASSOCIATIONS DES COMMERÇANTS D'ART DE LA SUISSE

THE NATIONAL ANTIQUE AND ART DEALERS' ASSOCIATION OF AMERICA, INC.

ART DEALERS ASSOCIATION OF AMERICA, INC.

ART AND ANTIQUE DEALERS LEAGUE OF AMERICA, INC.

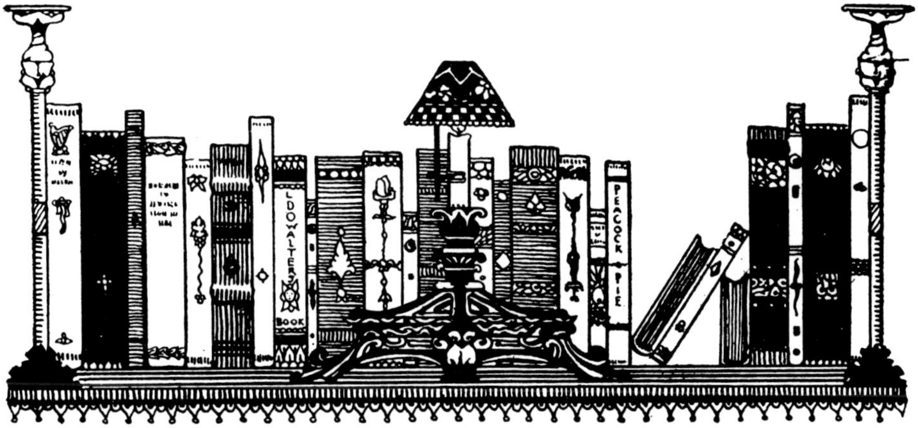

ACKNOWLEDGMENT

Of the many who have assisted in this book, by showing me work or manuscript material by Clarke, by helping me photograph it, by sharing their recollections and knowledge or by encouraging and supporting my research, I should like to mention the following people. It is very sad that a number are no longer alive to see the results of this study, in particular Ann Bourke, the artist's daughter, whose faith in me would, I hope, have been justified.

Br Tim Ahern, OMI; Veronica Aliaga-Kelly; Michael Archer, Victoria and Albert Museum; Keith Baker, Phillips, London; Sr M. Barbara, OP, The Dominican Convent, Belfast; Mary Barnard; The Rector and Rural Dean of Bedworth, Warwicks.; Dr Suzanne Beeh-Lustenberger; Mary Bewley; Victor Bewley; Bewley's Oriental Cafe, Grafton Street, Dublin; Charles Blakeman; the late Aileen Bodkin; the late Fr Matty Bodkin, SJ; the late Ann Bourke; Sara Bourke; Mary Boydell; the late Brian de Breffny; Peter Brennan; Charles Brett; Mr and Mrs J.G. Brickenden; the late Kathleen Bridle; Heather Brigstocke, former High Mistress, St Paul's Girls' School, London; the late Rose Brooke; Brigid Brophy; the Center for Advanced Studies in the Visual Arts, National Gallery of Art, Washington, DC; Bob Brown, the Archives of American Art, Boston; Keith Burns; A.P. Burton, Assistant Keeper of the National Art Library, London; John Butler; Tom Carr; Janice Hynes Chadbourne, Boston Public Library; The Rector, Church of Ireland, Donegal; the late Austin Clarke; David Clarke; the late Florence Clarke; John Clarke; Michael L. Clarke; the late Professor Nevill Coghill; Peter Cormack; Alan Cox, Clerk to the Worshipful Company of Grocers, London; Mary Crichton; Professor A.O. Crookshank; Frank Cruise; Dr John Cullen; Maurice Cullen; Kitty Curling.

David Davison; Donald Dean; Eileen Dempsey; Alan Denson; Dame Ninette de Valois; the late W.A. Dixon; Lamia Doumato and the staff of the Library, National Gallery of Art, Washington, DC; the late William J. Dowling; the late V.J. Drury; Dr Elizabeth Duane; Fionnuala Duane; Liam Dunne; Olivia Durdin-Robertson; Francis Farmar, Christie's, London; Mark Fiennes; R.R. Figgis; Alfred Fisher; Brian Fitzelle; Professor Aloys Fleischmann; Monsignor Flood, former Prior, St Patrick's Purgatory, Co. Monaghan; Frances-Jane French; The Earl of Gainsborough; Daniel and the late Sylvester Gilman; John Gilmartin; The Viscount Gormanston; Peter Gordon; Roderick Gradidge; Kenneth Grant, OTO; Robin Greer; Robert Guinness; the late Fr Aubrey Gwynn, SJ; Martin Harrison; Julian Hartnoll; Julian van Hassalt; Elizabeth Healy; Sr Francis Ellen Henry, SND; Michael Heseltine, Sotheby's, London; John Hewitt; members of the Hicks family; the late Nan Holland; Derek Hunter; John Hutchinson; Elizabeth Jameson; the late Ruth Jameson; Jeffrey B. Jenkins; Katharine Johnston; the late Seán Keating; the late Harry Kernoff; Elizabeth Kerr; the late Alison King; Peter Lamb; Rowan Le Compte; the late Polly Little.

Mercy McCann; Ciarán MacGonigal; the late Maurice MacGonigal; the late Norah McGuinness; the late Micheál MacLiammóir; James McNamara; Dr Edward McParland; Mairead McParland, National Gallery of Ireland; the late Lady Mander; Mary Manning; the late Hilda Marsh; Neil Marshall; George Meares; Rosemary Miles, Victoria and Albert Museum; the late Liam Miller; George Mott; Aideen Molloy; Niall Montgomery; Very Revd Séamus Morris, Carrickmacross; Rachel Moss; Ristéard Mulcahy; John Murphy; Peter Murray, Curator, Crawford Municipal Art Gallery, Cork; David Norris; the late J.E. Nuttgens.

The Revd P.R. Oades, Vicar of St Mary's, Sturminster Newton, Dorset; Cynthia O'Connor and Sir Robert Davis-Goff, Bt.; Cynthia O'Connor Gallery, Dublin; Angela O'Brien; the late Dr Brendan O'Brien; Lucy O'Brien; Professor Maurice O'Connell; Seán O'Criadáin; Dr John O'Grady; the late Cicily O'Kelly; Una O'Higgins O'Malley; William O'Sullivan, former Keeper of Manuscripts, TCD; Clare O'Toole; The Headmaster, Oundle School, Northants; Roger Parrish; the late Margaret Parsons; Peter Pearson; the late Lionel Perry; Patrick Pollen; the late Albert Power; John Poynton; Patricia Proctor; Susannah Pym; the late Nano Reid; the late Dora Allen Reeves; The Registrar, The Royal College of Art, London; Margaret Richardson, former Deputy Curator of The British Architectural Library: Drawings collection, London; Don Roberts; the late Dolly Robinson; Richard Robinson; Dr Frances Ruane; Hugh Salmond; Fr Superior, St Oswald and St Edmund's, Ashton-in-Makerfield, Lancs.; The Administrator, St Stephen's Cathedral, Brisbane; Orin E. Skinner; The Secretary, The Slade School of Fine Art; Fr Brocard Sewell, OCarm.; Jeanne Sheehy; Peyton Skipwith, The Fine Art Society; Jack Sharkey; the late Professor Walter Starkie; Martin Steenson; Ann Stewart, Librarian,

National Gallery of Ireland; Barry Sullivan; Norman Temme, former editor of the *Stained Glass Journal of America*; the late David Tierney; the late Stan Tomlin; Professor John Turpin; the late Arland Ussher; Aileen Vaughan; Ethna Waldron, Curator, and Patricia Flavin, Hugh Lane Municipal Gallery of Modern Art, Dublin; Seymour Hurndall Waldron; Leo Wallace; George Walsh; Helene Weis; Henry Wemyss, Sotheby's, London; Dr James White; the late Earl of Wicklow; the late Dr Henry Lee Willet; Brenda Williams; Jeremy Williams; Ernest Wood, SC; the late Victor Wood; Dr Moira Woods; Robert Woods; Dr Michael Wynne; Alan Younger.

Introduction

Harry Clarke, born exactly one hundred years ago, played a major part in the Arts and Crafts movement in Ireland early in this century as well as the international stained glass revival which arose from the movement in England. He can also be seen as Ireland's major Symbolist artist, whether in his illustrations or in his stained glass.

Earlier this year, John Christian described him as 'the most exotic of all the hot-house flowers' in *The Last Romantics* exhibition in which his work, with that of George (Æ) Russell, represented the Irish strain of the Celtic dimension in nostalgic British art in the earlier years of the twentieth century. However, his art displays a wilful decadence and an ambivalent religious mysticism of medieval intensity which ranges from the sublimely beautiful to the grotesquely macabre, rarely found in the work of his Celtic peers. While his contemporaries sought subjects appropriate to nationalist aspirations, or were tamely inspired by W.B. Yeats' complex and richly evocative images, Clarke's journey to the poet's 'holy city of Byzantium',[1] 'that gloomy apse gleaming with dull gold and gory purple, from which peer enigmatic faces, barbaric yet refined, with dilated neurasthenic pupils . . .',[2] allied him to his older European *fin-de-siècle* contemporaries. Just as Yeats' introduction of Symbolism to Ireland 'gave it a special accent which leads us to think of his poetry from the point of view of its national qualities rather than from the point of view of its relation to the rest of European literature',[3] Clarke — like Beardsley, who strongly influenced his early graphic work — 'typified the Wildean preciosity' which 'was transmuted on the Continent into something far more elemental and deep',[4] albeit a generation earlier. He has been described as 'the last of the Pre-Raphaelites . . . Ireland's only great Symbolist artist',[5] who 'virtually gave the Irish Renaissance its iconography' in a 'splendid afterglow'[6] of unearthly and eccentric genius. Æ called him 'one of the strangest geniuses of his time . . . who might have incarnated here from the dark side of the moon'.[7]

Like his fellow Belvederian, James Joyce's hyperaesthetic adolescent hero, Stephen Daedalus, 'a bat-like soul waking to the consciousness of itself in darkness and secrecy and loneliness',[8] Clarke's quest for the realization of his archetypical images through a scrupulously demanding and inventive technique began in the antithetical cloisters of Jesuit Dublin. From an early age he immersed himself in copious and extensive reading, which

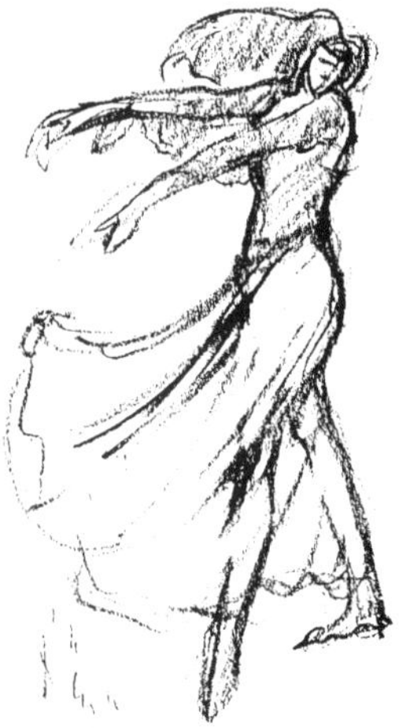

3 Drawing of Salome's dance, from a sketchbook, pencil, *c.* 1907; this shows the influence of Gustave Moreau's pencil designs

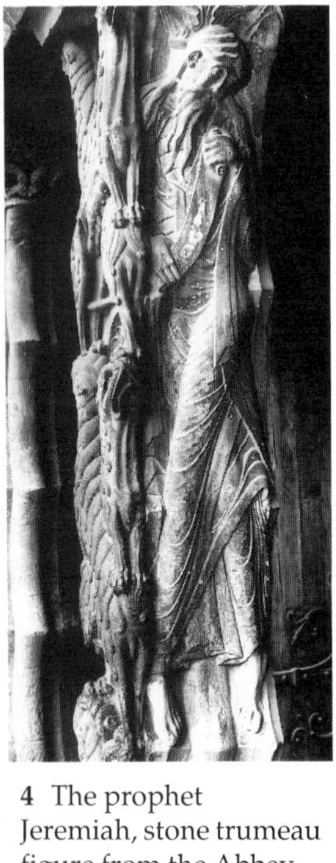

4 The prophet Jeremiah, stone trumeau figure from the Abbey of Saint-Pierre, Moissac, *c.* 1115; a figure whose stance Clarke would adapt in *The Rape of the Lock* and *The Ancient Mariner*

gave his work the strong literary interest common to those Symbolists with whom his art has the greatest affinity. Although a generation younger than many of them and with none of the social connections and confidence of his better known literary compatriots, his predilection for 'the poisonous honey of France'[9] is evident in a sketchbook as early as 1907, in a sketch of Salome's dance from Gustave Moreau (fig. 3). That year, the eighteen-year-old student was able to see in Dublin, as part of the extensive Irish International Exhibition, works by Burne-Jones (notably *The Depths of the Sea*), Rossetti, Watts, Walter Crane, Ricketts, Simeon Solomon, Khnopff, Jean Delmain and Beardsley. Strangely, it was not until 1913 that Beardsley's influence began to manifest itself, in a series of pen and ink illustrations, including *Salome with the Head of John the Baptist*, three to W.B. Yeats' 'Song of Wandering Aengus' and a series to Pope's *Rape of the Lock*. These also reveal the influence of the Japanese print and Romanesque stone trumeau figures from Moissac (fig. 4) and Souillac. Earlier that year his *Ancient Mariner* illustrations had recalled Gustav Klimt in their dramatic juxtaposition of mask-like faces and spiky white fingers with intricately patterned ornament, whereas a rainbow-coloured interpretation of Oscar Wilde's *De Profundis* (plate 11)[10] filled with etiolated spirits and severed heads, is reminiscent of Ensor, Kupka, Minne and Toorop (fig. 5).[11] The same year, his restrained Art Nouveau *Watchman of Ovada* poster allied him with his older Glasgow contemporaries, while his ominous *Judas* stained glass panel evoked a medieval precursor in Chartres Cathedral — 'a religious subject certainly, but seen from the sort of morbid and exotic sado-masochistic angle that Gustave Moreau and the French Decadents would have recognized and approved'.[12] Earlier work had demonstrated his sound training under William Orpen and Alfred Child of Christopher Whall's studio and the graphic influences of the English caricaturists and the Wiener Werkstatte, but none of the later idiosyncracies in which the Burne-Jones/Whall idiom is fused with an eclectic and decadent Symbolism of medieval richness and Byzantine splendour.

John Russell Taylor has written that 'of all the artists working in stained glass during this period of mostly rather pallid, ghastly-good-taste ecclesiastical design, he is the only one whose work is instantly recognizable, as much for its strong and subtle design as for its rich and barbaric colouring'.[13] That an 'astonishing number of his gaunt and decadent figures, worn out with the contemplation of strange sins, did in fact find happy homes in otherwise staid ecclesiastical surroundings' is all the more remarkable. In his graphic work, the same critic feels 'none of the artistic progeny of Beardsley managed quite such an individual note of dazzling nastiness'. Clarke represents the subversive side of Symbolism in his predilection for dreamed images invested with iconic substance, deliberately ambiguous nuances, enigmatic, fatalistic, sensual and ominous figures, drawn from eclectic and obscure sources and closely related to contemporary or recent literature, poetic and musical ideas. His art conforms with Baudelaire's definition of

> an ingenious complicated style full of shades and of research, constantly pushing back the boundaries of speech, borrowing from all the technical vocabularies, taking colour from all palettes and notes from all key-boards, struggling to render what is most inexpressible in thought, what is vague and most elusive in the outline of form, listening to translate the subtle confidences of neuroses, the dying confessions of passion grown depraved and the strange hallucinations of the obsession which is turning to madness. The style of decadence is the ultimate utterance of the Word — summoned to final expression and driven to its last hiding place.[14]

In its predilection for stylized two-dimensional, decorative mural-like work, frequently compared to precious jewels or stained glass, such art was analogous to Art Nouveau and anticipated the early expressions of abstraction which it outlived. Kandinsky's *Concerning the Spiritual in Art* (first translated into English in 1914) is still the best statement on colour in Clarke's work, although for comparative images reference should be made to Dürer, Otto Dix, Klee, Max Klinger, Böcklin, some of Grosz's outrageous caricatures and Franz Marc's pre-war apocalyptic chromatic visions in Germany.

It is ironic that although the non-figurative linear elements of Art Nouveau are seen as coinciding with the influence of early Christian art on the Celtic Revival[15] — with Ireland, particularly W.B. Yeats, central to the movement — Clarke is never mentioned, only the Mackintoshes and MacNairs (fig. 6) in Glasgow and Patrick Geddes, John Duncan and company in Edinburgh.[16] The search for an independent, national and vernacular style in a modern idiom was as much an Irish as a Scottish preoccupation, but Ireland never enjoyed the patronage and cohesion of Scotland during what was politically a more crucial period in her history. Clarke's symbiotic treatment of motifs favoured by Art Nouveau artists and craftsmen and

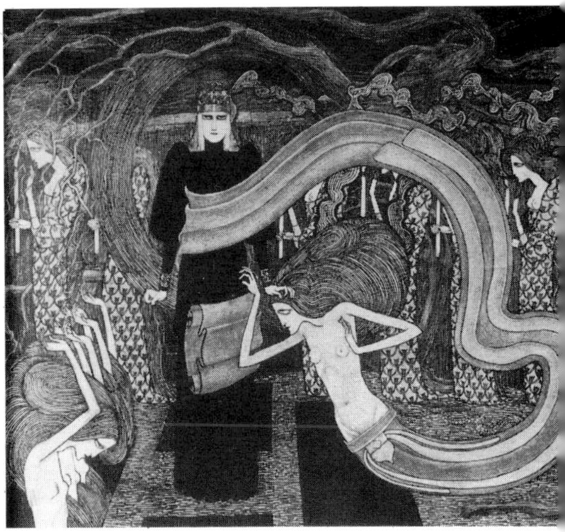

5 Jan Toorop, *Fatalisme*, 1893

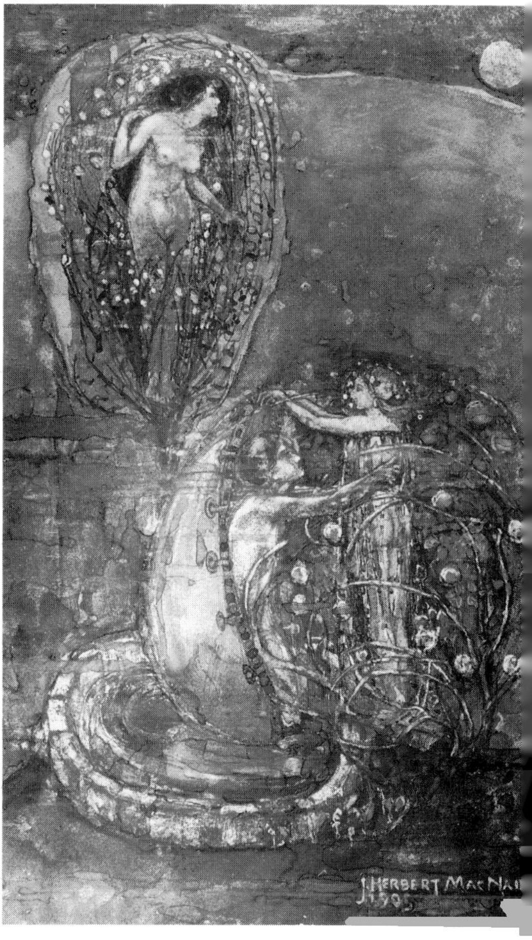

6 J. Herbert MacNair, *Tamlaine*, 1905

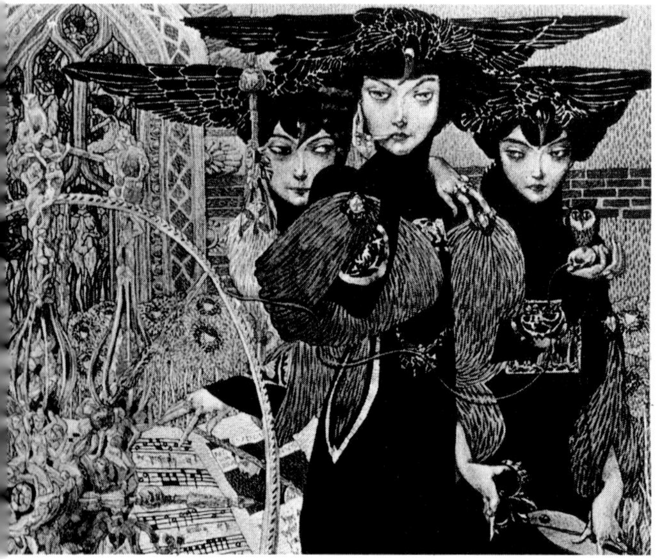

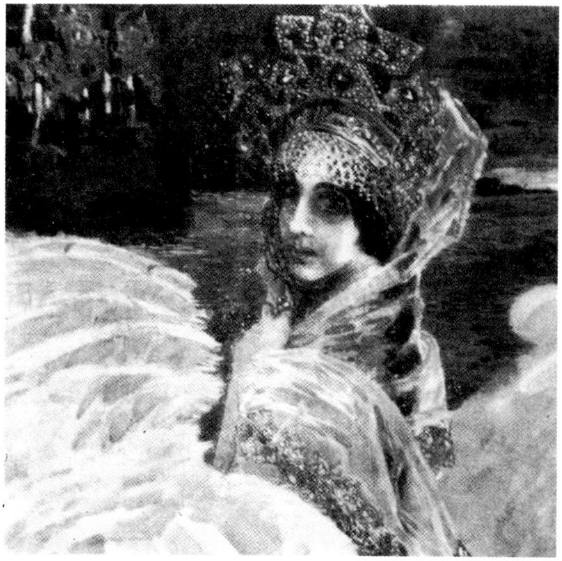

7 Gustav-Adolf Mossa, *Les Parques* (detail), 1905

8 Mikhail Vrubel, *The Swan Tsarevna* (detail), 1900

women, and his use of mythology, legend and a carefully constructed archetype, imbue his work with a recognizably Celtic character and can be found throughout his work in glass, graphics and textile design. The details in which Clarke frequently indulges in the borders of his stained glass windows correspond with those in the margins of a manuscript page. 'The intricacy, variety and humour of many smaller figures of animals and human beings, together with delicate plant designs, provide a wealth of detail that calls for repeated study', Dr George Otto Simms has written of the latter;[17] his description is equally applicable to Clarke's work and to that of his colleagues at An Túr Gloine, the stained glass co-operative.[18] At the same time, he was singled out at the four Arts and Crafts Society of Ireland exhibitions at which he showed as being the most consistently 'modern' artist, craftsman and designer.

He was also modern in his Baudelairean enjoyment of the city, of street life and a certain dandyish appearance. One of his greatest regrets was that he did not live to illustrate Baudelaire's allusive evocation of an exotic, drug-induced Heaven and Hell in *Les Fleurs du Mal* or Huysmans' *A Rebours*, which Wilde's Dorian Gray thought

> the strangest book that he had ever read. It seemed to him that in exquisite raiment, and to the delicate sound of flutes, the sins of the world were passing in dumb show before him. Things that he had dimly dreamed of were suddenly made real to him. Things of which he had never dreamed were gradually revealed. The style in which it was written was that curious jewelled style, vivid and obscure at once, full of 'argot' and archaicisms, of technical expressions and of elaborate paraphrases that characterises the work of some of the finest

artists of the French School of Symbolistes. There were in it metaphors as monstruous as orchids, and as subtle in colour.[19]

However, another Symbolist text, Edgar Allan Poe's *Tales of Mystery and Imagination*, gave ample scope for his sinister 'flesh-creeping' depiction of the macabre, the beautiful juxtaposed with the gruesome. Many critics have felt that Clarke is their ideal illustrator, that no one could do greater justice to their every aspect. He was able to penetrate deeply into the subconscious, mixing seemingly 'real' images and fantastic concoctions from his fertile imagination in a faultless graphic technique. His predilection for contrasting alluring, voracious, depraved sirens, as described by Swinburne, with credulous, virginal, ill-fated damsels, like Faust's Marguerite, is also found in the work of contemporaries like Gustav-Adolf Mossa (fig. 7), Mikhail Vrubel (fig. 8), Léon Bakst (fig. 9), Alastair (fig. 10) and Jan Toorop, to name but a few.[20] A dualistic medieval fascination with mystical, heavenly beauty contrasted with worm-ridden, rotten evil was as close to Clarke's work as it was to many of his Symbolist and Northern European Renaissance precursors. There is a wealth of material for the psychoanalyst in his more explicit imagery.

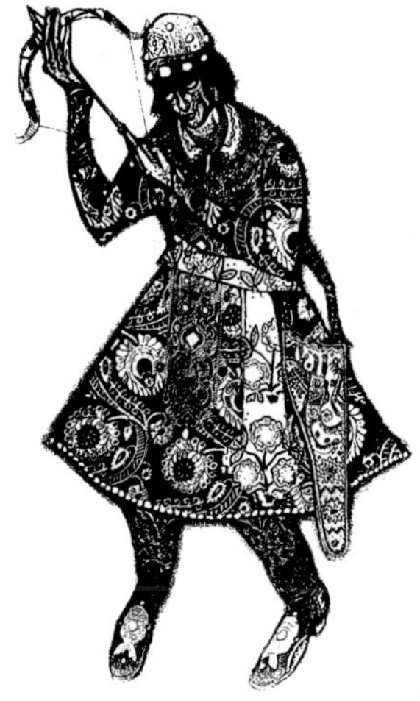

9 Léon Bakst, costume design for the Tsarevitch, *The Firebird*, 1910

The dual nature of his work first became apparent in his eleven superb windows in the Honan Chapel at University College Cork (1915-17), each portraying 'an ecstatic figure segregated from a human tower'[21] sumptuously orchestrated in a series of key colours. These and subsequent windows made over the next ten years encapsulate what has been termed Synaesthesia,[22] a stylized inter-relationship of abstraction and symbol, and lure us into his figures' bemused trances through their enigmatic expressions and hieratic stances. His hypersensitive painterly skills, idiosyncratic vision and religious sensibility, synthesizing a wide range of literary and art historical references, with an incomparable manipulation of the jewelled qualities of glass, give his work a dimension usually only dreamed of by the Symbolists. Such richness iconographically as well as technically appealed to patrons sick of conventional ecclesiastical and Celtic banalities. It is curious how few of the Symbolists turned to stained glass, despite the analogies frequently drawn between it and the hieratic, mystical and jewelled splendour of their work. Exceptions were Melchior Lechter (figs. 11, 12) and the Hungarian artists, Miksa Róth and Sándor Nagy,[23] who sought national romantic expression in glass, but rarely could one artist fuse artistic vision with technical skill as could Clarke and his contemporaries in Ireland, Wilhelmina Geddes[24] and Michael Healy.

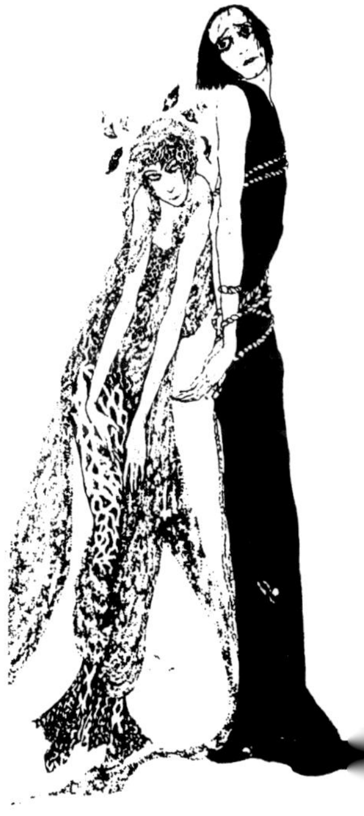

10 Alastair (H.H. Voight), *Salome and Iokanaan* (detail), *c.* 1925

There are interesting comparisons between the splodgy colour sketches of Moreau, the early romantic paintings of Kandinsky (fig. 13)[25] and Clarke's colour notations for glass, but direct influences are speculative. However, it is in the work of Gustav Klimt that the greatest closeness in mood, design, colour, line, even texture to Clarke's is found, even though

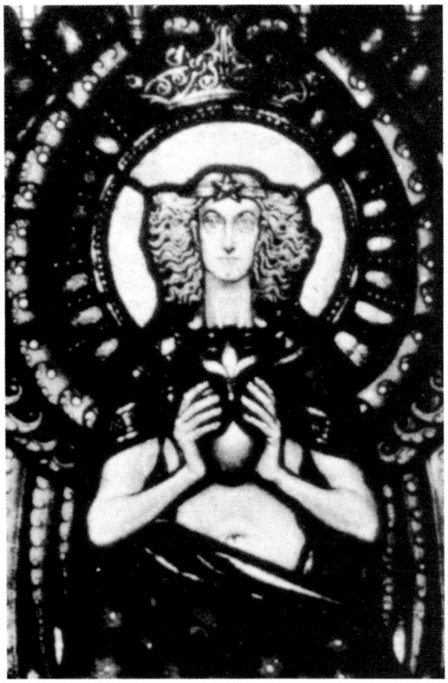

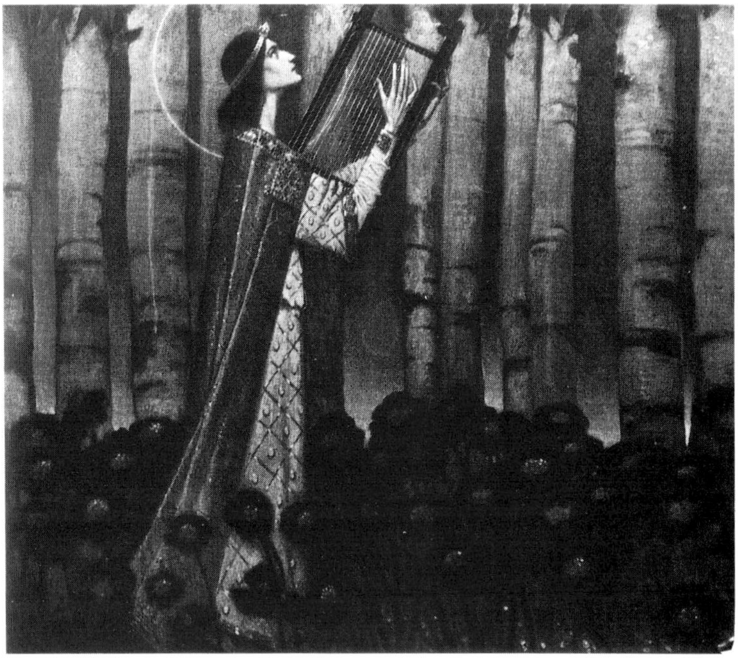

11 Melchior Lechter, *Christ* (detail), stained glass window, 1916

12 Melchior Lechter, *Orpheus* (detail), oil on canvas, 1896

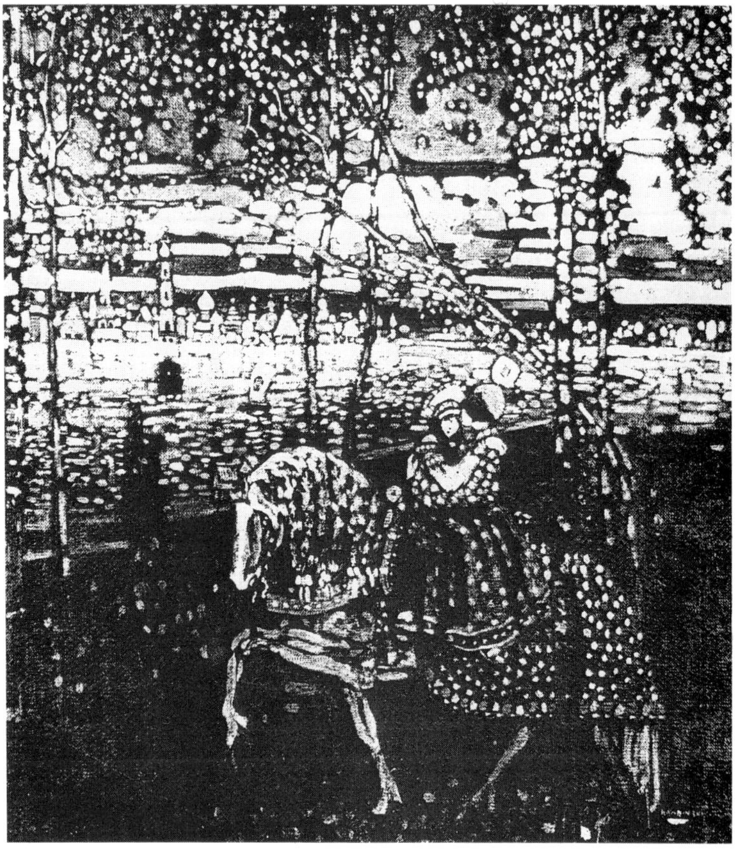

13 Wassily Kandinsky, *Riding Couple*, *c*. 1905

Klimt never worked in glass. They both favoured designs incorporating beautiful, slender, ecstatic figures or emaciated, agonized or grossly corpulent bodies, intent on their own mystical experiences. They both tend to present their subtly orchestrated figure compositions against an abstract, often symbolic, decoratively patterned backdrop devoid of dimension. There is little suggestion of form within the apparel — only an icon, a symbolic effigy; flesh has been transcended or spent, 'forms emerge from forms and others arise or descend from these' (fig. 14).[26] Klimt uses this device in his portraits, encasing the realistically painted human heads and hands in a decorative scheme, sometimes applying semi-precious materials as collage to enhance the ornamental effect, as the Byzantine mosaicists had done. His *Judith II* (1909; fig. 84), *Hope I* (1903) and *Sea Serpents* (*c.* 1904-7) are blood relations of Clarke's *Ligeia* (1918), *Little Mermaid* (1914) and *St Gobnait* (1915). Decadent as defined by Havelock Ellis,[27] both artists shared a fascination with Death, Sleep, Art for Decoration's Sake and an overt sexual element, at times morbid. The earlier analogies with the Elizabethan miniature and the book illustrations of Edmund Dulac and Kay Nielsen (figs. 42 and 44),[28] with Hoppé (fig. 15), George Sheringham and Jessie King (fig. 47) and E.A. Taylor, were absorbed by 1919, together with a variety of others described in the following text. This year marks his visit to Diaghilev's Ballets Russes season in London and the emergence of his idealized androgynous[29] archetype. Heavy lidded, ascetic, lost in reverie, with deathly pallor, red-gold hair, tapering fingers and elaborately stylized apparel, he/she may be an angel, a merman in a ballad by Heine, a soldier saint, the young St John, Lazarus, Elijah, Flaubert's St Julian or the Spirit of Time. The 'thin, clear gaze',[30] chiselled features, heroic but disturbed Wagnerian expression would soon become increasingly spectral as, with the onslaught of tuberculosis, he reduced his visual scale to ever-decreasing microscopic proportions. Dame Ninette de Valois justly rued the fact that he never designed costumes for the ballet or the theatre, which he enjoyed so much.[31]

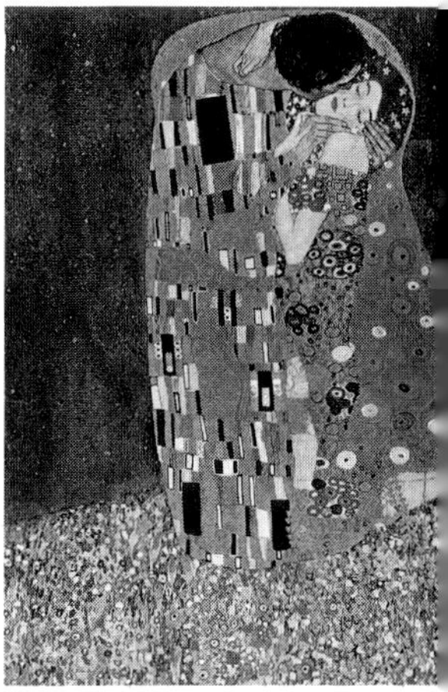

14 Gustav Klimt, *The Kiss*, 1907-8

In his short working life, he forged out an idiosyncratic style, aptly described by Sidney Sime, writing of one of his monsters for Lord Dunsany's tales: 'part is beautiful, part is complicated, part is unhealthy and the whole thing is unwholesome and intricate.'[32] Like Sime, in his Dunsany illustrations, Clarke in his Poe illustrations reached a rare point of artistic freedom, in which he had liberated himself from all influences to express his own images 'crammed with fine detail . . . filled in at incredible speed' (fig. 16).[33] One contemporary felt his genius to be 'so versatile and subtle that the beholder is at first more conscious of its dangerous facility than its solid achievement', and 'that such a talent . . . will not stand still, avid for new problems and the joy in solution that new situations create'.[34] His most consistently perceptive critic, Æ, was convinced that colour was his 'great gift', that 'Harry Clarke has a genius which manifests itself at its highest in stained glass', and that 'the full soul of the artist' could not be 'manifested until he can let light pour through his design. . . . I imagine that if one scraped a little the subconscious mind of the artist you would let in a flood of rich colour out of some inner luminous aether, where the fire is more brilliant than the eye can see, and the only way he could recreate that colour for us was by the art he practises.'[35]

Because Clarke's masterpieces are in the relatively inaccessible medium of glass and have to be tracked down in often remote churches or private collections, or have been lost after colour reproduction had done them little justice, the legacy of his short life has been insufficiently recognized.

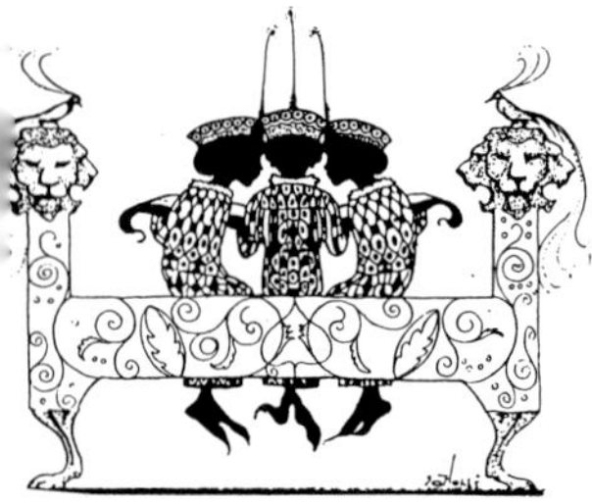

15 E.O. Hoppé, headpiece decoration, *c.* 1913

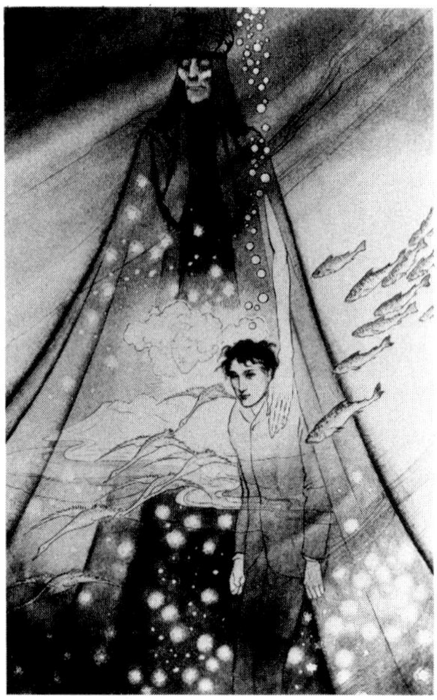

16 Sidney Sime, 'Goodbye', illustration from Lord Dunsany's *The Sword of Welleran* (1908); the compositions, figures and plant and bird detail in a number of Sime's illustrations to Dunsany's haunting tales bear similarities to those of Clarke.

1

The craft of stained glass in Ireland in the 1900s — An Túr Gloine — Joshua Clarke — Harry Clarke's formative years in Dublin and London and on Aran

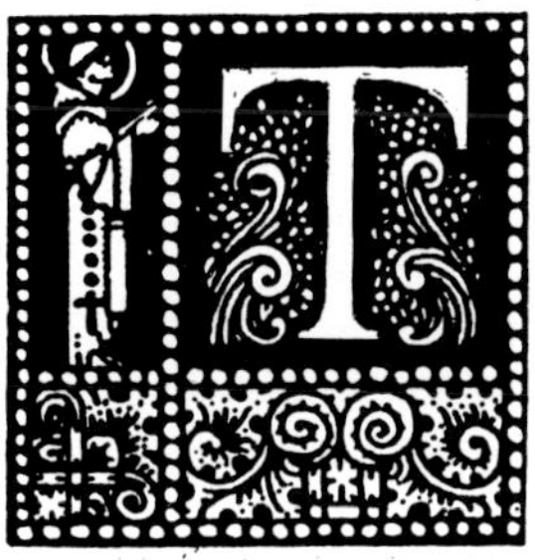

17 Initial T, from the introduction to the catalogue of the fifth exhibition of the Arts and Crafts Society of Ireland, 1917

The craft of stained glass had fallen to such a low standard in Ireland at the beginning of the twentieth century that Æ could write: 'We have bad stained glass . . . in our churches because there is no authority in matters of taste to indicate what is poor and is truly beautiful.'[1] Edward Martyn, co-founder of the Irish National Theatre, in his preface to a collection of critical essays by Robert Elliott[2] advocated the need to save church decoration from dirty colours, machine-made imitations in 'sham materials' and the 'crude paw of the tradesman'. He felt it was a pity that 'nice, clean plain white glass, letting in the wholesome and radiant light of heaven should have been hastily removed to make way for garish pictures . . .'. Denis Gwynn, writing on the Irish Revival,[3] describes Edward Martyn's role in freeing 'Munichized Dublin' from 'foreign purveyors of stained glass' with their 'crudely painted window blinds', dirty yellows and mass production. Martyn felt that stained glass had suffered more than any other craft and traced the general decay of the decorative arts 'back to the democratic educational movements of the early part of the [nineteenth] century, which sought to give everyone, irrespective of wealth, equal facilities of learning'. This had resulted in 'the speedy rise of cheap sham' and stained glass, being particularly 'delicate and refined', was 'the first to suffer and die under the clumsy hand of the Philistine'.

Martyn began his campaign to raise the standard of Irish stained glass in 1901 by inviting Christopher Whall from London to make a set of stained glass windows for the family church at Laban, near Ardrahan, close to his home at Tulira Castle, Co. Galway. By the end of the 1890s Whall had emerged as the most progressive stained glass artist and teacher in the British Arts and Crafts movement. Trained as a painter but self-taught in glass, he had absorbed the earlier nineteenth century investigations into medieval glass by Charles Winston[4] and Whitefriars, the theories of William Morris and Ruskin and his own contemporary fellow architects with whom he shared a common belief in a thorough 'knowledge of materials as a basis for style'.[5] E.S. Prior's invention of Norman slab glass was as essential to his work as Winston's and Whitefriars' rediscovery of

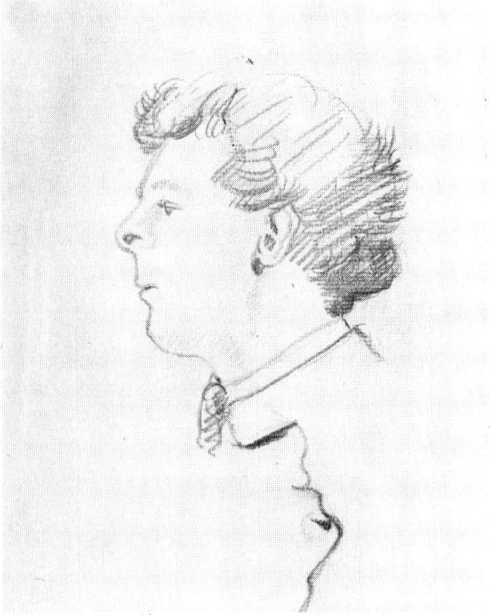

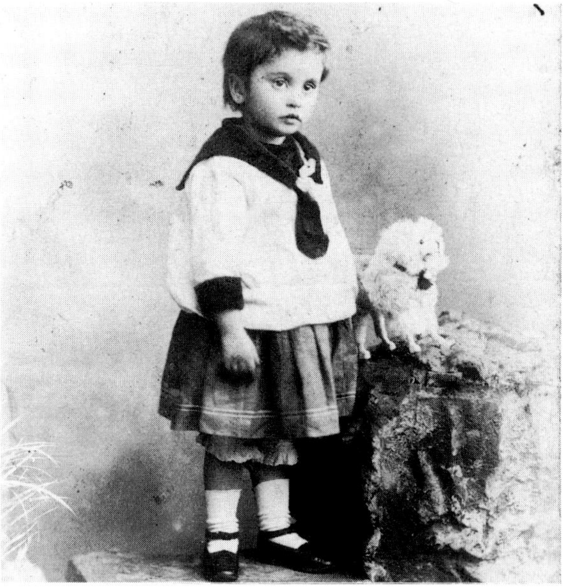

18 Kathleen Fox, pencil sketch of A.E. Child drawn in the stained glass studio at the Dublin School of Art, *c.* 1906

19 Studio photograph of Harry Clarke as a child

'antique' pot metal had been to the previous generation. Like Winston, he understood that the beauty of the glass 'lay not so much in its formal stylistic characteristics as in the way in which, through superb craftsmanship, light and colour were made almost in an abstract way the instruments of artistic expression.'[6] Whall was to influence the best of all the ensuing generations through his handbook, *Stained Glass Work* (published in 1905)[7] and his teaching at the Royal College of Art and the Central School of Art in London.

Until 1907 when he established his own studios and workshop in Ravenscourt Park, he designed and made windows with a devoted group of students and associates from Lowndes and Drury's workshops in Chelsea. Many of these would rent studios in the unique purpose-built Glass House which Mary Lowndes and Alfred Drury set up in Lettice Street, Fulham in 1906.[8]

When the glass commissioned by Martyn was ready Whall sent Alfred Ernest Child (fig. 18) to Ireland to oversee its installation. Martyn persuaded Whall to let Child stay in Ireland and, establish a new school of stained glass. In January 1903, with the active and financial support of Sarah Purser, the Dublin portrait painter, and Whall's invaluable advice, he set Child up as manager of a co-operative studio workshop at 24 Upper Pembroke Street in Dublin.[9] This was christened An Túr Gloine (The Tower of Glass), and its credo, as quoted by Sarah Purser in a silver anniversary address,[10] was that 'each window should be in all its artistic parts the work of one individual artist'. W.B. Yeats later wrote to Whall's daughter, Veronica, that her father 'did a great deal for the emotional life of this country when he helped Miss Purser to establish here her school of glass'.[11]

In 1900 the Dublin Metropolitan School of Art, formerly the responsibility of the Department of Science and Art and under the control of South Kensington, was reconstituted under the new Department of Agriculture and Technical Instruction.[12] This greatly enlarged the scope of the school, especially in the applied arts and crafts. Alfred Child was appointed as the school's first stained glass master in September 1901, to train a new generation of Irish stained glass artists. His first recruit was Michael Healy, who was followed by Beatrice Elvery (later Lady Glenavy), Catherine O'Brien and Ethel Rhind.[13] Harry Clarke was later to be a student and subsequently a teacher at the school.

At the age of eighteen Harry Clarke's father, Joshua, had moved to Ireland from Leeds, where his family had a thriving printing business: two spendthrift cousins had inherited the family business, which failed, and Joshua escaped to Dublin, where he found a job with a firm of ecclesiastical suppliers. However, he had far too much energy and initiative to work long for someone else, and in 1886 he set up his own business as church decorator, manufacturer of objects of art, and sanitary contractor. He married Brigid MacGonigal from Cliffoney, Co. Sligo and they lived at first on the North Strand, Dublin. By 1887 they had accumulated enough capital to take a lease on 33 North Frederick Street, a spacious Georgian house behind Parnell Square. They also kept a seaside house at Bray.

Joshua Clarke was ambitious for his business and, realizing that his efforts were only as good as his one other competitor in Dublin, in 1892 he brought over from England a draughtsman and stained glass worker named Pope. Harry Clarke later wrote: 'Pope was in his time one of the finest stained glass draughtsmen in these countries and worked with my father until about 20 years ago when his position was filled by William Nagle, who was contemporary with [William] Osborne and a Gold Medallist for Life in the RHA Schools. Nagle was 36 or 37 years here and worked with me until he died in 1923'.[14]

On St Patrick's Day, 1889, a son, Henry Patrick, was born to Joshua and Brigid Clarke, exactly a year after the birth of their first son, Walter (fig. 19). Mrs Clarke was consumptive, and both Harry and his elder brother inherited a tendency to weakness in the chest. The girls — Kathleen, the eldest of the four Clarke children, and Dolly (Florence) — were stronger. Mrs Clarke died on 11 August 1903 at Bray in her forty-third year, when Harry was fourteen.

Harry was educated first at Marlborough Street School, and then by the Jesuits at Belvedere College, round the corner from North Frederick Street. The school magazine recorded that 'his contemporaries at Belvedere remember Harry as a reserved and rather sensitive boy, a little aloof from the rough and tumble of school life, but well-liked by his companions and conspicuous among them for his skills in drawing'.[15] He left school in 1903, aged fourteen. It is clear that Joshua entertained hopes for his younger son as a stained glass artist. Before Harry left school, his father wrote to London to a Mr Payne, who supplied and serviced their kiln, asking him to look out for a good place in a Munich stained glass firm, where the boy could earn his keep for about three years as an apprentice.[16] Fortunately, this plan was never realized and Harry learned the basic techniques of his craft from William Nagle in his father's studios.

Joshua Clarke worked extremely hard in the early years to build up his business (fig. 20). Although nearly all his supplies were imported from different parts of Britain — his kiln, lead, glass and stained glass, paint, polish, glue, opus sectile, painting materials, brushes, even ladders — he preferred to use Irish labour and would employ men from the Metropolitan Painters' Hall in Aungier Street and from the Catholic Association. Because he was a strict taskmaster and the men were not paid very much, he sometimes ran into difficulties with his staff, but he always maintained a high standard of workmanship. His foreman throughout his life was his wife's brother, Frank MacGonigal, whom he despatched all over the country on decoration, glass installation and repair work. To attract patronage Joshua had to be on good terms with the different religious orders, and his work had to be superior to that of other firms. His main competitors were the Tower of Glass and Earley's of Upper Camden Street (who had links with the Birmingham firm of John Hardman & Co.). Because foreign firms, such as Mayer's of Munich and the English firms of Heaton, Butler and Bayne, Powell's and Hardman's, tendered for work in Ireland as well as in Britain, it was also essential to develop good relations with architects engaged on church design such as Ashlin and Coleman, R.M. Butler, Thomas McNamara, Professor William Scott, Sir Thomas Drew, A. Scott, T.N. Deane and C. Powell — to name some of the architects for whom Joshua Clarke worked in Ireland.

Harry seems to have done some stained glass work for the family firm before he left school in 1903. During the following year he worked, probably as a draughtsman, in Thomas McNamara's architectural office in Dublin. McNamara is reputed to have encouraged Harry to pursue the art of stained glass, rather than an architectural career.[17] Harry also travelled around the country taking photographs of stained glass for the Studios, while his brother Walter was seconded to the decoration, painting, repairing and opus sectile division of the business.

In the 1904 Art Industries Exhibition at Ballsbridge, Dublin the Clarke Studios won a prize,[18] and in November at the third Arts and Crafts Society of Ireland exhibition at the Institute of Civil Engineers in Dawson Street they showed a stained glass window.[19] Arthur Orr of Harrow made most of their original designs for stained glass, which Joshua insisted 'must be fully Celtic, original and quaint',[20] although, hedging his bets, he advocated a German facial type as being the most popular with his clients.

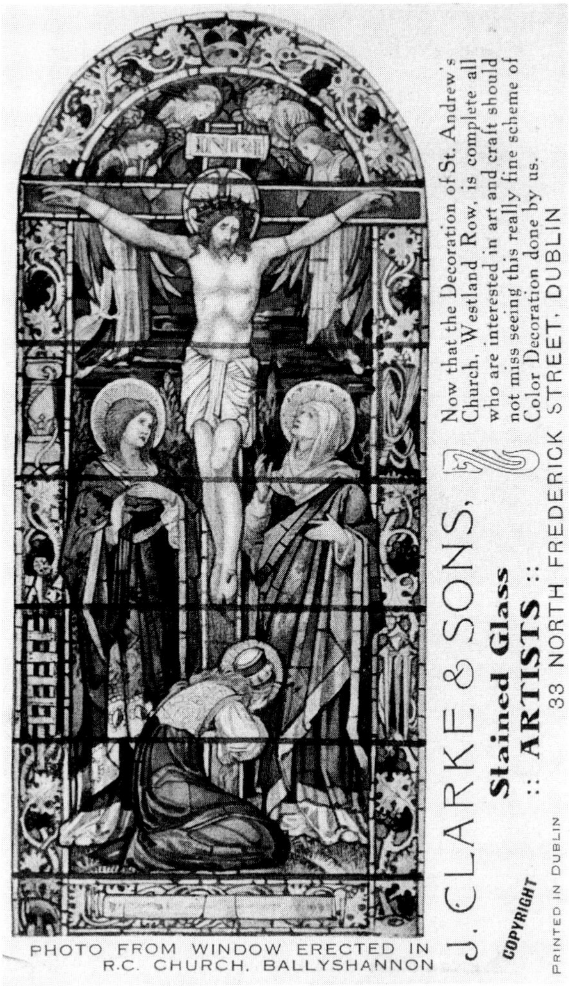

20 Trade advertisement for J. Clarke and Sons, *c.* 1908, issued as a coloured postcard and featuring a window adapted from a design by A.A. Dix

August 1905 brought bad floods to Dublin and, with a severe business recession and both boys on his hands, Joshua found himself in a precarious financial situation. However, he was still determined that his sons should gain experience abroad and asked Arthur Orr to try to secure an apprenticeship for Harry in England for a few years. As Harry had already begun night classes at the Metropolitan School of Art in Dublin, it was decided that he should attend the South Kensington Schools of Design while working in a London firm for a trial period of three months. His father described the work he had already done at the Dublin School as 'inexperienced but done with a certain amount of care, neatness and confidence'.[21]

In London, Harry lodged with Mr Orr's sister and her family and attended the Royal College of Art in South Kensington daily for two months.[22] However, despite the efforts of his father and Mr Orr, he was unsuccessful in getting 'placed' in any of the standard glass firms in London. Mr Dix's studio, where Arthur Orr worked, could not offer him a place; nor could Mr Salmond of Hetley's (the Clarke Studios' main glass supplier) find anyone to take him on. Harry was doing plenty of drawing but was rather homesick. The main problem, however, seems neither to have been Harry's youth nor his shyness, but the fact that his father could not pay the fee of about one hundred pounds required by anyone taking on a trainee apprentice. Eventually, Joshua arranged for Harry to spend a trial month in the stained glass department of Gasgoyne's in Nottingham; but within a few days Harry was back in London, 'disheartened and miserable', intending to give London one more week before returning to Dublin for Easter.

He returned to Dublin for Easter 1906, and for the next few months worked in his father's studios, still undecided on his future career; during this period 'his drawings . . . certainly improved'.[23] In the evenings he attended Alfred Child's classes in stained glass at the School of Art. Meanwhile, Joshua Clarke was struggling to keep the firm going. He was now using Hoffman's illustrated *Life of Christ* as a copy book, and instructed Mr Orr,

> Don't have as much of naked legs as you had in the other Holy Family. This is a great objection in stained glass as in the first place it never looks well and in the second place it's very objectionable when there is too much of it.[24]

In April 1907, along with Ward and Partners of Belfast and Catherine O'Brien and Ethel Rhind, pupils of Alfred Child at the Dublin School of Art, the Clarke Studios submitted their entries for the arts and crafts subsection of the home industries section of the Irish International Exhibition to be held in Dublin's Herbert Park. The Palace of Fine Arts section of this exhibition prepared Dublin for Hugh Lane's[25] generous gift of one hundred and fifty four works of art the following year. Oswald Reeves, appointed master of enamel and metal work at the Metropolitan School of Art shortly after Child, was one of the selectors for the exhibition who rejected two windows from the Clarke Studios but chose an opus sectile *Stations of the Cross*, a drawing for *The Nativity, Crucifixion and Assumption* and a design for *St Patrick baptising the Two Princesses*. Arthur Orr's part in these designs had to be kept quiet as he lived in England.[26] William Nagle of the Studios had a design for church decoration at Blackrock exhibited with his cartoon for the *St Patrick* window. The window of *St Patrick and the Neophyte Princesses*[27] (valued at £60) was erected just inside the left hand side of the principal entrance to the Grand Central Palace. James Watson & Co. of Youghal and Campbell Bros. of Belfast also had stained glass displayed in this section of the exhibition.

Joshua was delighted that R.M. Butler wrote about and illustrated his exhibits in the *Irish Builder*, and he wrote to Oliver Fry of the Exhibition

Committee asking if it would be possible to

> draw His Majesty's attention to my window . . the best work I have ever done, in fact, I think it's the best work that has been done in this country.[28]

This window, which won a silver medal the following year in the 1908 Franco-British Exhibition of Science, Arts and Industries in London, was illustrated in the 1909 *Irish Catholic Directory* inset advertising J. Clarke and Sons. Such exhibitions were a good way of giving a public showing of stained glass which might be inaccessible once installed, and it became standard practice for Joshua, and subsequently Harry Clarke, to show completed windows in the Studios before they were packed up and despatched.

In August 1907, during the Oireachtas Exhibition of Arts and Crafts in the Rotunda, Dublin, in which the firm exhibited two windows, Harry went back to London. This visit was purely for pleasure, probably to visit exhibitions. He seems to have stayed with the Orrs again. After his return later that month, Joshua insured Harry as a stained glass artist's apprentice at the Studios where he was alredy attending to some of his father's business correspondence during Joshua's absences.

Throughout the first half of 1908 Harry was quite seriously ill from a bad attack of 'flu. His heart was so weak that a nurse had to be brought in to look after him, and he had several relapses. In June he was sufficiently recovered to be sent off to Bray to recuperate in the sea air.

At the Studios, Joshua was beginning to favour an 'exact imitation of Hardman's style', which meant that figures were of prime importance in composition, garments were diapered, and there was very little paint or detail. However, by the end of July, the Studio style changed yet again, this time to that of Frampton or Dix, the studio for which Orr worked — 'very modern, all worked in water except a little tar to get extra strength of shades'. Although Joshua altered the style of his work in whichever direction he felt would be the most popular, there is no doubt he had a firm grasp of the properties of glass, 'rich in colour and mellowness in light'. He resented enamelled glass and muddy overpainting but was not above imitating Mayer's style out of sheer financial necessity. Even though the Studios were by now advertising banners and bannered paintings, fresco paintings on canvas and linoleum, Stations of the Cross in opus sectile (which had the advantage of being impervious to damp), regilding of frames, restoration of paintings, plain and ornamental leadlights, as well as housepainting, church decorating and stained glass work, business was not particularly good and overheads were heavy. Mr Orr, who seemed to be doing very well in England, was not producing designs as fast as Joshua wanted them, particularly when they were needed quickly for tenders.

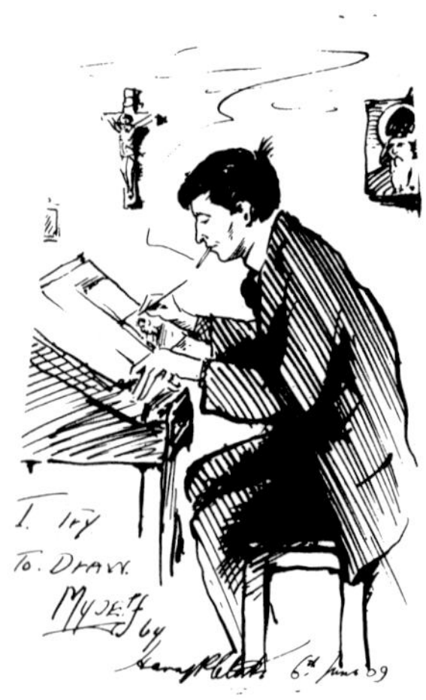

21 'I try to draw myself', pen and ink self-portrait from the autograph book of the Clarke Studios' secretary, Miss O'Sullivan, 6 June 1909, Hugh Lane Municipal Gallery of Modern Art, Dublin

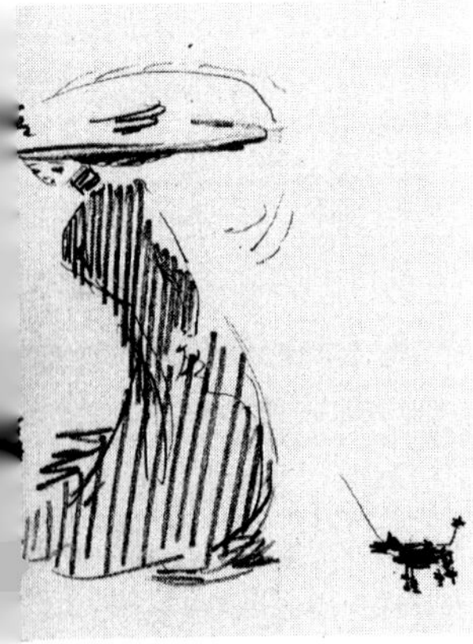

22 Drawing in pen and ink, after Phil May, *c.* 1909

On the eve of St Patrick's Day 1909, which was Harry's twentieth birthday, the Countess of Aberdeen organised the Irish Industries Pageant, held in celebration of the 1906 Trades Act which gave protection to those using the Irish Trade Mark.[29] Practically all the costumes were designed and made by students of the Metropolitan Art School, and the tableau representing stained glass showed a 'magnificence of apparel'. Perhaps Harry, as a student of the School of Art, was involved in this event (fig. 21).

On 1 April 1909 the Clarke Studios began their long association with Hartley Wood & Co. of the Portobello Glass Works, Sunderland, who, with W.E. Chance of Oldbury supplied all their standard glass and other sundries. James Hetley & Co. of Soho were the agents for the above and also for any French or German glass they took.[30] Norman slab glass was made by a very small firm, E. Claridge & Son of Homerton. Pigments, silver stain, kelp, staining sheets, ambetti, oxides and 'geet' — the coarse red- brown pigment they used to grind down in the early days — all came from Messrs Heaton of Cumberland Market in London. Joshua would order samples by post and then crates would be sent by boat and rail. He was in almost daily correspondence with Mr Salmond of Hetley's. Joshua was still in a quandary about Harry, who continued to suffer poor health. There had been further plans to send him to Germany, but Harry must have dissuaded his father, for Joshua announced at the end of July: 'Harry is going to Aran Island to study the natives and their habits, perhaps it may do him good as it will be a perfect rest and nothing between him and America.'[31] During the summer he had been reading as avidly as he always did and drawing, particularly caricatures in the manner of his favourite masters — Phil May (fig. 22), H.M. Bateman, Hanslip Fletcher and Heath Robinson.

He left for Inishere in the Aran Islands on 7 August, with his friend Austin Molloy, a fellow student at the School of Art, who was also talented at black and white illustration and stained glass. The weather was good and Harry filled several sketch books during his holidays, the first of a succession of annual trips to Inishere. Austin Molloy and he would go out every day with sketch books and painting and drawing gear strapped about them. There is a witty and deftly drawn caricature of himself and Molloy signed KLANK (or KLARKY?) in imitation of Phil May's signature, in which Harry depicts himself as an elongated, droopy figure, clad in pampooties, setting off to sketch, beside the diminutive figure of his companion. There were also a number of finely observed drawings of ships, harbour scenes, curraghs and Aran fishermen. One of the finest of these, dated 14 August 1909, is entitled *Bar Scene on Inishmaan*.

When Harry returned to North Frederick Street he found his father adapting the Studio style once more, to something 'between Hardman's and Mayer's', a 'rather German style after Hoffman's', to attract business from the Irish clergy. Joshua also wanted to go in for mosaic, probably because Mr Ward, the head of the School of Art, had started teaching wall decoration and mosaic that year. There was increasing competition from Sarah Purser's Tower of Glass, which by now was employing students of A.E. Child at the School of Art. The stained glass class had been the first art craft class to be established under the new régime, and all concerned were justly proud of its progress. In 1906, the first year Child entered his class for the Board of Education's National Competition held in South Kensington, six out of seven pupils were awarded medals and premiums. From its modest beginning, the work of Child's class was having a con- siderable influence on stained glass in Ireland. Their work was exhibited not only at the Dublin School, South Kensington, and the Royal Dublin Society exhibitions, but also at the Franco-British Exhibition and the Budapest Exhibition, and was written up in art journals.

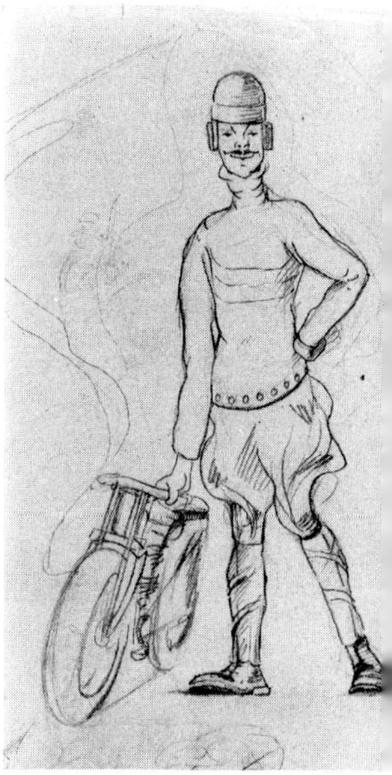

23 Pencil design for the *Irish Cyclist*, 1909

In January 1910 Harry was still attending Mr Child's night classes in the School of Art and helping in the business during the day. He was also doing some little drawings for Fr Fitzhenry, the administrator of St Aidan's College, Enniscorthy, and a coloured 'motor' sketch for a Mr Powderly of the Sackville Press.[32] Joshua wrote to Mr Orr that Harry was much more artistic than the new painter they had just employed from Smithwick's in Birmingham, who was so methodical that he spoilt any stained glass. 'Since Harry was in London you would not know his work, he is so much improved . . . the few months in South Kensington did him a great deal of good', his father wrote.[33] Harry, was, in fact, working in the Studios in the absence of a flesh painter and was doing so well that Joshua thought he might put him in that position and employ only an ornamental painter, who would be less skilled. This was Harry's first attempt at painting flesh — a deceptively simple task needing a light, steady touch and a good eye.

While Joshua was away in London interviewing prospective employees, Harry, now twenty-one, took over the running of the Studios. He had a small success in April when his cartoon of a window entitled *Tragedy and Comedy* was accepted for the Abbey Theatre. However, there is no record that the window was ever carried out. In May he entered a design for the Trinity Week poster competition at Trinity College, Dublin, but was not successful. In June a furious quarrel broke out when Joshua accused 'the contemptible puppy' (Orr) of slackening in his Irish work, to which Orr replied that he regarded these jobs as mere 'pick-me-ups'. This row may well have precipitated Harry's involvement in designing stained glass for the Studios. At the same time he was getting several small commissions of his own for black and white drawings, including some for the *Irish Cyclist* (fig. 23),[34] although he was seriously handicapped throughout that summer by the after-effects of a series of nose operations, which meant he couldn't bend his head and his eyes were sore and inflamed. In August his father decided to start him on painting a head, to test him, because 'if you never try you will never learn'.[35] He was pleasantly surprised by the result. Later that month Harry found time to return to Aran, where he did some oil sketches of the landscape and a good small oil portrait of an Aran girl (fig. 24), painted in a manner similar to, although less adept than, his friend Patrick Tuohy's *Aran Fisherboy* (1910).[36]

Before the opening of the School of Art on 4 October, there was great apprehension in the Clarke family as to whether Harry's application for the art scholarship in stained glass had been successful. This specialist scholarship, inaugurated the previous year, had become available in July, when Ernest Lakeman, the previous year's winner, had given it up. Until now Harry had only been attending night classes; a scholarship would mean not only that he could attend daytime classes free of fees, but also that he could participate in the various exhibitions and competitions open to day students. So far, he had only been awarded a second prize for ecclesiastical stained glass at an exhibition of student work at the Royal Dublin Society. On 20 September the Secretary of the Department of Agriculture and Technical Instruction informed Harry that he had been granted the stained glass scholarship for the 1910-11 session. Joshua was delighted at the news and, at the same time, at his great luck in signing on for a year 'the greatest artist as glasspainter it was ever my pleasure to meet', a 'thorough gentleman', and past scholar in portrait painting from the School of Art, late of Heaton Butler's.[37] This was William MacBride, who later founded the Craftworkers Guild in Harcourt Street and worked with Colm O'Lochlainn at the Sign of the Three Candles. At last prospects seemed more hopeful at the Clarke Studios, although MacBride was so 'quiet, respectful and steady' and generally excellent that Joshua was constantly worried he might leave. Harry, while relieved of some demands on his time by MacBride's appointment, found it hard to exist on the guinea a week he received from his scholarship and was glad to get small freelance commissions from Fr Fitzhenry and others.[38]

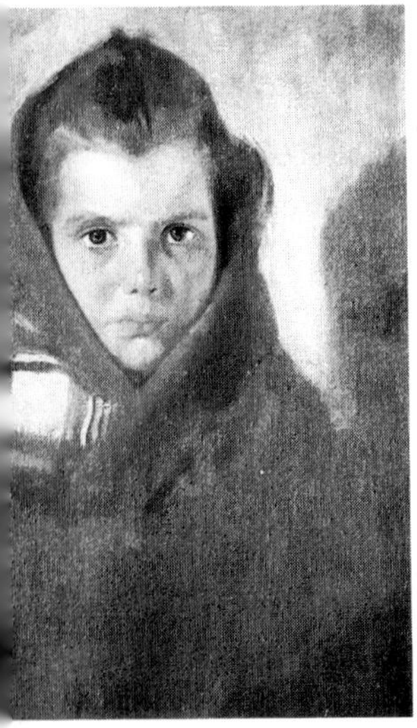

24 *Portrait of an Aran girl*, oil on canvas, *c.* 1910

25 *The Consecration of St Mel, Bishop of Longford, by St Patrick* (detail), stained glass panel, 1910; the first in a series of panels to win Clarke a gold medal at the National Competition in London for three consecutive years

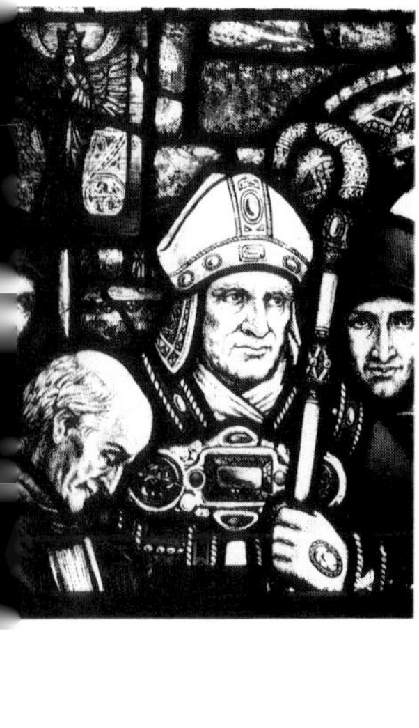

There seems to have been some tension between Harry and his instructor, Alfred Child, perhaps because they represented rival studios. Child must have realised that his trained pupil could never be recruited into the Tower of Glass team. Harry used to call Child 'Mr Meat' because of his small, squat, ruddy appearance, and would joke about the dapper suits that he always wore beneath his white slip and overall. Despite Child's uninspiring appearance, there is no doubt that he was a very sound craftsman and an unusually talented teacher of the basic techniques of stained glass. Before the year was up Harry had exhibited his panel of *The Consecration of St Mel, Bishop of Longford, by St Patrick* (fig. 25; plate 1)[39] in the Art Industries exhibition at the Royal Dublin Society, and at the Arts and Crafts Society of Ireland's fourth exhibition in Dawson Street, where he also showed his cartoon for a window he later submitted for the National Competition, *The Meeting of St Brendan with Judas Iscariot*. This exhibition marks the beginning of his involvement with the newly-founded Guild of Irish Art Workers and the Arts and Crafts Society of Ireland.

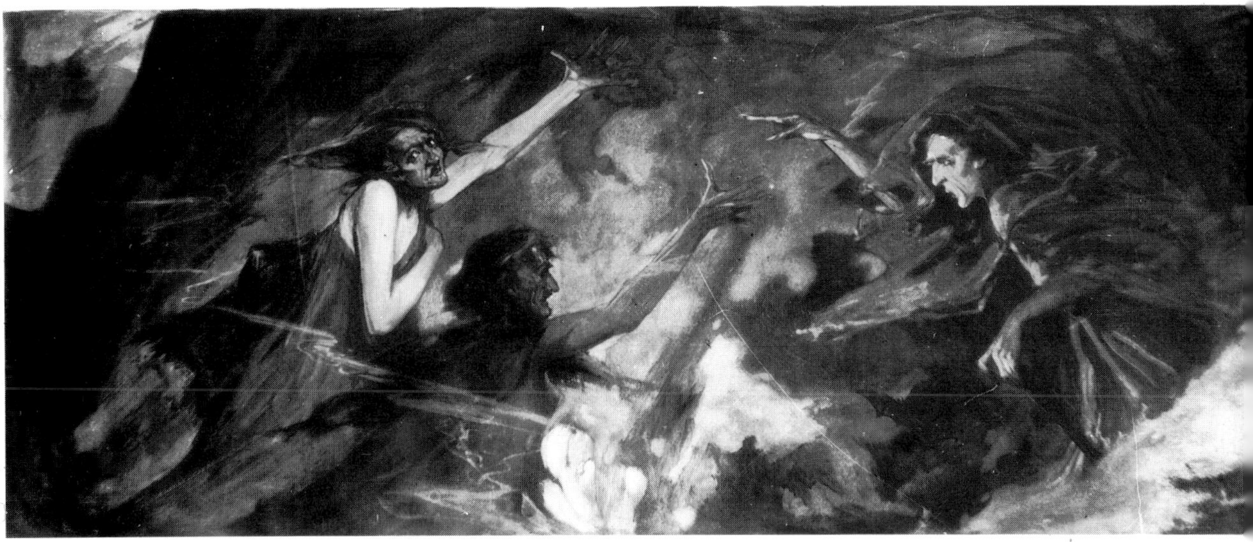

26 'The Three Witches' from *Macbeth*, oil on canvas, *c.* 1911; the first manifestation of Clarke's penchant for attenuated limbs and fiendish subjects

Harry was working hard both at the Art School, where he was preparing four cartoons for the National Competition with two accompanying sections worked out in stained glass, and also at his father's studios, where he assisted in the administration of the business as well as helping MacBride with stained glass work and photographing completed work. Joshua felt his younger son was not strong enough to spend all day working at the Art School and was afraid Harry was not used to being 'knocked about', although he agreed that his drawing was 'wonderfully improved' (cf. fig. 26).[40] In June Harry wrote to Leitrim Co. Council that he had 'given up illuminated addresses to devote my time to stained glass and decorative work'.[41] He was at this time in great discomfort after a nose operation, which may have contributed to his decision to concentrate his energy into what he felt he was best at.

Business at the Clarke Studios was gradually improving during the summer of 1911 when the heat was 'so intense you could hardly walk', the quarrel with Mr Orr was patched up and, at the end of July, to Joshua's great pride, Harry was informed that he had won a gold medal for his stained glass entries in the South Kensington National Competition. The examiners were pleased to see 'the quite remarkable advance that has been made in this class of work.[42] This coveted and, in Ireland, unprecedented, award was indeed justified. Harry's work already showed an impressive technical mastery and originality. One of his entries was a cartoon for a three-light window, *The Godhead Enthroned* (fig. 27).[43] The panel, which he worked out in glass to accompany the cartoon and a colour sketch, is a strongly designed and leaded composition, showing the head and shoulders of God, clad in a ruby robe and a great brass girdle with symbols of the four evangelists around his nimbus (fig. 29). The two small inset slabs beside the borders of the panel, which contain tiny monumental saints, etched and stained on

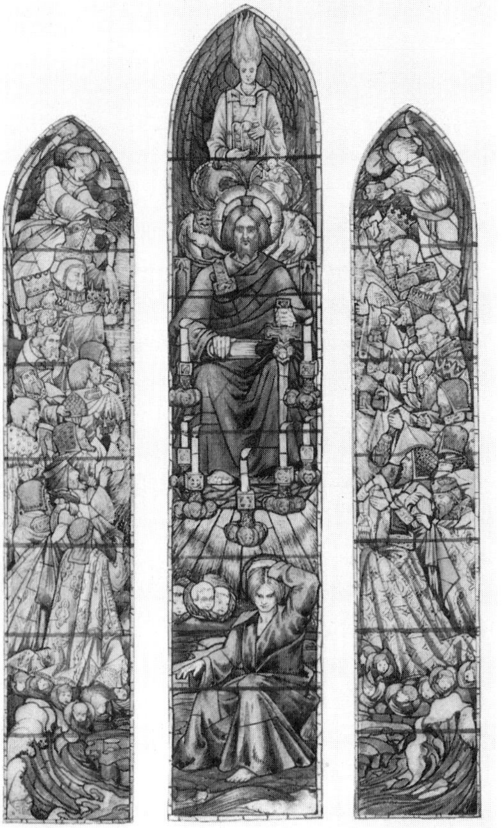

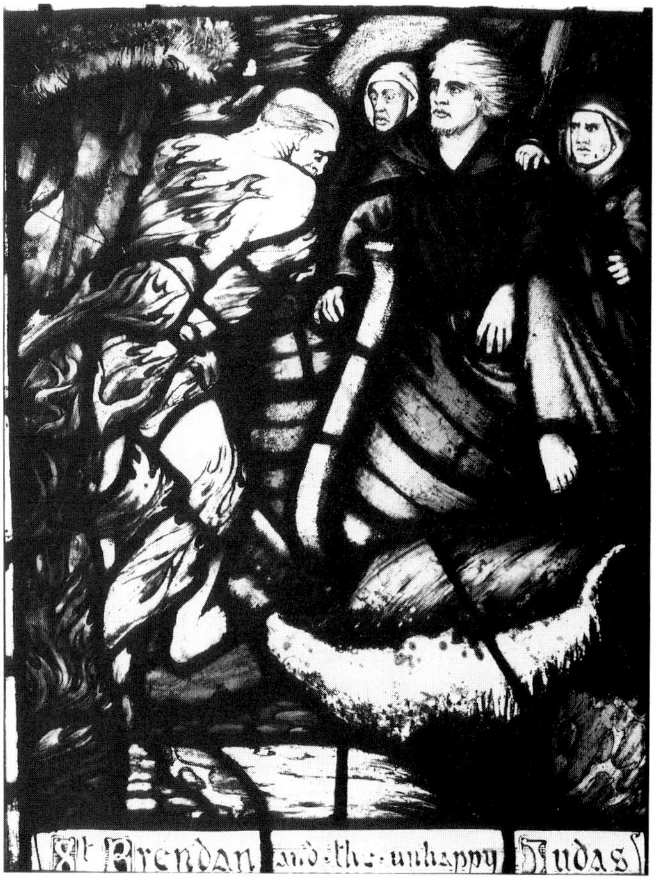

27 Cartoon for *The Godhead Enthroned*, 1911

28 *St Brendan and the unhappy Judas*, stained glass panel, 1911, Crawford Municipal Art Gallery, Cork

blue glass, reminiscent of figures found in illuminated manuscripts or stone carvings, contribute a feeling of antiquity to an early Christian subject. Harry had already inserted a miniature Queen of Heaven lozenge into his *Consecration of St Mel* panel. Several artists of this period in Ireland favoured this effect, inspired by Whall, as it echoed the tradition of Celtic illumination.

Harry's other stained glass panel illustrated the meeting of *St Brendan and the unhappy Judas*, a mythical moment of great drama and pathos which fascinated him and which he depicted several times (fig. 28). It is perhaps inspired by Matthew Arnold's poem 'Saint Brandan':

> At last . . .
> He sees float past an iceberg white,
> And on it — Christ! — a living form.
>
> That furtive mien, that scowling eye,
> Of hair that red and tufted fell —
> It is — oh, where shall Brandan fly? —
> The traitor Judas, out of Hell!

Palsied with terror, Brandan sate;
The moon was bright, the iceberg near.
He hears a voice sigh humbly: 'Wait!
By high permission I am here. . . .'

In rich, flickering colours, Judas is shown encased in tormenting flames with bald pate and wild, menacing eyes and stance not unlike that of Blake's *Ghost of a Flea* (1819) as St Brendan with two horror-stricken companions approaches him in his coracle across the foaming sea. The leading in the panel is particularly effective and there is a real sense of impending drama in the graphic narrative of this bizarre meeting. This panel, like the other prize-winning entries in the competition, would have been exhibited in August in the open square courtyard of what is now the Victoria and Albert Museum.

Work at the Art School went well for Harry, winning him a second class honours for design, first class for drawing of common objects from memory, and school prizes for his designs of given subjects from Irish history and for the best piece of stained glass. His life drawings of this period reveal the influence of Orpen's life drawing classes (fig. 30)[44] in drawings such as the head of a girl, dated 1911, or the subtly shaded linear studies of female nudes where anatomical accuracy has been over-

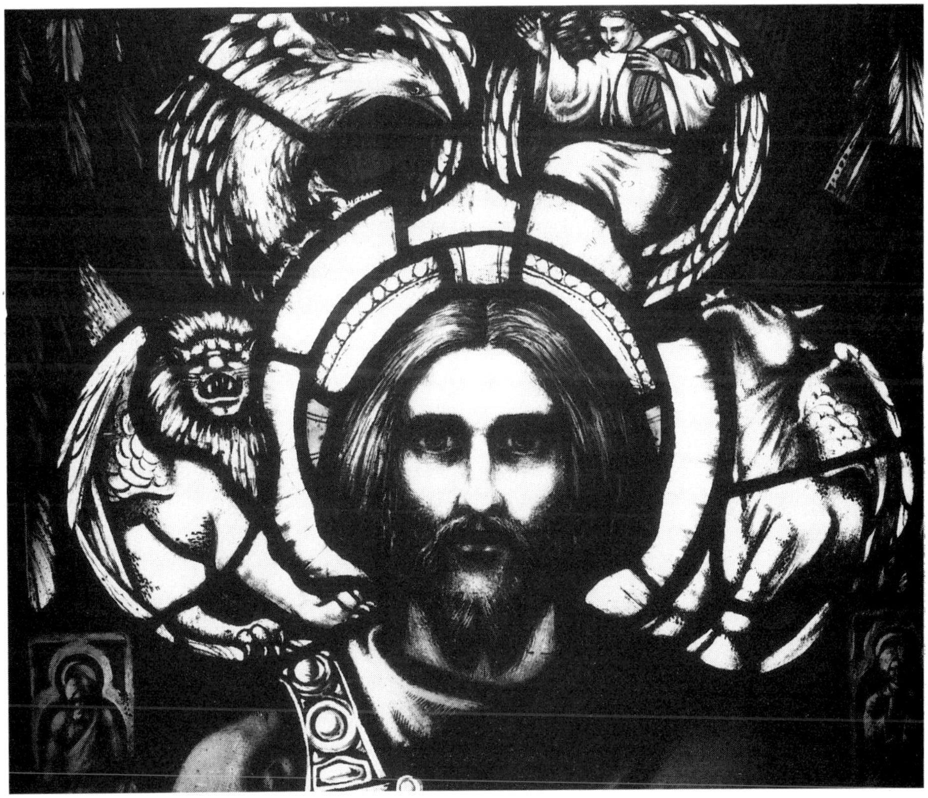

29 *The Godhead Enthroned* (detail), stained glass panel, 1911, Crawford Municipal Art Gallery, Cork

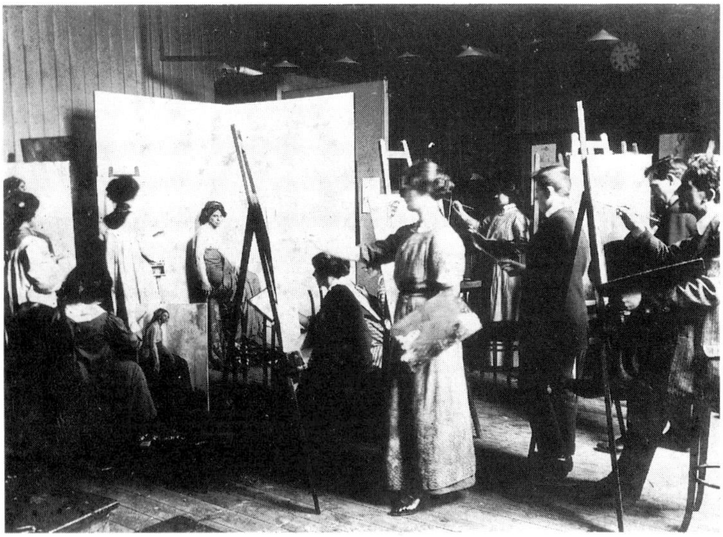

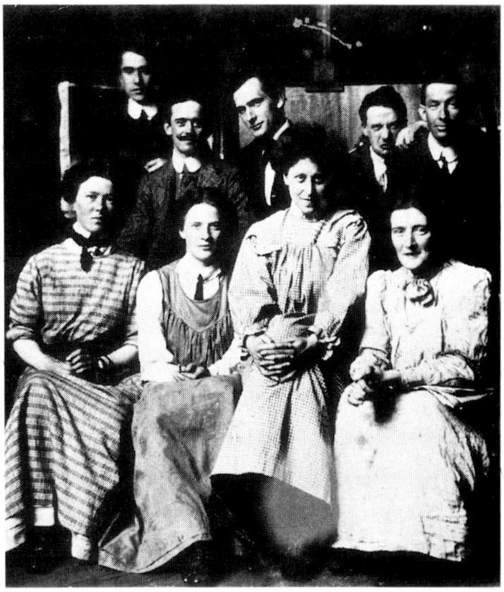

30 Photograph of Orpen's life class, Metropolitan School of Art, Dublin, *c.* 1911

31 Photograph of Harry Clarke (back row, far left), Margaret Crilley (front row, far right), and fellow students, Metropolitan School of Art, Dublin, *c.* 1911

shadowed by his sheer delight in the sinuous lines and tiny punctuated accents of his pencil. His scholarship was renewed on account of these successes (fig. 31). During 1912 work was beginning to come in fairly steadily to the Studios and, although Joshua had problems with Walter who was jealous of Harry's success and was not at all conscientious, he had electric lights installed in North Frederick Street and was sending albums of photographs and designs, many of them in colour, to prospective clients. He also appointed an agent to look for English work.

Harry submitted six pieces for the 1912 National Competition in South Kensington, which included the small coloured design for a stained glass window, the full-sized cartoon and a portion of the window made up. The judges' report reproduced a powerful coloured design skilfully composed, both in its strong leading, its softly glowing colours and its mysterious iconography. It shows a small inset quatrefoil with a moonlit Adoration of the Cross below a mosque-like temple from which water flows,[45] and small angels' heads with swirling hair, four helmeted archangels and a monumental early saint are bathed in brilliant rays. A panel above depicts a damsel pursued by a leering man on a charger. The panel executed in glass is more subdued and depicts the baptism of *St Patrick* (fig. 32). This is a development of Harry's *Consecration of St Mel* panel and features a series of strongly modelled heads, deep in meditation, in early Irish garb.[46] The full-length cartoon was reproduced in the examiner's report.

His six entries won Harry the only gold medal awarded to Ireland[47] that year for 'a fine imaginative design, which, however, would have been improved, had the drawing been more severe and searching'. The power and originality of his work was commented upon and, consequently, his scholarship at the School of Art once again renewed — for progress in stained glass design and craftsmanship. His father could scarcely contain his pride and felt the art of stained glass in Ireland was truly in the ascendant. Harry was also one of four students at the Art School to be awarded a £10 Taylor Art Prize from the Royal Dublin Society as well as being given an award for design and another for anatomy. Austin Molloy won the School prize for stained glass. That year, as in 1911, the two friends escaped for a month to Inishere.

Physically, Harry resembled his mother, who was tall, dark, and of a rather nervous, sensitive appearance. In photographs of this time he looks soulful, with large, shining black eyes, dark cropped hair and long, tapering fingers. His face was rather sallow and slightly marked from childhood illnesses: Joseph Hone was later to describe him as 'saturnine'. Harry was basically shy, despite his attractive nature and obvious gifts, and suffered from an inferiority complex, yet he was completely confident of his artistic potential. He greatly admired a fellow pupil, Margaret Crilley, principally because she had all the gifts which he knew he lacked, and because their different natures complemented each other. She was a Catholic from Newry and was short, with strong features, cropped brown hair, and steady steel-grey eyes (fig. 33). A quiet and self-possessed girl, she came to Dublin on a scholarship in 1905 and became one of Orpen's star pupils, winning medals and awards. Harry did a pencil portrait of her in 1907, when she had already qualified as a teacher, while he was still a student. Orpen greatly admired both her life drawing and her oil painting, whether figure, landscape or still life and also entertained a certain fondness for her. She acted as a model for several of his paintings, such as the *The Aran Islander* (fig. 34). The two men were reputed to have disliked each other for this reason, but it is more likely that Orpen thought most of Harry's work decorative and decadent. Through Harry, Margaret was commissioned by his father to paint a series of Gothic busts, and Joshua proudly referred to her as 'one of my artists'. She also exhibited a portrait of Harry's younger sister, Dolly, in the Royal Hibernian Academy exhibition in the spring of 1913.

In 1913, for the third time running, Harry's South Kensington entries won him a gold medallion for 'a remarkable original design, both as to the subject and treatment, admirably drawn and well carried out in glass. The colour is rich, sombre and of great beauty, while the very ingenious and beautiful arrangement of the leading makes a delightful pattern in itself'; this was the opinion of the judges, Walter Crane, Selwyn Image and Byam Shaw. They were referring to Harry's *Judas* window (plate 2), a long, thin, single- light leaded panel (48″ x 13¾″) in which his individual style

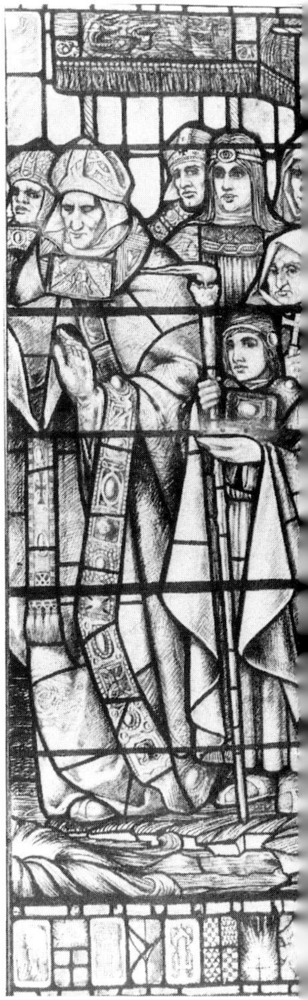

32 Cartoon for *The Baptism of St Patrick*, 1912; Clarke's panel, worked from the top section of this cartoon, was exhibited at the 1914 Louvre exhibition.

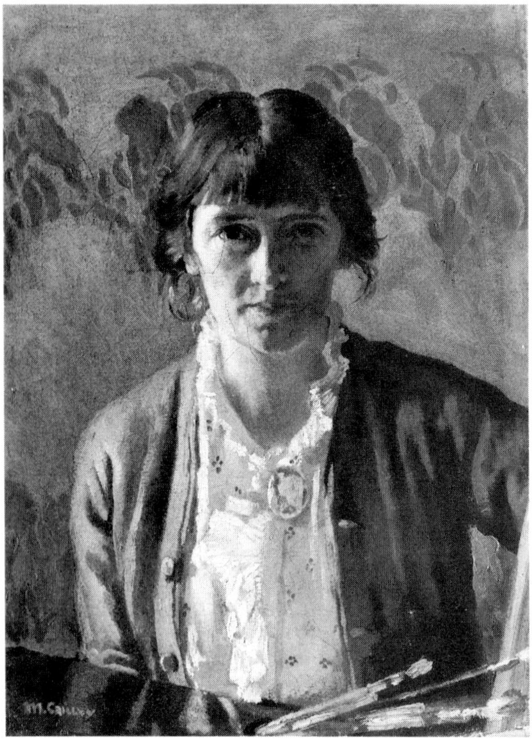

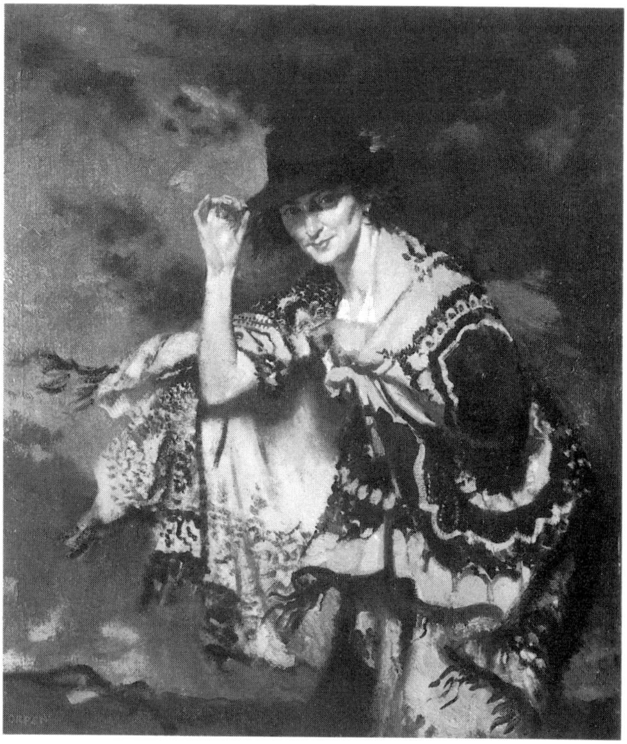

33 Margaret Crilley, *Self-portrait*, oil on canvas, 1914

34 William Orpen, *An Aran Islander*, one of several portraits by Orpen of Margaret Crilley (courtesy of Pyms Gallery, London)

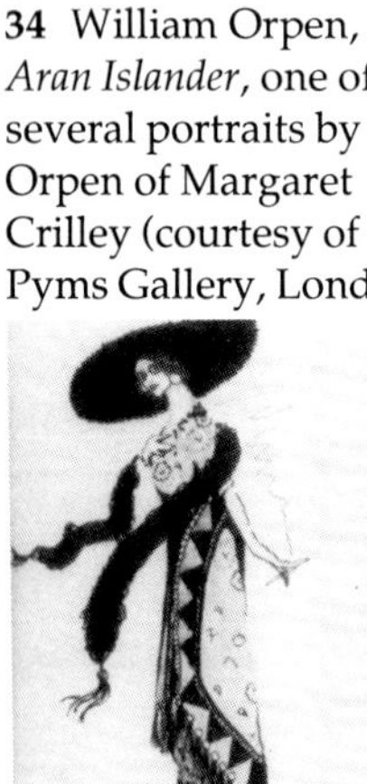

35 Fashion drawing in the Vienna Secession style, pen and ink, from Miss O'Sullivan's autograph book, October

is, for the first time, quite clearly manifested (fig. 36; plate 2). This window, in its decorative, iconographical and technical treatment is a direct precursor of the fine Honan Hostel series begun two years later. It is a marvel of intricacy. Leaded into Judas' symbolically yellow robe are the thirty pieces of silver, each bearing a minute image of Caesar's head. Although this window has never had to endure the ravages of time in an external position, it is remarkable how well it has survived. The narrow, intricate leads grip the tiny pieces of glass firmly, enhancing the overall design and the rich colours of the glass. The painting of the traitor's hypnotic features and the loose 'matted' brushwork on the glowing saffron yellow pieces which make up Judas' robe are particularly effective. It is interesting to note that one of M. Houvet's lumière plates[49] illustrates the thirteenth century *St Jacques* in Chartres Cathedral wearing a robe strewn with shells, just as Judas' is with the pieces of silver. In addition, the *St Jacques* has beading around his halo, a motif that Harry would often use and beneath the figure are four suspended orbs, such as Harry would subsequently adopt as Japanese-style roundels.

Harry also won a bronze medal at South Kensington for his designs for programme and book illustration. Among the latter may have been his undated and unpublished *Paganini*[50] illustration in pen and ink. In this the tall, cowled, barefooted fiddler has distinctive features similar to those of St Patrick in Harry's 1912 *Baptism of St Patrick* panel, as well as the small galactic explosions of his *Silver Apples of the Moon* (*c*. 1913; fig. 37). These drawings reflect the strength of his glass work of the time, without the black and white decadence of some of his early pen and ink drawings where Beardsley's influence is predominant.

Harry's scholarship was renewed and he was also awarded school prizes for designs 'adapted to technical requirements of various materials'. These designs probably included a poster he designed as a competition entry for a bazaar held at the Royal Dublin Society in 1913, *The Watchman of Ovada*, in strong blocks of black, viridian and yellow on buff with sweeping Jugendstil lines and lettering, interspersed with stylised roses. Other school prizes were for stained glass and for painting Irish historical figure subjects.

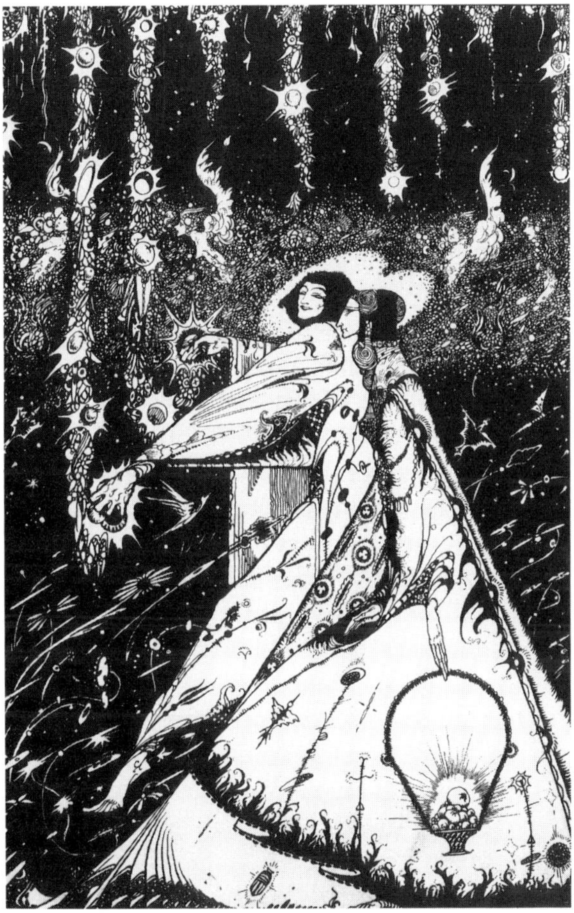

37 'The Silver Apples of the Moon, the Golden Apples of the Sun', pen and ink, 1913

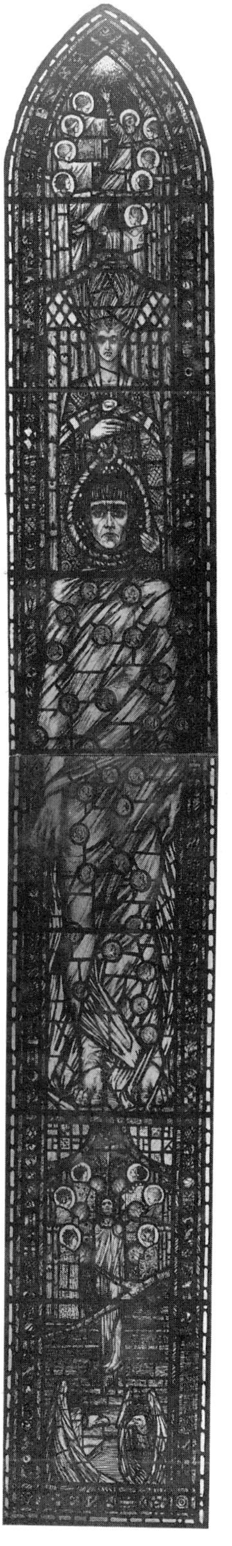

36 Contemporary photograph by Harry Clarke of the cartoon for his *Judas* window, 1913.The verso carries these notes in Clarke's hand: *'National Competition 1913* / Subject Judas Iscariot / Top panel. Judas received in heaven through the prayer of angels / At base of window. Judas martyrs himself. / Central figure Judas — behind him the angel of death holds the rope which forms his nimbus. The figure is diapered with the 30 pieces of silver.' The treatment of the thirty pieces of silver leaded into Judas' robe was inspired by that of the shells in the thirteenth-century *St Jacques* window in Chartres Cathedral.

2

First commissioned book illustrations — Laurence Waldron, patron — Studies of medieval glass in France and England — Marriage to Margaret Crilley — First major stained glass commission

Once again, in the summer of 1913, Harry went to Inishere with Austin Molloy. While they were there, Harry's *The Baptism of St Patrick* was awarded first prize in the annual Art Industries Exhibition held at the Royal Dublin Society in Ballsbridge in conjunction with the Horse Show. All three of Harry's entries had also been National Competition prizewinners, the other two being *The Godhead and St John* and the *Judas* panel, and were generally judged to show 'excellent design' and 'an artistic, spirited production'.[1] In addition, he received the first prize for a design for a stained glass window, Sarah Purser's studio being the second prize winner in this category.

While on Inishere, Harry sent a card to Sir Robert Woods, the eminent ear, nose and throat specialist. The drawing on it is particularly interesting as it is the first dated black and white illustration to show the manifest influence of Beardsley in Harry's work. It depicts three figures, cloaked and hatted, one with elfin ears, the other carrying a fish by the tail, with a veiled lady between them. Harry wrote on the other side, 'This is a very primitive place but very charming for a rest holiday. Will call and see you when I go back to town. I trust then you will have time for me. . .'.[2]

There are some other interesting black and white drawings dated 1913 and each revealing slightly different treatments evoking Beardsley's influence and that of the Wiener Werkstatte. There is only one extant pen and ink illustration, of the possessed figure of *Paganini,* which avoids such influences and whose powerful central figure is akin to St Patrick in the 1912 *Baptism* panel and anticipates the cymballing king and supernatural setting depicted in the 1913 *Silver Apples* illustration.

On a page in the autograph book of his fellow student and stained glass artist, Wilhelmina Geddes (1887-1955) he drew the unmistakable profile of their colleague Ethel Rhind as Salome — tall and willowy, in exotic garb. She is victoriously holding out the head of St John the Baptist, while three leering bumpkins gaze behind her, and beneath a siren with a huge naked nipple claws the hair of a befuddled gypsy.[3] Among other small heavily inked figures from this period are a profile drawing of a fat lady on a card, and another of a pregnant lady in profile, wearing only a corset.[4]

Also from 1913 are three fine black and white drawings, each drawn in a different manner, but all seemingly illustrations for W.B. Yeats's 'The Song of Wandering Aengus'.[5] The first, entitled *The Silver Apples of the Moon, the Golden Apples of the Sun,* is signed 'HC' and undated, but it must have been completed by June 1913, as it was reproduced in the *Irish Review* as the frontispiece to its July 1913 issue (fig. 37). The unearthly figures of a king and queen in this illustration are the precursors of the merman and mermaid in Clarke's later illustrated panel of Heine's *A Meeting*. They proceed through a fantastic landscape of whorling phosphorescence, perhaps below the sea or in outer space. Apart from the shining fruit suspended around them, the illustration would appear to have less reference to Yeats' poem than to a poem by Æ, 'The City', published in the same issue of the *Review*.[6]

The second illustration is signed Harry Clarke 1913 in the early *Rape of the Lock* and *Ancient Mariner* manner, on its surrounding mount. It was exhibited in the 85th Royal Hibernian Academy exhibition in 1914 entitled *A Decorative Fisherman* and was later known by its first owner as *The Little Silver Fish*. The composition, the stylized river banks, the spare, taut anatomy and strange langour of the Japonnist Aengus are strongly reminiscent of Beardsley's *Siegfried* (1892/3), a reproduction of which Harry would certainly have seen in *The Studio*.[7] It was later reproduced in *A Second Book of Drawings*, published by Smithers in 1899 and again in Marillier's *Early Work of Beardsley*. The treatment of the landscape and principal figure in Clarke's composition also recalls Beardsley's frontispiece to the first volume of Malory's *Le Morte d'Arthur* (1893).

The third illustration is inscribed 'The Song of Wandering Aengus' and is signed and dated in the same manner. Here, the errant Aengus is dressed as a Japanese youth in a long robe, regarding a gold moth metamorphosized into a sylph-like, grinning, garlanded damsel. The black ink is touched with gold and pale rose, and the composition is well-balanced, though still in the Beardsley style. It is probably this illustration which was exhibited in the 1915 Royal Hibernian Academy exhibition.[8] It is regrettable that Harry illustrated so little of Yeats' work, particularly in view of the symbolist nature of both men's imaginations.[9]

As Harry's course at the Metropolitan School of Art was finished, he went to London to 'finish his studies' after he returned from Aran. Joshua was worried as he felt sure that Harry would 'never get along in London by himself for some time.... However, it is experience for him and he would not be satisfied unless he went . . .'.[10] In London Harry took a studio at 6 Balcombe Street and stayed with cousins in Upper Gloucester Place, off Dorset Square in Paddington while he was waiting to hear if he had been awarded a scholarship to the Royal College of Art in Kensington, or a travelling scholarship to study on the continent.

The Belvederian, the magazine of Harry's old school, reported diligently on his development from 1912 onwards. His lack of academic and athletic prowess was compensated for by the fact that he was 'advancing steadily in the art world'.[11] His unique success in being the only Irish stained glass designer ever to be awarded a gold medal, let alone three, in the National Competition was reported with justifiable pride. Several old Belvederians, too, were to be extremely helpful to Harry's career, principally Laurence ('Larky') Ambrose Waldron, solicitor John Robert O'Connell, the barrister and art connoisseur Thomas Bodkin, and several Jesuit patrons.

'Larky' Waldron, a governor of Belvedere College, had taken a special interest in Harry Clarke since the summer of 1912. He became Harry's first patron and remained his patron until he died in December 1923. Born in 1858 of a landed Tipperary family, Waldron became a member of the Dublin Stock Exchange in 1881. In the remaining four decades of his life he accumulated considerable wealth and a notorious reputation for lavish entertaining at his sumptuously furnished and book-lined house overlooking Killiney Bay. His guests at dinner included the cream of the artistic, legal and literary world of the time. 'A lucky person might have met Mahaffey, T.M. Kettle and Hugh Lane at one of his dinners, for he was a connoisseur in talk even more than in pictures, books or wine', wrote his obituarist.[12] Walter Starkie described how 'the beloved portly Maecenas of Dublin'[13] would stagger on foot into Dublin behind his chauffeur-driven Delaunay-Belville, his corpulent dog perched encouragingly on the back seat. Gogarty graphically evoked his hospitality[14] and love of quotations, while Enid Starkie was more struck by his 'enormous white bulk' sighted at a men-only bathing party.[15]

The young Harry must have been amazed and amused — not to say educated — at these gatherings. He was attractive, intelligent, well-read and quick to learn. While he was originally patronised by Waldron they soon became firm friends. Although he was shy at first in company, Harry became a popular and witty conversationalist, a regular favourite of Waldron's friends and eventually one of Larky's inner circle.[16] Joshua Clarke could not begin to understand such a milieu but presumably felt (rightly) that Mr Waldron would help Harry.

In the first half of 1913 Waldron commissioned Harry to do a set of six illustrations for Alexander's Pope's *The Rape of the Lock*. A comparison with Beardsley's nine illustrations 'embroidering' Pope's poem[17] is inevitable, and may even have been intentional (figs. 38 and 39). Harry's six illustrations are executed in pen and ink, with the initial pencil sketches clearly visible beneath. There are witty pencil caricatures on the back of each drawing which are more original and less derivative than the illustrations themselves. Not only do Clarke's six illustrations depict incidents also drawn by Beardsley[18] but he adopts many of Beardsley's pen and ink idioms — squares of cross hatching, dotted 'ersatz eighteenth century'[19] rococo work, and parallel lines to suggest graining and other textures, as well as myriad tiny spirals. Compared with Beardsley's drawings Harry

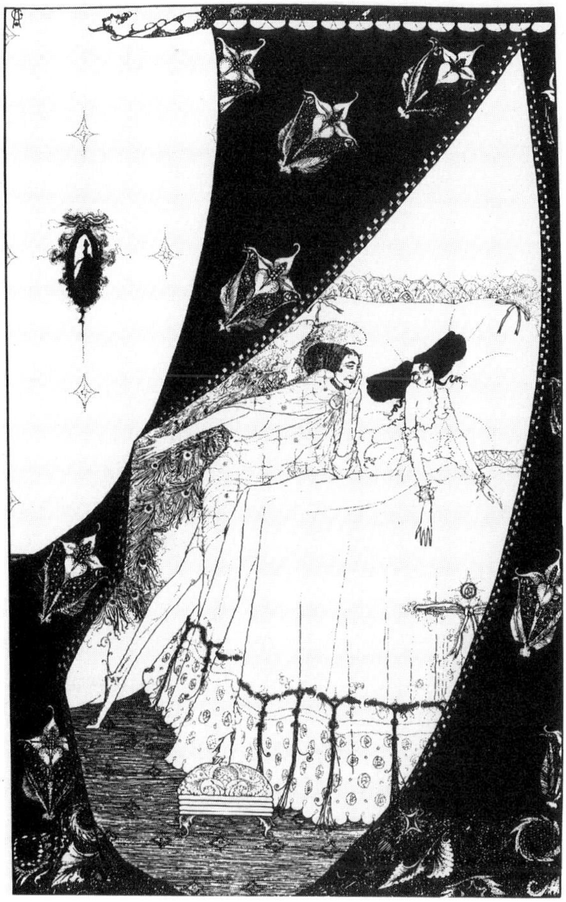

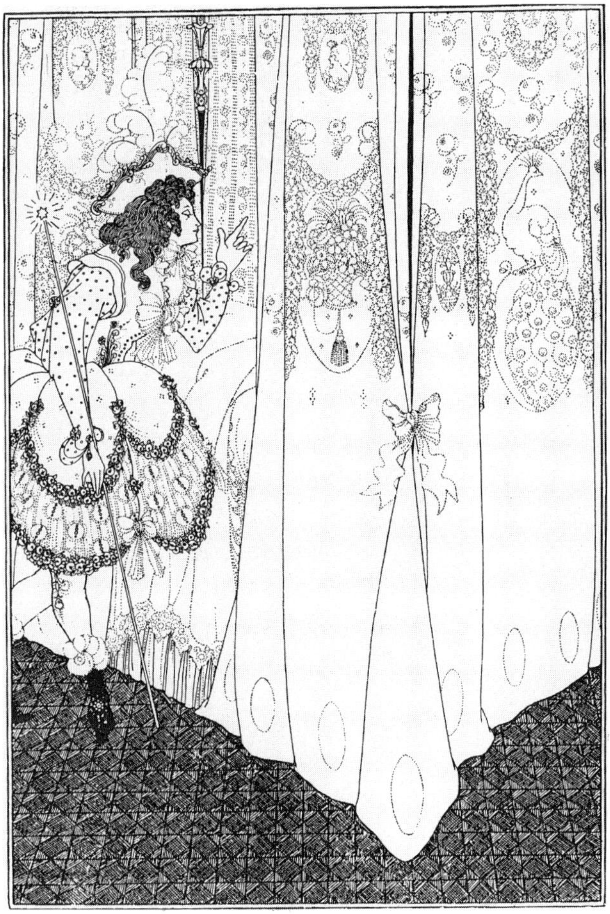

Clarke's appear fussy, effete and insubstantial: the puppet-like characters are feverish and wraith-like. Only in 'The Cave of Spleen' drawing, where he applied his powers of imagination to the shades of darkness, evil and boredom does his pen become spirited and convincing.[20]

38 'The Dream', opening illustration to Pope's *The Rape of the Lock*, pen and ink, 1913; cf. fig. 4.

39 Aubrey Beardsley, 'The Dream', opening illustration to *The Rape of the Lock* (1896)

It was at Waldron's Killiney house that Harry met most of his future patrons. Through Joseph M. Hone Harry was introduced to the publishers Maunsel & Co., for whom he produced a series of black and white full-page illustrations for *The Rime of the Ancient Mariner* by Samuel Taylor Coleridge.[21] These illustrations are much more mature and effective than those for *The Rape of the Lock*. Stylistically, they are strongly vertical and reminiscent of Klimt in that the expressive features and hands of the protagonists dominate their flat but sumptuously decorative attire. They rely for their effect on contrasted often intricately worked areas of black and white and on the haunted faces of the Mariner and the characters he encounters. The second and seventh in the series[22] were drawn two years later and much more than the previous six express an almost physical terror, heralding Clarke's later horrific illustrations to Poe (figs. 40 and 41). His imagination seems very much in tune with Coleridge's as he depicts the hypnotic gaze of the accursed 'bright-eyed Mariner'[23] as the dreadful penalty for his killing of the albatross unfolds. There is an element of self-portraiture in the Mariner's features, which also seem to bear a strong resemblance to those of *Richard II holding the Red Rose of Lancaster*, as painted by Norman Wilkinson (*c.* 1895).[24] This haunted face with huge staring eyes and the wheeling astral bodies behind would become recurrent features of Harry's work; it is also interesting to find him already stylizing fingers and toes.

In the last *Ancient Mariner* illustration the Hermit's robe bears a huge patchwork butterfly, a Beardsleyesque motif often used by Clarke in these early years, as are the cliffs and tiny white ripples in the black sea behind. All eight *Ancient Mariner* drawings were acquired by Sir Robert Woods, a contemporary and friend of Waldron's, and a knowledgeable collector and connoisseur in the best Dublin professional tradition. He became an admirer and friend of Harry's. He was a talented sculptor himself and made beautiful little wax heads of many an eminent Dublin friend; his wife, for whom Harry designed a bookplate the following year, made rugs and carpets.

In the first week of November 1913, partly due to Waldron's efforts on his behalf, the Department of Agriculture and Technical Instruction awarded Harry a special scholarship to travel on the continent for a few months. He planned to take this up after Christmas, but meanwhile he was trying to get work in London to supplement the bursary. Joshua went over to visit him in November, and they 'had a really good time . . . visiting most of the principal theatres, Music Halls and Restaurants'.[25] Father and son also made a special trip to Hetley's to choose glass and were particularly interested in the streaky ruby they saw there.

A week before Christmas Harry gave up the London studio, which his father felt he would not require again for at least twelve months. He returned to Dublin and made Joshua immensely proud as he brought back with him a commission for 200 guineas to illustrate the *Fairy Tales* of Hans Christian Andersen for the London publishers, George G. Harrap & Co. Clarke had unsuccessfully shown his portfolio to twelve London publishers before he visited George Harrap as his last attempt. Harrap recalled, 'But for me, so he said, he would probably have abandoned the idea of illustrating books. . . . It is not often that a first book by an unknown and untried author is given the distinction [of being issued as a signed limited edition].'[26] There can be little doubt that Harrap's decision to publish such an illustrated edition was influenced by the enormous success of Edmund Dulac's colour plate illustrations and decorations to an edition of *Stories from Hans Andersen*, published by Hodder and Stoughton in 1911 (figs. 42 and 43),[27] as well as the first English publication (by the same publishers) in 1912 of illustrations by the young Danish artist Kay Nielsen (1886-1957) to *In Powder and Crinoline, Old Fairy Tales*, retold by Sir Arthur Quiller-

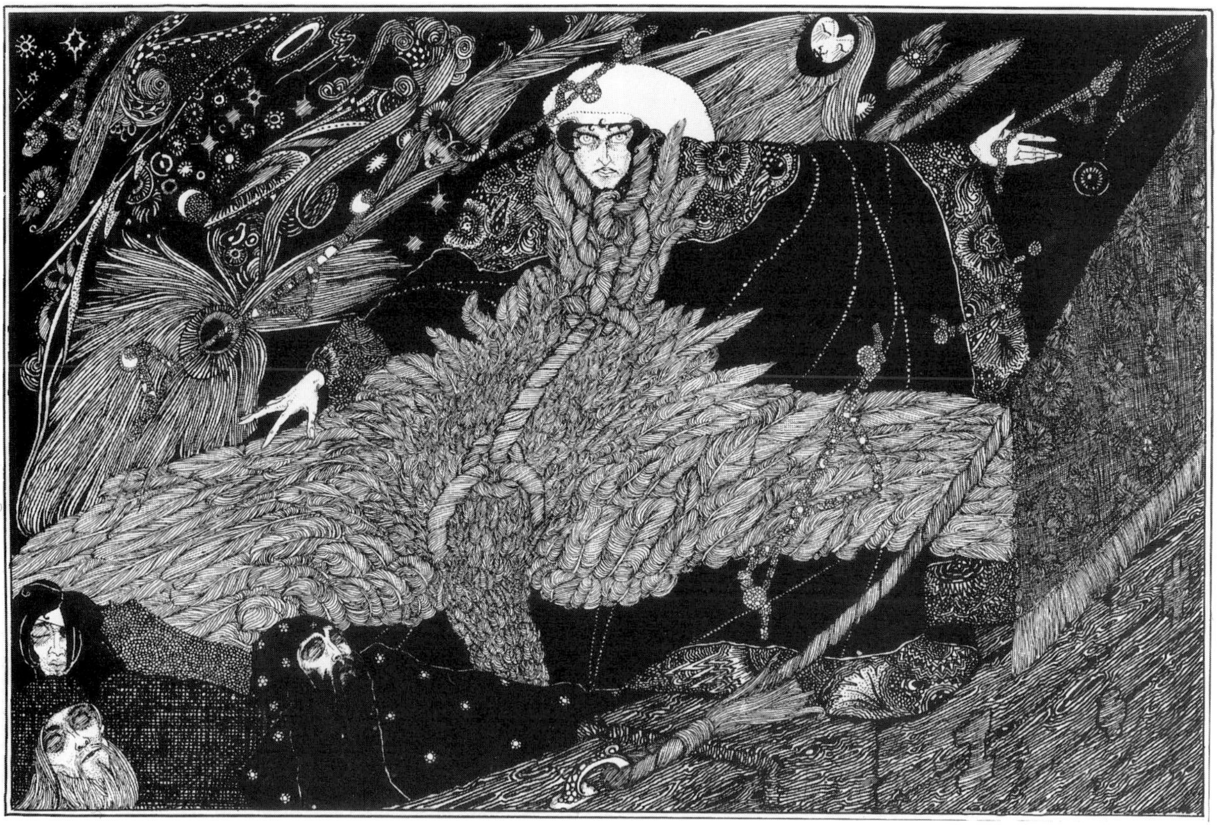

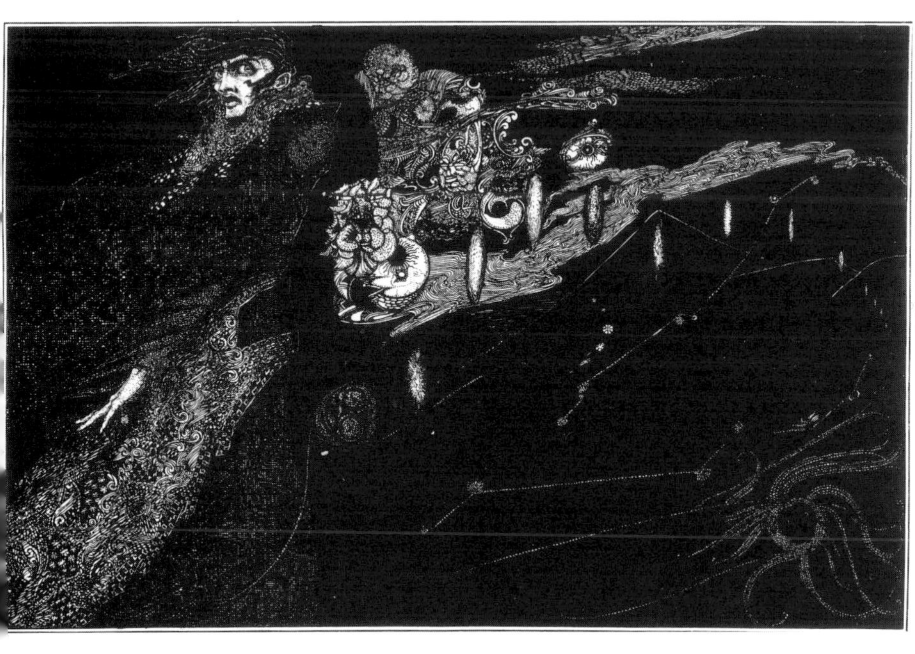

40 'The souls did from their bodies fly', illustration to Coleridge's *The Rime of the Ancient Mariner*, pen and ink, 1913; when reproduced in *Modern Book Illustrators and their Work* (1914), this illustration proved influential.

41 'Like one that on a lonesome road / Doth walk in fear and dread', illustration to *The Rime of the Ancient Mariner*, pen and ink, 1915; one of Clarke's two later illustrations to Coleridge's poem

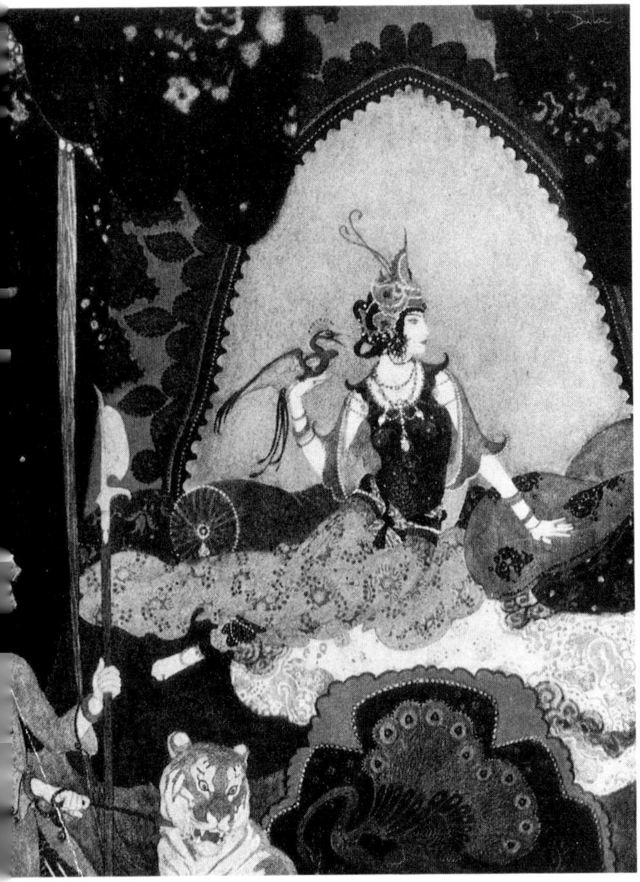

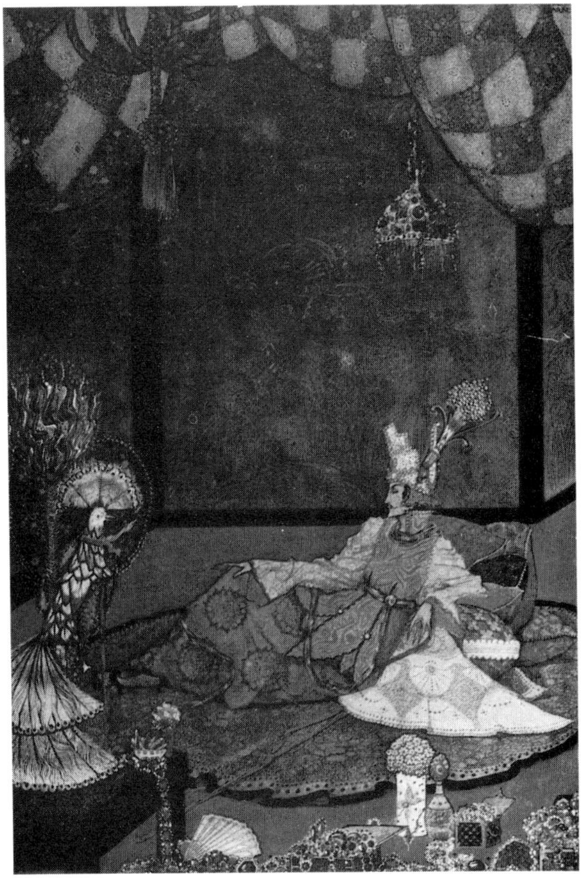

42 Edmund Dulac, illustration to 'Laylá and Majnún, A Persian Love Story', originally published in *Vanity Fair*, then in *Edmund Dulac's Picture Book for the French Red Cross* (1915)

43 'The Nightingale', illustration from *Hans Andersen's Fairy Tales*, watercolour and ink, 1916; this shows Clarke's debt to Dulac.

Couch (fig. 44). In 1914 Hodder and Stoughton published Nielsen's 'vigorously patterned',[28] exotically costumed illustrations to *East of the Sun, West of the Moon* by P.C. Asbjørnsen and Jorgen Möe. In these drawings the influences of oriental miniatures, Japanese prints, Beardsley, the Ballet Russes and Norse imagery are all to be found. There are marked similarities between Nielsen's illustrations of this period and Harry's subsequent Hans Andersen designs, not only in their similar treatment of unworldly marionette-like figures whose gestures seem motivated by a supernatural power, but also in the decorative treatment of costume, landscape, ornament, pattern and pictorial space. It was probably these very similarities in respective Slav and Celtic treatments that appealed to George Harrap. He had recently 'discovered' Willy Pogany as a competitor to Dulac; Harry Clarke was to be the answer to Nielsen.

On 13 January 1914 Harry left Dublin for Paris to begin his continental tour, intending to work on the Hans Andersen drawings during his trip. He stopped off at Hetley's in London with some designs that he wanted Mr Salmond to have executed in glass for him as a special favour. These were for four small stained glass panels (7″ x 5½″ each) to fit into a lantern for

Larky Waldron. Presumably Harry felt that no one in Ireland could make them sufficiently well. One panel shows the Waldron arms ornately embellished, another a swag of shamrocks, small brown and gold chequers and a sun with rays bursting out, and each of the other two a stylized thistle on a bed of fish scales, with a background of wriggly lines.[29] Whoever Hetley's found to execute the panels did not do a very good job, despite the carefully finished drawings given to them.

Harry arrived in Paris on 20 January and spent the following Sunday at Chartres Cathedral. He was fortunate to visit Chartres during M. Etienne Houvet's guardianship of the cathedral as he was permitted to climb up scaffolding to examine some of the glass closely.[30] Not only did Houvet write extensively on French medieval and Gothic architecture[31] but he also made an extensive series of innovatory lumière plates of the stained glass, which were the only available means at the time of recording the windows in colour — hence the scaffolding. Harry was to learn much from this visit, principally the importance in stained glass of a rich depth in colour that Ruskin called 'the glow of controlled fire'; the juxtaposition of one colour against another so that the eye of the onlooker would mix and harmonise them; and the importance of clear, sinuous brush strokes and 'matting' with clear highlights, which would give further depth to the glass and control the light playing through its surface. He also saw the use of decorative borders, often filled with rows of small painted beads or long rectangles to further break up the light, as part of the design of each panel, and the need for a clearly legible iconography and dramatically portrayed figures with powerful facial expressions.[32]

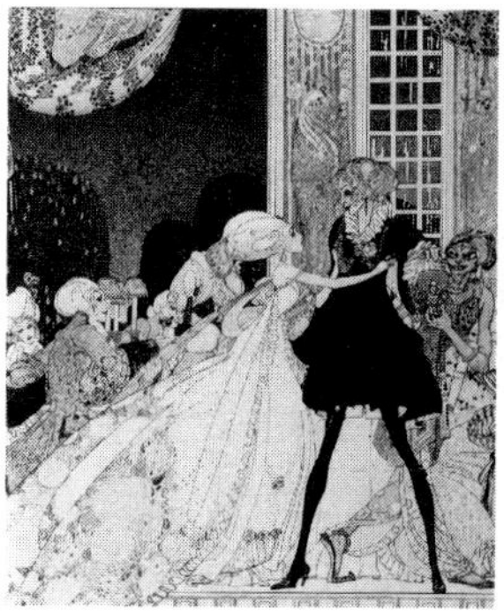

44 Kay Nielsen, illustration to 'The Twelve Dancing Princesses' from A. Quiller-Couch, *In Powder and Crinoline* (1913); Nielsen greatly influenced Clarke's *Hans Andersen* illustrations (1916).

Perhaps it was from the famous window, *La Belle Verrière*, that he became aware of the medieval convention of varying the scale of the figures according to their importance (fig. 45); he certainly used the unusual seated, enthroned position of the Madonna for his *St Albert* window (1915) in the Honan Chapel series, as well as figures of small attendant thurible-swinging angels in a number of subsequent designs such as his window at Sturminster Newton (1920). But one of the most important lessons that he learned at this time was to enhance each piece of glass by the lead line which surrounded it,[33] although his *Judas* panel (1913) — made before he went to France — shows that he had already begun to make use of this vital element, which he would have studied from reproductions of medieval glass or the actual examples in the Victoria and Albert Museum.

Harry could not stand the severely cold weather in France, he caught a bad chill, he could not eat the food or speak the language and was altogether so miserable, despite his visit to Chartres, that he decided to retreat to London. He arrived back in England at the home of his friend Karl Parsons[34] after being only ten days away. Harry had met Parsons earlier in 1913 through Joseph Nuttgens at the Harrow studio of Arthur Orr. Nuttgens had been with Mr Orr since he was sixteen and was then studying

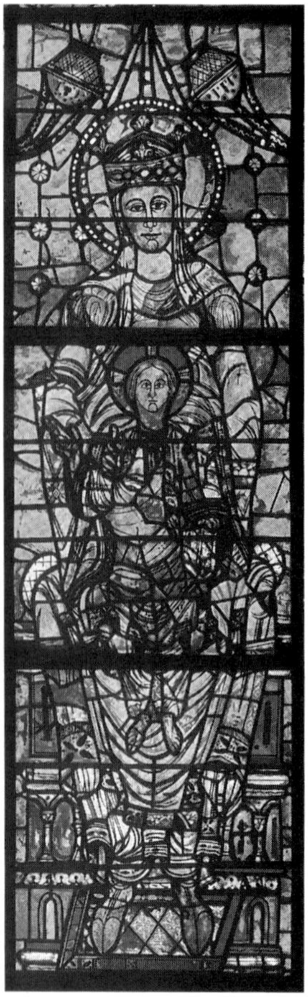

45 *Notre Dame de La Belle Verrière* (detail), stained glass window in Chartres Cathedral, twelfth century; one of the medieval windows which Clarke studied and which altered the course of his Whall-based attitude to stained glass

under Parsons at the Central School.[35] Karl Parsons was five years Harry's senior, and the two men remained close friends until Harry's death. As well as being an extremely competent designer and excellent draughtsman (frontispiece), Parsons was a keen believer in the integrity of artists and craftsmen, a belief which he instilled in Harry. Through Parsons and his wife Bunny, Harry met other stained glass workers such as Edward Woore, poets such as W.H. Davies, and musicians. Harry felt happy and comfortable at the Parsons' home and, once he had been nursed back to health, he took a room in their house as their paying guest, an arrangement financed by the Harrap commission.

From the Parsons' Harry wrote to the Department of Agriculture and Technical Instruction in Dublin requesting permission to postpone his scholarship until the summer, when the weather would be milder. He commenced work on his first black and white illustration to Hans Andersen's fairy tale 'The Emperor's New Clothes'. He worked solidly at his Harrap illustrations and on 4 February sent off *The Emperor's New Clothes* and *What the Moon Saw*.[36] The next day he worked from 10.30 a.m. to 7.00 p.m. on his first (published) colour illustrations to 'The Swineherd'. He worked the same long hours every day for four and a half days (Sunday included) until he had finished the illustrations, and then spent another four and a half days working on 'The Tin Soldier'. On 13 February Margaret Crilley arrived in London, and his schedule was interrupted as they explored London together, including a visit to the National Gallery, and a social call on William Orpen.

When Margaret returned to Dublin, Harry resumed his strict routine, working on 'The Swineherd' and 'The Mermaid'.[37] On 25 February he sent off the last designs of the first completed batch and received a cheque from Harrap's for £25, which he immediately lodged in Karl Parsons' account. He allowed himself no respite and set to work at once drafting 'The Wild Swans' and 'The Tinder Box'. He usually worked at the illustrations in pairs, to avoid becoming 'stale'. Occasionally, he met his cousin Beatrice, or Arthur Orr's son Murren, visited galleries, Hetley's and Whall's, or attended Hugo's life studio in Oxford Street. However, his life revolved around the illustrations for Harraps, not least because he was very poor and Harrap's payments were his sole means of subsistence.

In the middle of March, shortly after he had illustrated 'The Garden of Paradise' and 'The Nightingale', he sent two coloured designs to his father to be sent to Oswald Reeves as part of his submission for the Exhibition of Decorative Arts of Great Britain and Ireland, organized by the British Government, to be held in the Louvre from April to October 1914.

Harry's diary reveals that already, on his twenty-fifth birthday, 17 March 1914, he was reading Edgar Allan Poe's *Tales of Mystery and Imagination* with a view to illustrating them. His earlier treatment of Oscar Wilde's *De Profundis* (plate 11) had demonstrated his singular aptitude for these haunted stories. While he was still working on 'The Nightingale' and 'The Little Mermaid' for Harraps, an interview with Duckworth's, the publishers, resulted in his spending three days illustrating Poe's gruesome tale, 'The Facts in the Case of M. Valdémar'. When he had completed this he resumed work on 'The Emperor's New Clothes', and 'The Tinder Box'. He also visited another publisher, William Heinemann, and drafted illustrations for further Poe tales — 'The Fall of the House of Usher' and 'The Tell-Tale Heart' (for later coloured versions cf. plates 33 and 34).

He decided to go home for Easter and on his way back visited Bath, Salisbury, Lacock and Fairford, where he was greatly impressed both technically and iconographically by the great fifteenth-century seven-light *Last Judgment* west window in the church of St Mary. When he reached Dublin he found that his prize-winning stained glass panel, *The Baptism of St Patrick*, had been selected for the Louvre exhibition to appear in distinguished company there, beside the stained glass of Douglas Strachan, Anning Bell, his colleague Wilhelmina Geddes, and Karl Parsons.

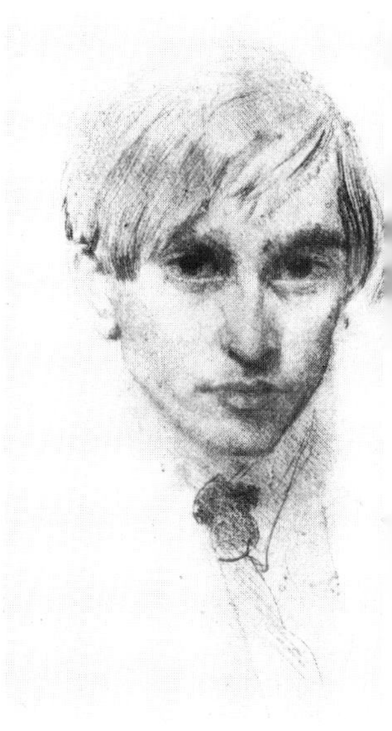

46 Margaret Crilley, portrait sketch of Harry Clarke, pencil, 1914; drawn shortly before her marriage to Clarke and given to his sister Florence

When Harry returned home he found that Joshua's main interest lay in the acquisition of 'a rather pretty place' in Shankill, a cottage on the coast in south Co. Dublin. He felt it was 'an ideal spot, just the sort of thing we should all be very happy in'.[38] He very much wanted Harry's approval on it before the purchase went ahead.

During Easter week in Ireland Harry visited Larky Waldron and other friends, such as Lady Woods and Miss Jane French, for whom he made a stained glass panel bearing a flamboyant heraldic device painted in enamel and stain. Although he was ostensibly on holiday, his diary entries include daily notes to read particular issues of contemporary magazines on decorative art, especially German periodicals like *Deutsche Kunst und Dekoration* and *Innen-Dekoration*.[39] Throughout his life he was a voracious reader, always seeking material to stimulate his imagination. He also enjoyed the theatre, music and cinema.

He returned to London, once more as the Parsons' paying guest, and resumed his life classes at Hugo's in Oxford Street and work on the Harrap illustrations. He began with 'The Butterfly' and 'The Ugly Duckling'. He delivered these to George Harrap, together with 'M. Valdémar', the Poe illustration which Duckworths had presumably returned. He seems to have been working on further black and white illustrations to Poe and was negotiating a fee of 100 guineas for the entire Poe set with both Harrap's and Duckworth's. The first half of May was taken up with these negotiations, illustrating 'The Old House', 'What the Old Man Does' and 'The Garden of Paradise' and attending Hugo's studio every few days. When these drawings were delivered on 14 May he received another cheque for £25 from Harrap. On the same day he wrote to Dublin, asking that his scholarship be renewed from that day. He left for Paris on 19 May.

In Paris Harry, probably with an introduction from Parsons, contacted

Jessie M. King (1878-1979) and her husband E.A. Taylor (1874-1952),[40] the Glasgow artists whose Shealing Atelier of Fine Art was renowned as a meeting place for young artist-craftsmen and women. Here, between 1911 and 1915 at 16 rue de la Grande Chaumière, they both taught and worked at book illustration, batik, watercolours, china paintings and designing of all kinds. Harry would certainly have known Jessie King's book illustrations (fig. 47); these had been widely published and her work had been featured in *The Studio* from 1898 onwards. There are a number of parallels between the work, interests and lifestyles of the Taylors and of Harry and his subsequent wife. Both couples spent their honeymoons on their respective country's western islands; both loved the native crafts of their lands. The Taylors collected Yeats' books and had volumes by Lady Gregory, James Stephens, Frank Harris, and Padraic Colum.[41] They also had a large collection of the British and European decorative arts magazines Harry so much enjoyed. Jessie King designed invitation cards, catalogue covers, posters, bookplates, greeting cards, booklets and textiles as well as her book illustrations. Taylor worked at stained glass in Glasgow, Manchester and London with George Wragge and in Paris with George Rhind. His conviction that 'the success of modern stained glass in a domestic environment depended on the versatile inventive faculty of the designer' and his own romantic panels would have disposed him well towards Harry.[42]

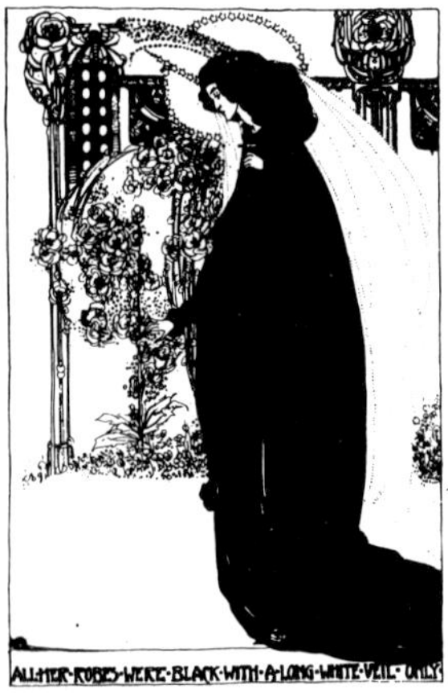

47 Jessie M. King, 'All her robes were black ....', illustration from William Morris, *The Defence of Guenevere* (1904); both Jessie King and her husband E.A. Taylor were good friends and early supporters of Clarke and influenced his work.

Taylor was the Paris correspondent of *The Studio*, which probably accounts for the publication of two of Harry's *Ancient Mariner* illustrations in its special autumn 1914 number *Modern Book Illustrators and their Work*.[43] Other illustrators represented in this issue included Phil May, Kate

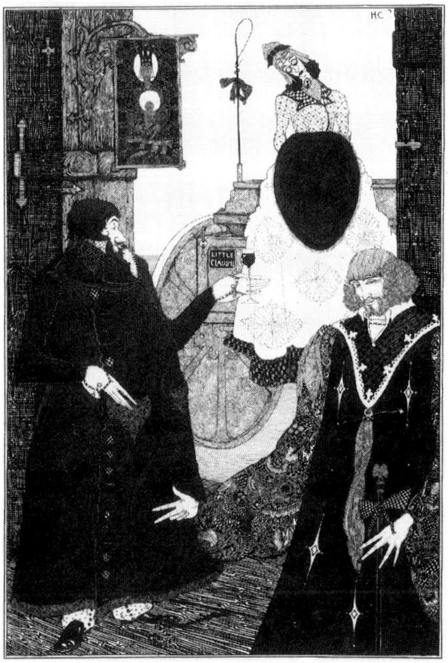

48 'Great Claus and Little Claus', unpublished illustration to Hans Andersen's *Fairy Tales*, pen and ink and watercolour, 1914 (courtesy of Sotheby's)

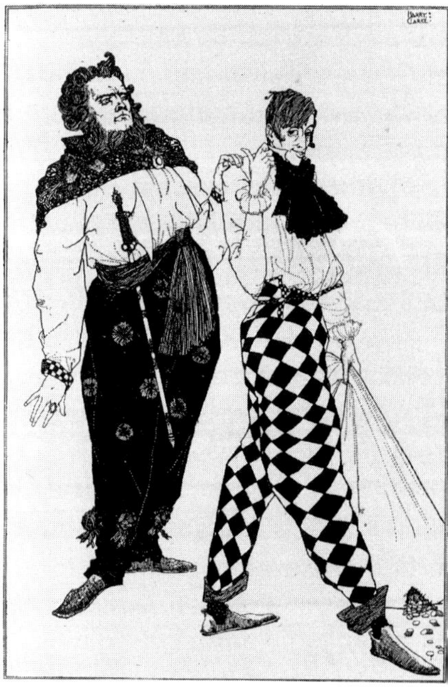

49 'Great Claus and Little Claus', illustration from Hans Andersen's *Fairy Tales* (1916); a self-portrait of the artist with Victor Wood

Greenaway, Walter Crane, Beardsley, William Morris, Burne-Jones, Heath Robinson, Hugh Thomson, Jack B. Yeats, Edmund Dulac, Arthur Rackham, T. Sturge Moore and Charles Ricketts. Interestingly, only Harry's illustrations and those by Jessie King are finely reproduced on thin creamy paper. This publication marks the beginning of Harry Clarke's long association with *The Studio*.

He settled in Paris at the Hotel Windsor in the rue de S. Petersburgh and immediately resumed work on his Harrap illustrations. The first drawing he made was one of the black and white illustrations depicting the treacheries of 'Great Claus and Little Claus' (figs. 48-50), which included a witty selfportrait, showing himself in a chequered harlequin pantaloon suit, and a semi-caricature of his friend, Victor Wood, the hefty, rugby-playing son of Albert Wood, KC, another friend of Waldron's and a future patron.

Joshua joined him at his hotel in Paris for the Whit weekend. The two of them visited Versailles, Saint Cloud and Chartres and generally had 'a real good time'. Joshua had hoped to bring with him his old friend from Glasgow, John Duthie, his paint supplier, especially because Duthie wanted Harry to design a picture for his firm's annual calendar, a commission which Joshua was carefully negotiating for his son. When Duthie eventually decided he could not travel to Paris, a long correspondence began over the calendar.

When Harry had completed *The Little Match Girl* he wrote to Harraps for another £25 instalment, which was duly sent. He then took some time off to visit places in Paris, such as the Panthéon, the Madeleine and the Beaux Arts. It must have been a special pleasure for him to go to the Louvre and see his own work on exhibition there. However, much of his time was spent studying and copying the stained glass in a hidden locked room within the old Trocadéro Museum on the Colline de Chaillot with its comprehensive collection of French stained glass windows and fragments, a 'superb introduction to the sturdy anatomy of the ancient craft' (fig. 51).[44] He made fluidly watercolour studies of several of the many stained glass fragments he had copied there, such as a late twelfth century lunette of *The Money Changers* and a twelfth century fragment from Châlons-sur-Marne, *The New Law and the Old Law*.

He also visited the Cluny Museum, which had an 'excellent collection of legendary medallions, some said to be the original glass from the Sainte Chapelle'.[45] He would naturally have visited the cathedral of Notre Dame and the Sainte Chapelle, 'the jewel box of France',[46] the walls of whose upper chapel are almost entirely composed of lancet windows of ruby and blue stained glasss, still impressive despite their extensive restoration by Viollet-le-Duc over 600 years after the chapel's consecration. All the experiences and influences on this French visit were to be richly drawn on in Harry's Honan Chapel windows less than a year later.

When the second instalment of his bursary came through, Harry spent

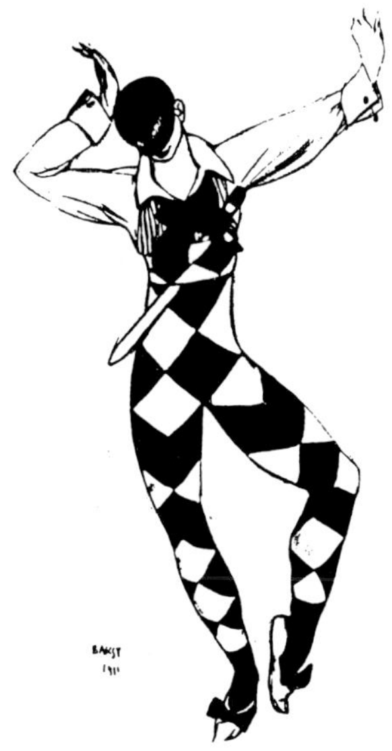

50 Léon Bakst, costume design for Nijinsky as Harlequin in *Carnaval*, 1911, the source for Little Claus' pantaloons

51 Copy of a fourteenth-century stained glass panel from Châlons-sur-Marne, ink and watercolour, 1914; one of a number of fragments which Clarke copied in the old Trocadéro repository in Paris

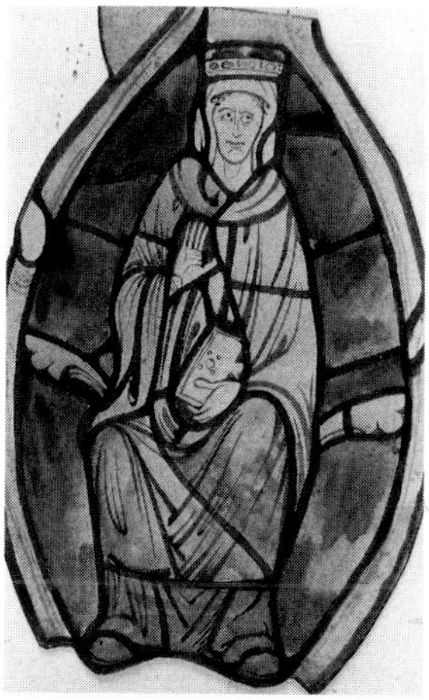

four days in Rouen, looking at the examples of thirteenth and sixteenth century glass in the museum, and at the splendid glass of St Ouen and Notre Dame.[47] The expressive use of leadlines, the intricate juxtaposition of ruby and blue glass and the inclusion of humorous, symbolic or pathetic narrative detail, particularly in the borders or around the principal figures in medieval windows was to radically affect him on this visit. It also taught him that no amount of reading or looking at reproductions of these medieval masterpieces can replace the experience of witnessing the changing light filtering through the jewel-like colours of the glass. Here the magnificent north aisle ambulatory window depicting the legend of *St Julian the Hospitalier* in glorious ruby, blue and yellow medallions and the poignant beribboned signature in the thirteenth century *Story of Joseph* window in the lady chapel would provide him with ideas for his own work.[48]

From Rouen he went on to Fécamp in Normandy where he spent another five days exploring the countryside and visiting the fine abbey church of the Trinity (twelfth and fourteenth century) with its long lancet stained glass windows in the lady chapel.[49] Harry also visited Amiens Cathedral before his return to London on 6 July. In London he contacted stained glass colleagues like Mr Orr and Mr Salmond before returning to Ireland.

In Dublin his father had been busy on his behalf. Joshua had promised the architect R.M. Butler that Harry was by now 'in a position second to none in the U.K. for stained glass art and craft' and would be prepared to carry out an entire scheme of stained glass at Balla Church, Co. Mayo, all 'except the mechanical part'.[50] Unfortunately, as Harry's price was 50 per cent above Mayer's, Mayer got the commission. Joshua had also applied to the registrar of the Art School on Harry's behalf for the return of his prizewinning National Competition *Judas* window and its accompanying cartoon, as Harry wanted them to be exhibited in the forthcoming Art Industries Exhibition at the Royal Dublin Society. Harry also found that the 1914 *Catholic Directory* featured a rather poor reproduction of a richly coloured design he had done at the end of the previous year for the Studio's advertising inset, depicting a Belliniesque *Madonna and Child* decorated with crimson floral ornament.

52 Sketch of Tom Conneelly of Inishere, pencil, *c.* 1911

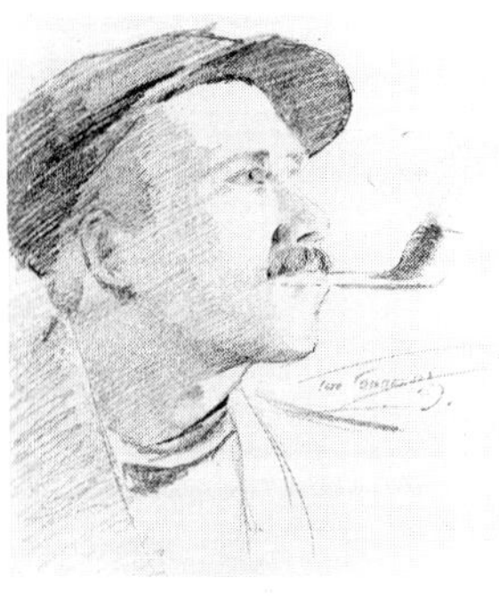

Harry lost no time in seeing his Dublin friends, among them Waldron and Joseph Hone, and his art school friends Austin Molloy and Seán Keating. He was soon at work on a bookplate commissioned by Waldron; there is no evidence that this plate was ever printed though the design was no doubt appreciated by the bibliophile. He visited various friends of Waldron's, including Dr William Starkie and the Kirkwoods at Clondalkin, and borrowed several books from the library at Marino, mostly by Thomas Hardy and Samuel Butler. It is interesting to note from his diary that he was reading Frazer's mythological work *The Golden Bough* at this time. For Dr Starkie, the father of Walter and Enid and brother-in-law of Arthur

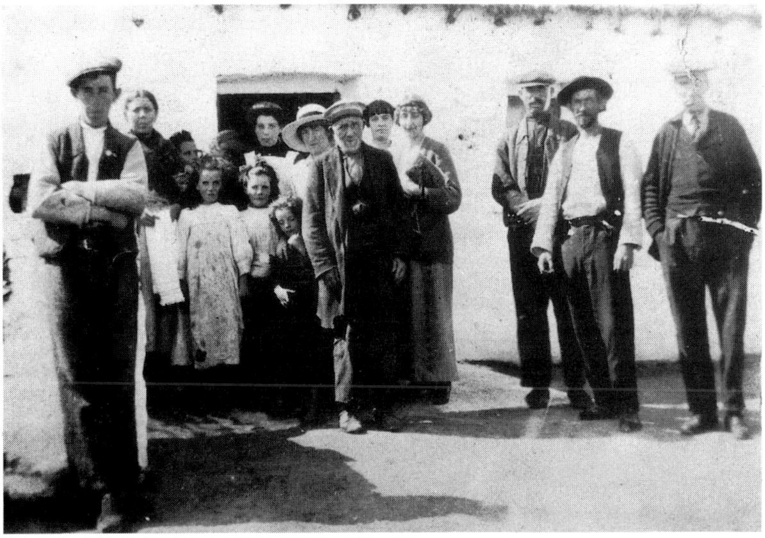

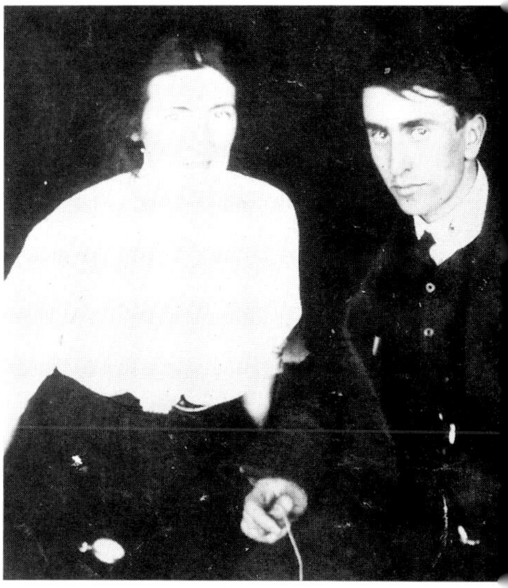

Rackham, a privy councillor and resident commissioner of education in Ireland, he designed a higher certificate to be awarded by the commissioners of national education to national school teachers for a specially high standard of scholarship and efficiency.

On 4 August 1914 war was declared. A few days later, after Harry finished a further Hans Andersen illustration in colour, 'Paradise', he set off for Inishere with Austin Molloy and introduced Seán Keating, whose painting owes so much to the West of Ireland, to the Aran Islands. During this holiday Keating painted his *The Aran Fisherman and his Wife*. Harry apparently greatly admired this picture, although he would tell people in later years of the painter's unwillingness to part with the fish depicted until it had fully served its purpose as a model, despite its gradual putrefaction during the process![51]

The three friends went sketching every day and were soon joined by Margaret Crilley and Johnny Doran, the piper, who had first taken Harry to Aran and who had also visited him in London. A number of photographs, mostly taken by Harry (fig. 53), and a sensitive sketch of Harry by Seán Keating[52] date from this holiday. In turn, Harry incorporated Keating's unmistakable features into his unpublished Poe illustration to 'M. Valdémar' (1918; fig. 90) and, in 1917, into *The Mad Mulrannies* (fig. 86), an illustration to J.M. Synge's *Playboy of the Western World*.[53]

In Dublin, the war was affecting business, especially the import of supplies by ship. Despite Joshua's precautions in buying several loads of scrap lead from the Mining Company of Ireland to keep the Studios in materials, due to shortages he found himself in financial straits. There was a general falling off in business and he decided to have the upper part of 33 North Frederick Street altered to take a tenant. While he helped his father out at the Studios, Harry continued to work at the illustrations and sent

53 Photograph taken by Harry Clarke on a visit to Aran; it includes Margaret Crilley, Seán Keating and Ethel Rhind (fellow art students in Dublin), 1914; Clarke was a keen amateur photographer.

54 Photograph of Margaret Crilley and Harry Clarke on their engagement, 1914

seven more drawings to Harraps, for which he received a further advance of £25.

The RDS annual Art Industries exhibition was cancelled, as the premises were taken over by the military. All 941 exhibits were returned and the catalogue, already printed for the exhibition, had to be scrapped. Harry appears to have submitted nothing for the Taylor Art Scholarship that year; his colleagues Keating, Whelan, Tuohy and Bowe divided the prize money between them. He had, however, exhibited ten unpriced 'decorative illustrations' at the annual Royal Hibernian Academy exhibition in Abbey Street earlier in the year, one of which was *A Decorative Fisherman*.

Harry's diary entry for 19 October records his meeting that day with Sir John O'Connell at which he had undertaken to submit designs in five weeks for several windows in the Honan Chapel in Cork which was then being built out of bequests made in 1913 by the Honan family of Cork City. The chapel was situated beside the hostel which also bore the family name, in the grounds of the Royal University (now University College, Cork), and was to be a unique exposition of the Irish Arts and Crafts movement, following the precedent of Loughrea Cathedral twelve years earlier, where the work of outstanding native craftsmen had been used. Larky Waldron had probably arranged Harry's introduction to Sir John, the trustee of the last Miss Honan's will. Sir John was a neighbour in Killiney and, like Waldron, a governor of Belvedere College, Harry's and Sir John's old school. Another closer friend of Waldron's was the president of University College, Cork, Sir Bertram Windle.[54] Sarah Purser had already accepted a commission for some of the Honan Chapel windows before Harry was approached and she was under the impression that her studio would do all the windows, a conclusion which led to considerable resentment and ill-feeling on her part towards Harry. Although Harry did not receive a formal order from Sir John until the beginning of the following year, his first design submitted, for the *St Brigid* window, was so well liked that he was asked to submit a further four designs, and he was assured that a number of the Chapel windows would be commissioned from him.

Joshua was naturally delighted at his son's success, especially as he was having to lay off men because there was so little work. The price of lead had increased dramatically since the outbreak of war and was in any case in short supply as it was needed for ammunition.

To everyone's amazement, Harry announced that he was getting married to Margaret Crilley, seven months his senior (fig. 54). The wedding on 31 October was a quiet affair with only close family present. On the following day the young couple moved into the new flat in North Frederick Street and throughout the following week Harry worked on a calendar design for John Duthie, which he called 'The Lady of the Decoration'. This was completed by 10 November and was posted off to Glasgow.

The illustration (fig. 65) shows a heavy-lidded, redheaded lady, clad in

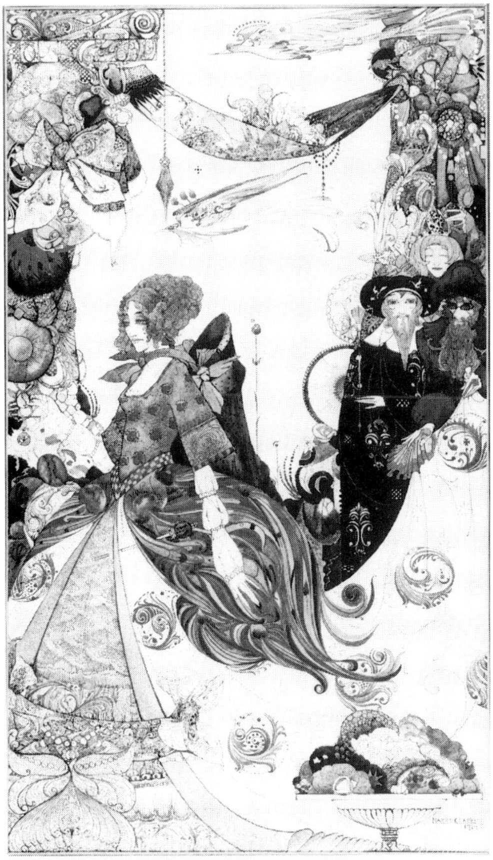

55 *The Lady of the Decoration*, pen and ink and watercolour, 1914; a calendar designed and painted for the Glasgow paint manufacturer John Duthie

an elaborately swirling eighteenth century costume of turquoise, green and white set against a venetian yellow background. Japanese and Persian decorative devices are synthesized with a new delicacy, control and subtlety of colour. The juxtaposition of the yellows and greys which predominate recall the exotic grisaille windows in Rouen.[55] There are two companion watercolours to *The Lady of the Decoration*; one, 18″ by 8″, in deep shades of emerald, viridian and jade washed with ultramarine, crimson and madder, is untitled, unsigned and has never been reproduced (plate 10). In the foreground is a queen, probably Hibernia, crowned in green, with Celtic symbols including a cross around her. Arranged above and behind the queen are Old Man Time and four menacing men, each holding a symbol of the passing of Time or Fate.[56] Harry's sister Dolly later recalled that this picture was commissioned by an insurance company for a calendar.

The other picture, slightly larger and later in date was commissioned by W.A.R. Cruise, the managing director of the Hibernian Fire and General Insurance Company, to be reproduced as a calendar design, though it is not clear if it was ever printed. It depicts a graceful young Hibernia with her Irish harp against a turquoise ground, standing before a round tower, a full moon, and a medley of fantastic flowers and butterflies. Harry was paid fifteen guineas for this design in January 1915.[57]

Before the end of the year Harry designed and assembled four glass panels in the porch of his father's house in Shankill (fig. 56). Composed of cullet pieces collected in the Studio, some painted (ears, eyes, noses, hair) and some unpainted rubies, purples, greens and blues, they are leaded up with pieces or irregular ambetti and clear glass into rectangular lozenges, on which Harry painted whimsical Celtic symbols, sharks' fins and whatever took his fancy.[58] At the same time he was working on further illustrations to Hans Andersen, for 'The Snow Queen' and 'The Travelling Companions'. His diaries record titles of books to read and characters to illustrate. Beside a reminder to draw a bookplate for Lady Woods, he noted Keats' *La Belle Dame Sans Merci*[59] and *Faust*, as well as a reminder to complete *The Ancient Mariner* and to deal with the copyright of the *Ancient Mariner* drawings which at some stage passed from Maunsel and Roberts to the Woods. Other reminders refer to 'Queens', J.M. Synge's poem which he would subsequently illustrate in nine miniature glass panels for Waldron.

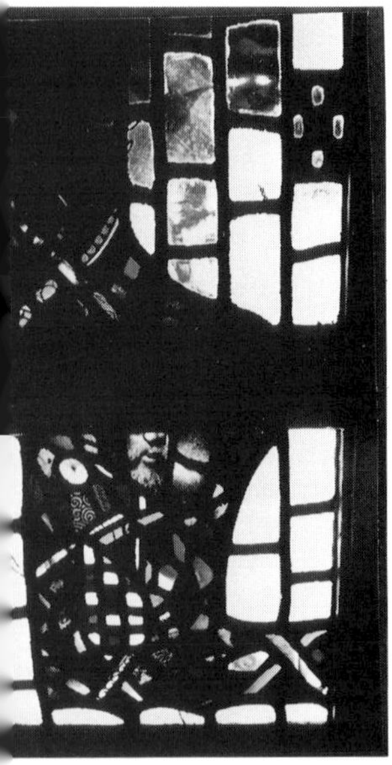

56 Stained glass cullet panels assembled by Harry Clarke for the porch of his father's house, Cluan-na-Greine, Shankill, Co. Dublin, in 1914

The official order for his first five windows for the Honan Chapel came from Sir John O'Connell before the middle of January 1915. As well as the five openings initially allotted to him, he could expect to compete for the rest of the work. The commission came as a result of his submission of five intricately drawn and coloured scale drawings of windows depicting Sts Patrick, Brigid, Colmcille (plate 3), Gobnait and Ita. Every line of lead is drawn in, even the thickness of the coloured glass suggested, and the flesh and features of each saint are shaded in finest pencil tones.

Harry did not begin work on the Cork windows until mid March, as he had to finish three colour plates and three black and white illustrations to Hans Andersen for Harrap, for which he was paid £25. He also worked on the further two illustrations to *The Ancient Mariner* from passages chosen by Sir Robert Woods' elder children, as well as some smaller additional ornaments. However, on the eve of his twenty-sixth birthday Harry was ready to begin his magnificent series of windows in the Honan Chapel, arguably his greatest achievement in glass.

3

A major monument of the Celtic Revival —
The Honan Chapel windows in Cork (1915-17) establish Clarke's reputation —
Publication of his Hans Andersen's Fairy Tales *—*
His Ancient Mariner *project is destroyed during the 1916 Easter Rising*

Harry began the full-scale cartoons for the first of the Cork windows, *St Patrick*, on 18 March 1915, and two months later finished cutting the glass. The glass would next be painted, acided and stained by him, and then fired and leaded up by the Studios, who were to be paid by Harry for supplying, glazing and fixing each window at a rate of 25 shillings per foot.[1] With the *St Patrick* window, Harry went to London in April because, as his father wrote to Mr Salmond, he was 'anxious to get some sixteenth century glass for his windows — blues and greens is what he wants it would be well to get them out before he calls. I will want some sharp greens also you might let him see what you have and charge it to Chance's as he may not have time to go [there]'.[2] (He eventually had to go up to Chance's in Birmingham for some of the glass he needed.) During Harry's absence, Austin Molloy, the 1914 silver medallist in the South Kensington National Competition, was helping with the Honan Chapel work and went to the Studios every afternoon.

The *St Patrick* is the centre light of a three-light window representing the *Trias Thaumaturga* (the three wonder-working saints of Ireland), in the west wall of the Honan Chapel. On his return to Dublin Harry worked steadily on the cartoons and glass for the *St Brigid* light in glowing reds and blues, on the right side of *St Patrick*, and on the third light of the window, which depicts *St Colmcille* and and is the same size as the *St Brigid*. The cartoon for this was begun on 27 June, but the glass was not ready for cutting until the middle of July, as Harry was ill and had to recuperate at his father's house in Shankill.[3]

At the Studios Joshua felt he had to keep his non-Irish transactions private, in response to the national fervour for home-grown products; most of his materials came from Britain because of 'the great run on Irish manufactured goods' and, as he wrote, he found that most 'Irish ones don't please the Studios or their clients'.[4]

Business at the Studios had picked up recently, even though Mr Orr had let Joshua Clarke down in June and consequently he had lost a tender because the design was badly finished. Orr's standards seem to have slumped, certainly where the Clarke Studios were concerned, perhaps because he felt their financial rewards did not warrant too much effort.[5] MacBride was kept busy gilding halos and painting, the usually dependable Nagle was fully occupied (he was now working part-time at the Dublin Technical Schools as well) when not succumbing to the attractions of alcohol, a continual threat in the Studios, and Fitzpatrick was begrudgingly given a halfpenny a week rise. Walter travelled round on his bike, exhibiting pictures and sending back illegible telegrams. He astounded his father at the beginning of June by announcing that he was to get married in a fortnight's time to Minnie Crilley, Margaret's younger sister, who had come down from Newry to housekeep for Harry and Margaret in North Frederick Street. After the marriage Joshua decided to give Walter more scope, especially in domestic and convent contracts, to encourage him to take more interest in his work.

Harry made three more lamp panels for Larky Waldron at this period, painted with the family crest. These are quite orthodox except for the convoluted lines, like unravelled knitting, which fill the space behind the heraldic bull and motto.

When the first three Honan Chapel windows were ready they were exhibited at the Studios. Joshua wrote to the architect R.M. Butler, editor of the *Irish Builder and Engineer,* that Harry's work was 'looked upon by some of the great art critics who have seen it as the best work that's been seen in this country or even England', although 'of course it's very expensive and it is only occasionally one has chance of getting such work'.[6] Harry would always charge what he felt he should get for his work, which was more than anyone in Ireland, and did not try to undercut other artists. He preferred not to quote a price until the design was finished, when he could estimate the real value of his work. Despite his poor health he managed to complete the cartoon for the first window on the north side of the nave of the Honan Chapel before his summer holiday. This was to measure 10′ 11″ x 2′ 5″, like the other nave windows, and depicted *St Finn Barr,* the first in a series showing the patron saints of Munster. On Monday 26 July Harry and his wife left for Aran on their belated honeymoon. They were away until 1 September.

On his return Harry spent most of September making drawings for an edition of *The Ancient Mariner* which Maunsel and Co. planned to publish. In addition to eight full page black and white illustrations, he completed a pen drawing for the cover design, a decorated title page, eight pieces of lettering for the full page drawings and fourteen small illustrations for the text.[7].

On 24 September he resumed work on the cartoon for *St Finn Barr,* which he finished on 6 October. He also completed a design for a screen of clear glass and yellow stain with decorative leadlines for Mr Lander of Lafayette's, the photographers, in Westmoreland Street. His father contemplated getting him to do a calendar design, similar to Mr Duthie's, and obtained estimates from the Grange Printing Works in Edinburgh, who had printed Harry's design for Duthie's calendar the previous year, for an ecclesiastical design in three colours, either 4½" x 7" or 9½" x 7".

By now the Studios had twelve months' work in hand. Harry completed his cartoon for the *St Ita* window on the south side of the Honan Chapel nave by 22 October. When he had done the research necessary for each saint's life, personality and symbolism, he would sketch out the composition and colour scheme, and then work up each cartoon with comparative speed: however, in the case of the *St Ita* design, there are considerable changes in composition, iconography and details between the cartoon and the final window.[8]

Early in November he had been given another window to do, the *St Albert*, on the north side of the nave. Even though he had to have a small nasal operation performed by Oliver St John Gogarty, the throat specialist, the detailed colour sketch of *St Albert* was finished by 11 November. He had to make further alterations to the *St Ita* cartoon before commencing the *St Albert* cartoon (fig. 57). By December he was at a standstill, waiting for sheets of staining glass, and had his father so 'worried daily looking for it' that Joshua wrote to Hetley's asking for a few feet cut small to keep him going.[9]

Although wartime conditions slowed the passage of materials from London and there was a glaziers' strike in progress, Joshua could write to his patrons that the firm 'was second to none in the U.K.' and in a position to do 'modern pictorial or medieval English or modern 13th century, any of these styles we are quite familiar with'.[10]

While London suffered the Zeppelin raids, Ireland's churches, described by Edward Martyn for the most part as 'unshapely as sacks of potatoes,'[11] were enjoying a wave of redecoration prompted by the fervour of the Celtic Revival: the exhortations of aesthetic arbiters like Martyn, Robert Elliott, George Russell (Æ), R.M. Butler and W.B. Yeats in the wake of Newman and Pater were usually in vain. Joshua conducted an ardent campaign seeking commissions from the clergy in Ireland. To one bishop he described Harry as 'an artist who stands alone in the United Kingdom for his creative powers and originalities and his artistic abilities which he has proved . . . he is no amature [*sic*]'.[12] What effect such letters had is not recorded, but certainly Joshua built up a valuble network of contacts for the firm; as time went on Harry's work earned a reputation in its own right, yet the commercial success of the firm was principally due to the clientèle built up by his father. With the increase in work Joshua was persuaded to make long-discussed improvements in the Studios, which were still under way in April 1916. Harry was 'snowed under with work', according to Walter, and 'would not be moved under any circumstances'.[13] He was finishing off the illustrations and decorative devices for the *Hans Andersen* which was to be published for Christmas of that year and also working at his Honan

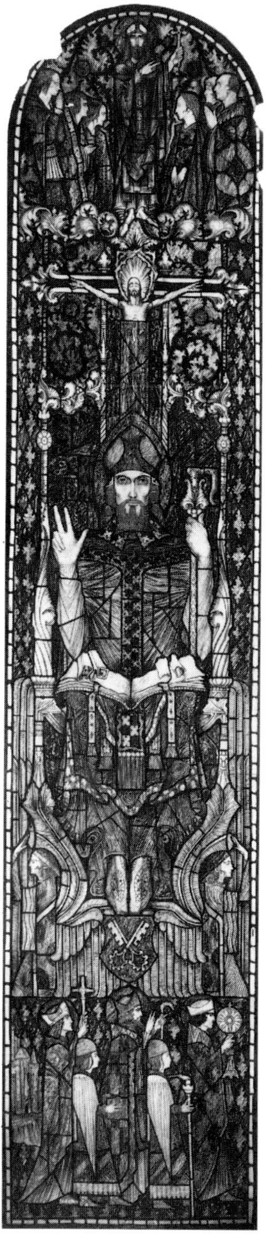

57 Cartoon for the Honan Chapel *St Albert*, 1915, showing the intricate monochromatic beauty and detail of each of these Clarke cartoons

Chapel windows, aciding, staining and painting the glass, making alterations, and having the glass cut.

Thomas Bodkin (fig. 58), a new friend introduced by Waldron, visited the Studios in April and saw the Honan Chapel windows in progress. Afterwards Harry wrote to him that he had 'inserted the small queens to modify the hands in the window', as Bodkin had suggested, but that, as he had not had it erected yet, he did not know if he was 'out of [his] difficulties'.[14] The small 'queens' are the three little female figures at the base of the *St Ita* window, whose hands are elegantly joined parallel to their feet (plate 6). Harry had already radically altered this panel, inserting two male saints and substituting a golden bird for an altar.

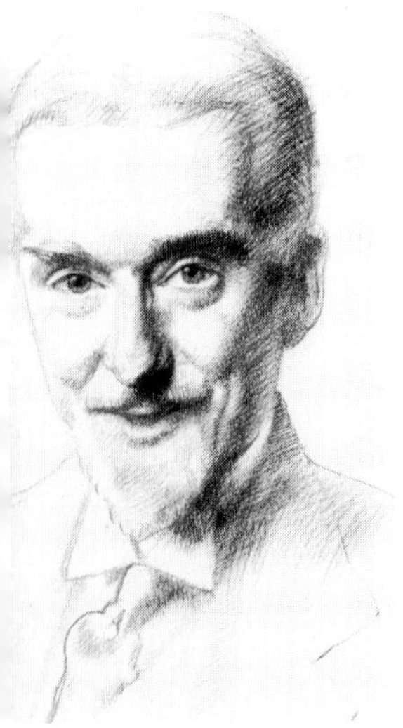

58 Seán O'Sullivan, *Portrait of Thomas Bodkin*, pencil, 1935; for many years Clarke's closest friend and critic, Bodkin's goat-like features are here captured after his appointment as director of the National Gallery of Ireland.

From an early stage he found ears and hands troublesome and would invent some excuse to cover ears and 'to connect hand and wrist nicely together' by carrying the sleeve 'along the back and front of the hand, tapering to meet between the thumb and index finger'.[15] Traces of this 'gadgett,'[16] as he called it, first appeared in his early 1913 Beardsleyesque profiled pen and ink Queens but did not become a characteristic of his work until the end of 1917.[17] In all his work the hands and tapering fingers of his figures are remarkable for their slender, sensitive beauty. His penchant for exotic and imaginatively inventive head- and footwear is already noticeable at this stage, used as an aesthetically appealing component of his decorative art rather than as the resolution of a problem.

Thomas Bodkin had initially been attracted by some drawings that Margaret Clarke had done of Waldron's little nieces, and Harry's letter quoted above marks the beginning of a close friendship which lasted until the end of Harry's life. Bodkin, who was less than two years older than Harry, had also been educated at Belvedere and subsequently at Clongowes and University College, Dublin. He was called to the bar in 1911 and practised until 1916, when he became secretary to the Commissioners of Charitable Donations and Bequests in Ireland. In 1917, Bodkin's interest in art was recognized by his being appointed a governor and guardian of the National Gallery in Dublin, and in 1927 he became the gallery's director. He was a generous and helpful critic of young Irish artists, a knowledgeable and perceptive collector and dealer, buying work little known or appreciated at the time, and an upholder of various causes connected with the arts.

During the armed rising of the Irish Volunteers in Easter Week 1916 (fig. 59) the Studios in North Frederick Street were in the area of central Dublin affected by the fighting. The military refused permission for the men to leave the building, so they were held there for four days, and work was at a standstill until 8 May. Joshua Clarke, confined to his house out in Shankill for twelve days, had to endure the anxiety of not knowing 'whether my house was blown down or my sons killed in Dublin'.[18] Luckily, North Frederick Street was some distance from Sackville Street, the centre of the

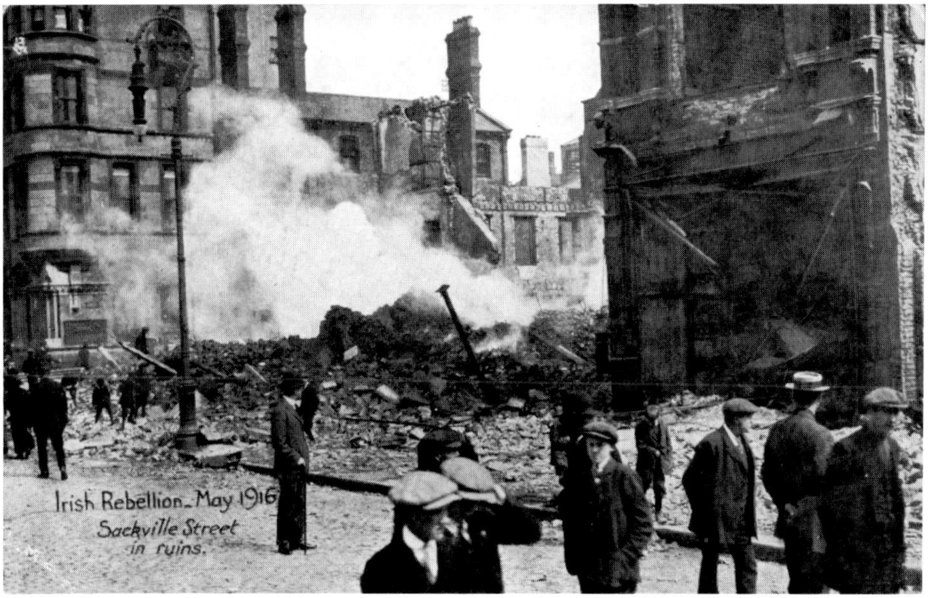

59 Photograph of Sackville Street in Dublin after the devastation of the 1916 Easter Rising

action, although a few bullets grazed the walls of No. 33 and struck the balcony.

One unfortunate result of the rising was that the premises of Maunsel & Co. at 96 Middle Abbey Street was razed to the ground and most of Harry's drawings for *The Ancient Mariner* were destroyed. Only the eight full page illustrations escaped because they were not on the premises, but the blocks made from them were lost. As a result the publication was abandoned.[19] Harry claimed compensation but had to agree to the assessors' valuation at a lower figure than his claim, which was paid in November. The abandonment of the project was a deep disappointment to him. Fire also destroyed the premises of the Royal Hibernian Academy nearby. The many pictures housed there were burnt, including some of Margaret Clarke's portraits. Some felt that this was a symbolic event, as the Academy had lost the revered position it had held in the nineteenth century. Bodkin had criticised the Academy severely three years earlier, when he had written, 'The death of all fresh talent and slow development of those few newcomers from whom great things were expected depresses the visitor. . . . Entering the gloomy door of the Abbey Street premises, one seems to recognize dimly on every side, half forgotten pictures which were once familiar in the pages of magazines, or on the walls of other galleries.'[20] The burning also marked the occasion of Orpen's formal resignation from the Academy.

On 29 and 30 June Harry exhibited at the Studios the windows he had completed for the Honan Chapel *Sts Patrick, Brigid, Colmcille, Finn Barr, Ita* and *Albert*. He invited Bodkin and mentioned that Larky Waldron had suggested he might give them a small write-up. Short notices appeared in most of the Dublin papers, and Bodkin wrote an appreciative article, though Harry was disappointed it was not in the *Irish Times*. He told Bodkin he was glad he had sincerely liked the work, as 'I seldom know where I stand and good criticism is welcome. Yours is to me most encouraging'.[21] Harry was always extremely modest and welcomed informed, sensitive and constructive appreciation or criticism of his work. He always maintained that, of the two of them, his wife was the real artist. As a result of the exhibition Harry was given a commission for six more windows for the chapel, making a total of eleven. According to Joshua, Miss Purser had been given an assignment of eight windows for her firm, the Tower of Glass, before Sir John O'Connell discovered Harry, on the understanding more would follow; they never did.

By September, Harry's illustrated *Hans Andersen* was printed and the prospectus sent to bookshops and purchasers. Harry sent Bodkin a copy of the book asking how it struck him. Bodkin consequently wrote a short review in the *Irish Independent* which was so laudatory that Harry said he 'blushed' at the 'jolly things' Bodkin wrote about his facility of line. He was rather wary of letting Bodkin write another review so soon after his glowing Honan Chapel piece, which had caused 'a disgruntling in certain quarters' (probably Sarah Purser's). Nonetheless, he was glad he had not been 'churlish' and stopped Bodkin from going ahead.

Harry and Margaret decided to move out of town and to rent a house near the sea — 36 Mount Merrion Avenue, in Blackrock (fig. 60). As Walter now had a baby he presumably needed more space in North Frederick Street where he was managing the Studios during Joshua's trips to England. The house in Blackrock had a mews cottage at the end of the garden, which faced north and which Harry readily adopted as his studio for doing cartoons and drawings.

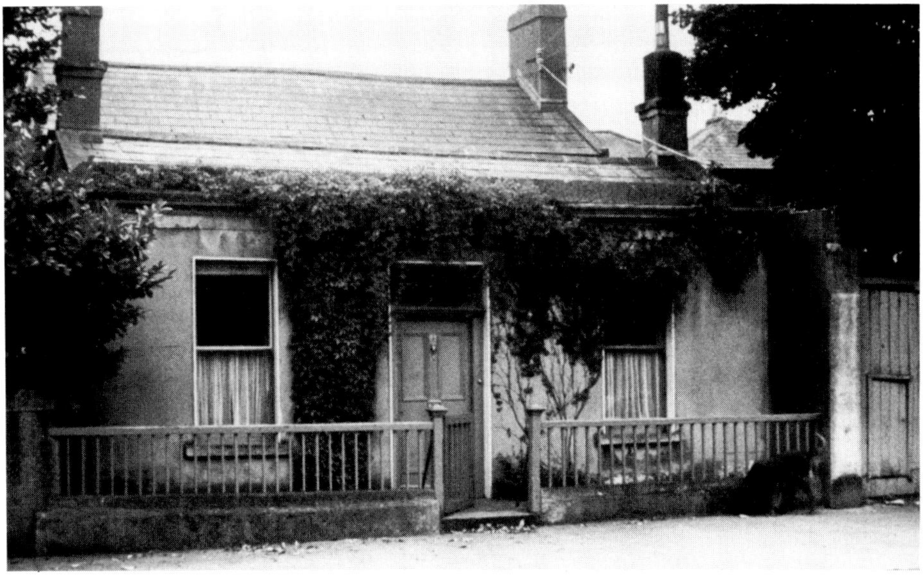

60 Photograph of No. 36 Mount Merrion Avenue, Blackrock, taken *c.* 1978; Clarke's studio was at the bottom of the long garden.

He began work on his next series of Honan Chapel windows in July, when the commission was formally extended. The first window depicted *St Gobnait* on the south side of the nave. The next was *St Brendan*, and for this window Harry had to get some unusual brown glass flashed on blue from Hetley's, as well as extra flesh. Because of wartime manpower problems Hetley's were slower than usual, and by the end of September Harry was desperate for the brown flash and the flesh, as the windows had to be completed and ready to be fixed by the end of October. He also needed specially wide-grooved lead to hold the thick glass (especially the blue slabs) he was using. The *St Declan* (fig. 61) was not begun until the beginning of October, so there was tremendous pressure to have the three windows ready for the consecration of the chapel on 5 November. However, Fitzpatrick had them fixed in time for the ceremony, at which the Bishop of Ross preached the union of creeds, followed by a lunch in the hall of residence next door with some bad speeches and a toast to 'the King, the Pope, and O'Connell'. Sir Bertram Windle, who had inspected Harry's windows in the Studios before they were installed, thought they were 'quite wonderful beyond all',[22] and Professor Patrick Abercrombie, who had come to Ireland to work on the new Dublin town plan, wrote,'These windows are amazing, the best modern glass I have ever seen. They knock the William Morris and Burne-Jones windows hollow.'[23]

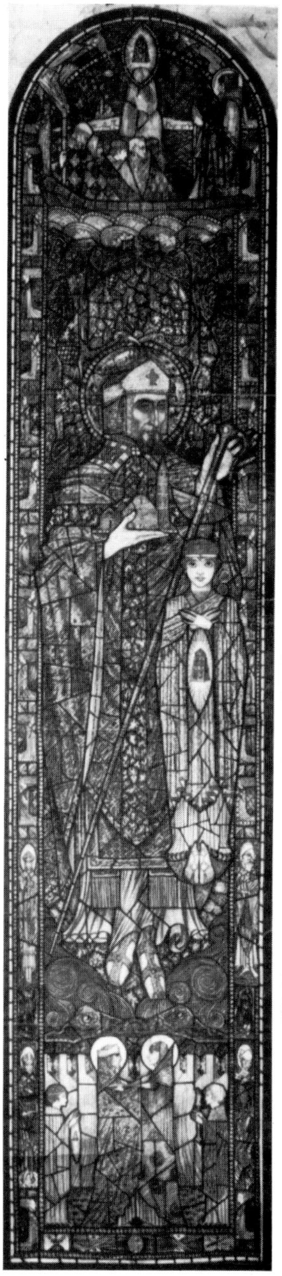

61 Cartoon for the Honan Chapel *St Declan*, 1916

Although Sir John O'Connell published a booklet on the Honan Chapel in 1916 (*The Collegiate Chapel*), Harry's final windows, depicting the *Blessed Virgin* and *St Joseph* for the south wall of the chancel, were not completed until March 1917. The *St Declan* window, which had been temporarily erected for the offical opening, had to be refixed in January 1917.

While he was finishing the Honan Chapel windows, Harry designed for his father a small black and white Christmas card of a decorative Madonna and Child, similar in style to the figure of a lady on the box label of the limited edition of his illustrated *Hans Andersen*, which had come out in October. The book, *Fairy Tales by Hans Christian Andersen,* had sixteen full page colour plates, twenty-four full-page black and white drawings as well as decorated chapter headings and tailpieces and was issued in three editions at 20 shillings in grey cloth, 30 shillings in full leather, and in a limited signed edition of 125 copies for England and the United States bound in vellum at three guineas . Harrap's gave the book an impressive spread in the Christmas 1916 supplement of *The Bookman*, introducing

> a new Irish artist . . . whose work will certainly command extreme admiration. Mr Clarke brings to Hans Andersen an entirely fresh interpretation and he appeals to the intellectual emotions of art lovers, who will find in his work satisfaction of their craving for new and unconventional treatment of themes which may never be exhausted while the spirit of life exists in Art. He is a craftsman who devotes to

each drawing an infinity of pains which is little less than marvellous, and it is difficult to know which to admire most, his fresh conceptions or his delicate and intricate details.[24]

The *Irish Builder* was pleased to review the *Hans Andersen* as they claimed to have been the first to publish Harry's black and white work in their pages, while he was still studying at the Art School.[25] The Christmas issue of *The Studio* carried an unsigned review, which must have irritated Harry, as it dismissed him as yet another of Beardsley's disciples, adding that none of Beardsley's followers 'has ever attained his exquisiteness of line and his art was so essentially the product of his peculiar temperament that emulation of his methods almost inevitably has the appearance of affectation'.[26] The review concluded that 'Mr Clarke is a clever draughtsman and possesses a fine sense of colour as well a a good deal of imagination . . . [but] his work would have been more agreeable if his admiration for Beardsley had been less pronounced.' Such comments must have prompted Harry to develop his own graphic idiom and break away from the influence on his early work not only of Beardsley but also, equally notably in these illustrations, of Edmund Dulac and Kay Nielsen. There is no doubt that in the *Hans Andersen* illustrations his individual style has begun to emerge, and that his already subtle use of colour puts part of his work in a category incomparable with Beardsley. Bodkin's review, not published until June 1917, regretted the effects of photo process reproduction in the reduced colour plates so that admirers of his stained glass would scarcely recognize 'Mr Clarke's jewels'.[27]

On 28 April 1917 Harry had a private show in the Studios of the two last Honan Chapel windows before they were sent down to Cork. The *Irish Builder* reported the progress of the chapel's construction, noting its similarity to the early stone-roofed churches, divided into nave (72′ long x 28′ wide), chancel (26½′ long x 18′ wide) and sacristy. It stated proudly that with two exceptions (the mosaic floor and the opus sectile) everything was Irish made: the Cork limestone, marble, furniture and fixtures were all local, and the stone workers had been selected from the Cork Technical School and from local building firms. Members of the Dun Emer Guild had worked the banners, sanctuary carpets and cloths and bound the missals; Oswald Reeves had wrought the enamels for the tabernacle and altar furniture, and Joseph Tierney had illuminated the altar cards; Professor W.A. Scott had designed the grille at the porch of the chapel, the monstrance, altar candles and cruets; and the Irish poplin vestments were made in Cork. The statue of *St Finn Barr*, to whom the chapel was dedicated, was made by Oliver Sheppard, and the stained glass came from the Clarke and the Tower of Glass studios.[28] The Ruskinian sincerity and integrity of purpose in the conception of the chapel, and its optimistic revelation of fresh Irish talents and skills, inspired unanimous hope and praise.

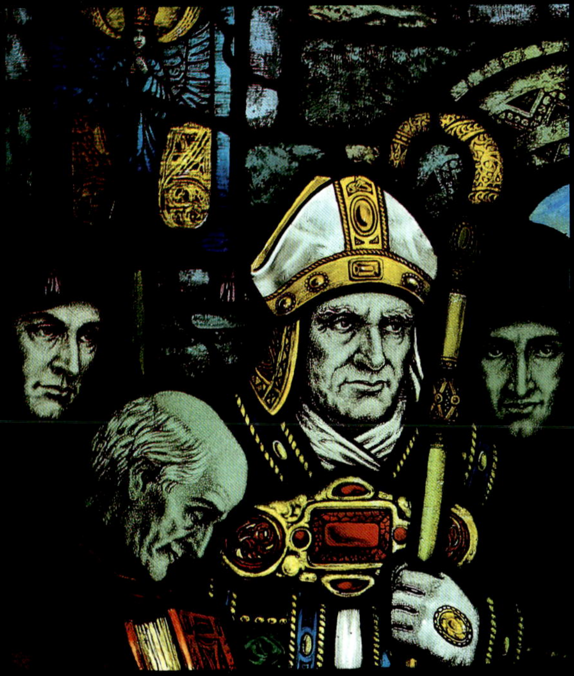

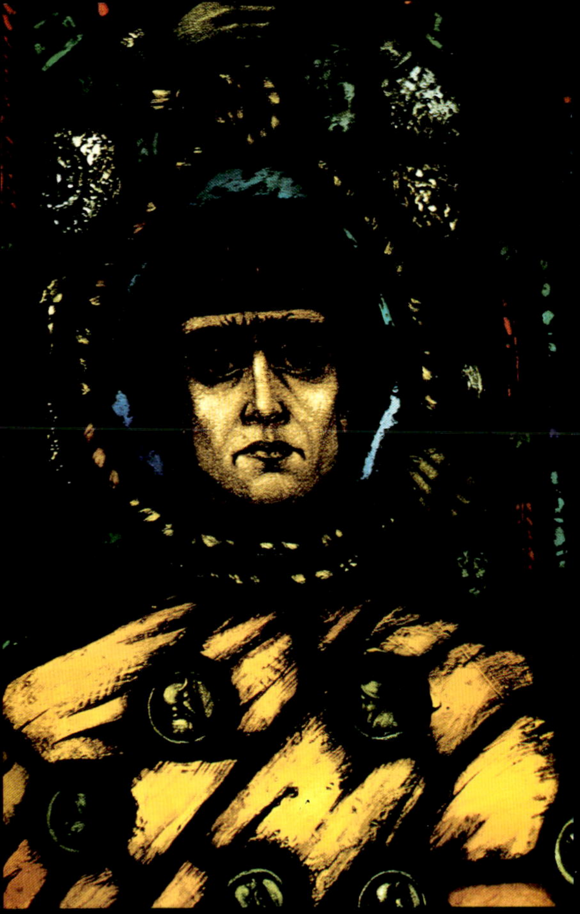

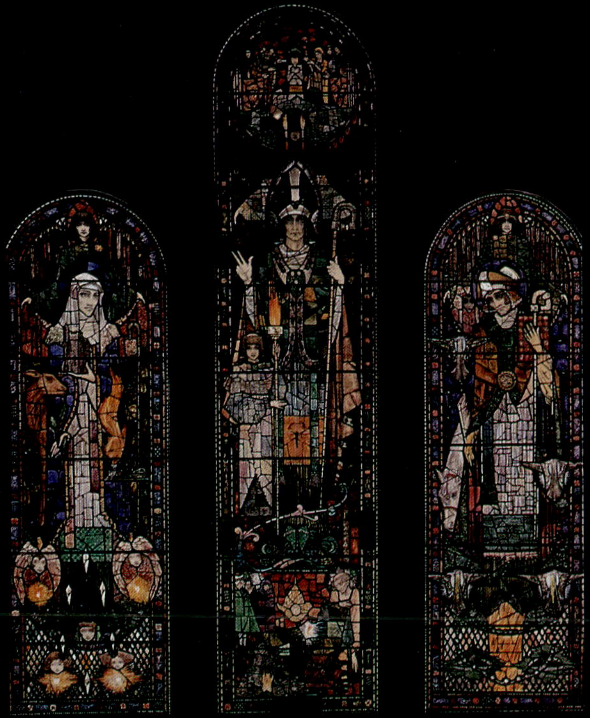

1 The Consecration of St Mel, Bishop of Longford, by St Patrick, **1910; detail of the stained glass section worked from a full-length cartoon, Clarke's earliest extant work in glass**

2 Judas, **1913, detail of the stained glass section worked from a full-length cartoon (fig. 36)**

3 Sts Brigid, Patrick and Colmcille, **the three Wonder-Working Saints of Ireland, 1914, small-scale pencil, ink and watercolour designs for the three lights made in 1915 for the west window of the Honan Chapel, Cork. These designs led to Clarke's first major commission, which established his reputation.**

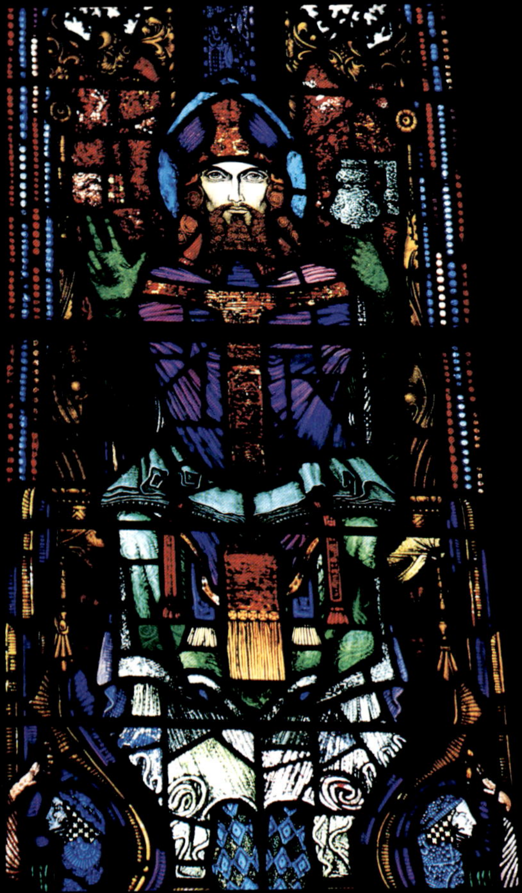

4 St Albert, detail of the enthroned figure of the great Dominican theologian in the window of the Honan Chapel, Cork, completed early in 1916; at his brocaded feet two acolytes appear.

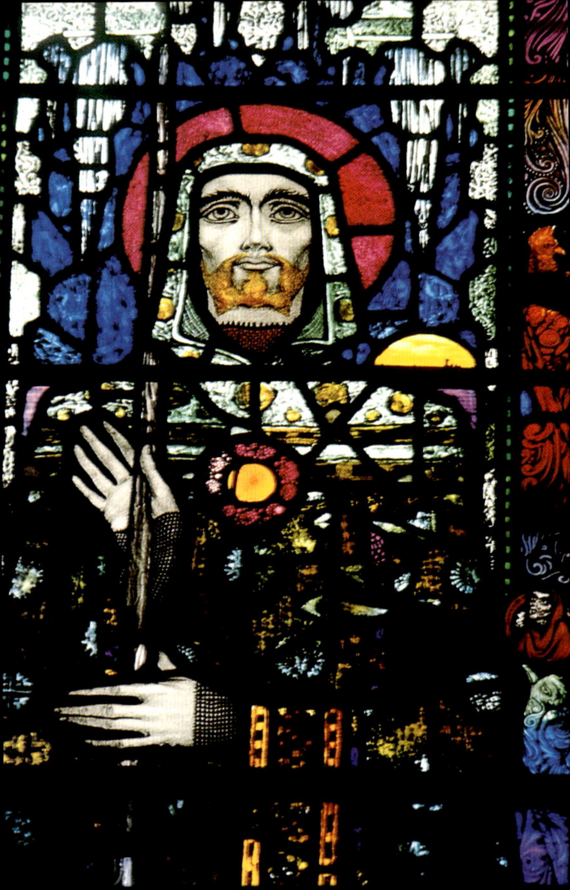

5 St Brendan, detail of the commanding figure of the seafarer, adapted from Klimt's Hygeia (fig. 74), Honan Chapel, Cork, 1916; at his shoulder is the setting sun, in his hand an oar, and framing his head the fantastic stalactites he encountered.

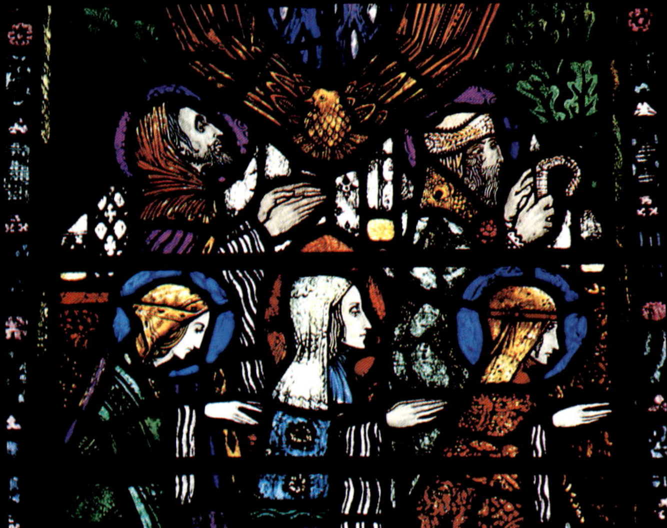

6 Detail from the base panel from the St Ita window, Honan Chapel, Cork, 1916; the saint is depicted as a young woman (in a royal blue mantle studded with the three jewels of the Trinity) with her two holy maids and St Colman and St Brendan on a missionary journey. Their prayers are symbolized by the gilded bird above them.

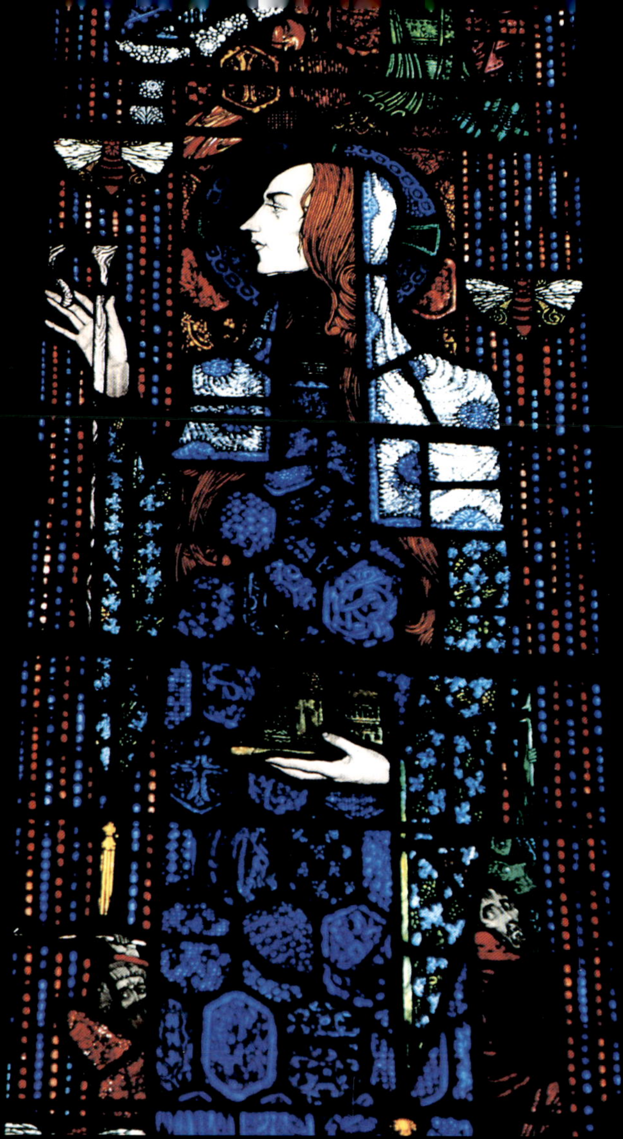

7 St Gobnait (detail), the patron saint of bee-keeping, Honan Chapel, Cork, 1916; her lace shawl frames a red-headed profile adapted from fifteenth century images by Donatello and Baldovinetti.

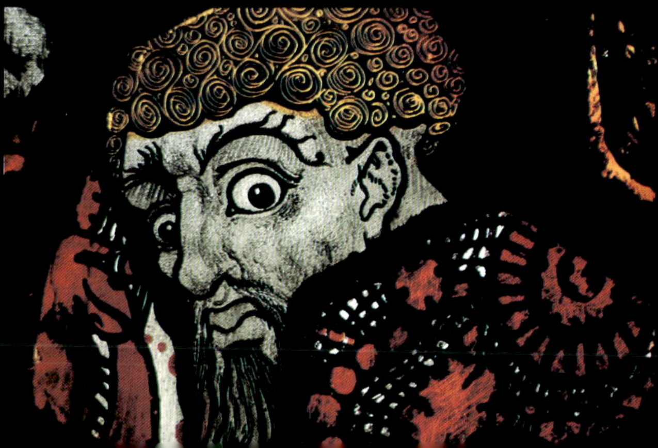

8 A robber, detail from St Gobnait; this tiny figure is one of several on to whom the saint released her avenging bees to prevent the theft of her beehive.

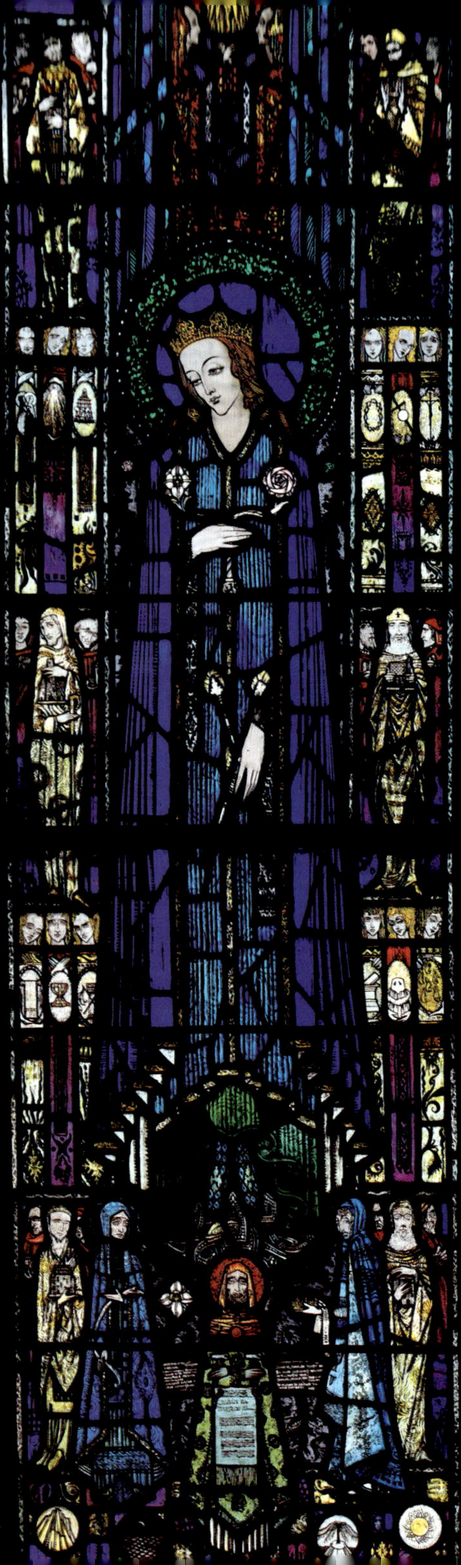

9 The Virgin Mary, Mother of Sorrows, Honan Chapel, Cork, 1917, all but the top lunette of the window. The wealth of subordinate figures, dolefully seeking intercession from the Virgin, as well as symbols of her life, and her son's passion, are woven into a rich golden tapestry.

10 *Hibernia*, calendar design for an insurance company, 1914, pencil, watercolour and ink on board, depicting the Celtic queen and symbols of the transcience of life

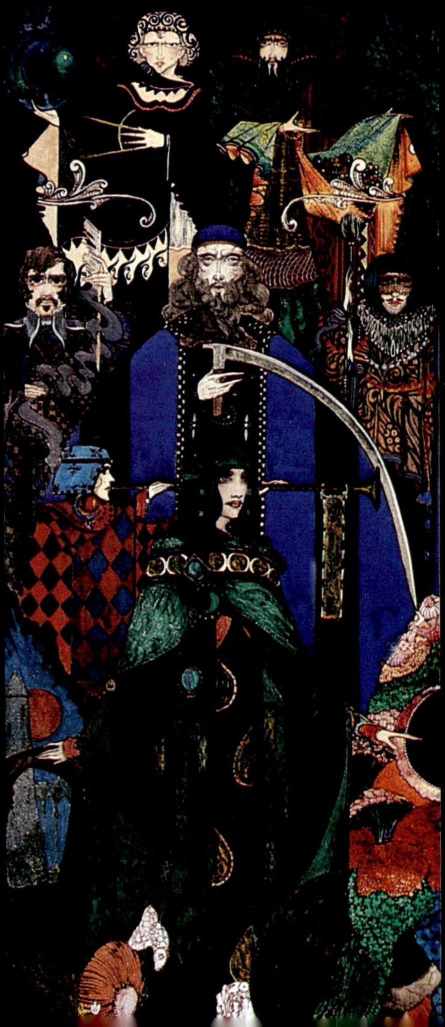

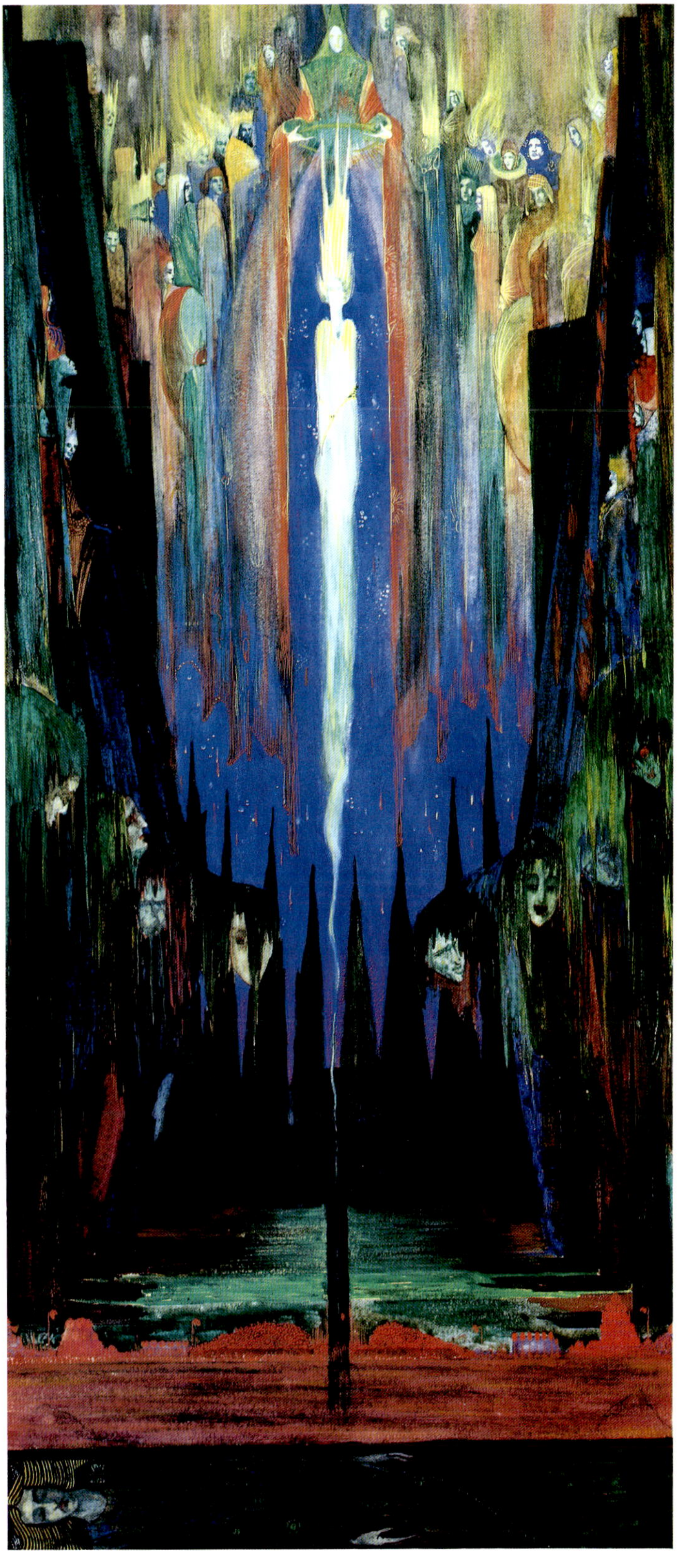

11 *De Profundis*, illustration to Oscar Wilde, 1913, watercolour on paper on board. This illustration to Wilde's tragic epistle written in gaol is a dramatic expression of the antithetical nature of Clarke's imagination, while placing his work in a firmly European Symbolist context.

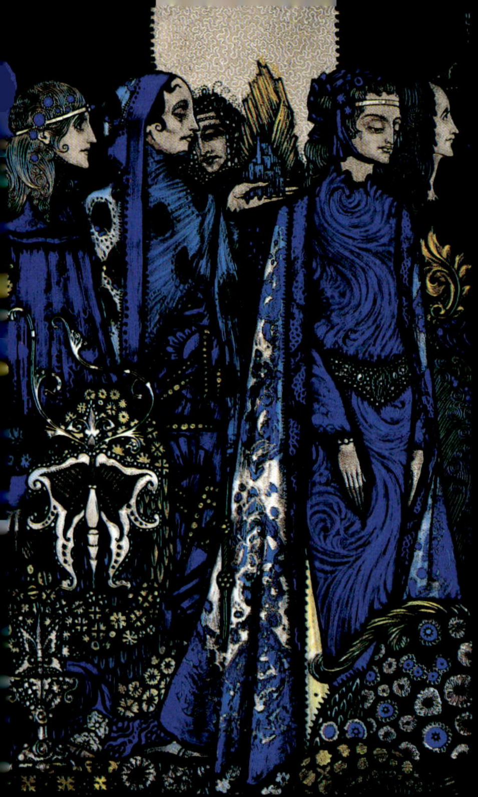
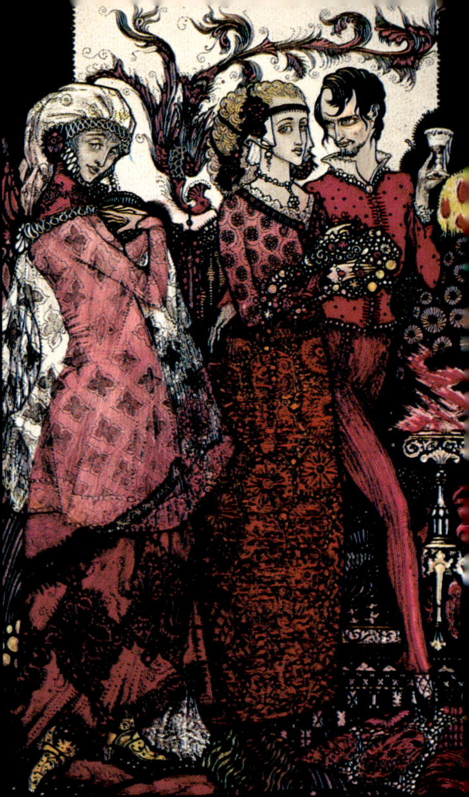
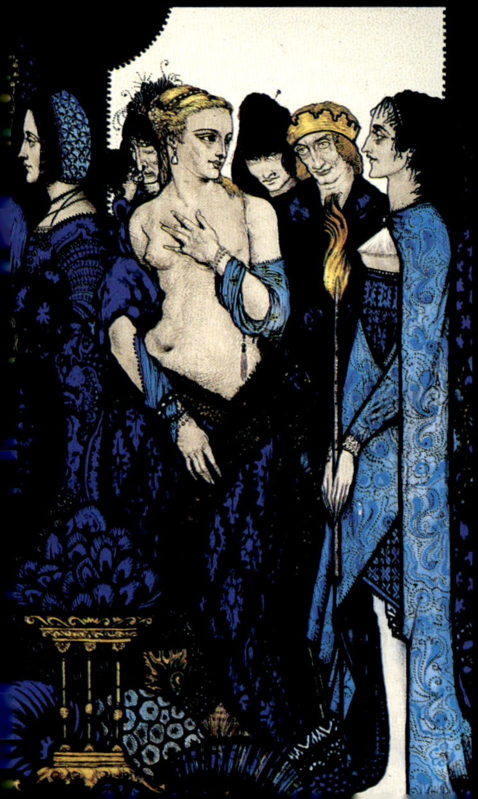
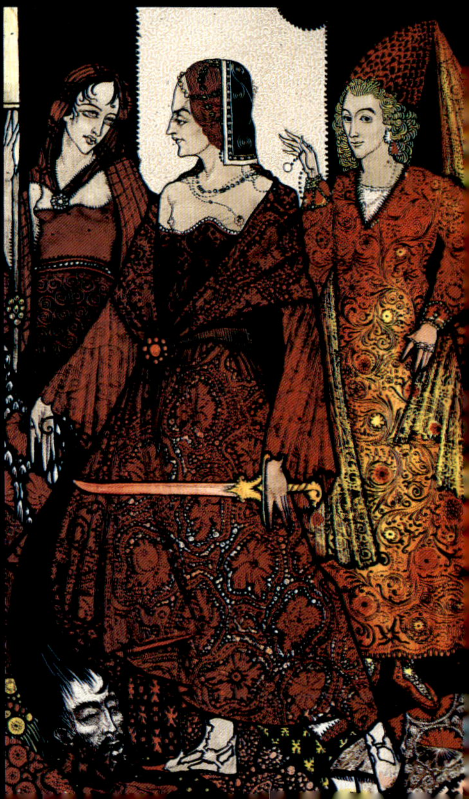

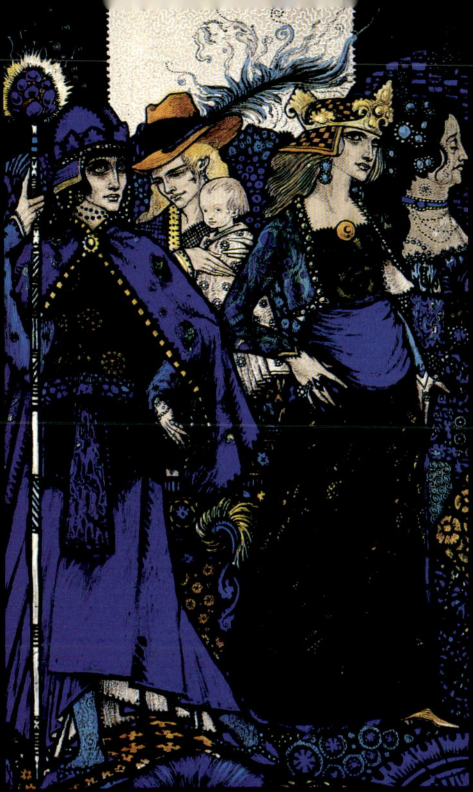

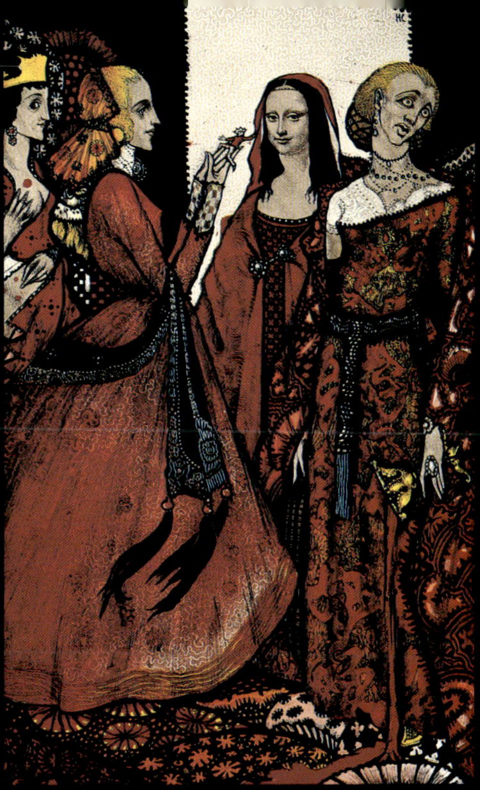

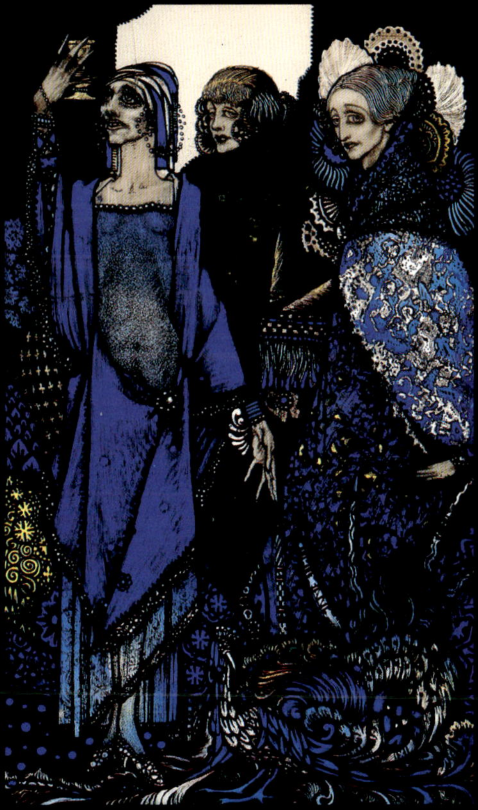

12-18 The central *Queens* suite (cf. figs. 82 to 85); for the prologue and epilogue panels see figs. 80 and 81.

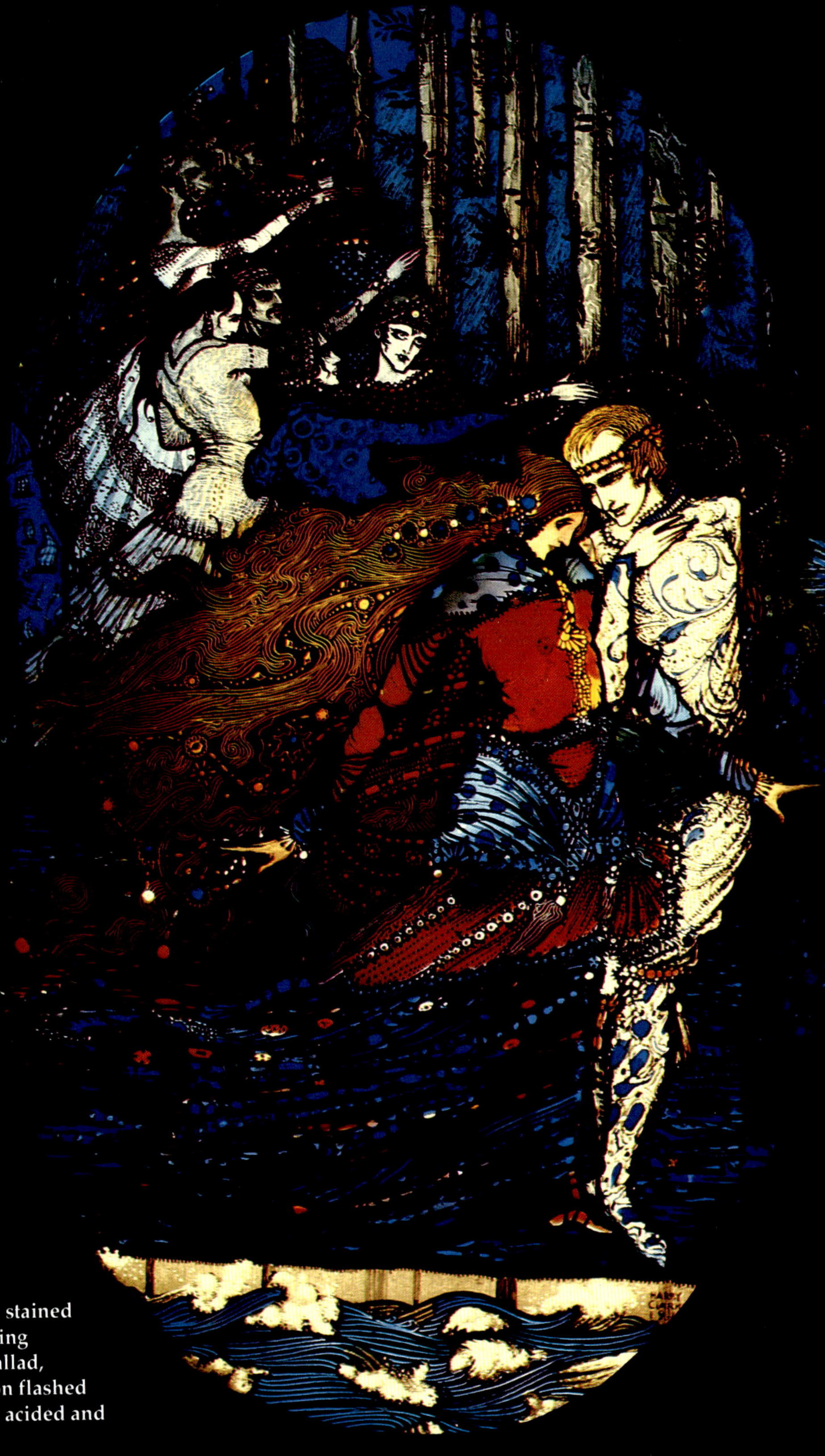

19 A Meeting, 1918, stained glass panel illustrating Heinrich Heine's ballad, flashed blue glass on flashed ruby glass, painted, acided and stained

Bodkin later wrote, 'Nothing like Mr Clarke's windows in the Honan Chapel had been made or seen before in Ireland. Their sustained magnificence of colour, their beautiful and most intricate drawing, their lavish and mysterious symbolism, combine to produce an effect of splendour which is overpowering.'[29] Oswald Reeves wrote that

> no one has ever before shown the great beauty that can be obtained by the leads alone, nor the mysterious beauty and 'liveness' that each piece of glass receives at the hands of this artist, nor the jewelled gorgeousness of 'pattern' that may be given to a window that teems with subject, interest and meaning. These windows accept their 'architectural place' to a fine degree, with an ease and and certainty that would suggest that rendering of the subject held no temptation to pictorial excess. The light as it passes through them is marvellously transformed, not alone by the colour . . . but by ingenuity of individual craftsmanship, and it is this transformed, glorified and vitalized light in all its varied and 'live' qualities that holds the surpassing beauty and significance.[30].

Ruskin's tenet that windows should be 'serene, intense, brilliant like flaming jewellery', that 'we are always trying to get colours bright when their chief real virtues are to be deep, mysterious and subdued' is fully met.[31]

On entering the chapel, the three single lights of Ireland's wonder-working saints glow richly above — *St Patrick*, in the centre, attended by *St Brigid* on his right and by *St Columcille* on his left (cf. plate 3). The name of each principal saint is inscribed in the border of the relevant window in Celtic script and often in its Irish form. The dominant colour of the *St Patrick* light is green. Clad in deep green cloak, brooch, stole, mitre and boots, the saint raises his right hand in blessing and holds a shamrock; the left hand holds his bishop's crozier; at his right his acolyte, Benignus, holds a flaming torch, symbolic of truth, light and awareness. A medallion above (a traditional medieval device), referring to his childhood, is linked to his mandorla-shaped halo by an angel whose halo is in the form of St Andrew's cross suggesting a Scottish origin for the saint. Beneath his feet, poised symbolically over some serpents, his death scene is shown against the paschal fire lit by him on the Hill of Tara. Light also comes from the blazing torch held by one of the group of mourners around the death bed. The borders are filled with symbols of his learning, dignity, majesty, justice and faith; at the centre of the bottom border is a golden missal, whose open pages read

Pray for Harry Clarke who made this window	And for Austin Molloy who helped him June 1915.

In the *St Brigid* light, blue is dominant. 'The wide-eyed Bridget with her lamp and spray of oak' left Thomas Bodkin 'groping for adequate words with which to describe the wonder'.[32] In preparing the design Harry consulted the ancient lives of the saint in the *Book of Lismore* and the *Leabhar Breac*: Brigid is reputed to have been so ethereal and other-worldly that she once absent-mindedly hung her cloak on a sunbeam; thus in the window she gazes in St Patrick's direction, bearing in one hand a model of the cathedral and abbey church that she founded and in the other an oak leaf symbolic of Kildare (*Cill Dara*, the church of the oak tree) and also reminiscent of the pre-Christian cult of Brigid the druidess. Against a glowing ruby background of plaited osier reeds, an angel holds a cloth behind her head. A calf nuzzles her arm suggesting her dairy. The flame of a lamp is symbolic of her faith and healing power, and her staff indicates her dignity and spiritual strength. At her feet four angels carry torches, emblems of her prayers, prophecies, miracles and charities,[33] and five lilies beneath her brocaded slippers symbolize the provinces of Ireland, over which she had spiritual control. Other symbols connected with her ancient cult fill the border. The overall effect of this and the other Clarke windows in the chapel is of sparkling, glowing kaleidoscopic richness, continually changing with the light outside, a veritable symphony of prismatic harmonies reflected onto the mosaic floor and the stone walls. Harry was a great music lover and it is not improbable that he would have been aware of Haydn's use of each instrument to symbolize a particular colour, as in *The Creation*, for example.[34] The colours of stained glass, enlivened by the evermodifying light which shines through them, are particularly analogous to music, a point stressed by Whall in his book.[35] Relevant to this window is Kandinsky's observation that

> the use, side by side, of red and blue, colours in themselves of no physical relationship, but from their very spiritual contrast of the strongest effect, is one of the most frequent occurrences in modern choice of harmony . . . It is interesting to note that this very placing together of red and blue was so beloved by the primitives both in Germany and Italy that it has till today survived, principally in folk pictures of religious subjects.[36]

Harry Clarke's windows reveal his instinctive understanding of the essential qualities of his medium, not only in his skilful treatment of the leadlines, but also in the way he fragments the daylight by breaking up the surface of the glass, painting the whole surface with devices, such as strings of little beads, so that the light sparkles through, filtering kinetically — one of the many skills he would have appreciated in the glass of the medieval masters. He preferred to use irregular, thick glass, often Norman slab,[37] or unusually flashed blues, rubies and gold-pinks, so that the light would appear to be captured within the very texture of the glass. Æ commented in one of his valuable assessments of Harry's work:

> Looking at [his] windows, I imagine that if one scraped a little the subconscious mind of the artist, you would let in a flood of rich colour out of some inner luminous aether, where the fire is more brilliant than the eye can see, and the only way he could recreate that colour for us was by the art he practises. There is not a square inch in these windows which is not invented. Everywhere one looks, one sees the creative faculty at work. It is an art where the designer is limited in many ways by the necessity of leading — and he might easily fall into an inspired convention, but the limitations of the technique only seems to inspire Clarke, and from jewelled crowns to shoe buckles, there is endless invention. The glass glitters like the breastplate of jewels made for Aaron the High Priest. Prophet and Saint wear the robes of paradise who, while living, wore the robes of poverty. They are resplendent in purple and sapphire, in rose, silver and azure. Here is ruby smitten through with gold and emerald, twinkling with silver lights. Starry points of colour break through everywhere, but one has to *see* the colour.[38]

Harry was aware of the colour symbolism which dictated the schemes of the early Gothic artist-craftsmen. He used a jaded yellow as the background to his 1913 *Judas* panel, this being the traditional colour of faithlessness, deceit and jealousy, thus associated with Judas in medieval glass. In the Honan Chapel windows he gave a dominant colour to each saint, as already seen in the *St Patrick* (green) and *St Brigid* (blue) windows, to accentuate symbolically his or her essential characteristics and to provide a key to each window.[39] In the *St Columcille* light a pure yellow, symbolizing brightness, goodness and faith, is dominant. The design is akin to that of *St Brigid*, with an angel above holding a cloth of heaven behind the saint's inclined head. Columcille holds a staff in one purple-gloved hand, and a quill and his book in the other. By his right arm is the blessed white draught horse who used to comfort him and who even shed tears on the abbot's breast when his earthly end was near. To the right of his head is the profile of the guardian angel who accompanied and guided him. The two doves shown were his messengers on Iona: his name means 'The Dove of the Churches'. The predella below his feet, with its two praying angels in ruby, shows the saint on Iona and his followers in Derry; the tossing waves between the two islands are spanned by chains of beaded stars in the sky above, symbolic of the spiritual communication between the two. Other symbols fill the border, including a high cross sacred to the saint, his mitre and the flames of ardent faith.

In the *St Finn Barr* window, Harry's first in the nave, scarlet dominates in a northern light, reflecting on to the stone floor beneath. The sixth-century saint hovers mitred and red-headed (fig. 62), robed in a red silk mantle,

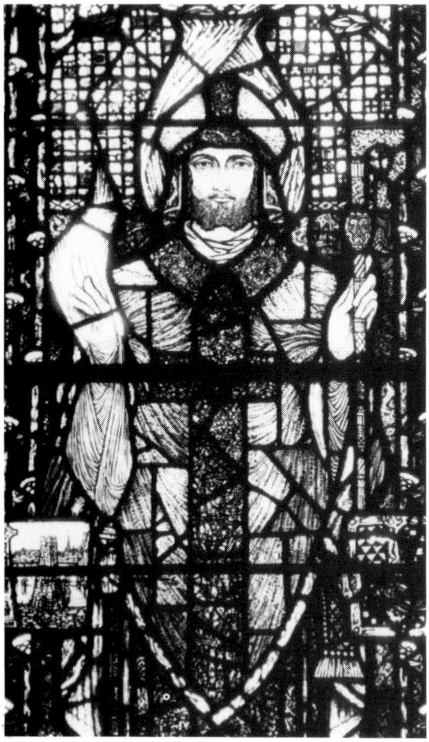

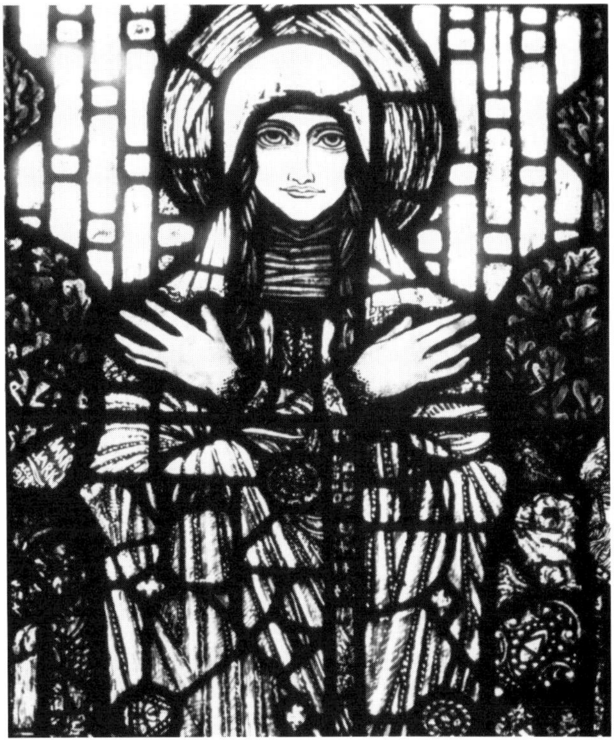

62 *St Finn Barr* (detail), stained glass window, Honan Chapel, 1916

63 *St Ita* (detail), stained glass window, Honan Chapel, 1916

trimmed in ruby and gold; his ungloved left hand holds a golden crozier, while a lambent flame surrounds his right hand, gloved in gold and raised in blessing. Legend has it that the young saint encountered Christ in a vision and, when he fell to his knees, Christ bade him arise and helped him up, taking hold of his right hand; ever after, this hand glowed so brightly that it was always covered by the divinely donated glove to dim the radiance of the hand. On Finnbarr's right is a vignette of Cork city of which he is the patron, with the spire of St Finnbarr's Cathedral, and the monastery and school he founded after an eagle had led him to Corcach-mor-Murnhan, the great marshy place of Munster. On his left is his book decorated with the arms of the diocese and fastened with a golden buckle. The lower sides display emblems of the see and the saint's name in Gaelic script on a vertical parchment-like strip is reminscent of Dr George Otto Simms' description of the 'wealth of detail' in the *Book of Kells* pages that calls for repeated study.[40] The borders of the window show a flowering hazel tree in snow, recalling one of Finnbarr's miracles. The lower panel, framed in floral garlands, shows St Finnbarr and St Maccuirp, the Master of Barras, kneeling on either side of an angel in front of which is a shining white vesica, encasing their two mitres. Here, the flames depicted refer to the saint's miraculous consecration. The flame motif is repeated in the halo above the main figure and carries the theme into the top panel of the design, which shows the fiery legend of the saint's birth. His noble mother rejected her betrothed Tyagerlach and eloped with the man she loved, Amergin, the father of the saint. The unborn Finnbarr is depicted crying out from his mother's womb as his hapless parents face fiery death from the vengeful Tyagerlach, resulting in the wicked chieftain's conversion and his family's salvation.

Across the nave from the *St Finn Barr* is the *St Ita* window. In this the dominant colour is a deep royal blue, a colour which Harry loved more than any other[41] and which he used with powerful effect in this and in the *St Gobnait* window. This blue was to become associated with his work in the minds of many people, particularly when he used it in thick irregular slabs. A quotation from Kandinsky, nearly contemporary with the making of these windows, seems apposite:

> The power of profound meaning is found in blue, and first in its physical movements 1) of retreat from the spectator, 2) of turning in upon its own centre. The inclination of blue to depth is so strong that its inner appeal is stronger when its shade is deeper. Blue is the typical heavenly colour. The ultimate feeling it creates is one of [supernatural] rest. . . . In music a light blue is like a flute, a darker blue a cello; a still darker a thunderous double bass; and the darkest blue of all — an organ.[42]

Blue is the colour associated with St Brigid, and St Ita was known as the Brigid of Munster. She lived in the sixth century and was born Deirdre, the daughter of a chieftain of the Decies, directly descended from high kings of Ireland such as Felim the Lawgiver and Conn of the Hundred Battles. On her conversion to Christianity despite strong opposition, she changed her name and became a fervent ascetic and devoted teacher, qualities reflected in the window by her lean face, veiled head, crossed hands and the stark, checkered background to her head, symbolic of the miraculous manna bestowed upon her while fasting (fig. 63).[43] The heads of four of her pre-Patrician disciples are shown in tiny ruby and gold medallions on either side of her — Sts Brendan of Kerry (her foster child), Colman of Cloyne, Finnbarr and Carthage. Her nimbus, like that of Finnbarr, is made up of tongues of flame crossed above her head, and symbolizes her ardent love of God. Behind her mantled figure the golden background is composed of emblems of her royal birth (crown, sceptre, orb) discarded by the saint, and at her feet those emblems of the Holy Trinity which she adopted in their stead.

Harry Clarke used wings, flames or fire to symbolize mystical, spiritual, supernatural or metaphysical elements as in the flaming nimbus and the golden wings wrapped round the cross and the triad. The Trinity is particularly associated with St Ita because in a vision she was presented with three priceless jewels, symbols of the Trinity. In the window jewels are set into the seemingly throbbing thick slabs of her blue robe, and there are triads of jewels in the border, interspersed with sacred oak leaves. In the tableau at the top of the window the Queen of Heaven, crowned in gold, envelops Ita in a magnificent wheatsheaf of plaited ruby and sapphire as the three priceless jewels are absorbed into her radiating nimbus.[44] The lower panel of the *St Ita* window is linked to the rest of the window by a burnished golden dove rising from the figures in the tableau which represent St Ita as a young woman, praying with her two holy maids, and St Colman and St Brendan, as they proceed from Killeedy, Co. Limerick, the seat of her cult (plate 6).

Next to the *St Finn Barr* window, that of St Albert of Cashel shows the only seated saint in the chapel, reminiscent in attitude of the Chartres window, *La Belle Verrière*, and the twelfth century *Osias* in Canterbury Cathedral. In a dominant colour of green, the saint is dressed as a bishop, the keys of the holy city at his feet, one green gloved hand raised in blessing, the other holding a silver crozier, decorated with Celtic interlacing (plate 4). His face, framed in curls of red hair, appears to gaze beyond us into some beatific vision. Strings of ruby, sapphire and pearl beads decorate the border, and sparkle around the sculpted golden baroque throne of the saint; behind him rises a golden crucifix, bearing the dimly discernible figure of Christ. Little is known of this eighth-century saint, although his legend concerns visions of the Cross. Harry used himself as the model for the figure of Christ in this window and had himself photographed in a loin cloth for the purpose. He worked from these photographs when designing this window and, a couple of years later, used the same photograph when he designed the *Crucifixion* window in Terenure, Dublin. Above the crucifix in the *St Albert* window a thick horizontal bar of dark green glass forms the arms of a larger, dark cross. From this the standing figure of St Albert rises, a golden crucifix in hand, preaching to the converts of Ratisbon in Germany, in which city he died. Beside the saint's feet, two of his fellow missionaries are ingeniously worked into the composition each facing solemnly outwards and bearing a standard. The lower panel shows Albert setting off from the grim battlemented gate and cliffs of Ratisbon, in a sumptuously attired procession, led by St Erhard, bearing a golden bell and monstrance, accompanied by a dark young man, St Hildulph, with a cross, and two young acolytes with bible and staff. The saint's name is inscribed in the lower border in Irish and in Celtic script.

St Gobnait (or Gobinett, or Judith) of Ballyvourney (fig. 64) on the south side of the nave is radiant in blue, with shimmering strings of vertically strung ruby and blue beads, into which are set five large crimson and black bees, in honour of the patron saint of beekeepers (plate 7). The ruby background and the blue robes of this saint are composed of large honeycomb-shaped lozenges,[45] on which are painted tiny figures and decorative devices. The composition of the window is strongly vertical, following a serpentine line from the top scene, in which St Gobnait raises her crozier as she inscribes a white line across which the plague cannot pass into her community and affect those who have taken refuge there. Behind the line three gasping, terrified, unprotected men, are gripped by the plague, one of them bearing the artist's initials and date, 'HC 1916'. Harry here shows the delight he took in depicting deformity, disease and the macabre. This fascination with the poles of the beautiful and of the ugly and grotesque is a propensity he shared with many medieval artists.

Beneath, St Gobnait stands regally, her head turned in profile to the east, her abbess' wooden crozier held in the tapering fingers of her right hand and in her left a model of her abbey and high cross at Ballyvourney. Born in Ballyvourney, Co. Cork at the beginning of the sixth century, Gobnait lived her whole life there and a strong cult developed around her. Her face is delicately and sensitively painted, reminiscent of the striking, pale-skinned beauties of the West of Ireland; her fine features are offset by her deep red hair, which falls in long wavy strands to her waist.[46] A lacy shawl falls from her head onto her shoulders. Her nimbus, which incorporates a local stone cross once associated with her cult, is dulled deliberately, to

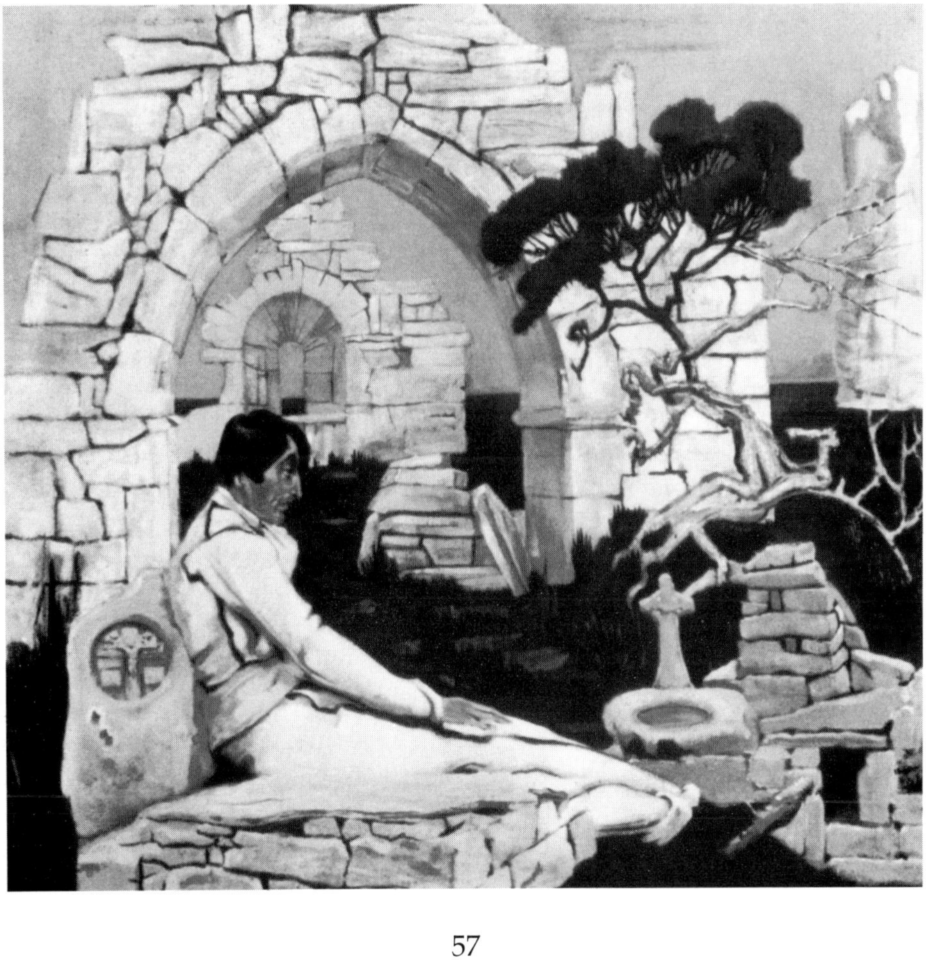

64 Seán Keating, *Thinking out Gobnet*, oil on canvas, 1917 (inscribed on verso: 'John Keating to Harry Clarke 29 Aug 1917'); Clarke in the báinín cloth and pampooties of the West of Ireland considering his *St Gobnait* window, which he completed in 1916

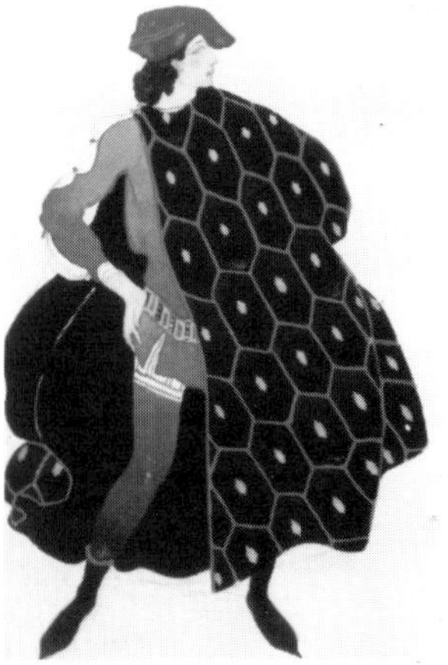

65 Léon Bakst, costume design for Ida Rubinstein in *The Martyrdom of St Sebastian*, 1911; the blue honeycombed cloak in Bakst's design is analogous with the intricately worked robe worn by Clarke's *Gobnait*, patron saint of beekeeping.

enhance the contrast between the rich colouring of her hair and the pallor of her face. Her tunic is intricately patterned in sapphire lozenges in a honeycombed arrangement that seems to pulsate in the light. Behind her impassive figure a band of tiny robbers is creeping; on the right, a frightened man and two green-faced spectres bearing cudgels look back in terror; lower, on the left, a barefooted robber, clad in ruby, runs for his life (fig. 71), beating off a huge bee, whose body is larger than the man's head. The painting of the tiny head of this man warrants careful examination. In accordance with medieval tradition, two lead lines cut across the terrified face, accentuating the pathos of the man, rather than blandly following the contours of his head. Clarke's choice of flesh tones for his glass, and his painting of detail, is seen to great effect in this window. Beneath the saint's exquisitely buckled shoes the last robber, a shield inscribed with a Celtic cross at his arm, escapes in panic from another huge bee (plate 8). According to legend, robbers tried to break into the abbey one night and were foiled when St Gobnait's beehive, a miraculous bronze relic, was used to ward them off. Another version says that St Gobnait turned her bees into men to give chase to the robbers. In the bottom panel of the window Gobnait, setting her bees on the robbers, stands behinds a cleric who holds the beehive. One of the blue lozenges of her cloak (fig. 65) is inscribed with a miniature mitred bishop, holding a crook and a child, signed 'HC 1916'; on another, a miniature gravestone bears the inscription 'HC RIP'. The techniques, choice and treatment of glass and imaginative and expressive detail of the three figures of St Gobnait, the little novice (fig. 70) and the curly-

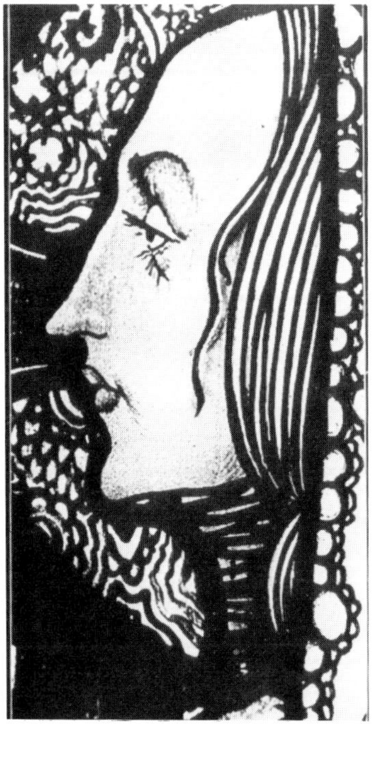

66 *St Gobnait* (detail), stained glass window, Honan Chapel, 1916; this is the profiled head of the saint which corresponds most closely to the Waldron *Madonna* roundel of 1915 (fig. 69).

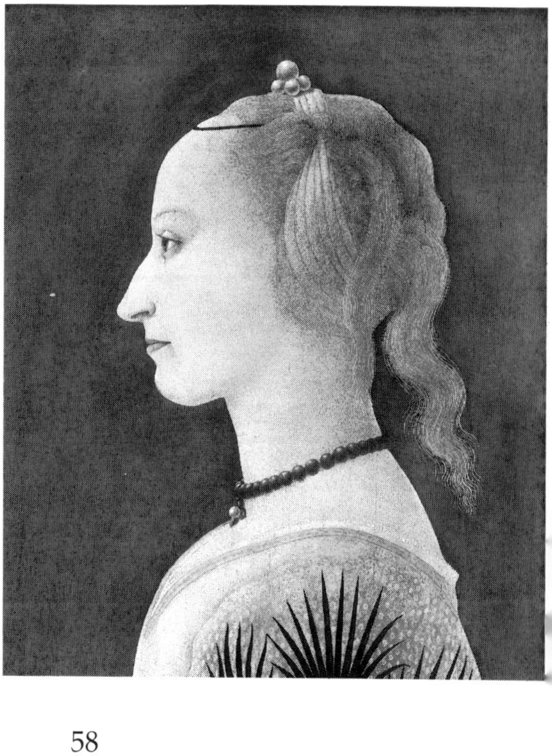

67 Alesso Baldovinetti, *Portrait of a Lady in Yellow* (detail), fifteenth century (courtesy of the National Gallery, London); the sitter's profile was synthesized by Clarke with that of Donatello's Virgin (fig. 68) to create one of his idiosyncratic archetypes.

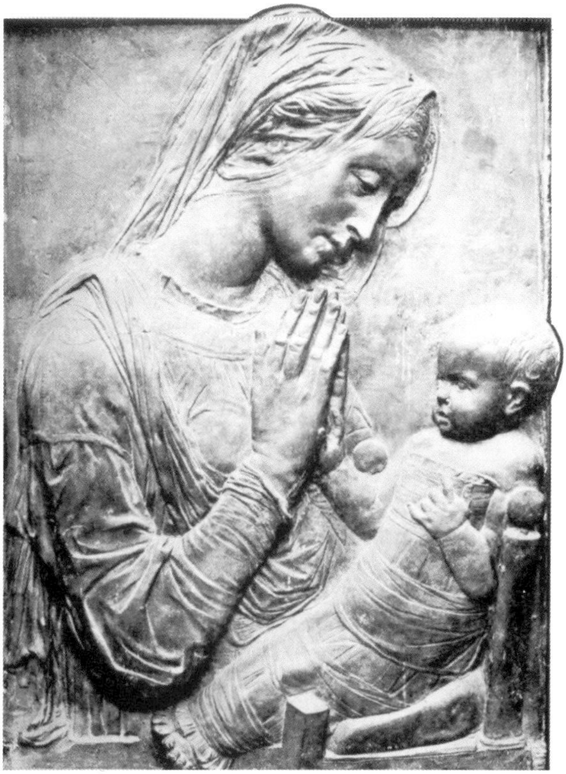

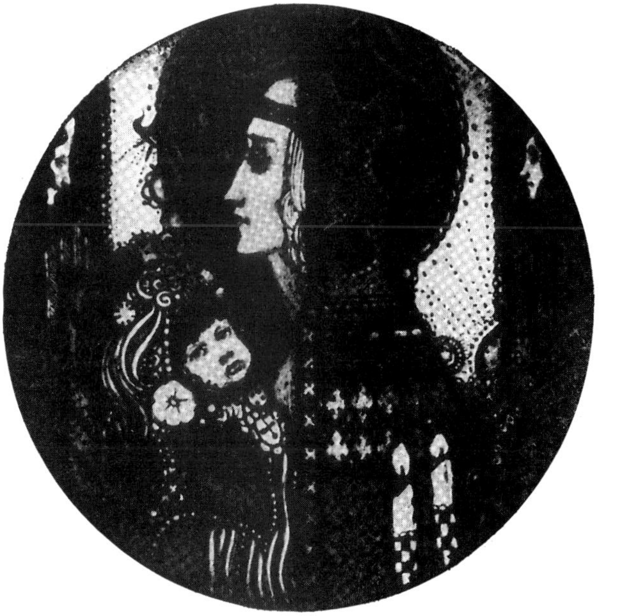

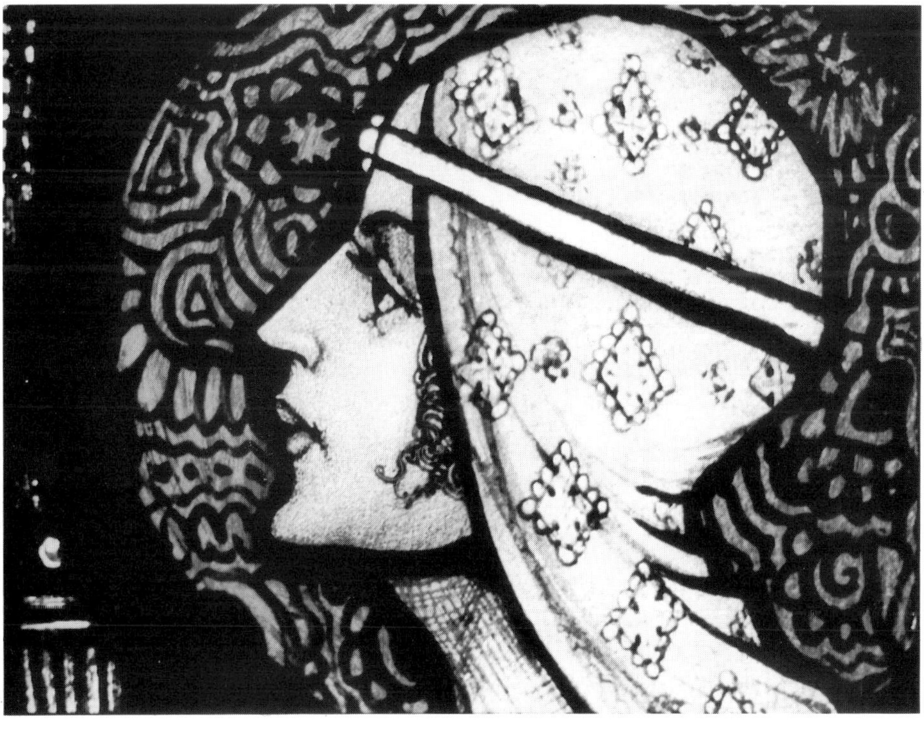

68 Donatello, *The Virgin and Child*, relief in terracotta and gilt, fifteenth century; in the collection of the Victoria and Albert Museum since 1867 and thus known to Clarke during his formative years as a student in London

69 *Madonna and Child* roundel, stained glass, 1915; a tiny panel made for Clarke's first major patron, L.A. Waldron, demonstrating the technique he would evolve for his miniature panels over the next few years

70 A handmaiden (detail from the *St Gobnait* window, Honan Chapel, 1916)

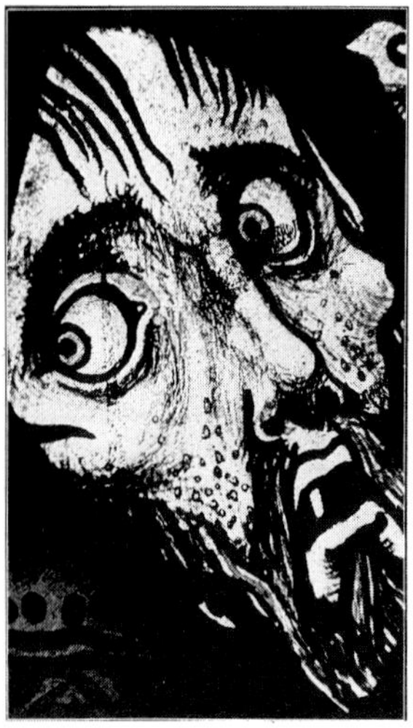

71 A robber being chased by bees (detail from the *St Gobnait* window, Honan Chapel, 1916)

haired robber are amongst Clarke's finest works in glass. They recall Charles Connick's comment on the windows at St Mary's, Fairford in Gloucestershire depicting the history of the Christian religion in the Old and New Law: 'The master glassman who designed this series of windows evidently enjoyed the opportunity given to him to celebrate the wicked persecutors. They have a picturesque and striking air of wickedness that is rare in the stained glass windows of the world.'[47]

The head of St Gobnait in the lower panel (fig. 66-68) is interesting for two reasons. First, because this is the first time we see Clarke using a feature which became characteristic of his work — a high-necked collar of minutely ruched material, which runs from the collar bone up to the chin, completely covering the neck; and secondly, in relation to a little roundel of flashed blue glass in shades of bright turquoise and green (achieved by using silver stain in varying degrees) Harry had made slightly earlier for Larky Waldron. Signed 'H. Clarke to Laurence Waldron, Dec. 1915', it is just under five inches in diameter and depicts a profiled head of the Madonna whose features, hair and veil are exactly the same as the small Gobnait profile (fig. 69).[48] This little Madonna holds a tiny bambino. There are two white candles acided out in the foreground and two angels in profile, one on either side of the Madonna. The date reveals that the roundel was made while Harry was working on the *Gobnait* window; perhaps Waldron was so taken with the head of *Gobnait* that he asked for a copy, which Harry made into a Madonna and Child as a Christmas present.[49] It is a fine example of Harry's experiments with small cabinet panels, using minute aciding and staining techniques with subtle effect; the little roundel would seem to be the first successful piece of this kind that he made.

The next window in this series of Munster saints depicts St Declan of Ardmore of the Decii on the north side of the chapel. Yellow is the dominant colour in this window, which shows Declan as a seafarer, despite the brocaded slippered feet hovering over spiralling waves. The sensitive, strongly chiselled features, the shaggy dark eyebrows and spirals of red hair, like those on ancient Irish jewellery, suggest that this face determined but bemused, may be based on one of the portraits of the fishermen Harry drew on Inishere (fig. 72). The reddish-gold patchwork of his cloak is echoed throughout the window, complemented by an unusual jade green. Behind the figure, small glittering pieces of highly wrought rubies and blues make up a sumptous patchwork which creates an overall richly decorative effect.

The scene at the top of the window shows Declan, cross in hand, preaching to his small band of disciples, seated in the boat which is taking them from Wales to the land of their new mission.[50] The face of Ruanus, his young acolyte, is pale green, perhaps reflecting Harry's first trip to Aran, when he was violently seasick. The expressions on the face of each man, tossed by heaving, spiralling waves, deserve attention; one man holds a flaming torch and a tiny Madonna and Child adorn the prow of the boat.

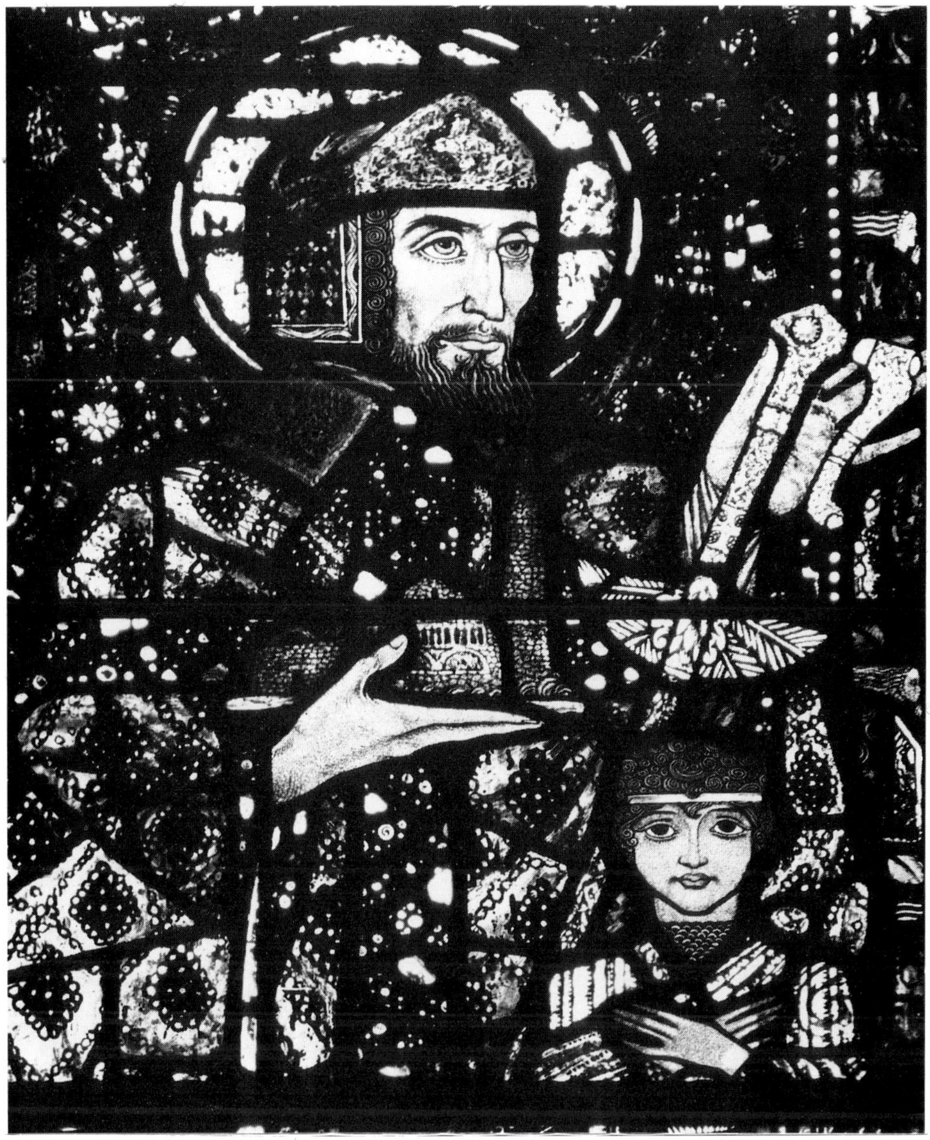

72 St Declan with Ruanus (detail from the *St Declan* stained glass window, Honan Chapel, 1916)

Behind them is the bell which was miraculously presented to Declan. Legend tells how Declan, originally from Ireland, embraced Christianity in Wales and vowed to spread the Christian message in his native land. When he was already some distance from the Welsh coast, he realized that the bell had been left behind on a rock. In response to Declan's prayers the bell, still on the rock, appeared before their boat, and sped before them to an island known as High Sheep's Island on Decii territory in Waterford. Declan landed and there he founded his city and bishopric. He named the place which the king granted him Ardmore.

St Declan holds a carefully detailed model of his monastic settlement with its cathedral and round tower. The silver staff he carries is covered in

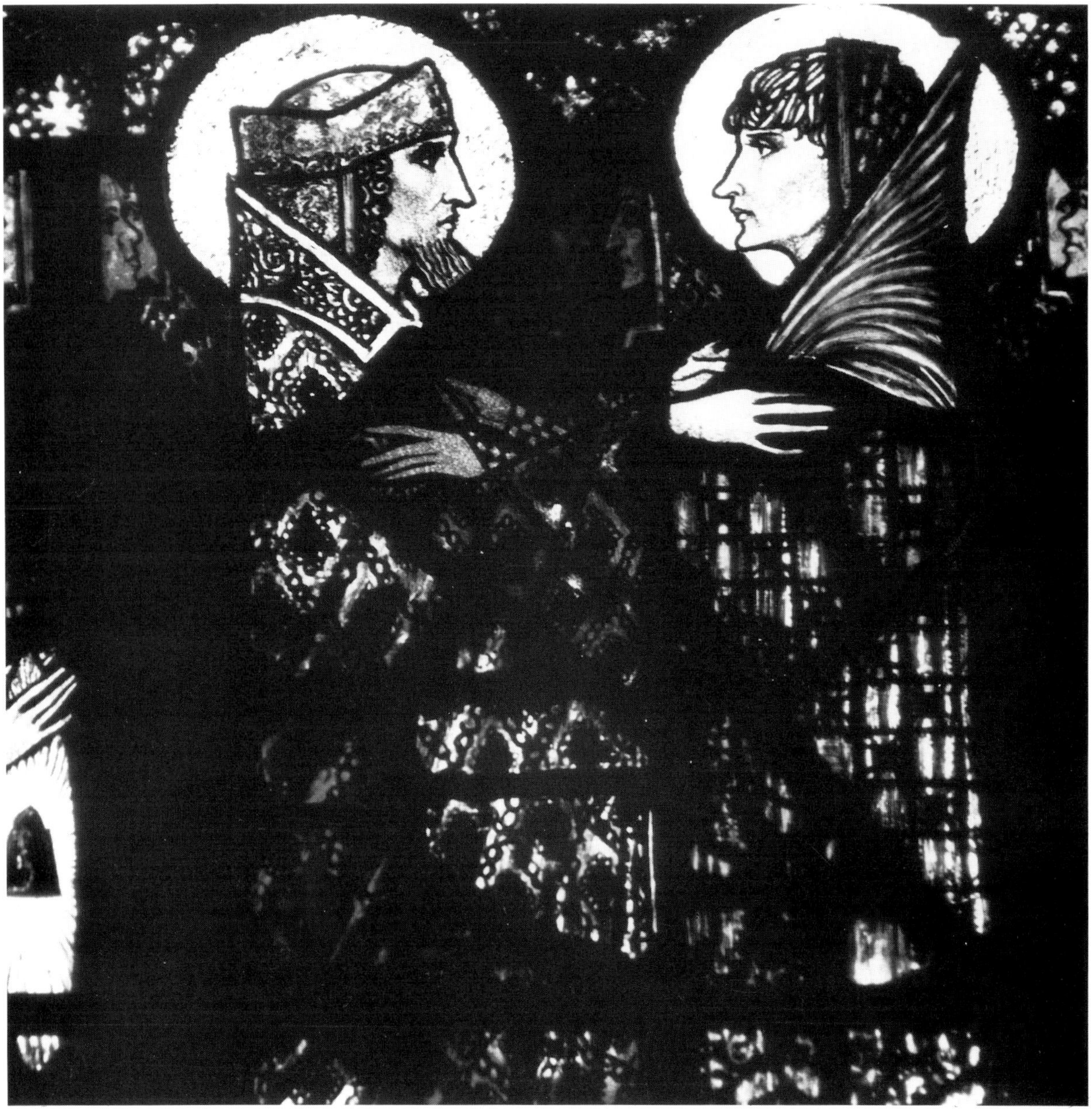

73 St Declan meeting St Patrick (detail from the Honan Chapel *St Declan*); note the embracing figures of monks discernible behind the two men.

Celtic motifs, and a flame motif reflects another legend in which Declan flung his staff at a burning chieftain's residence, miraculously extinguishing the fire. Ruanus stands with the bell, looking penitent at the memory of its near loss. In the border tiny angels with windswept hair (fig. 74)[51] accompany the ecstatic figures of Declan's four pre-Patrician companion saints, Ciaran, Ibar, Ailbe and Colman. A rich ruby passage leads to the lower panel in which St Declan is depicted returning from his consecration by Pope Leo in Rome, and meeting St Patrick, as yet unconsecrated, on the road from Ireland to Rome; they embrace and look into each other's eyes (fig. 73). Each is accompanied by his acolyte — Ruanus with the bell, Benignus with a flame. Behind them, dimly visible on blue glass, are painted the profiled heads of seven pairs of early Christians embracing each other in solemn brotherhood. Sheaves of flaming corn are interwoven beneath. In the original cartoon, eight witnesses stand clearly behind figures of Declan and Patrick as they greet each other.

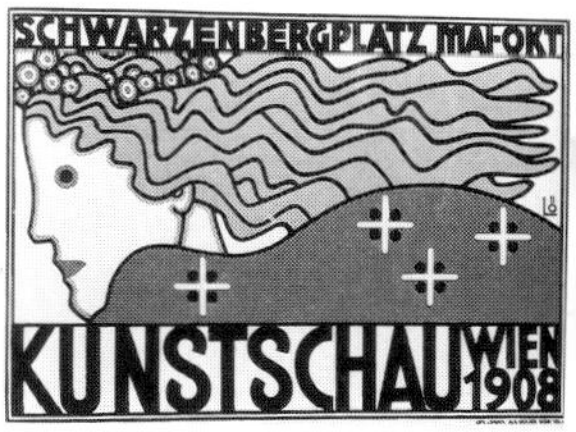

74 Berthold Löffler, *Kunstschau Wien*, 1908; probably the source of the tiny wind-blown angels in the border of the *St Declan* window

On the south side facing St Declan, is the window of *St Brendan* of Kerry and Clonfert (plate 5). Here the dominant colour is green, although deep pinks, reds, golds, and blues abound. In this window, as in Clarke's other windows in the chapel, the overall effect is of a replendent unity of colour and line before the many details emerge. The commanding figure of Brendan the Navigator, famed for his adventurous spirit and his learning, is shod in glowing red pampooties (the rawhide shoes of the west of Ireland, such as Harry and Molloy wore on Aran), leggings, heavy leathern cloak, alb, stole and brooch. His large eyes gaze up and outwards, suggesting his learned wisdoms. His red beard is trim; his hooded head-dress looks somewhat Assyrian and is surrounded by a pink halo. He is reminiscent of Gustav Klimt's *Hygeia* (1901; fig. 75) from the *Medicine* frieze (destroyed in 1945). He holds an oar, to symbolize his sea-faring. At his shoulder is the golden semicircle of the setting sun, towards which he sailed; at its base, the minuscule silhouette of his coracle and a rock. The ultramarine sky behind him is framed by stalactites of white marble and crystal, encrusted with Celtic interlacing, which he encountered on one of his journeys.

75 Gustav Klimt, *Hygeia* (detail), 1901; the source for the imperious figure of *St Brendan* in the Honan Chapel

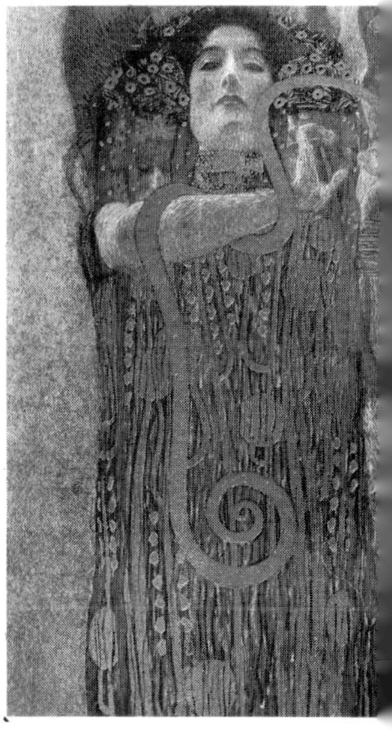

The upper panel, which perhaps represents Brendan's vision of Paradise, is spanned by a golden hemisphere and depicts the saint at sea in his coracle preaching to his companions as they approach the skull-ridden coastline of America in their search for the Islands of the Blessed. On board is the Host and a crucifix. In the ruby-toned borders, exotic plumed birds and cockatoos and metamorphosized fallen angels — which Brendan saw at the Fountain of the Birds — alternate with tiny medallions, inscribed with the portraits of Brendan's contemporaries — St Ita the Wise, St Brigid, Erc, Jarlath, Finian, the blind Addagh and a mysterious tonsured figure, around whose head is written in minute script, 'the poor monk with the Iron in his Head'.[52] The birds may recall Brendan's arrival at the island called the Paradise of Birds, when the birds sang out Latin hymns and welcomed the seafarers with their music.

Beside the crest of the arms of the diocese of Ardfert, framed by Brendan's pampooties, is a silvered arch of Celtic interlacing. From its murky depths glows a pillar of flickering flame supporting the ravaged figure of Judas Iscariot; behind, in their coracle, their faces lit by fire, are three awe-struck monks, horrified by the vision before them (fig. 76). Beside them Brendan looks steadfastly ahead, deep in prayer. Brendan is said to

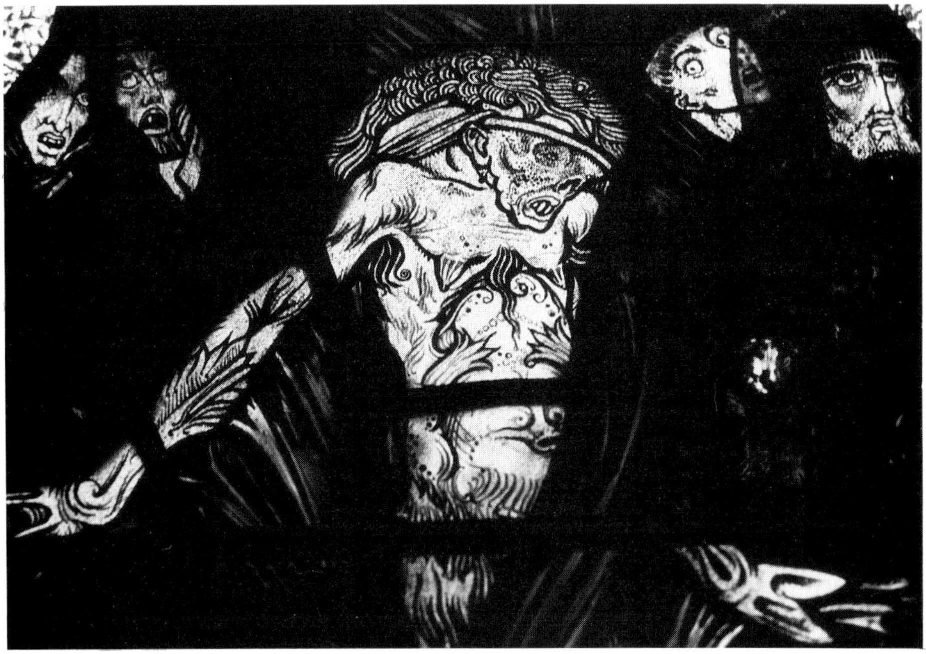

76 Judas discovered by St Brendan and his companions (detail from the Honan Chapel *St Brendan*, 1916); the influence of Clarke's visits to English and French medieval glass is obvious, but it is effectively assimilated.

77 Late twelfth-century head in profile, stained glass (detail) in the collection of the Victoria and Albert Museum; this fragment shows the sort of pitting Clarke wished to emulate when painting the ravaged features of Judas in the *St Brendan* window.

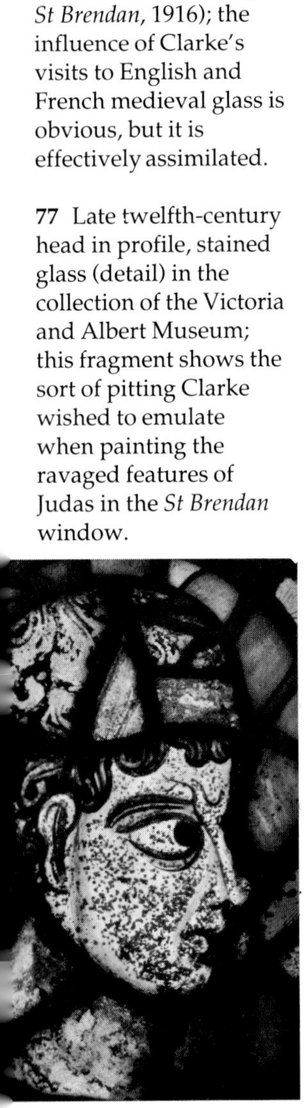

have found Judas, one Christmas night, suspended between two bars, fastened to a rock in the middle of the ocean, holding only a javelin and lashed by the sea. When Brendan enquired who he was, Judas told how he had betrayed Jesus some six hundred years earlier, how he was tortured by fire day and night in the middle of a mountain Brendan had sailed past. Every Sunday, during certain Christian festivals, he was shown mercy and allowed to spend the day on the rock where Brendan had found him. Brendan interceded for him by prayer, so that the unhappy traitor could have extra respite from his fiery torture until sunrise the next day. Judas told Brendan that the rag he was permitted to wear round his head referred to his one act of charity on earth, when he gave a piece of cloth to a leper at Joppa; this, he explained, protected his head and face from cutting winds and biting fish. The pathetic, agonized figure of Judas, his face ravaged,[53] his body shrivelled, plumed and hooved, his calves sprouting fins so that he appears part Pan, part devil and part spectre, is an unforgettable image and a masterly realization of Harry's imagination. This Judas panel is a medieval vision of terror and misery, vivid both graphically and chromatically.

Harry's diary reveals that he consulted Matthew Arnold's moving poem[54] as well as the mediaeval *Navigatio Sancti Brendani Abbatis*, which was well known throughout Europe, both for the *Judas* incident and its other fabulous adventures. In the story Brendan and fourteen monks voyaged for seven years into the Western Ocean in a wicker and hide vessel. Harry would have been inspired by the descriptions of enchanted isles with their supernatural delights alternating with those of the shrieking multitudes of demons, who came to claim their victim, Judas, when Brendan's intercession had proved futile.

He must surely have been affected by the depiction of fiendish torment in the medieval seven-light *Last Judgment* window, in the west end of St Mary the Virgin, Fairford. As noted in Chapter 2, Harry had made a special pilgrimage to Fairford, the only church in England to have retained a complete set of medieval stained glass windows. Not only do these windows express the terror and mortal dread of Judgment and eternal hell fire, which the medieval masters captured so vividly and which Harry is among the very few modern masters to emulate (for example, the faces of Brendan's companions, Judas and the honey thieves in the *Gobnait* window), but they also employ elements of the stained glass technique which Harry was to develop along his own lines in subsequent years. They used rich rubies, often abraded (which Harry would acid instead) and painted with half tone matts, taking full advantage of the texture and quality of each piece of glass, to suggest the inherent forms and features of their caricature-like monsters. Harry had the additional benefits of hydrofluoric acid, silver stain and adjustable firing methods to obtain the effects he sought (fig. 77).[55]

Harry's two single-light windows representing *St Joseph* and the *Virgin Mary, Mother of Sorrows* in the south wall of the Honan Chapel chancel are on a smaller scale than the others and, as they are set at eye level, can be seen close up. In the *Joseph* window beside the altar, towards which the main figure is turned, the dominant colour is red, with a secondary emphasis on blue. On Joseph's head there is a gold Jewish cap and in one of his crossed hands he bears a stem from which two white lilies grow, symbols of purity. He also bears a mallet, representing his carpenter's craft. Beneath his feet there is a silver panel of Celtic interlacing. Above his figure, a golden crown is set over a vignette in which Joseph shows Jesus how to hammer nails into a wooden beam, which crosses a vertical stake, while Mary kneels beside him holding a taper. The border of the window is composed of figures of angels bearing symbols of Joseph's virtues as worker, father, husband, man of faith and craftsman. The lower panel shows the death scene of Joseph with Jesus at his head and Mary at his feet and four haloed figures, St John, St Finbarr, St Columcille and an old woman.

Both this window and its companion, the *Virgin Mary* window beside it, are later than the other ten windows by Harry Clarke in the chapel and are painted in a more delicate style than his previous work. The change of style may have been deliberate to show Christ's parents 'living in the world and fulfilling the daily round and civic life, yet not of it'.[56] These windows show the refinement of the delicate and elegant style which is characteristic of Harry's later work.[57] It may be that Molloy had some hand in the Joseph window because here the colours, the leading and the composition seem less subtle than usual, particularly in the drawing of the face, which is weaker than those in the nave windows and appears somewhat insipid by comparison.

Blue predominates in the *Virgin Mary* window (plate 9). The central figure (fig. 78) is crowned in gold, and her exquisite Celtic face is surrounded by long red hair. Her lapis lazuli blue mantle hangs in folds over a Fortuny-like pleated tunic in turquoise, trimmed in gold. One hand, across her breast, holds a lily, symbol of purity, and a rose. Her other hand, extended downwards, holds crossed tapers (or perhaps sponges on rods, symbols of the Passion). As in the St Joseph figure, the feet, in brocaded slippers, rest on a panel of Celtic interlacing in silver. The wide borders are filled with forlorn figures bearing symbols of Marian devotion and the Passion. Above the central figure a pair of angels, surrounded by palm branches in blue and green, cross hands beneath the dove of the Holy Spirit, from which golden light radiates. The Nativity is represented by stars, one more brilliant than the others, above the dove, and groups of smaller figures at the sides of the panel — what appear to be three shepherds on the left

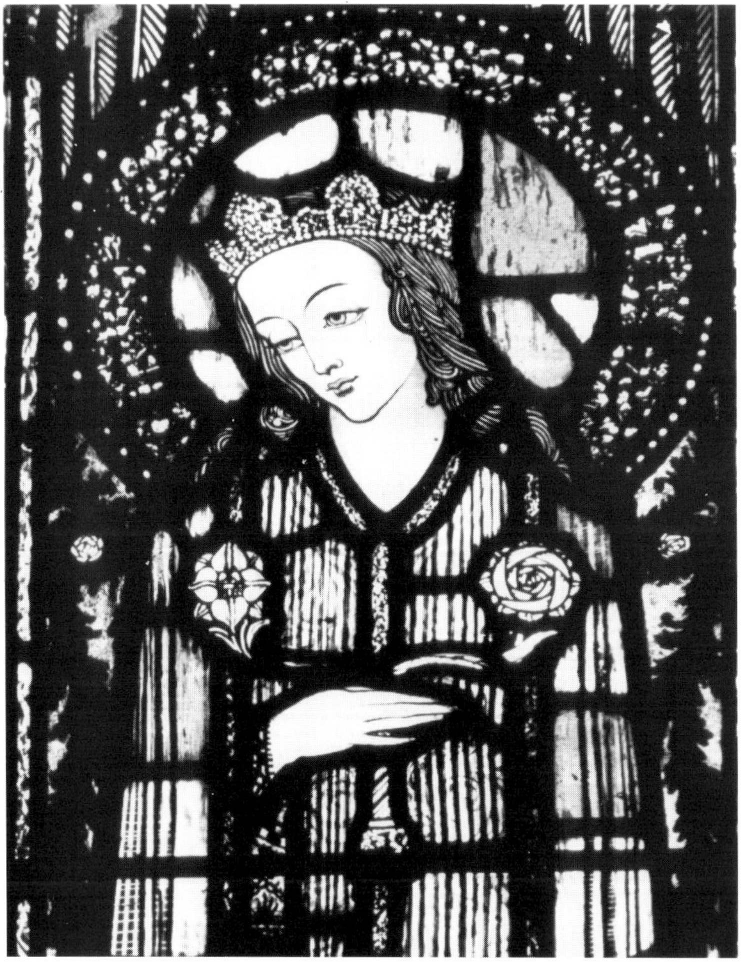

78 *The Virgin Mary* (detail), stained glass window, Honan Chapel, 1917

and three kings on the right, one identified as 'Brendan' in minute script, in a coracle, perhaps to give an Irish dimension to the Christmas story. The face of the ruby-robed shepherd nearest the central star anticipates in style some of the haunted figures in his drawings for Poe's *Tales of Mystery and Imagination* and Goethe's *Faust*. It also recalls *The Ancient Mariner* drawings. Like many similar faces in his work, the features are based on his own.

In the bottom panel of the window a haggard Cronan of Roscrea, from whose ancient church the architectural style of the Honan Chapel was derived, holds a sheet of music strung on a cord. The title, *Cronan na Magdine,* and four lines of minute musical notation are inscribed on the sheet and beside the figure the words of 'The Lullaby of the Maiden' are inscribed in Irish on the left and, on the right, in English; the text seems to read:

> Sleep! Hush O! my treasure
> is my child
> My jewel without deep
> [y] shore of the great world
> Sleep! Hush O!
> isn't he the great pleasure
> ye treasure in his bed
> sleep without sorrow!

On St Cronan's right stands St Ita holding a lily and, on his left, a surreptitious hooded figure carrying a crown. Beside each of these a gold-clad ascetic bears a model of an ancient monastery and behind each group stand two dark ruby figures, popes perhaps, one of which has a strong facial resemblance to Lorenzo the Magnificent. This group of mysterious figures foreshadow the figures in Clarke's series of panels illustrating Synge's poem 'Queens', which he began in 1916 for Waldron's study at Marino. These figures carry the viewer into the secret haunted world of Clarke's vision, reminding one perhaps of the creations in a Fellini masquerade, disturbing images such as Kokoschka or Bacon might create. Below them, at the very bottom of the design four roundels are leaded into a patchwork of symbolic patterns. These resemble Japanese seals[58] and depict a sunflower-like golden sun, a palm tree on an island, a crescent moon on a black sky over a seascape, and a steep rocky crag with steps leading to its summit, possibly representing the elements of air, earth, fire and water. The window is signed 'Harry Clarke March 1917' (the month of its completion) on the music scroll beneath the title of the lullaby. This window shows Harry Clarke's stained glass at its finest. Its overall effect, similar to that of a Gothic altarpiece, is of a composition in gold and lapis lazuli, studded with precious stones. It has been compared[59] to the turn of the century painting by V.M. Vasnetsov, the late nineteenth-century Russian Revivalist

(1848-1926), in St Vladimir's Cathedral in Kiev entitled *The Joy of All who Sorrow* which also depicts the Virgin; but there is no evidence that Clarke was influenced by the Russian work.

These two windows ended the Honan Chapel work. They were sent to Cork by train and fixed and storm-glazed in April 1917 by Fitzpatrick, who was warned by Joshua Clarke not to leave any finger marks on them! The completion of the commission was a great achievement for Harry, who had not reached his twenty-eighth birthday. Ever since, these windows, emanating the 'glow of controlled fire'[60] have been regarded among the masterworks of Irish glass, as famous as the great east window of St Canice's in Kilkenny, erected in 1553, for which the Papal Nuncio offered £700 in 1648 but which in the next decade fell to Cromwell's troops, and so escaped comparison with Clarke's.

4

Clarke's commitment to the Arts and Crafts Society of Ireland — The first of his unique series of miniature stained glass panels illustrating scenes from literature by Synge, de la Mare and Heine

Harry Clarke's reputation as an outstandingly talented and original stained glass artist was firmly established by the Honan Chapel windows, and his illustrated *Hans Andersen* manifested his gift for spirited book illustration, both in ink and watercolour. Despite the influences of Nielsen, Dulac, Beardsley and Sime, his individual style and idiosyncratic sense of line and colour ensured that his graphic work generally bore his distinctive hallmark.[1]

In the summer of 1917, his old school magazine, *The Belvederian*, reported in their 'News of Our Past' the prominence into which their former student's work had recently been brought. Beneath Seán Keating's study of Harry's head, his progress was described:

> He has already won an enviable reputation as a brilliant and original worker in stained glass and [as] a remarkable exponent of delicate and original pen and colour work. In both of these branches he has won widespread and well earned recognition within the past year. As an illustrator, he has produced a volume of Hans Andersen which on its appearance commanded widespread attention. He brought to his work an entirely new inspiration and treated his subject in an artistic and highly decorative fashion. The drawings have a wonderful wealth of detail which testify to the painstaking care with which this artist deals with his work. But it is in stained glass that his inspiration finds truest expression. The windows which he has designed and executed for the Honan Hostel Chapel attracted considerable attention when exhibited in his studio and have been written about extensively since they have been placed in position in the Cork Chapel. It is difficult to know what to admire most in Mr Clarke's windows, whether the colour scheme, the marvellous use of symbolism or the entire originality of treatment. There is a complete departure from the common unattractive window so often erected at a fixed price per foot, Mr Clarke has given us real works of art. His windows are to most others in this country what the oil painting from the brush of a great artist is to the common oleograph. We hope that his windows will be

examined and studied by those who are best competent to judge the real value of such work and that those who wish to leave in their churches lasting memorials of themselves will not send orders out of the country until they have seen the work of this remarkable craftsman.[2]

Such supportive comment was invaluable to Harry's career, issuing as it did from the influential Jesuit school magazine.

The next major work which Harry undertook represented a fusion of his talent for book illustration with that for stained glass, in a series of miniature stained glass panels, each no larger than the page of a book, on which he would illustrate in minute detail scenes from literature. The idea for these panels is directly related to his work on the tiny details worked into the Honan Chapel windows, but his attraction to very small scale detail was evident as early as the tiny head painted on the medallions leaded into his *Judas* window (1913) and the tiny effigies painted on the lozenges incorporated into his *Baptism of St Patrick* (1912). Working on the Honan windows he had discovered the magical effects to be achieved by aciding, plating, staining and painting. It must have been a great challenge to him to translate his ideas for illustration into such small pieces of glass, as breakages were bound to occur when working on such a small scale, and the risk of damage was high, particularly in the firings.

Two years earlier he had made the 5″- diameter *Madonna* roundel for Laurence Waldron which so resembled the head in the *St Gobnait* window, and he had also made an undated heraldic panel for Waldron, signed 'H . . . C', where the coat of arms was painted in stain and terra cotta coloured painting medium on a clear glass panel 9″ x 6½″, set into a border of green glass 13″ x 10″ in size. He also made Waldron a tiny grisaille panel 9″ x 3½″, signed twice, of a ghoulish, gypsy-like Harlequin with three teeth, playing a lute, in which the colours were limited to black, tones of grey and yellow stain (i.e. grisaille).[3] Another 7½″ x 6½″ panel, still in the Waldron family collection, unsigned and undated, has a border of opalescent glass, painted with abstract designs; its corners are made of green glass squares and it contains a rectangle of pale lime 'seedy' glass on which a thin wash has been laid and a Botticelli-like Madonna painted.[4]

That June, a week after the birth of Harry's and Margaret's first child on the 17th, the fifth exhibition of the Arts and Crafts Society of Ireland opened in the Metropolitan School of Art. Harry's committed involvement with the society took up much of his time. A member of the Guild of Irish Art Workers, he served on its council and executive committee which included a number of Waldron's friends and Harry's contemporaries from the School of Art.[5] Also, at the request of the executive committee, he designed the cover and initial letter of the foreword of the catalogue, which was finely printed on handmade paper from blocks made from the Irish Photo

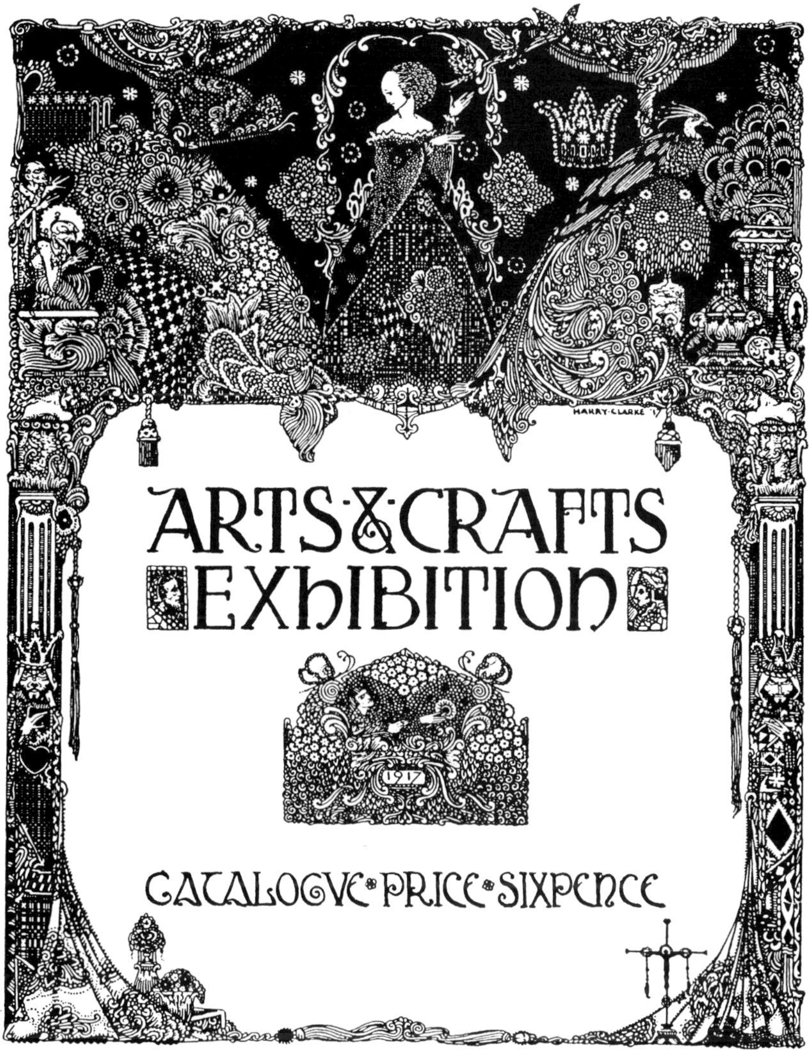

79 Cover of the catalogue for the fifth exhibition of the Arts and Crafts Society of Ireland, 1917

Engraving Co. His design for the cover measures $7\frac{3}{4}''$ x $6\frac{1}{4}''$ and depicts a fanciful and intricately decorated frame with a large upper panel in which a doll-like queen in a garden frees some doves, watched by laughing hobgoblins and two mischievous caryatid kings (fig. 79). Floral ornament and swirling patterns abound; a little crucifix and pots dripping with flowers, both recurrent details in Harry's work, appear beneath the decorative lettering. Two tiny vignettes portraying heads are set into the lettering, and butterflies adorn the vignette, which includes a further figure surrounded by flowers and the date, 1917. The initial letter is a scarlet T ($1\frac{5}{8}''$ square) printed in a black square with a white beaded surround and a tiny haloed monk standing in profile.

Harry's other contributions to the exhibition were designs for a book plate lent by Laurence Waldron, his 1916 Christmas card, with copyright for sale, priced at £5, an illustration in black and gold, *The Miners* (a strong graphic portrayal of Aran fishermen, transposed into a liftshaft, also lent by Waldron) and a reproduction of an illustration by colour process. Several cartoons for the Honan Chapel windows were shown — *Our Lady* for sale at £15, *St Gobnait* at £21 and *St Brigid* at £15; Waldron also lent his tiny *Madonna* medallion in glass.

The Studio magazine, in its regular reports on the activities of art students, societies and exhibitions working in the applied and decorative arts and crafts, published a long article by Oswald Reeves, 'Irish Arts and Crafts', written while the exhibition was in Belfast in the autumn of 1917.[6] In this he described the constitution of the society and the 'evidence of a steady striving towards peace and beauty, serious and sincere,on the part of a widely spread number of men and women . . . in a land too apt to be thought one of unrest alone'. He pointed out how fortunate England was, where the movement was born, to have had the 'genius and force' of William Morris's example and teaching, as well as men like Burne-Jones, Madox Brown and Walter Crane and what became a 'world-centre of genius and riches'. Ireland had never had similar advantages, he felt, but at the peak of the Morris movement, 'when Irish craftsmanship was at its lowest ebb', Lord Mayo had founded the Irish Society. He drew a parallel between the Irish literary revival and that in the Irish Arts and Crafts and hoped a similarly strong national character would emerge. After a modest mention of the distinctively Celtic yet modern craftsmanship in enamelling, he continued:

> There is one artist represented in the exhibition . . . who has gone further in achievement than any of his fellows, and whose work illustrates more clearly than any of the foregoing how a genuine Celtic character marks the best Irish Applied Art. Harry Clarke, of Dublin, exhibits drawings for reproduction, stained glass, and cartoons for stained-glass windows. His drawing for reproduction in black and white and colour is already very well known. It is in his stained glass, however, that the full scope of his undoubted genius is to be seen, and his best efforts, so far, now enrich the chapel attached to the Honan Hostel. . . .

The first direct reference to an extremely important series of nine cabinet panels, *Queens*, which Harry was working on immediately after the Honan windows had been completed, occurs in a letter to Bodkin dated 4 March 1917. In this Harry wrote how very much he was enjoying himself on the drawings and asked Bodkin's help on two points of information about the queens described by Villon and Ronsard. These are referred to in Synge's poem, 'Queens', written in 1902 and published in a Cuala Press edition in 1909,[7] which, probably at Waldron's suggestion, inspired the series.

The *Queens* series was made to hang in the window of the library of Laurence Waldron's house, looking out over Killiney Bay. The window was

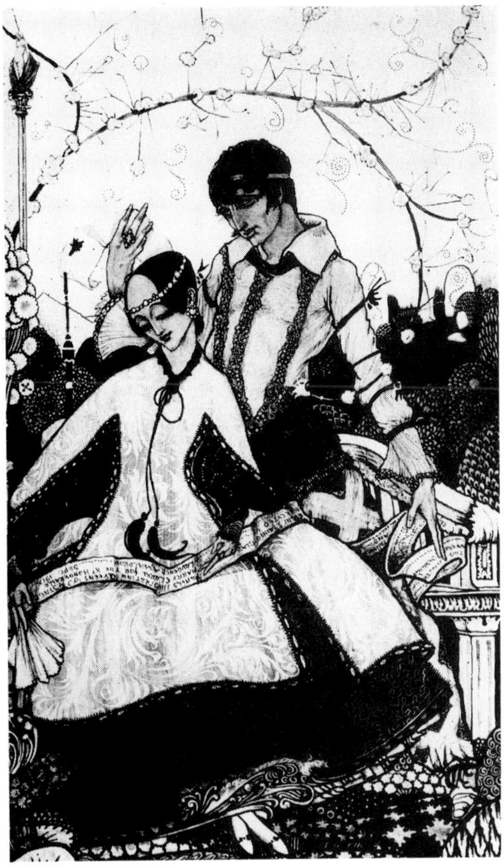

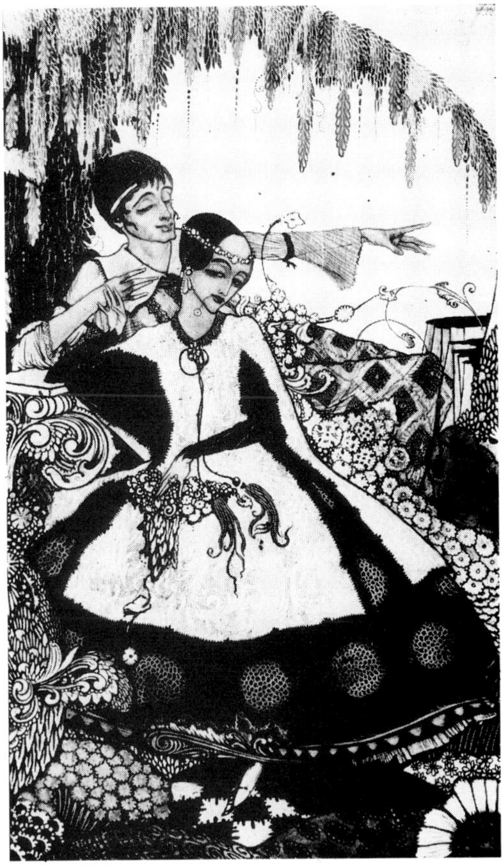

80 Prologue painted in grisaille from the series of stained glass panels illustrating J.M. Synge's *Queens*, 1917

81 Epilogue panel for the *Queens* series

composed of seventy-seven small panes of glass into which the nine little panels were set in a horizontal line, as though in procession across the window. Beneath, on tiny slip panels of clear glass, each measuring 2" x 6" and framed in lead, the lines illustrated in each panel are inscribed in Harry's hand. Each panel is painted in a sepia-coloured painting medium in fluid, deft and intricate lines. Flat washes of diluted painting medium are also matted on with decorative motifs scratched onto this, and extensive use is made of yellow stain in its different strengths and of hydrofluoric acid, used with impressive control and variety. On 24 July an urgent order was sent to Chance's for 'a very important job', enclosing samples to be matched up exactly for three sheets of antique flashed blue, three of flashed ruby and one of flashed gold-pink, each to measure 11″ x 7″.[8] A week later, Heaton's were asked to send by return an ounce of each of three prepared silver stains. By 4 August Harry was trying to get the first painting of the *Queens* finished so that he could have a week off before he began the second painting.

The first panel acts as a prologue and the last as an epilogue to the series in the manner of Japanese Shunga prints (figs. 80, 81). In the next seven panels the strange company of Queens named by Synge are clustered into groups and framed by dark draperies with fringed edges. Flowers, sumptuous brocades and architectural ruins are strewn across the foreground. The queens seem to process over heaps of embroidered cushions and their exotic headdresses, hairstyles and profiles form a rich frieze beneath the curtained outline, before closer examination reveals the identities of the individual characters. The clear space behind the heads, between the curtains, is covered with a light badgered matt[9] on which a motif like unravelled knitting has been worked.

The title and first four lines of the poem are written in Harry's hand on the accompanying clear glass panel:

> Seven dog-days we let pass
> Naming Queens in Glenmacnass
> All the rare and royal names
> Wormy sheepskin yet retains.

The panels run from left to right in a frieze and were never joined, as they were separately inserted into adjoining astragals.[10]

The first panel in the series (fig. 80) is painted on glass, flashed with a thin coat of kelp, which contains extract of seaweed ashes and holds stain very well. The smooth painting on this grisaille panel could as well be on paper, parchment or ivory as on glass. It depicts a romantic scene where a dark gypsy-like lady, garlanded and dressed in white damask over a deep golden crinoline, is seated on a stone in a graveyard beside a raven-haired swain in a golden shirt, crossgarters and hose. Her eyelids are lowered and arms outstretched as she unravels a scroll across her lap. The young man's attitude, as he kneels poised behind his lady, is one which Harry often used. The wilting heroine and her harlequinesque hero recur in Harry's earlier book illustrations. A carefully placed arabesque of wintery branches fills the clear glass background rising from a heap of 'fleurs du mal' and, on a little eminence behind, a mysterious tiny lady unshrouds herself. The scroll unfurled by the beloved is inscribed,

> This and the following stained glass panels illustrating Queens by J.M. Synge executed by Harry Clarke for the Rt. Honourable Laurence A. Waldron. . . . Sept 1917.

The panel is signed 'HARRY CLARKE' above the date, 1917, in the bottom corner.

The second panel (plate 12) illustrates Synge's lines

> Etain, Helen, Maeve and Fand,
> Golden Deirdre's tender hand.

Here the figures are depicted on a sheet of deep blue glass. As Harry would acid each panel as many as six times, he has used the thickest possible rectangles of glass to allow as many tones of blue as possible to emerge as the acid bit into the layer of flashed colour. Most of the heads are in profile; Deirdre's is identifiable, a gold band binding her forehead and golden curls. One queen holds a little church, and butterflies and flowers adorn the group. The panel is signed 'HC 1917', the letters and figures vertically over each other.

In the third panel (plate 13),

> Bert, the big-foot, sung by Villon,
> Cassandra, Ronsard found in Lyon

are illustrated in rich tones of the beautiful and costly flashed gold-pink glass Harry used whenever possible. The colours in this panel range from a deliciously rich pink to a pale rose. The exotic arabesque made by a glistening bird of paradise decorates the background. Ronsard's 'belle Cassandre' from his erotic ode, 'Ah! Je voudrais, richement jaunissant'[11] steps on to an embroidered cushion while being offered a wine glass by a beguiling bearded beau (perhaps the wishful Narcisse of the poem), clad in deep pink shimmering satin, who dances temptingly beside her. Villon's Bert, the 'Berte au grant pié' in his *Ballade des Dames du Temps Jadis*,[12] reputedly Charlemagne's mother, stands, golden slippered, in equally exotic garb, on further piles of patterned cushions. This panel is signed 'HC'.

In the fourth panel (plate 14),

> Queens of Sheba, Meath and Connaught,
> Coiffed with crown, or gaudy bonnet

follow, on blue glass. On this panel Harry has acided away the glass surrounding his signature, written as an autographed 'Harry Clarke', so that his name stands out in relief in delicate blue handwriting. Here we see a bizarre, brooding collection; a monstruously ugly queen, a queen in a plumed hat with a baby, an androgynous queen with a peacock and crozier and a young fair, crowned queen in fashionable brocaded sapphire gown. None is readily identifiable.

The fifth panel, the first in ruby glass, signed 'HC' (plate 15), illustrates the next quatrain,

> Queens whose finger once did stir men
> Queens were eaten of fleas and vermin,
> Queens men drew like Monna Lisa,
> Or slew with drugs in Rome and Pisa.

To illustrate the first line, a profiled queen with golden hair and a fantastic headdress very characteristic of Harry's later work, wearing a fine shawl and a rich ruby crinoline, holds a tiny puppet of a king in her hands, as a plaything. The second line is illustrated by a queen on the left of the panel who glides along in golden crown, her neck and bosom bared to reveal big red scabs. Next, Harry's copy of Leonardo's *Mona Lisa* is vested and gowned in sumptuous ruby. She stands behind a queen of Rome or Pisa whose long girdled dress of figured velvet falls from her shoulders to reveal her lace chemise, her expression agonized as she casts back her head, eyes rolling. In her left hand a golden goblet hangs limply, poison dripping on to the ruby flowered carpet on which these four queens stand.

The sixth panel, on flashed antique blue glass is signed 'Harry Clarke' in Harry's ordinary handwriting in blue glass (plate 16), raised in relief from the etched background:

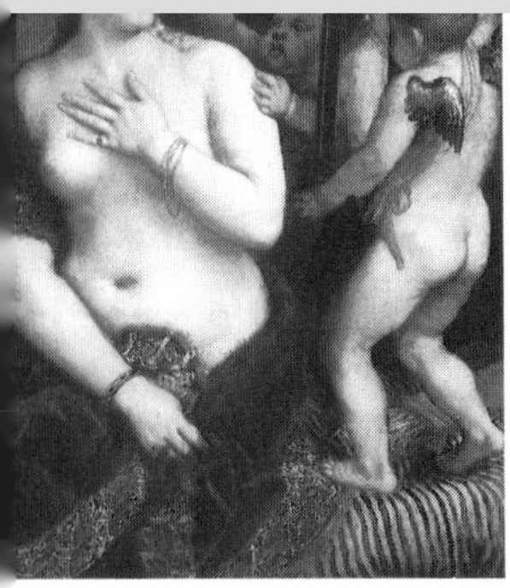

82, 83 Titian, *Venus with a mirror* (detail), courtesy of the National Gallery of Art, Washington, DC; and Giovanni Ambrogio Preda, *Profile Portrait of a Lady* (detail), fifteenth century (courtesy of the National Gallery of London), believed, in Clarke's day, to be a portrait of Lucrezia Crivelli; adapted by Clarke in the sixth *Queens* panel, 1917

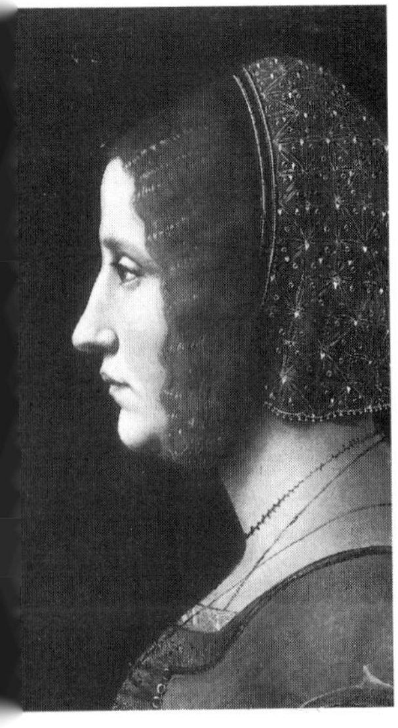

We named Lucrezia Crivelli
And Titian's Lady with amber belly,
Queens acquainted in learned sin,
Jane of Jewry's slender shin.

The panel is dominated by Harry's interpretation of the figure from Titian's voluptuous *Venus with a Mirror* (fig. 82).[13] Immediately recognizable with 'amber belly', traditional *pudica* hand position, golden hair, bracelet, rings, pearls and a diamond drop ear-ring, Harry's lady is slimmer than Titian's and her arms are swathed in a royal blue drape which falls in heavy folds to the ground; here it is strewn with decorative flowers and extravagantly patterned cushions. Unlike the original version she is unattended by *amorini*. Her eyes meet those of 'Jane of Jewry', shown in profile on the right of the panel, whose 'slender shin' and bosom emerge through her draped costume of sky blue. The procession is led by Lucrezia Crivelli, a subdued, bonneted queen, in a Renaissance gown of deep blue. She is another adept transcription from Ambrogio Preda's *Profile Portrait of a Lady* (fig. 83).[14] Between 'Titian's Lady' and 'Jane of Jewry' stands an older scheming queen, crowned in gold, clad in a dark cloak, accompanied by a hooded crony, accomplices 'acquainted in learned sin'. Another wasted, malevolent looking androgyne lurks behind.

The seventh panel (plate 17) illustrates

Queens who cut the bogs of Glanna
Judith of Scripture, and Glorianna.

On a rich body of deeply glowing ruby, three queens are portrayed. It is signed 'HC'. On her right is the bedraggled figure of a queen 'who cut the bogs of Glanna', with large watery eyes. Her tapering fingers caress a silver turf-cutting spade and she wears a deep crimson halter-necked dress and plaid shawl. In the centre of the panel, in strong profile and bare breasted, the dramatic figure of Judith is poised, the head of Holofernes at her sandalled feet, her blooded sabre cutting a strong horizontal line across the lower half of the panel (fig. 84).[15] Her head, with its thoughtful, intelligent expression, finely delineated against the curtained background and the pale background space, is reminiscent of an early Italian Renaissance portrait. Beside her, quizzically peering at us, stands Gloriana, with golden curls decked in richly diapered brocade, one hand smoothing the folds of her gown, the other silhouetted as it plays with a little monocle. Gloriana's costume is taken from Marcus Gheeraerts the Younger's portrait of Elizabeth I as *A Lady in Fancy Dress* (*c.* 1590-1600), in the Royal Collection at Hampton Court, where she 'is disguised as a Persian Virgin, a costume derived from the figure of a Virgo Persica in Boissard's *Habitus Variarum Orbis Gentium*' (fig. 85).[16] There are interesting analogies between Elizabethan miniature and portrait paintings and Harry's coloured illustrations on glass or paper. Both favour small scale, intricate and symbolic detail, glowing jewel-like colours, the two-dimensional use of an elaborately attired hieratic figure set against a decorative setting with any chiaroscuro reserved for the face and hands of the figure, 'a reduction of modelling to decorative simplicity'.[17] Both frequently include a minutely inscribed cartouche in their designs, and Harry's figures often evoke the 'sabre-coloured' melancholy cultivated by the Elizabethans, his men in particular, dressed according to his own eclectic system of gallant beauty, analogous to that of the Elizabethan beau.[18]

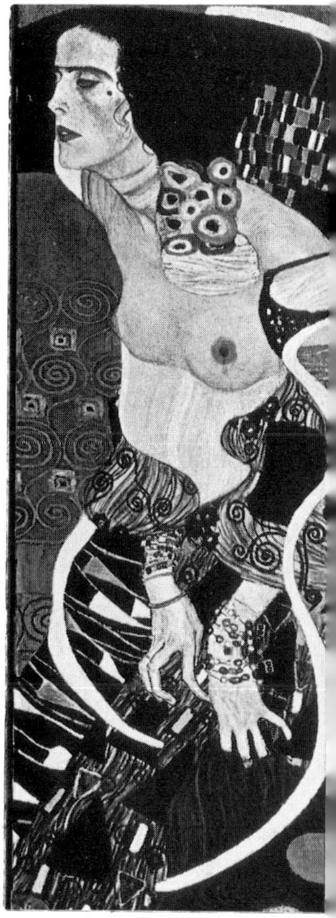

84 Gustav Klimt, *Judith II*, 1909; this darkly profiled figure was adapted by Clarke for 'Jane of Jewry' in the sixth *Queens* panel and 'Judith of Scripture' in the seventh, and in a number of smaller details elsewhere

The eighth panel, on blue glass, is also signed 'HC' (plate 18). It illustrates

> Queens who wasted the East by proxy,
> Or drove the ass cart, a tinker's doxy

and shows a haggard queen gazing at her golden goblet, an apprehensive, lavishly clothed queen whose ballooning sleeve is freely acided, and a vampish beaded queen with ass's ears. The blues are rich and deep and inventive decorative details fill all but the top of the panel.

The ninth and final panel (fig. 81) returns to the poet and his lady, painted on clear glass in grisaille; above them are written the final four lines of the poem and the poet's name:

> Yet these are rotten — I ask their pardon —
> And we've the sun on rock and garden,
> These are rotten, so you're the Queen
> Of all are living, or have been.
>
> J.M. Synge

They sit beneath a bower of fairytale confection, in a garden strewn with huge unreal flowers and foliated classical ruins. The cliffs behind resemble those of Bray Head and the garden could well be based on Waldron's own. In his gold harlequin costume the poet's spiky fingers indicate the procession of queens, while he eyes his coy Columbine queen, crowned with daisies. This last panel is signed 'HARRY CLARKE 1917'.

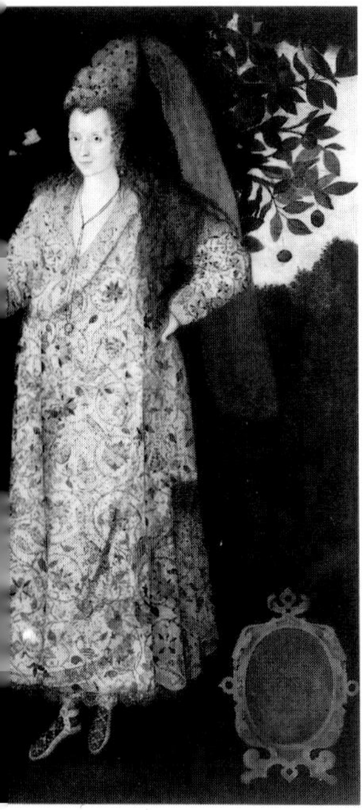

85 Marcus Gheeraerts the Younger, *A Lady in Fancy Dress*, c. 1590-1600 (courtesy of Her Majesty the Queen, the Royal Collection, Hampton Court, London); the source for 'Gloriana' in the seventh *Queens* panel, 1917

Even on a dull day the *Queens* panels sparkle and glimmer and must have effected an enchanting transformation of Waldron's library, while their art historical references would have appealed to his more literary colleagues. They are also a major technical achievement, being so intricately worked on such tiny areas of glass; and they are innovatory in that they are part fantasy, part illustration, using single sheets of thick unleaded flashed glass, acided, stained and painted (although not plated). As Bodkin wrote, 'Mr Waldron's panels have no exact precedent in the history of stained glass'.[19] Their nearest counterparts would be those domestic panels which were hung against windows in domestic interiors in the seventeenth century. Thomas Bodkin, who was to be a vitally important source of encouragement, guidance and constructive, educated criticism to Harry, much admired Waldron's *Queens* and soon commissioned a panel of his own. While working on this, Harry inscribed to Bodkin a pen and ink illustration for J.M. Synge's *Playboy of the Western World* illustrating 'The Mad Mulrannies' (fig. 86). This drawing was reproduced in Bodkin's article on Clarke in the November 1919 issue of *The Studio*[20] and in Crampton Walker's *Irish Life and Landscape* (1927). It was also exhibited at the Royal Hibernian Academy and the 1924 Aonach Tailteann exhibition in Dublin. It depicts a reference by Pegeen Mike in the first act of Synge's play to the grotesque characters of the neighbourhood including 'the mad Mulrannies, who were driven from California and they lost in their wits'. Harry has

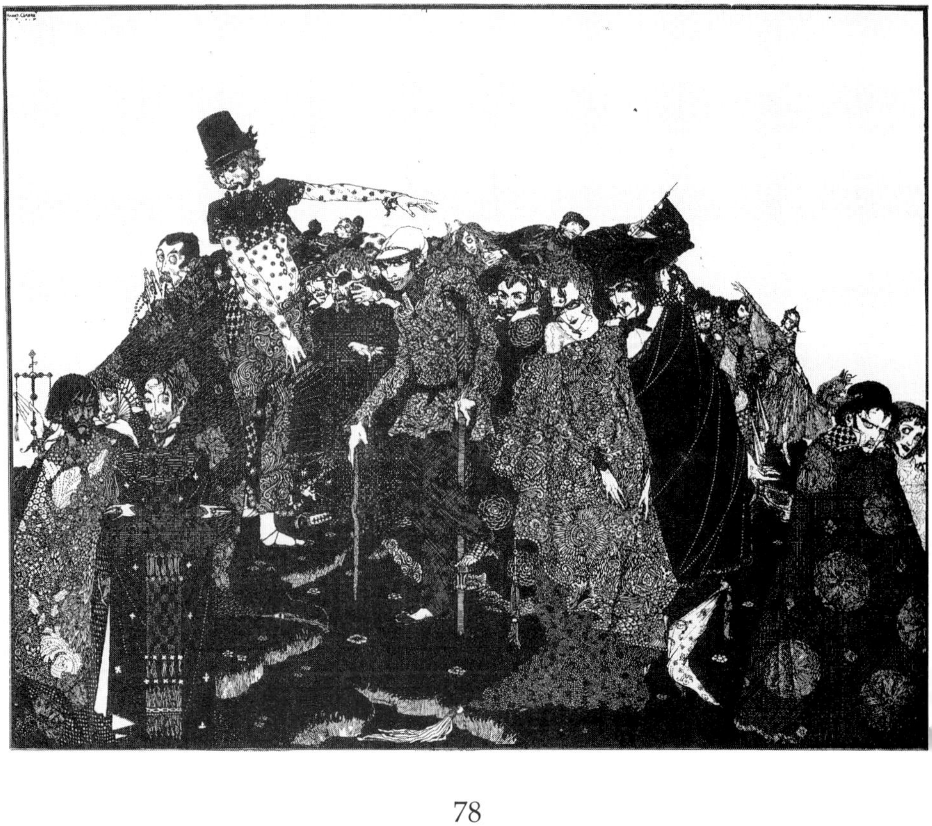

86 'The Mad Mulrannies', illustration for J.M. Synge's *The Playboy of the Western World*, pen and ink, 1917

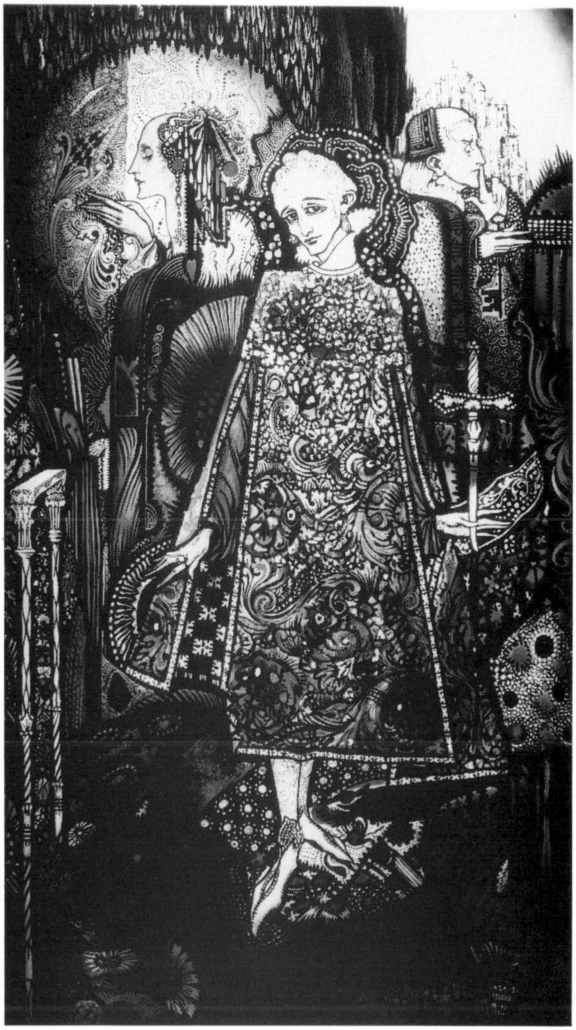

87 *The Song of the Mad Prince*, illustration to Walter de la Mare's poem, stained glass panel, 1917

used the text to draw a rich composition of caricatured figures piled on top of each other beside the jagged coastline. These include a self-portrait, the face of Seán Keating in several different guises, and the face of Judith from the *Queens* which resembles a face already seen in the background of the Honan Chapel *Virgin Mary* window, which would reappear in the second, unpublished illustration to Edgar Allan Poe's 'M. Valdémar' (fig. 90).

For Bodkin's glass panel (fig. 87), Harry decided to illustrate Walter de la Mare's 'The Song of the Mad Prince', a poem he was to illustrate again in watercolour in April 1920 for *The Year's at the Spring*, an anthology of poetry Harrap published later that year. The figure of the Mad Prince in Bodkin's panel is reminiscent of the Prince in Harry's illustration to 'The Swineherd' by Hans Andersen. Bodkin described the technique used by Harry in this panel:

> by plating two pieces of glass, ruby and blue, aciding each to as many as six various shades down to transparency, working on them with stain, and drawing on them with a pen in hot wax, he has produced effects, and in a technique undreamt of by his predecessors. A clear

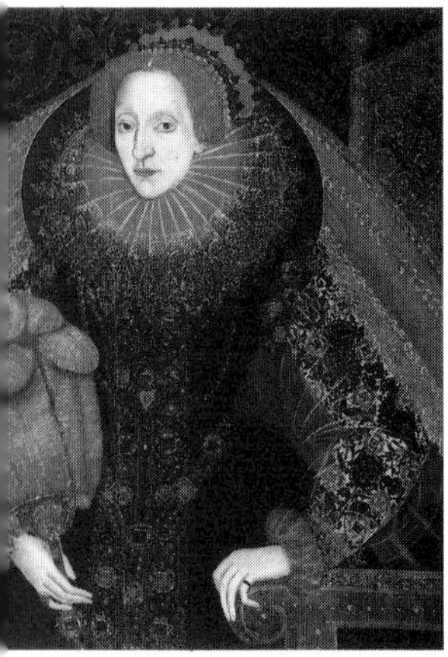

88 John Bettes the Younger (attrib.), *Portrait of Queen Elizabeth I*, c. 1585-90 (courtesy of the National Portrait Gallery, London); Elizabethan portraiture, particularly of the Queen, is an important source for Clarke's work at this period, with its predilection for detail, jewel-like colour, small scale and melancholy.

surface, unbroken by leading, shows every imaginable combination of primary colours.[21]

The Song of the Mad Prince (13" x 7") consists of a sheet of blue glass plated against a sheet of ruby. Both were intricately worked on with pen and acid until 'registered', rather like two colour-process blocks. The two pieces of glass were then inserted, blue in front of ruby, into a small four-sided cabinet made mostly of walnut. This contains a light bulb behind another sheet of opaque unstained glass which, when turned on, diffuses a rich light making the double-sheeted panel glow deeply and richly, while at the same time protecting it and ensuring the image may be viewed at any hour. Bodkin commissioned the little cabinet from the Dublin master cabinet maker, James Hicks, after rejecting an ornate container of his own design. The panel[22] is signed 'Harry Clarke 1917', and the title of the poem and Harry's name are engraved on a copper plaque on the cabinet. The Prince stands, head cocked to one side, distractedly watching us with a melancholic but quizzical expression. Reminiscent of a melancholic figure in an Elizabethan miniature (fig. 88), he wears a richly decorated tabard and hose with pointed toes and a ruff, and holds a dagger in the shape of a crucifix in one hand and a fan in the other. As in the *Queens* panels, the background and foreground are filled with lavishly patterned patchwork shapes and cushions. He is lamenting at the side of his beloved's freshly dug grave, strewn with flowers. On either side, behind him, in exquisite profile, stand his father the King, tapering fingers bidding silence in the cool blue moolight, and his mother the Queen, a swan-necked echo of the profiled Gobnait, in a swirling aura of ruby gold light (plate 21). The panel was later reproduced as a special colour supplement in *The Studio*[23] and was exhibited in the Arts and Crafts Society of Ireland's sixth exhibition in 1921. Harry regarded the panel as a successful experiment.

Another panel, commissioned by Miss Jane French, a friend of Waldron's, was based on Heinrich Heine's ballad, 'A Meeting', and was made in July 1918 (plate 19). This employs the same technique and is of similar size to *The Mad Prince* but in an oval shape (12¾" x 7½"). Miss French was one of several sisters devoted to the Arts and Crafts movement in Dublin. She lived beside An Túr Gloine in Upper Pembroke Street and was a keen and generous patron of Harry's as well as being a miniaturist in her own right. Apart from *A Meeting* and an early heraldic panel, she owned the 1913 drawing *A Decorative Fisherman* (Aengus), *The Maelstrom* from the Poe illustrations (1919) and a *Faust* endpiece (1925). Discussions about her panel had begun in 1917, and once Harry started work on it on 20 July 1918, he had it finished in a few days, so that it was exhibited with *The Song of the Mad Prince* in the Studios at the end of the month. There is a finely detailed preparatory watercolour design for the panel in golden ochre, touched with a pale blues and pink and highlights of white bodycolour, from which he worked.[24] Although the ballad illustrated is entitled in translation 'A Meeting',[25] Harry sometimes called this panel *The Mermaid* or *The Merman*; it is likely that he chose Heine's haunting poem as his subject because of his lifelong fascination with mermaids, mermen and underwater life.[26] The beshawled mermaid wears a brilliant red dress, dissolving into pebbled spangles at the knee, her mane of flowing golden hair unfurling behind her, while the pale, balletic figure of the androgynous merman is clothed in exquisitely figured doublet, breeches and hose of Harry's imaginative confection. He knowingly salutes her as they prepare to part at the water's edge, abandoning the dancing gypsy couples behind them to their watery fate.

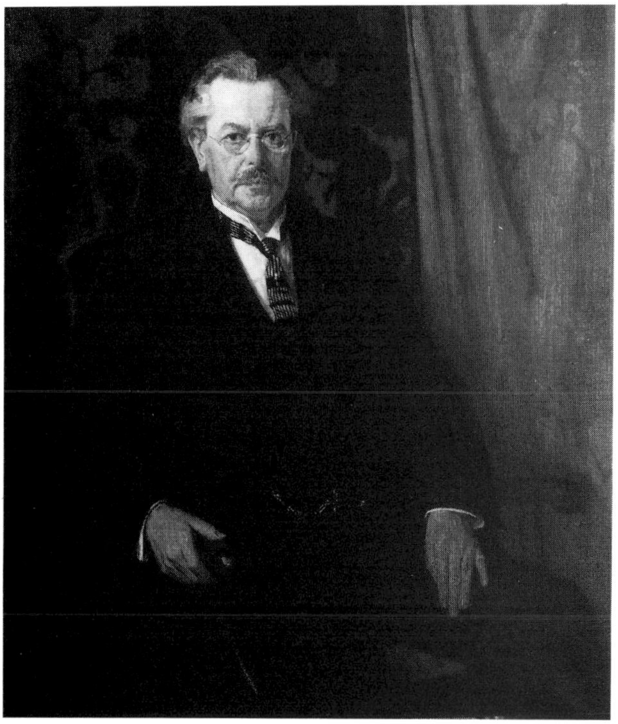

89 Margaret Clarke, *Joshua Clarke*, oil on canvas, 1917, National Gallery of Ireland; painted in February and probably included in the artist's 1917 Royal Hibernian Academy submission, as well as that for 1923, this portrait confirms Orpen's high regard for his former pupil.

Before the end of 1917, Harry designed a stock certificate for the Dublin United Tramways Company which has a good initial T, similar to that for the Arts and Crafts catalogue foreword, much stylized floral ornament, some charming contemporary scenes of Dublin including Nelson's Pillar and the tramway premises on the corner of College Green. Certificates for preference stock had the heading overprinted in red and those for ordinary stock in blue.

The Art Industries Exhibition at the Royal Dublin Society did not take place in 1917 because the premises were being used by the military; and, because of the Easter Rising in 1916, the Royal Hibernian Academy Exhibition had to take place in the Art School in 1917. Margaret Clarke had work exhibited (fig. 89), including a portrait of Madeleine Hurndall, commissioned by her uncle Laurence Waldron.

Harry's Christmas card design for 1917 shows an attenuated angel setting free a haloed dove of peace, while hovering over Killiney Bay. Beyond the horizon, the silhouettes of Bray Head and the Sugar Loaf mountains are discernible, while a tiny Nativity is poised on a cliff face beneath Sorrento Terrace. Around the angel's head is an elaborately spiked, eight-pointed halo. The androgynous body of the angel follows a sweeping, inverted 'S' shape, and wears a high-waisted chemise whose long sleeves are inscribed with unfurling tendrils and merge with feathery fronds and a sumptuous train packed with tiny decorative details.[27] The card is signed, dated and finely printed on rag paper.

5

Symbolism developed in a series of major commissions in stained glass and in critically acclaimed illustrations to Poe — The Ballets Russes influence on textile designs and on a panel for Lutyens illustrating Flaubert

In 1917, shortly after he had completed the Honan Chapel windows, Harry was commissioned to make a three-light east window for St Barrahane's church at Castletownshend in west Cork as a memorial to Dr Thomas Somerville of Drishane House and his wife Henrietta (née Townshend). On behalf of Dr Somerville's grandchildren Harry was approached about the window by Sir Egerton Coghill, a cousin of the family (and also of Sir Bertram Windle of Cork), but it seems to have been the writer, Edith Oenone Somerville, one of the partnership famous as Somerville and Ross, who took charge of seeing the work through on behalf of the family.

St Barrahane's, described by Dr Simms as 'that beautiful little church on the hill',[1] was designed by James Pain in 1826, a classical building of elegant proportions. However, the old east window, referred to by another grandson, Nevill Coghill, as the 'hideous patterned Victorian window known to the family as the Berlin Woolwork',[2] was so gloomy that in 1915 Dr Somerville's grandchildren were given permission to have it removed and sold, and a new window more pleasing and fitting in design made to replace it. A preliminary plan for the window was prepared by Nagle at the Clarke Studios in June 1917, but Miss Somerville had not made up her mind by the following February, when Harry wrote to her, presumably to confirm the commission and to ask her what her plans were for the work.

Harry was almost fully occupied during the first months of 1918 with his illustrations to *Tales of Mystery and Imagination* by Edgar Allan Poe for Harrap. The drawing for 'Ligeia' took up the first week in January, that for 'The Cask of Amontillado' the following week, and during the third week he finished the drawing for 'The Masque of the Red Death'. After a short break to pursue his stained glass business, submitting an unsuccessful tender for a window at Reading, he resumed work on the illustrations and completed 'Landor's Cottage' on 26 January[3], 'Berenice' on 5 February, 'Lionising' on 13 February, 'Assignation' on 22 February and his second, unpublished drawing for 'M. Valdémar' (fig. 90) on 1 March. By 12 March he had produced a new version of his illustration to 'The Cask of

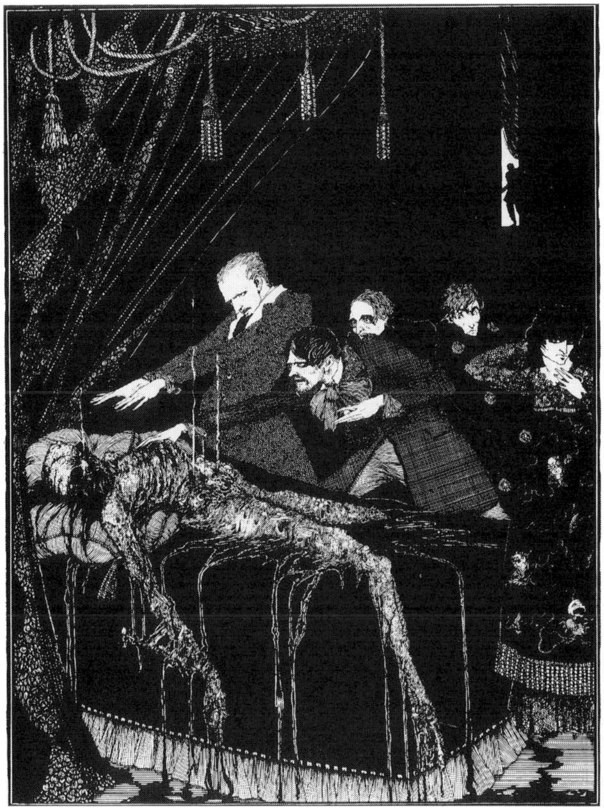

90 'Upon the bed there lay a nearly liquid mass of loathsome — of detestable putridity', illustration to Poe's 'M. Valdémar', 1918; this unpublished version features Seán Keating and tiny embryo motifs on the dress of the female figure not used in the published version; the tiny figure silhouetted in the background is derived from Velasquez's *Las Meninas* (fig. 172)

Amontillado' after which he celebrated his twenty-ninth birthday before revising and touching-up this group of black and white drawings. This period of drawing was followed, during the latter part of March, by the preparatory coloured design for a three-light window depicting the Sacred Heart, St Margaret Mary and St John Eudes, to be erected for the Vincentian Fathers in St Peter's Church at Phibsborough in Dublin. The sketch and costing for the window took him about a week and were submitted to Fr Comerford, who was responsible for the commission, by the beginning of April.

As the detailed measurements had come from Castletownshend, he began the cartoon for the *Nativity* window on 5 April. By the 26th of the month he had completed the cartoon for the three main lights, three main tracery lights and eleven small tracery openings.[4] Meanwhile Joshua had worked out an approximate costing at £2,300, which was a very large sum at that time. He suggested that Harry should prepare the colour designs and draw the openings for the figures, adding that he was sure Mr Nagle would draw 'any other ornament' and thus bring the price down — a suggestion Harry would never have accepted at this stage in his career. By the end of April Harry had the cutlines for the window under way, and a month later Duane, the Studios' glazier, had cut the glass, much of it specially ordered from Hetley's, and Harry had commenced the aciding staining and painting of the pieces. His design incorporated a considerabl amount of Prior's white slab glass to allow as much light as possible to filte through without overpowering the richer colours, and he was speciall careful in his rendering of the flesh tones in the design.

During June he interrupted work on the Castletownsend window t prepare coloured designs for a small *Angel of Peace* window,[5] for Mrs Lloy of Victoria Castle, Killiney in Co. Dublin, commissioned as a war memoria to her son in Holy Trinity Church, Killiney, and for his panel, *A Meeting* for Miss French. The first and second paintings on the glass for th Castletownshend *Nativity* occupied the middle of July, and the leadin must have proceeded quickly for, at the end of July, the window was show in a small exhibition of Harry's recent work, held in the Studios at 33 Nort Frederick Street for two days only, so that the work routine would not b disturbed. The exhibition was announced in the press and was an effectiv way of showing the work to the general public as well as invited patron and clients. Other pieces exhibited included the nine *Queens* panels, *A Meeting*, and *The Song of the Mad Prince*. In his review of the exhibition i the *Dublin Evening Mail* Bodkin said, of the Castletownshend *Nativity*,

> It has not the sumptuousness of colour which we are accustomed t associate with [him], for it is especially designed to hang in th comparative dimness of an eastern light. But it has an appropriat beauty of colour second to none of his earlier works and a suavity o design and strength of drawing that shows, if that be possible, a advance in the artist's power.[6]

Bodkin also wrote articles on Harry's work in the *Dublin Evening Telegraph* and another in the *Freeman's Journal*, which Harry felt was instrumental i persuading his vacillating client to give him the Phibsborough commission

In the Castletownshend *Nativity*, Harry's widespread use of vertica white slab quarries, alternately linked by a minute oval of coloured glass is impressive. In the tradition established by Whall, A.E Child often use this device, as in the north wall of the Unitarian Church, Dublin;[8] Harry' choice and treatment of glass, however, warrants closer inspection. No only has he taken full advantage of every irregularity in the white sla quarries, enhancing them with matt washes, stipples and semi-abstrac lacework sequences so that each differs from its neighbour without de tracting from the overall effect of a subtly embroidered quilt in which th light lingers: he has also acided quarries of gold-pinks, greens and blues t the barest skim of colour. The principal scene appears strung like a heav tapestry across the three trefoil-headed lights; jagged indigo rocks descen on either side of the Holy Family, who stand before a screen of flora ornament, similar to that used at the foot of each *Queens* panel, at the fee

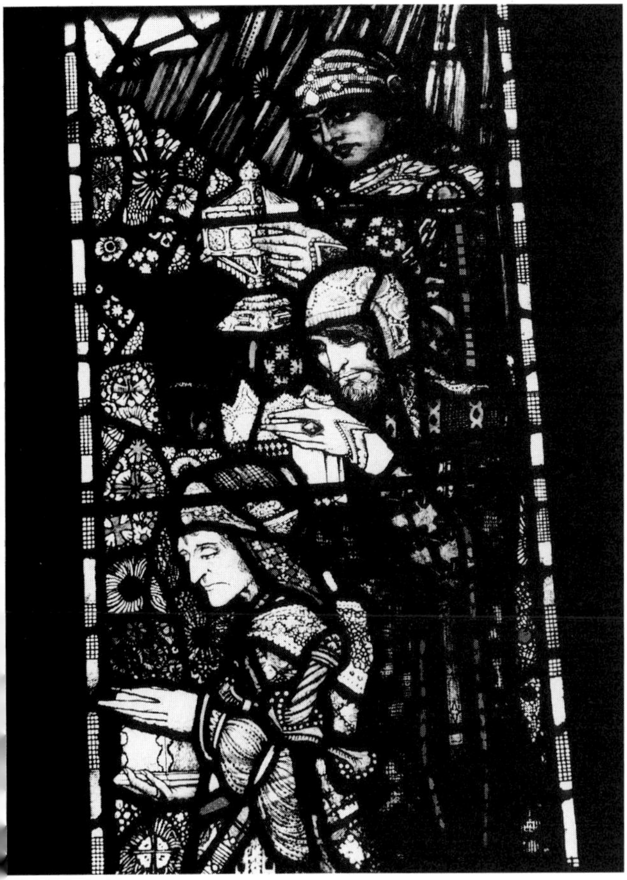

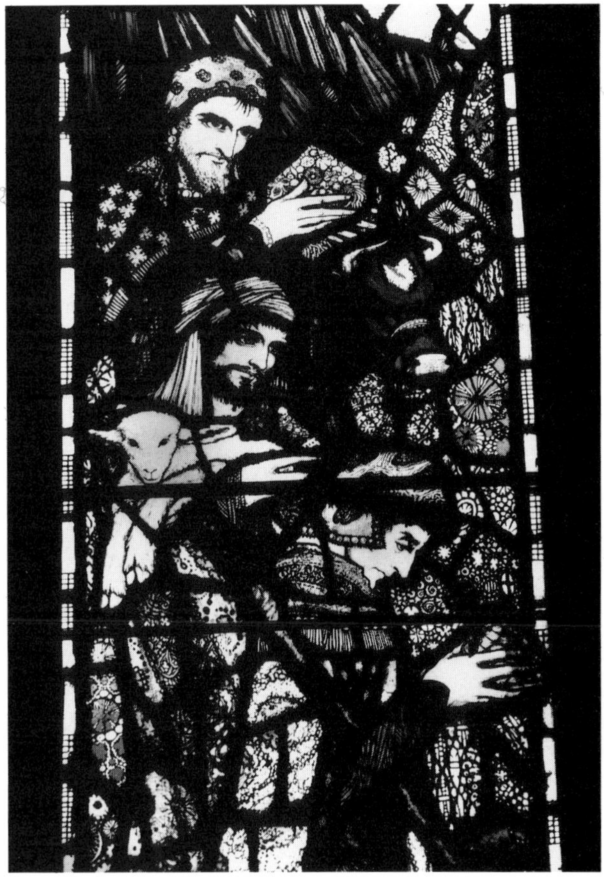

91 The Three Kings, a detail from the *Nativity* window, Castletownshend, 1918

92 Three shepherds, a detail from the Castletownshend *Nativity*

of the *Mad Prince* and in many of the Hans Andersen illustrations. The screen tapers to a point three quarters of the way up the central light behind the head of St Joseph. It is a mosaic of glass of every shape and size, flashed greens, blues and rubies acided to reveal a lot of clear glass, painted with fantastic flora. These stylized flowerheads became a hallmark of Harry's work, both in his pen and ink and watercolour illustrations, and painted or acided onto his glass. The device succeeded brilliantly when executed by himself but was too often repetitive and lifeless when imitated by his followers. Such floral decoration became commonly known as 'FOs', or even 'Fried Onions' by the men in the Studios and became a characteristic of Harry's decorative treatment, but in his hands never hackneyed. The stylized approach sometimes geometrical, sometimes floral in pattern, which Harry used to such effect, is also found in the work of a number of decorative and applied art workers and designers contemporary with him.[9]

The centre opening of the *Nativity* window depicts Joseph in delicate grisaille, wearing an embroidered helmet, similar to the one worn by Rebecca West in her photographic portrait by E.O. Hoppé of that year, and obviously inspired by Ballets Russes costumes. His halo is a rich emerald green painted with a lace-like pattern in black. His pale, tapering fingers hold the chain of a golden lantern, which burns with a scarlet flame. Before him kneels our Lady, a gentle portrayal on a slightly larger scale than the other figures. St Joseph looks out firmly at us, as though protecting her. In the centre of the light, on a bed of straw in front of the Virgin, painted entirely in grisaille, lies baby Jesus in a white chemise and golden bodice, his head and hands raised, his black halo decorated in minute pearls and gold filigree.

This central scene is linked to the *Adoration of the Kings* on the right, and the *Shepherds* on the left by a semicircular cusp of silver whose diameter reaches its lowest point beneath the Child and then ascends to support the two adoring groups, leaving space for the respective arms of the Somerville and Townshend families. The kneeling cloaked figures of the two lowest men on each side (respectively a king and a shepherd)[10] are perhaps the most striking feature of the whole window (figs. 91, 92). The heavily brocaded folds of their cloaks sweep to the edges of their respective lights, deliberately overlapping the silver arc to avoid too glib a geometric plan. The treatment of these two figures is remarkable from a linear, decorative and material point of view, the use of gold-pink flashed glass being most original. The effect is Byzantine, reminiscent of the style of Gustav Klimt's work. Both Clarke and Klimt rely on the faces and hands of their figures to convey human expressiveness, and only here does any attempt at modelling occur. Both artists are equally unconcerned with perspective, reality or a third dimension. In the tradition of the best purely decorative work, background and foreground, figure and setting are equally important and integral. Any light is reflected from within the fabric of the design. Movement is created by the way in which the light affects the surface of the picture, and by the symbolic fluidity of line. This is what W Hoffman has termed *Synaesthesia*[11] — a stylized, ornamented style, where people are statues, backgrounds are wallpaper, and interchangeable linear formulae are used as arrangements for figures and settings in different colour relationships, so that abstraction and symbol interrelate. Harry seems to have already firmly rooted himself in this Symbolist idiom.[12]

In terms of Harry's treatment of glass, it is worth noting that the French in particular were experimenting with decorative glass at this period mostly for use as art objects rather than in windows. Lalique had abandoned a brilliant career as a jeweller to make glass objects, and Maurice Marinot was so inspired in 1911 by what he saw in a glassmaker's studio that he stopped being a Fauve painter and began a twenty-six year long experiment with glass. Like Harry, he was intrigued by the impurities, bubbles and irregularities in the medium, which to him suggested new and strange beauties of texture. The work of the French Decuper-Delvaux and Quenvit with enamelled glass can be seen as parallel to Harry's use of floral ornament on stained glass; bouquets of stylized rosebuds, sunflowers

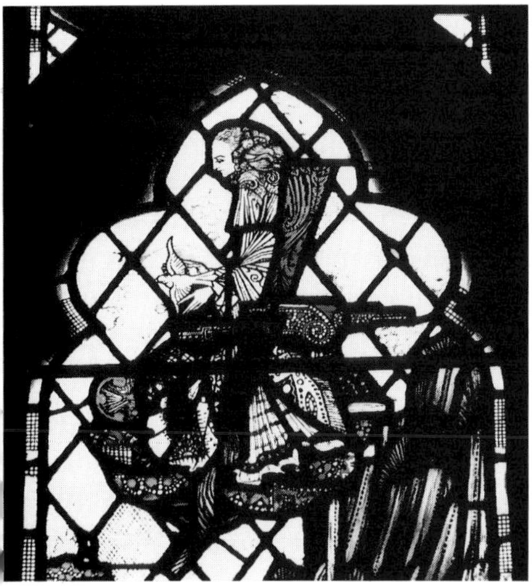

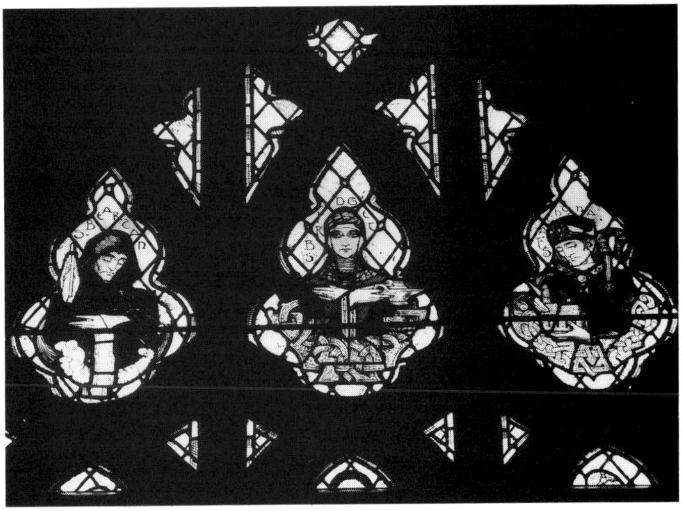

ribbons and spots, clusters of daisies and tiers of tiny leaves and branches recur. Technically closest to Harry's aciding on thick flashed glass are pieces inscribed 'Le Verre de France'.

The fashionably dressed idiosyncratic angels (fig. 93) at the head of each light and the three major tracery lights, depicting Sts Bridget, Bearcan and Fachtna, abound in exotic decorative detail (fig. 94). Hardly surprisingly, the Castletownshend window cost so much to make that Joshua reluctantly advised Harry that he would have to charge him 30/- per foot if the Studios were to make even the smallest profit. Despite the welcome absence of German competition, the constraints of war had resulted in serious shortages of lead, firewood and hydrofluoric acid, and Joshua was annoyed to discover that William MacBride was not working exclusively for the Studios[13] and Orr was tendering against him for English firms. The lead situation was temporarily solved by stripping a deconsecrated church and sending its lead down the canal on a barge.

During the summer of 1918 Harry became involved in a long-drawn-out affair which demonstrates the sort of administrative difficulties he had to contend with, and also clarifies his position in relation to his father's Studios. In June 1918 Fr Thomas of the Fr Matthew Church in Cork, had, on the strength of the Honan Chapel windows, asked Harry if he would design and make a two-light window, *Christ, Prince of Peace, and St Francis*, to be donated to the church by local trade unionists and the Labour Council. Harry accepted the commission at £250, subject to certain conditions:

> Firstly, that in the event of any of the windows in the church being filled with stained glass later on that [*sic*] I will be given them at an ordinary current price — this might be calculated by the cost of the window I now propose to do for £250. The cost of this window should be £400 and windows larger or smaller could be approximately priced

93 A modish angel, from the upper register of the Castletownshend *Nativity*

94 Sts Bridget, Bearcan and Fachtna, the three tracery lights in the Castletownshend *Nativity* window. One of the hallmarks of National Romanticism was its search for vernacular heroes; in Ireland a number of early little-known saints were revived and researched.

> from this.
>
> Secondly, I will require accurate templates and measurements of the present window sent to me.
>
> Thirdly, the inscription as it is at present is much too long and cannot go into the base of the window. I suggest that a short inscription be put in the glass and the full matter be engraved or cut in a brass or marble tablet and fixed in the wall directly under the window — this question of the inscription is of some importance.
>
> Fourthly, I would also ask that the price I now accept should not generally be spoken of as I could not generally work to this scale. I hope you will forgive my suggesting these points but you can understand that I am going to do you a good window, the materials for which I have to pay irrespective of my clients — it simply means much longer hours and harder work in this window for which I do expect a return eventually.[14]

This commission led to a long series of misunderstandings; Mr McMullen, the architect of the Fr Mathew Church (as for the Honan Chapel) is shown by the extensive correspondence about the window to have been as obstinate (about his own authority) as the clients during the quibbling that ensued. Harry refused to be bound to his original sketch, which was substantially altered by McMullen, and was adamant that any changes in the design, colour and arrangement of the scheme should be those he thought necessary. If the clients insisted on having the entire wordy inscription on the window, 'I cannot promise that this inscription will be readable from the ground.'[15] Harry asked them to consider an inscribed tablet 'in case anyone might want to know what the long written matter in the window was all about'! The traceries also presented problems, so Harry asked if Sisks could, as they had done with the Castletownshend window, 'set out the whole tracery full size, showing the width of the mullions and the actual relation of each piece of tracery to the rest'.[16]

He refused to give this commission priority and delay his other work as a consequence. In August, he found that the actual size of the window exceeded McMullen's original size by 25 square feet and that the committee were trying to include a Crucifixion in the design for the same price. Consequently, Sir John O'Connell was called in, as Harry could hardly be expected to do this Crucifixion work for nothing.[17] Stalemate followed — Harry refusing to do the window unless the donors would pay him for the work done over and above the original commission, 'upon which we based our agreement'.[18] He was sorry for the unpleasant position in which he and McMullen were placed and assured him 'mine . . . would be still less so if I had to pay £50 for extra materials on a job I'd already dropped £20 on'.[19] He did not want to appear ungrateful but he reminded McMullen that he was not connected with the firm. My father and brother run these Studios. They supply me with all materials and I use their kiln etc., but my windows are my own work from start to finish and I have to personally bear whatever loss there is on my glass work. This is only mentioned because you allude to *my firm.* Had I partners to share a risk or loss I could act differently in the case which has now arisen. I take it for granted that the matter is now closed between us and in conclusion offer a suggestion. I will give my design to the Studios here, will select the glass and generally supervise your window. In this way you would be sure of a good window for the money at your disposal. But the window will not be mine although this fact will not, I imagine, trouble your clients very much.[20]

He suggested McMullen reply to him at the Studios. In November Joshua wrote to McMullen, offering to take over the work:

> I will give you as good work as you would get from my son or anyone else, it will not be the same style as my son's but it will be as good in quality, design and execution. I will take the window at £250 and guarantee to have it fixed within 5 months.[21]

In fact, Joshua was prepared to do absolutely anything Fr Thomas and the donors wanted to secure the commission, although he did feel it was unfair to use Harry's drawing when he stood to gain nothing from this arrangement; he therefore offered to get out a new design, while Harry oversaw the whole procedure, without actually working on it. He again emphasized that Harry was not a member of his firm. Eventually, Harry handed over the design — by now in a poor state as someone had written all over it (to Joshua's outrage) — and undertook to superintend the selection of the glass and the execution of the work. Joshua wrote to McMullen, 'Altogether I think Harry has been magnificent over this, as he loses all and gains nothing',[22] and insisted that Harry's design be returned when the work was completed. The final result is not unattractive, although the inscription is still too big and the painting and treatment of the glass lack his special touch.

Despite these problems, the window was so admired that another window, to be designed and supervised by Harry and made by the Studios, was ordered in 1920. Walter Clarke described this window as depicting angels of peace flying over Shandon steeple, apostles and advocates of peace holding myrtle and olive branches, and saints of Cork with the Blessed Virgin and St Francis. It was he who supervised the erection of this window, as Joshua was not well and could not travel so far from Dublin. Joshua was also determined that it was time that Walter should start taking a major role in the business, as his own health was failing.

As well as his work in stained glass and illustration, Harry was at this time deeply involved in the cultural life of Dublin. At the public meeting held at the Mansion House on 29 January 1918, he was elected to the 'illustrious Committee' formed to effect the return to the Municipal Gallery in Dublin of the thirty-nine modern masterpieces claimed by Britain as a result of an unresolved codicil in Sir Hugh Lane's will.[23] He served on the committee of the Dublin Industrial Development Association, the Arts and Crafts Society of Ireland's council and exhibition committee, and the committee of the Guild of Irish Art Workers; he also taught black and white illustration at the School of Art every Monday morning, an activity he continued until the end of November 1923 and which was a major influence on illustration in Dublin during the early 1920s.

Among his friends at the time was Ellie Duncan, pioneer of the Arts Club and first curator of the Municipal Gallery of Modern Art, then at 17 Harcourt Street. She was a sister of Hester Dowden, the fashionable medium, whose daughter Dolly Travers-Smith would, in 1930, marry Lennox Robinson, the playwright and close friend of Harry's from the early 1920s; Robinson and Ellie's son, Alan, would become his most faithful friends. Alan Duncan married Belinda Atkinson, the sister of George, who became the Principal of the Dublin School of Art after John Ward. They were all supporters of the Dublin Drama League, which was founded by Lennox Robinson, James Stephens and W.B. Yeats in 1918 'to secure the production of plays which in the ordinary course of events would not be likely to be seen in Dublin'.[24] Later both Harry and George Atkinson designed covers for some of the League's productions. Also in 1918, at the production of a Greek play at Robinson's house, Sorrento Cottage, in Killiney,[25] he met the actor and co-founder of the Dublin Gate Theatre, Micheál MacLiammoir, who was struck by Harry's exquisite dress and charming manners but worried by his abnormally high complexion. He christened Harry the 'Master of the Heavily Encrusted Detail'.[26]

Early in August, after the Studios' exhibition, Harry took a week off at Shankill to rest. He was pleased by Bodkin's laudatory reviews, but while writing to thank him he was, he said, 'mighty sorry that it should be necessary for [Bodkin] to fortify against the attacks of Miss Purser through your having given me a favourable notice but unless she is hopelessly poisioned against me I think if she saw your panel, she would admit that it is unique in its way.'[27] On his return to work he began another small panel of a crest and sun for Waldron, which developed into a coat of arms. This filled his time until he received confirmation of a major commission, for the east window in St Joseph's Church, Terenure in Dublin, whose subject was to be the Crucifixion.

Negotiations about the Terenure *Crucifixion* had commenced in February 1917, while Harry was working on the *Queens* panels. He had gone to see the parish priest, Fr Healy, to discuss the commission. Joshua too, was interested in the job and wrote to Fr Healy asking if he could quote for it, adding

> My writing now to you has nothing to do with my son Harry as of course you know our work is entirely different, if you have decided to give the work to him it would be no use I wasting any further time of yours and mine but I should certainly like to do that window myself if it was possible.[28]

By the end of March, Joshua had resorted to proferring alms for the poor of Terenure and sending tentative designs.

Harry must not originally have been keen to do the window, perhaps because of the price, or because of its huge scale, about 200 square feet, as, by May, Joshua was working out a design 'of the richest colour'[29] and assuring Fr Healy that 'Harry has promised to superintend [the window], that is, if the work is not given to him'.[30] By October, Joshua still had not heard what Fr Healy thought of his design. It was adventurous of him to quote for such a large window as he was still having great problems getting lead and kelp (staining sheets). He had a cart sent out at regular intervals to fetch firewood from houses being demolished along the quays. However, he was so involved with doing the *Father Knapp* memorial window in West Kensington Carmelite Church in London — 'rather a swagger church'[31] — that he was not as aggrieved as he might have been when the commission for Terenure went to Harry.

From 15 August to 9 September Harry worked continuously on the design for the *Crucifixion* window. The centre light was to be 22′ x 3′ 11″ and each of the side lights 19′ x 3′ 1″.[32] Although the subject was *The Crucifixion*, Harry thought of the design as an *Adoration of the Cross by Irish Saints*. Once the designs were completed, they were sent off to Fr Healy to discuss with the donor, Major Verdon Corcoran of Rathgar.

Harry then spent a couple of days on a design, of which there is now no trace, for a stained glass window in the Catholic church in Church Street, Dublin. The coloured design for this was exhibited together with that of *The Crucifixion* in the 1919 Royal Hibernian Academy exhibition. In the same exhibition his wife's work was represented by seven portraits. On 14 September he met Mrs Lloyd at Holy Trinity Church, Killiney, to discuss the lancet window he had designed in June in memory of her young son Clifford, killed on active service in 1915. That afternoon he met a Mrs O'Keeffe of Wexford whose son, Lt William Henry O'Keeffe, had also been killed in action in France the previous year. From 18 to 26 September he did further work (probably alterations) on the design for the Killiney window, and worked on the O'Keeffe design, of a two-light window for the Church of the Assumption in Bride Street, Wexford. On the 27th, he sent off the O'Keeffe design with an estimate of £125 for the window; and the revised Lloyd design with an estimate of £70 for that. From then until 2 October, he alternated work on the Somerville arms and the Waldron arms. He was still working on a sun design, perhaps the little panel which became part of a lantern for Waldron in the following year.

Next he began setting out the design for the Phibsborough three-light window and transferring it to the cartoon stage. His treatment in the initial coloured designs, drawn to a scale of roughly an inch to a foot, was more or less the same as that he had used for the Honan Chapel windows. The leadlines, painting and modelling lines, facial, decorative and symbolic details as well as colours were all meticulously suggested.[33] As the Phibsborough window measured fifty-three square feet, he worked at the cartoons in North Frederick Street.

On 4 November he attended a meeting at the request of James Stephens, the writer and registrar of the National Gallery in Merrion Square, to meet the sub-committee appointed to choose a design for a corporate seal for the gallery. Harry submitted two designs but neither was accepted.[34] Both of these, one of which Harry gave to Bodkin, show a medievalized *St Luke*, patron saint of painters, poised in a vesica decorated with references to the arms of Dublin City. Work on the cartoon for the left hand opening of the Phibsborough window took eleven days. Three more days were spent on the cutlines and a further day on the tracery cutlines. It is hardly surprising that, by Harry's standards, the cartoons for this window took such a comparatively long time; like all his best cartoons, they are masterpieces of chiaroscuro, subtle modelling and detail. Although the initial small-scale coloured designs often bear little resemblance to the cartoon, each cartoon became an exact monochrome (or grisaille) version on paper of the finished window, drawn to the same scale and finished to the minutest degree. Each is impressive in its own right, worked in fluid, sensitive but unfaltering charcoal tones, before being finally fixed to prevent the lines being rubbed off. The taking of the cutline would have been a speedy and easy task, and the painting-in straightforward, as all the work was so clearly set out in the cartoons.

Work on the Phibsborough cartoons was finished just after Armistice Day, and then Harry began the cartoon for the memorial window in Killiney (fig. 95). As this was only fourteen square feet and he was not feeling well, he decided to work on this in his studio at 36 Mount Merrion Avenue. His wife Margaret was expecting their second child the following April, and this meant they could both work at home, he in his den at the bottom of the garden, she in her studio in the house. The Killiney cartoon[35] was finished in less than a week, on 22 November. This shows the *Angel of Peace*, or Hope (Harry referred to her as both), a variation of his 1917 Christmas card angel, holding a haloed dove, appropriate both as a war memorial and as a prayer for peace after the horrors of war. Next, he began to set out the two-light O'Keeffe memorial window, which shows *Our Lady and Child* in the left light *adored by St Aidan of Ferns and St Adrian* in the right (fig. 96). He then alternated work on the Killiney cutline and the Wexford cartoon until 13 December and worked on the Wexford cutlines from 14 to

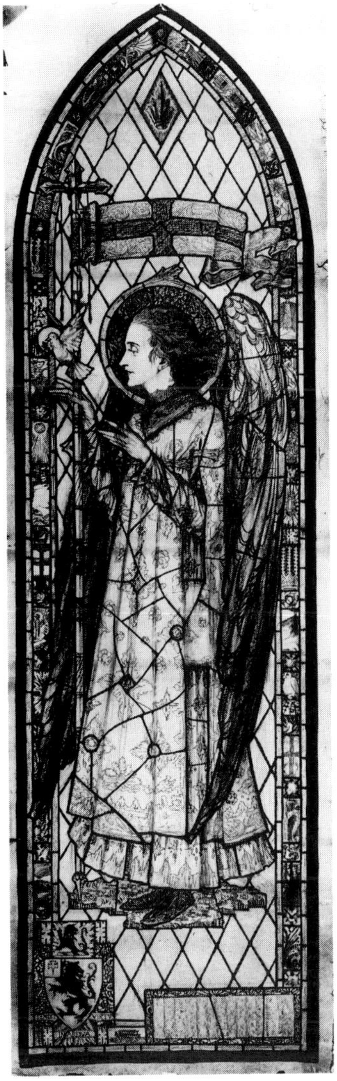

95 Cartoon for *The Angel of Peace and Hope* window for Killiney, Co. Dublin, 1918

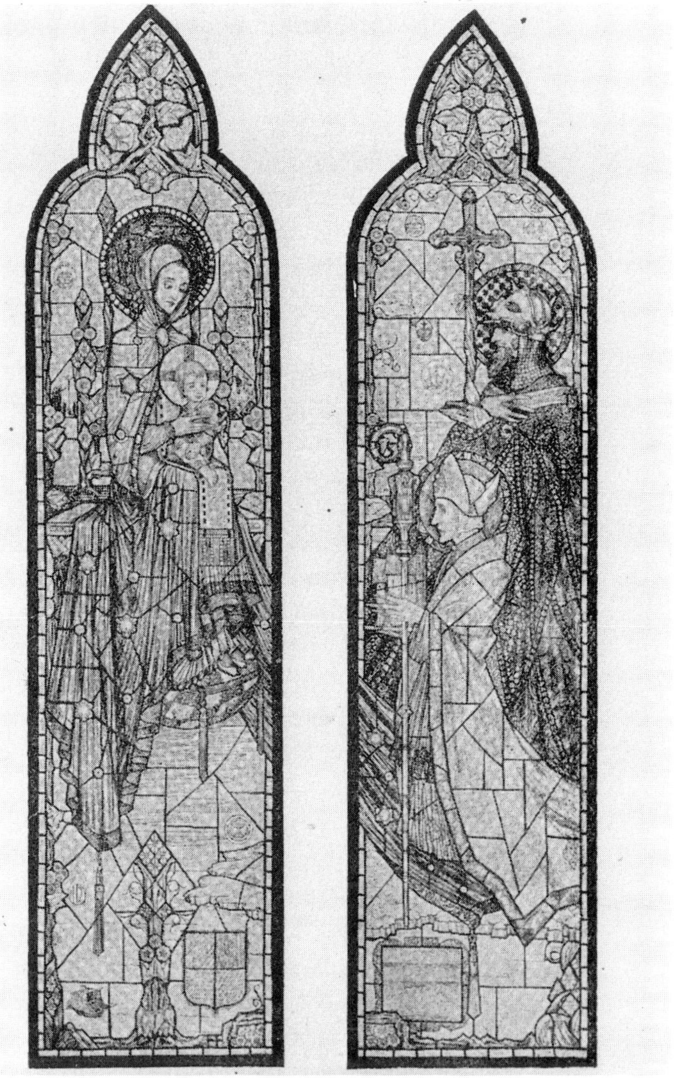

96 Cartoon of the O'Keeffe memorial window, Wexford, 1918; here the intricacy of detail is never sacrificed to the fluid integrity of the composition.

17 December. It is interesting to see how he seemed to work best when keeping several jobs going simultaneously. As early as 5 December, he was in communication with the Revd Lewis Vaughan about a further memorial window proposed for the parish church of St Mary at Nantwich, in Cheshire. Also, about this time, there is the first reference to Doctor Faustus in his diary, but no allusion to any proposed illustration.

On 26 December he attended Bodkin's Hermione Lecture, which he enjoyed, particularly the slide of Sir Martin Shee's self-portrait: 'I never saw such a dangerously handsome man'.[36] He and Bodkin were both involved in trying to get two Irish representatives elected to the Committee of Industrial Design, which had been written about at length in the latest Royal Society *Journal*. In a letter to Bodkin written about this time, concerning a production at the Abbey Theatre, Harry expressed his views about W.B. Yeats:

> I know exactly how I feel about Yeats and would not consider the business for one instant if I thought I would have to conform in any way to his 'Art' views and guff about composition and colour. He made me want to cat. I had great happiness to come home to my wife and Ann after listening to that bruiser. How Mr Waldron would love him.[37]

He was later to change his opinion of Yeats. Harry is barely mentioned in Yeats' correspondence, though their paths must have frequently crossed. Yeats certainly visited the Studios to see work on exhibition,[38] and Yeats and Clarke would often meet through Lennox Robinson, who in subsequent years was a close friend to both. [39]

The O'Keeffe window design was finished on 17 December, after three weeks of continuous work, except for one day, 3 December, when he went to Belfast, to meet the handkerchief and textile manufacturers, Sefton's. Walter William Sefton (d. 1952), who ran the firm, was married to the graphic artist Ann Harriet Fish, or A.J. Fish as she usually signed herself, whose 'Eve' cartoon pictures deftly drawn in black line were, at that period, 'clamoured for abroad by publishers' and whose 'impersonations of war-time soldiers . . . brightened many a gloomy hour'[40] during the 1914-18 War. Harry may have met Ann Fish in London where she had a studio[41] and thus been introduced to Walter Sefton, or vice versa. In 1915, Fish had designed a *Marionette's Calendar*, which would have appealed to Harry. In 1918, the Bodley Head published rhymes, with Fish's drawings. At this juncture Harry met Fish.

The outcome of Harry's meeting with Walter Sefton was a commission to design two sets of eight handkerchiefs in decorative boxes, which he would also design, and two sets of their *Sherevoile* dress fabrics. He began work on this commission at the end of December and worked on it through January and into February.

On 6 December, he designed his 1918 Christmas card, the original of which he gave Mrs Bodkin as a Christmas present. The little card measures 5′ 3½″ and was printed inside a folded leaf of handmade paper in black and white; it shows the tiny silhouette of a sailor standing and two seated figurines on the deck of a ship with patchwork sails on a black swelling sea, speckled with white dots. Despite the small scale the whole effect is of a rich pattern fluently expressed.[42]

Harry's extraordinary ability to work on a variety of jobs is shown by his commissions at the end of 1918, which included his illustrations to Poe's *Tales of Mystery and Imagination*, a set of eight handkerchiefs and two fabric designs for Sefton's, his own Christmas card, windows at Killiney, Wexford,

Phibsborough, and two others for which he had tendered, at Terenure and at Nantwich. He was also involved in a projected anthology of poems to be edited by Walter de la Mare which would feature colour reproductions of his *Mad Prince* and other panels in the same technique together with some of his book illustrations; the publishers were to be responsible for any damage to the panels and to obtain the permission of the original publishers of works he had illustrated. Harry was to oversee the colour reproductions and the general setting out of the book. If it were too short, he or the publishers were to select one long poem for which he could do an extra glass panel; each poem was to be printed in full as well as the quotation illustrated, and copies were to be sent to the publishers and to de la Mare. Unfortunately this project never materialized, despite Bodkin's intent and close involvement. The only comprehensive article illustrating his work in various media at this period appeared in the November 1919 issue of *The Studio*, when *A Meeting* and two of the panels in the *Queens* series were illustrated in colour.

Harry was so busy at the end of 1918 that any new work with which he could not cope was handed on to his father. Harry certainly helped, when necessary, with advice on stained glass and, in February 1919, is recorded[43] as assisting T. McNamara (the architect to whom he had been apprenticed in 1904) with the stained glass windows depicting scenes from Shakespeare in the front entrance to the Scala Theatre, Dublin (since demolished). Joshua, who was not feeling 'up to the mark', thought Harry's resolution of the Scala windows magnificent.

At the beginning of January 1919, Harry heard that his tender had been accepted for a three-light memorial window at St Mary's Church, Nantwich for Arthur Knowles of Alvaston Hall nearby, and added this design to his already crowded work-load. On 20 January he sent off seven tailpieces, the cover design, an altered illustration to 'The Pit and the Pendulum' and the original (1914) drawing for 'M. Valdémar' to Harrap for the Poe book. Once these were dispatched, he went into the Studios to get on with the Killiney *Angel*. Kathleen Quigley, a contemporary of Harry's, trained at the School of Art under Child, who sometimes worked at the Tower of Glass, began work at North Frederick Street, to assist Harry with his own stained glass. She had sound technical experience and was also skilled at illumination. Her first job for Harry was to acid the Killiney *Angel*, while Harry was selecting the glass for the Wexford *Adoration*, some of which had been specially ordered from Powell's of Whitefriars. He also had to meet Mrs Lloyd about the coat of arms to be inserted into the Killiney windows, and oversee the Fr Mathew window in Cork, as well as completing his Poe illustrations. The jacket design for the Poe was drawn on 26 and 27 January, the illustration to 'The Manuscript in a Bottle' on 28 and 29 January, and that to 'Monos and Una' commenced on 31 January and finished between 13 and 16 February. He noted that he had sent off a total of twelve drawings for the Poe in 1918. Time had also to be found for meetings with Jane French, the hon. treasurer of the Arts and Crafts Society of Ireland, whose sixth exhibition was being discussed, although it did not eventually take place until the autumn of 1921.

By 13 February, he had completed his first set of handkerchief designs, which he duly sent off to Sefton's together with five variant designs for their *Sherevoile* dress fabric. These were painted with ink and watercolour onto card or tissue: one design was a small magenta and black chequered pattern; another, arabesques of rich orange, pink and crimson; and the other two, floral motifs in shades of indigo, blue, mauve and crimson. Perhaps these were rejected as too intense, in favour of his much lighter daisy-head

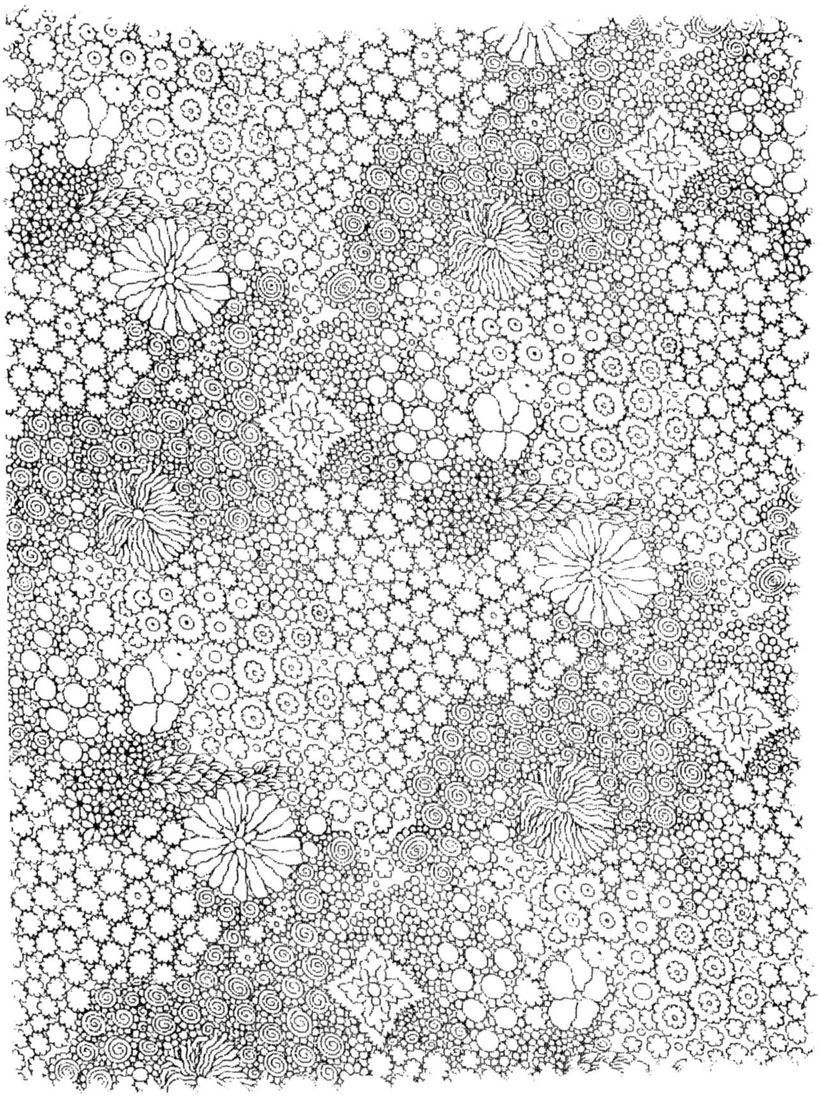

97 A sample of Sherevoile fabric, printed by Sefton's of Belfast, 1919

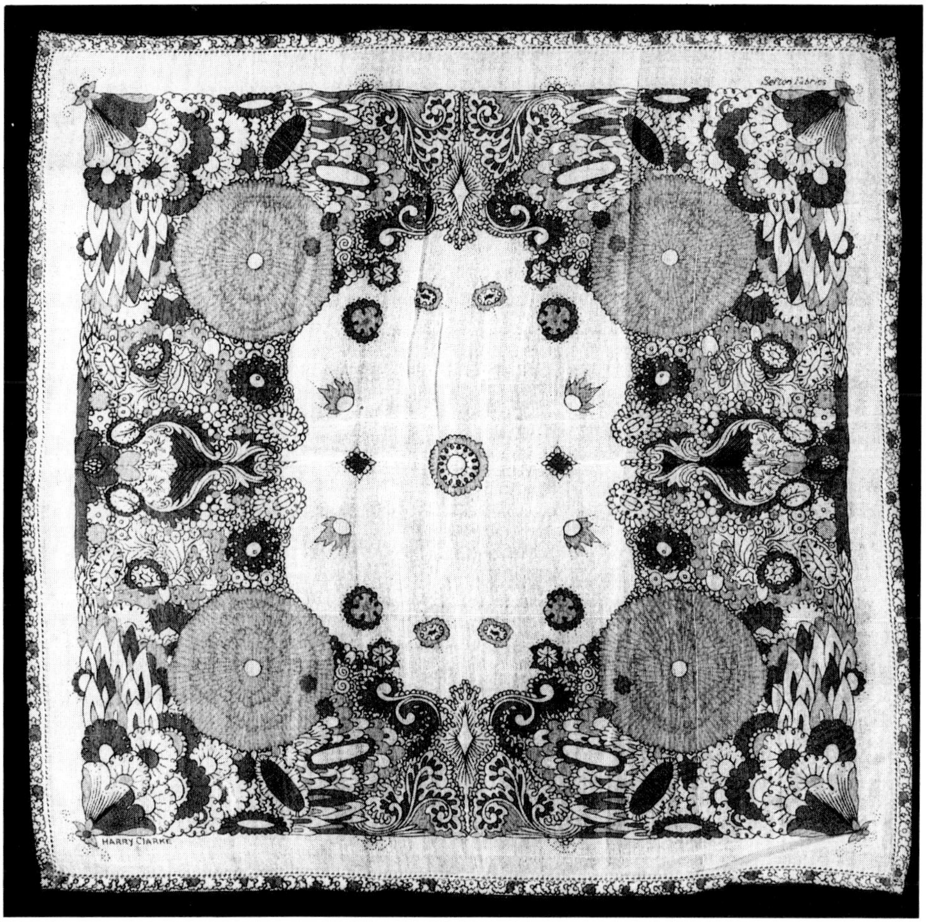

98 One of the first series of handkerchiefs Clarke designed for Sefton Fabrics; each handkerchief carried his printed signature or colophon; 1919.

motifs, which were used (fig. 97). The first handkerchief box design was sent to Sefton's on 5 April, when the project was approved.

Harry's handkerchief designs are fanciful and imaginative; the handkerchiefs were printed in Belfast[44] on small squares of fine cambric, roughly 11′ 10½″, each with ¼″ decorative border, separated from the main design by the stitched hem. The first set are all signed 'HARRY CLARKE/Sefton Fabrics', and the second with Harry's adopted monogram.[45] The designs of the first set (fig. 98) in their use of exotic and imaginative floral motifs, butterflies, jellyfish, sea urchins, sea anemones, gherkins and enlarged microscopic organisms echo the Hans Andersen illustrations.[46] In the second set (plate 29) the decorative motifs include seedpods, cockatoos, strutting cockerels, arabesques, huge petunias, seaweeds and crazy paving.

The colours are used in distinctive combinations and very much reflect the taste of a young man of aesthetic and decorative bent, slightly ahead of the 1920s' Art Deco period, but in the wake of the Ballets Russes. The earlier set tends to be composed of more subued colours, oxbloods, madders and chocolates, although there is pale rose, beige and an orange-brown Bakst had made popular, later known as 'Tango' ; this Harry juxtaposes effectively with pale grey, lime and chocolate.

It would seem that there was one trial handkerchief, signed in the manner of the first series, as there is a ninth in the series, bigger than the others, too big to fit in their box, and with no hemmed decorative border, like the others. On a mauve-grey background, it has a central circular ball of 'FOs' bound with a ribbon and is edged with jellyfish, garlands of flowers and sea anemones in warm plum, untramarine and raw umber.

The second set of handkerchief designs followed over a year later, in the summer of 1920. In this set, Harry often uses a shrill cyclamen pink, later popularized by Schiaparelli as 'Shocking Pink' and, again, first used distinctively by Bakst (plate 29). This was to become a favourite colour of Harry's; he often used it lavishly in his initial coloured sketches for stained glass and in his book illustrations, although when it was printed it never seemed to show up to full effect, as it does in the handkerchiefs. It should be remembered that Harry worked on this set and their box lid immediately after returning from a memorable visit to London to see Diaghilev's Ballets Russes season at the Alhambra Theatre, where Bakst's *Schéhérazade* and *Cleopatra* were included in the programme.

Each design in the second set is roughly based on a central mandala with much use of stylized organic motifs: underwater flora and fauna, butterflies, seed pods and ribboning tendrils recur; some give the impression of having been evolved from an initial splodge made on the crease of a folded piece of paper, pressed and then opened out. The designs are often reminiscent of the geometric formations to be seen in a kaleidoscope. They are intricate, inventive and never repetitive or stereotyped; Harry's innate empathy with diminutive organic forms is manifest, so that at times one is reminded of a fish tank or the vision at the end of a microscope.

Harry made a design for a decorative box lid, ten inches square, to accompany each set of handkerchiefs. The first (fig. 99), on which he worked from 8 to 13 April 1919, is signed 'HARRY CLARKE' in the bottom corner and inscribed in the bottom left corner 'HANDKERCHIEFS FROM DESIGNS BY HARRY CLARKE (Sefton Fabrics)'. In soft pastel colours, it depicts a lady in stylized Venetian costume with a little doll tied on a string round her waist and a young man in brocaded matador costume bearing her voluminous lace shawl and, in the other hand, a garland of roses which he drapes about them. A huge pink jellyfish spreads its tendrils in the foreground and other outsize marine creatures are arranged from left to right in pale pinks, blue-greens and beiges.

The second lid, designed more than a year later, took him five days. It is less decorative and only signed with a 'c' device in the bottom left hand corner; 'Handkerchiefs from designs by Harry Clarke' is inscribed in the white border around the picture, which in turn is surrounded with a black line and a grey border across which magnified microbes in blue and pink

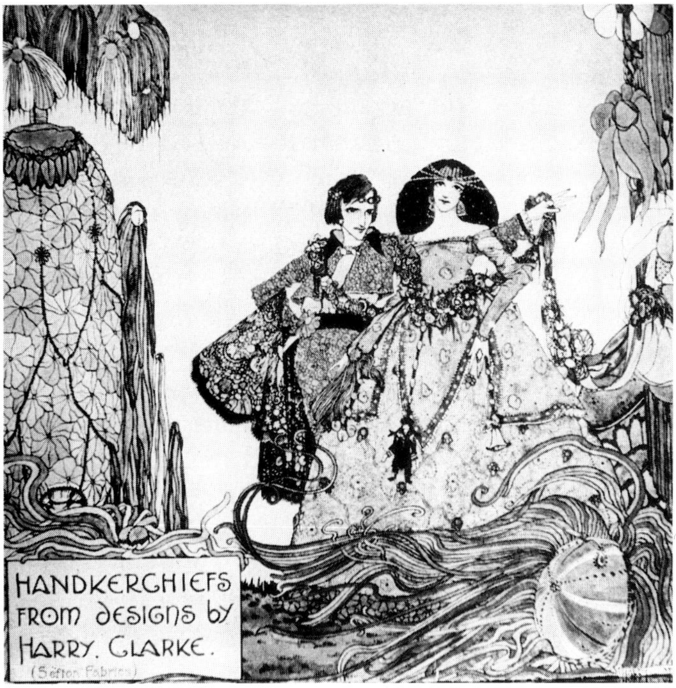

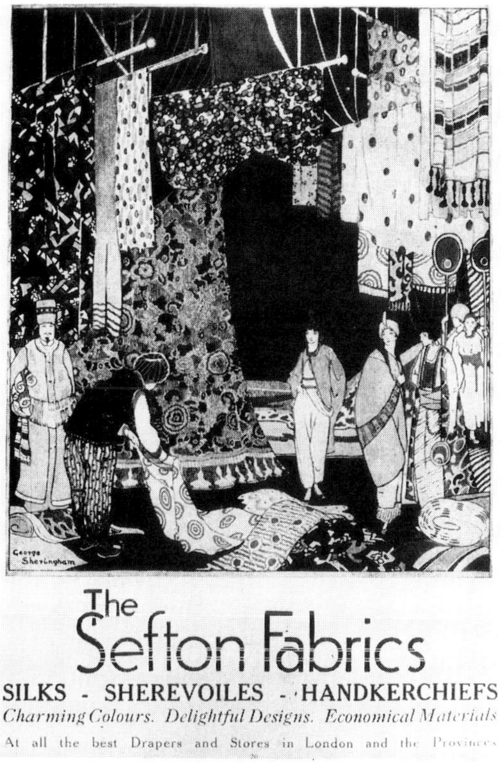

99 The box lid Clarke designed for the first set of handkerchiefs, 1919

100 'Aladdin's Cave'; advertisement from *Eve* (1919) designed by George Sheringham for Sefton Fabrics to display some of their current range

are swimming. The picture[47] is reminiscent of a Russian fairy tale; set against a white background, a small, elegantly decolletée lady in a black Erté gown and red cloak waits to be rescued from a beaded dragon by an effete plumed knight on a jade rocking-horse. The colours are of an earthy tone, darker than the sugary, pastel tones of its predecessor.

Both of his designs for *Sherevoile* printed linen dress fabric owe less to the Ballets Russes influence. Twelve differently coloured versions of each were printed. The first design (no. 248) is made up of overlapping linear daisy flowerheads and printed in a subdued array of soft colours (fig. 97). The second, more intricate design (no. 257) is composed of geometrically stylized small flowerheads arranged diagonally across the fabric. For this the colour combinations are mostly dark, with an emphasis on black, white and grey. These materials were most effective when made up into dresses; Harry's daughter had several dresses made from them by her aunts. It should be remembered that geometrical stylized flowerheads were devised not only by artists at that time but also by textile designers like Poiret's Atelier Martine and by Bénédictus (1878-1930). Like Harry, two exquisite colourists, Bakst and Erté, both Russian, worked in grey rooms with neutral backgrounds, restricting all glowing colour to the creations on their drawing boards.

The note Harry made in his diary to have 'the Half title Eve' ready at the beginning of December 1919, and his reference in a letter to Bodkin on 21 November that he had been invited to contribute to 'Eve', would seem to refer to *Eve*, a new illustrated ladies weekly, directed by the editor of *The Tatler*, as a sister publication to that magazine. This was named after Fish's immensely popular heroine, regularly featured in *The Tatler*, *Vanity Fair* and *Harper's*. Unfortunately, there is no sign of Harry's half-title, which he drew at home on 4 and 5 December (1919). Perhaps he missed the deadline of 1 December; nor does any of his work appear in any issue of *Eve* during the year after it first appeared on 11 March 1920. However, the early numbers of *Eve* magazine [48] featured several fine full-page coloured advertisements for Sefton's *Silks, Sherevoiles and Handkerchiefs*. The first advertisement [49] by George Sheringham, showed an Aladdin's cave festooned with *The Sefton Fabrics* (fig. 100); the second,[50] a selection of *Sefton Novelty Handkerchiefs*, featured four box lids, one of which was Harry's first lid design, and a selection of handkerchief designs by Harry, Sheringham, Mabel Lucie Attwell etc. The designs featured reflect the Russian Ballet influence on the new Art Deco design — a fusion of the geometrical with the ornamental — and the motifs and colours then coming into vogue, which were at the same period being taken up by the Bauhaus and purified into essentially well-designed, useful, while decorative, objects. To read through the pages of such magazines as *Eve* and look at fashionable designs for textiles, clothes, scent bottles and powder puffs is to realize the widespread eclecticism that had developed in the previous five years.[51] In several issues[52] *Sherevoile* designs radiate out from a central motif, among which Harry's first daisy design is illustrated. *Eve* included a number of illustrations by John Austen,[53] perhaps the first Harry had seen by this artist whose work he admired and who became one of his greatest friends, as well as work by Brunelleschi, Sheringham, Rzewuski, Lorenzi, E. Lord and Gordon McColl. These usually frivolous illustrations are interesting to compare with Harry's, as regards both colour and design. For example, E. Lord's *Cocktails*[54] was undoubtedly the source of Harry's *Autumn* illustration, reproduced in his 1920 anthology. Harry's impeccable and subtle sense of colour and design should also be compared with the work of George Sheringham, often remarkably similar in design. *The Studio Year Book of Decorative Art*, 1920, which featured their work together,[55] also featured some no less fanciful designs by E.O. Hoppé, well known as the photographer of the Ballets Russes dancers[56], who also ran the Dorien Leigh Galleries in London and the magazine, *Colour* ('the most fascinating magazine in the world'), which he founded, edited and controlled 'for the pleasure of picture lovers' for most of the period 1914-32. Harry would have read this, as it reviewed not only his own books but also the work of those artists he most admired. As an amateur photographer, he would have known Hoppé's photographic portraits[57] and it is possible he even met Hoppé in London, as Hoppé lived next door to Lavery in Cromwell Place, and we know from Harry's diaries that he made a note of Lavery's address and telephone number several times. A drawing of Hoppé's which appeared in *The Tatler* in 1913 is remarkably similar to Harry's illustrations of the 1914/15 period.[58]

Harry's next Poe illustrations, *Monos and Una* and *Morella* (fig. 101), on which he embarked when he had sent off the Sefton designs, predictably depict figures swathed in Sefton-like floral ornament. The former, illustrating 'Flowers, fantastic flowers, far more lovely than any of the old earth'

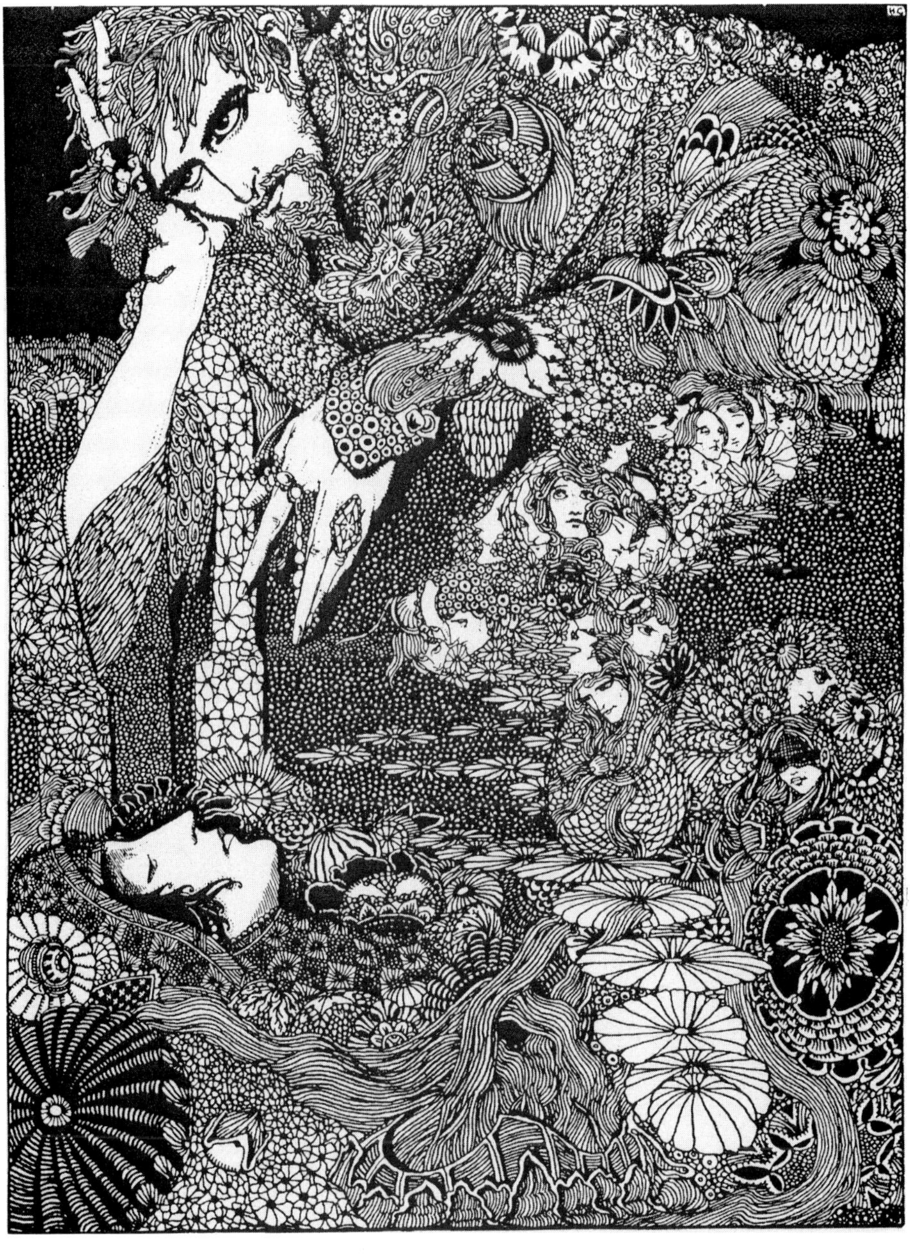

101 'The earth grew dark, and its figures passed by me, like flitting shadows, and among them all I beheld only — Morella', illustration to Poe's 'Morella', 1918

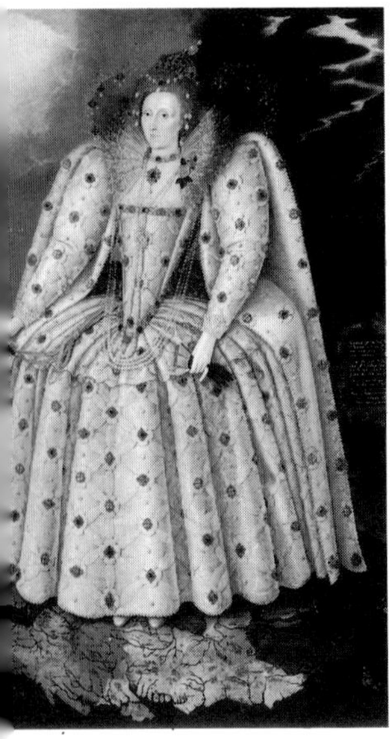

102 Marcus Gheeraerts the Younger, *Ditchley Portrait of Elizabeth I, c.* 1592 (courtesy of the National Portrait Gallery, London); a key image to Clarke (for example, in the Killiney *Angel*) in its iconic depiction of the ashen-faced, red-haired, bejewelled queen, clasping a fan and gloves while poised on an outline map beside a cartouche of tiny script

portrays Monos and Una as though on a sea bed, with a huge jellyfish waving its tendrils towards them. *Morella* also appears to be set on a sea bed, but whereas the *Monos and Una* flowers are restricted to variations on the daisy, in *Morella* spiralling, tiny, overlapping leaves and all manner of exotic 'fleurs du mal' engulf Morella and her brooding lover; mingled with these are the tiny faces of the 'figures that passed by me'. These illustrations manifest his imaginative adaptation of Japanese *katagami* stencil designs, of which he has recently been described as a 'leading exponent'[59] in Europe. The Japanese and Russian Ballet influences and a 'horror vacui' are as remarkable as Harry's frequently microscopic vision and predilection for marine flora and fauna. Sources for these submarine forms must surely have included the extensive Blaschka collection of glass models in the Dublin Natural History Museum (of which there were 530 by 1886).[60]

At the same time, Harry was working at the Studios to finish two windows; the Killiney *Angel* was fired on 20 February 1919 and finished by lunch time the following day. That afternoon and over the next two days, Harry did one of his simplest but most powerful black and white illustrations to Poe's 'Maelstrom', a whirling vortex into whose spiralling depths a tiny man and his boat are being sucked.[61]

The Killiney *Angel* window (plate 24) is a single lancet in the south wall of the little church of the Holy Trinity and consists of thirteen square feet of glass, for which Harry paid the Studios £22.15s, at their new rate of 35/- per square foot. The large ambetty diamond-shaped quarries in this window glow with a pale opalescent light. The border is composed of a string of tiny white pearls, set inside a thicker border where long, painted grisaille rectangles alternate with tiny squares of green glass. Each rectangle is filled with miniature emblems, such as a cross, a crown, pansies and other flowers, a lantern, lighthouses, a little galleon and other ships, an ornamental H (for Harry?) and other abstract devices. The emerald squares are painted with single flowers, St Brigid's crosses and abstract motifs. In the right hand bottom corner a wide rectangle of parchment-coloured glass, edged with golden swirling floral motifs is inscribed, 'TO THE GLORY OF GOD / and in loving memory of / Clifford B. Lloyd who / died January 27th 1915'. The lettering was painted by William Nagle under Harry's instructions. To the left of this is a tiny Noah's ark beneath the pearl beading, and in the bottom left corner the coat of arms of the family is suspended between two rose-pink sticks and a black floral edged scroll, inscribed 'VIRTUS IN ARDUA'.

The sandalled feet of *The Angel of Hope and Peace* stand on a green island, edged with white cliffs and festooned with large flowers; it looks like a small raft being navigated through the parchment quarries. This is a borrowing of Harry's from Elizabethan iconography — a device borrowed from Gheerhaerts the Younger's *Ditchley* portrait of Elizabeth I (*c.* 1593; fig. 102), where the Queen is poised on a detailed coloured coastline map of

England.[62] Other features of this portrait adapted by Harry are the minutely inscribed laudatory cartouche beside the Queen, transposed in this case to bear the inscription, the tiny galleons on the sea and the distinctive colouring of the Queen, with her deathly pale face, pointed features and red, curly hair recognizably transposed to the Angel. This ashen-faced Angel with tapering fingers and sumptuous gold-pink wings is Harry's archetypal androgynous creature, developed from the Saints of the Honan Chapel, the *Queens*, the *Mad Prince*, the Mermaid and Merman in *A Meeting*, and many of the smaller attendant figures in these works. She will reappear in other guises in his later work in various media, but it is in stained glass that she reaches her apotheosis. However suggestive the watercolour or black line or tones of grisaille, colour has its full power in Harry's stained glass. In this window, he has synthesized this image into form and its material expression (plate 24). He was a decadent in the decorative, symbolist, Gothic sense, an evocative illustrator with a strong literary bent, but without Yeats' prophetic Symbolism.[63] The window was exhibited in North Frederick Street for one day before it was installed on 3 March. It became known as the 'Beardsley' window between Harry and Bodkin.

By the end of February, Harry had to resume work on the Poe illustrations and he was fortunate to have an able assistant in Kathleen Quigley, who undertook the preliminary work on the war memorial window for Wexford, beginning on 24 February. On the same day he began the illustration for the 'Marie Roget' story, but had to interrupt his work on this the following day to do a glass design for a commission of his father's at the Carlton Cinema. The *Marie Roget* drawing took two further days and was followed by that for 'The Premature Burial', over the next three days, interspersed with aciding work in North Frederick Street on the Wexford window. As he drew the illustrations at home, he tried to keep a whole day to work in each medium. The *William Wilson* drawing took two days, *The House of Usher* took three days, *The Gold Bug* two and a half days, *King Rat* three days, *Man of the Crowd* two days, and *Silence* three days. This completed the Poe commission, although Harraps had still not decided whether to use the 1914 or 1918 version of the *M. Valdémar* drawing.

Before he resumed work on the Wexford window, Harry took a well-earned holiday on 22 and 23 March, as he was exhausted by the burst of activity at what is widely regarded as his illustrative masterpiece. However, the strain of this concentrated work on the Poe illustrations took its toll, and he was out sick until the end of the month.

On 31 March he resumed work on the Wexford window and continued until 7 April. During the afternoon of that day, Harry's first son, Michael, was born at the family home in Blackrock. Since Harry wanted to be at home with his wife, he spent the next week there, working on the second Sefton box lid, *The Princess being rescued from the Dragon*, which he duly sent off before he returned to the Studios to work on the Wexford window. Glazing began on 21 April and the painting of the two lights was completed a week later. The last two days of the month were spent on the tracery lights.

For the 90th Royal Hibernian Academy exhibition, held at the School of Art during the week after Easter, Harry borrowed his drawing of *The Mad Mulrannies* from Bodkin and two stained glass designs, for Terenure and Church Street, Dublin, but had considerable trouble in finding suitable frames for his work.

Despite his hopes of a respite, Harry continued to be busy through April and May. He managed to complete the Wexford window by the beginning of May, ready for the Studios to have it fixed. This two-light window employs a lot of clear and ambetty glass, lightly matted and painted with small grisaille devices. It is set in the south wall of the side aisle in the church and signed 'Harry Clarke 1919'. The trefoil tracery light above depicts the bust of a male saint, possibly St Aidan, in yellow with a turquoise halo. Beneath, a smaller inset tracery light shows a golden dove hovering over an inverted golden triangle. The two main lancet-headed openings show the *Madonna and Child adored by Sts Aidan and Adrian*. A clear border surrounds each, interwoven with the stems of twisted briars, and spiralling tendrils from this border meander into the central part of each light, where the tiny symbolic devices painted on the subtly modulated tones of leaded clear glass include miniature galleons, crucifixes and crosses, lighthouses, Noah's arks, perfectly detailed Crucifixion and Ascension scenes, the letters WOK and H, chalices, temples and flowers, often set in tiny grisaille medallions. The patchwork-sailed galleon depicted in such detail on Harry's 1918 Christmas card appears in the bottom left corner, as though sailing on the high seas;[64] sharks' fins swim in her wake. Another vignette depicts the Puginesque church in which the window is set. The arms of the O'Keeffe family are suspended at the foot of the left light, and a cartouche commemorating the young Lt William Henry O'Keeffe is edged in black filigree lacework at the foot of the right light. The two lights are gracefully and artfully linked by the downward sweep of the Madonna's blue silk cloak, which falls diagonally away from the opening in which she is seated, to overlap that of the two saints, while providing a cushion for St Aidan to kneel on.

The Madonna and Child hover above the sea, lightly suggested by grisaille ripples. St Aidan of Ferns and St Adrian worship her from the grass green, daisy-strewn outline map of a coast, similar to that at the feet of the Killiney *Angel*. The O'Keeffe arms are treated in an unexpectedly grainy Whall manner — four shields depicting a silver lion rampant on gules, a winged horseman on a pacing charger, a golden eagle with silver stars on azure and three salamanders on vert.

This window is Harry's most Art Nouveau design, its borders framed in a sinuous canopy of intertwining branches and stalks, punctuated by tiny roses and lilies. It is restrained, delicate and exquisitely painted. The colouring is grisaille, or more or less clear apart from dramatic splashes, like the Virgin's deep gold-pink halo edged with green, the diapered ruby and gold cushion on which she rests her slippered feet, and the horizontal flashes of gold beneath her, the areas of deep ultramarine on her mantle, and patches of crimson and silver on St Aidan's cope. His frail ascetic frame and silver emblems (plate 22) contrast with the exotic, Symbolist portrayal of the knightly St Adrian, resplendent in a lemon and black cloak crossed with crimson bands, jewelled accoutrements and turquoise and ruby halo framing his chainmail balaclava and foliate helmet (plate 23).[65] The cartoons for the two main lights of the window were reproduced in sepia in the 1922 *Catholic Directory* advertising inset.

On 2 May, Harry began work on his Phibsborough window and carried on with it for the next week. On Sunday the 11th, he took a day off to design a headpiece for the special Diamond Jubilee issue of the *Irish Builder and Engineer*.[66] Signed 'H' and 'C', it depicts St Brigid in the centre, with St Patrick on the left and St Columcille on the right above the lettering; underneath, between an interlaced design, a monk with a hammer is on the left and a cowled monk with a scroll inscribed with a cross and a pair of compasses on the right. A round tower rising beside early monastic buildings suggests the first Irish builders on the Skelligs; there are further silhouettes of a round tower and a high cross, the whole design being framed by columns with Celtic motifs. The following week was again occupied by work on the Phibsborough commission, while Sunday was spent designing a bookplate, 3" diameter, in black and white, for Florence Anne Howden; he then resumed work on the Phibsborough window for a third successive week.

During the weekend of 24 and 25 May Harry worked on the zodiac panels to be arranged as a lantern around the sun panel he had completed for Waldron in September 1918, together with two armorial panels. He had, in 1914, made an earlier lantern with thistles and the Waldron arms which was not entirely successful. The *Zodiac Lantern* is six sided, eleven inches tall and set in a bronze case made by McGloughlin's Art Metalworkers, its peaked top gathered to a point on which a bronze loop has been welded. A small rim, pierced with circular holes, rises at an angle to the upper perimeter of the lantern, and a similar pierced border at the base acts as a frame for the glass panels which form the sides, separated by bronze dividing pieces. Each side contains five pieces of glass; the upper half (5" x 5") is edged in black with a golden stained rim between two further black lines inside which is painted a central emblem, either a butterfly or a stylized sunflower set on a background of light matt, etched with the 'unravelled knitting' motif. On one side, the monogram, ornately inscribed, replaces the central emblem. The two halves are divided by a bronze frame; the lower half (also 5" x 5") is subdivided vertically into two by a thin lead line and, again, an inch from the base, by a horizontal decorative bronze

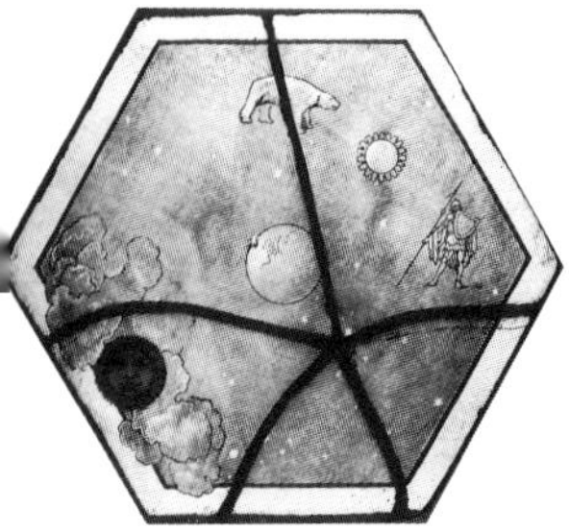

103 Hexagonal base panel, stained and painted glass, from a lantern commemorating the first non-stop transatlantic flight by Alcock and Brown, who left St John's, Newfoundland, on 14 June 1919 and landed the following day in a bog near Clifden in the west of Ireland. The panel is dated '20.6.29' and depicts the tiny aircraft breaking into the Atlantic from the outer surface of Earth; outlines of America, Ireland and England are suggested, as are Mars, the Sun, Polaris and other planets.

line. In these small lower panels the twelve symbols of the zodiac are painted beneath their signs in shades of silver stain, ranging from deep amber to pale lemon and a greyish painting medium; the brushwork is loose, full and fluid. A seaweed motif recurs as a decorative background. The zodiacal symbol is written on a small *trompe l'oeil* notice seemingly pinned to the glass, similar to those favoured by fifteenth century Flemish painters.

The hexagonal panel at the base of the lantern (fig. 103) is perhaps its most original aspect, since it commemorates the first non-stop transatlantic flight by Alcock and Brown, who landed in a bog near Clifden in Connemara on 15 June 1919. Harry's panel is signed 'H.C.' in a box and dated 20.6.1919, less than a week after the historic event. It depicts the tiny aircraft breaking into the Atlantic sea from the outer surface of a globe on which the outlines of Ireland, England and the edge of the American continent are sketched in; other planets and constellations are deftly suggested.

The entry in the catalogue of the 1921 Arts and Crafts Exhibition catalogue states that the lantern (no. 312) was designed by Harry but executed by Kathleen Quigley.[67] It is interesting to note that it was Kathleen Quigley, skilled as an illuminator and miniaturist, who painted most of the stained glass in Sir Neville Wilkinson's miniature masterpiece, *Titania's Palace* (1907-22). It is surprising that Harry did not contribute work to *Titania's Palace*, as he must have known Sir Neville through their mutual involvement with the Arts and Crafts Society. In 1921-2 he made a miniature stained glass panel depicting *Titania and Bottom*, which was mounted in a mahogany cabinet by James Hicks, who had made the mahogany structure of *Titania's Palace* for Sir Neville. Lutyens, for whom Harry also made a stained glass panel in the summer of 1919, designed the palace's belfry. The stained glass inside the palace was by Alfred Child and Kathleen Quigley, who also made the Byzantine mosaics in the chapel; this contained an exquisite miniature copy ($1\frac{1}{8}$" in diameter) in silver and enamel of the Ardagh Chalice made by Mia Cranwill, the jeweller and enamellist, who was, with Oswald Reeves and some of his pupils, the only other craftworker contemporary with Harry in Ireland to produce work of a consistently Symbolist nature.[68]

On 28 May, Harry left for London with Bodkin, a visit planned to coincide with Diaghilev's season at the Alhambra. This was the second phase of Diaghilev's Ballets Russes, following the 1917 Revolution and the War. Nijinsky and Bakst had been succeeded by Massine, Larionov and painters such as Picasso, Dérain and Balla, although this season marked the reappearance of Tamara Karsavina, now married to an Irish diplomat. The most popular ballerina was Lydia Lopokova, subsequently Mrs Maynard Keynes; she was certainly Harry's favourite.[69] This was the end of the Bakstian era, of which Harry had long been an avid admirer. Proust[70] later recalled being told, during the Paris season in the following May, the sobering news that Bakst was in hospital with general paralysis, and Nijinsky diagnosed insane. Micheál MacLiammoir remembered meeting Harry at this Alhambra season and thinking how well he fitted into the artistic ambience, exquisitely attired and looking not unlike Massine.[71] On their first night he and Bodkin saw *Papillons*, whose Pierrot costume by Bakst Harry had adapted in his Hans Andersen illustrations, *The Good Humoured Ladies* and the chromatic extravaganza, *Cleopatra*. On the second night they saw the original, sumptuous production of *Firebird* and *Les Sylphides* and, on their last night, *Petrouschka* and the exotic, hugely in-

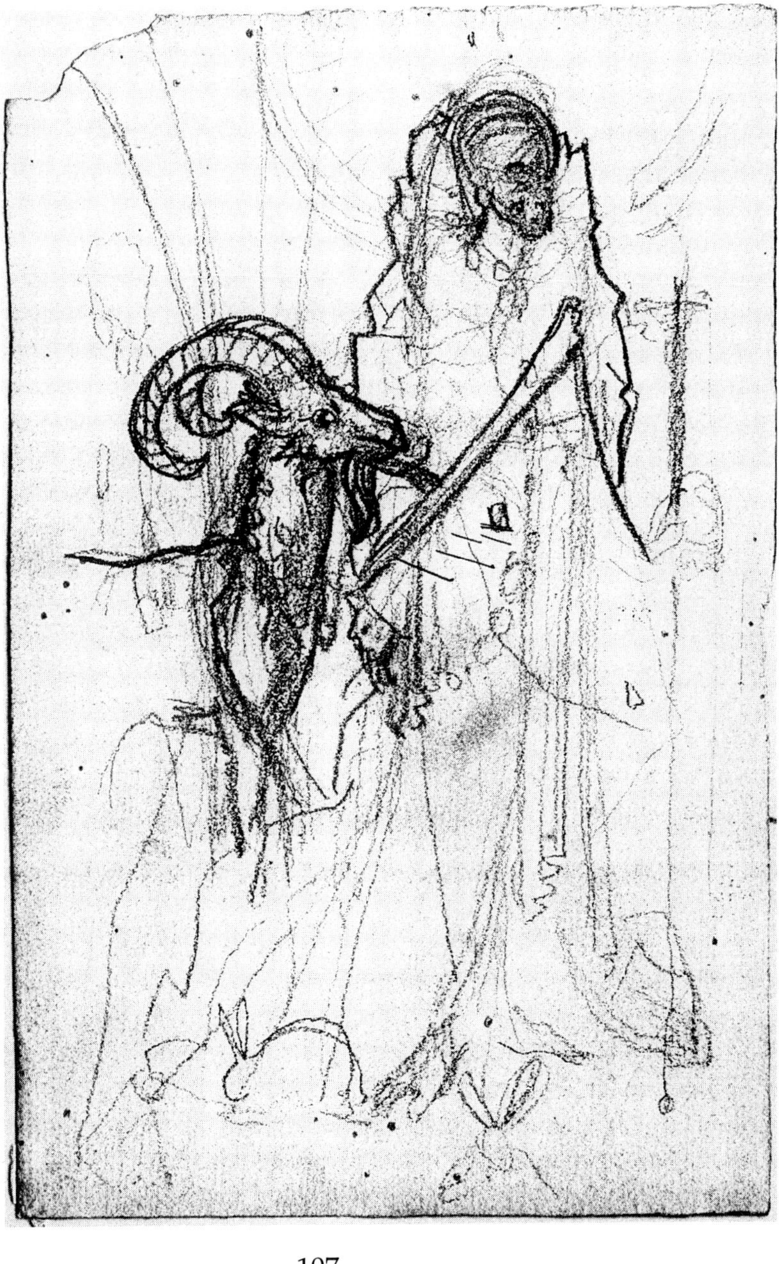

104 An early, mostly rejected, design for *Julian*, 1919

fluential succés de scandale, *Schéhérazade*, whose original designs by Bakst he could have seen in Paris in 1914, as the Musée des Arts Décoratifs had bought them during its first season in 1910.

Harry had taken to London some of his 'small glass panels — something new, and wonderful in design and craftsmanship — a treat'[72] according to his father, who was very keen that Mr Salmond should see them. Harry had an appointment to see Harrap, partly about the illustrated *Poe* and with Bodkin he had a project to help his work become better known which in some way involved the publishers, *The Studio*, Sir Edwin Lutyens and Sir Cecil Harcourt-Smith. Waldron wrote to Bodkin on 1 June, saying how he was 'burning with curiosity — to give it no worthier name — to hear how you and he succeed in your enterprises. . . . Best regards to you both and hoping soon to see you returning in a blaze of glory and success.'[73] The obvious outcome was Bodkin's comprehensive article in 'The Art of Mr Harry Clarke', which appeared in *The Studio* in November 1919.

In London, a letter awaited Bodkin at their hotel, The Berners — Sir Edwin Lutyens giving him and Harry an appointment on 2 June.[74] On the afternoon of that same day Bodkin and Harry visited Sir Cecil Harcourt-Smith at the Victoria and Albert Museum, where he had been director since 1909. Harry would certainly have known of him, if not have actually met him, while he was at South Kensington or when his prizewinning gold medal entries were exhibited there three years in succession. It seems, from Harry's diary and the Bodkin and Clarke manuscripts, that Harry made two panels for Lutyens and Harcourt-Smith, commissioned after he had shown them the small panels he had already made.

After his return from London on 5 June his diary shows that he worked for ten days on a project named *Julian* (fig. 104). From 18 to 27 June he worked on *Gideon*, and on 30 June *Gideon* was sent to Sir Cecil Harcourt-Smith. One can conclude, from his letter of 15 June to Bodkin, that the *Julian* panel was made for Lutyens.

The *Julian* panel (plate 20) was eventually never boxed, just framed in a thick, 6″ wide ebonized wood mount; it measures 8½″ x 5″, is signed 'H. CLARKE. 1.9.1.9.' and is constructed of three pieces of glass plated between a lead frame. The clear panel is to diffuse the light through the intricately acided and painted flashed blue and unusually thick, irregular ruby. Flaubert's *Légende de S. Julien*, which the panel illustrates, was first published as the third of *Les Trois Contes* in 1877. Flaubert concluded his short story by explaining, fancifully, that his tale was 'telle à peu prés qu'on la trouve sur un vitrail d'église dans mon pays',[75] that is, the thirteenth-century window, *La Légende de S. Julien Hospitalier*, in Rouen Cathedral which Harry would have seen on his 1914 visit. Harry's panel synthesizes various episodes in Flaubert's vivid tale around the principal figure of the saint, who is seen full length, facing us, gloved hands clasped at his breast head turned sideways to the left, cutting a strong, Donatello-like profile against his black, golden-scalloped halo.[76] He has chosen to show Julian reflecting on his past life of unquenchable desire for slaughter, when he used to feel sadistically 'a savage tumultuous delight'[77] at his victims' death agonies; relics of his torture, his crusading banner, his palace in Occitania and symbols of impending doom surround him. One could quote any number of extracts from Symbolist literature to put this design in context, perhaps as an evocation of Yeats' 'Byzantium' and a vision into an interior lost world, coloured by the impossible.

The *Julian* panel was never reproduced in Harry's lifetime, nor did Lutyens buy it.[78] On 16 December, Edmond Lupton, a barrister and magistrate and friend of Bodkin's, bought it from Harry on Bodkin's advice and, according to his widow, treasured it all his life. Bodkin seems to have arranged for Lupton to see the panel on approval, once it was known that it was to return to Dublin. Lupton subsequently 'made or rather converted a container with a light to show it off'.[79] *Julian* was exhibited in the sixth Arts and Crafts Society exhibition (no. 293), held in the autumn of 1921 at the School of Art, where Harry stated in the catalogue that, although he would do no replicas, panels 'in this manner' would cost from £25. Early in January 1921, he had still not given up the idea of illustrating *Julian* in black and white, to complement the panel illustration.[80]

As yet, the *Gideon* panel is untraced, although it would seem that it still belonged to Sir Cecil Harcourt-Smith in 1943; there is no record of its having returned to Ireland. The subject of this panel would suggest that it was a companion piece to *Julian*, especially as the two panels were conceived and executed at the same time. The exploits of Gideon, whose name means 'destroyer' or 'one who cuts off the hand', are described in the Bible in *The Book of Judges*, chapters 6 to 8. His miraculous, avenging and lustful adventures would have given Harry as much scope for illustration as the Bible's detailed descriptions of his accumulated riches. The panel's disappearance is the greatest gap in a catalogue of his work.

The rest of July and the first week of August were occupied with the Phibsborough window, followed by a rest, before finishing the work on 28 August. The window is one of Harry's early masterpieces, although the present window now in St Peter's, for which it was commissioned, has been substantially altered. The three-light traceried window was designed to face north east in the north aisle of the church; inexplicably, the window was removed in the 1950s, the opening bricked up and a statue put in its place, and Clarke's window moved to an inconspicuous place over a confessional which juts out at least three feet beneath it, blocking the base of the window. As the opening to which it was moved differed in measurement from the original opening, a section was cut out of each of Harry's three lights, a mauve border inserted and seven new tracery lights and a trefoil in brown were added above the tracery light; dotted lines were scraped onto their matted surface, a tasteless inscription added and the top third of the window plated in blue/mauve cathedral glass. This insensitive treatment was also responsible for the destruction of three sections of the main lights and all Harry's tracery work from the original window. Luckily, the original cartoons survive. Each of the main tracery lights was in the form of a pointed quatrefoil and portrayed the bust of a nun holding a scroll, surrounded with a border of Celtic ornament. The nun on the left's reads 'Behold this Heart'; St Gertrude's (her name is inscribed around her halo), 'Which hath'; and St Mathilde's, 'So loved men', on the right — a reference to the fact that St Peter's is the home of the Arch-Confraternity of the Sacred Heart in Dublin.

Despite the adverse conditions of light, structure and design, what remains of Harry's window is still a wonder. It is basically composed of areas of rich ruby, sapphire and emerald, with touches of gold, very pale green and gold-pink. Its rich colouring and the dramatic expressions of the three principal burnished red-haired figures are more in the style of the Honan Chapel windows than the lighter, more delicately grisaille Wexford and Killiney windows. The two side lights, in the manner of the Honan windows, are filled with tiny evocative portraits of attendant saints and symbols. The original window contained 53 square feet of glass. The draped figure of Christ evokes French Romanesque sculpture, while the entranced profiled figures of the androgynous St John (fig. 105) and equally beautiful, elegant St Margaret Mary[81] are further variants of Clarke archetypes, Wagnerian in essence.

Harry allowed himself a few days 'mucking about and taking photos'[82] at the end of August before he began his first sketches for Nantwich on 4 September. Arnold Bennett in his *Journal*, writing of his visit to Dublin for the Horse Show 1919,[83] described the morning of 31 August when 'we [he, Bodkin and Sir John O'Connell] saw a few pictures in the Gallery and then off somewhere to see young Clarke's stained glass. Then lunch at the Dolphin and O'Connell and I joined X and his wife and a friend for Phoenix Park'. Bennett does not comment on the work he saw, nor in his own diary did Harry mention meeting Bennett. Bennett also tells of the things he bought with Bodkin in Dublin and recalls a good dinner, where the star was 'old Miss Purser who had known Marie Bashkirtseff intimately and was now 75, owns a stained glass factory in Dublin and bosses it herself'.[84]

During the summer, Harry would accompany Larky Waldron, Bodkin and other members of Waldron's circle on car jaunts to Ashford, where they would have tea at Miss Gillettlie's famous Hunter's Hotel after a visit to the Walpole gardens at Mount Usher. They all contributed doodles to the visitors' book at the hotel.

By 16 September Harry had finished his initial coloured design for the Nantwich window and posted it off to Arthur Knowles. This was to be a three-light window depicting the *Virgin and Child with St Cecilia and Richard Coeur de Lion*, in memory of Mr Knowles' wife Clare, and of his son Richard,

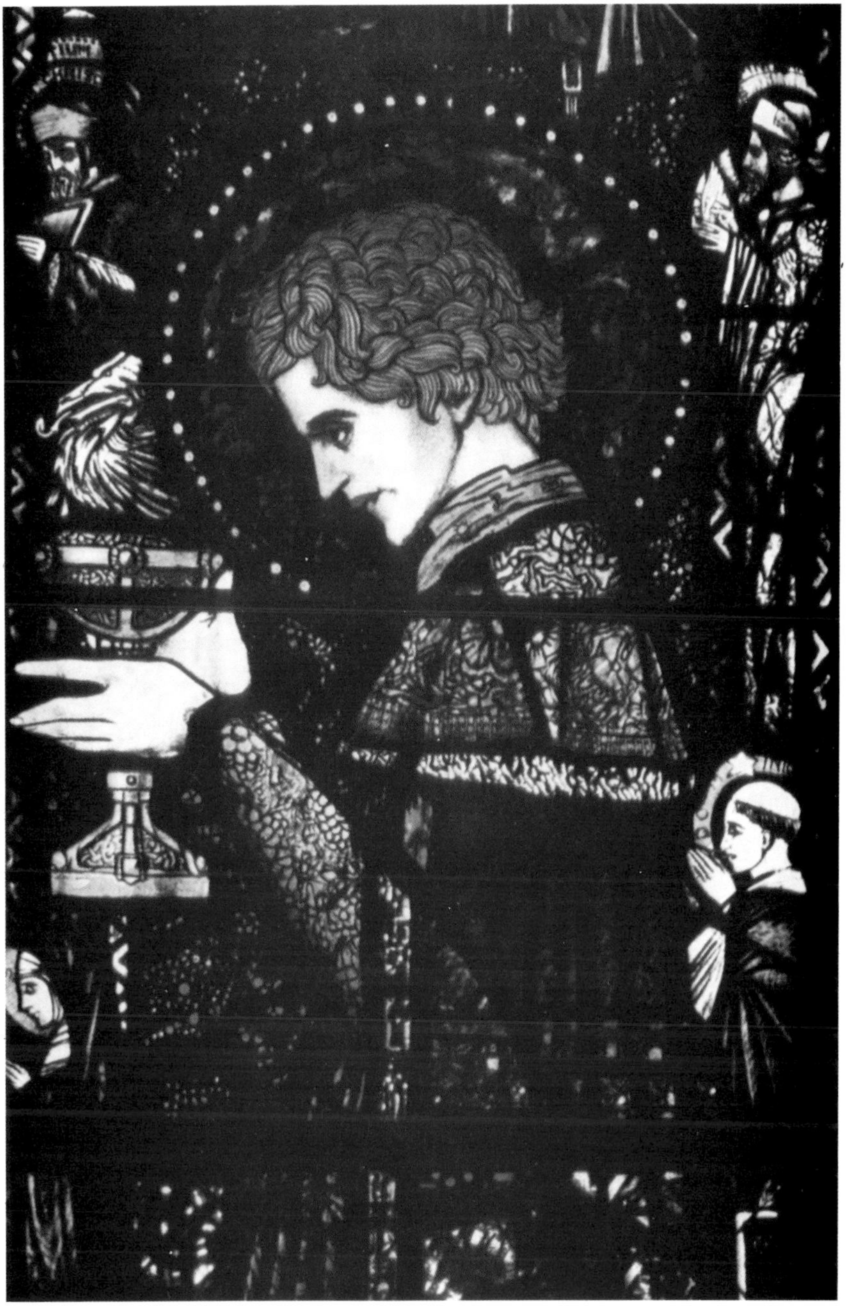

105 St John, detail from *The Adoration of the Sacred Heart* window, Phibsborough, 1919; a Clarke archetype

killed in the war. On 17 September he began work on the cartoon for the huge Terenure window which had been hanging over him for some time. He began with the right hand opening (partially reversed for the left hand opening) and by the 25th, had started on the centre opening. He diverted himself by going to Charlie Chaplin films and reading H.G.Wells. On the 29th, he designed a policy heading in pen and ink for the Irish National

Assurance Co.; signed 'HARRY CLARKE '19', it measures 4½" x 9¼" and shows the name and address of the firm in English and Irish on a decorative background, composed of variations on the usual themes of floral motifs, jellyfish, overlapping leaves, hairlike coils and swirling tendrils. Each corner is punctuated with a shield bearing the arms of one of the four provinces of Ireland and beneath the lettering are four vignettes. As his father had suffered a fall after a race meeting at the Curragh, he was called upon to submit a detailed coloured design on the four-light *Pietà* war memorial window over the altar in the Presbyterian church, Clontarf, Co. Dublin. A fine, albeit conventional, design, Harry's idiosyncracies are restrained, as the window was to be made by the Studios once it was approved.

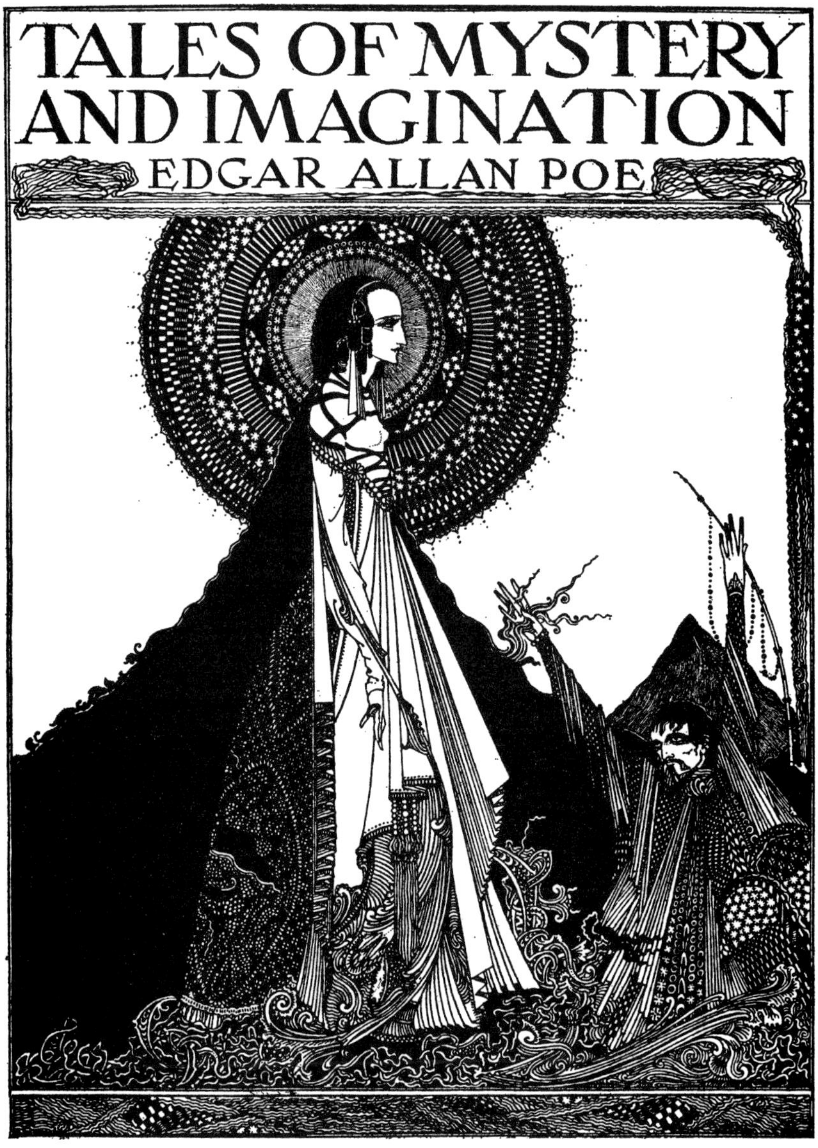

106 'In the excitement of my opium dreams (for I was habitually fettered in the shackles of the drug), I would call aloud her name', illustration to Poe's *Ligeia*, 1918; incorporated into Harrap's advertising folder for Poe's *Tales of Mystery and Imagination* (1919)

When the central opening for Terenure was completed, Harry spent a few days on a mysterious *Peacock* sketch. Could this have been for the little Peacock Theatre attached to the Abbey Theatre, founded by Lennox Robinson? He was working so hard that he had to refuse several invitations from Bodkin: 'I only have a few hours each day now and Sunday work is off for me for present until November at any rate'.[85] He needed every hour of daylight he could get. On 23 October he was working at the left hand opening for Terenure, which he adapted from the right hand opening; he worked solidly at this until 4 November. By 11 November he had completed the cartoons for the three lights. On 17 November he set off to London to select more glass from Hetley's as the glass stock in the studio could not supply all his needs. While in London, he visited Harrap's to discuss his next book for them and collected a picture for Bodkin from the National Gallery, before investigating a job in Sussex and visiting Nantwich. It was all a 'dreadful rush . . . without even one Russian Ballet or Charlie Chaplin . . . and not much joy news . . . this trip is not pleasant I assure you',[86] but he must have been happy to hear that, on the strength of his initial drawing, he had been given a commission to do a large three-light window in the parish church of St Mary in Sturminster Newton in Dorset.

On his return he immediately started work on the Terenure cutlines, which took him about ten days. As another potential commission was being offered him, from Castletownshend, on 6 December he suspended his work at the Studios to spend three days at home making a preliminary coloured design. He returned to work on the Nantwich window, setting out the measurements and making alterations, on the strength of his recent visit to the church, before beginning the cartoons, starting with the traceries and proceeding to the centre light, the Blessed Virgin. He worked on this right up to Christmas eve, only taking a day off to make some Christmas cards. He had not had time to do a black and white design and have it printed, so he sent small watercolour sketches to close friends only. He often made little drawings for place names at his children's parties and on notes to friends. Bodkin's card was a tiny watercolour (5″ x 3½″) — a sparse Japanese composition in which a silver birch tree painted parallel to the edge of the white card contains the figure of an angel hovering in a red robe, with black feathery wings and blue halo; the tree is dotted with red blossoms and on a lower branch a dark bearded figure kneels praying in a red and black gown. The end of 1919 saw Harry back at work on the cartoon for the *St Cecilia* light at Nantwich.

Joshua continued to help Harry by ordering glass for him, mostly from Hetley's, with the odd consignment from Powell's — opalite flesh, antique, flashed and streaky rubies, flashed blues, gold-pinks and some seedy ambers. He was enormously proud of Bodkin's long illustrated article in the November *Studio*.[87] Not only did it give a detailed account of Harry's career up to date; it also featured full-page reproductions of Miss French's

A Meeting, two of Waldron's *Queens* panels in colour; and, in black and white, Bodkin's *Mad Mulrannies* and the Poe *Morella*. Illustrated within the text is a three-light cartoon for stained glass, *The Immaculate Conception*, reproduced by permission of Sir John O'Connell. This was the first time Harry's work had been assessed and illustrated in a critical article, published in an internationally read magazine rather than in a short newspaper review. The *Studio* article was reprinted with excerpts from Bodkin's 1916 *Studies* review of Harry's illustrated *Hans Andersen* and inserted into a folder advertising his illustrated *Poe*; his *Ligeia* illustration was reproduced on the front (fig. 106).

Tales of Mystery and Imagination with Harry's illustrations was published by Harrap in October 1919, page size 10½" x 8" in four editions, cloth extra with 'a tasteful jacket lithographed in Biscuit and Green' (15/-), velvet Persian yapp (30/-), full morocco (3 guineas) and in a 5-guinea full vellum limited de luxe edition of 170 copies on hand-made paper, signed and numbered. Twenty-four full page black and white line drawings, each 8" x 6", were supplemented by additional drawings on the front cover, spine and dust jacket and ten ornamental tailpiece drawings, two of which had already appeared in the *Hans Andersen* volume. The original 1914 version of *M. Valdémar* was eventually used in the book (five years had already elapsed between this first illustration of M. *Valdémar* and Harry's completion of the drawings). Harrap's publicity campaign for the *Poe* was extensive, and the book achieved lavish notice in the Christmas Supplement of *The Bookman*, which devoted a double spread to the *Marchesa Aphrodite* illustration, while their advertising illustrated the cover of the folder and announced the book at the top of their seasonal list.

Following the critical acclaim[88] and record-breaking sales of the illustrated *Poe*, Harry submitted a dummy for a new anthology — Lettice d'Oyly Walters' selection of contemporary poetry, *The Year's at the Spring* — and within a week had formally accepted George Harrap's commission to provide line and watercolour[89] illustrations for the book.

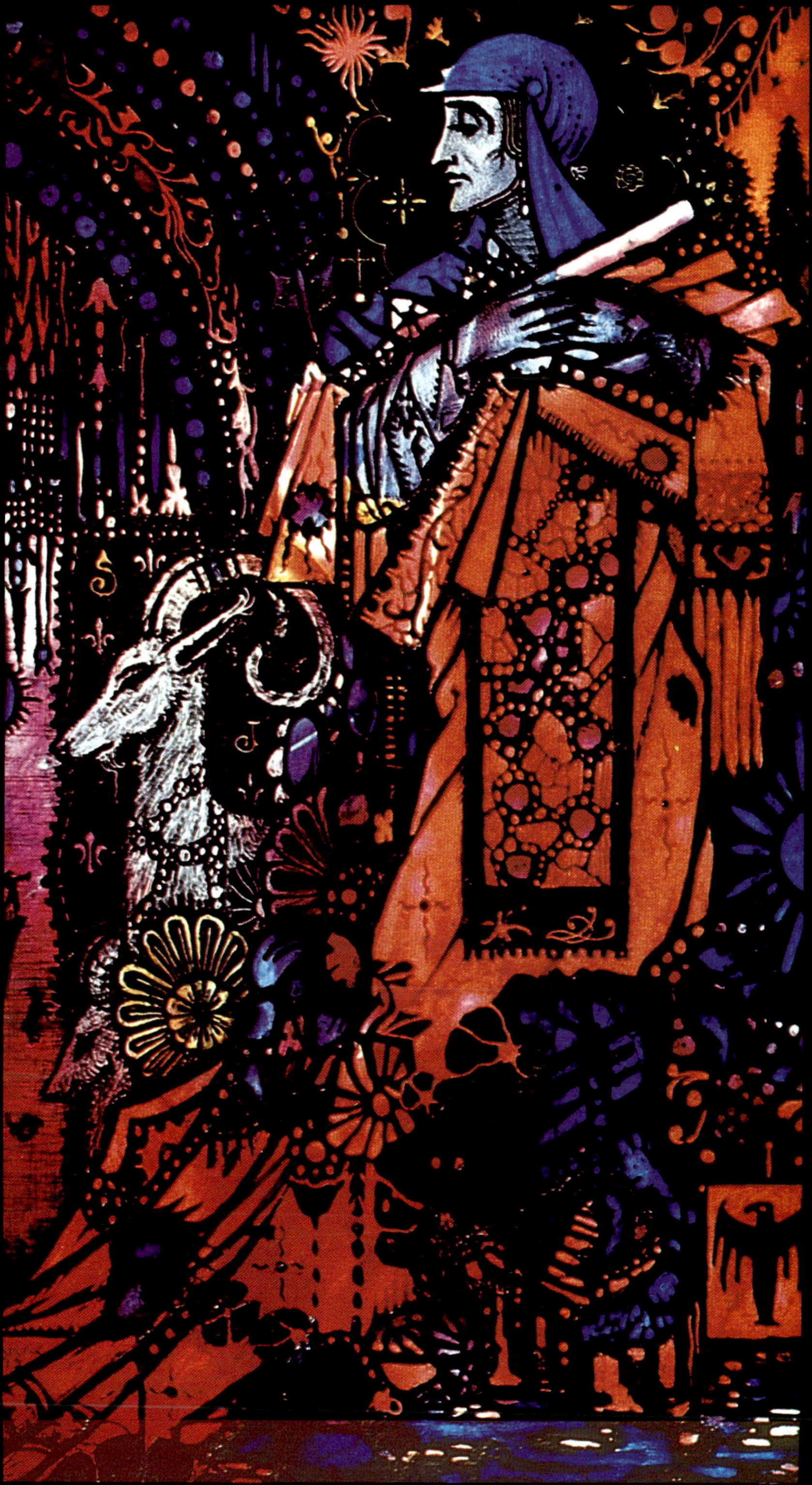

20 Julian, **stained glass panel illustrating Gustave Flaubert's** *Légende de S. Julien*, **1919, flashed seedy ruby glass plated behind a panel of flashed blue glass, painted, acided and stained**

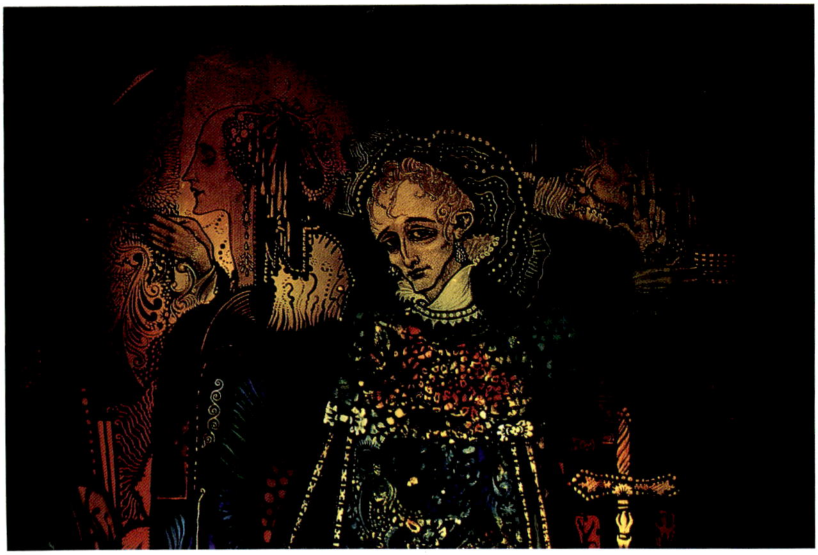

21

21 **Detail of the king and the queen from** The Song of the Mad Prince **panel, 1917, flashed ruby glass plated behind a panel of flashed blue glass, painted, acided and stained**

22 St Aidan, **detail from the O'Keeffe memorial window, Wexford, 1919; the local saint is portrayed as a frail old bishop, treated almost totally in grisaille but for the deep ruby of his brocaded cape and mitre.**

23 St Adrian, **detail from the O'Keeffe memorial window**

22

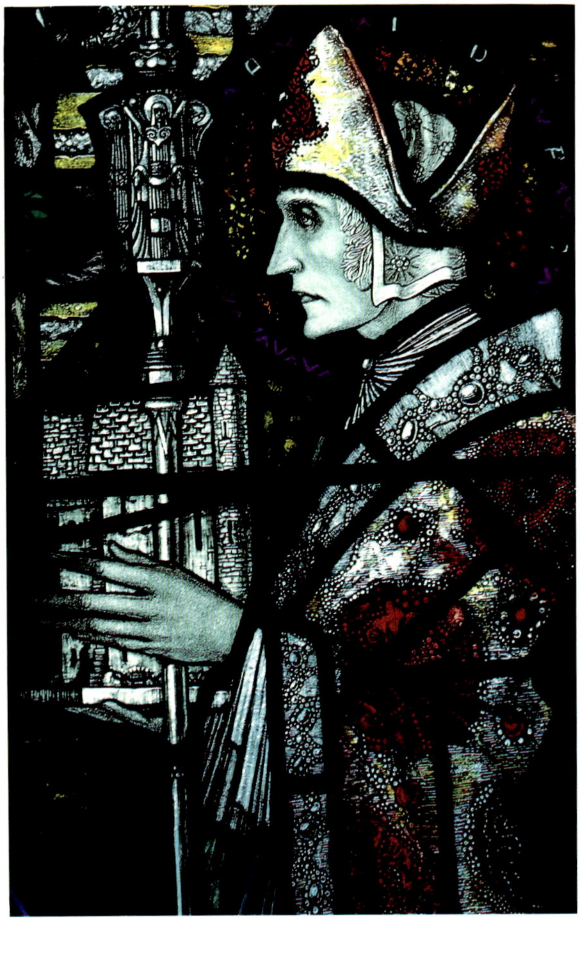

23

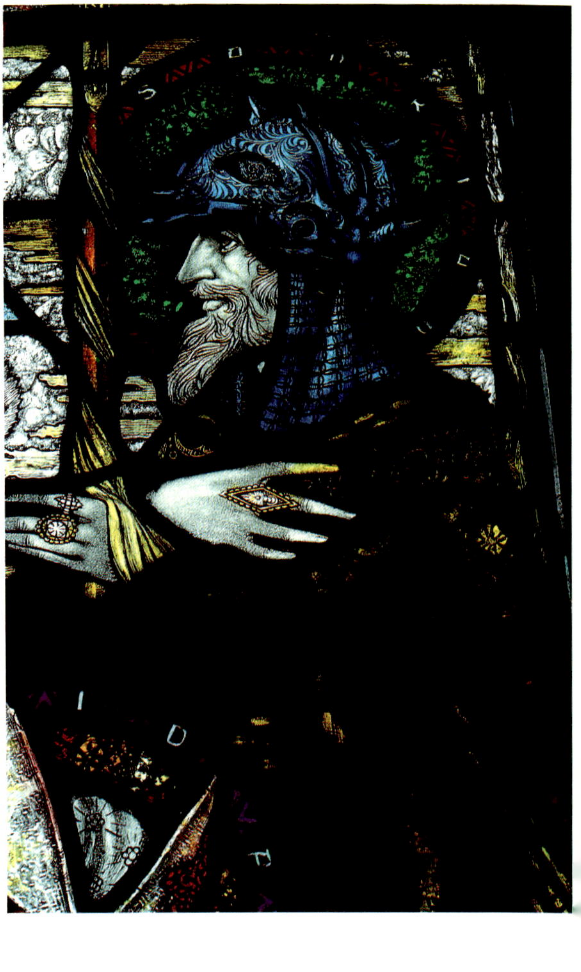

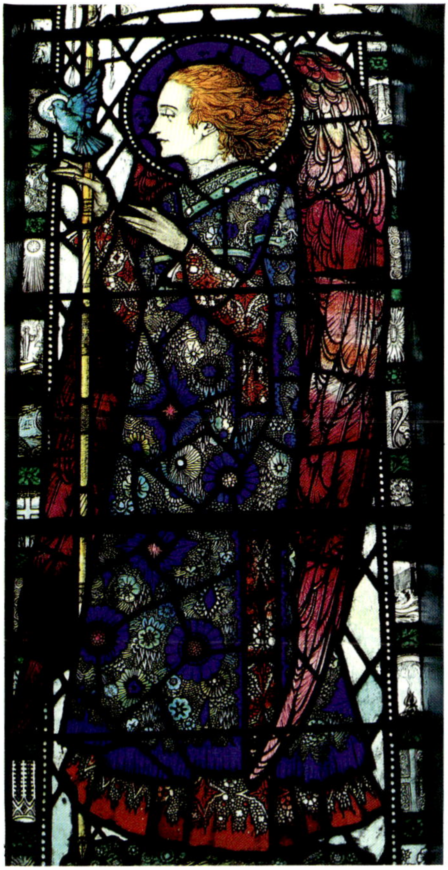

24 The Angel of Peace and Hope (detail), Lloyd memorial window, Killiney, 1919; exactly contemporary with the Wexford window, its design and treatment display a rare sensitivity.

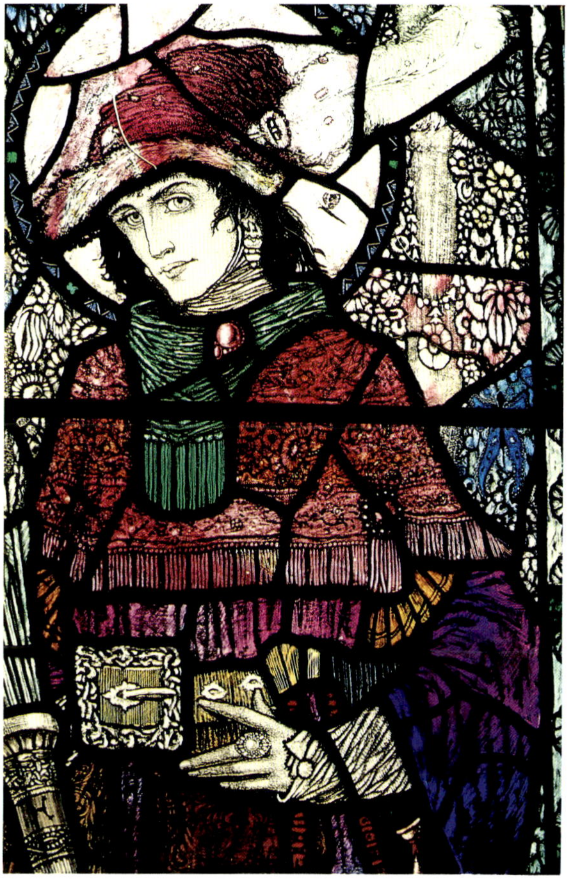

25 St Hubert, patron saint of huntsmen, detail of the La Touche memorial window at Carnalway, Co. Kildare, 1921

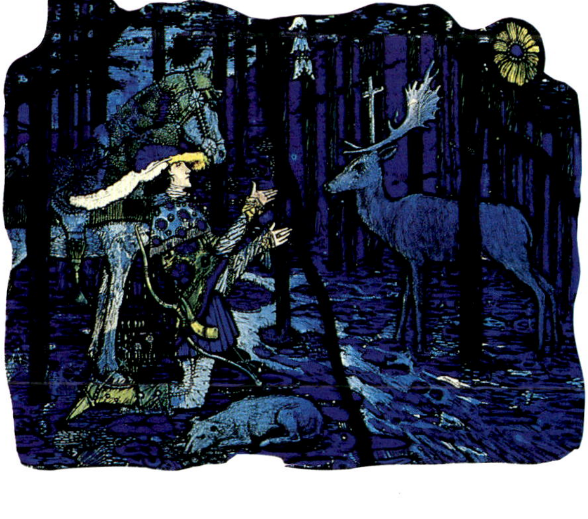

26 The conversion of St Hubert, from the St Hubert window, Carnalway, 1921; this small leaded panel at the base of the window is painted, acided and stained on a single piece of flashed blue glass.

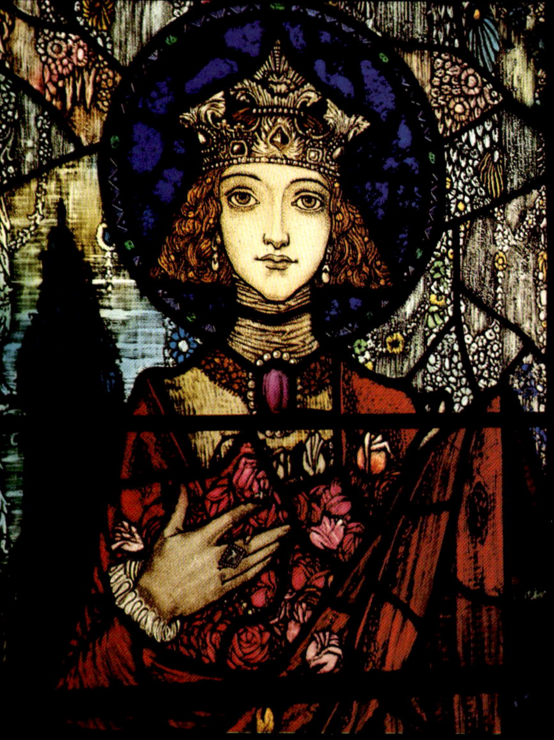

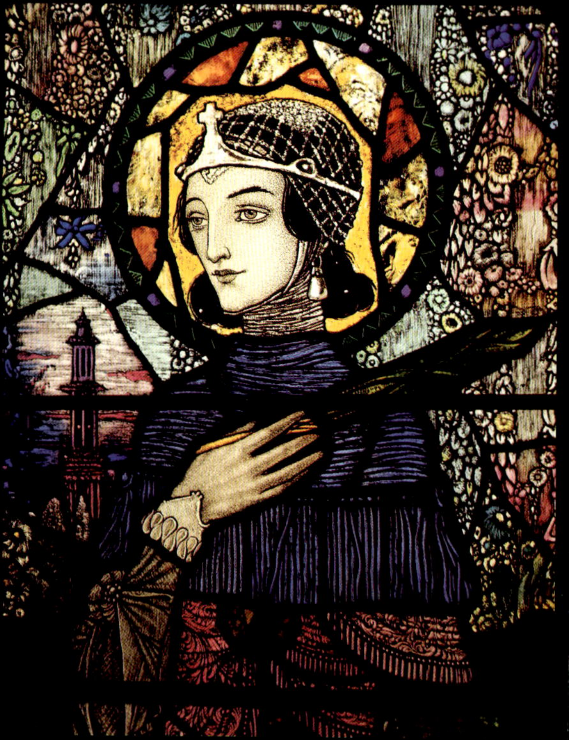

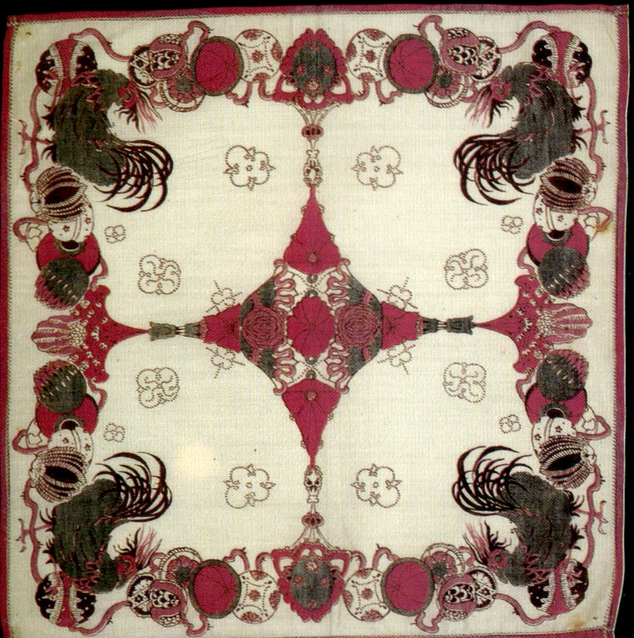

27 St Elizabeth of Hungary **(detail), Sturminster Newton, Dorset, 1921**

28 St Barbara, **a Syrian virgin and martyr and patron saint of artillery (detail), Sturminster Newton, 1921**

29 Handkerchief designed by Clarke and

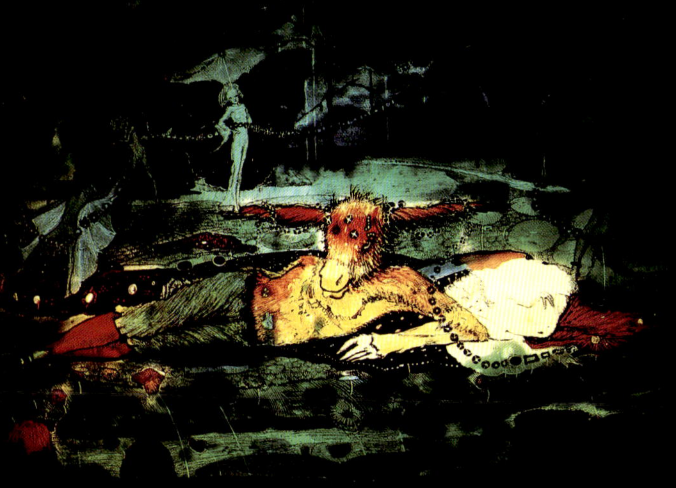

30 'Titania and Bottom', stained glass panel, flashed blue glass plated on flashed ruby glass, painted, acided and stained, illustrating Act IV.i. from Shakespeare's A Midsummer Night's Dream, **1922 (see fig. 122)**

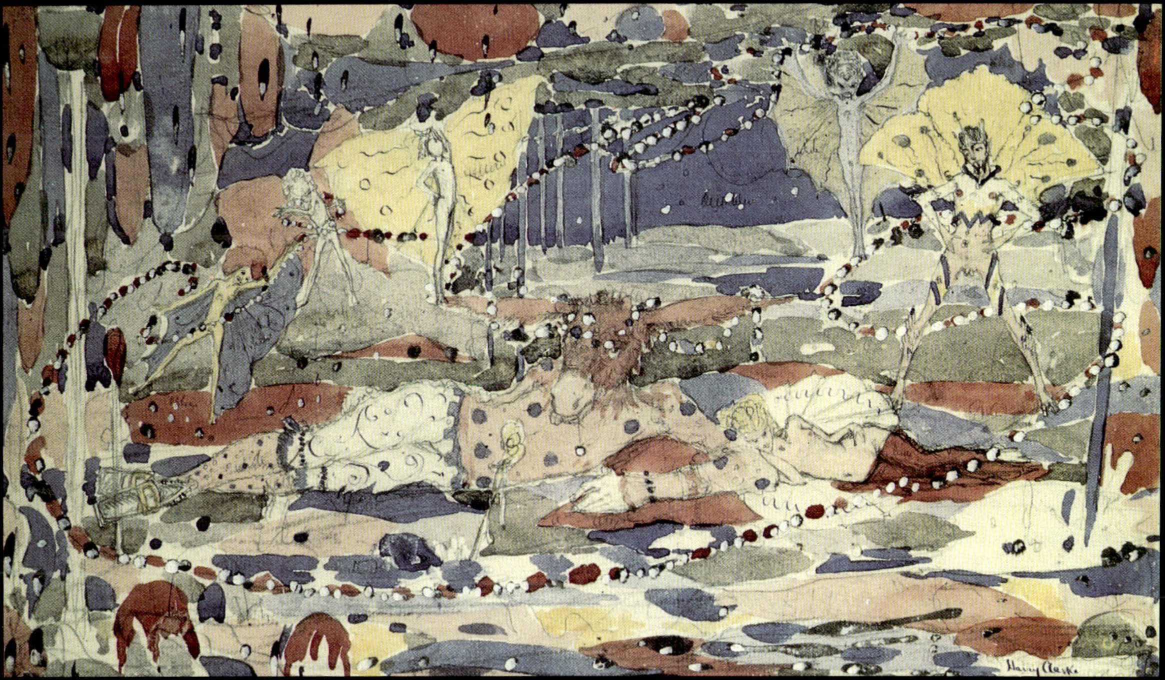

31 Design for a stained glass panel, illustrating A Midsummer Night's Dream, **1921, pencil and watercolour on paper**

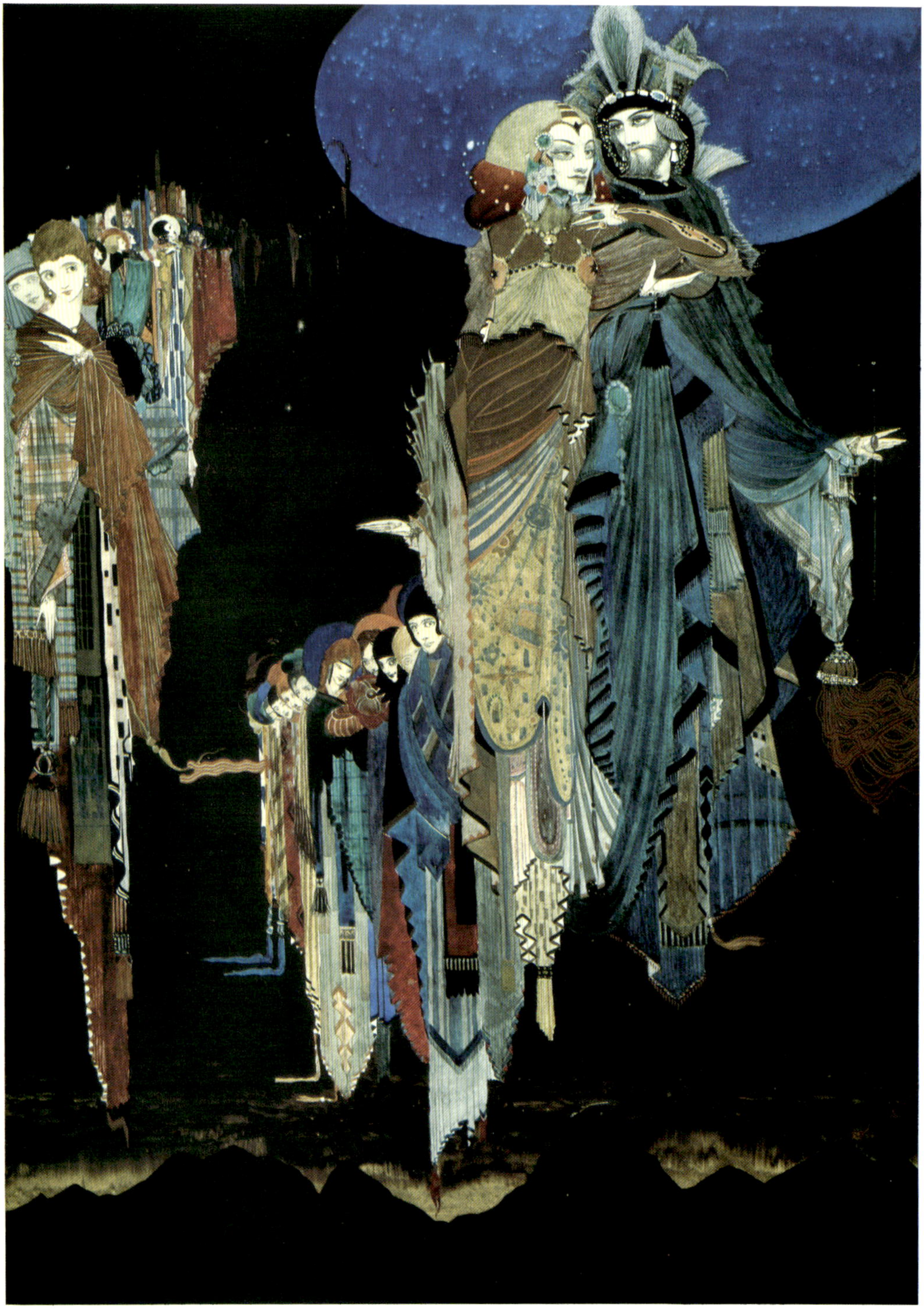

32 'In death we have both learned the propensity of man to define the indefinable', illustration to Poe's 'The Colloquy of Monos and Una', pencil and watercolour, 1923

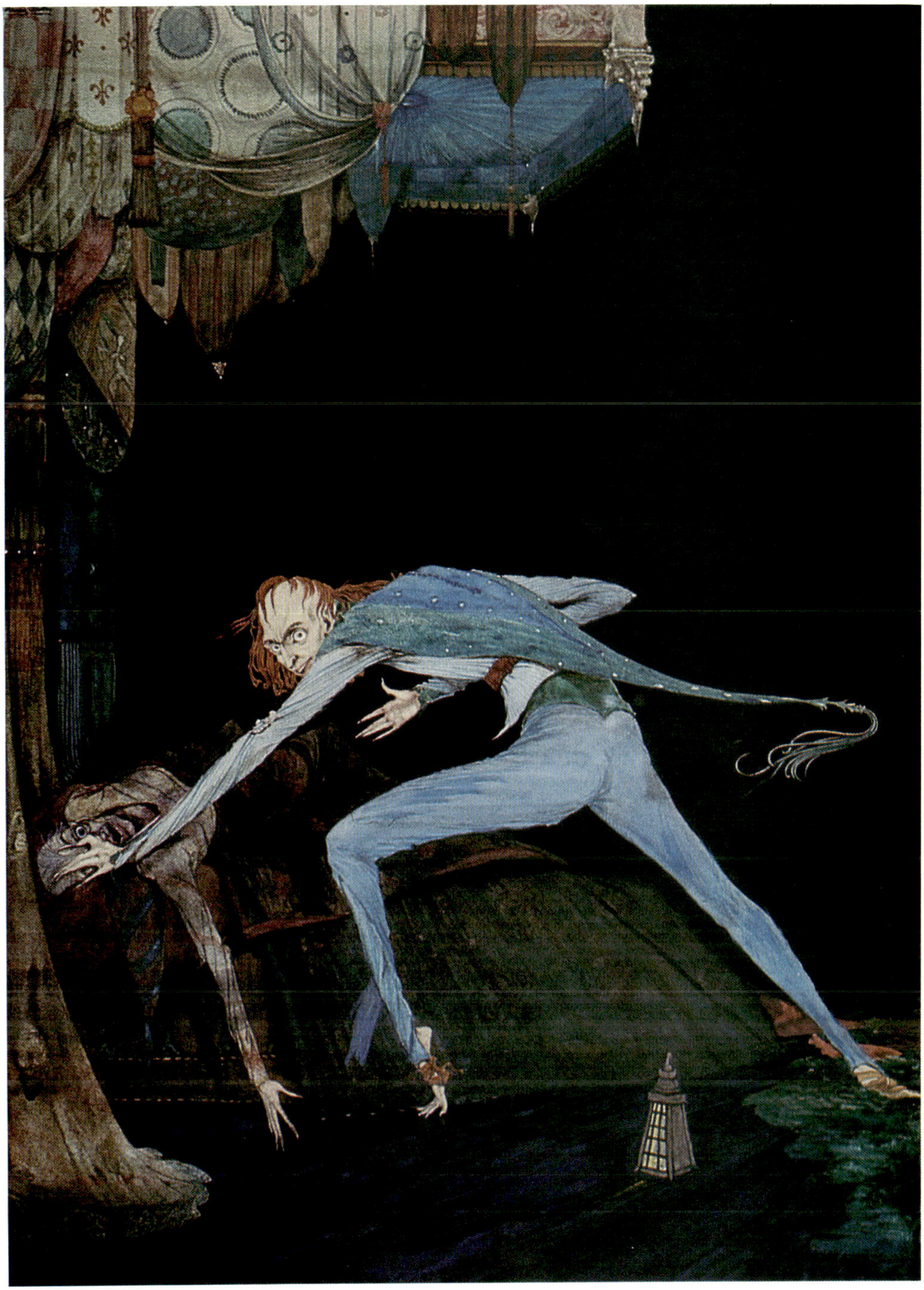

33 'He shrieked once — once only', illustration to Poe's 'The Tell-Tale Heart', pencil, pen and ink and watercolour, 1923

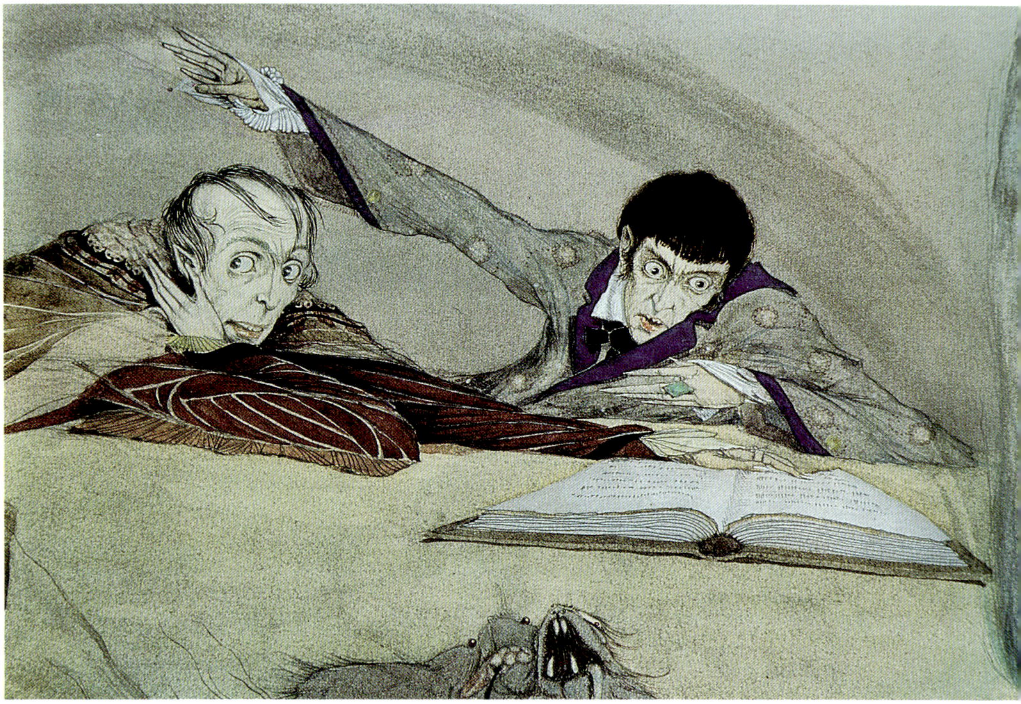

34, 35 Details of illustration of 'The Fall of the House of Usher', pencil and watercolour from Poe's *Tale of Mystery and Imagination* (1923); inscribed on the reverse in Clarke's hand, 'Yes, I hear it, and have heard it, long-long-long — many minutes — many hours — many days have I heard it'.

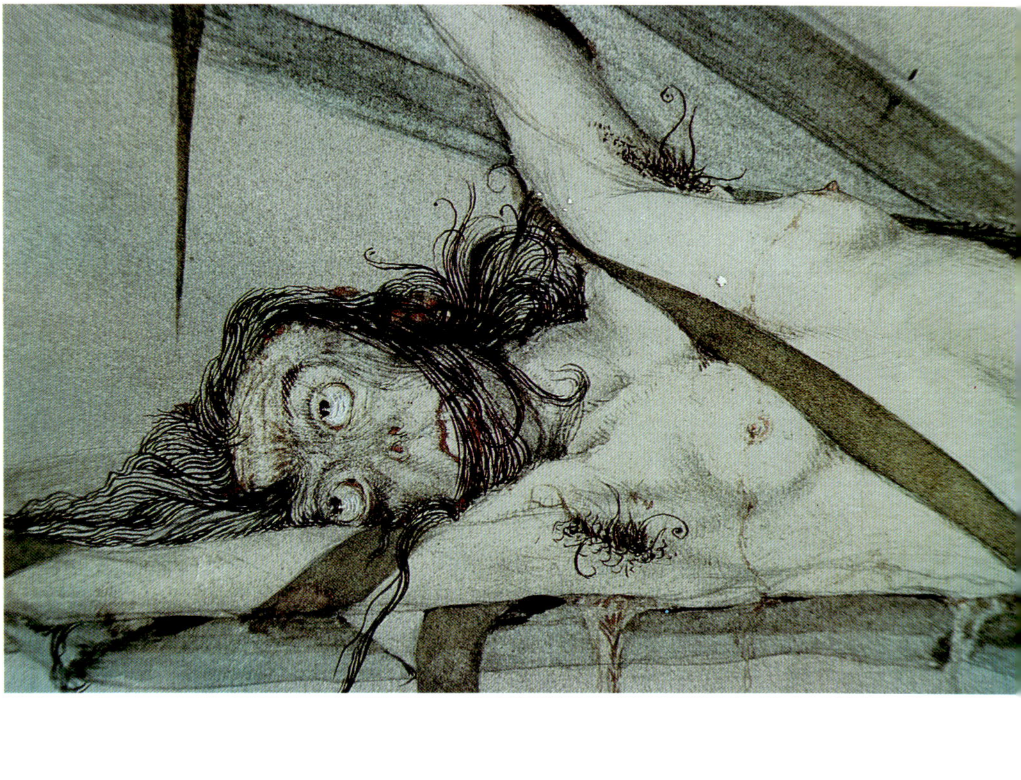

6

Windows in Cheshire and Dorset — A post-war illustrated anthology — The full-scale Terenure Crucifixion *— Joshua Clarke's death*

Harry's pocket diary for 1920 included a list of the eight steps needed to make a cigarette. Harry was an incessant smoker and many of his self-portrait sketches showed a cigarette drooping out of one corner of his mouth. Friends of his remember that he had a *sfumato* brown line running up his left temple because, when he worked at his desk, he would rest his left hand, his lighted cigarette smouldering between his fingers against the side of his brow, supported by his elbow on the desk, while he drew with the other.

In January, while seeing a lot of Bodkin and Waldron, he continued to work on the Nantwich cartoons. He completed the *St Cecilia* panel (fig. 107) during the first days of the month and worked on the *Richard Coeur de Lion* design from 4 to 9 January.[1] He commenced work on the anthology for Harrap on the afternoon of 23 January and at the same time made an initial sketch for a further window for the church of St Barrahane in Castletownshend, which was to be a two-light depicting *St Louis IX, King of France, and St Martin of Tours*. However, his most concentrated work was devoted to the Terenure *Crucifixion* window, whose cutlines he had completed the previous month. On 12 January, he started on the left hand opening of the three long lights, working from top to bottom. This involved several paintings and a considerable amount of aciding and staining, and they were not completed until 13 February.

107 St Cecilia, detail from the cartoon for the left-hand light of the Knowles memorial window, Nantwich, 1919

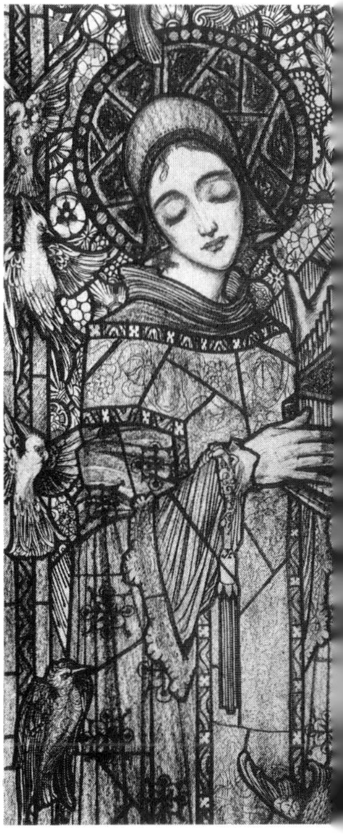

Joshua was not well and work at the Studios was hampered by Nagle's protracted absences from work, by a faulty kiln and by the lack of an additional young glass cutter; nor did trade union disputes and a 15 per cent rise in the price of glass help. However, he was anxious to be given the job of erecting Harry's Terenure window and was glad to take on commissions rejected by Harry, whose tenders he automatically undercut.[2]

To meet his deadline for *The Year's at the Spring*, Harry decided to devote his time to this in early February, despite being 'badly stuck on the job'.[3] He seems to have had considerable problems with this book right from the start: normally he worked well under pressure but perhaps the pressure at this time was too great, or he was not inspired by many of the poems. By 21 February he had ten drawings ready, which he sent off to Harrap's, including the jacket design, cover, title, ornaments and one illustration in colour. On 22, 23 and 27 February he did the bizarre colour illustration to Rupert Brooke's 'The Dead' (fig. 108), followed by that to Walter de la Mare's 'Mad Prince', also in colour, which he then decided to scrap. He then had to return to the Terenure window, for which he painted and fired the top of the centre light in the first weeks of March. He was sick on 17 March, his birthday, but resumed work the next day on the Terenure right hand opening, aciding, staining, painting and repainting, working from top to bottom, as on the other two lights. However, before he had finished this, he was sick once more, from 25 March to 6 April. He was back at work again on the window next day and ten days later, to his great relief, the whole window was completed. He also spent two days cutting for the Nantwich

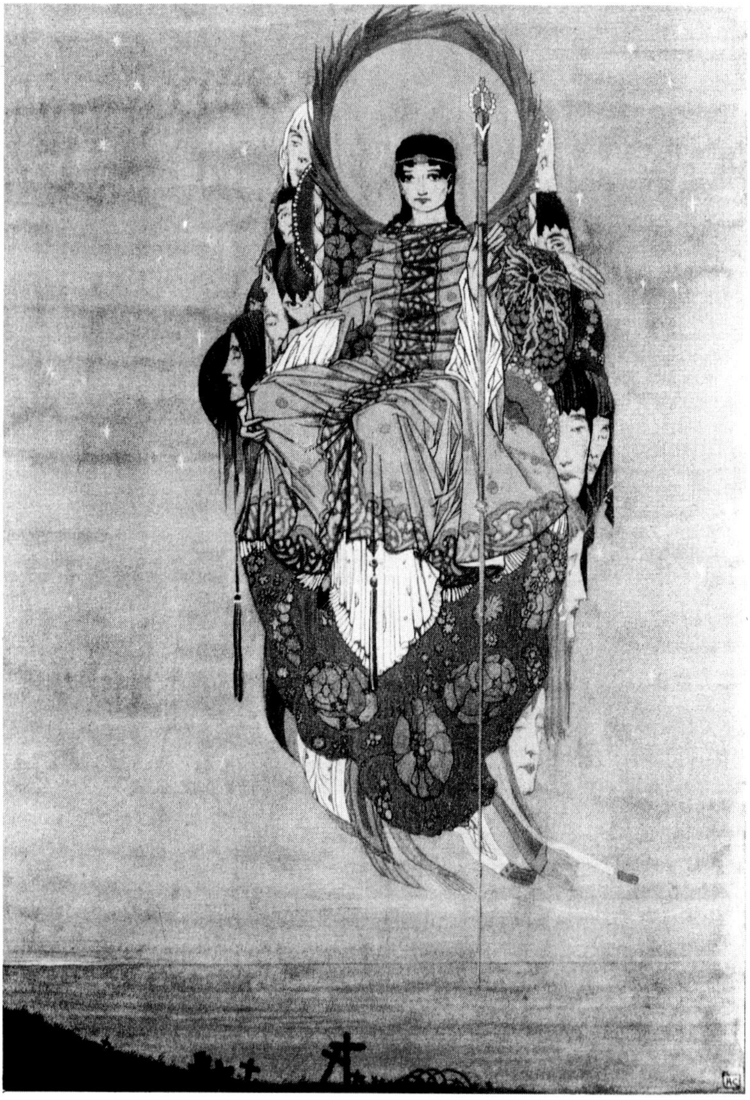

108 Detail from 'Honour has come back, as a king, to earth', pen and ink and watercolour illustration to Rupert Brooke's poem 'The Dead' in *The Year's at the Spring* (1920)

window to avoid a general strike on 13 and 14 April and to see how much glass he would need for the job.

Only four of Harry's pictures were selected for the Royal Hibernian Academy exhibition that April, all of them for sale — *Morella* (10 gns.), *Landor's Cottage* 10 gns.), an untitled illustration (5 gns.) and *Mr Hyde* (7 gns.); the latter is interesting as it may refer to the unrealized project for the volume illustrating passages from literature. Robert Louis Stevenson was immensely popular at the time and was constantly featured in literary reviews; his gruesome story, 'Dr Jekyll and Mr Hyde' would have held obvious attractions for Harry.[4]

The correspondence between Harry and Bodkin at this time shows how frequently they met, and how much Harry relied on Bodkin's advice, support and criticism, while Bodkin evidently greatly admired Harry. One note from Harry is in the form of a dashed-off pen caricature of himself rushing to hand the postman a note after he had overslept, while Bodkin is seen standing impatiently on the steps of his house in Wilton Crescent; others are dashed off on cards; some are long, carefully pondered letters.

On 19 April, Harry returned to *The Year's at the Spring* illustrations with a second attempt at the colour illustration to 'The Song of the Mad Prince'. On 22 April, he wrote in his diary that he had finished it 'D.V.' The drawing is loosely based on his stained glass panel illustrating the poem, without the King and Queen. His Prince is more like a playing card Knave than a highly strung, pining, romantic swain. From the 23rd until the 29th, he worked on the decoratively Japonnist coloured illustration to de la Mare's 'Arabia'. On the 30th, he began Harold Monro's *Overheard on a Saltmarsh* in colour and had it finished by the next day; one of the most unearthly of the series, it too employs Japanese motifs. The influence of the Japanese print is more noticeable in these illustrations than in any of Harry's others,[5] in his decorative use of composition and pattern and in the muted blue, grey, soft yellow, rust, jade and black he arranges geometrically. It is likely that he would have looked at pattern books of Japanese floral ornament, common enough at the time,[6] or absorbed elements from the many reproductions in art periodicals. There is an elusive, silvery quality in the colours of these illustrations, and the pen and ink illustrations are often sparingly and geometrically placed in their plain cream surrounds against the white backgrounds of the pages. E.J. Brady's *Ballad of the Captains* (in colour) took two days to complete, in similarly muted colours, incorporating one of Harry's favourite galleons brightly decked and sporting a languishing odalisque. By 6 May he had four tailpieces finished and sent off; on the same day, he began a coloured illustration to G.K. Chesterton's 'Donkey' — a lugubrious but apposite illustration in dingy colours, of creepy monsters, a bloodshot black sea and the pathetically grotesque, braying donkey, set above three small predella pictures of clear blue, touched with minute scenes of the Flight into Egypt, Palm Sunday and the Nativity. Harry was ill for a couple of days while working on this and did not complete it until 10 May.

On 11 May he went into the Studios to do some work on the Terenure *Crucifixion* and, in the afternoon, began *The Shepherdess*, a rather uninspired colour illustration in keeping with Alice Meynell's poem. On 12 May he worked on the Nantwich *Richard Coeur de Lion* opening and had this finished by the 14th. The next day he completed *The Shepherdess*. The oval black and white illustration to William Watson's 'April', reminiscent of Jessie King's work, took two and a half days and was followed by another galleon design in black and white to illustrate John Masefield's 'Sea Fever'. Each of these illustrations was preceded by a very rough pencil sketch.

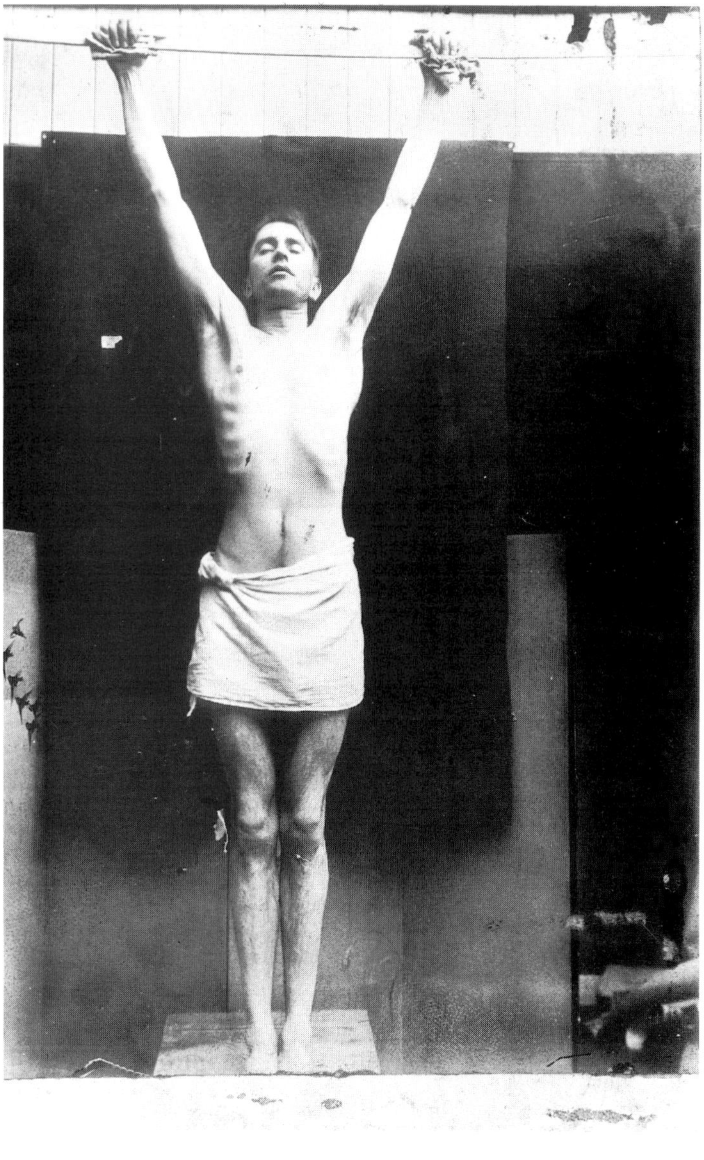

109 One of a series of photographs of Clarke posing for the figure of Christ in the Terenure *Crucifixion* window, 1919-20

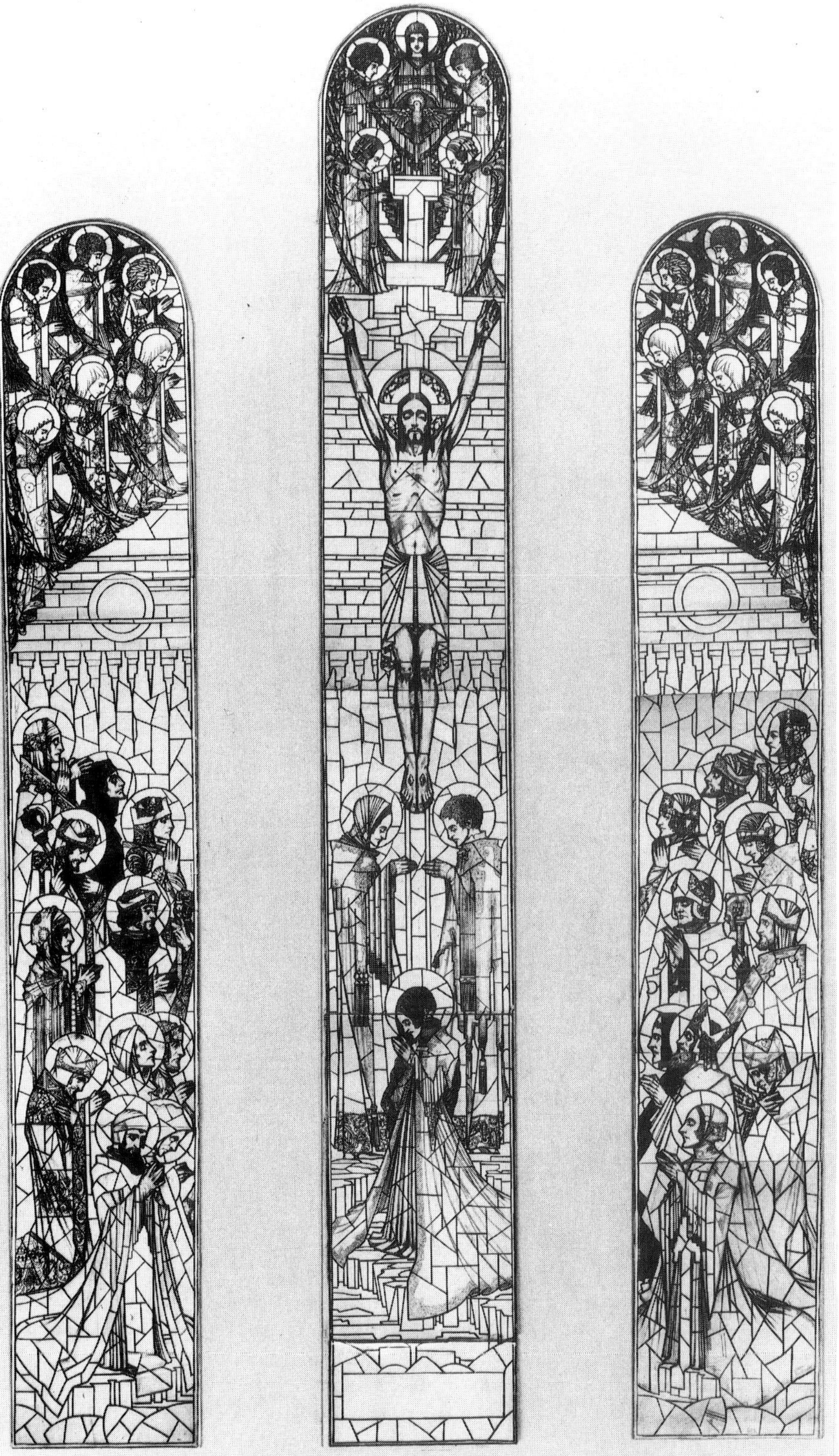

110 Cartoons for the Terenure *Crucifixion* window

After another day spent cutting the Nantwich *Richard* he drew a black and white illustration of mermaids and marine creatures for 'Very Nearly', a weak poem by Queenie Scott-Hopper. Reading the poems selected for the anthology it is not hard to wonder why Harry lacked inspiration.

On Whit Sunday, 23 May, the east window above the high altar at St Joseph's, Terenure, was consecrated and unveiled. Major Lawrence Gorman of Brighton Road, Rathgar had left £500 for the erection of a stained glass window, which he stipulated must depict the Crucifixion in memory of himself and Edward and Jeannie de Verdon Corcoran. Miss Fanny Andrews of Terenure Road East gave the balance required, and so the window was erected free of debt. As the cost of the glass and materials alone was £300 (200 superficial feet at 35/- per foot), that left Harry £200. As Brian MacGiolla Phádraig has written, 'It is to Father Healy's everlasting credit that he entrusted the work to a young Dublin artist and gave him a free hand. The window was dedicated by the Bishop of Johannesburg during a High Mass at which Fr Healy preached a sermon, later printed as a Discourse with an Appendix[8] together with appreciations by Thomas Bodkin,[9] Captain Stephen Gwynn,[10] Sir John O'Connell,[11] Kathleen Fox,[12] and a short excerpt from the Irish correspondent's page in *The Athenaeum*.[13]

For his powerful portrayal of Christ, Harry used three photographs of himself, dressed only in a towel as a loincloth, hanging on to a wire, poised on a box (fig. 109); one of these he squared up, as he seems to have had some difficulty in drawing the upper part of the torso, not least because of the angle from which it would be viewed *in situ*. The cartoon shows some hesitation and a not entirely satisfactory resolution of this. The drawing is firm, angular, simplified and somewhat Byzantine, even Assyrian, and the drawing of the whole window is unaccustomedly bold with modelling like stitching rather than his usual subtly *sfumato* shading, probably because of very large scale. In the cartoon (fig. 110), Harry only drew in the outlines of the figures and the leadlines (none of the modelling). As noted above, the crucified figures in the Honan Chapel *St Albert* and the Phibsborough *Sacred Heart* are the precursors of this larger than life-size figure, while the landscape in the latter window anticipated the dramatically shot background here. This window, of which Sir John O'Connell commented, 'Even if the sermon were wholly bad, Harry Clarke would take a text and preach beauty', is Harry Clarke's most striking large-scale window. In its depiction of twenty carefully researched Irish saints[14] incorporated into an imposing tiered design in a kaleidoscope of smouldering colour, it anticipates iconographically and stylistically a number of his subsequent windows. Years later, Austin Clarke, who described Fr Healy as 'a man of culture, who met with much opposition in the parish but persisted', wrote:

> Sometimes I steal past the holy water font into Terenure Church to see the stained glass window by Harry Clarke above the High Altar. Its

hues are in delicate violet, green, purple; a glittering Celtic twilight in which long-forgotten princesses and their lovers seem to sigh.[15]

It is sad that, apart from enlightened patrons like Fr Healy, few of the clergy realized Harry's potential. Edward Martyn, Robert Elliott, Æ, Yeats, Sarah Purser and Bodkin, among others, tried to enlighten them. The 1919 *Catholic Truth Annual and Conference Record* printed a lecture[16] on 'The Interior Decoration of Churches' which Bodkin had read to the Bishop of Achonry. After decrying the 'Jesuit style, the most base of all conventions, the classic vulgarized', he pointed out that 'our most remarkable present development is perhaps in glass — but our buildings give little scope for its adequate display'. The same publication reported that Sir John O'Connell, vice-president of the Catholic Truth Society, was currently trying to establish a chair of ecclesiastical art at the National University. He and Evelyn Gleeson of the Dun Emer Guild reiterated that 'The future of art in Ireland lies with [the clergy] . . . but they must be prepared to pay generously and not adhere to the fetish of cheap work.'

On 26 December that year the Catholic newspaper *The Universe* carried a long piece in its Dublin Newsletter on 'A Notable Irish Artist'. Their correspondent referred his readers to Bodkin's Catholic Truth Society address and to his article in the current issue of *The Studio*, where 'the distinguished art critic' drew the attention of those outside Ireland to 'the conspicuous merits of a young Catholic artist'. Although the article is written from a strong nationalistic and Roman Catholic viewpoint, it makes some interesting points. It reminds the reader that 'until recently' the artist 'has worked without even the one assistant whom he now employs'; that his visit to see French stained glass, 'valuable as it was, did nothing to limit his originality or influence him to imitation of other work, however great. He has an astonishing fertility of ideas and an amazing power of unconventional expression'. It revealed that 400 copies of Harry's illustrated *Poe* had already been sold in Holland, and concluded, 'for a young man of 30 Mr Clarke's record is certainly one of great achievement. He has many skilled admirers in Ireland who, like Mr Bodkin, believe that he will do even greater work in the future.'

Harry, meanwhile, continued to work solidly at his anthology illustrations. He began the haunting *All is Spirit* in colour on 26 May and had it finished in three days. Set on a grey background, its white underbellied triple whiplash fuses with two naked raven-haired nymphs, attenuated clusters of flowers and angelic heads suspended over a seaside cliff. Flecker's *The Dying Patriot* (fig. 111), another colour drawing, followed — a beautiful and moving Symbolist illustration, of the 'dead robed in red and sea-lilies overhead' swaying 'when the long wind blows'. On 30 May he began Yeats' *Lake Isle of Inisfree*, a colour illustration in warm pastel tones of a slender, hooded figure with a lantern and a purse, meditating in a misty

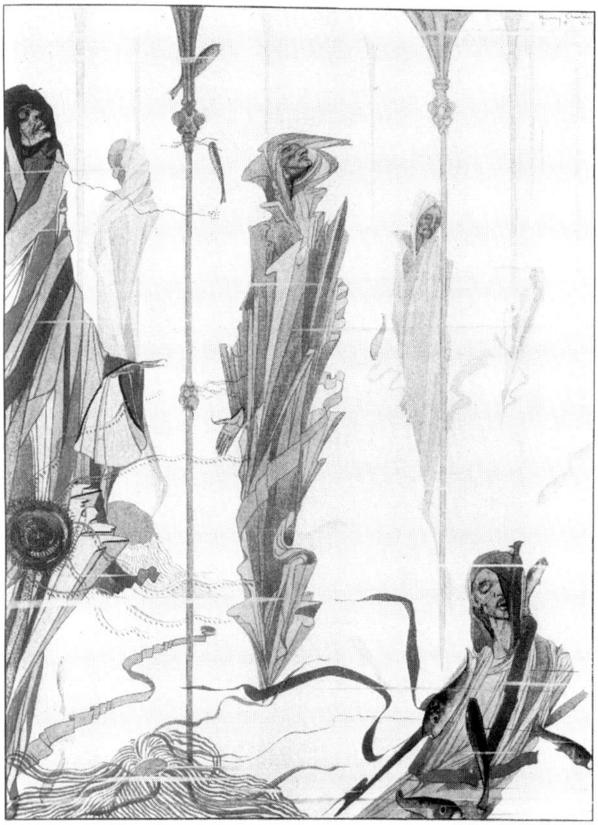

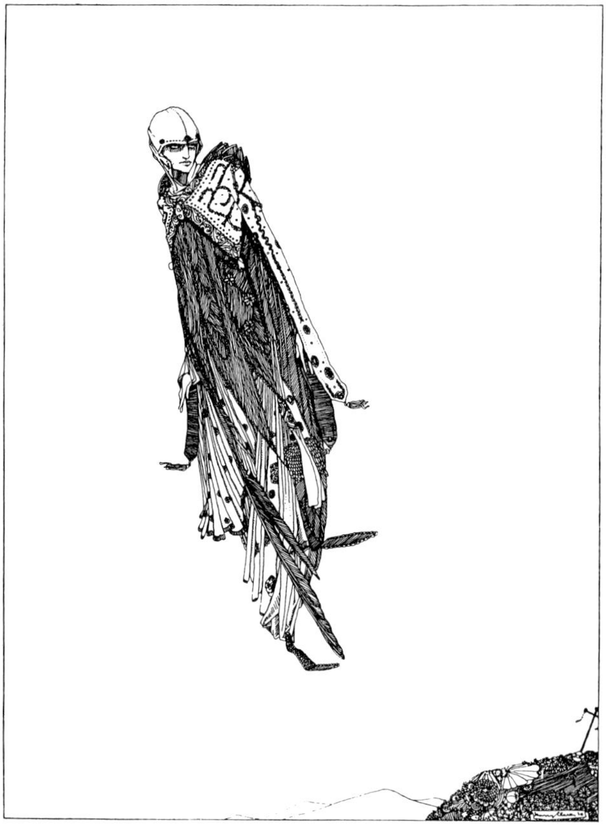

111 'And the dead robed in red and sea-lilies overhead / Sway when the long winds blow', illustration to James Elroy Flecker's 'The Dying Patriot' in *The Year's at the Spring* (1920)

112 'Out on the wind of Time, shining and streaming . . .', illustration to Rupert Brooke's 'The Great Lover', in *The Year's at the Spring*

lakeland overhung with willows, whose islands and mounds of fantastic flowers contrast with the thin dark verticals of tree trunks, mooring posts and the stick of the lantern. A day and a half later he began *Alms in Autumn*, also set in a fantasy landscape with strange flora of unrecognizable proportions in warm pastel shades. This illustration only took a day, and was followed by the delicate little black and white oval, *To the Coming Spring*, in which a tiny fairy unlocks rosebuds 'with magic key'. Two days later, on 3 June, he began the black and white *The Fiddler of Dooney*, for Yeats' witty poem. This was followed by *The Broomstick* and a day later by his black and white oval illustration to Rupert Brooke's 'The Great Lover'. On 6 June, he took a well-earned rest; he wrote to Bodkin, 'I am depressed but working very rapidly and well. Next week will see the end of the book and the week after I hope to be in Frederick Street again'.[17] On 10 June he resumed the illustrations with Robert Graves' *Aquarius*, a good composition showing a smiling boy in exotic garb bearing two pails on a stick which he swings and spills as he is catapulted through space. On the next day, he completed Rupert Brooke's *The Great Lover* (fig. 112), having scrapped the previous drawing; this is one of the most sublimely imaginative illustrations Harry ever did. 'Out on the wind of time, shining and streaming', the spirit of all those who have sacrificed their lives and lie buried in the flowered graveyard just visible in the bottom right corner of the frame, soars through the sky, bearing their names and the love they have given. The exotically plumed, behooded apparition propelled across the white page is an unforgettable image. The next day Harry completed *Black and White*, to a poem by H.H. Abbot, a curious drawing of a pale young man, bearing Harry's own features and akin to those of the *Ancient Mariner*, hatted and coated against the cold, peering out warily from a menacing crow-lined roadside.[18]

The next two days were taken up with the black and white illustration for Flecker's 'The Dying Patriot', a powerful composition using strongly silhouetted, undecorated black shapes, the mirage of a black Kentish coastline on which are grouped the tiny silhouettes of a band of monks, a hooded monk in the foreground bearing a Cross, and the striking, stern but haggard profiled figure of Augustine praying in the centre.[19] This was Harry's final illustration for the book; he celebrated its completion on 12 June by taking a couple of days holiday.

June 14 to 18 was spent painting the centre opening of the Nantwich *Madonna and Child*, and then he took another couple of days off while it was being fired and cooled. He spent a further three days on the centre opening, which was finished by 23 June. On the 24th, he worked on the six Nantwich tracery lights, which were fired two days later and finished by the 29th. The *St Cecilia* panel took from 1 to 12 July, with a short break, before he took up the right hand opening, *Richard Coeur de Lion*, which was fired on the 23rd. By 26 July, the Nantwich window was 'finished complete'.[20] He was just within his deadline, since he had promised the window to Mr Knowles for the following day. This three-light window is erected in the south aisle of the historic church of St Mary, described in its guide book as the 'Cathedral of South Cheshire'[21] and is in keeping with the architecture in which it is set; the rich blues of the Virgin's robes, the rich gold-pinks of St Cecilia's, and the pale greens and golds of Richard's enhance the deep plum of the Cheshire stone in which the church is built; indeed, they brighten up its rather sombre tones. The window is inscribed 'To the Glory of God and in loving memory of Mildred Clare Knowles, died December 2nd 1913, and of her son Lieutenant Richard Arthur Lees Knowles M.C., K.R.R.C., killed in action near Salonica, February 24th 1918, aged 19 years'. The figure of Richard, in particular, had undergone radical changes between the coloured design stage and the cartoon.[22] The cartoon designs for *St Cecilia* and the *Virgin* were published in *The Studio*,[23] and the initial colour designs for *St Cecilia* and *Richard* were well reproduced in colour in the Clarke Studios' *Church Directory* advertising inset in 1930.

While Harry was in the middle of painting this window, a Mrs Prentice of Waterford House, Welwyn Water in Hertfordshire arrived in Dublin, as she had commissioned Harry to make a window to commemorate her daughter Rachel, who had died in March 1919, aged only nineteen. It is not clear how either she, Sir Drummond Spencer-Smith of Sturminster Newton or Mr Knowles of Cheshire knew of Harry's work; Harry had sent her twelve photographs of his work on 9 June 1920. He gave up a morning just before he had finished *St Cecilia* to show her his glass in Terenure and in the Studios.[24]

There was no respite from work. He had to commence the window for Castletownshend for which he had made an initial sketch in January, and he had to make drawings for the second set of Sefton handkerchiefs, a task he interrupted only to show his Nantwich window and to supervise its dispatch to England. He worked on his second Sefton box lid from 6 to 9 August. The following day he had to move his wife into a nursing home in North Frederick Street[25] for the imminent birth of their third child. His diary records his search for possible names for the child. On 11 August he commenced the sketch design for the Dorset window commissioned the previous November. He continued at this until the 19th when he returned to the Sefton designs, at which he worked intermittently until he had the box lid and whole set completed on 1 August and posted to the manufacturers. Harry's and Margaret's last child, to be named David, was born on 25 August. Harry sent his wife and children to Greystones for the healthy sea air, where he would visit them whenever he could. A couple of weeks later, the Bodkins had another child, and Harry expressed 'very real regret' he had not asked Bodkin to be David's godfather, as Bodkin asked Harry to be godfather to his new child — a reflection of the esteem in which Bodkin held Harry.

By 1 September Harry had begun drawing the cartoons for the two lancet lights and four long tracery lights topped with a small diamond-shaped quarry of the Castletownshend window. The subjects chosen to commemorate Col. Kendall Coghill, CB, a veteran of the Indian Mutiny, were *St Louis IX, King of France*, an ancestor of the colonel's, and *St Martin of Tours*, patron saint of soldiers. Both soldier saints were compassionate men, as Col. Coghill had been; 'Colonel Coghill was a most generous man, always helping the less fortunate, so St Martin was a most appropriate subject' and 'St Louis had fought in Egypt just as Colonel Coghill had, some 600 years later.'[26]

Harry had the cartoon for *St Martin* finished by 9 September; *St Louis* and the traceries took another eight days. It is interesting to note that Harry drew these cartoons loosely in thick charcoal, the design boldly expressed with detailing and shading minimal, but still conveying a good idea of how every part of the window would look.

Without a break he began the three-light window commissioned for Sturminster Newton, which was to depict the thirteenth century queen, *St Elizabeth of Hungary* at left, a *Madonna and Child* in the centre light, and the third century virgin martyr *St Barbara* at right. He completed the cartoon for *St Elizabeth*[27] on 8 October, that for St Barbara on the 16th and the *Madonna and Child* on the 26th (fig. 113). By the end of the month, he had

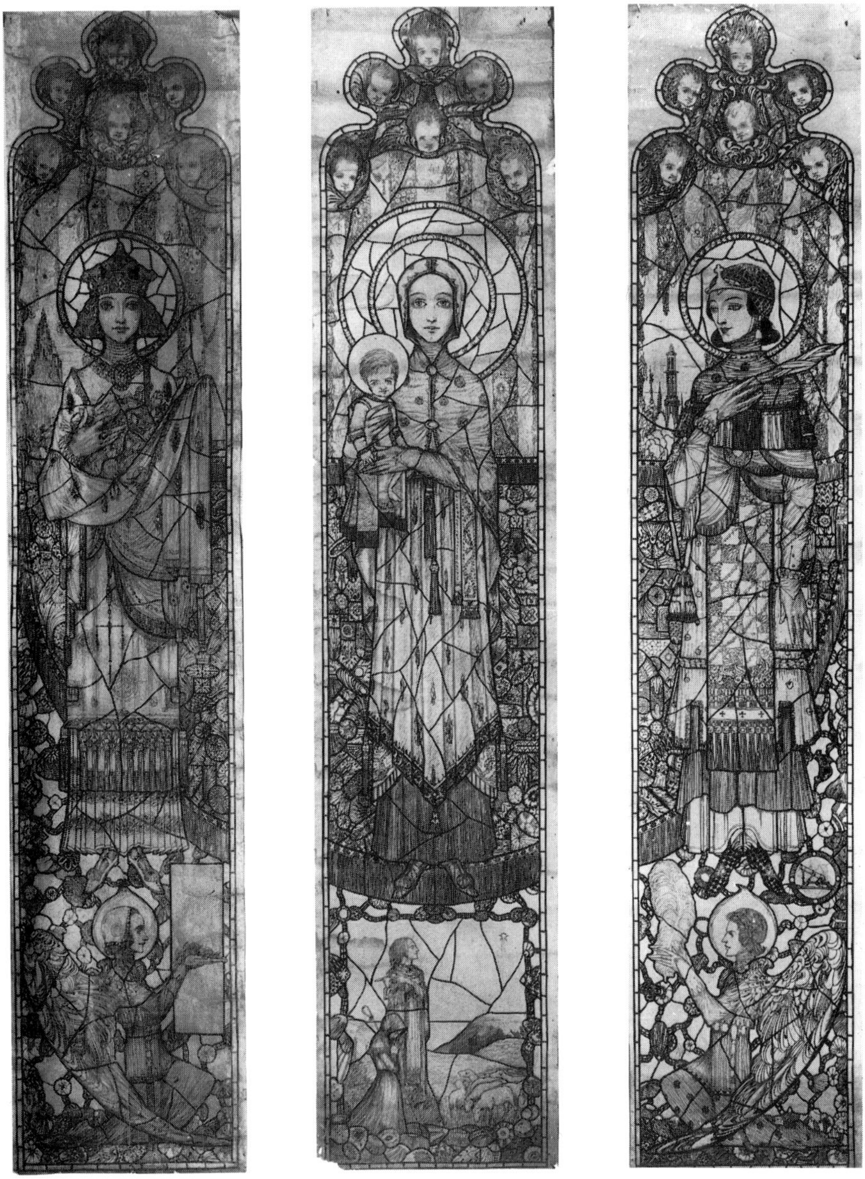

113 Cartoons for Clarke's 3-light window, Sturminster Newton, 1919

completed the tracery cartoons. He used the same loose, bold, charcoal lines for these Dorset cartoons as he had for the Nantwich and Castletownshend ones; however, there are areas of detail in the decorative floral surrounds and in the faces of the three figures, particularly that of St Barbara, whose features are based on those of his wife, Margaret.

The anthology, *The Year's at the Spring*, selected by Lettice d'Oyly Walters, was published by Harrap at the end of September with Harry's illustrations, twelve colour, twelve black and white full-page plates and twenty-two decorative drawings in black and white. There was a signed, limited edition of 250 copies at five guineas bound in vellum imprinted with a gold, mauve and yellow girl angel on the cover beneath the title and a golden decorative device on the spine; and a buff cloth-covered edition with the same oval vesica on the spine printed in turkey red and a red Art Deco bowl of flowers in a square on the front beneath grey lettering and a dust jacket bearing the girl angel printed in indigo. It was priced at 16/-, while an issue in a similar design but in antique leather cost 30/- shillings. *The Bookman*'s Christmas supplement had a full page reproduction of *Midst of all was a cold white face* (Harry's self-portrait from H.H. Abbot's *Black and White)* in their special feature, Harrap's *Books Beautiful*,[29] and commented: 'The subjects [of these poems] provide an admirable field for the genius of Harry Clarke . . . his colour pictures are particularly interesting; their delicacy . . . will be much admired'.[30] *The Studio* did not review the book until the following May,[31] accompanied by a full-page reproduction of the black and white illustration to E.J. Brady's 'A Ballad of the Captains' and wrote:

> Mr Clarke, who has illustrated this selection with some two dozen drawings of which half are in colour, exclusive of head and tail pieces and other decorations, is an artist of marked individuality, and the imaginative faculty which he possesses in a high degree is well shown in these drawings as it is in those stained glass creations of his of which several examples have been reproduced in this magazine. As showing the quality of his black and white work, we give here an example. . . .

Joseph Maunsell Hone, in his regular letter from Ireland published in the *London Mercury*,[32] advised his readers that, 'Supposing an absent Irishman were trying to collect a comprehensive Irish library, how many of the new books could he order on sight without waiting for a reviewer's or friend's advice?': he should go for Lady Gregory's *Life and Achievement of Hugh Lane*, Thomas Bodkin's *Four Irish Landscape Painters*, W.B. Yeats' *Plays for Dancers* and his new volume of poems on Ireland, James Stephens' *Irish Fairy Tales*, Maunsel and Co.'s *Occupation of Land in Ireland in the Early 19th Century*, 'and an Anthology of modern English poetry for its illustrations by Mr Harry Clarke, a talented young Irishman'.

In November, Harry spent a week working up a coloured drawing for another illustration project, Perrault's *Fairy Tales*, which Bodkin was anxious to translate. On 20 November he travelled to London, probably with Bodkin, and proposed the book to Harrap's who were not enthusiastic because, since 'the cost of book production is so heavy' there would be no room in the illustrated book for payments for a retranslation'.[33] At Bodkin's suggestion an approach was made to Hodder and Stoughton, and an interview with Sir Ernest Hodder Williams was arranged for the morning of 22 November. The following day Sir Ernest wrote to Bodkin at Berners Hotel that he had 'given very careful consideration to our talks yesterday' and was 'distinctly interested in this artist' but was afraid he might be 'too decorative and not simple enough for our purpose'. He was therefore 'not inclined to commission his Perrault illustrations on the strength of one specimen picture. If I could see two others I would say yes or no in 5 minutes.' He even went so far as to suggest satisfactory terms — '15 guineas to Mr Clarke for each picture' and one guinea per thousand words for Bodkin's translation, concluding that 'in these most difficult days, we must have illustrated books to appeal to both the Gift Book and Childrens Book public'.[34] While Harry was in England he travelled to Nantwich to see his window installed, as there had been a few breakages in transit. He spent a night in Dorset, taking notes as to how he should treat the window in relation to its future situation. He also visited Hetley's, Harrap's and Mrs Prentice in Hertfordshire (after whose name there is a string of exclamation marks in his diary). Whether or not he visited G.K. Chesterton before he left for Dublin, the great man's name and address in Buckinghamshire are noted in his diary.[35]

On his return to Dublin Harry immediately started on three sample illustrations for the Perrault, to send to Hodder and Stoughton. Taking only Sundays off, he worked at them from 29 November to 14 December, even noting the exact time he finished work on each one. It must have been most disappointing when Bodkin received a reply, in Sir Ernest Hodder Williams' absence in America, that the latter 'has distinctly stated we must have illustrated books which appeal to the big children's public, and as we are very doubtful whether the three pictures submitted, beautiful as they are, comply with these requirements, we shall be forced to say "no", if you require an immediate decision, although it might be advisable to await Sir Ernest's return.'[36] The following month, Sir Ernest's secretary wrote to inform Bodkin that he was very sorry he could not proceed further with the scheme for the Perrault and was therefore returning Harry's *four* illustrations by post. The project was then dropped until negotiations reopened with Harrap towards the end of the year.

Finishing the Castletownshend window occupied the second half of December and the early weeks of 1921, interrupted by a week of illness at the beginning of the New Year. There is no record of the exact date on which the window was erected, but it is evident that the job was finished in Harry's usual burst of concentrated work. The window reveals a new freedom of treatment, the painting on the glass reflecting the free drawing of the cartoons. The right hand lancet-headed light is occupied by St Louis, beneath a pattern of sunflowers in red, yellow and shades of blue and mauve. The border,[37] made of floral and decorative motifs, is abstract and multi-coloured, encased in a thin outer rim of clear glass and an inner one painted to resemble beading. The face of St Louis is rather wooden and seems to copy a presumed likeness beneath his ornate gold crown with long ear flaps. Dimly visible behind the halo of the purple and mauve glass which predominate in this window edged with green painted beads and tiny gold crosses, is a small procession of the heads and shoulders of the poor and diseased who used to feed at his table (fig. 114). These again show Harry's unique ability to depict the gruesome, macabre and palsied in an exquisite manner; they seem to be derived from the gaping throng in Pieter Bruegel the Elder's *Adoration of the Kings* (1564; fig. 115) in the National Gallery, London. The seven men depicted, old, bereft, angry, or leprous, are painted on shades of sea-greens and blues, mauves and grey-greens, in fine detail with strong lines and a few brilliant touches, like the grotesque green man's profiled head capped in fiery ruby, the leper helmeted in clear turquoise with silver carbuncles, and the aged cripple on the right in ruby and gold chequers.[38]

The touches of ruby in this right hand opening are picked up on the left by the richly mottled ruby cloak which the entranced St Martin is dividing with his golden-handled sword for a sensitively portrayed beggar (fig. 116) kneeling at his feet. His armour merits close examination — overlapping fish scales, chain mail, a green underskirt of overlapping leaf patterns and a beautifully decorated niello helmet, topped with a tiny chimera/sphinx (fig. 117), whose exquisite head is raised above her bosom, with lavish wings and a seal-like winged tail. The miniature landscape in which the fourth century city of Tours, Martin's bishopric, is painted against a livid sky is equally notable, and the tracery lights are filled with symbolic detail.

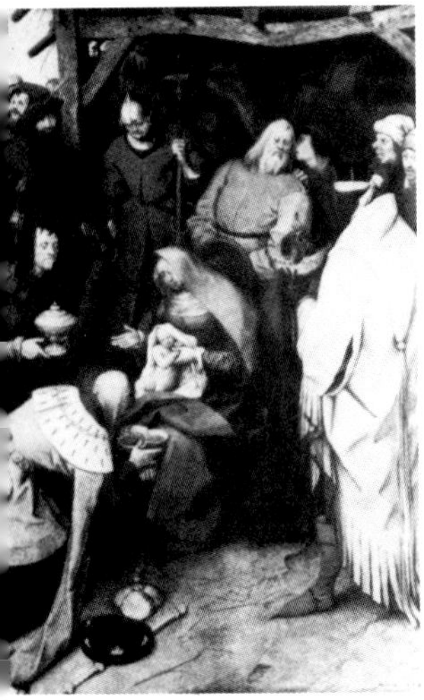

115 Detail from Pieter Bruegel the Elder, *The Adoration of the Kings*, 1564; Clarke's marked admiration for Bruegel is expressed in the Castletownshend *St Louis and St Martin* through his emulation of the gaping throng in a painting he knew well from visits to the National Gallery in London

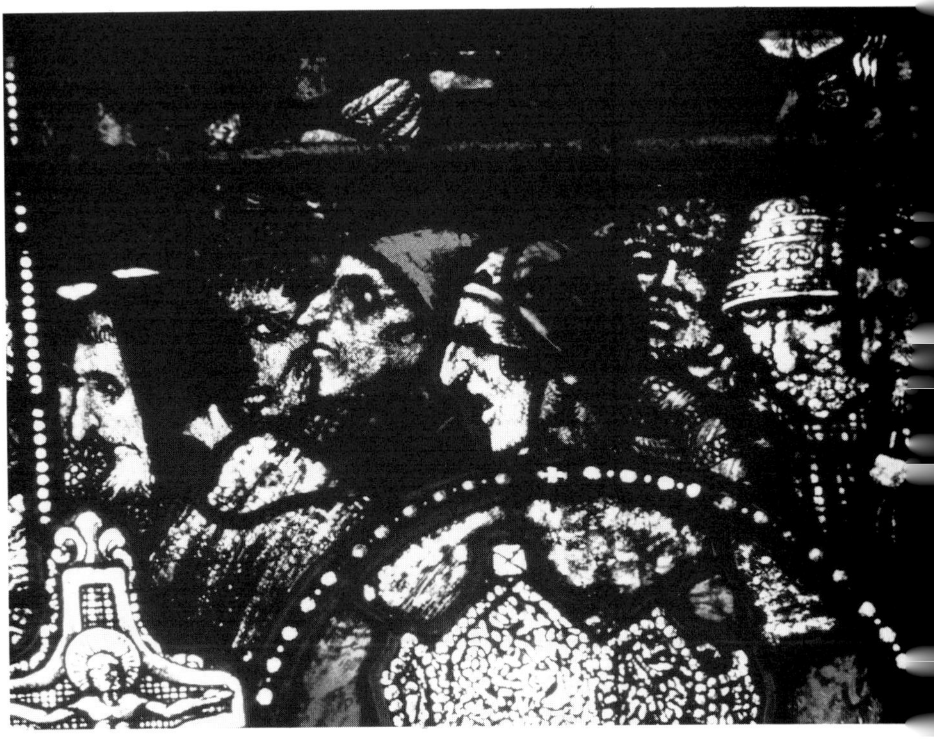

114 The Afflicted at the court of St Louis, detail from the *St Louis and St Martin* window, Castletownshend, 1920

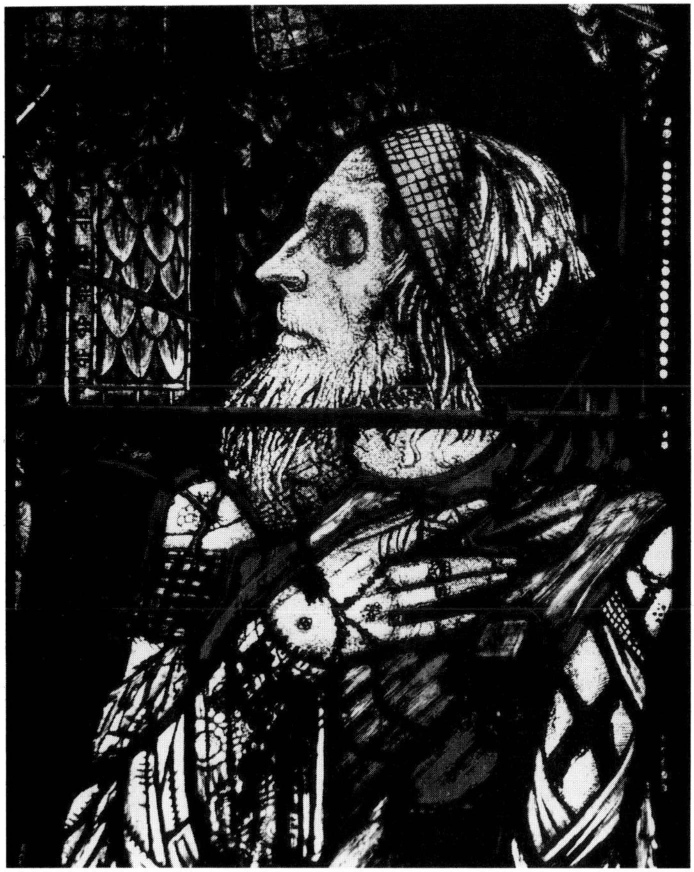

116 The Beggar, a detail from *St Louis and St Martin*; the dignified features of the decoratively patched beggar were based on life studies on the streets of Dublin

Commissions continued to come his way. About the end of March, he was asked to make a single-light memorial window for Canon J.O. Hannay (the writer George A. Bermingham) at the delightful little church at Harristown, Carnalway, near Kildare, and early in April he wrote to Waldron, who was taking the waters in Bath, that the Lea Wilson window in Gorey, for which he had done a preliminary sketch in January, was confirmed. Waldron wrote to Bodkin, asking why there was no work by Harry or Margaret Clarke in the current Royal Hibernian Academy exhibition catalogue. Harry, perhaps as a protest at the poor showing given him the previous year, decided not to exhibit that year, and did not exhibit again until 1924, when he was elected as an associate of the RHA. As the years went by and Harry was constrained by his deteriorating health, his frustration at the ineptitude of bodies with which he would associate increased. His was the classical dilemma of a highly sensitive, articulate, talented and informed Irishman with a metaphorical foot on either side of the Irish sea. Although Irish by birth with a deep love of the country, especially Dublin, he felt more in tune artistically with the atmosphere of London. He had a vision of his glass being sent out to enhance all the corners

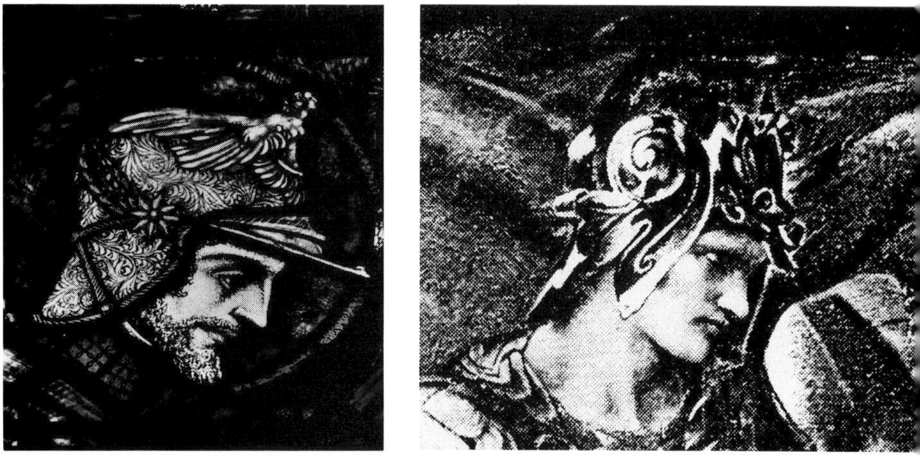

117 Detail of St Martin's helmet from *St Louis and St Martin* compared with that of Perseus in Burne-Jones' *The Doom Fulfilled*, 1884-8; see also St Adrian's helmet (plate 23) in the O'Keeffe memorial window, Wexford, 1919.

of the earth, and yet he realized with increasing anguish that there was a limit to how much he could do alone, and that it was he, rather than the Studios, who bore the mark of genius. It was with such hopes that he consciously threw his lot in with the Arts and Crafts Society of Ireland rather than the Royal Hibernian Academy. Throughout 1921, he worked hard on the council of the society to make sure the exhibition to be held that autumn would comply with the high standards he always set and expected of others.

Joshua Clarke had been 'in very indifferent health for some time — in fact since his visit to Glasgow'[39] the previous winter — and, as the Studios badly needed a first-class stained glass artist to paint figures and flesh and a similarly good decorator to do figure work in the various theatres they were decorating, Harry had to give up a certain amount of his time to help. Nagle's drinking had Joshua 'worried to death'[40] and, all in all, he did not feel the man he used to be. Therefore, at the beginning of May, he decided to hand over the deeds of 33 North Frederick Street to Walter. The political situation, moreover, was highly unstable. Joshua was in favour of Home Rule, but the political unrest made business relations difficult. Although he had to hand the business over to Walter, he was not really satisfied with his elder son's efficiency, while he thought 'Harry the cleverest man in the U.K.' At the end of the month, he was relieved to engage a new stained glass man via Hetley's, from Peckham, at £5 for a 44-hour week.

Meanwhile, Harry had been working away at the three-light window for Sturminster Newton and had it finished by the end of May. It is signed 'Harry Clarke Dublin 1921' and there are 56 feet of glass in it. It is described in the church guidebook as 'notable'[41] together with its counterpart on the north side of the church, *St Martin dividing his cloak* by Christopher Webb (1911), and as 'a window of deep and rich colouring . . . signed by the distinguished Dublin artist Harry Clarke'. The church of St Mary is quite different from that at Nantwich, being light, graceful and mellow ensitively restored in 1825 in local stone, with large plain leaded windows, nore like those of an orangery than a church.[42] The three saints in the vindow hover before an exquisitely worked background of clear glass ainted with cascading floral motifs in pale golds, blues, corals, and greens, et with small exotic butterflies, birds and submarine creatures. At waist evel a line is drawn across the three openings and bolder motifs and lecorative geometrical shapes appear, regular, round and in bright pangled colours. The Madonna wears a pink robe and brownish skirt of ortuny-like pleats beneath a deep blue mantle hemmed in green. Her hawl of turquoise and mauve is closed at the neck by a golden collar, and tasselled girdle falls from the waist; the Christ child, clad in white and old with a small beaded halo, rests on her right arm. The pale ompassionate face of the Virgin is enhanced by the high, ruched scarf, the V' of the golden collar, the blue headdress and the halo of rich gold-pink, dged with tiny Celtic chevrons inside a large outer halo of speckled greens lso bordered with tiny chevrons. This huge nimbus is intersected by that f the Child and is almost as wide as the opening.

St Elizabeth, Queen of Hungary and patroness of nurses, occupies the eft light (plate 27). Harry has depicted her with the same pale, oval face as he Virgin, but with deep red hair, which forms two triangles at either side f the face. She wears a golden crown, long earrings and tiny pearls in her air. Her halo is deep blue with a rim of chevrons interspersed with green ewels. The lap of her ruby cloak is filled with roses, to hide the bread she ecretly distributed to the poor. Behind her appears the tiny vignette of her othic castle of Wurtzburg perched high in a dramatic landscape. lizabeth's dress is of gold, decorated with deeper gold discs and edged vith long golden tassels. Beneath it she wears a brown skirt of tiny pleats; er exotic shoes hover above a slender angel in long, pleated white silk and ace robe and bonnet, kneeling in profile to face the Madonna, to whom she ffers an armful of flowers.

St Barbara, a Syrian virgin and martyr, is shown in the right hand light vith a plaited reed, symbol of martyrdom in her gloved right hand (plate 8). Her other hand holds a book, symbol of her studious life spent in the ower where she was imprisoned by her father who feared she might be bducted for her beauty. She refused all suitors and had three windows nserted in her tower as a symbol of the Holy Trinity. These three lancet vindows are visible in the top of the miniature folly-like tower behind her ight shoulder, beautifully depicted on pale ruby glass, shot with a ramatic sky behind and framed with foliage and flowery swags, complementing the castle shown in the St Elizabeth light. Other symbols of her niracles include the feather borne by the androgynous angel beneath her legantly booted feet. Uncharacteristically, Harry was pleased with this vindow: 'It's good I think'.[43]

Joshua arranged for his own glazier to go to England and fix Harry's

Sturminster Newton window at the beginning of July even though the Studios were very busy; a lot of decorating jobs were in hand, yet they were still badly in need of a glass painter and lead glazier.[44] It was decided in the middle of July to incorporate the Studios as a limited liability company because Joshua was evidently very much aware of his failing health, and Walter had to take responsibility for running the business, which now employed one glass cutter, two lead glaziers, two glass painters, two scaffolders and three painters. On 3 August, Walter wrote, 'I am sorry to tell you that Father's illness has become very serious and critical and he is being operated upon this evening'.[45] After the operation for appendicitis, which had deteriorated into peritonitis, Joshua's condition was critical but over a week later he suddenly took a turn for the better. This meant that Harry had to look after the Studios whenever Walter was away on business, as it was obvious that it would be a long time before their father would be able to work again. Miss Quigley was still helping Harry on special work, but she came in on her own terms until, at the beginning of October, she was entered in the Studio books as an employee.[46] Harry and Walter expected their father would need a couple of week's rest after his time in hospital, but that he would be back by the end of September. Harry went over to London, during the first week of that month, to select glass for the Studios' stock at Hetley's — mostly opalescent flesh, neutrals and seedies. Walter wrote to a client on the 12th, apologizing for Harry's not being able to accept a certain invitation: 'As far as Harry is concerned he is up to his eyes in work and father has been seriously ill for the past six weeks and with the quantity of work we have in hand we are very pressed for time.[47]

On the next day, 13 September, Joshua Clarke died, aged 63. He was buried in Glasnevin cemetery. Harry designed a memorial card in pen and ink, signed 'c' and dated 'September 13th 1921'. It is on white with a narrow black border and shows a black curtain, hanging on a rod, against which are a small crucifix, a flaming heart in a vesica, and the banner of St Patrick. At the foot of the Cross are two heaps of tiny flowers which trail across the inscription beneath. The card is poignant in its simplicity. The two brothers were stricken, both by the suddenness and grief of their father's death, when he was thought to be improving, and by the huge gap his absence left in their lives. Walter wrote a couple of days after their bereavement: 'It will be our endeavour to live up to the reputation which our dear father has created for his work',[48] and Harry wrote to Arthur Orr: 'I would like to tell you that I am, in conjunction with my brother, carrying on the Studio here.'[49] Harry was to tell W.B. Yeats a couple of years later that he owed much of his success to 'the fine knowledge of the technique of stained glass which I learned from my father during the five years I worked with him as a stained glass worker'.[50] He too was determined to try to carry on both his own work and that of the Studios as smoothly and successfully as possible.

7

Clarke assumes control of the burgeoning Clarke Studios while producing his finest work in glass and graphics

A fortnight after Joshua Clarke's death, the sixth exhibition of the Arts and Crafts Society of Ireland opened at the Metropolitan School of Art, Dublin, where it ran from 30 September for four weeks before transferring to Cork. The catalogue was similar to that for which Harry had designed a cover in 1917, and his initial T to the foreword was retained, but this time Wilhelmina Geddes provided a powerfully expressionist cover design. Harry was a council member of the society, with Evelyn Gleeson, Thomas Bodkin, Lily Yeats, Sir John O'Connell, Mrs Joseph Hone and Major Dease; Jane French was honorary treasurer. Harry was also one of the thirty or so members of the Guild of Irish Art Workers who were listed in the catalogue, several of whom were stained glass artists. In his introduction George Atkinson referred to the outstanding work of both Harry and Oswald Reeves. 'Despite a time when the whole structure of civilisation appears to be shaken to its foundations', he wrote, the exhibition was remarkable in its emergence 'out of a period of more closely concentrated travail within these island shores':

> Some of our craftworkers, without any sacrifice of fine traditional qualities, notably Harry Clarke in stained glass and P.O. Reeves in enamelling, have, by the introduction of new methods and a fine personal quality of rendering, so developed their craft and invested it with a delightful vitality that it becomes in their hands a fresh mode of artistic expression.

He had harsh words for any 'naive insolence of slavish imitation' and for 'any scanty treatment'.

Among Harry's exhibits was 'a book bound in vellum designed for George Harrap Esq.', of which copies were on sale at five gns. This was one of the signed limited edition of *The Year's at the Spring*. His drawings in colour included a fine roundel of *The Madonna and Child with Sts Brigid and Patrick*, priced at £15, and a pencil and watercolour illustration of a crinolined lady plucking a lute, much in the style of the *Perrault* illustrations and possibly one of the drawings submitted to Hodder and Stoughton with the project but omitted from the Harrap *Perrault* of 1922. This drawing, *Hilda*

Luvia, also priced at £15, was, according to Harry's friend Victor Wood,[1] named from an incident when Harry was walking across Butt Bridge and saw a barge tied up below with the inscription 'Hilda I Luv Yer' painted on her side. The title of the drawing is a blend of this with 'Anna Livia', the river's Dublin name, later adapted by James Joyce in *Finnegans Wake*, where his Anna Livia is described as 'just a young thin pale soft shy slim slip of a thing then, sauntering, by silvermoonlake. . . .' Harry loved to hear friends trying to decipher the odd name of this fey watercolour, with its watery Japonnist landscape. Several watercolours for *The Year's at the Spring* were also included and, in the black and white section, two of the *Poe* drawings, *The Tell-Tale Heart* and *The Red Death*, as well as five from *The Year's at the Spring*. Four pieces of Harry's stained glass were shown, the most recent being the Percy and Lady Annette La Touche memorial window commissioned by Canon Hannay for the church of St Patrick at the gates of the La Touche estate, Harristown, Co. Kildare, where he was rector. The window was quite small (6′ 0″ x 1′ 9″) and could be easily transported and mounted in the exhibition. In his review of the exhibition Bodkin described this window, which depicted St Hubert, patron of huntsmen, as Harry's most important stained glass exhibit (fig. 118).[2] The upper part of the design shows the standing figure of the saint (plate 25). Below, a small panel, about eighteen inches square (plate 26), shows Hubert as the young protegé of the Duke of Aquitaine in a moonlit forest beside a brook, kneeling before a stag which bears an incandescent crucifix between its antlers (fig. 119). This panel is worked on two pieces of sapphire glass, fired and acided, perhaps a dozen times, and wrought into a microscopic delicacy of detail; iconographically it is derived from Dürer's engraving of St Eustace.[3] This little painted panel anticipates the wonderful 'revel in blue' Harry would create two years later in his *Eve of Saint Agnes* window. Nowhere in Harry's work is one so aware of the influence of Ballets Russes design as in the brocaded, plumed, gloved, belted, booted and spurred figure of Hubert who stands, one breeched leg relaxed, hand on hip beneath a huge ornate belt buckle. The figure recalls Jean Cocteau's note to d'Annunzio's ballet *Le Martyre de S. Sébastien* that there was 'the same awkwardness, the same precise breadth of treatment, the same shy charm' about Ida Rubenstein as the androgynous Sébastien: 'She suggests some saint from a stained glass window who, suddenly called to life, and still trammelled by the thought of his translucent immobility, has not yet grown accustomed to the newly bestowed gifts of speech and gesture.'[4]

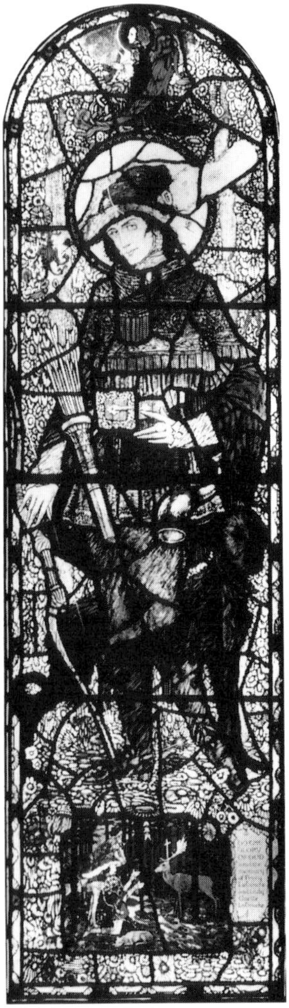

118 *St Hubert*, the La Touche memorial window, Carnalway, 1921; commissioned by Canon Hannay (the writer, George Bermingham) and shown at the sixth exhibition of the Arts and Crafts Society of Ireland (see plate 25).

Hubert's pale face is framed by long black wisps of hair, a green silk scarf outside a tight white pleated balaclava and pendulous silver ear-rings beneath a crimson fur-brimmed chapeau with a white ostrich plume. A moth is framed against the acided pink of the plain nimbus, with its chevroned border. The background of miniature floral motifs painted on a rainbow of colours, acided to vary their tonal values, is reminiscent of

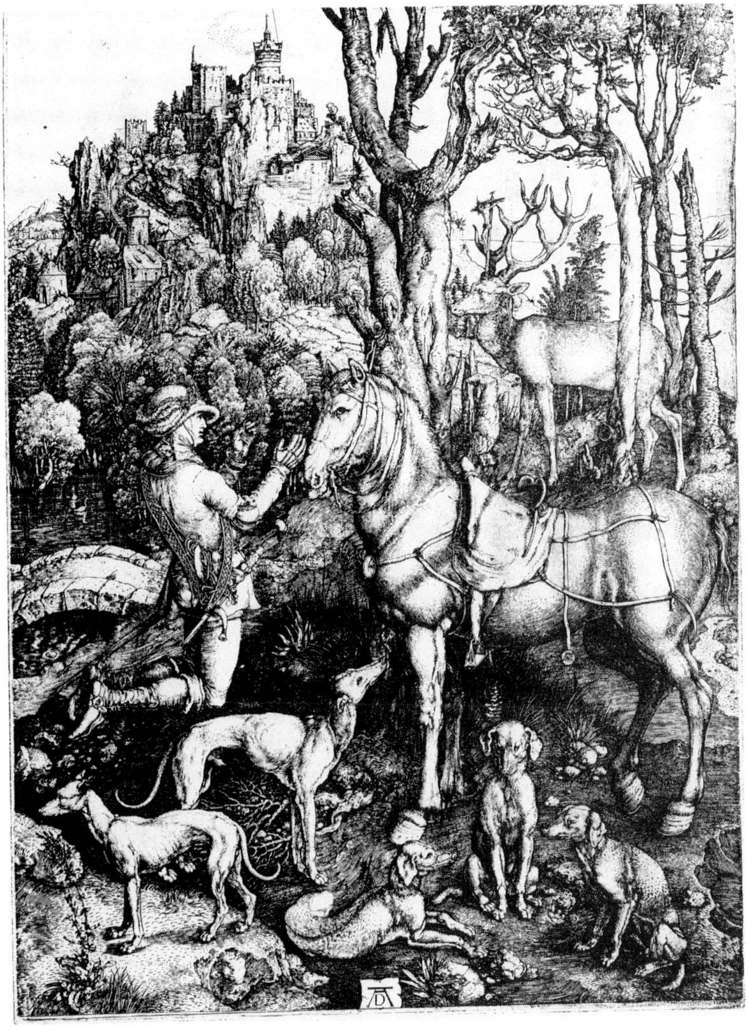

119 Albrecht Dürer, *St Eustace*, engraving, *c.* 1500, the source of the composition in the tiny conversion panel at the base of the *St Hubert* window at Carnalway (see plate 26).

Harry's treatment of the backgrounds in the Sturminster Newton window. An Irish wolfhound stands at Hubert's feet,[5] above the square panel so admired by Bodkin. At the base the memorial inscription, painted as if in sepia on parchment, has a floral border and below it the signature 'Harry Clarke Dublin 1921'.

Harry also included three 'panels for domestic decoration' in the exhibition. These were three of his miniature panels, *The Song of the Mad Prince*, lent by Bodkin, *Julian* from Edmond Lupton's collection and *Bluebeard's Last Wife*, which was offered for sale at £25. The catalogue stated that panels 'in this manner' would be made at £25 each, but the artist would not make replicas. Albert Wood, the well-known KC, who lived in Northumberland Road, bought the *Bluebeard* panel and had it mounted in a mahogany cabinet inlaid with walnut and tortoiseshell specially made for it by the Dublin cabinet maker James Hicks.

This five-sided cabinet, 17″ x 15″ x 11″, accommodates a light bulb to illuminate the panel. *Bluebeard's Last Wife* (fig. 120) is 11″ x 5¾″, a panel of flashed blue glass plated onto flashed ruby, acided and stained. The panel is signed and dated 1921 in the bottom right hand corner and illustrates one of Perrault's tales. It may have been planned as one of a series on literary themes or specially made to augment Harry's entries in the stained glass section of the exhibition, but no records of the circumstances of its making have survived. In the rather involved design an Eastern maid, with a large nimbus encircling her head, shoulders and waist, is dancing over a draw-bridge supported on thin poles over inky green water (fig. 121).[6] Her dress seems composed after Bakst's costume designs in an Oriental vein, with Hindu-Siamese elements. The sadistic Bluebeard lies in wait, helmeted in blue, with a long golden-bladed scimitar. Ominous shapes occupy the background, sinister bird forms against a sky which fades through shades of gold. At the bottom, the red sphere suggests decapitation.

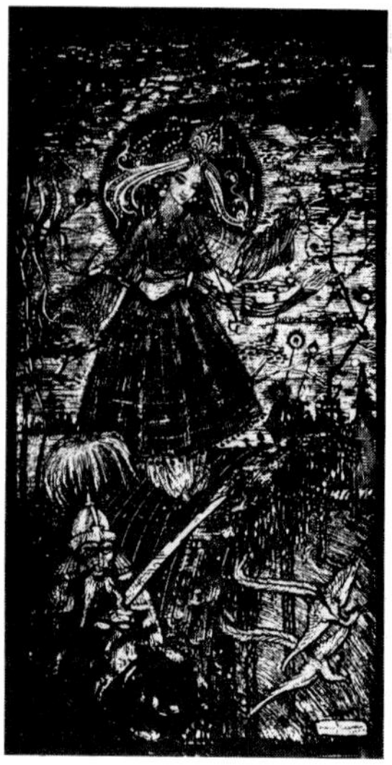

120 *Bluebeard's Last Wife*, miniature stained glass panel for domestic decoration, 1920, made for the sixth Arts and Crafts exhibition

121 Ivan Bilibin, *Oriental Woman*; the painting was reproduced in *Jar-Ptitza* and is a traditional image of a dancing maid in Russian popular art and seemingly the source for Clarke's *Bluebeard's Last Wife*.

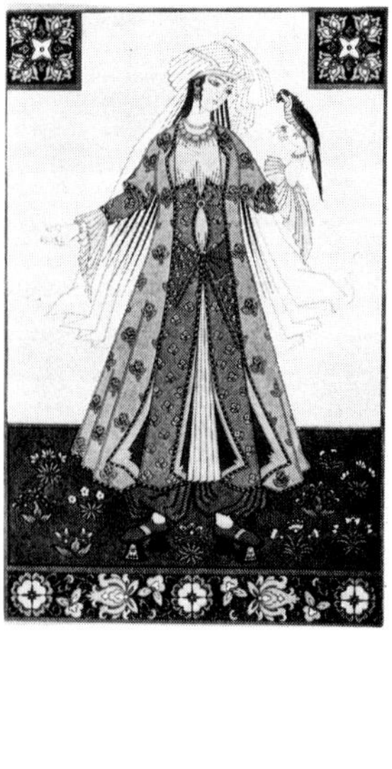

An unremarkable head of an angel was shown in the stained glass section listed as being by Harry Clarke and Kathleen Quigley 'after Botticelli'. The *Lamp with the Signs of the Zodiac* which Kathleen Quigley had made for Laurence A. Waldron to Harry's design was also shown, but this was too late for classification in the catalogue. As 'Designs and Cartoons' he showed the cartoon for the Sturminster Newton window and the coloured design for Nantwich. His handkerchief designs were lent by Sefton's, and a rejected seal design for the National Gallery of Ireland completed his twenty-two entries. Bodkin's laudatory *Studio* review of the exhibition included a coloured reproduction of his *Mad Prince* panel.

Much of Harry's time was now occupied with the day-to-day business of the Studios; this pressure on his time was to increase over the next few years and eventually to contribute to the decline in his health. While his great concern was that the Studios show a lead in the improvement of standards in Irish church decoration, competition for each contract was fierce and he had to compete with constant price-cutting by his competitors. 'Cash is of the essence of the contract for the parish priest',[7] he wrote. On the recommendation of Arthur Orr he added Philip Deegan of Worthing to the staff at the Studios in October, and offered new terms to his most valued assistant, Kathleen Quigley, to whom he wrote asking if she would consider his 'proposing new terms in her salary as from October 29 — 2/2d. per hour while working on the present commission[8] . . . and a further advance of 1d per hour when you start on my Gorey work. . . . I hope you will consider this favourably as it is the utmost to which we can go.' He also hoped she might be able to set regular working hours for each day, 'say 10 or 10.30 to 5 or 5.30',[9] as this would be to their mutual advantage. The increase in work led to the Studios' running short of glass and he had to arrange with Chance's to make two pots of opalescent flesh specially. Placing this order, he confessed to Mr Salmond, 'I need not tell you we miss the poor Gov. terrible'.[10] And, when he could not get anyone to finish six of the figures in the Stations of the Cross for a Scottish order he had to finish them himself with Nagle's help. The annual insets advertising the Studios in the *Catholic Directory* were ready in mid-November. These illustrated the cartoon for the O'Keeffe memorial window in Wexford and stated, 'all work is produced by or under the personal supervision of Mr Harry Clarke.' The negotiations for the mural decorations in the Catholic cathedral at Carlow commissioned by Dr Foley, Bishop of Kildare and Leighlin, proved difficult. The work was postponed until spring 1922, and Walter had to assure Dr Foley that 'Harry will superintend all the colour schemes and decoration when in progress'.[11] To a request from the Convent of Notre Dame at Dowanhill near Glasgow for a prospectus of his windows, Harry responded with some photographs but stated, 'I personally do not do any replicas of my work'.[12] He was recommended to the Novitiate of Notre Dame at Ashdown Park in Sussex and wrote seeking a commission, the first of several to come through the influence of Major Gerald Dease.[13]

The peevishness of certain clerical patrons had not prepared him for his first substantial problem with church authority. His design for a two-light window, *St Cecilia and a Listening Angel*, commissioned by Mrs Prentice of Welwyn Water for the church of St Michael and all Angels at Waterford in Hertfordshire was turned down by the Diocesan Advisory Committee.[14] His first cartoons were not accepted, nor were the changes made at the committee's request. The order was cancelled and no fees paid. The committee felt that Harry's design was out of keeping with the predominantly Pre-Raphaelite windows by, among others, Burne-Jones, Morris, Ford Maddox Brown, Philip Webb and Selwyn Image already in the church. Ten years later, in 1929, Karl Parsons made a single-light window for the church after Harry's design, but the work is unmistakably Parsons'.[15]

Harrap's took up the proposed Perrault edition which Hodder and Stoughton had rejected, but could not afford a complete new translation of the tales. George Harrap wrote to Bodkin early in November:

> Mr Harry Clarke has informed me that the proposal which I asked him to make to you on our behalf is acceptable, namely, that you should write an introduction to a set of Perrault's *Fairy Tales*, which Mr Clarke is to illustrate — *c.* 2500 words against a fee of 7 gns. Probably Mr Clarke has told you we are to use the quaint 18th century translation of eight of these stories to be found in the enclosed book. We have thought that this translation would appeal in a book of this kind which would be bought by adult readers.[16]

Publication was planned for August 1922 and the book was to be a companion volume to *The Year's at the Spring*, so, although he had made some preliminary drawings when the project was being considered by Hodder and Stoughton, Harry had an unusually short time in which to complete twelve watercolours, twelve black and white full-page drawings,

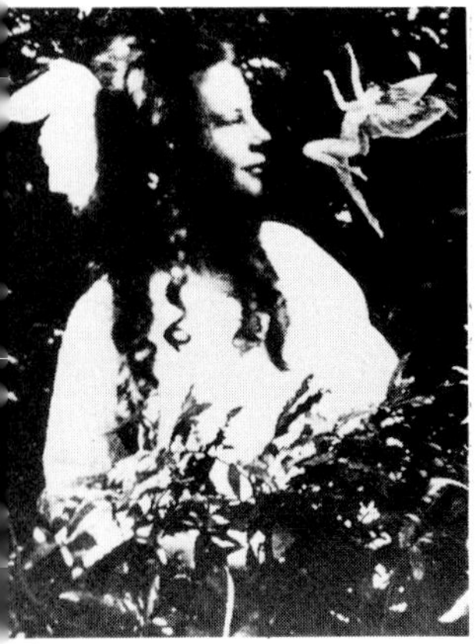

122 Detail from a photograph of a Cottingley fairy reproduced in the *Strand Magazine* 1920), a likely source for Peaseblossom, Cobweb, Moth and Mustardseed menacingly teasing the comatose Bottom and Titania in the 1921 and 1922 *Midsummer Night's Dream* panels

tailpieces, cover designs and other minor decorations, as well as plannin the general layout of the volume. He received an advance of £180 as ar outright payment for the full-page illustrations when he signed the contrac with Harrap's in November.

He also found time to make a miniature acided, stained and painted panel for Sir Robert Woods, which was ordered on 28 November at £21 The subject was Bottom and Titania from *A Midsummer Night's Dream*, IV.i His first attempt, on a sheet of ruby glass, was 'badly smashed in the kiln'[17] just before Christmas, but he leaded into a panel (fig. 123) the seventeen intricately acided and painted pieces into which the glass had broken and, ir the New Year, made Sir Robert an entirely new version, this time plating sheets of ruby and blue glass together. It is evident from the original sketcl design for the panel that ruby and blue elements were always intended ir the image. This sketch (plate 31) is in a dappled technique similar tc Gustave Moreau's and the thick cartridge paper is splashed with touches of cobalt, pink, white, crimson, olive and lemon yellow, reminiscent of the early effects achieved by Kandinsky in his romantic mythological pictures.[18] The second (unbroken) version of *Bottom and Titania* is a technica marvel (plate 30, the plated sheets of ruby and blue each extensively acidec and stained to produce a wide range of greens, mellow ruby and gold overpainted with areas of black. The scene depicted shows how fantasti Harry's imagination could be. The viewer is transported into a fairylanc realm where Richard Dadd would have been at home. Bottom, dressed ir a golden brocaded jerkin and breeches, with ruby hose and buckled shoes reclines on black pearl-bound cushions in the centre. His long ears stick ou at each side of his ass's head and are hung with daisies; a little bird perches on one of them. He looks dreamy as he chews on a daisy. The diminutive Titania, the Fairy Queen, propped up by a white shell, languishes a Bottom's left elbow, her hair brushed up on end, naked except for a wisp of red material at her loins, a large cherry-like nipple revealed at the end o a tiny upturned breast. Behind her, phosphorescent flowers glow in a dar rock pool. The unlikely lovers recline on the flowery bank of a swift stream Titania's discontentment perhaps prompted by the menacing fairies (fig 122), Peaseblossom, Cobweb, Moth, Mustardseed and Puck,[19] who are linked by a chain of daisies and seem to be teasing the translated Bottom Fronds of fantastic flora hang along the top of the picture and the glade is strewn with exotic pansies, nasturtiums, sea-anemones and other indeterminate flora and fungi. A dead tree-trunk looms at the left of the uneas scene. In the foreground of the river is the signature 'Harry Clarke 1921'.

Harry hung the repaired first version of *Bottom and Titania* in the Studic This reveals the sheer virtuosity of his technique with its shimmering gre washes, hair-fine lines, minute stipple and great variety of tones of ruby Producing these put the panel at great risk as the resultant thickness of th glass varies accordingly. In August 1924 Lord Holmpatrick saw this firs

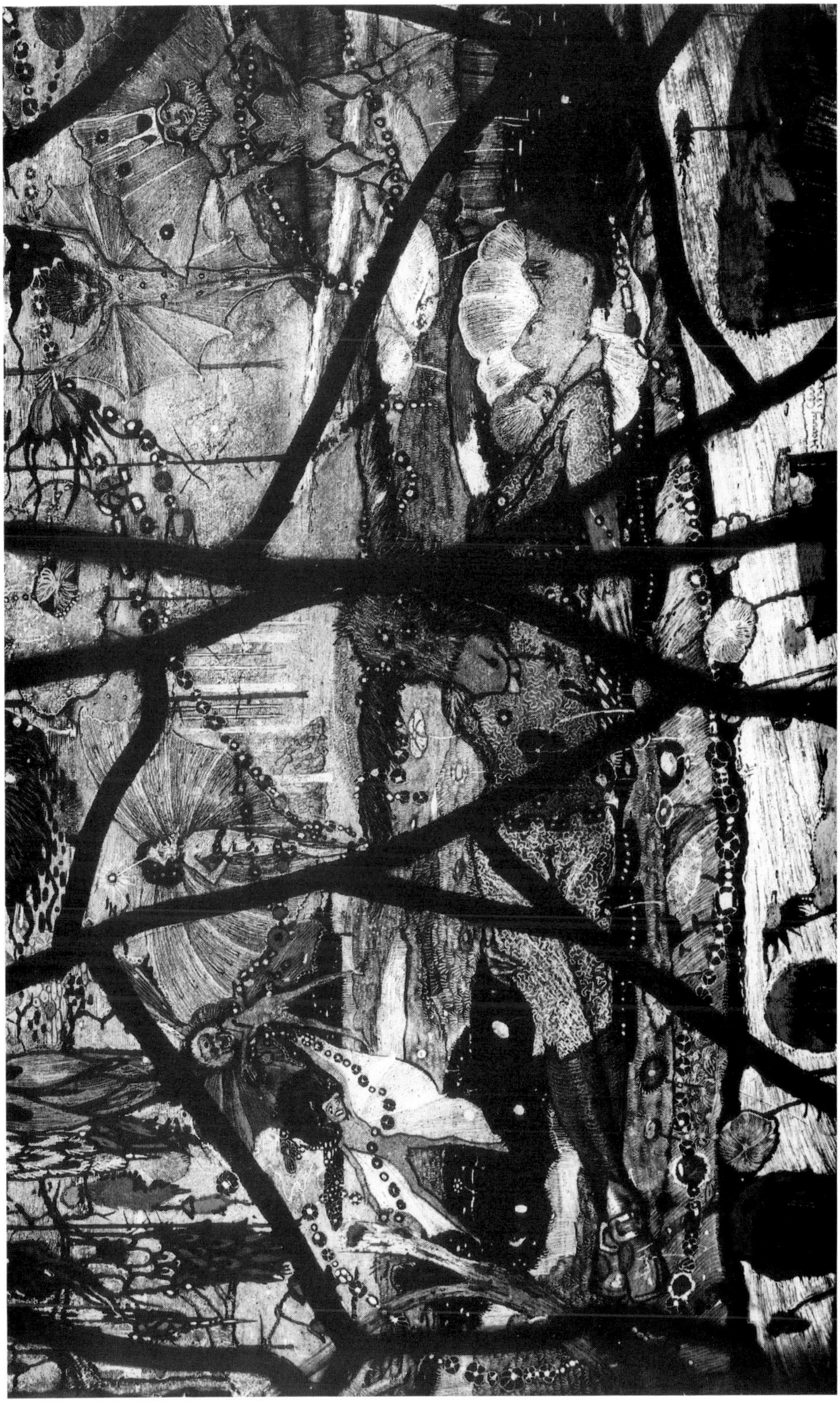

123 *Titania and Bottom*, painted, acided and stained on flashed ruby glass, in illustration to Act IV.i. from Shakespeare's *A Midsummer Night's Dream*, 1921; the first version, leaded up after it had shattered in the kiln

version at the Studios and offered to buy it, but Sir Robert Wood asserted his prior right and persuaded Harry to let him have it as a companion to the other panel, paying a total of £40 for both. Like *Bluebeard* and *The Mad Prince*, it is encased in a mahogony cabinet expressly made by James Hicks.

Up to Christmas Harry was working with Kathleen Quigley to finish the St Stephen window for Gorey. He wrote to Miss Lea-Wilson, the donor, that he expected to be through with it by mid-January, when he would contact the rector, the Revd Gahan, about fixing it: 'The window has come out extremely well and you will be pleased to hear that I have successfully carried out your views with regard to the crest and coat of arms'.[20] He had no time to make himself a Christmas card and so was glad to send friends copies of the Christmas issue of *The Studio* which contained Bodkin's review of the Arts and Crafts exhibition. However, he did feel obliged to send the many Christmas gifts, mainly to religious institutions, that his father had been in the habit of sending from the Studios. He also had to prepare exhibits for the Exposition d'Art Irlandais at the Galeries Barbazanges in Paris from 28 January to 25 February, organized as part of the universal Congress of the Irish Race which opened in Paris on 21 January 1922, the anniversary of the establishment of the Irish Republic by Dáil Éireann. He showed fifteen drawings for Poe's tales, eight illustrations from *The Year's at the Spring* and other black and white 'designs'. In colour, his work included three from *The Year's at the Spring* and one Poe subject as well as *Hilda Luvia*. He also included an 'assortiment de douze mouchoirs imprimés', lent by Sefton's, among 'Dessins pour Tissus' and, among 'Projects pour Vitraux' five cartoons and the little *Femme de Barbe-Bleu* panel. His work was singled out in Arsène Alexandre's rather gushing catalogue introduction.[21]

He visited Glasgow in January 1922, where he stayed with Dr Phillimore, Professor of Humanity at Glasgow University and an old friend of Sir Bertram Windle in Cork. Phillimore accompanied him to meet Sister Wilfred, Superior of the Convent of Notre Dame at Dowanhill to discuss a window for the chapel, *The Coronation of our Lady*, to commemorate those who had fallen in World War I. He also managed to spend a few days with E.A. Taylor and Jessie King at their home in Kircudbright, where they let the cottages in the cobbled close around their house, Greengate, to artists in the summer. A postcard to Bodkin, sent on 7 January, indicates that he was 'having a splendid time amongst the best artistic folk I've met for years. Glasgow was a little dull but here is fine. Back early next week'.

When he returned to Dublin he wrote to Sr Wilfred asking for measurements so that he could give a precise estimate for the window. On 1 February he sent the estimate, and the order was confirmed on 2 March. He was supervising stained glass schemes for the new church at Finglas, the Franciscan church at Carrick-on-Suir, and for Twomilehouse in Co. Kildare. Business was thriving, and stocks of glass could not keep up with orders coming from England as well as Ireland. However, by the end of February Harry had to take sole command of the business as Walter was ill with pleurisy. He found it necessary to find a more convenient home for his family and managed to buy 48 North Circular Road,[22] not far away, and had moved them there by mid March. On 24 and 25 February he had a showing of the Gorey window, which was to be despatched after the weekend even though a strike prevented the storm glass being ready in time.

The single-light *St Stephen* window in Gorey is treated on a comparatively large scale (fig. 124). The cartoon was drawn in the loose, bold charcoal lines that Harry had begun to develop in the Castletownshend window. The window was erected by Mrs Lea-Wilson in memory of her husband, a prominent member of the Royal Irish Constabulary who had been shot by Republicans outside his home. Thus the scroll held by the angel in the window reads, 'Lord, lay not this sin to their charge.' Similarly the subject is St Stephen, the first Christian martyr, whom Harry has shown carrying the symbolic palm of martyrdom and bearing a book in his left arm while his right hand is extended, palm forward, suggesting his innocence. The stones by which he was slain are shown leaded into the rich purples, mauves, rubies and pinks of his simple vestments, contrasting with the emerald green of the book he holds. His face is pale and angular, the head inclined to the left with a long nose and sad, pensive eyes. This soulful Celtic face is reflected in the equally direct unstylized treatment of the hands and sandalled feet. The two girl angels above and below the Saint are gentle and child-like, treated in the Whall tradition, as is the whole window.

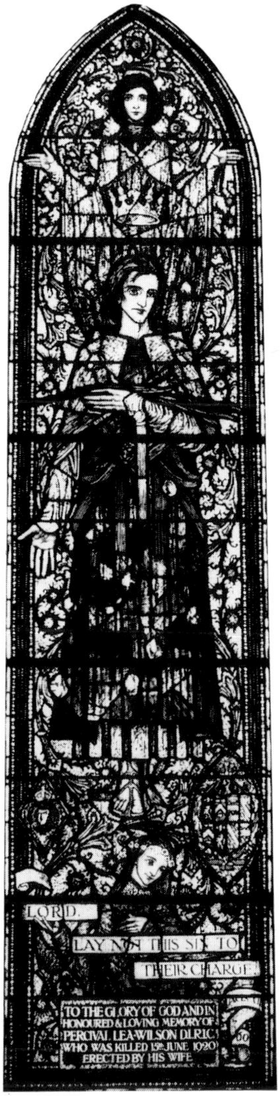

124 *St Stephen*, the Lea-Wilson memorial window, Gorey, 1922

On 16 February an estimate was sent to Fr Healy for a further two-light window in the Lady Chapel at Saint Joseph's, Terenure. The Glasgow design was in hand and, at the same time Harry was planning to move house and trying to meet the deadline for the Perrault illustrations. A further commission arrived to design and illustrate *Ireland's Memorial Records*, a set of eight large quarto volumes to contain the Roll of Honour of men in Irish regiments and Irishmen in British regiments who had been killed in the 1914-1918 War. These volumes were produced for the Irish National War Memorial Committee by Maunsel and Co. The eight volumes were printed on handmade paper in a limited edition of one hundred copies issued in 1923 with a set enshrined in four special granite pavilions at the Irish National War Memorial at Islandbridge, Dublin, designed later by Lutyens. For these books Harry made a particularly fine title-page border (fig. 125) which is repeated in each, seven page borders which appear, sometimes in reverse, throughout the books, and a tailpiece for the final volume. The designs incorporate Celtic and Art Deco motifs, battle scenes in silhouette,[23] medals, insignia and religious and mythological themes, all drawn in pen and ink.

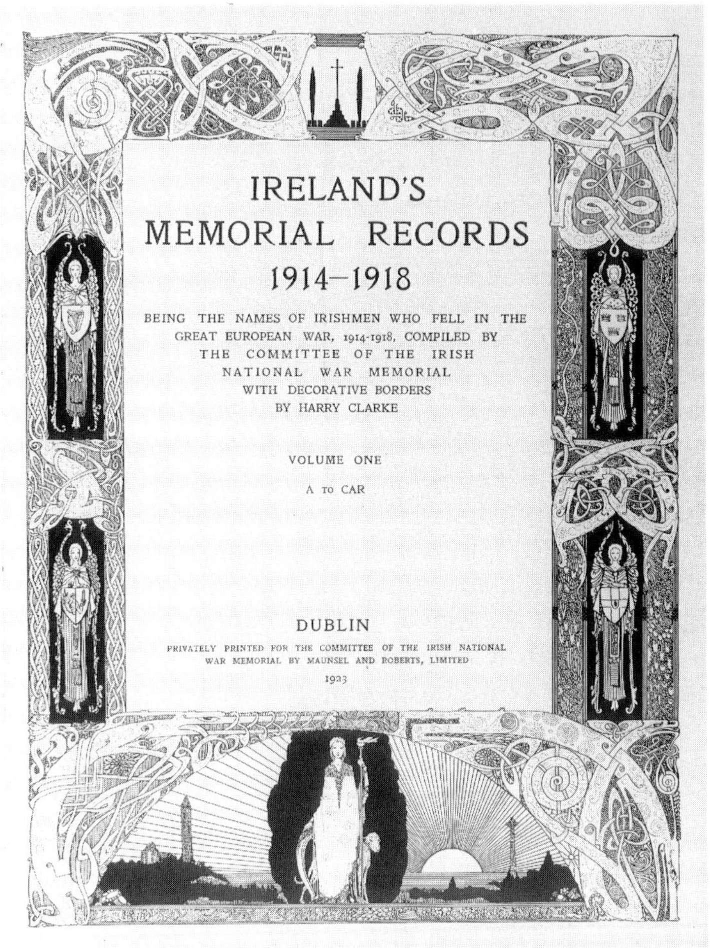

125 Title page from *Ireland's Memorial Records* (1923), a limited edition commemorating men from Irish regiments and Irishmen from British regiments; one set was later enshrined in the Irish National War Memorial in Dublin designed by Sir Edward Lutyens.

Life in Ireland at this time was very unstable because of the Civil War which divided a country already ravaged by the five-year struggle for Independence folllowing the 1916 Rising. The Civil War saw those Irishmen who upheld the Treaty concluded with Britain in December 1921 at war with those Republicans who opposed it. There were great tragedies on both sides. Arthur Griffith died on 12 August and, ten days later, Michael Collins was shot in an ambush. Harry designed the cover of the memorial booklet which commemorated both leaders. This quarto, *A Pictorial Record of the Lives and Deaths of the Founders of the Irish Free State*, is unremarkable except for the cover, for which Harry made at least six drafts. The final design is simple and incorporates a squarish vignette printed in black and viridian on buff paper showing a mourning woman kneeling by a lake; behind the mountains on the horizon shafts of light spread out.[2] Parallel with her straight back are steep black cliffs above which two crosses appear in silhouette. The design is signed 'HC'. A further symbolic ring device appears on the cover.

Irish art was also going through a troubled time. The National Gallery was closed for almost two years pending the appointment of a new director, and was only partially reopened in the spring of 1924. Even the School of Art was closed during most of 1923. The Municipal Gallery was 'still lodged in a decaying private house, badly lit and in imminent danger of destruction by fire'.[25] After the burning of several of Dublin's finest buildings in 1922, adding further to the existing destruction in the centre of the city, the Civics Institute of Ireland decided to publish a new plan for the capital. This had resulted from a competition funded by Lady Aberdeen, the wife of the Lord Lieutenant, which the Institute had organized in 1916. The first prize was awarded to *Dublin of the Future*, a scheme submitted by Patrick Abercrombie, professor of civic design at Liverpool, and his colleagues Sydney Kelly and Arthur Kelly. The adjudicators found this

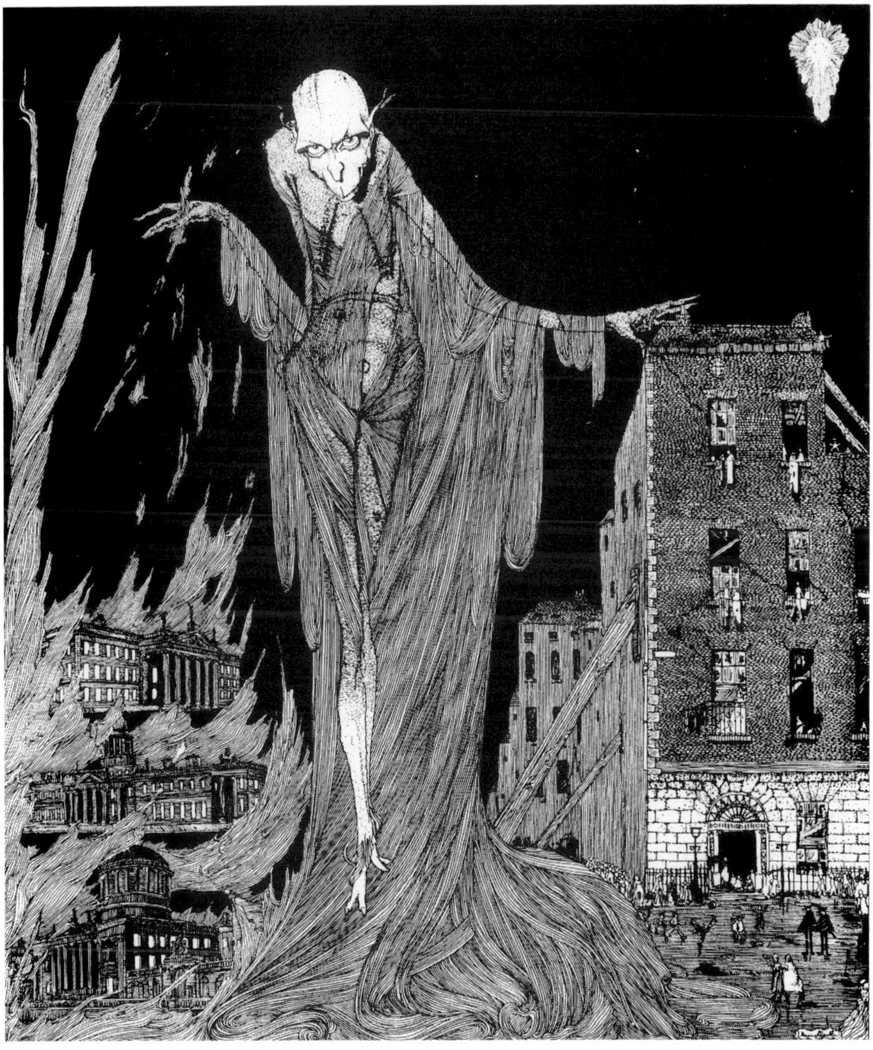

126 *The Last Hour of the Night*, frontispiece illustration to *Dublin of the Future*, published in 1922 by the Civics Institute of Ireland as the new town plan for the war- and poverty-stricken city

> A well-reasoned scheme, outlining an economic system of scientific, artistic and hygienic municipal reconstruction and development, providing specially for the conservation of citizen life and natural resources and the total abolition of slum conditions.[26]

When *Dublin of the Future* was published in 1922 by the Institute, in association with Liverpool University Press and Hodder and Stoughton, Harry contributed a fine but eccentric pen and ink frontispiece, *The Last Hour of the Night* (fig. 126), one of the stranger expressions of his imagination. A bald, emaciated creature swathed in translucent strands of hair-like drapery stoops commandingly in the centre of the picture, cloven toes emerging from tapering stubbly shins, and spindly hands extended on either side.[27] On the left is a montage of Dublin's finest buildings, all casualties of the Troubles — the Four Courts, above it the Custom House and, on top, the General Post Office, all encased in flames. On the right of the figure a row of Dublin Georgian town houses stands, fallen into the decay typical of the twentieth-century state of so many of these once proud dwellings. Beneath the houses two policeman watch as children play on the street and weary-looking figures pass by. Above, in the top right corner a blazing star in the jet-black sky perhaps heralds some new hope for the city. Harry was deeply concerned at the indifferent attitude of the new Free State government to matters of Art and Design exemplified in 'the horrid designs for the first issue of stamps' and lack of vision in rebuilding Dublin or supporting the Art School. While caring deeply about the future of Ireland, he and Walter were 'actually neutral in their political opinions'.[28]

At the Studios, still named 'J. Clarke and Sons', Harry began to restyle the typography of the advertising and produced, in the 1922 *Catholic Directory*, the first of a new series of small insets which continued annually until he became too ill to direct their design and content. This illustrated the two-light Wexford window, and on the back he addressed the firm's clients:

> We beg to thank our many clients for their kind consideration and patience whilst awaiting the completion of their commissions, and at the same time to inform them that we are reorganising our Studios which are now adequately staffed, thus enabling us to work more promptly and to definite dates.... All work now entrusted to us shall be produced by or under the personal supervision of Mr Harry Clarke.

A list of some of the stained glass and decorative schemes produced by the Studios followed, for clients in Ireland, England and Scotland.

At the 1922 art exhibition of Aonach Tailteann, the Gaelic Revival festival, which replaced the Royal Dublin Society's annual Art Industries show, Harry won first prize in the stained glass section for the left light, *The Annunciation*, of the lady chapel window at Terenure (fig. 127). He was also awarded silver medals for fabric design and black and white drawing. He seems to have asked Waldron to lend the *Queens* panels for the exhibition, but no catalogue has come to light.

Stained glass continued to occupy most of his time, whether his own designs or studio work being made under his supervision. On 7 June the Presentation Convent in Dingle, Co. Kerry ordered a set of twelve lancet lights and at the same time he was supervising a window depicting *St Catherine of Siena* to be shipped to America for the First National Bank building in Paterson, New Jersey (since destroyed) and another series of two-light windows for the Sacred Heart Chapel in Leeson Street, Dublin. In October his friend, W.A.R. Cruise, general secretary of the Dublin Hibernian Fire Office, asked him to make a panel 15″ x 9″ for the firm's London offices, for which he was charged £21. Sadly there is no trace of this panel; as Harry wrote in 1924,[29] it was his only piece of domestic glass in England.

The Fairy Tales of Perrault, prefaced by Thomas Bodkin's introduction, with twelve colour plates, twelve full-page black and white drawings, twenty-two decorations and cover title-page decorations was published by Harrap in August 1922. The book appeared in various binding styles — in ivory cloth at 15/-, 'in full Persian Levant leather', tooled in gold on front and back at 25/-, or with the same design but only gold on the front in cobalt buckram, or 'tastefully bound with French paper sides of rich design'.[30] In format the *Perrault* is uniform with *The Year's at the Spring*, published two years before. Neither book seems to have sold well, nor did *Perrault* receive the usual enthusiastic welcome from the reviewers. G.S. Layard observed that 'Mr Clarke's skills and artistry [are] far more fitted to the satires of Pope or Swift than to tales consecrate to the days of our innocence'.[31] *The Studio* review,[32] with which two black and white drawings from the book were reproduced, was mildly appreciative. It was the *Poe* illustrations that had established Harry's reputation, 'his tremendous imagination vitalizing pictorially with amazing power and invention the *Tales of Mystery and Imagination*'.[33]

The *Perrault* drawings abound in idiosyncratic and fantastic detail and were perhaps too weird for a generation attuned to the illustrations of Rackham, Dulac and the Robinsons. They parallel Harry's approach in the miniature glass panels, such as *Titania and Bottom*, to a microscopic fairyland, often grotesque, peopled, landscaped and decorated entirely from his imagination. The deep, rich colours of his *Hans Andersen* pictures have given way to warm corals, sandstones, grassy greens, beige, forget-me-not blue and grey. Tapered limbs, cloven feet, vestigial limbs, hobgoblins, marionettes, fantastic frock coats, perruques and scanty crinolines, all appear to a tiny scale (figs. 128-130). Pinnacled cities loom in misty landscapes, reminiscent of the miniatures of the Limbourg brothers; tiny birds, toadstools, fantasy flowers, wispishly clipped poplars and willows mingle

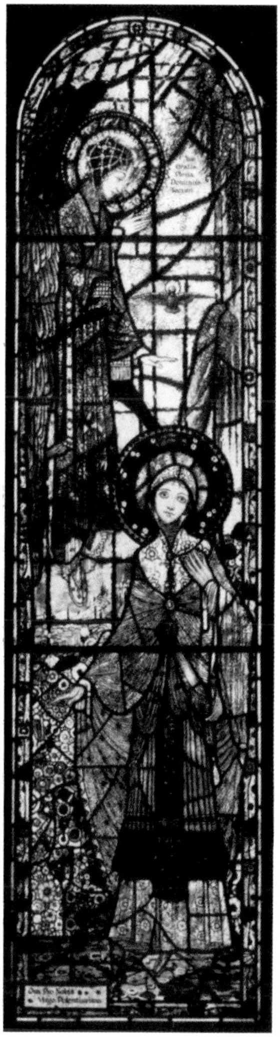

127 *The Annunciation*, 1922, left-hand light of the Terenure lady chapel window

128 Marionettes, decorative illustration in pen and ink from *The Fairy Tales of Perrault* (1922)

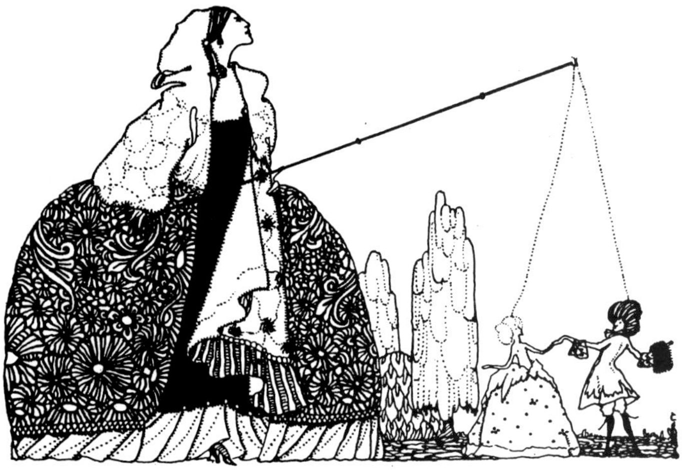

129 A lady and a beggar, decorative illustration in pen and ink from *Perrault*; this illustration was used as a Christmas card for 1922 and was originally heightened with gold ink.

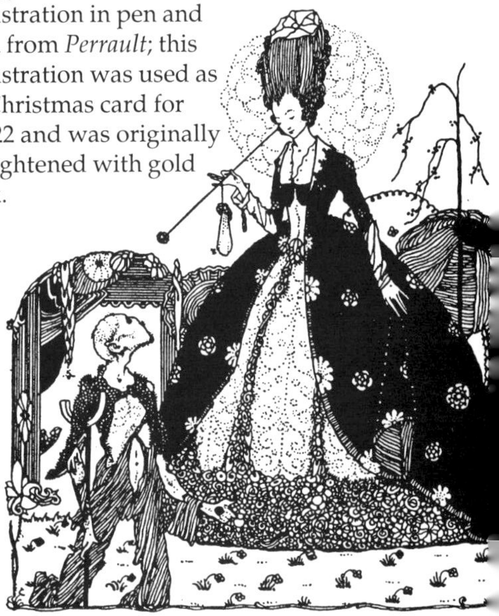

130 'Bluebeard', title illustration in pen and ink from *Perrault*

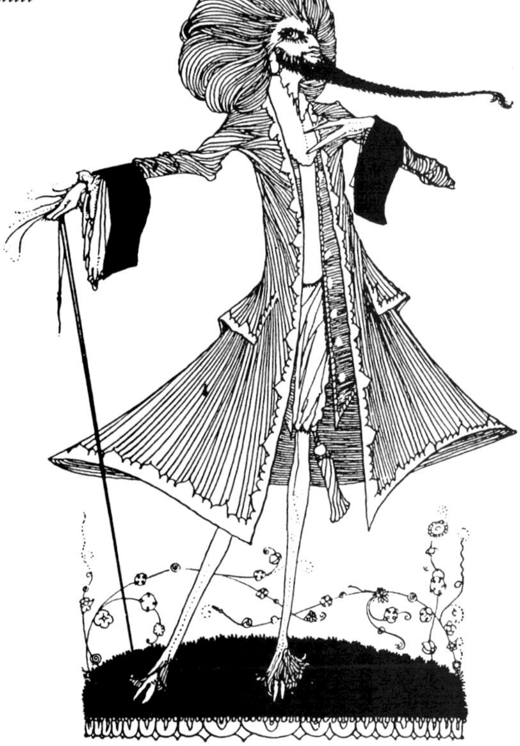

131 'The Ridiculous Wishes', title illustration in pen and ink from *Perrault*; Clarke's use of silhouettes in this book was particularly effective.

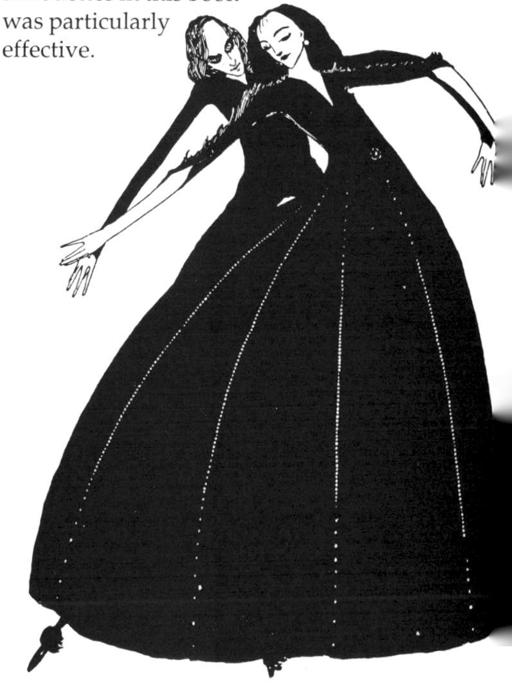

with jellyfish, sea-urchins and sea-anemones. Some of these pictures, such as 'This man had the misfortune to have a blue beard' are reminiscent of Watteau's *Fêtes Champêtres* both in their pale colours and in details such as the naked mandolin-playing lady, sprayed silver to become a statue. There is the haunting silhouetted waltzing couple of 'The Ridiculous Wishes' tale (fig. 131), the frankly erotic damsel wrapped in her donkey skin and the naked 'Sleeping Beauty' swathed in muslin lying on her bed before a sea of sleeping faces. Certainly it is more a book for adults, as Harrap predicted. Private jokes appear, such as the caricature of Victor Wood as the ogre Queen who wants to eat Beauty with a sauce Robert and, in *Cinderella and the Ugly Sisters*, one of the sisters is a caricature of Harry's elder sister, Kathleen, with whom he had quarrelled when he was drawing the illustration. A disturbing element seems to lurk beneath the playfulness of these illustrations, decorative, inventive, and beautiful as they are. The colour plates in *Perrault* have lost a lot in reproduction, as have some of the black and white, both plates and tailpieces. Only the silhouettes have been perfectly printed, and these are superb. In its review the *Westminster Gazette* thought Harry

> succeeded admirably in his treatment of Perrault. Not only has he entered thoroughly into the spirit of the tales, but his firm yet delicate line work, his composition and his use of silhouette are excellent, while his colouring is original but pleasing.[34]

The *English Review* admired the 'unearthliness' of his work.[35]

In December, when Harry visited Harrap's in London, they decided to prepare a new edition of the *Poe* and commissioned a further eight illustrations in colour for which he accepted £100. He was also asked to make twelve colour and twelve black and white drawings to illustrate *The Arabian Nights*, to be published in 1924, for which he would receive £180. However, this project was later cancelled and an illustrated edition of Goethe's *Faust* produced instead. At the end of 1922 *The Studio*, in its special number, *Drawings in Pen and Pencil from Dürer's Day to Ours*, with notes and appreciations by George Sheringham, reproduced one of his 1915 *Ancient Mariner* drawings, *The very deep did rot, O Christ*, considerably reduced, but on a fine paper.

Stained glass work continued to come in. The Revd Gahan ordered another window for the church in Gorey, a two-light of *St Luke and St Martin of Tours with the Beggar* and an ornamental rose window which was made at the Studios to Harry's design. The two-light window was a memorial to a local surgeon, and was erected in the autumn. This striking window, signed 'CLARKE/DUBLIN' and undated, has its long narrow lights set closely together. It is treated in a vertical geometrical fashion with clear painted glass forming a glowing background to the figures of the two saints, who are identified by their symbols and richly glowing tones of turquoise, rust, deep pink, gold and grey. Also, resulting from the *St Stephen* window in Gorey, he was asked by the Earl of Wicklow to design a Resurrection for the little church of Eneriley and Kilbride, near the Earl's estate, Shelton Abbey in Co. Wicklow.

Early in 1923, despite his heavy work-load both in glass and illustration, Harry decided to enter the competition for a very large window (45′ by 7′) at Bristol University. On 2 March he wrote to Bodkin that he had decided to 'go hard' for this and was therefore spreading his other work to gain an extra fortnight to prepare the design. He thought he was 'on to a new "Gadgett"'[36] for this and felt optimistic about the result. He wanted to show Bodkin what he had in mind as Thomas MacGreevy had dropped in to see him and it. He wished Bodkin knew MacGreevy better 'because he loves a picture almost as much as you do yourself.'[37] MacGreevy seems to have joined Harry's circle of friends about this time. The beautifully executed coloured scale design (23¾″ x 8½″) for the Bristol window is signed and dated March 1923. The design has four layers of seven lights, twenty-eight in all, with tracery lights above, topped by armorial bearings. Four figures occupy the centre, among them Anselm, Dunstan and an ancient king presenting a tablet to two soldiers. Figures of a jester and a lady with a lute also appear as well as a courtly medieval scene. Below, the punning inscription 'As God Wills' with coats of arms refers to the Wills family, owners of the Imperial Tobacco Company and benefactors of the university, to whom the window was planned as a memorial. Harry did not succeed in winning this competition, the winner being a pupil of Whall's, Arnold Robinson.

During the previous August Archbishop Sir James Duhig of Brisbane had visited 'the Irish manufacturing house of Clarke's (Stained Glass)'[38] as he put it in his diary, to commission a window for Dr and Miss Mayne in memory of their brothers Isaac and William. He had been recommended by a Brisbane resident, Joe Kelly, who later became the Studios' Australian agent. Harry probably showed the Archbishop the three-light *Crucifixion* at Terenure, for the window which the archbishop ordered on 22 August at £775 has several similar features. However, the Australian order must have posed severe problems for Harry who had not visited the site and had to work from reports as to the quality of light in which his work would be seen. The schedule for the work too was tight, as the window had to be delivered to Brisbane and installed for its unveiling on 10 June 1923.

In composition the Brisbane window resembles the Terenure *Crucifixion*. Three tall, narrow lights, topped by a quatrefoil and two small tracery lights show a robed Christ, the stigmata of his Passion displayed, ascending against a horizontally leaded sunset sky pierced by vertical evergreen cypress trees. Below, robed in rich blues and reds, the Madonna kneels in a rocky garden. Apostles occupy the lower halves of the side lights, five on the left and six on the right, with brightly coloured robes and winged and plumed haloes. Angels, also in brilliant colours, hover bearing Passion symbols in incandescent badges, seven in each light. Further angels with badges occupy the quatrefoils, complemented by three more badges held over the Christ in the centre light, where another six brightly coloured angels hover, two in the centre, four at the side. In the intermediate tracery lights little angels' heads peep from behind the borders: from a distance each of these small faces looks like a self-portrait of Harry. The window is more colourful by far than Terenure, and is arguably somewhat garish, only held together by the blues, rubies and golds. It bears the hallmarks of Philip Deegan's work. The inscription is unexpectedly distracting as the lettering is stark white against the dark background. The Studios' name appears in the bottom right corner.

The archbishop was delighted with the window, and cabled Harry,

> Window unveiled Apostolic Delegate Sunday. Artistic triumph. Brisbane most favourably impressed. Posting bank draft, Press notices. Sincere congratulations.[39]

Harry at once sent copies of the cable to Bodkin and MacGreevy who had both seen and liked the window before it was despatched, adding that he was 'tremendously bucked' by it. The window had been dedicated and unveiled by the Apostolic Delegate before a Mass at which Archbishop Duhig preached to the text 'I have loved, O Lord, the beauty of thy house and the place where thy glory dwelleth'. On the following Saturday, 16 June, the *Brisbane Age* wrote enthusiastically of this 'glorious masterpiece of the glazier's art':

> You are face to face with one of the finest examples of stained glass work that has ever been imported into Australia. It has come from the Island of Saints and Scholars, the isle of artists and of religious-minded people. In the Irish capital by a young Irish artist, this window was designed and worked especially for this Cathedral.

Harry celebrated this success by buying a Darracq, a source of great pride and indispensable for driving to an ever-increasing number of clients all over Ireland.

In north Co. Dublin, Canon Byrne, parish priest of Balbriggan, ordered two two-light windows to be fixed by November 1923 and, on 27 April, Harold Jacob ordered a domestic window, 62" x 20½" for the landing of his father's house. Harry suggested several subjects for this (Bluebeard, Sleeping Beauty, the Playboy of the Western World) and on 4 May Jacob wrote expressing a preference for a window based on Keats' poem *The Eve of St Agnes*.[40] Three days later Harry replied, 'I shall get to work on *The Eve of St Agnes* and submit my first coloured draft for discussion', but he 'had to clear off an accumulation of work' during May and June 'to get a clear run on your window'. He was also planning an exhibition at the Studios in late July when he would show the Terenure and Glasgow windows as well as some book illustrations. This would be his first show since he had taken on the running of the Studios and, despite the rush to get it mounted in time, it proved a great success as Bodkin's piece in the *Irish Times* indicates:

> In his exhibition . . . Mr Harry Clarke excels himself. Such is his pleasant custom, he never recedes, he never stands still. With each fresh work he shows a power that grows steadily deeper and stronger. 'Genius' is the only word in my vocabulary which does full justice to the measure of his gifts as an artist in stained and painted glass.

He went on to describe the two windows, one of which would soon

> be leaving Ireland on its way to the Church of Notre Dame in Glasgow. It is a large representation, in three lights . . . of the Coronation of the Blessed Virgin, and contains no fewer than twenty-five half life size figures. Mary kneels on a flight of shallow grey steps down which her girdle spills in exquisite waves to receive her Crown from the Christ triumphant. Her robe is woven of a melting emerald; her mantle made with all the molten hues of flowers and skies and waters.[41]

In the *Freeman's Journal*, George Atkinson wrote of this window, as

> a work of exceptional beauty as notable as it is different of treatment, for instead of the method of division into panels, the artist has designed an arrangement that covers the whole field of three lights and has secured an effect that is at once homogenous, rich and solemn. Above the central subject and in the tracery are the figures of SS. John and Luke and angels in adoration, while below and around are grouped the figures of Saints, including those having special significance in Scotland. The great nimbus passing across the window localises the chief subject of the Coronation, while outside and merged within its compass are the figures of the Saints; but there is no detachment, each figure and the group of angels lead to the main theme, and emphasise a sense of reverence and mystery that pervades the treatment of the subject.[42]

Thomas MacGreevy wrote a long appreciative piece for the *Irish Independent* in which he appealed for a halt on the export of such native treasures and the introduction of an import tax.[43] Bodkin also wrote of the two lights for the Terenure lady chapel — *The Annunciation* and *The Blessed Virgin in Glory*:[44]

> Though they form an entirely harmonious whole, they are treated in different manners. *The Annunciation* is a simple, if wholly spiritual, pastoral. *The Virgin in Glory* has a quality of hierarchic mysticism and grandeur. Her halo is of lambent flame. About her drift a multitude of little foreshadowing figures, Ruth, Rachel, Deborah, Rebecca, Judith and Esther. These are drawn with such amazing delicacy of detail that they demand inspection at the closest quarter; and yet when seen from a distance they sink into a background swirl of lovely hues enhancing the majestic figure of their queen. The destined site of this window allows for its examination at all ranges for the full exploration of all its wonders. It does much to reconcile us to the imminent departure of the larger window to Glasgow.

The Annunciation, a subtle work with shimmering pale colours, gossamer lines and finely laid-on tones shows Mary, innocent, wide-eyed, gazing into space, one hand clasping flowers to her breast. Her blue silk boots are poised on an inventive crazy paving patchwork of acided green flowers, while the tapestry of warmly modulated flower heads behind her terminates in a miniature grisaille depiction of a Palestinian hill town framed by the angel's stylish slippers. The window is signed 'Harry Clarke 1922'. It was reproduced by E.L. Armitage in *Stained Glass — History, Technology and Practice* (London, 1959), who wrote:

> The rarest prerequisities are the intuition and insight undergirding knowledge by which the artist or author is able to relate his subjects to the life and destiny of his fellow human beings. Some men know how to make things; they deal deftly with the transitory (rather than the eternal). A few also know why they make them and they are also in touch with the eternal.

He then quoted Viollet le Duc's insistence on the hazardous importance of decoration and ornament in controlling colour and sunlight. He felt Harry's work 'always has a beautiful decorative quality emphasized by glowing colour and imbued with religious sensibility'.

As Bodkin suggests, the other light of this window, *The Blessed Virgin in Glory*, is in a different mood (plate 42). The Virgin, robed in turquoise, with emerald girdle and white mantle, in a cloak of deep ultramarine, and with a golden halo around her silver diadem, occupies the centre of the light, full-face. She holds a sceptre and an orb and a scroll unfolds across her breast. Her feet are poised over a fork-tailed serpent coiled around the horns of the moon from which sprout the leaves of a great tree bearing golden fruit. On either side of the tree the naked figures of Adam and Eve cower, clasping their bodies in shame (fig. 132). These figures are surely derived from those in Paul Klee's etching *Two Men Meeting, Each Presuming the Other*

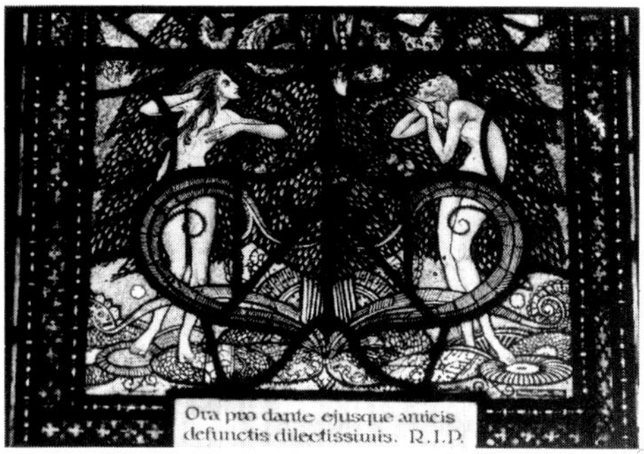

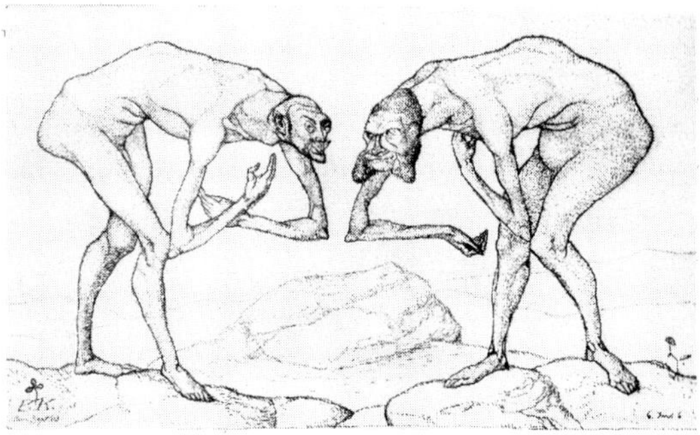

132 Adam and Eve and the Tree of Life, detail from *The Blessed Virgin in Glory*, 1923, right-hand light in the Terenure lady chapel

133 Paul Klee, *Two Men Meeting, Each Presuming the Other to be of Higher Rank*, 1903, from Klee's early figurative period, which bears obvious affinities with Clarke's work of the early 1920s; the source of the cowering attitudes of Adam and Eve at the base of the Terenure *Blessed Virgin in Glory*

to be of Higher Rank (1903; fig. 133).[45] Characteristic floral motifs, etiolated archangels and five minute grisaille scenes from the Life of the Virgin inside the deep blue border edged with white beads, frame the deeply jewelled screen studded with graphic portrayals of characters from the Old Testament. Particularly notable are Ruth and Deborah on green glass and Judith in crimson beside Holofernes 'under a canopy . . .woven with purple and gold, and emeralds and precious stones';[46] in another scene Judith's maid in mauve grimaces at her gruesome trophy (fig. 138), the decapitated head of the Assyrian general. The window is signed 'Harry Clarke 1923'. Of it Stephen Gwynn wrote that Harry Clarke 'is a designer who obviously owes a great deal to Beardsley, but more to his native gift, and a colour-worker in glass who reaches a brilliancy that I have never seen equalled in modern work'.[47]

The studio exhibition also included illustrations, among them *The Pit and the Pendulum* for Poe (fig. 134)and his drawings for Rupert Brooke's 'The Great Lover' and for James Elroy Flecker's 'The Dying Patriot', which he presented to MacGreevy. He also took the opportunity to begin a visitors' book for the Studios and among the names in this are those of his patron, Revd Dr Healy of Terenure, who wrote, 'a marvel of workmanship and rich detail',[48] Albert Wood, the architect R.M. Butler, the Bodkins, Sir John O'Connell and his wife, Major and Mrs Dease, W.B. Yeats, Lennox Robinson, Beatrice Campbell, Tilly Fleischmann and Stephen Gwynn.

The end of the Civil War brought a period of optimism in Ireland and one result was the emergence of two new publications which regularly featured articles on the arts — the *Irish Statesman*, founded by Horace Plunkett and edited by Æ, which would prove influential in directing national opinions, and, devoted to the literary field, Seumas O'Sullivan's *Dublin Magazine*, which first appeared as a monthly in August 1923. Harry, who was still teaching black and white design at the Dublin School of Art, designed the first cover for the *Dublin Magazine* and also advised O'Sullivan on layout and design.[49] His cover design is simple and striking, designed to be printed in black, blue and gold on a matt white paper. The decorative element is a rectangular vignette within a classical fluted border showing a smart couple in stylized Regency garb promenading against a Dublin panorama in silhouette. This cover was used for three years while the magazine ran as a monthly. Subsequent issues featured illustrations by his students from the Art School and the Studios, all very much in his style. In autumn 1926 publication was changed to quarterly and the cover was redesigned as a typographical layout.

Other graphic work at this time included a bookplate or Christmas card design for R.M. Butler, for which he prepared several trial sketches. One

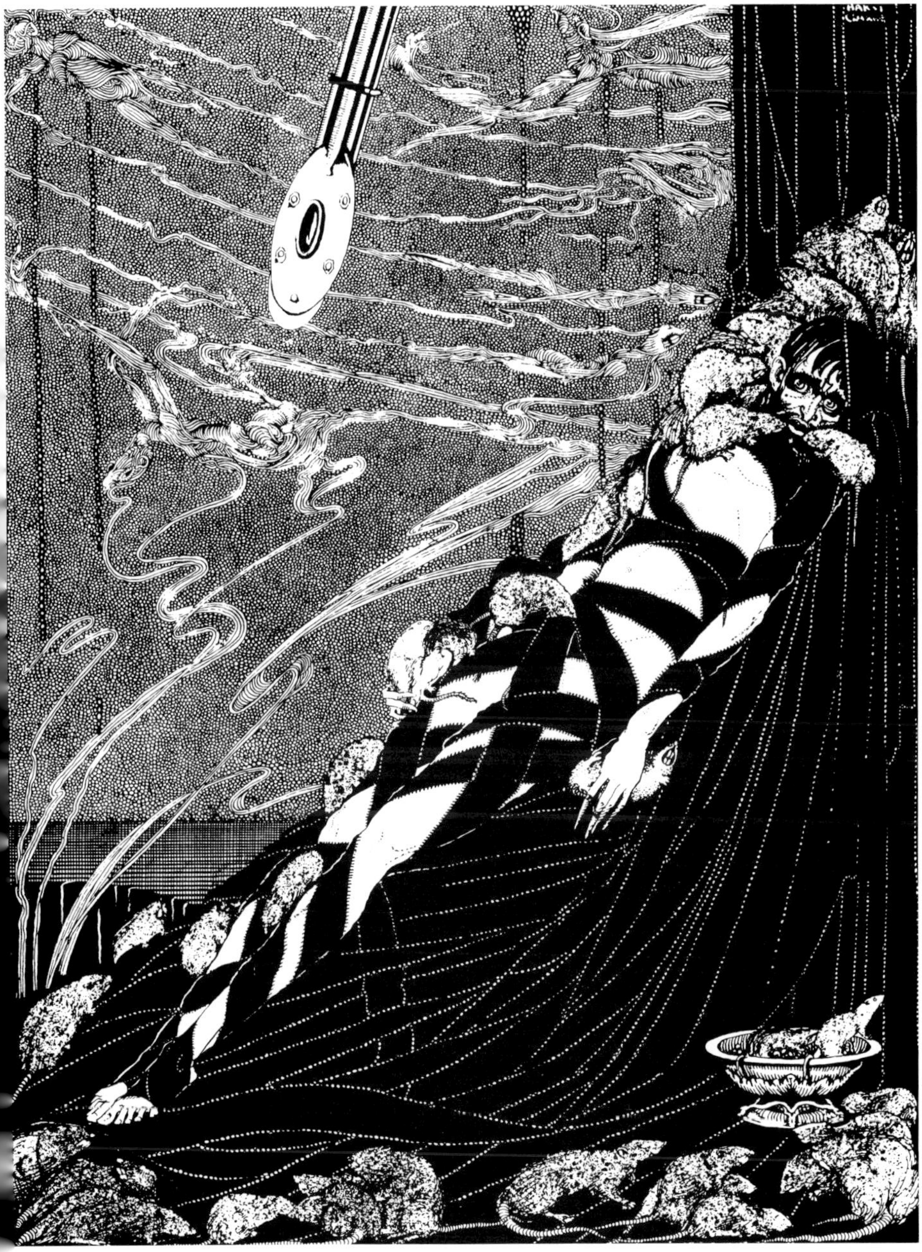

134 'I saw them fashion the syllables of my name', pen and ink illustration to Poe's 'The Pit and the Pendulum' in the 1923 edition of *Tales of Mystery and Imagination*

135 Cover design for Lennox Robinson's plays, pen and ink, 1923

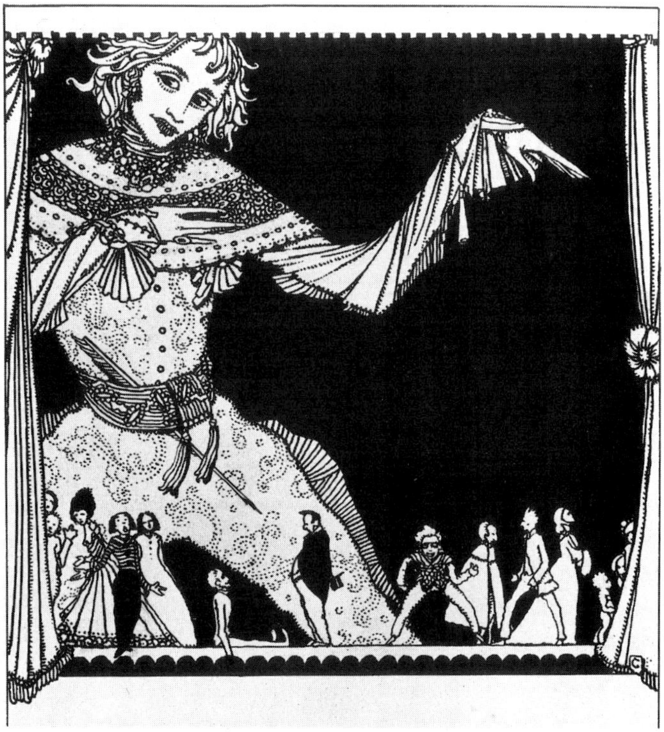

136 Austin O. Spare, *Portrait of the Artist*, 1907; an occult illustration by the co-editor of *The Golden Hind* and Clarke's co-exhibitor at the 1925 St George's Gallery exhibition, it depicts the idea of the creative artist's supernatural powers to transfer his energy into inanimate objects. The concept is embodied in Clarke's illustration of the dramatist and his characters in the cover design for Lennox Robinson's plays and in his vignette of Lizst composing the 'Vivace Scherzando' for his *Valse Impromptu in A Flat* (both 1923).

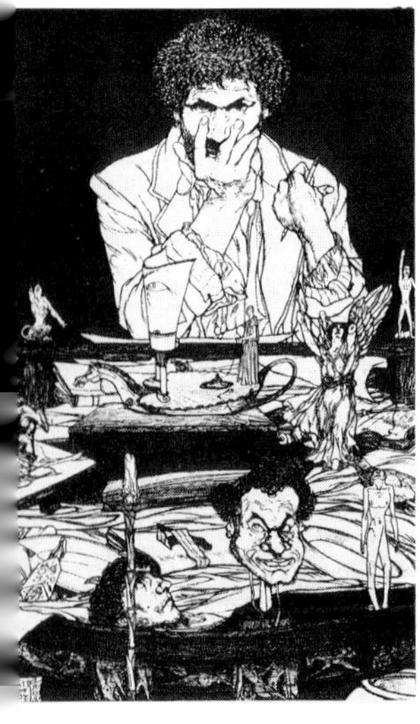

features the Hiberno-Romanesque church recently built to Butler's design at Newport, Co. Mayo, another a cowled monk drawing at a high desk. The chosen design (4" x 2") shows the garden front of the house Butler designed for himself at 73 Ailesbury Road in Dublin. It is a night scene and the lights of the house contrast with the inky sky. Two crinolined ladies and a frock-coated man occupy the foreground of the scene, which is framed by weeping willows and enclosed in a fluted border similar to that on the cover vignette of the *Dublin Magazine*. For Putnam's, the publishers, Harry designed a cover for the plays of Lennox Robinson, *Crabbed Youth and Age* and *The Round Table* which they published in 1924. Later, the same design was used by the Talbot Press in Dublin for other Robinson plays, including *The Whiteheaded Boy* and *The Blackbird* (1926). Preliminary drafts of this design indicate that he originally thought of a specific design for each play (an old woman and a baby under a round table; the same figures dancing on top of the round table) before producing the stylish and witty drawing of a stage framed by curtains, with a crenellated pelmet and footlights. The figure of the exotically dressed 'dramatist' directs the little creatures of his imagination in their antics before the footlights (fig. 135).[50] The composition anticipates a later programme cover which he made in 1925 for the Dublin Drama League. Another drawing from the same period and illustrating a similar concept (fig. 136) is in watercolour heightened by gold. It was done on 23 August 1923 after he had heard his friend Tilly Fleischmann of Cork play Lizst's *Valse Impromptu in A Flat* for him at her sister's house in Sutton. She had studied with Lizst's last pupil. Harry's little picture (5″ x 3½″), which he presented to her, shows Lizst's head and shoulders. He tears at his hair as he struggles with the composition — a tiny crinolined figure tied to his outstretched baton. Above, before a painted curtain a girl personifying the *Vivace Scherzando* dances on a black stage, naked except for the large cloak which billows behind her; her wild mop of hair is picked out in gold paint. The drawing is initialled and inscribed 'Franz Lizst *Vivace Scherzando* — Dublin'.

Harrap's published the new edition of Poe's *Tales of Mystery and Imagination* in time for Christmas, described in *The Bookman* as 'a new and handsome edition . . . with more of Mr Clarke's admirable and terrible illustrations'.[51] The publisher's announcement listed the eight new plates in colour and twenty-four full-page line drawings. The book was published at 21/- in cloth or at 31/- in antique leather. This edition had new cover and

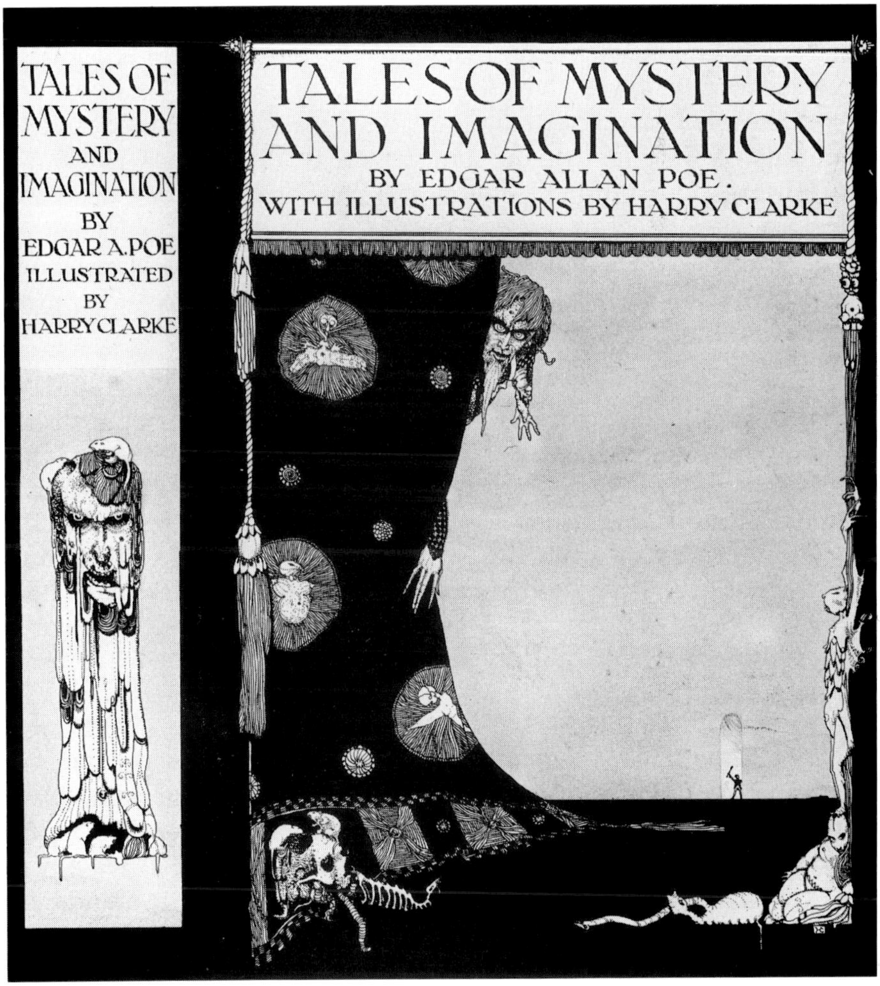

137 Jacket design for the 1923 edition of Poe's *Tales of Mystery and Imagination*, pen and ink and watercolour

jacket designs, the latter a grotesque and sinister scene arranged around a heavy curtain and its pole, a device Harry favoured in the early 20s (fig. 137).[52] This 1923 edition proved very popular and had already gone into a third printing by 1928.

The eight colour plates, which were printed separately from the text and tipped in on thick grey paper leaves, added a new dimension to Harry's illustrated *Poe*. They show an extraordinary advance in his graphic work and reflect the imagery he had been creating both in glass and on paper since he made the monochrome drawings four to six years previously. The subjects chosen for the colour plates were 'The Tell-Tale Heart' (plate 33), 'The Manuscript Found in a Bottle', 'Metzengerstein', which incorporates a self-portrait, 'Ligeia', 'The Fall of the House of Usher' (plates 34, 35), 'Man of the Crowd', 'The Mystery of Marie Roget', a reflection of the stylish 1920s in the costume and attitudes of its figures, and 'The Colloquy of Monos and Una' ('In death we have both learned the propensity of man to define the indefinable': plate 32), a Symbolist vision and one of his most beautiful illustrations, rich and sombre in colour.[53] The menacing precision of these plates, revealing the technique of a miniaturist, is sadly not reflected in the reproductions which, even by the standards of the time, are only average. The *Monos and Una* colour plate replaces a black and white design in the first edition, so, to make up the complement of illustrations, Harry made a new full-page illustration to 'The Pit and The Pendulum' as well as six new tailpieces.

The Special Winter Number of *The Studio* reproduced Harry's unpublished drawing of Poe's *M. Valdémar,* and M.C. Salaman wrote, comparing the Poe drawings to those for Perrault:

> Never before, I think, have these marvellous tales been visually interpreted with such flesh-creeping, brain-haunting illusions of horror, terror and the unspeakable. In black and white Mr Clarke sets pictures before us that glimpse for us fresh meanings in the tales and at the same time give us artistic satisfaction. Here is an unpublished design for the horrible ending of 'The Facts in the Case of M. Valdémar'and it is not so ghastly as the version in the book. Mr Clarke has a pen and ink style of his own and it is interesting to compare this with [the delicate fairytale idyll reproduced on the following page from the Perrault, *Riquet with the Tuft*].

Thomas Bodkin was appointed Irish correspondent of *The Studio* in the summer of 1923. He reported how much 'attention and admiration' Harry's exhibition at the Studios had attracted, and generally gave more prominent coverage to Irish art than it had previously had in the journal. He welcomed the advent of the new magazines, the *Irish Statesman* and the *Dublin Magazine,* and invited applications for the vacant post of director of the National Gallery of Ireland.

As lack of space at the Studios had become critical, especially as Walter and his family were now occupying 33 North Frederick Street, Harry negotiated the purchase of two houses across the street, Nos. 6 and 7, which had previously been a nursing home. The lower floors of these houses would provide the extra studio space needed, and the upper floors could be converted into self-contained flats. The extra demands on his time necessitated his resignation as teacher of design at the Dublin School of Art, where he was succeeded by his old friend Austin Molloy. On 11 December he wrote to Tilly Fleischmann:

> I move myself to my new studio quite soon and am involved in the beastly consequences of painting and carpentry work. The blooming house is full of workmen, although I was assured when purchasing that the houses were in perfect repair.[54]

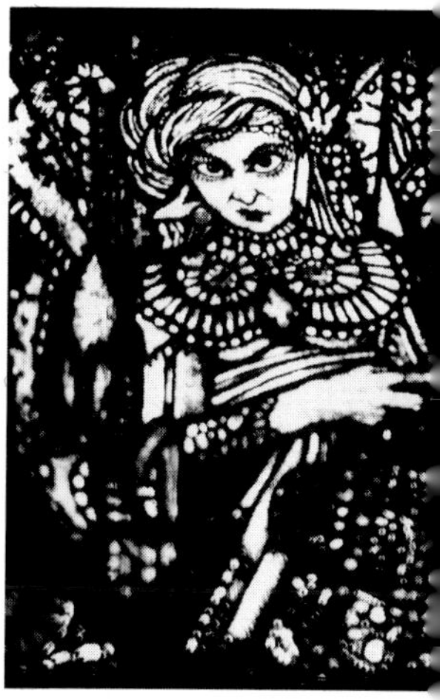

138 Judith's maid grimacing as she holds the head of Holofernes in a bag, detail from the *Blessed Virgin in Glory* in the Terenure lady chapel, 1923; a tiny detail on mauve glass from the rich tapestry of female Old Testament characters around the central figure

Because of the reorganization at the Studios the two windows commissioned in April by Canon Byrne for Balbriggan, one of which should have been installed in November, were delayed for several months, so that, on 19 March 1924, eleven months after the order had been confirmed, Harry had to write to his client:

> I do feel utterly ashamed of myself for not having your windows in by now. My only excuse is that we are transferring our Studios from 33 to 6 and 7 North Frederick Street and this has been a slow business, for we were hung up by Corporation committees, officials, dilatory contractors — in fact every conceivable form of brake has been applied to our efforts. I know you have not pressed me and I am duly grateful and this is really to say that your windows are drawn, the glass cut, the heads and hands painted and that the bulk of the work should be through in say another six weeks. Kind regards and renewed thanks for your patience.

Shortly after this Canon Byrne died and erection of the windows was further delayed as the commission had not been settled at the time of his death. However, all was eventually sorted out and these windows, which are among Harry's finest, were erected. When placing the order, worth £116, Canon Byrne had written:

> With much pleasure I give you the commission for the erection of the two stained glass windows measured by your brother last Saturday. The subjects you submit are admirable [*The Widow's Son* and *The Visitation*]. May I suggest for the altar beside the Sacred Heart *The Widow's Son* and for the altar beside Our Lady's altar the *Presentation* or *Visitation of the BVM* — whichever you prefer.[55]

Neither the cartoon nor the finished *Visitation* window (pl. 41) is dated, but it seems safe to date the two cartoons for both lights of the window in

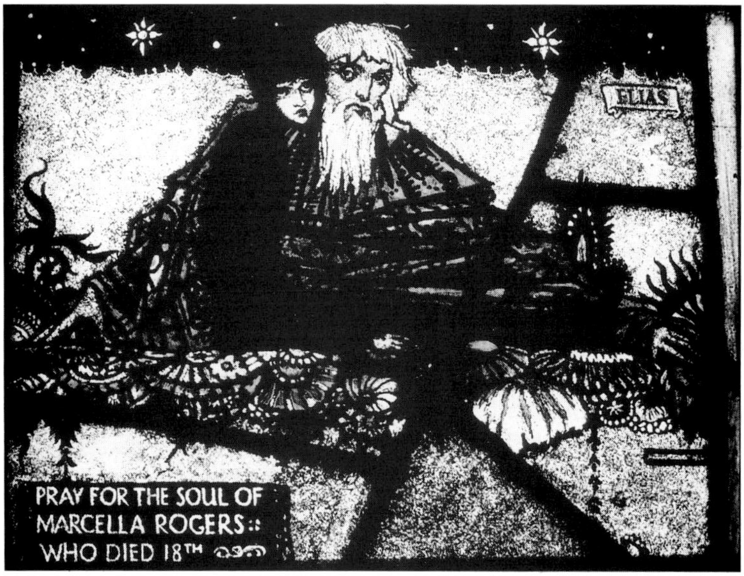

139 Elias and the revived child, predella panel painted, acided and stained on flashed blue glass, from *The Widow's Son*, Balbriggan, 1924

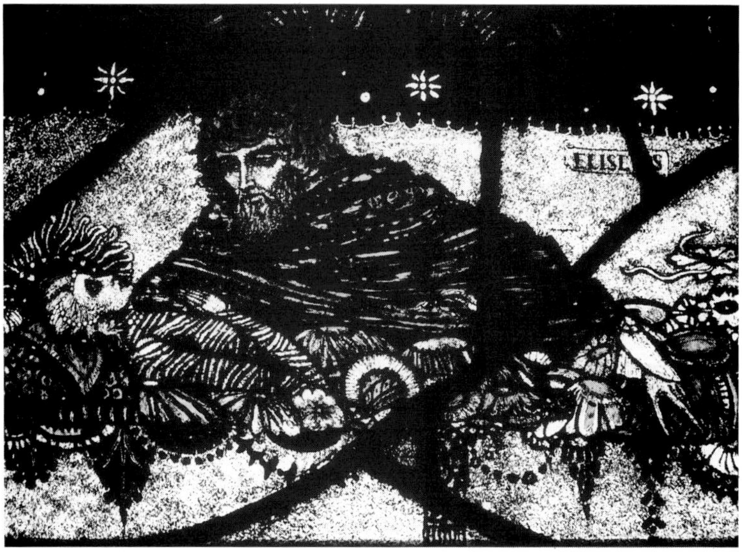

140 Eliseus reviving a figure, predella panel, painted, acided and stained on flashed ruby glass, from *The Widow's Son*

1923, as both are reproduced in the Studios' inset in 1924 *Catholic Directory*, which would have gone to press the previous November. These drawings, with their fine detail and coloured washes laid over a base drawing in pencil, are similar in technique to the Terenure lady chapel cartoons, and bear Harry's signature. The two slender lights, across which the design runs continuously, like Japanese pillar prints, show the elegantly dressed Virgin in profile on the left being greeted by St Elisabeth, also in profile, on the right; behind, Simeon peers out towards us. At the onion-shaped head of each light, sulky, decadent angels are poised on ornamental chariots among exotic details in miniature grisaille landscapes. The idiosyncratic treatment of the figures, their features, gestures, dress and symbolic settings and accessories here are very characteristically Harry's. At a first glance the window seems a delicate collage of finely cut jewels, lace and silk, set on a white-gold background, in the manner of the Honan Chapel *Our Lady* window, the overall design predominantly blue and gold (plate 41). In contrast the other window in Balbriggan, *The Widow's Son*, erected in memory of Marcella Rogers, and signed 'Harry Clarke 1924' is predominantly red and gold and has the same characteristic finely detailed painting as well as two arcane predella panels on heavily acided ruby and blue glass symbolizing resurrection (figs. 139, 140).

In the midst of all this turmoil, Harry still managed to design a 1923 Christmas card for himself, a small, delicate design 4" x 3½" of two angels beside a vesica containing a Madonna and Child with a halo of tiny interlaced leaves, set against a semi-circular lunette decorated with fine stripes, tendrils and floral ornaments (figs. 141). The card, signed 'Harry Clarke / 1923', was printed on handmade paper.

The end of the year was saddened by the death of his great friend and patron, Laurence Waldron, on Thursday 27 December, at his Killiney home. He was sixty-six, but his health had been failing for some time and he had not been able to attend his office for over a year. The *Irish Times* described him as 'one of the men whom Dublin circles most grieve over'.[56] His butler, Brown, broke the news of the death to Waldron's circle of close friends. Harry designed a memorial card (4½" x 3")[57] which depicts the view across Waldron's garden, over Killiney Bay to Bray, in an oval vignette; beneath a bowl of flowers, an extinguished candle, a book and a cross balance the words 'Missed by those few who loved his company'.

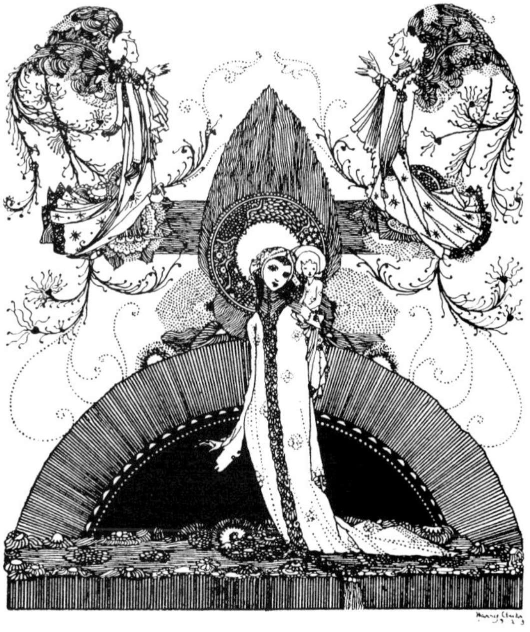

141 Christmas card, from a pen and ink design, printed on hand-made Irish paper, 1923

8

Clarke at the peak of his career, 1924 —
The success of The Eve of St Agnes *— His health deteriorates —*
Desire to escape to London — Election as Academician by the RHA

At the beginning of 1924 Harry Clarke was at the peak of his career, in both stained glass and illustration. However, his health was beginning to deteriorate, among the causes being the extreme pressure of work, the extra responsibility his father's death had put on him, and the upheaval in his life caused by the reconstruction of the Studios and the conversion of the two extra houses acquired in North Frederick Street. Nor was there any hope of a respite; in fact the next two years would be the busiest in his life.

In January he went to London; among other business calls, he travelled down to Sussex to Ashdown Park to meet Sr Bernard, Superior of the Convent of Notre Dame. Sr Bernard asked him to quote for the windows in the new chapel of our Lady and St Richard and introduced him to Mr Smart, the architect, who showed him the plans for the building. On his return to Dublin on 17 January he sent a proposal and an estimate of £1500 for seven two-light windows with traceries on the theme of *Scenes from the Life of our Lady with Emblems from her Litany*. A week later his tender was accepted, with the stipulation that the work be completed in eighteen months. He replied to Smart, 'I shall do my very utmost to produce a fine series of windows.'[1]

As Walter was unwell, he had to take charge of all work in the Studios, where he improved facilities by ordering a large kiln and by having iron frames fitted on which to assemble the glass, as well as having large north-facing windows fixed in the new premises to improve the lighting of the working areas. He employed one of his former art students, Millicent Girling, as an extra assistant, originally for a three-month trial period, and also engaged Austin Molloy to help him with cartoons, probably those required for a series of windows illustrating the *Life of Christ* at the Presentation Convent, Dingle. Added to this, he had discussed a further commission with Oliver Andersen of Harrap's, but the subject was not decided; this led to his declining a commission from Macmillan of New York and Padraic Colum for illustrations because he felt he could not meet the deadline they proposed.

New stained glass projects continued to come in. Lord Mayo invited him to visit Palmerstown to discuss a window for Kill church. He spent 9

February with Lord Wicklow discussing a further window for Shelton. The last of the cartoons for the Dingle windows were sent to Sr Ita and the architect R.M Butler early in February; the only modification they requested was in the face of our Lord. Sr Bernard of Ashdown Park ordered an additional three-light window for the memorial chapel tower which caused him to worry about time on the Ashdown Park work as this extra window could extend the time-scale by two to three months. He suggested making a pencil sketch for this new window when the others were being made, but Sr Bernard insisted that he do the tower window, *The Immaculate Conception with St Anne*, before the seven sanctuary windows, *Scenes from the Life of the Virgin*. He wrote that he needed exact templates first and that it would take him six weeks to clear a backlog of work before he would have a clear run at her commission. He was anxious, he wrote, to maintain a unified iconographic scheme, derived from Anna Brownell Jameson's *Legends of the Madonna as represented in the Fine Arts*.[2] He sent Sr Bernard this book, adding that 'the authoress is the most interesting and reliable source for sacred and legendary art that I know of'.[3]

The Dublin distillers, John Jameson and Sons, commissioned an illustrated booklet, *The History of a Great House*, as part of their contribution to the International Advertising Convention in London in July.[4] Harry designed the layout and twenty-one two-colour line illustrations to the text by Geoffrey Warren, which was subtitled 'The Origins of John Jameson Whiskey, containing some interesting observations thereon together with the Causes of its Present Scarcity'. The printing, by Maunsel and Roberts in Dublin, was so disappointing, particularly in the inaccurate two-colour register, that Harry specified, in the next job he did for Jameson's, that another printer should be used. However, as he did not draw in the second colour on the originals until the key blocks had been etched, the fault may not have been entirely the printer's.

The extra small lancet window made for the transept of Kilbride Church near Shelton was ready at the beginning of March and he despatched this with the bill for the *Resurrection* window, £250. In the three-light *Resurrection*, the figure of Christ in the centre light stands at the foot of a staircase, robed in ruby and crowned with thorns, bearing the palm of martyrdom. The ruby glass is carried into the border, into the side traceries where it is neither painted nor acided, and it is echoed in the medallion showing the Crucifixion in the centre of the rose tracery above. It is also used in the figure of Christ, which appears in each of the quatrefoil panels of the side lights which, set in rich borders of ruby, blue and green, seem inspired by medieval glass. A rich blue dominates four medallions showing miracles of the Lord; that in the lower right hand light features a self-portrait of the artist, a halo over his untidy hair, and huge eyes giving him a haunted look (plate 43) while, above, the resurrection theme is evocatively illustrated by the miracle of Lazarus. This window is much enhanced by the rough, unplastered wall in which it is set. The 'quite unique'[5] little window is an experiment in abstract glass by Clarke, and has no figurative elements. Lord Wicklow wrote of this, 'The small window above the door by Harry Clarke is made of scraps of glass he had left over — an experiment, he told my father'.[6] Harry described it in this way:

> It is an experiment that *has* come off and the first time I am near Shelton I shall call in to see it. . . . In the case of the transept window I have charged only for materials and the man's time fixing — my own time was not of great consequence and moreover I learnt a little on the experiment.[7]

The window is based on two large thick slabs of blue glass, which seem to shimmer amid the magenta and pink surrounding pieces. They are separated by a golden vesica containing a green circle. At the top of the lancet is a crimson circle. The background is a thick cobweb of lines on green, beige and clear glass. Harry had earlier used these thick 'Norman' or 'Early English' slabs in some of the Honan Chapel windows, particularly in those of *St Ita* and *St Gobnait* in emulation of current Arts and Crafts interests in these slabs' 'deliberately uneven texture and properties of intensifying light and colour', which 'emphasized the importance of materials as the basis for style'.[8] The two Shelton windows display a new freedom of approach in his glass: matts are washed on, stippled and badgered to give a rough even scratchy effect, chevrons are only suggested, and leaf and flower forms are simplified making the window appear unusually open and grainy. Perhaps the reason he waived his fee on the small window was that he hoped Lord Wicklow might

> say a word in my favour regarding the larger window in the left transept in St Patrick's [Cathedral in Dublin]. I am keen — superlatively keen — to do this work — it is the last window available in the finest structure of its kind in Ireland.[9]

In the event neither he nor his older contemporary from An Túr Gloine, Michael Healy, was given the commission in St Patrick's; the job went to Frank Brangwyn.

With the Ashdown Park commission in hand, Harry wanted to spend more time in London and, with the reconstruction work completed at the Studios, he felt Walter could manage the work in Dublin, assisted by Kathleen Quigley, Leo Cartwright, Philip Deegan and Millicent Girling as designers. He hoped, in collaboration with John Austen, whose graphic work he admired, to establish a London base, as he wrote to Bodkin:

> He and I are keen to start a stained glass show in London and, as I cannot 'swap horses crossing a stream', I must get my new show

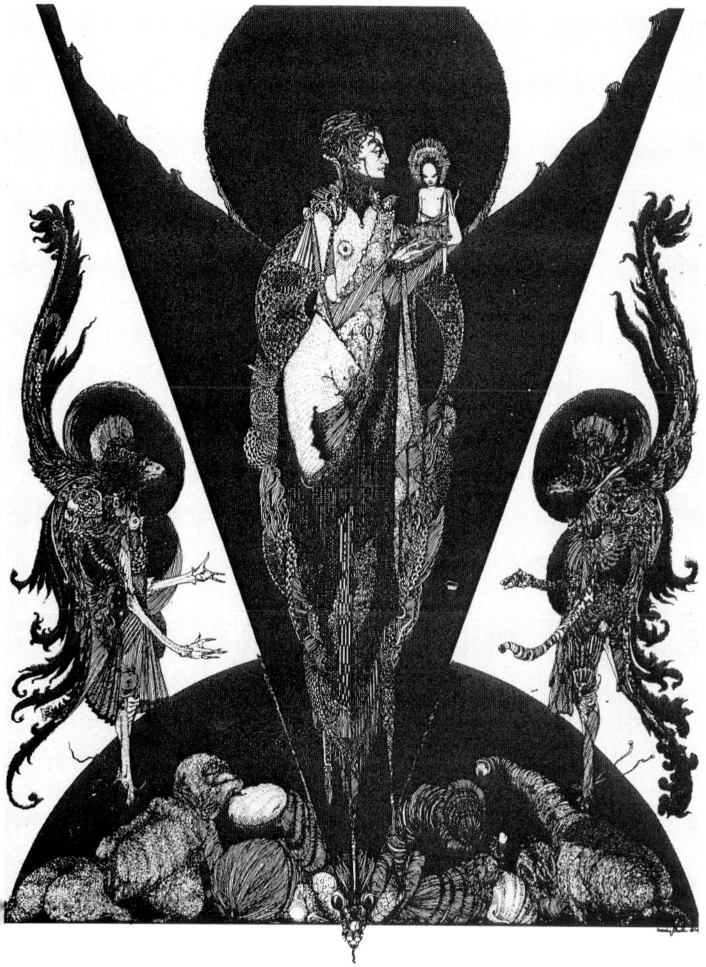

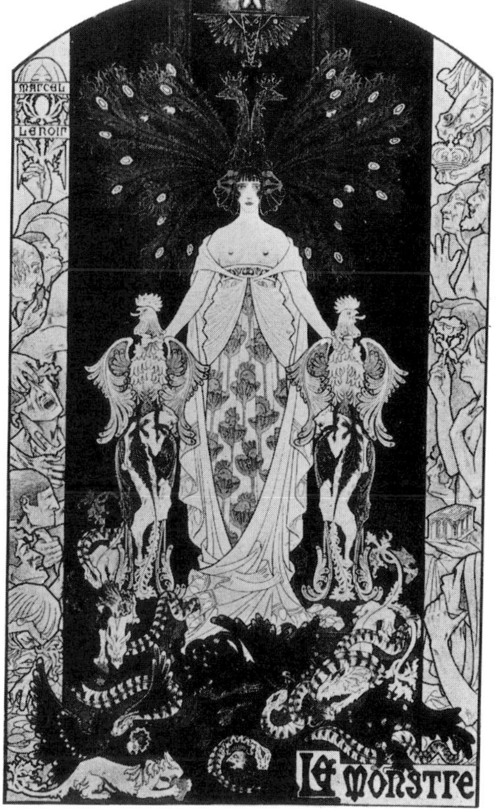

142 *The Devil's Wife and her Eldest*, pen and ink, reproduced in *The Golden Hind*, July 1924

143 Marcel Lenoir, *Le Monstre*, 1897; surely the source for the composition in Clarke's *The Devil's Wife*.

> running nicely here before our venture starts in London. Now I am driven here all the time and want Austen on this side to help me to get things going. You could tell him much more about me — my studios and my glass, and further about my purpose in being alive, than I could. . . . I would like you to see some of his originals and in his house he has some remarkable drawings by Odle which to me were of extraordinary interest. I think I told you that J. Austen started absolutely from scratch. Lordy — but I wish you were not a civil servant for with you as manager, my brother Walter as interviewer and traveller and Austen and I as designers and workers with a suitable staff — why we'd be rich in a few years.[10]

While John Austen was a successful illustrator,[11] he had no stained glass experience, and it is strange that Harry should have chosen him as his London partner. Austen was described at this period as 'the perfect

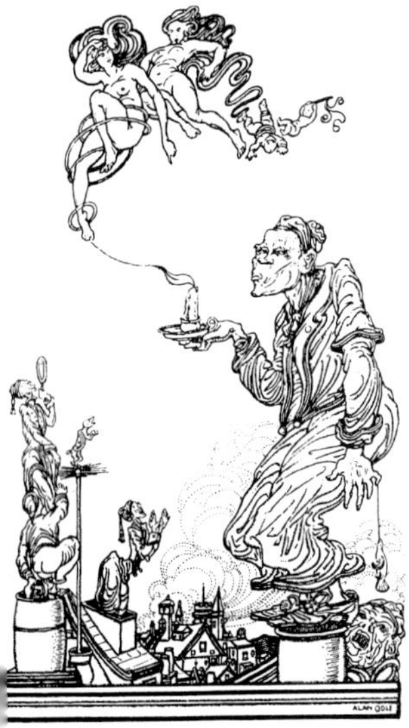

144 Allan Odle, pen and ink drawing reproduced in the July 1924 issue of *The Golden Hind*; John Austen, who with Odle and Spare exhibited with Clarke at the St George's Gallery in July 1925, also had a pen and ink drawing in the same issue

145 *The Eve of St Agnes*, stained glass window in two sections and twenty-two panels illustrating Keats' poem, 1923-4, Hugh Lane Municipal Gallery, Dublin

aesthete, precious, even in appearance, to the finger tips; and a trifle cynical . . . the long-haired studio exquisite' living in Regent's Park and still admiring Beardsley's 'static vitality'.[12] However, they were firm friends, and in July, with Austen's encouragement, Harry exhibited two drawings at the Graphic Arts Society's annual exhibition in London. A year later he was elected a member of the society. There are many similarities in the work of Clarke and Austen and it is interesting that a black and white drawing in the collection of the Victoria and Albert Museum, *Judith and Holofernes* (or *Salome and John the Baptist*) is catalogued as by Clarke while it is more likely by Austen.[13] Probably due to an introduction from Austen, Harry's drawing *The Devil's Wife and her Eldest* (fig. 142) was printed as the frontispiece to the July issue of the *Golden Hind*, the fifth issue of the short-lived quarterly of art and literature edited by Clifford Bax and A.O. Spare. This grotesque parody of an entranced Madonna[14] attended by plumed fiends like Balinese puppets (fig. 143) heralds a group of insidiously ambivalent drawings, drawn in intricate detail, the later examples on vellum, which Harry was to make during the remaining years of his life. The obsession with sexual grotesqueries (fig. 144) reflects a similar obsession evident in Beardsley's final years and Paul Klee's early, Beardsley-influenced, period (*c.* 1905).[15]

During March he supervised Philip Deegan's work on the six two-light windows for Dingle while, assisted by Kathleen Quigley, he was working on *The Eve of St Agnes* in a technique she could refer to in Bodkin's miniature panel, *The Song of the Mad Prince*. *The Eve of St Agnes* (fig. 145), which is signed 'Harry Clarke April 1st 1924', was made in two sections, each headed by a decorative lunette (plate 37) in which the leadlines are concealed by leafy fronds enclosing fantastic floral and marine images inside fascicled borders of green and clear glass, filled with tiny elfin and foliate forms. These lunettes were originally erected with the window in its original site in Ailesbury Road, Dublin, later set aside, but now restored to their original positions above the window. They are interesting as forerunners of the windows illustrating the Orders of Architecture which Harry designed in 1927 for Bewley's Cafe in Grafton Street, Dublin. A colour sketch exists for the lunettes with instructions in Harry's hand to Kathleen Quigley.

The nineteen preliminary pencil, watercolour and gouache drawings (figs. 146, 147) for the twenty-two panels in *The Eve of St Agnes* are in the Crawford Art Gallery in Cork, for which they were bought later in the year, together with six of the *Poe* designs, three in colour. The features of the figures throughout these drawings are delineated in detail, while the backgrounds are loosely filled in, indicating that in working on these panels Harry made precise definitions of the characters and their expressions, before allowing the glass to suggest the detailed effects of the background settings. Detailed drawings also exist for the fluted borders of the main

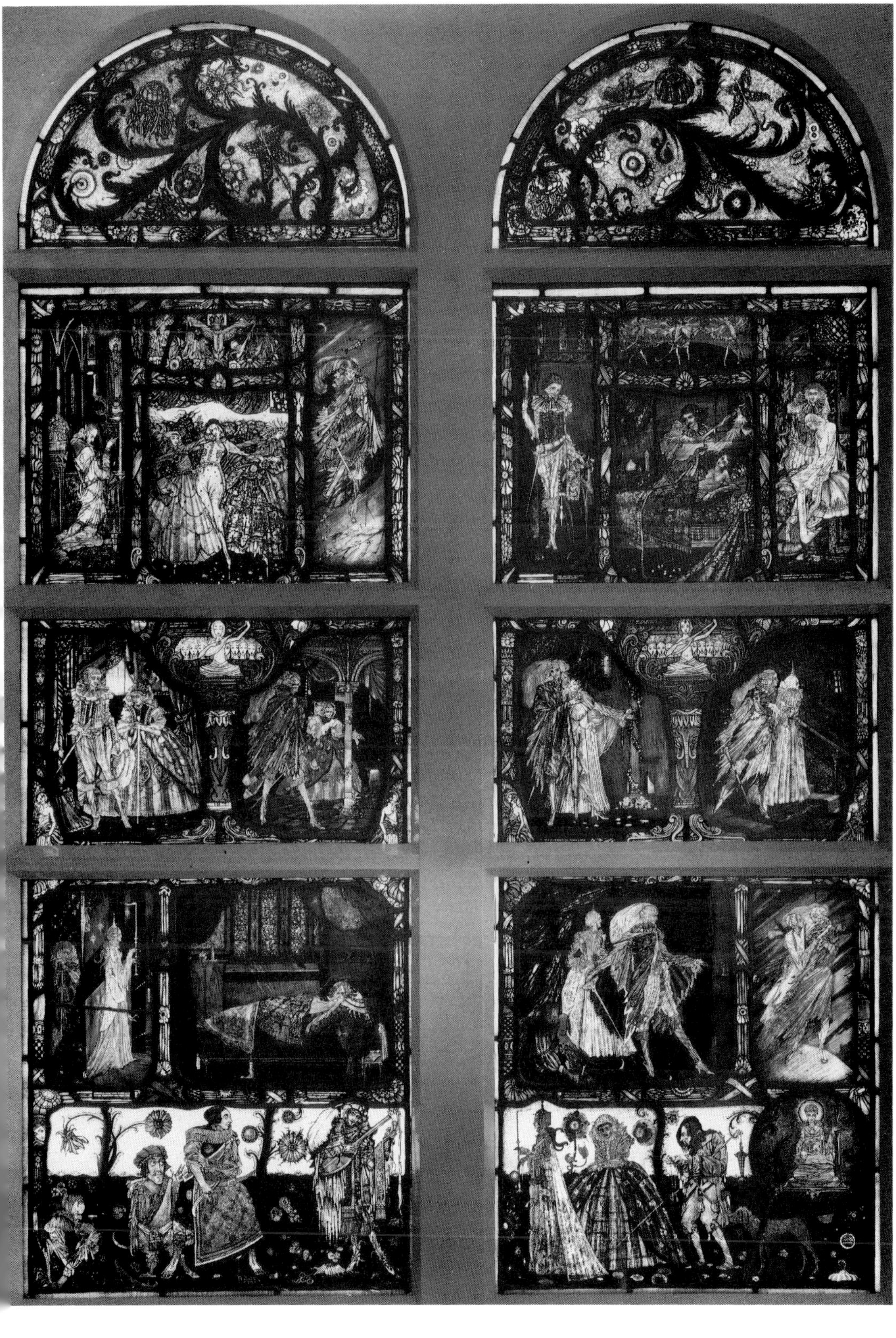

146 'Numb were the Beadsman's fingers / While he told his rosary . . .', pencil, watercolour and gouache design for a panel in *The Eve of St Agnes* window, 1923

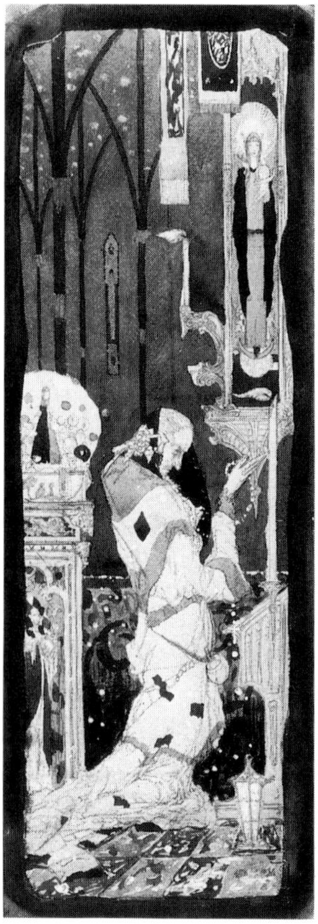

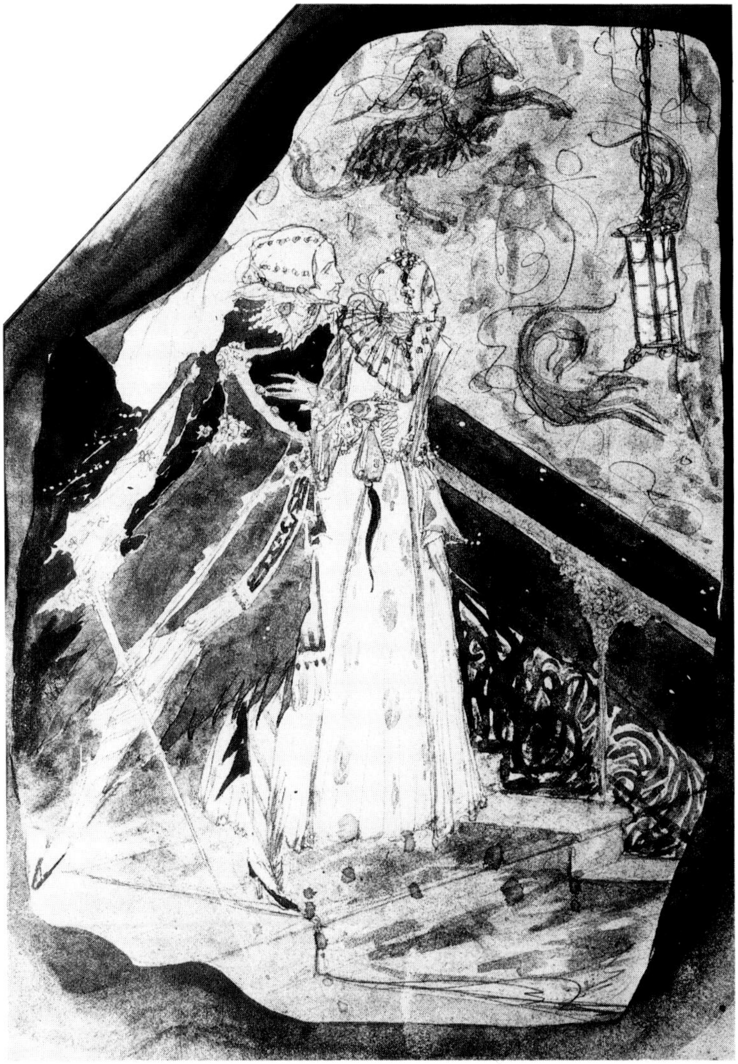

147 'The arras, rich with horseman, hawk and hound / Flutter'd in the besieging wind's uproar', pencil, watercolour and gouache design for the panel depicting the lovers' escape in *The Eve of St Agnes*, 1923

panels, bound with green ribbons and with miniature figures and grotesques.[16] The window is probably the finest expression of the technique which Harry made uniquely his own. He saw the commission as an opportunity to do something never done before. When placing the order, Harold Jacob had asked for 'something out of the usual run of domestic stained glass' and Clarke responded that he would use every method he knew on the whole surface of the window. Certainly, for the £160. 7s. 6d charged, the client received a work which expressed the full range of Clarke's artistry, both as illustrator and as artist in glass.

The Eve of St Agnes presents an extraordinarily evocative series of illustrations to Keats' poem [17], composed into a unified whole by the borders and other compositional devices which surround them (plate 36). The relevant passages from the poem are inscribed in minute script below the fourteen scenes they illustrate, beginning in the top left hand corner descending from left to right. This depicts the icy-cold Gothic chapel where

> Numb were the Beadsman's fingers,
> While he told his rosary. . . .

the first of a series of haunting images in shades of blue and jewel-like colour, in perfect harmony with the fancifully medievalizing romance of the poet's tale. At the base, running across each light of the window, a pair of panels in blue and ruby presents a curtain call of the characters from the poem, reading from left to right — a 'drunken wassailer', which is a small self-portrait of the artist, 'dwarfish Hildebrand', Lord Maurice, Porphyro, Madeline, old Angela, the Bloodhound and the Beadsman with, on the right, a small roundel of St Agnes seated cross-legged with her lamb, above a tiny roundel etched with the signature and a moonlit scene in which a witch and cat on a broomstick fly over a lighthouse.

The window created a sensation at the Aonach Tailteann art exhibition in August, where it won the trophy gold medal for arts and crafts and art industries. The *Irish Times* of 11 August wrote that it was exciting

> the eager admiration of visitors, many of whom return again and again to examine its wonderful qualities . . . . At first glance a revel in blue, study of the details brings out, one by one, the many beauties which go to make one beautiful whole — the tiny yellow light of a flickering candle, for example.[18]

And Bodkin commented in *The Studio*,

> It is executed in the technique which Mr Clarke has made peculiarly his own — superimposed panels of different coloured glass, flashed and stained to produce an effect of microscopic delicacy and dazzling richness of hue.[19]

THE EVE OF ST AGNES

Key to the narrative panels

1 Numb were the Beadsman's fingers,
While he told his rosary . . .

2 At length burst in the argent revelry
With plume, tiara and all rich array (plate 38)

3 Meantime, across the moors,
Had come young Porphyro

4 Behind a broad hall-pillar, far beyond
The sound of merriment and chorus bland

148 'Awake! Arise! my love, and fearless be, / For o'er the southern moors I have a home for thee', stained glass panel from *The Eve of St Agnes*, 1924

149 'Ages long ago / These lovers fled away into the storm', stained glass panel from *The Eve of St Agnes*, 1924

5 Follow me child, or else these stones
Will be thy bier . . .

6 Madeline, Saint Agnes' charmed maid (plate 39)
Rose, like a mission'd spirit, unaware
With silver taper's light, and pious care

7 Full on this casement shone the wintry moon,
And threw warm gules on Madeline's fair breast, (plate 40)

8 These delicates he heap'd with glowing hand

9 She still beheld,
Now wide awake, the vision of her sleep (fig. 148)

10 'Tis dark; quick pattereth the flow-blown sleet
This is no dream, my bride, my Madeline!

11 Awake! Arise! My love, and fearless be,
For o'er the southern moors I have a home for thee.

12 The arras, rich with horseman, hawk and hound,
Flutter'd in the besieging wind's uproar

13 The key turns, and the door upon its hinges groans

14 Ages long ago
These lovers fled away into the storm (fig. 149).

In autumn 1924, Harry was elected an associate of the Royal Hibernian Academy, which established him firmly in the world of Irish art. Earlier in the year, just after the *St Agnes* window was finished, his wife had held her first public exhibition of paintings, which included her portrait of Joshua (fig. 89). About the same time Harry had to defend his father's reputation in a reply to a Senate speech by W.B. Yeats on the relationship of the arts to industry, in which the poet had stated, speaking of the progress of the revival in stained glass,

> About twenty years ago . . . the stained glass made in Ireland was the worst in the world. Now some of the best glass in the world is turned out in Dublin. Then the maker of the worst glass in the world was a Dublin man named Clarke; now the acknowledged best glass in the world is made by his son Harry Clarke.[20]

Harry wrote to defend

> the genuine effort my father made to do good stained glass in this country, which efforts were in the nature of spade work of which his successors have, and are, reaping the benefit. . . . Nobody could be more aware of the shortcomings of some of the work which left here at one period than I am, but I say in all sincerity that the very worst which left here was superior to the best work turned out of other

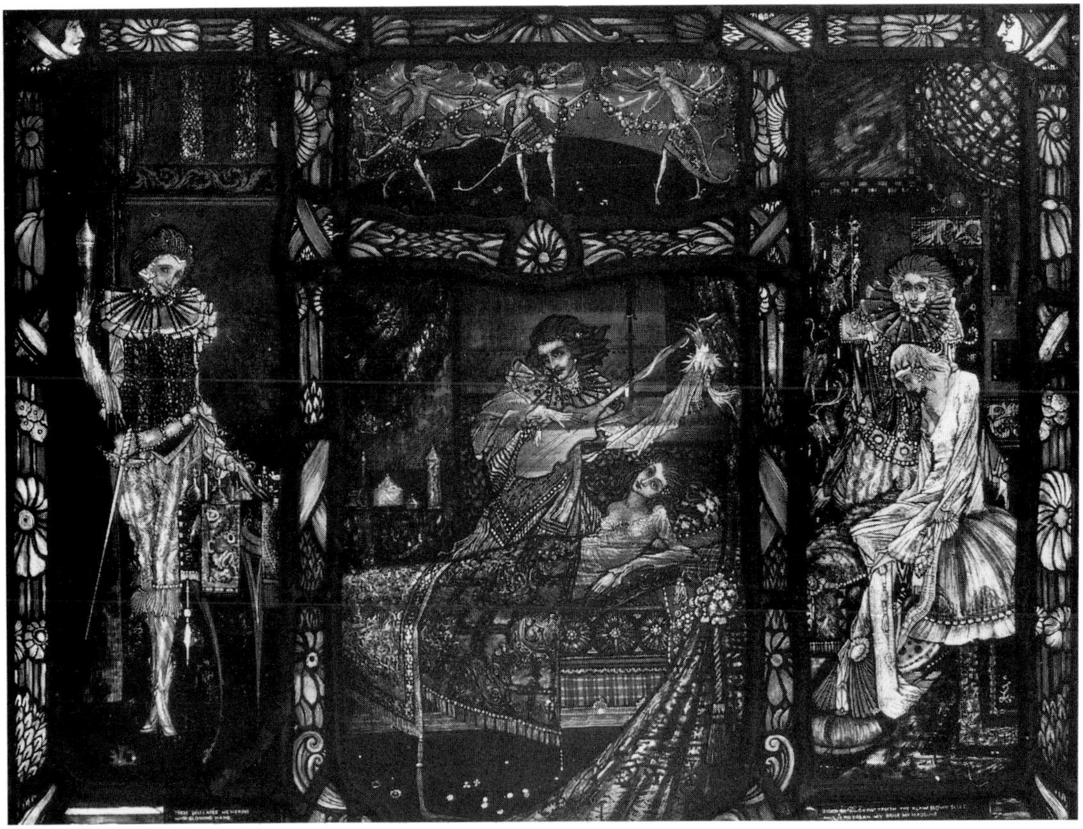

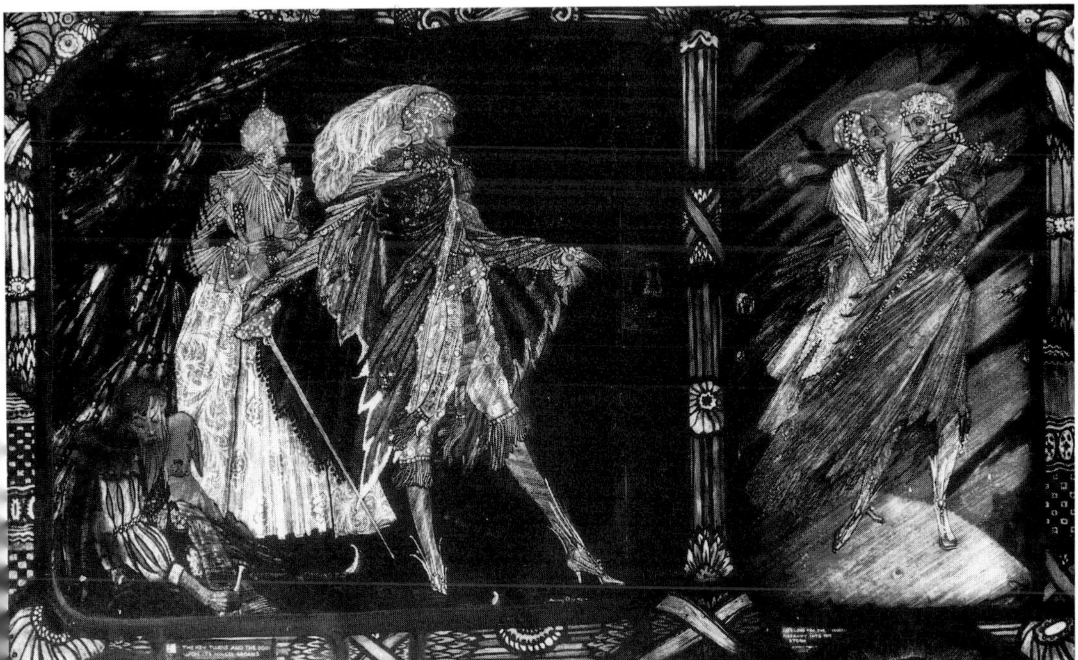

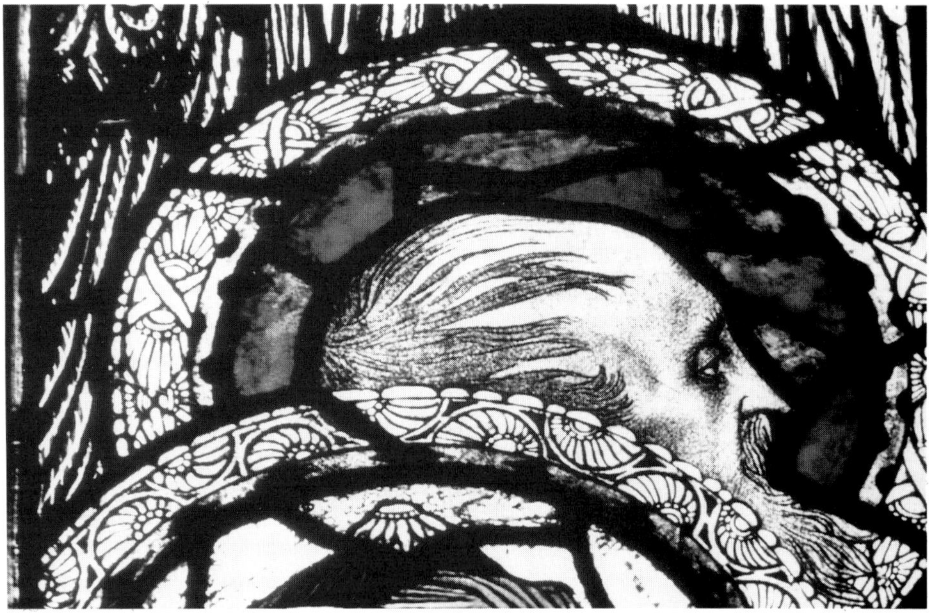

150 Detail of the head of one of the Three Wise Men from *The Nativity* window, Dingle, 1924

> houses in Ireland during that period. . . . I am most grateful for your recognition of my efforts, the success of which is due to a very real desire always to do my best, backed up by the fine knowledge of the technique of stained glass which I learned from my father. . . . In common with many others I recognize fully the value of your word and influence to applied art and I am duly grateful for all you can and have done for us here in Ireland.[21]

Later in the year he was again in correspondence with Yeats, this time to enlist his support of an application to the Fiscal Enquiry Committee to have a twenty per cent import tariff levied on 'completed or partly completed continental' stained glass coming into Ireland. He also had to defend his stand on the prices charged by the Studios, which were higher than those of his competitors, because he felt it necessary to work with materials of the highest quality if he were to 'produce stained glass of a very high standard with very skilful workers and lavish raw materials'.[22]

Although the Studios were responsible for most of the work on the Dingle windows, which were fixed in time for the consecration ceremony on the second Sunday in April, this series of six pairs of lancets is notable for some passages either worked or directed by himself. These include a sensitively painted head of the oldest King in the *Nativity* light (fig. 150), the head of John in the *Baptism* scene, details in the bizarre Gethsemane tableau showing the comatose disciples engulfed in exotic flowers, and a tiny pinnacled city set on a cliff, gazed at by a minute company of elegantly robed pilgrims. Most of the background quarries are painted with elaborate flowered lacework patterns, and generally the treatment of these windows displays the use of clear bright colours and a deft linear precision.

The major stained glass commission in hand at this time was the series for Ashdown Park, for which Harry sent Sister Bernard an initial design for the three-light tower window, to represent *The Immaculate Conception*, on 11 April. He had also commenced work on the sanctuary windows, but was waiting for inscriptions for these. Sister Bernard approved the *Immaculate Conception* sketch design quickly while suggesting amendments to the hands and to the heads, for she did not like the elongated features which Harry so often drew, a fact he had to keep in mind when he designed the other Ashdown Park windows. By 30 April he had completed the *Immaculate Conception* cartoon, except for the base, where the vent measurements were still unresolved. He suggested Sister Bernard hang the cartoon on the wall to view its proportions as, due to the length of the ultimate window, any other viewpoint would present a foreshortened, distorted view.

Harry saw the Ashdown Park job as the key to success in London, for the location was near the city and should consequently attract considerable attention. As he wrote to Sr Bernard, he was more than usually interested in the scheme, and the drawings and cartoons were sent backwards and forwards between Dublin and Sussex to receive the comments of his most demanding-ever client. The work took much of his time and energy for the next year, so that other jobs fell behind, among them a two-light window for Knock in Co. Mayo, *Christ with the Woman of Samaria* and a five-light *Ascension* at Cloughjordan, Co. Tipperary, for which his quotation had gone to the Bishop of Killaloe in October 1923. Pressure of work led to an unfortunate exchange with a Mr M.J. Kerner Greenwood of Vyse Court in Bishop's Stortford, who wanted twelve drawings similar in style to those in the booklet for Jameson's Whiskey, as well as some stained glass for his billiard room. Harry suggested inserting small abstract decorative panels or scenes of St Swithin and eventually sent the sketches for four ideas on 28 June. These were returned with adverse comments on 5 July, and the work did not go ahead. To another enquiry, from a Mr Frick in Essex, he replied,

> I have only one piece of domestic stained glass in London and it I have not had photographed. It can be seen any time during office hours at the Fire Offices Committee, Watling Street. The general opinion of this panel is [that] it is superior to the twenty odd panels by different Studios operating in England.[23]

Sadly, both this window (of 1922) and Harry's decorative panel in the Hibernian Fire and General Insurance building in Dublin have vanished with the buildings in which they were sited.

A gas strike in May added to his difficulties and meant that parcels of flesh tinted glass had to be sent over to Hetley's to be fired. Nevertheless he completed the scale drawing and colour scheme for the Cloughjordan window, a five-light showing *The Ascension with Five Irish Saints and Sts Michael and James* rather than the five subjects initially discussed with the client, for which he had sent an alternative scale drawing. The Bishop accepted his advice and the Studio staff were set to work on the job, while Harry worked at the designs for Knock and for the long narrow Dempsey Memorial lancet window at Lusk, Co. Dublin. This was to represent the old Irish saint Maculind, whom he portrayed in a striking small but detailed colour design, juxtaposing clear quarries with the deep blue slabs which had almost become his trademark.[24] He wanted to get ahead with the drawings Harrap expected for their proposed illustrated English edition of Goethe's *Faust*, but wrote that he was 'anxious to make a good dummy and plan the book more carefully than I have done before'.[25] He had also finished in April a series of mural decorations for St Mary's, Haddington Road, Dublin, showing angels hovering amidst eucharistic emblems, painted on fine canvas in pastel shades of jade, salmon, pink, blue, ochre and grey tempera (fig. 151).[26] Similar muted colours occur in a design dated June 1924 for mural decoration of the chancel arch in St Michael's, Ballinasloe, Co. Galway, depicting *Our Lady, St John and two Angels attending the Trinity*, where the hieratic Father is robed, wearing a pontifical crown, above the Dove of the Holy Spirit and the figure of Christ on the Cross.[27]

151 Angel, fragment from the mural decoration formerly in the chancel, St Mary's, Haddington Road, Dublin, tempera on canvas, 1924 (courtesy of the National Gallery of Ireland)

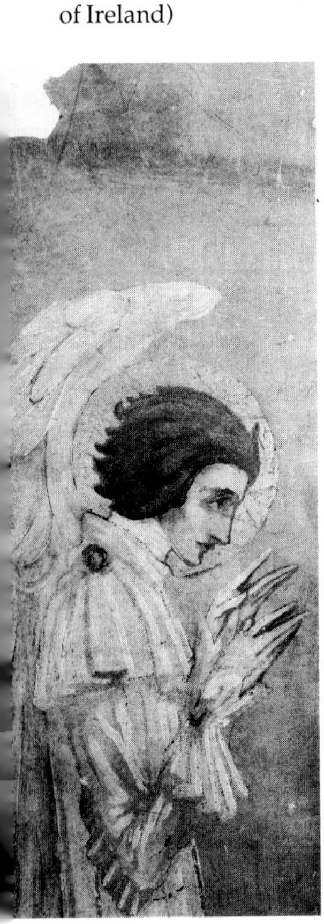

Despite the fact the Studios now had thirty-five employees, who all worked a sixty-hour week, Harry had to decline an additional window for Donnybrook parish church:

> We regret it would be impossible for us to have this window completed under twelve months. There are so many orders before it, and of course they must be taken in rotation.[28]

However, he was prepared to make exceptions for longstanding patrons, and agreed to make a window for the Countess of Gainsborough, sister of Major Dease, at the family chapel at Exton Park in Rutland, to whom he wrote:

> Now I am keen and anxious to do it for you and propose the following for your kind consideration. After you have sounded the other members of the family and know the sum available, if you come to me I would see what could be done. The window is fine for the subject (Blessed Oliver Plunkett and Blessed Thomas More) and as well I would like to repay you for all the kindness and interest you have given me — in the only way in which I can make a return — by means of my work.[29]

His own graphic work also had to be fitted in where possible. In July he was invited to illustrate a piece for *Good Housekeeping* — 'Women Voters and the Death Penalty' by Clemence Dane — and replied to the editor:

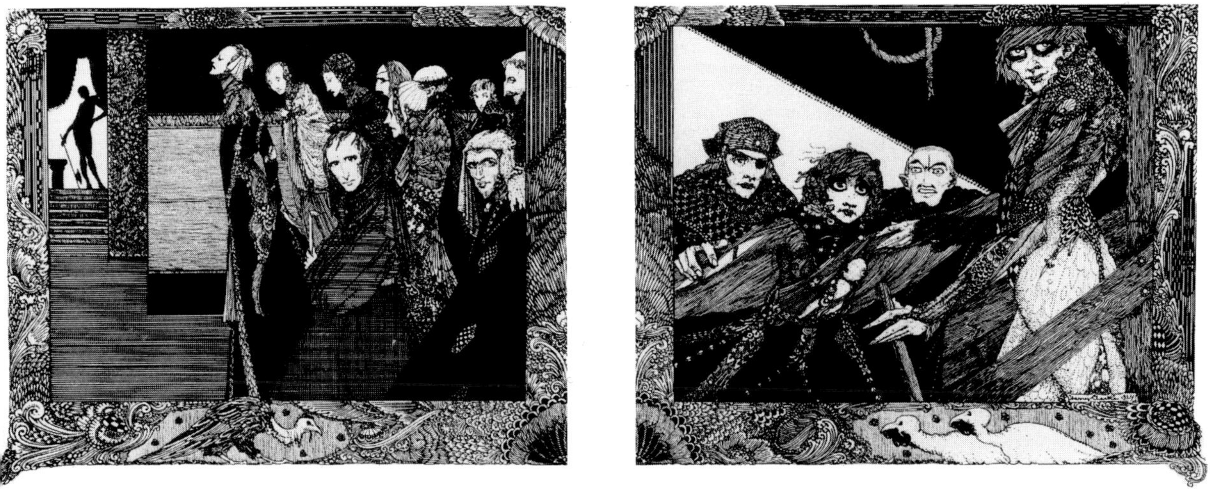

152 Pen and ink double-page illustration to Clemence Dane's 'Women Voters and the Death Penalty', published in *Good Housekeeping*, November 1924

> I have so far not done very much work for magazines, my principal reason being that work of this kind I found was usually required in a very great hurry. I would however be glad to contribute to your Journal and would ask you to consider the sum of twelve guineas and the original to be returned to me as a fair offer. If you consider this, I will be obliged if you will let me have the manuscript and date that the drawings are required and any other particulars you may think necessary.[30]

On agreement, he set the deadline at the end of July, but did not in fact finish the illustrations — which would appear around and above the text across a double spread — until 13 August, but still in time to appear in the November issue. These two pen and ink drawings, each within its geometrically floriated and grotesque border, make a graphically theatrical accompaniment to the writer's plea for women's rights and the abolition of the death penalty (fig. 152), the characterization of the dramatically contrasting figures, especially their faces and gestures, being idiosyncratically Clarke's. A more restrained design, similarly idiosyncratic but apt and spread over a double-page layout, illustrated 'The Portrait', a poem by Thomas Hardy; this appeared in the December issue of *Nash's and Pall Mall Magazine* (fig. 153). It incorporates devices from his earlier Poe and Perrault illustrations while anticipating features of the *Faust* and Jameson Whiskey designs.

At the art exhibition held as part of the huge Aonach Tailteann in August, where he showed the *Eve of St Agnes* window to such acclaim, he also won silver medals for his mural scheme for Ballinasloe, for a group of black and white drawings which included Bodkin's *The Mad Mulrannies* and eight *Poe* illustrations, also for the preliminary studies for *The Eve of St Agnes*, the cartoons for the Balbriggan *Visitation* and Ashdown Park *Immaculate*

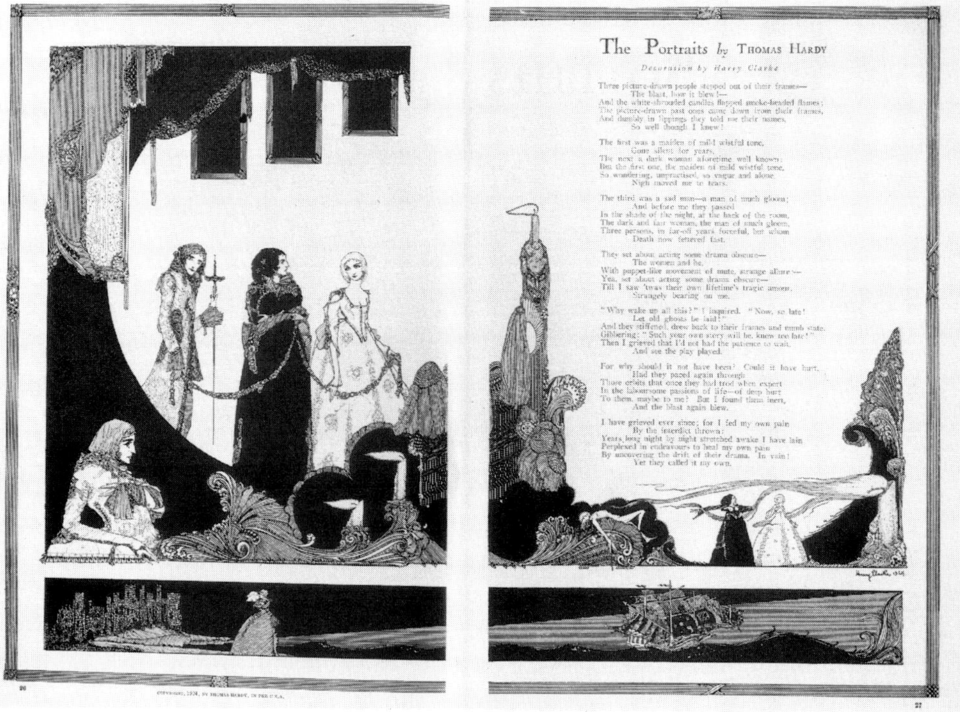

153 Pen and ink double-page illustration to Thomas Hardy's poem 'The Portrait', published in *Nash's and Pall Mall Magazine*, December 1924

Conception and for a set of colour illustrations selected from the Perrault and the Poe series.

Towards the end of July he had 'got badly knocked about'[31] as a result of an accident in which he was thrown from his bicyle, but continued to work at the frenzied pace that had become a condition of his life so that, in August, according to Walter 'it was found necessary to pack him off . . . as he had worked himself almost to a standstill'.[32] He informed *The Studio* that he had nothing to submit for their 1924 Year Book of Decorative Art as most of his glass was ecclesiastical and he did not think it would be of interest. 'Need I add', he wrote, 'had I any domestic work I would have been very glad to have it reproduced.'[33] He decided to spend about two months in London to meet old friends and follow up contacts which he wished to pursue. He took with him a commission for a memorial window to his former patron, Sir Egerton Coghill, at St Barrahane's in Castletownshend. In London he rented a studio in St John's Wood where he could work, and he also made plans to exhibit his work the following year in a group show with John Austen, Allan Odle and A.O. Spare at Arthur Howell's St George's Gallery off Hanover Square.[34]

He worked at jobs whose clients had been promised his own work. These were sent over by Walter — windows in the chapel of St Mary's, Belcamp, Dublin, and the mortuary chapel at Phibsborough, and cartoons for several of the Ashdown Park windows, which, however, he took the precautions

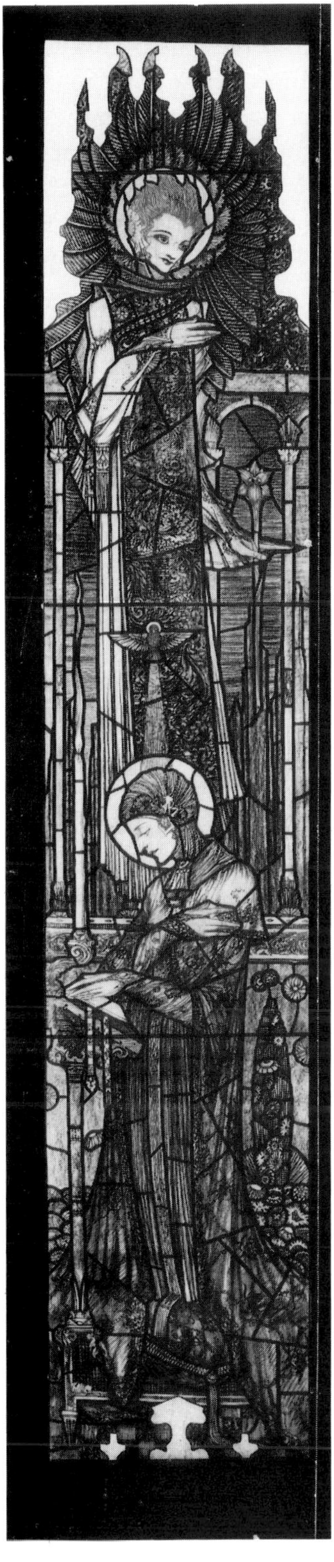

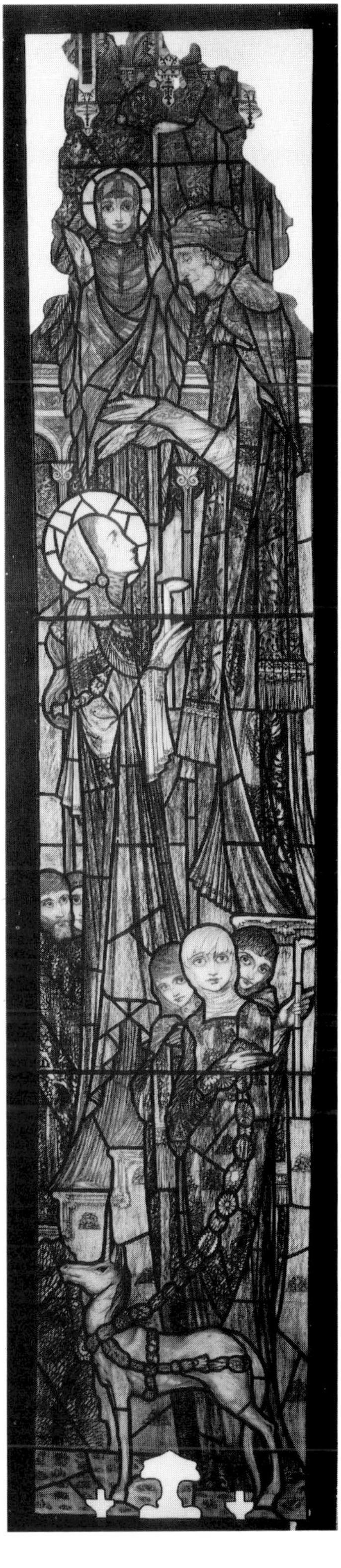

154 Cartoon for *The Annunciation* window, Convent of Notre Dame, Ashdown Park, 1924

155 Cartoon for *The Visitation* window, Ashdown Park, 1924, featuring the stylized hands, Virgin's face and the unicorn which Clarke managed to retain despite objections of sending back to Dublin so that Walter could forward them to Sr Bernard, rather than have her discover how close at hand he was to East Grinstead in his London studio. He felt unable to submit work for the extensive Exposition des Arts Décoratifs et Industriels being planned for the following spring in Paris, for financial reasons and for lack of suitable secular work available. The London interlude restored his spirits and he wrote to Bodkin early in October, 'I am doing well — very fit and the work comes nicely — not easily which I suppose is as it should be. I may be back by the . . . end of this month'.[35]

There was no respite when he did return to Dublin. Sr Bernard's criticism of the face, halo and wings of the angel in *The Annunciation* cartoon (fig. 154) had to be dealt with firmly, and Harry pointed out that no design on paper could ever adequately represent the effect of the glass *in situ*. She also objected to the 'emaciated' face of the Virgin in *The Visitation* (fig. 155) and to the elongated hands, and took a particular dislike to the Unicorn which Harry had included in the drawing and which he was loathe to remove. Other new commissions awaited on his return a series of two-light windows for Monsignor d'Alton at Ballinrobe, Co. Mayo, and another series of two-lights for the Catholic Church at Carrickmacross, Co. Monaghan. Two stained glass portraits of General Mulcahy, one rectangular, one oval, were ordered as a result of his work on the Griffith and Collins memorial book.

Two fine pen-and-ink drawings which appear on the Studios' 1925 *Catholic Directory* inset were made at this time, one of the Lourdes apparition to Bernadette, the other of St Rose of Lima, from which he used a detail for his Christmas card.[36] He also drew a headpiece for the inset, showing a cathedral, drawn in much freer style than the other two designs.

The third pair of Ashdown Park cartoons, sent on 10 November, showing *The Visitation* and *The Espousal*, were, much to his surprise, accepted by Sr Bernard except for the detail of the High Priest's face. He had also made up his dummy for the *Faust* book and begun work on the illustrations. He declined to advise Jameson's with their advertisements and felt he could not undertake a set of drawings for a further booklet they proposed before May 1925, but if they were in a great hurry he would try to find the right people to do the letterpress and the drawings. However, as Jameson persisted, he did supply nine pen and ink drawings in January for a planned brochure, granting them the copyright but insisting on the return of the original drawings after the blockmaker had finished with them.

E.M. O'Rorke Dickey, the art master at Oundle School in England,[37] wrote through Bodkin to ask if Clarke would collaborate with him on a series of windows for the school chapel and received a most enthusiastic response to the proposal. On 24 November Harry wrote that two forms of collaboration seemed possible. One was that Dickey would do a colour sketch, full-sized drawings and cutlines, which could be sent to the Studios and the very utmost that experts can do will be done to carry out the ideas embodied in your coloured drafts and cartoons — but I do not come in — in any capacity — other than that of a worker who is endeavouring to carry out another artist's ideas.

In this arrangement the windows would be entirely Dickey's. Alternatively Harry proposed that

> You produce the drafts and cartoons with me (we can fight every inch of the way), then we both deal with the raw material — arranging of the glasses, cutting, aciding, painting, staining, firing, second painting and leading. I will willingly impart to you all I know of the craft, you will be fresh on the work — we may strike new ideas. For designing and cartooning stained glass and not working in the material, and not having a good working knowledge of the craft is a rotten affair — no fun in it at all — and if when things do not turn out well one does not know quite how to set them right, besides the craft is a never-ending source of interest — and the best work is done by the man who designs, arranges and paints his own glass. . . . If we agree to carry out the second idea of collaboration it means a Studio in which to carry out the work — these are already here and available for you at any time — if on the other hand you are anxious to carry out the second idea of collaboration and not come to Dublin, obviously some other arrangement will have to be made. I have an enormous pressure of work here — but would be willing to discuss the possibility of opening Studios in England — in view of this present commission.

He planned to meet Dickey when he would be in England in January and discuss the project, which he found enormously exciting, and perhaps the much-desired opportunity to extend his work to an English base.[38] However, at home, the full responsibility of the Studios had again fallen on him as Walter was sick. He saw to the erection of the windows at Lusk — the *St Maculind* and the nine lancets which had been made to his designs. Clients all too often had ideas at variance with his, such as the rector in Jersey who disliked the 'eye' emblem in his window, or the parish priest of Ballylooby who was doubtful about the *St John the Baptist* design where Harry had shown Salome being presented with the Saint's head, above a decapitation scene in miniature. This client also felt the ornamental background of richly toned glass was inferior to one with figures, to which Harry replied:

> This is in no respect an inferior material — but *veritable* stained glass produced in exactly the same manner as our other work. We have successfully carried through commissions in it for the Earl of Wicklow, Lusk, Belcamp and are at present making eight windows for

Phibsborough. It will *not* look patchy or incomplete.[39]

The eight windows in the mortuary chapel at Phibsborough are perhaps Harry's most successful stylized floral motif designs. The eight lights are arranged as four two-light windows, each headed by a quatrefoil tracery light containing a large, untreated slab of amber glass. The irregularly thick, richly coloured glass is leaded in small cutlet pieces into an unusual jigsaw, providing a richly textured window which is almost as interesting viewed from outside.[40] Each light contains two tiny vesicas depicting symbols of the Passion and a Station of the Cross painted in shades of yellow stain.

Windows for Ballinrobe and Belcamp were at the drawingboard stage and for these drawings Harry seems to have developed a new technique to suggest the coloured effects he sought in glass. This is first seen in the design for the two-light *Sts Malachy and Brendan* at Belcamp. The openings are fluently drawn in ink on buff-toned tracing paper and the colours loosely washed in with watercolour and body colour, then overglazed with coloured inks. The effect is richer and seems more translucent than in the earlier minutely detailed watercolour studies or splodged colour notations and, accompanied by an detailed inch scale drawing in pencil, would have given a good idea of the job to the client.[41]

Although Harry designed a letterheading for himself at this time set in type rules, plain and decorated by a chevroned border, with widely spaced type, printed in black and yellow on a cream paper, he modestly regarded it as 'an amateur idea'.[42] He therefore decided to consult the noted designer Ashley Havinden[43] in London about stationery for the Studios. He sent Havinden his 'own small design for envelopes, which I considered at the time was too fine for that special purpose'.[44] Havinden produced a three-line typographical heading, incorporating a small vesica of Harry's design, which was printed at the Curwen Press.

While in England at the end of January 1925 he saw Anderson at Harrap's and agreed the proportion of wash and line drawings for *Faust* as eight in wash and four in black and white as well as the full-page colour and text decorations. He informed Bodkin that *The Studio* had agreed to 'give me a good show on *Faust* in the autumn'.[45] He also went to Oundle to meet O'Rorke Dickey about their proposed collaboration. On his return he wrote to the headmaster at Oundle, expressing his keen interest in the scheme what a fine and rare opportunity the chapel presented to a stained glass worker; if his quotations were accepted, he could begin the inch-scale drawings early in the summer. The commission would be Harry's and Dickey would act in an advisory role. His letters to the headmaster and to Dickey were delayed and at the end of February he wrote again to Dickey apparently still with the idea of establishing an English studio in mind,

> Let us hope enough work will be given us to start a Studios [*sic*] . . .

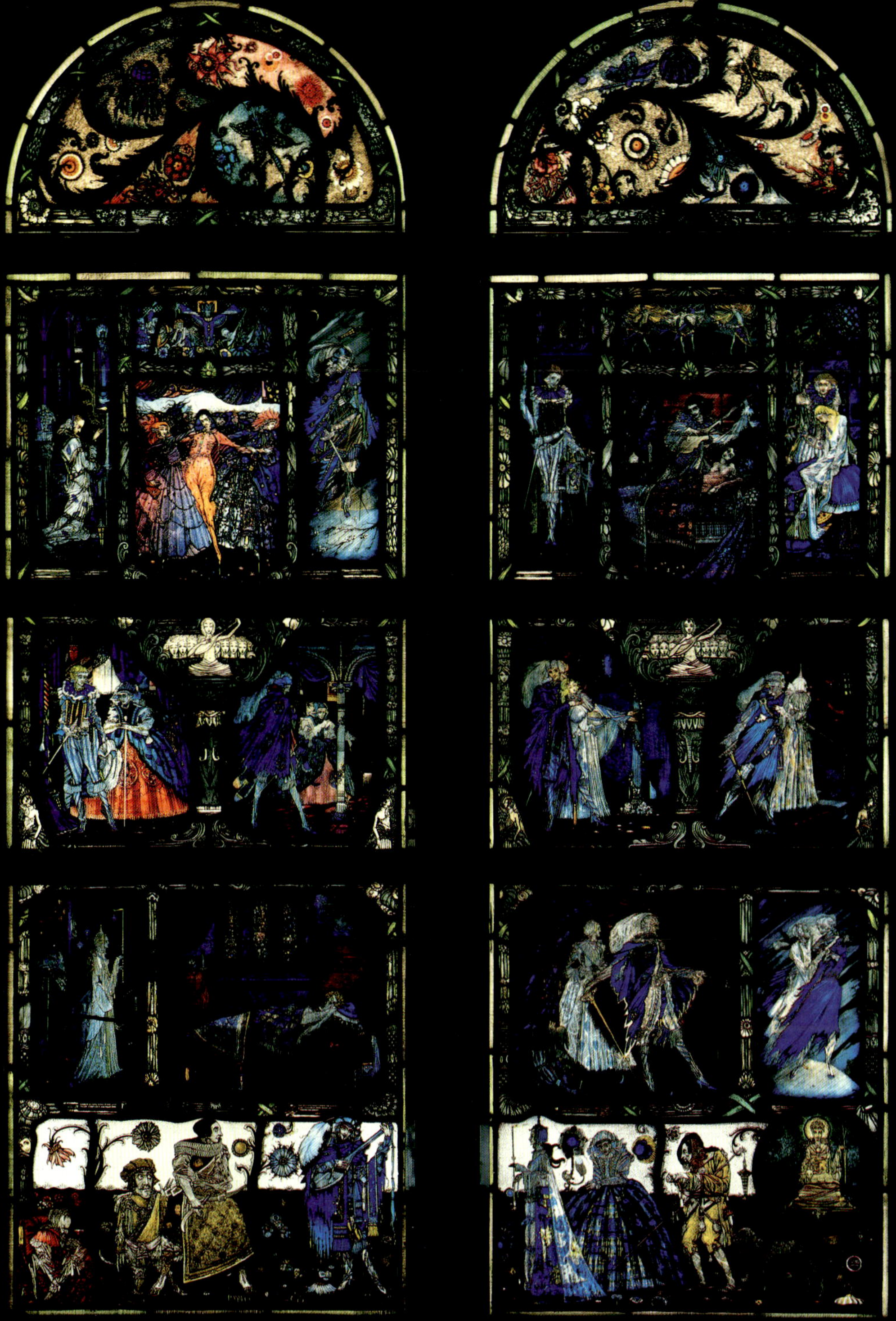

36 The Eve of St Agnes, **stained glass window in six sections, consisting of twenty-two small leaded panels, illustrating Keats' poem, 1923-4**

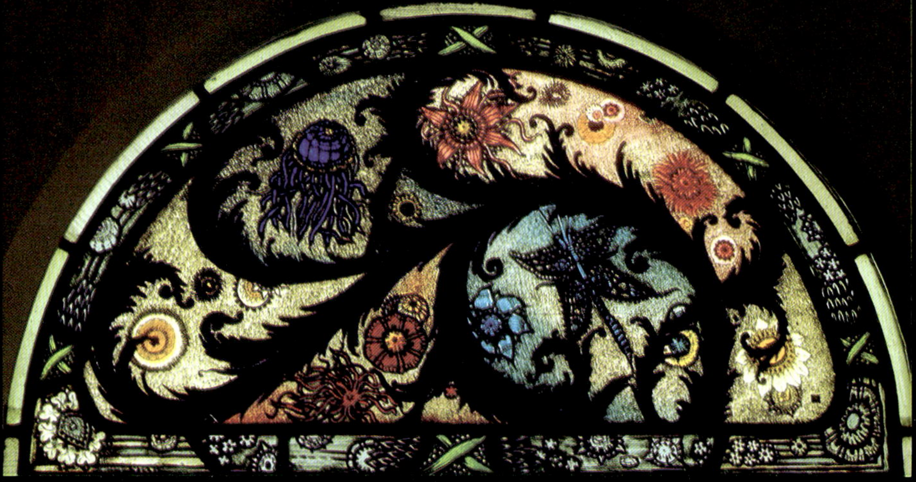

37 Decorative lunette from The Eve of St Agnes **window, 1923-4, showing Clarke's disguise of the lead lines as feathery fronds, a device he would repeat in the Bewley's Cafe windows**

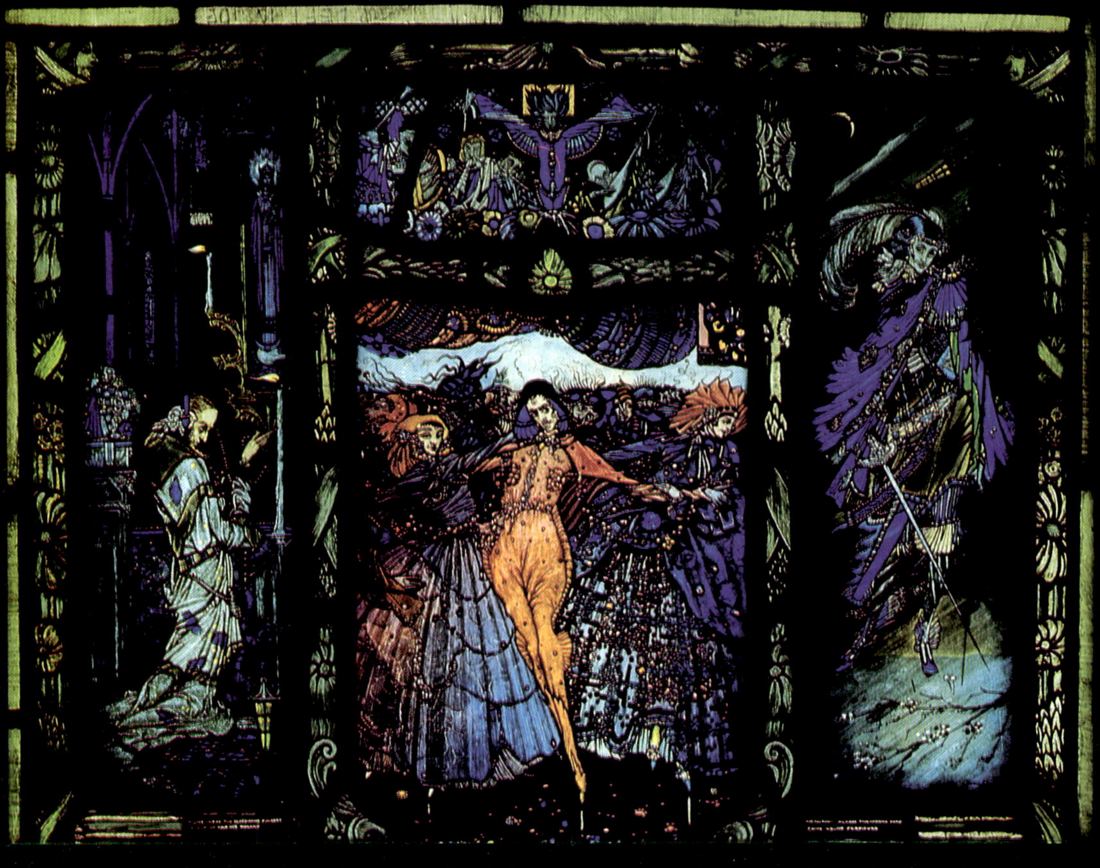

38 'Argent revelry . . . and all rich array', the second scene from the Eve of St Agnes **window, painted, acided and stained on flashed blue glass plated on gold-pink**

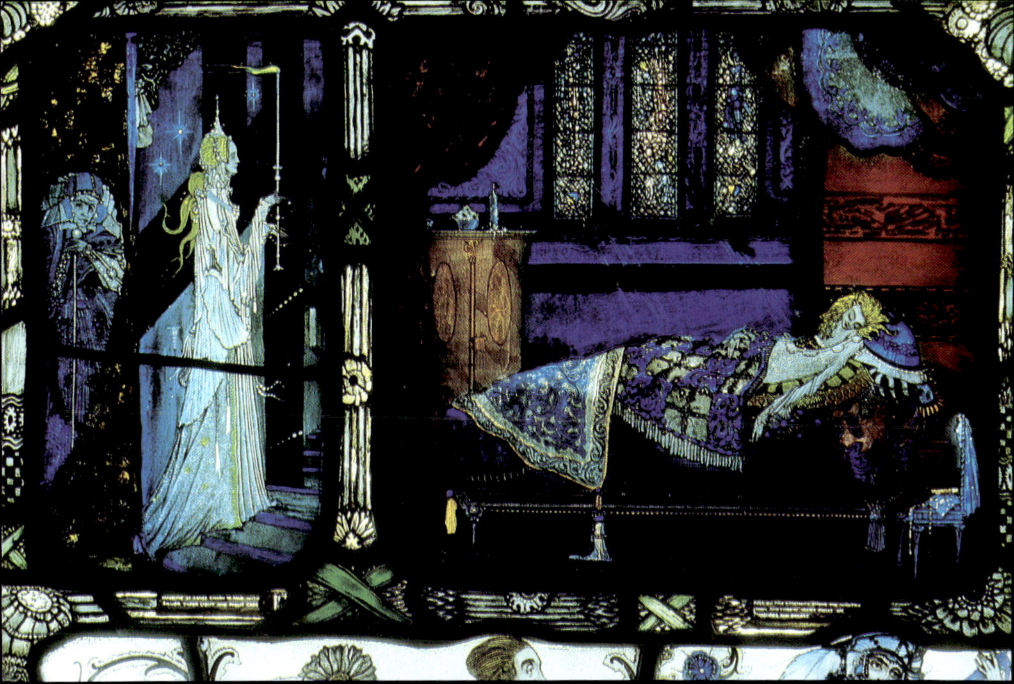

39 **Panel from the** Eve of St Agnes **window: 'Madeline, St Agnes' charmed maid'**

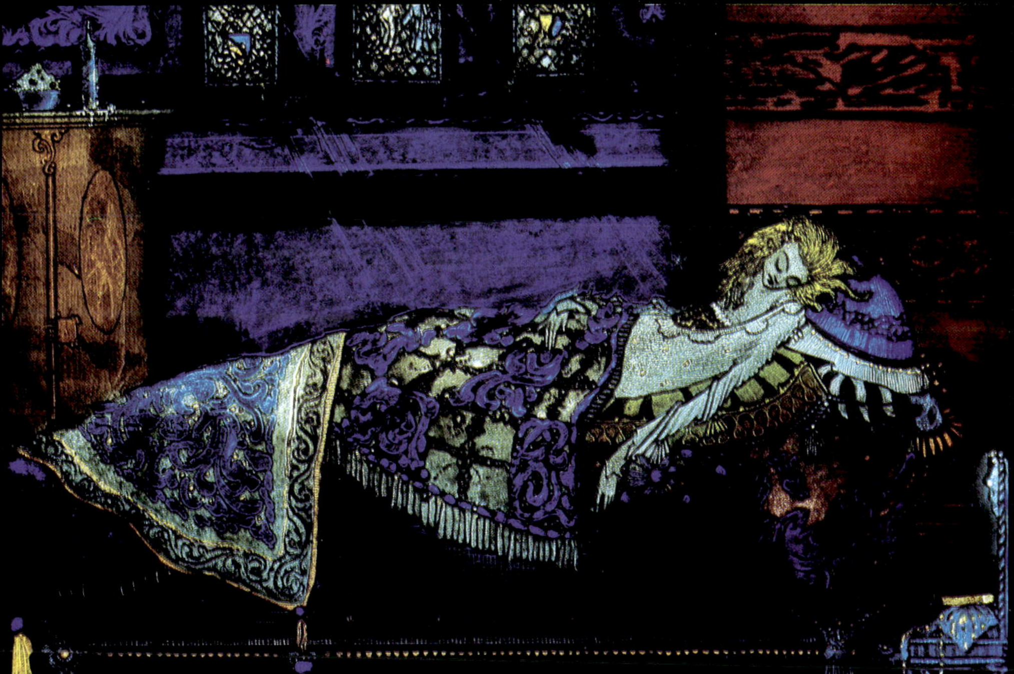

40 The Eve of St Agnes, **a detail of the entranced Madeline as the moonlight streams through the stained glass above her bed**

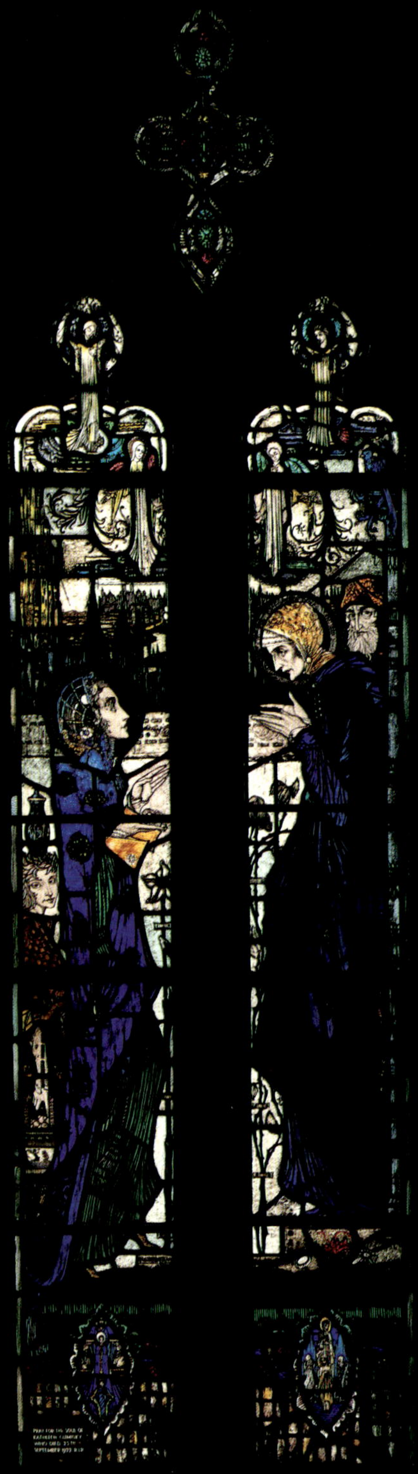

41 *The Visitation*, **Balbriggan, 1923; a window whose composition is based on the slender verticals of the Japanese pillar print**

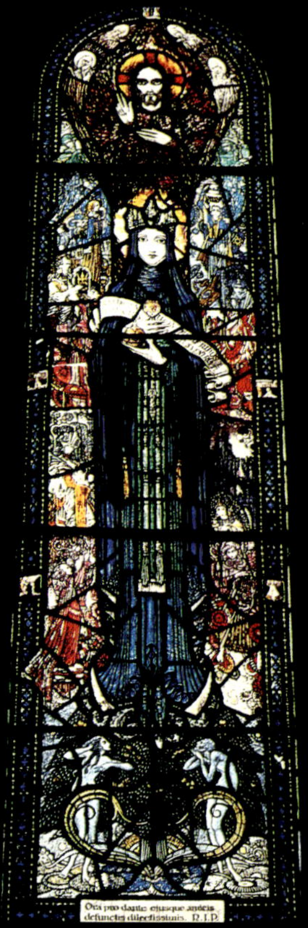

42 *The Blessed Virgin in Glory*, **right-hand light, 1923, of the lady chapel window, Terenure; the Queen of Heaven soars aloft, oblivious to the earthly tribulations of the female characters from the Old Testament woven into a richly coloured tapestry behind her.**

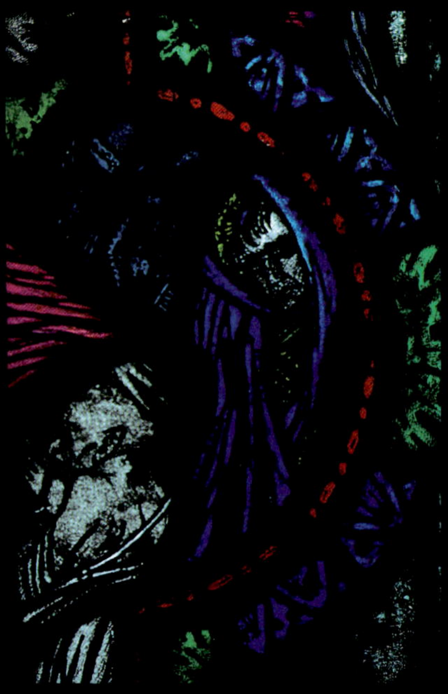

43 Harry Clarke's self-portrait, detail from his *Resurrection* **window for Lord Wicklow in Eneriley and Kilbride church, 1924**

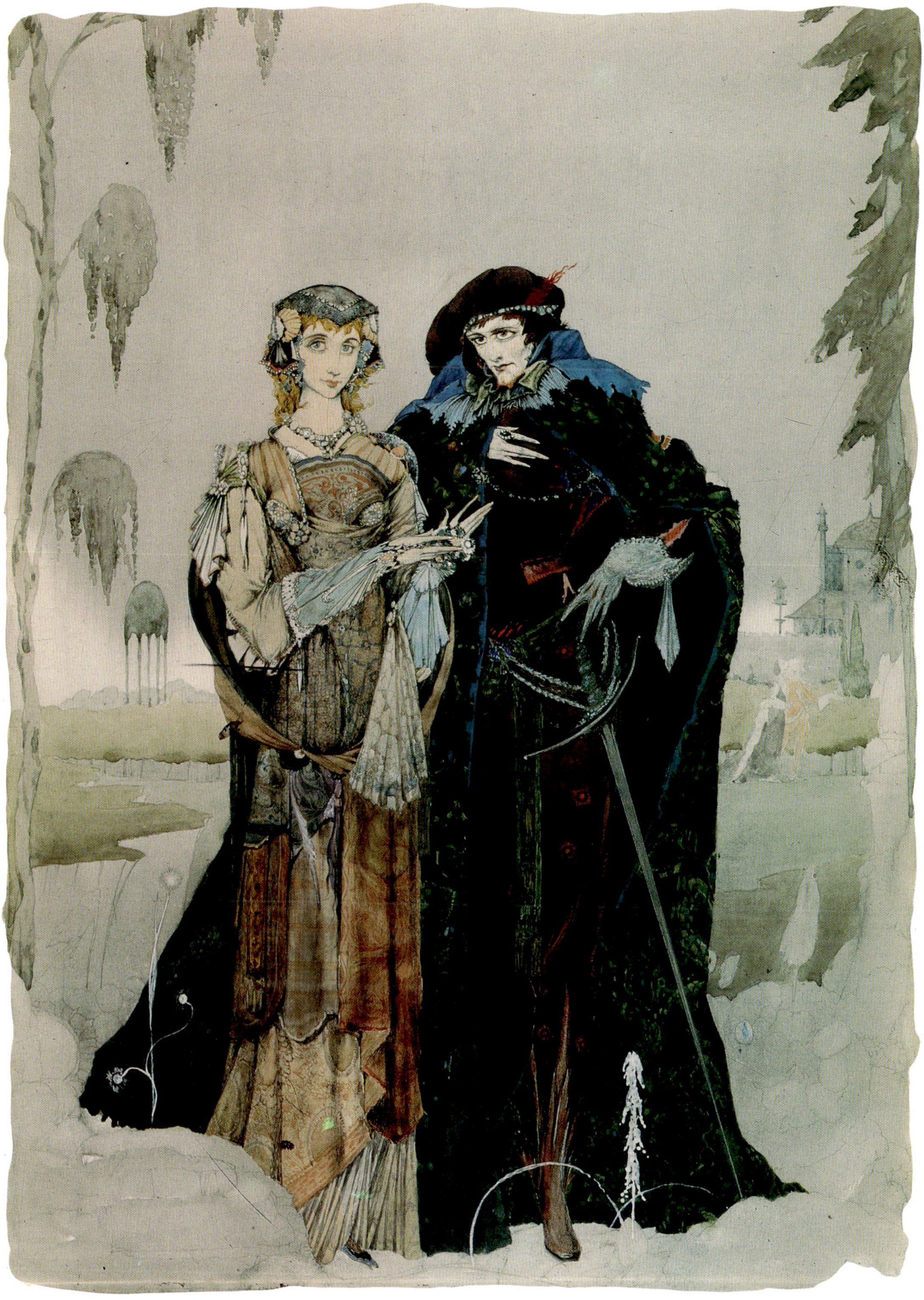

44 Unpublished watercolour illustration of the 'Garden' scene in Goethe's *Faust*, 1925

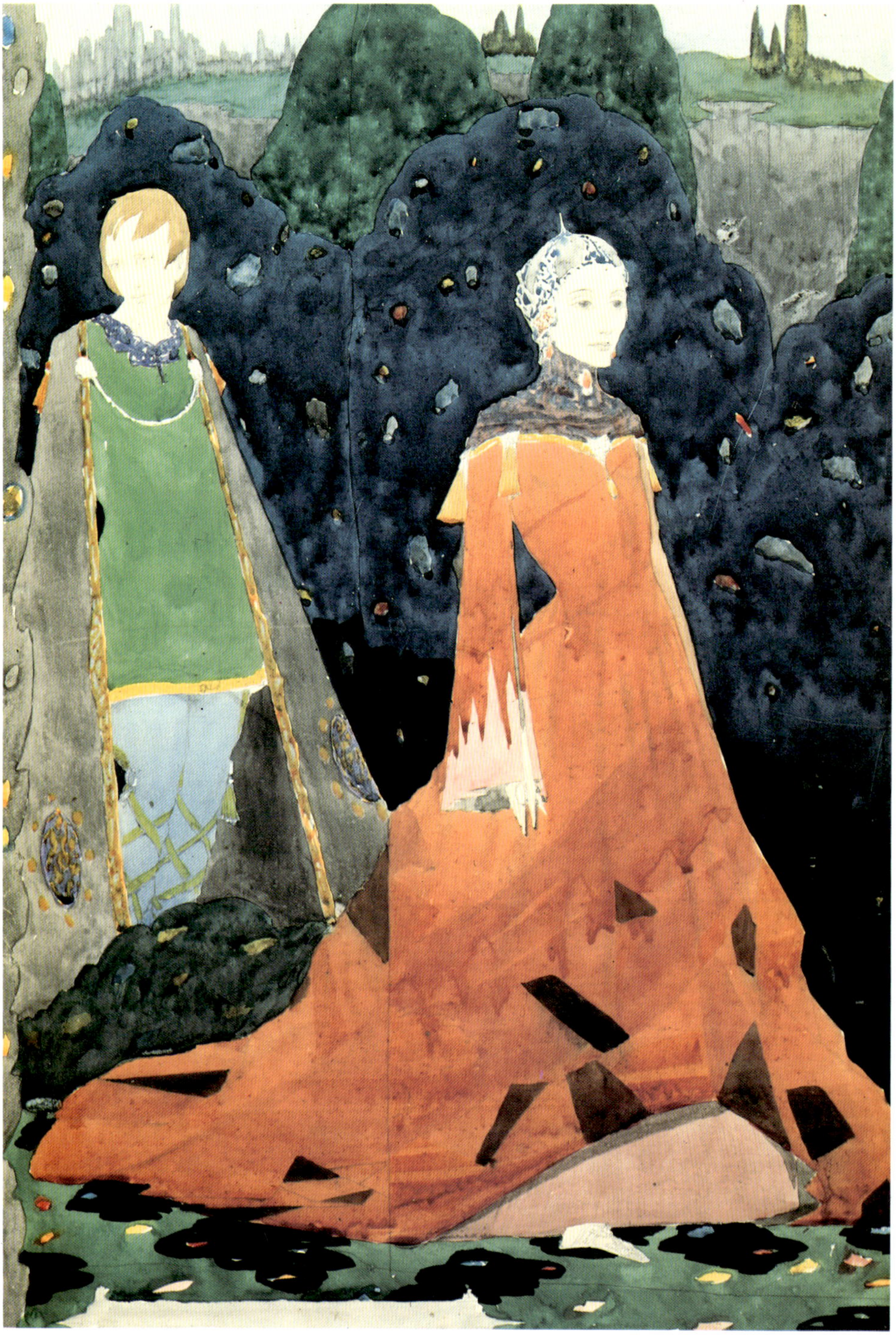

45 'I have heard a sound of wailing in unnumbered hovels, and I must go down, down I know not where', design for a stained glass panel illustrating W.B. Yeats' poem 'The Countess Cathleen' in the *Geneva Window*, *c.* 1928, pencil and watercolour

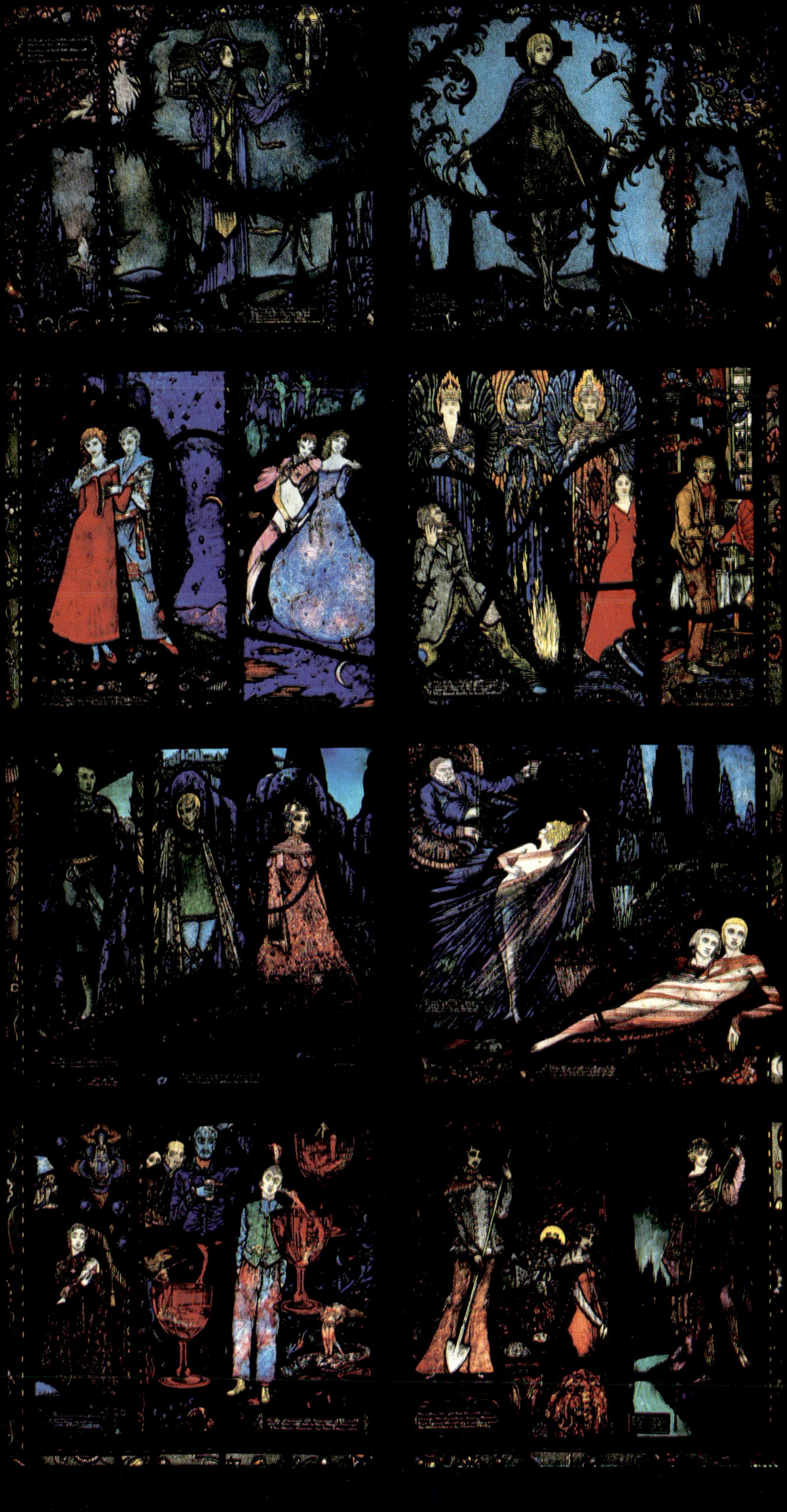

46 The *Geneva Window*, consisting of eight stained glass panels illustrating scenes from twentieth-century Irish literature, 1929; commissioned by the Irish Government to represent Ireland at the International Labour Organization in Geneva

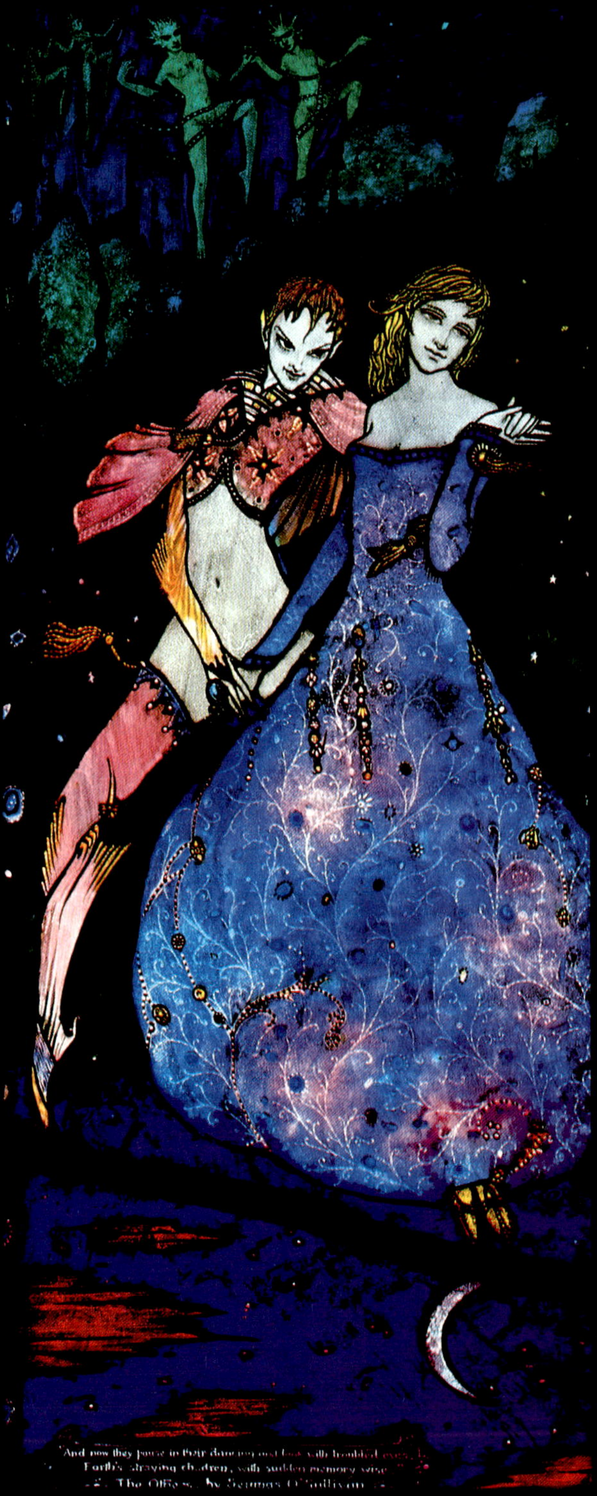

47 'And now they pause in their dancing and look with troubled eyes, / Earth's straying children, with sudden memory rise' from Seumas O'Sullivan's poem 'The Others', detail from the Geneva Window

48 The miraculous apparition of our Lady on St Luke's palette, detail from the Egerton Coghill memorial window, Castletownshend, 1926.

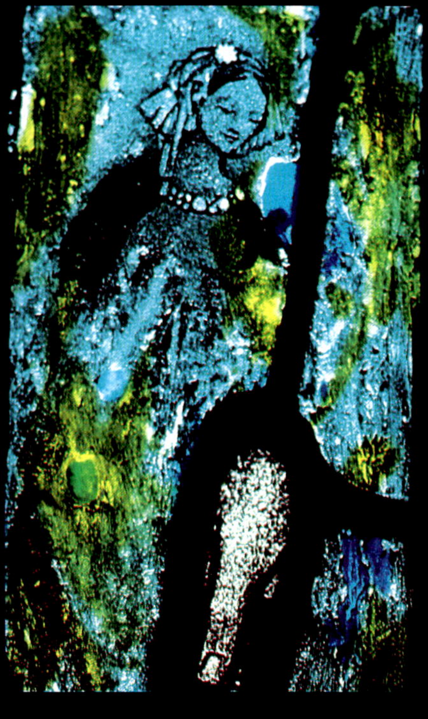

think of leaving here quite soon for a month or six weeks and will likely go to my sisters in London. I want more time for my own work which is getting very much in arrears. I mean I expect to be more available for you at Oundle should you want me to run up there again.[46]

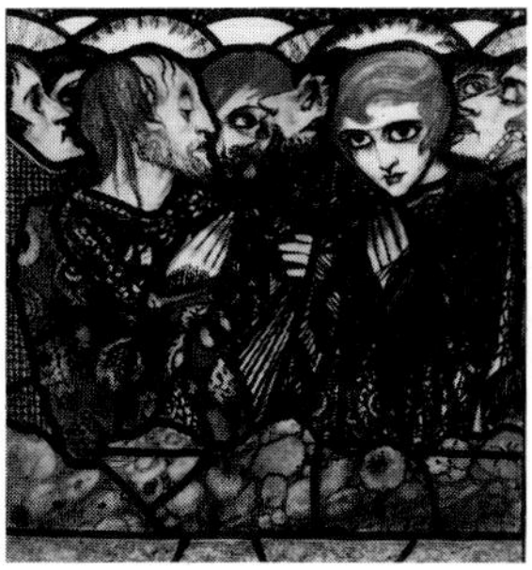

156 The Apostles, detail from the cartoon for *The Assumption* window, Ashdown Park, 1925

He needed time to work at the *Faust* colour illustrations,which he promised Harrap he would make 'not quite as gruesome as the first I sent you',[47] and Jameson's were still keen that he do another booklet. Harry insisted that Ashley Havinden would design the format into which he would fit the drawings, for which he would be paid a reproduction fee of £100, granting Jamesons an option to buy the originals at £5 each.

The work load at the Studios showed no sign of slackening and Walter was enlisted to do some of the background research on the more obscure Irish saints who would figure in the Carrickmacross windows, *St Ceara* of Monaghan, for example. Harry was behind schedule with the cartoons for the Ballinrobe windows of which only two of eight subjects were drawn, and, through Major Dease, came a new enquiry for a memorial window for Miss Martin Edmunds to be designed for the Church of the Sacred Heart at Edge Hill in Wimbledon. He made a proposal for the work, adding that he would be very rushed until August, but he did want to do his best. In March he went to London for a month, staying with his sisters in Hampstead, leaving the Studios to work on the Ballinrobe and Belcamp windows. He visited the Wimbledon church to see the location of the proposed window, and ordered templates and measured drawings from which to work.

Back in Dublin he was elected a full Academician by the Royal Hibernian Academy, and disappointed Bodkin by his 'comparatively slight exhibits'[48] at the academy's annual exhibition. These included his colour design for the Lusk window. The flow of cartoons to Sr Bernard for the Ashdown Park windows continued (fig. 156) and he hoped she would not pass judgment on his work until the chapel was completely filled with stained glass. By the end of May the tower window was fitted to Sr Bernard's satisfaction.

His group exhibition with Austen, Spare and Odle opened at the St George's Gallery on 21 May, thanks to 'the unfailing friendship and sympathetic support of Haldane McFall, to whom thanks are due for bringing about the exhibition', as the catalogue acknowledged. Harry showed twenty-three works including illustrations mostly for Poe, three for Perrault, the *Golden Hind* frontispiece and other often exotically entitled drawings as well as a delightful *Madonna* on vellum.

The exhibition attracted considerable attention. *The Bookman* felt that all four artists were 'united in one common defiance of the mundane',[49] and *The Studio* found Harry's work:

> distinguished by great technical mastery . . . in the minute style of

decorative composition. When he uses colour, he does so with a rare delicacy of feeling, and his work as a whole is remarkable for the depth and truth of its imaginative penetration.[50]

Bodkin was in Paris and could not attend the opening, but Harry wrote to him about his exhibits:

> I have some drawings on vellum in our show and wonder what you will say of them. They are a new medium and I would like to do some big ones of more ordinary subjects.

And about *Faust*:

> Holme has definitely fixed my *Faust* article for October and I am trying to quit the arranging of the whole matter but as this was in the hands of Oliver Anderson of Harraps and he was in Liverpool I have no details as to what he actually done. . . . I wonder if you would not hate this book — or its drawings; Harraps do not like it — full of stench and steaming horrors and they say 'leave you open to charges which we are sure you would indignantly repudiate'. But there it is: I felt queer and I did my best to convey what I felt. Harraps are bringing it out beautifully — photolitho' for the black and whites and it is a limited edition of 2000 — 1000 for England.[51]

It was at this time he first referred to his enthusiasm for Bruegel: 'He's a great great fellow. . . . I'd like his influence. Lord if only I had even a little bit of his mental attitude'.[52]

Pressure to complete the Faust drawings was great, so he reluctantly had to return to Dublin after only two days to work on these. On 27 May he sent the final large drawing — an illustrated wrapper, which was eventually used as an endpaper design — but had then to finish some forty head and tailpieces which he planned to send off in batches of six as they were completed. In these he endeavoured 'to illustrate . . . in a simplified manner . . . with decorative arrangements incidents in the Poem not covered by the full-page drawings' (fig. 157).[53] He was able to send off the final consignment of these on 24 June. At the same time he was making the nine two-colour drawings for the Jameson booklet, with the separations for the yellow blocks drawn to register with the proofs of the black subjects (fig. 158). This booklet, *The Elixir of Life*, with Ashley Havinden's typography was printed in Dublin with much better results than the previous booklet and published in June.

Harrap passed the final illustrations for *Faust*, and as soon as the blocks and plates were made all ninety of the drawings were sent to Holme at *The Studio* to select illustrations for the planned review article. Bodkin had

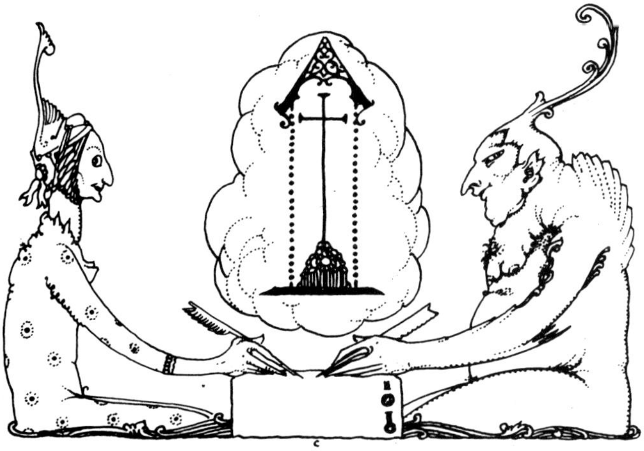

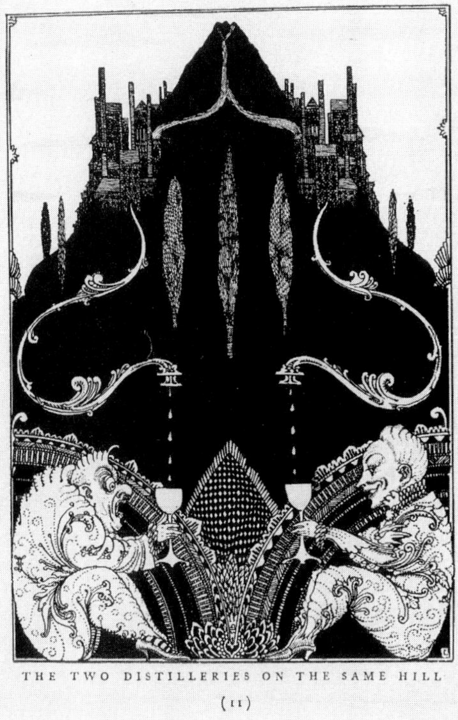

hoped to be invited to write this, but Dorothy Richardson was chosen as a literary reviewer.[54] She, too, was sent all the drawings for her selection.

Harry was also under great pressure to complete the Ashdown Park cartoons, and on 18 June he sent the last one to Sr Bernard, who was still volleying back her criticisms of the facial details. Harry responded,

> I am aware the drawing I put into the heads of my figures is often criticised — what I am really endeavouring to get into the heads is an element of humanity — or in other words get to away from the rather stuffy meaningless faces usually put into stained glass by the 'Trade houses'.[55]

But even the completion of this marathon task did not provide any respite. He wrote to Monsignor d'Alton at Ballinrobe on 11 June that as the client wanted 'the work to be designed and drawn by myself', he hadn't 'been able to take up the commission as early as hoped.' The subjects chosen were scenes from the New Testament and the life of our Lady on the south side, and a series of eight Irish saints with their emblems set in predella panels at the base of each light on the north side. On 2 July he sent drawings for the Irish saint windows — Jarlath and Enda, Kieran and Gormgail, Brendan and Colman (fig. 159), Fechin and Fursey — with a covering letter in which he said,

157 *The Street*, pen and ink title illustration from Goethe's *Faust* (1925); directly comparable with Clarke's illustration of two impish spirits from rival distilleries in *The Elixir of Life* (fig. 158)

158 'The Two Distilleries on the Same Hill' (that is, Jameson's and Power's), illustration from *The Elixir of Life (Uisge Beatha), being a Slight Account of the Romantic Rise to Fame of a Great House*, by Geoffrey C. Warren (1925)

> The little predella subjects at the base of the windows are all of great interest to me — but I would like your views thereon, especially *The Meeting of Saint Brendan and the Hermit Paul* could be changed for a more interesting subject. *The Meeting with Judas* and *The Paradise of Birds* I have done too often to do again with enthusiasm.[56]

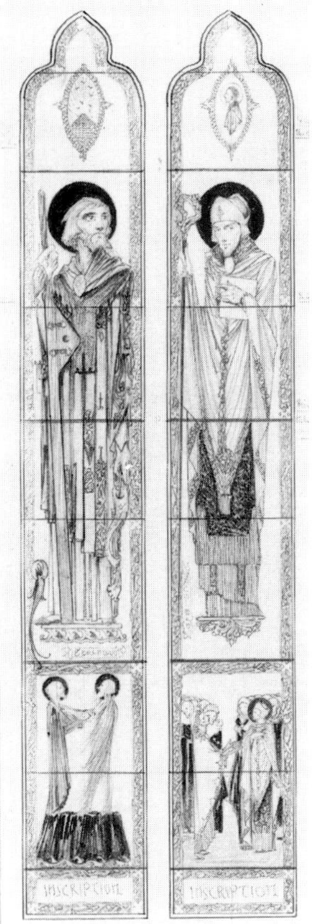

159 *St Brendan and St Colman*, small-scale annotated pencil design for the window at Ballinrobe, 1925; Clarke's minutely inscribed instructions would become clear to the Studio craftsmen when a drawing such as this was photographically enlarged at a scale of one inch to a foot and thus used as a cartoon.

He also wanted to experiment with alternating dark figures on white and vice versa, to give more light and strike 'a new note'. By early July he was able to begin the cartoon for *St Luke*, commissioned by Lady Coghill for Castletownshend, and prepare further drawings for Carrickmacross while at the same time planning a substantial exhibition of glass at the Studios. For relaxation he was reading Gauguin's *Journals* and Gerald Heard's *Narcissus — An Anatomy of Clothes*, published in 1924. Walter was trying to persuade a friend to secure President Cosgrave to open their exhibition in Horse Show Week: 'otherwise we'll have to get the Governor General to rise to the occasion.'[57] In the middle of the month, Harry began to experience difficulties with the job at Wimbledon. Fr White, the Jesuit rector of the church, professed not to know of Miss Edmund's intention to have the window erected until the Clarke Studios man arrived to take measurements. Then he insisted that the openings and bars on the two-light window and tracery should not be altered. Harry wrote to Miss Edmunds (who assured him that she had fully explained her wishes): 'Father White may be a bit difficult . . . he has a preconceived idea of the glass he thinks I ought to do',[58] and suggested she should persuade Fr White to go to Ashdown Park 'where I shall have seventeen opes in position by mid September and these he can compare with the work of Hardman's and one or two other English trade houses'.[59]

However, Fr White did not approve of Harry's pencil design and colour scheme depicting *St Frances of Rome and her Angel* and stated his objections in a critical letter to Miss Edmunds. Harry then decided he could not go ahead with the work. He begged Miss Edmunds' forgiveness but had 'no wish to involve [her] in a wordy war between Father White'[60] and himself. With great regret, he asked to be released from the commission and that he be refunded for his time and his visit to Wimbledon. This was not only a great disappointment but yet another blow to his hopes of building up a practice in England.

Harry's work was on show in two major exhibitions in Dublin during Horse Show Week in August 1925. At the Studios a finely printed card in red and black invited guests to an *Exhibition of Stained Glass Designed and Made by Harry Clarke RHA and His Assistants*, which was opened on Monday 3 August by President Cosgrave. This included work for Ashdown Park and Belcamp as well as 'pictures and drawings in colour and line' by Margaret and Harry Clarke. The *Irish Times* reported that

> The quantity . . . is scarcely less remarkable than its quality. The great

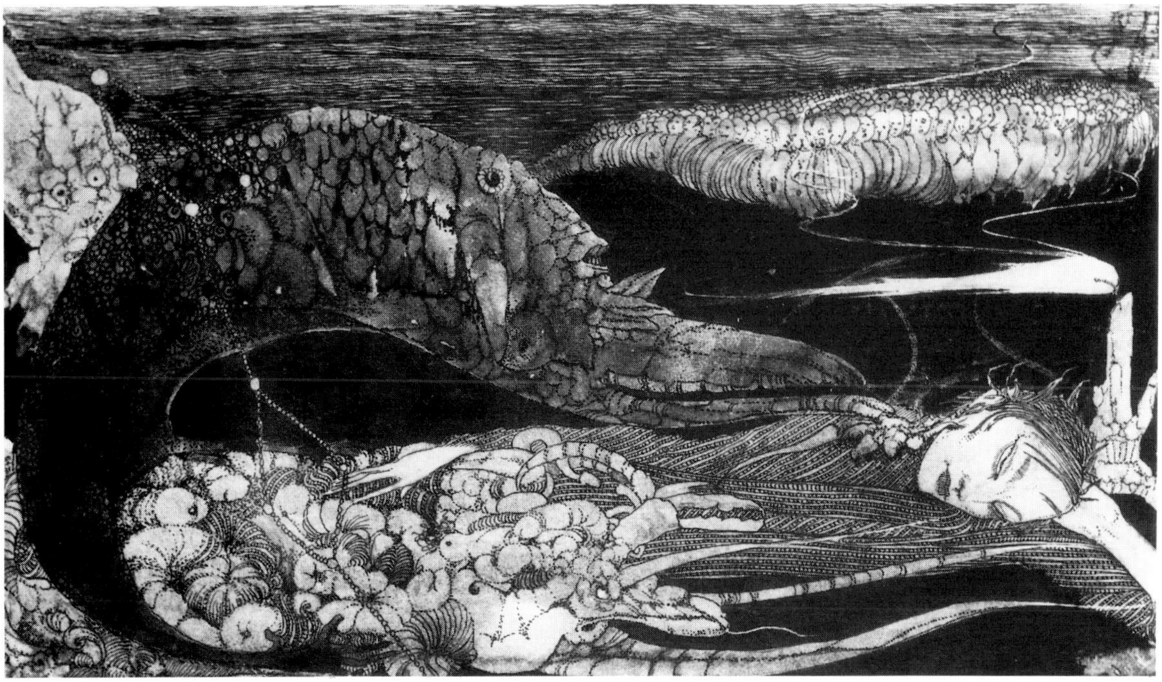

artist tends always to be lavish of his gifts. . . . Mr Clarke is in the right tradition in this as in so many other aspects. Since his last exhibition held a few months ago, he has conceived and completed a series of works which in mere labour of execution would seem to rival the industry of an average lifetime. In the fine Georgian house which shelters his workshops, five large rooms are now crammed with exhibits comprising seven immense church windows, twelve full sized cartoons and several dozen drawings of the most minute and exquisite delicacy. No single item is unworthy in any respect of the great reputation which Mr Clarke has won in his own country and, to an even wider extent, abroad. This being so, it is impossible to single out anything for special mention. His drawings range from suave, idyllic fancies to weird unearthly visions of degraded horror. The technique of all is equally impeccable (fig. 160) and so there is something among them to suit every taste. The windows are, of their nature, more uniformly inspired and in their mode, no whit less masterly. Many of the drawings have already been acquired by collectors from abroad and one series of windows is destined to adorn the Church of Notre Dame at Ashdown Park in Sussex. It is consoling to remember that the sixteen windows now being done for . . . Ballinrobe and the twelve for the Oblate Fathers in Raheny can never leave the country of their origin.[61]

160 *Ophelia* (or *Lobster*), pen and ink, 1925; derived from an erotic print by Hokusai, *The Amorous Octopus — A Female Fantasy*

In the *Irish Statesman*, using his pseudonym 'Y.O.', Æ wrote,

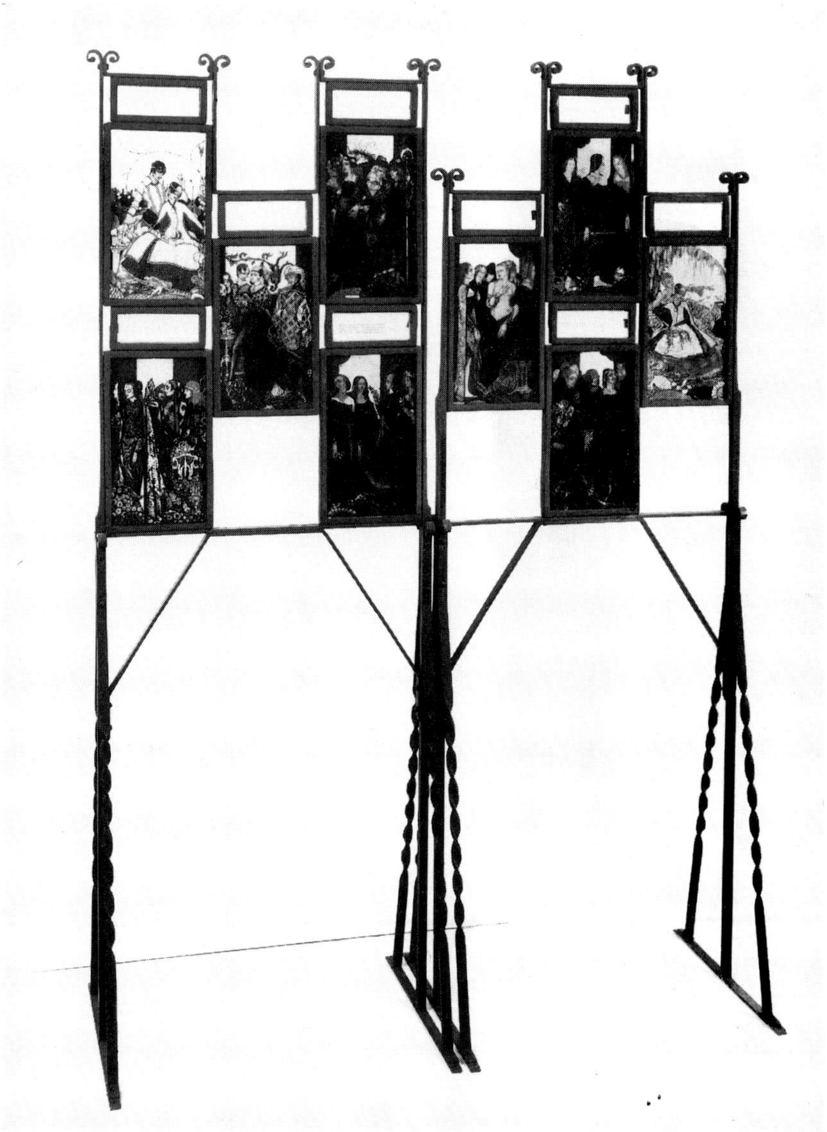

161 The *Queens* panels displayed on a wrought-iron stand designed by Clarke and made by James Hicks for display in the Municipal Gallery of Modern Art, Dublin between the years 1925 and 1927

162 'Three of the Separate Processes in the Production of a Stained Glass Window', advertising folder inserted in 1926 Church directories, featuring stages in Clarke's design for the *St Doulough* window, Belcamp, 1925

> There can be no doubt that Harry Clarke has a genius which manifests itself at its highest in stained glass. Interesting as the morbid imagination in the drawings and paintings is, I do not feel the full soul of the artist is manifested until he can let light pour through his design.[62]

At the Art Industries Show at the Royal Dublin Society, he showed drawings for reproduction in black and white and in colour, a window, and among his designs the twelve sketches for the Belcamp windows. That he could show so extensively in two exhibitions at the same time reflects the enormous amount of work, both in graphic art and in glass, that he had

THREE OF THE SEPARATE PROCESSES IN THE PRODUCTION OF A STAINED GLASS WINDOW

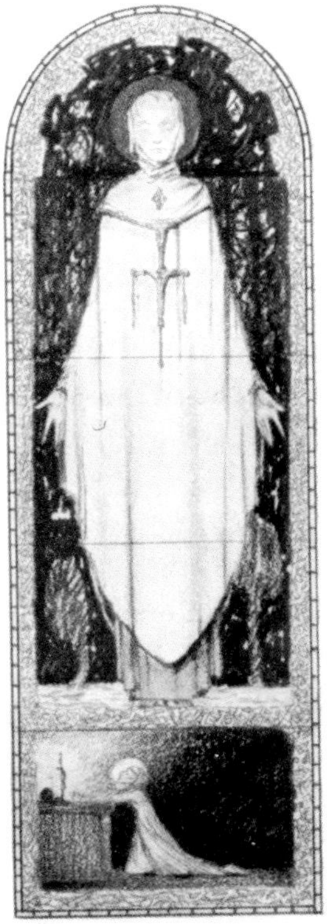

(1) *Working Drawing*

When the sketch has been approved, the next step is cartooning the window full size. A 'cutline' is then made, and the glass is cut to the different shapes.

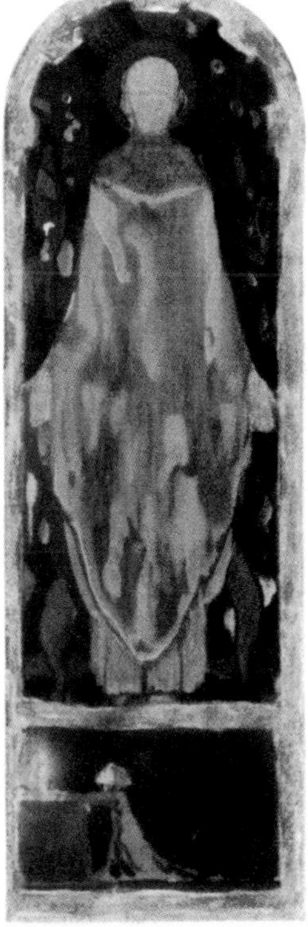

(2) *The Colour Scheme*

The different pieces of glass are stuck to a glass easel with hot beeswax; should no alteration be necessary the process of painting in with pigment, and a 'matte' and outline begins.

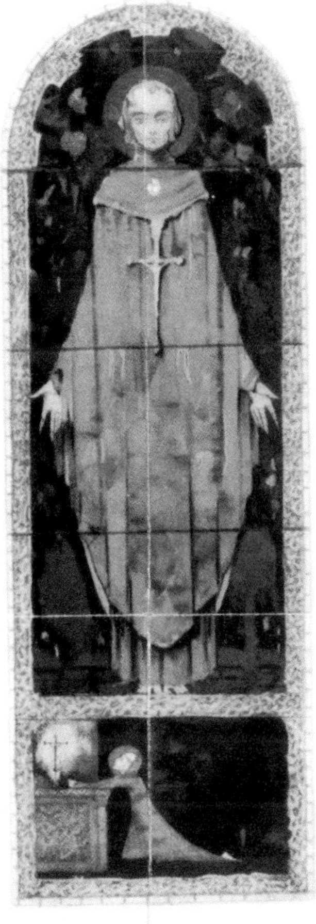

(3) *The finished Window*

After painting, the glass is fired in a kiln, cooled, stuck up again, and second painted and fired. It is again stuck up for final inspection, and then goes to the glazier, who leads it up, cements it, and the window is completed.

Stained Glass Commissions in Progress at Present

One Window: Repeat order St. Stephen's Cathedral, Brisbane.

Four Windows: Rt. Hon. Lord Rathdonnell, Rathvilly.

Four Windows: Parish Church, Drumcar, Co. Louth.

Two and Four Light: St. John's Church, Blackrock, Dublin.

One Window: Lady Coghill, Skibbereen, Co. Cork.

Decoration Commissions in Process of Completion

Oblate Fathers, St. Joseph's, Colwyn Bay, N. Wales.

Sisters of Charity, Mount St. Anne's, Miltown, Dublin.

Oblate Fathers, St. Mary's College, Belcamp, Raheny, Dublin.

St. Jarlath's Cathedral, Tuam, Co. Galway.

St. Agatha's Church, North William Street, Dublin.

J. CLARKE AND SONS

accomplished in a year. In August, too, the nine *Queens* panels were loaned to the Municipal Gallery in Dublin and remained on show for over two years in a specially made wrought iron stand which Harry designed to hold them and which was made by Hicks (fig. 161). After his August exhibition he dispatched a consignment of his unsold illustrations to the Brick Row Bookshop on New York's East 47th Street since its owner Mr Byrne Hackett had earlier sold 'a considerable amount' of his drawings.[63]

Ashley Havinden was invited by Harry to plan the layout and typography of the annual Studios' advertising folders which were, as usual, inserted in the *Catholic Directory*, the Latin *Ordo* and the *Church of Ireland Directory*, making a print run of eighteen thousand leaflets, which were printed under Havinden's supervision at the Curwen Press in Plaistow, London. This layout, aimed at brightening up 'the atmosphere of musty sacristy',[64] included a description of the process of stained glass illustrated in colour by Harry's designs for the *St Doulough* window at Belcamp (fig. 162).

In September the editor of the *Illustrated Country Review*, a London-published journal, invited Harry to contribute an article on his work as part of a series on the arts. Harry's piece, 'Some Notes on Stained Glass' (which is reprinted as an appendix to the present volume) appeared in the November issue with six illustrations of his glass and presented his *Credo* on his craft.

At the beginning of October the seventh exhibition of the Arts and Crafts Society of Ireland, which was to be the last in Harry's lifetime, was held in the Dublin Metropolitan School of Art. Harry was represented by the eight volumes of *Ireland's Memorial Records* and the first Jameson booklet, *The History of a Great House*, ten black and white drawings, of which six were Poe illustrations, two drawings in colour and schemes for decoration and cartoons. This exhibition marked the swan song of the Arts and Crafts Society of Ireland as it existed in Clarke's time and the emergence of a new generation of artists who were influenced by his work, among them Millicent Girling, Maurice MacGonigal, Colm O'Lochlainn and Hubert McGoldrick.

9

Constant demands for his work, and publication of his Faust *and* Swinburne *despite increasing ill health, force him to abandon long-cherished hopes of a London studio*

Although Harry was utterly exhausted and his health had not been at all good, he decided to go to England in October 1925 to see the installation of the windows at the convent at Ashdown Park; on his way he stopped off at Colwyn Bay with the pencil drawings for three pairs of chancel lights and traceries. In London, where he would stay for the next two months, only returning to Dublin for Christmas, he took lodgings in Tregunter Road in Fulham, conveniently near the Glass House in Lettice Street. While there he saw the Ashdown Park windows *in situ*: the Tower window depicting the Madonna surrounded by angels in a sea of rich blue, signed 'CLARKE/DUBLIN' and the sanctuary windows in deep rubies, blues, mauves and olives, signed 'J. Clarke and Sons, Dublin'. He was keen to use this commission as a basis for further work in England. In the hopes of being considered for Liverpool Cathedral he contacted Sir Giles Gilbert Scott, after an introduction from Lady Lavery. When he wasn't 'working and drawing' he was 'drumming all England' seeking jobs.[1] Disappointingly, after the detailed proposals he had sent to Oundle earlier that year, the school had only 'recommended' he get one small window and a scheme of ten as donors appeared.

Faust was published in October in an edition of two thousand copies — one thousand for England with the Harrap imprint and another thousand with an American imprint but otherwise identical. The 256-page book on fine Van Gelder paper had twenty-two full-page illustrations of which eight were in full colour, eight in line and wash lithographed in two workings, and six in black line. There were also sixty-four decorative drawings[2] in the text and as endpapers (figs. 163-165). The volume was quarter bound in vellum with grey boards.

The October issue of *The Studio* reproduced two full-page and a half-title black and white illustrations and a colour plate to accompany the long-planned review by Dorothy Richardson, who related the illustrations to Clarke's glass:

> There is from first to last in these pictures no sunlight, but rather light filtered, coming as through a glass darkly. And it is this quality of

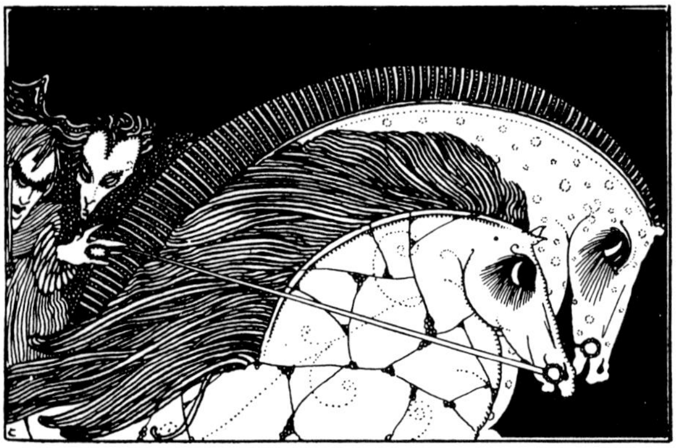

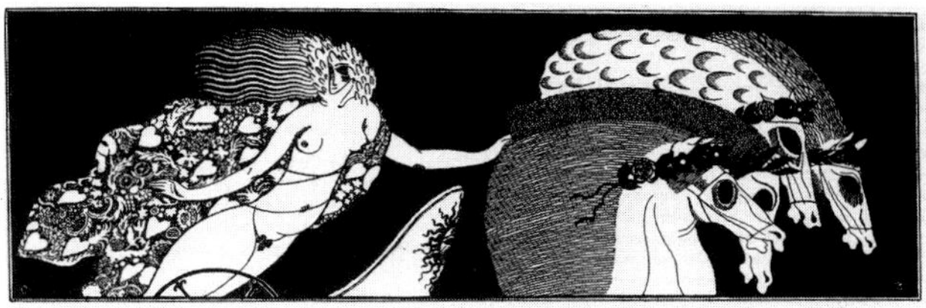

163 'Night — Open Plain', title illustration in pen and ink from the 1925 edition of *Faust*

164 An obvious source for *Night — Open Plain*, from an early unnumbered issue of the Russian emigré periodical *Jar-Ptitza*

filtered light, helping to make him so interesting a commentator on Goethe's tale, that is one of the distinctive charms of Mr Clarke's work. It is not for nothing that he is by choice a designer of storied windows richly dight, and in the case of these Faust pictures, the dimmed light is truly religious, binding together as in a single medium this wealth of fantastic invention and remaining in the mind when the book is closed and the illustrations flow together until the detail is lost in the whole.

Æ, who reviewed *Faust* in the *Irish Statesman* with customary perception and at considerable length, observed that in many of his 'imaginative marginalia . . . pencilled about Goethe's masterpiece', Harry had escaped from the influence of Beardsley. He felt that as

> the ideal interpreter of . . . Poe . . . wherever the imagination of Goethe conjures up the macabre, the witch, the imp and the devil, Clarke will add a shudder which is congruous with the drama. For the rest, he is himself unchanged. But what does this matter? The collector will buy this volume because of Harry Clarke's part in it, not because of Goethe's. . . . Nothing in these drawings represents anything in the visible world: all come from that dread mid-world or purgatory of the soul where forms change on the instant by evil or beautiful imagination. . . .
>
> Clarke's fertility of invention is endless. It is shown in a multitude of designs less elaborate than the page plates, but no less intense. Take the little drawing which illustrates the heartrending meditation of Marguerite, who has been listening to the girls' chattering scandal about Hannah and who is all the while conscious of her own secret. Here the distraught soul looks out from a misery from which there is no escape. Long quivering hands with fingers like sharpened fires waver in the air and point to the piteous figure. The hands have eyes

in them like vipers that know everything and will forgive nothing. We would like to close the eyes of the soul to shut out that piteous image. How awful, too, is the Despair with head like a bird of prey, which holds the fainting girl in the *Cathedral* [fig. 166], while the choir chants the Dies Irae. It is the soul inside the body rather than the external form which is symbolized in the decoration to the scene in *Auerbach's Cellar*, where one can almost hear grunt or whinny, from creatures already become half animal to the spiritual vision [fig. 167]. Clarke is not the artist of men and women, but the seer of forms which their passions and imaginations assume.[3]

The reviewer in the *Irish Times*,[4] however, was not so favourably disposed to the book. Probably the most perceptive contemporary notice was that signed 'WGR' in the quarterly *Artwork* which described the volume as 'probably the most notable illustrated drama of this century'; its reviewer saw 'the world of the psychoanalyst made visible' in

a dream-world of half-created fantasies; the powerless fancies of senile visions; misshapen bodies with wormlike heads [fig. 168]; staring eyes of octopuses and reptiles gaze like ponderous saurians of the lost world, while half-finished homunculi change like 'plasma' in forms unbound by reason. The treatment ranges through a Rabelaisian humour in Beardsley and Doréan forms, with a touch of Chaucerian gusto, while a voluptuous undercurrent is here, in the erotic line of semi-Gothic grotesque and there, as duplicates of Shaivaite emblems as used in S. France at Easter, a century ago.[5]

This perceptive analysis of a 'sublunar world of phantoms' and 'hermaphrodisiac figures' who 'stalk through the pages . . . in a gargantuan satire of mirthless laughter' is close to a more recent evaluation of these drawings, by Brigid Peppin in her *Fantasy — Book Illustration 1860-1920*. Here she observes that Harry's contemporaries,

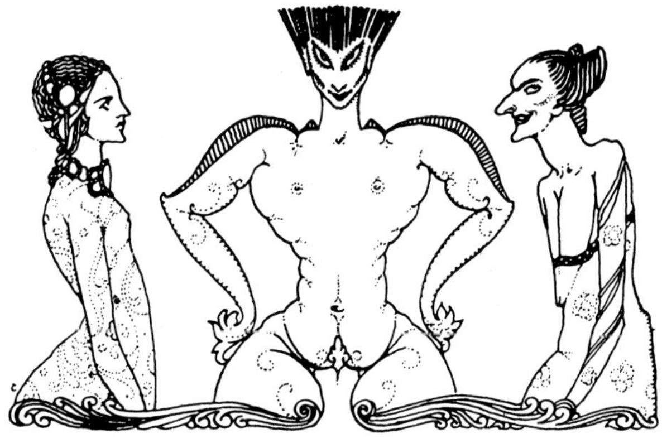

165 *The Neighbour's House*, title illustration in pen and ink from the 1925 *Faust*

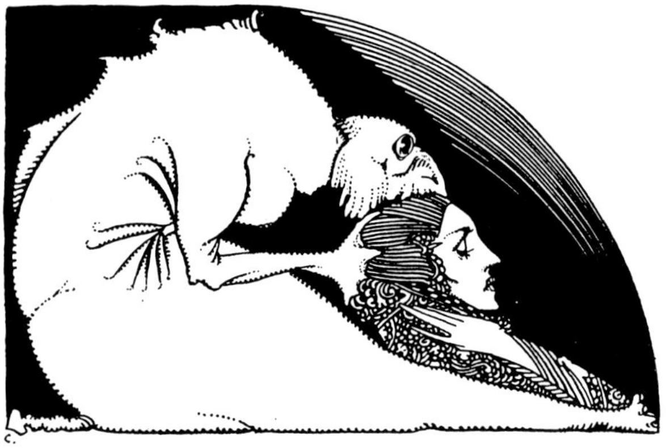

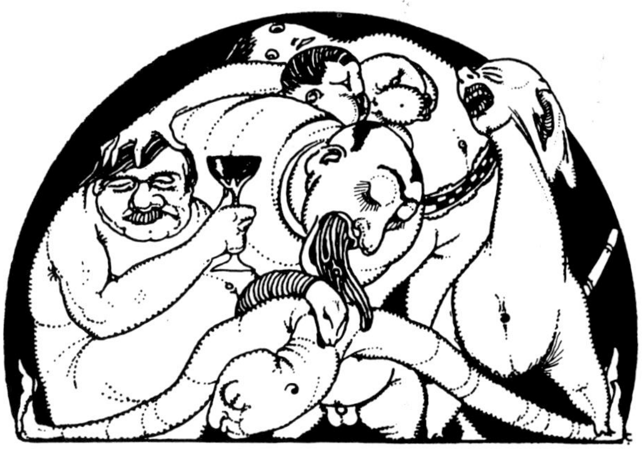

166 *The Cathedral*, title illustration in pen and ink from the 1925 *Faust*

167 *Auerbach's Cellar*, title illustration from the 1925 *Faust*; for Æ's description of figs. 167 and 168, see p. 188f.

like Beardsley's, overlooked or at least avoided mentioning the sexual implications of his imagery. . . . Particularly in his illustrations of Goethe's *Faust*, [Harry Clarke] invented figurations of evil that recall the paintings of Hieronymous Bosch. The *Faust* series includes drawings . . . peopled with hosts of grotesque and mutilated monsters and various fungi. There are multiple breasted, cadaverous demons which may be headless or armless with tufts of armpit hair, bird-headed and eye-tipped penises, rats crawling from mouths and other orifices (an echo here of Gillray's cowpox vaccine cartoon), and decrepit, naked witches with chopped wings and with claws for hands and feet. Clarke's Mephistopheles is in the same mould as the figure of Ill Nature in Beardsley's *The Cave of Spleen* and as *la Salomé Tatouée* in Gustave Moreau's painting; he is an elegantly bejewelled, sexually ambiguous creature with cloven high-heeled boots [fig. 169]. . . . Many of his images seem to contain bizarre perversions of religious iconography: diabolical gestures parody those traditionally ascribed to saints; flying witches and monsters with truncated or skeletal wings appear as the antithesis of angels. . . . In his perverse and satanic imagery, which often had strong homosexual overtones, Clarke exceeded the Decadents of the 1890's. Obscenity, though, was kept at bay by a dimension of comedy which invited the spectator to participate in the inversion of accepted notions of propriety and in the transmutation of the symbols of religious faith.[6]

The imagery in *Faust* anticipates the psychedelic, drug-induced fantasies of the 1960s, when his graphic work enjoyed a considerable revival, particularly in America and the later balletic extravagances of Michael Clark and Leigh Bowery; it may also in part be due to the onset of the long illness which would afflict his few remaining years. A contemporary, Ernest Keegan, who met Harry shortly after *Faust* appeared, recalls being told that many of the gruesome, deformed figures were derived from the victims of malnutrition, disease, inbreeding and neglect commonly seen on Dublin's streets and, explicitly, in the Public Baths at Tara Street.[7]

Although the booksellers were saying the book was 'lewd and stinking — you know the kind of stuff — "sisters" and "wifes" and "nasty-taste-in-the-mouth" kind of stuff', Harry thought it his 'best book — 'tis horrid I know — in fact I had to laugh at my creations or I would have become morbid. I think I shall illustrate no more T. Bodkin'.[8]

In another letter to Bodkin he wrote:

> I feel I do not do a book as it should be done. I see my drawings and there is only a hazy background of Book, whereas the drawings should, as you have *so* many times said, be subordinate to the whole — or an item in a complete scheme. Unless I am tempted by a good offer, which seems unlikely, I shall just do drawings of such ideas and things that strike me when I am alive; and try and sell them.[9]

Two unpublished drawings for *Faust* should be noted. The pen and wash drawing on vellum, *Prelude at the Theatre* is a grotesque fantasy, peculiarly Clarke's, in which three tiny gesticulating figures performing under a proscenium arch contrast with the foreground horrors of a deformed bare-bottomed dwarf attached by a nostril to the finger of a cellulitic, jock-strapped, worm-headed monster.[10] The other, a delicate romantic

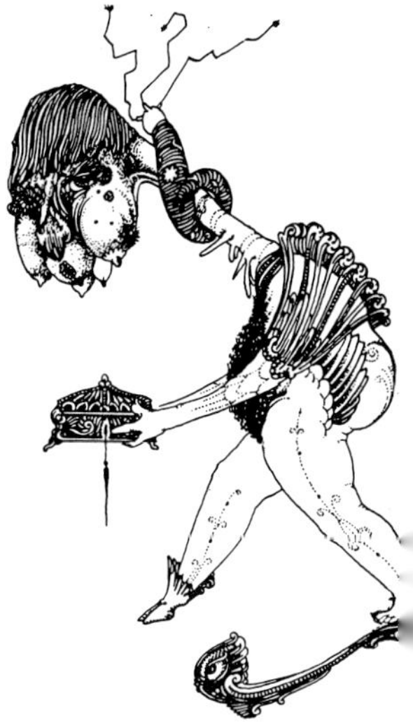

168 Mephistopheles, endpiece illustration in pen and ink from the 1925 *Faust*: 'misshapen bodies with wormlike heads' (cf. p. 189)

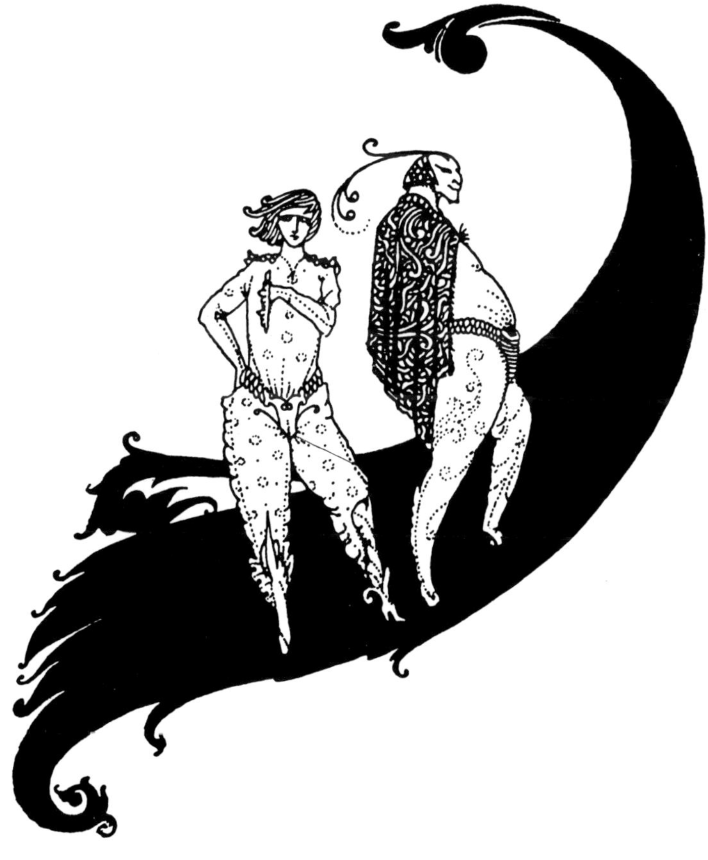

169 Faust and Mephistopheles, endpiece illustration in pen and ink for the 1925 *Faust*: Mephistopheles an 'elegantly bejewelled, sexually ambiguous creature with cloven high-heeled books' (cf. p. 190)

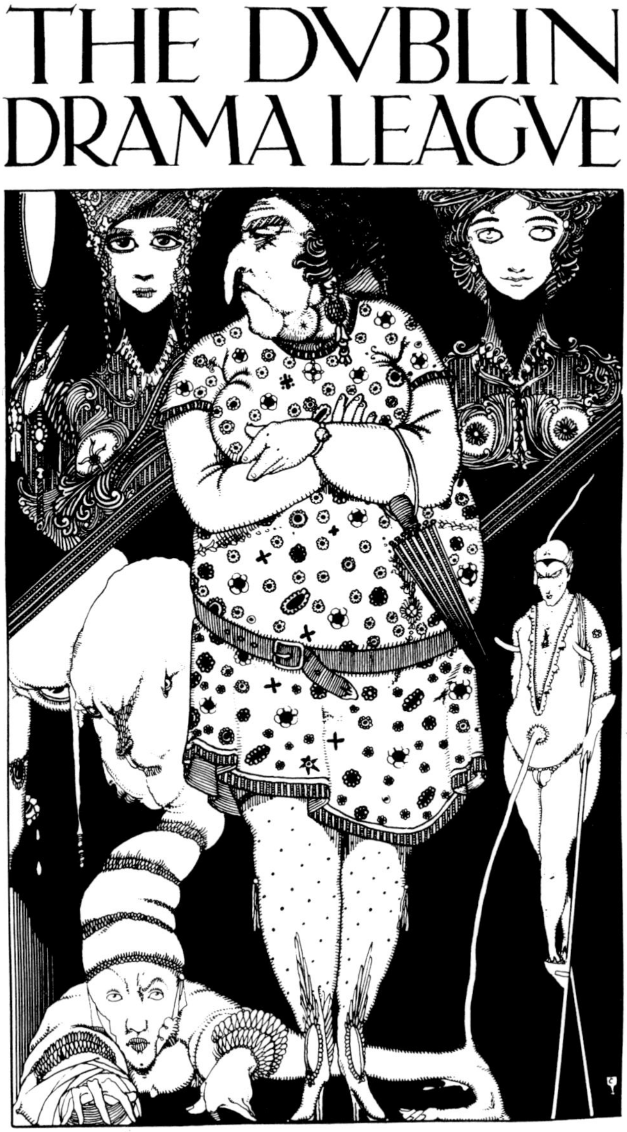

170 Short-lived cover design for the programme of the Dublin Drama League, pen and ink, November 1925

watercolour (plate 44), depicts Faust and Margaret from the Garden scene, attired in richly coloured and textured costumes which suggest the influence of stage design, set in an idealized lakeside landscape evoked by loose washes of pale colour and exotic detail. Perhaps Harry thought this fine drawing might lose too much in the colour process used by the publishers and left the setting unfinished.

A cover design for the Dublin Drama League programmes drawn in November at the request of Lennox Robinson is akin to the *Faust* drawings (fig. 170).[11] This was first used for the League's production of Strindberg's *Dance of Death*. The embryonic shapes and umbilically connected figures in this grotesquerie did not find favour and the design was abandoned after a couple of productions. This drawing was probably done in London, where Harry was being kept in touch with urgent matters by Walter, who would explain to anxious clients that his brother's absence from Dublin was necessitated by his need for rest and recuperation in view of his protracted poor health.

One of Harry's eyes had become so seriously infected that he could not read or draw during the resultant painful and slow treatment. On his return to Dublin before Christmas, he therefore entered into a two-year contract with Leo Cartwright to supervise the work on glass, cartoons, canvas and sketches at the Studios.[12] However, he planned to return to London in January and rent the studio Wilhelmina Geddes had been using at the Glass House once his eye trouble and severe headaches had cleared up. After spending Christmas in Dublin, he went to Ballinrobe to see the series of windows he had designed for Monsignor d'Alton in place. These had been made up in the Studios during his absence and they show how well his intentions had been carried out. On his return he wrote to Monsignor d'Alton, who thought the church had been darkened by the windows: 'The glass looked to me extremely fine and although you may think it's darkened the church, I think you'll agree it's enriched it with its deep colouring'.[13]

He also continued work in short spurts on the preliminary design for a three-light window for a Mr L.A. le Personne (a Belgian glass stockist in the City of London) for Caterham-on-the-Hill in Surrey, which he had begun in London. Despite his client's difficult demands, he tried to incorporate a number of disparate figure subjects into what promised to be an intricate design minutely treated.[14]

On 9 January 1926, while he was preparing to return to London, he had a severe fall from his bicycle in Dublin and suffered serious injuries — fractured ribs, as well as a compression at the base of the skull which led to meningitis. He was in bed for almost six weeks and when he was allowed up in mid February his friend Lennox Robinson persuaded him to stay with him and his wife at their home, Sorrento Cottage in Killiney, where Harry would have plenty of rest in the sea air and be away from the concerns of the business. However, Harry soon insisted on going in for an hour each day and by the end of the first week in March he was, very shakily, attending to correspondence at the Studios. Business prospects looked good; the Dowanhill sisters had ordered another window among the other new commissions, and Bernard Rackham, head of the ceramics department at the Victoria and Albert Museum, had written looking for reproductions of Harry's domestic glass for an article he was writing on contemporary stained glass.[15] Harry wrote to Seumas O'Sullivan that he was 'almost better again now tho' I stagger with my weakness and not with fire water'.[16]

'To encourage him to live when he was very bad',[17] Lennox Robinson, who was anxious to see the Holy Week processions in Seville, had suggested that he and Harry should go to Spain [18] for a holiday, and, when

Harry felt well enough in March and was still enthusiastic about the trip, they decided to go; as Robinson wrote to MacGreevy, whom he hoped would join the party:

> Off we go on the 19th by P. & O. to Gib. It's absurd of me to go with an overdraft instead of a balance but I always think something will 'turn up' . . . and anyhow, if it sets Harry up it will be worth it.[19]

Harry, conscious that he had lost several commissions through his eye trouble and his illness, wrote to several clients[20] before he left for Spain, apologizing for delays in their work. Before he left Karl Parsons wrote that he had rented studio space for Harry at the Glass House which would be available for him to start work on the new Glasgow window when he returned. It was a great relief to send off some of the Carrickmacross order, long overdue, and all Studio work from his detailed designs, except for the evocative *St Ceara* base panel (fig. 171). The Studios' work was greatly facilitated by his employment of the services of Messrs Raines, a photographers in Ealing, to make accurate inch-to-a-foot scale enlargements of his designs for use as cartoons.[21]

On 18 March, Harry travelled from Dublin to London, where he met Lennox Robinson and the next day the two friends boarded the P. & O. liner at Southampton for Gibraltar. From there they went on to Tangier, which they greatly enjoyed. Harry sent Bodkin a postcard of Arab pavement mosaicists:

> I simply am amazed all the time — 'tis so strange — in fact the painter who paints here and comes back to Ireland with his 'stuff' is a Fraud — for 'tis 90% picture and 10% painter. Wish you were here with us — 'tis terribly amusing [22].

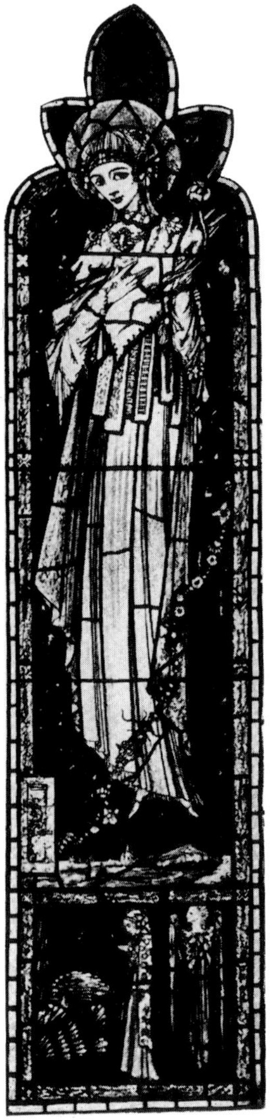

171 *St Ceara*, the only window (1925) in the extensive Carrickmacross series to be wholly designed and partly painted by Clarke; its base panel is particularly evocative.

And Robinson wrote back to MacGreevy that Tangier was 'very wonderful' —

> difficult to believe in. Harry loved it as I guessed he would. We had a long rolling six hours on the sea on a perfect moonlit night from there to [Cadiz] and got in a few minutes before 1 a.m. After a struggle with porters and the customs, as we arrived at the hotel, the coachman gaily suggested a 'senorita' to us. 'Es la Noche!', says I. 'Si', says he. 'Not on your life!', says I . . . Harry, after daily improvement, complains today and yesterday of headache which may be just ordinary, but frightens me a little as headache was so much one of his symptoms. I never properly envisaged what it would be like to have him ill in so foreign a country.[23]

From Cadiz the friends went to Seville for Good Friday and Easter where they were properly impressed by the Holy Week services in the cathedral, and Harry liked the glass there very much. He 'rejoiced in the bright Andalusian colour'[24] and was particularly taken with the jewel-encrusted effigy of the Santa Señora of Hope carried high in the processions. On Easter Monday they moved on to Madrid where they visited the Prado, where Harry at last saw the *Las Meninas* of Velasquez, a picture whose background figure had influenced figures in his own work since at least 1914 (fig. 172). They parted company at Madrid, Robinson to return to Dublin while Harry went on to Paris via Geneva, where he saw the proposed locations for a window at the International Labour Office which the Irish Goverment proposed to present to the League of Nations. He was in good spirits and loved his stay in Paris before returning to Dublin, via London.

While he was away the annual Royal Hibernian Academy exhibition had opened, with his wife's portrait of Lennox Robinson and with seven of his *Faust* illustrations included, among them the pen and wash drawing on

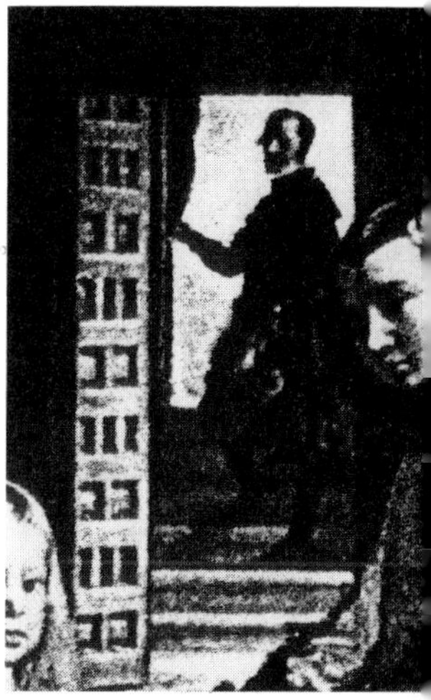

172 A detail from Velasquez' *Las Meninas*, 1656, showing the small background figure which Clarke had adapted in his Poe 'M. Valdémar' illustrations of 1914 and 1918 and the 1923 jacket design, as well as in *The Eve of St Agnes*, 1923-4; Clarke finally saw the painting on his visit to the Prado in Madrid in 1926.

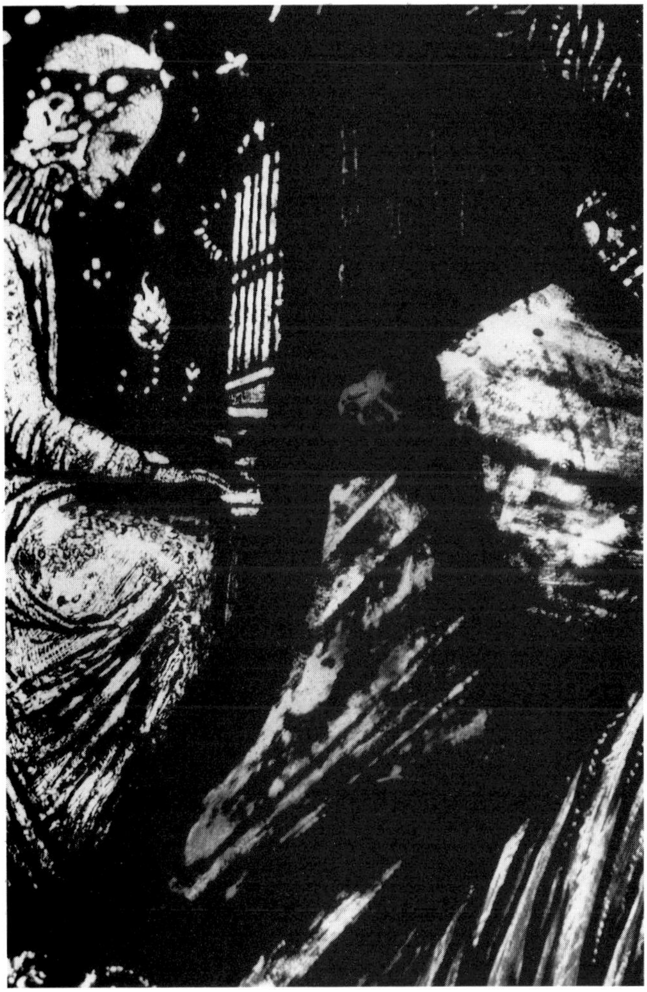

173 Detail of St Cecilia playing the organ in the *St Luke* Egerton Coghill memorial window, Castletownshend, 1926; it should be remembered that Coghill's cousin, Edith OE. Somerville, was for many years the organist in this church.

174 Pencil design for the *Nativity* window, Kilmaine, 1926, a window made by the Studios under Clarke's supervision

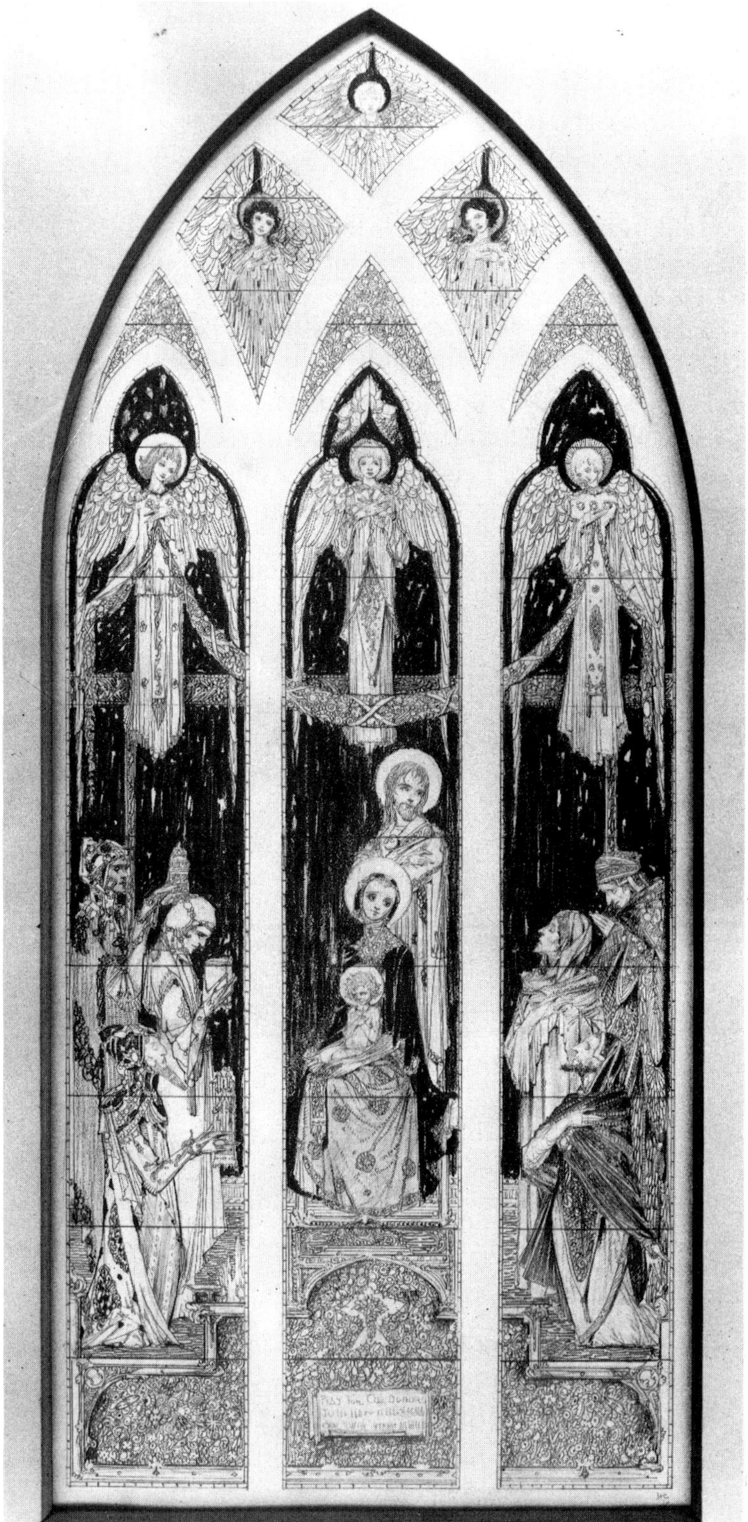

vellum, *Prelude at the Theatre*. His little *St Luke* lancet window, commissioned by Lady Coghill for St Barrahane's church at Castletownshend (4′ x 14″), which he had conceived and designed,[25] was executed during his absence from the Studios; this is evident, particularly in the grainy painting of the rather grey flesh passages. The design is highly imaginative and the langourous, exotically clad central figure of St Luke, with crimson jewelled cap framed against a turquoise halo and finely modelled face with large watery eyes, furrowed brow and forked beard is typically Harry's work, as is the tiny figure of St Cecilia, seated at an organ (fig. 173), and the minute, androgynously profiled St John. St Luke, in an elaborate, girdled blue tunic with silver collar and cuffs under a magenta cloak, holds a paintbrush in his right hand, and in his left three more brushes and a palette on which the Madonna's head is magically suggested in suffused blues and yellows (plate 48).[26] Level with this, painted on pale gold-pink opalescent streaky glass is the miniature figure of St Fidelio, in cope and mitre. At the base of the window, set in the richly coloured inventive abstract ornament which provides a sumptuous backdrop to the figures, are Sir Egerton Coghill's coat of arms and a memorial panel. The window is signed 'Harry Clarke' on a silver scroll beside the saint's remarkable sandals[27].

Although he was not fit for any strenuous work, Harry resumed the full range of his activities at the Studios, answering correspondence, supervising work in progress and preparing sketches and designs for new projects. His seven-light *Ascension* window for Hollymount, Co. Mayo, commissioned at the suggestion of the architect R. M. Butler, was being assembled, as was his two-light window for Donabate Catholic Church. His new designs included a three-light traceried east window for St Patrick's, Kilmaine (fig. 174) and, for Major Dease, a detailed pencil drawing and a colour scheme for the Exton memorial window showing Bl. Oliver Plunkett and Bl. Thomas More, both family connections. Other projects included a reworking of his twelve designs and two coloured cartoons for the Oundle *Moses* window, and schemes for the baptistery windows at Carrickmacross, decorations for the church at Cloughjordan and for the Mercy Convent at Nenagh, both in Co. Tipperary. By mid June he had to seek exemption from jury service and was out sick for about a month. Walter had to pursue the delicate matter of the windows at Belcamp, which the Oblate Fathers still thought too dark (fig. 175), even after the rapturous critical acclaim at the Studios' exhibition of the first four windows the previous summer. Despite his efforts, and the appearance of a piece by John Hunter praising the windows which appeared in the *Irish Statesman* of 17 July,[28] the problem was not resolved before the end of November.

Welcome distraction came in attending Lennox Robinson's rehearsals of the Dublin Drama League's production of *The Cyclops* by Euripides which was performed on the lawn of Sorrento Cottage 'to shock good people who

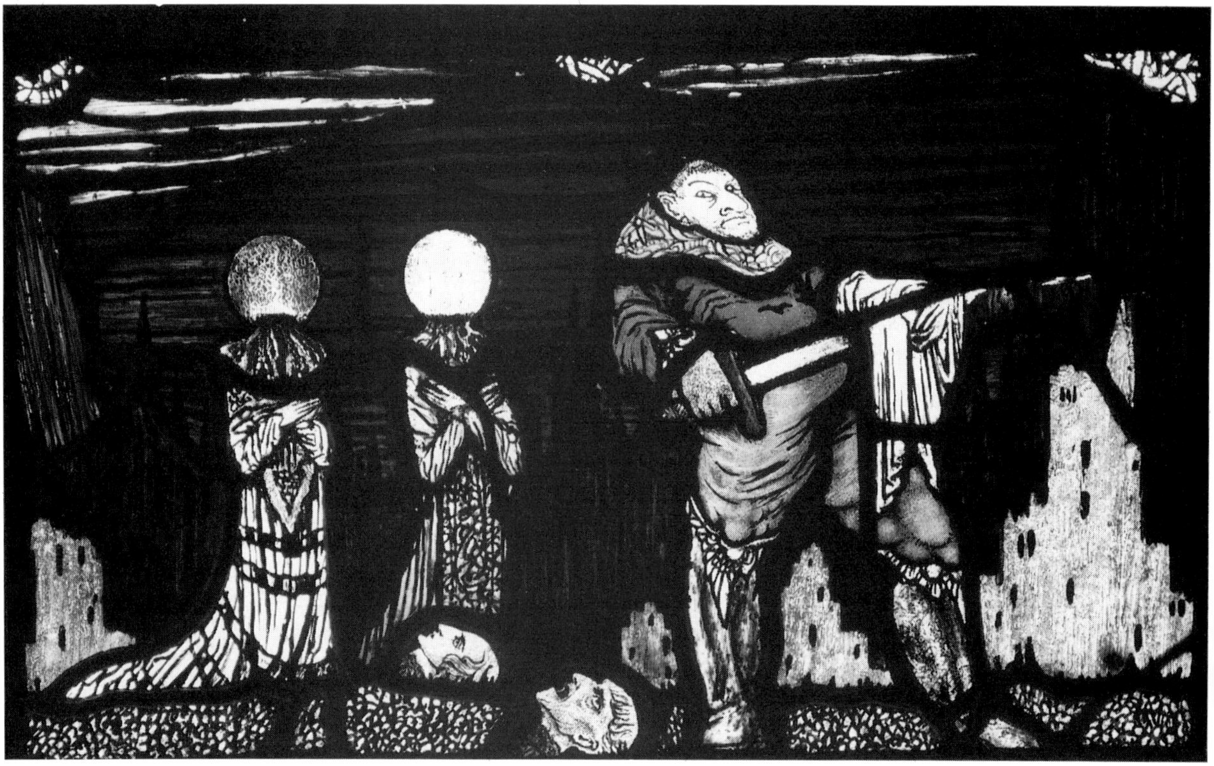

175 The Martyrdom of St Dymphna (patron saint of the insane) and St Gerebern, base panel in the *St Dymphna* window, Belcamp, 1925; this subject was repeated in the Carrickmacross *St Dymphna*. Its treatment is adapted from Fra Angelico.

think Greek plays always enobling and top lofty',[29] as Robinson wrote to MacGreevy. In the first week of August, Harry joined Paul Henry and Jack B. Yeats on the judging panel for the Royal Dublin Society's National Art Competition. But the demand for his work was insistent, and throughout August he was in sole charge of the Studios, supervising at least seven jobs. In September he travelled to Newport in Co. Mayo to make notes for the large east window commissioned, again at R.M. Butler's suggestion, for Butler's new church there. Canon MacDonald, the parish priest, had sold his life assurance policy to pay for the window, which was to depict *The Last Judgment*. Harry found him pottering about his rose garden with a basket and large straw hat, to his delight.

Harry took the sketches for the Newport window with him when he left for London for three months on 14 September.[30] He rented rooms in Bedford Park and contacted his sisters in Highgate. His friend Karl Parsons offered to share his studio at the Glass House with him (fig. 176), and Walter kept him posted on the progess of work at the Studios in Dublin. He was so impressed with the range of 'special' glasses available at Hetley's that he asked Michael Dunne, his head glazier, to come over and 'level up' the Studio stock: opalescents, streakies, unexpected flashed combinations and slabs. He gave Parsons part of a special pot of flashed glass he had had Hartley Woods make up, in gratitude. Despite all his work in hand, Harry was very depressed during this stay in London and only his assistant, Leonard Potter, who helped him with glazing, and visits to such friends as MacGreevy, the Odles, the Parsons family and the poet Austin Clarke, a fellow old-Belvederian and friend of the eccentric Odles,[31] helped to relieve his melancholy. Austin Clarke recalled Harry as a striking, considerate, kind but melancholic man,[32] who

> came round every week to visit me. He brought his own noggin of Whiskey for I could not afford him such hospitality after I had left *Argosy*. . . . I had suggested he should illustrate merrily *The Intoxication of the Ulsterman* based on an ancient mock-saga, *Mesca Uladh*, a long poem which I was writing. Unfortunately, the poem went wrong, for my technique had spread out too quickly. . . . The artist was tall, dark, handsome and consumptive. I have forgotten those evenings and can only remember the second last of them. When he arrived he told me excitedly that he had discovered a tank in the back garden of his lodgings, full of tiny wriggling monsters, some of them scarcely visible. He was exalted for he saw in these microscopic shapes new forms for experiment in art. He would develop in ornamental design these fantastic germ-shapes which had been almost hidden from the human eye for aeons.[33]

In November he was asked by the Minstry of Industry and Commerce in Dublin to prepare sketch designs of 'selected subjects' for Ireland's proposed window in eight panels for the suggested staircase site in Geneva. This was located in the International Labour Building of the League of

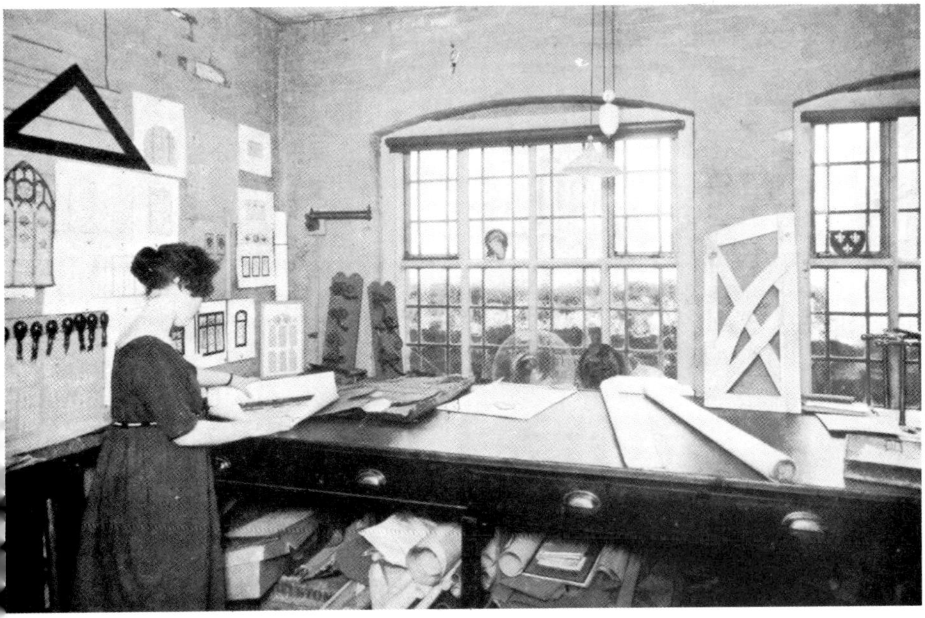

176 Photograph taken *c*. 1920 of a studio such as Clarke would have rented in the Glass House in Lettice Street, Fulham

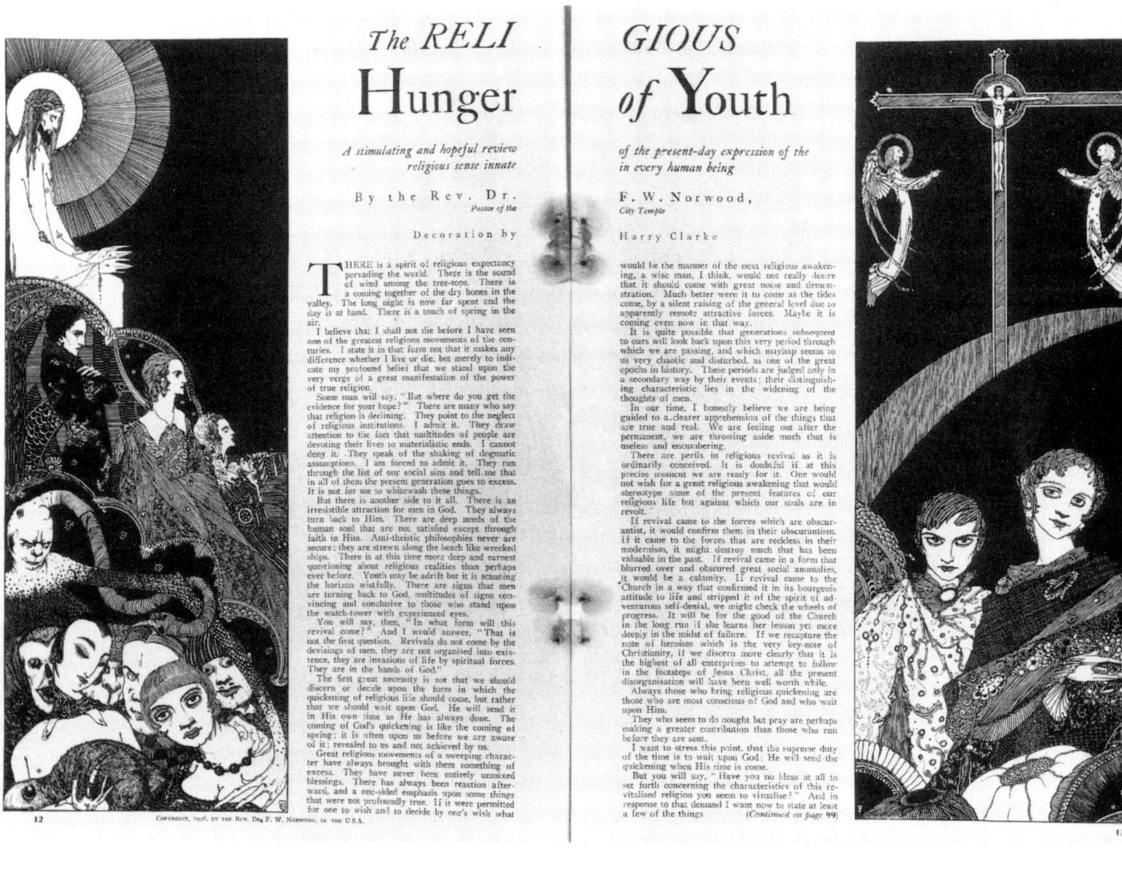

The RELIGIOUS Hunger of Youth

A stimulating and hopeful review of the present-day expression of the religious sense innate in every human being

By the Rev. Dr. F. W. Norwood,
Pastor of the City Temple

Decoration by Harry Clarke

THERE is a spirit of religious expectancy pervading the world. There is the sound of wind among the tree-tops. There is a coming together of the dry bones in the valley. The long night is now far spent and the day is at hand. There is a touch of spring in the air.

I believe that I shall not die before I have seen one of the greatest religious movements of the centuries. I state it in that form not that it makes any difference whether I live or die, but merely to indicate my profound belief that we stand upon the very verge of a great manifestation of the power of true religion.

Some man will say, "But where do you get the evidence for your hope?" There are many who say that religion is declining. They point to the neglect of religious institutions. I admit it. They draw attention to the fact that multitudes of people are devoting their lives to materialistic ends. I cannot deny it. They speak of the shaking of dogmatic assumptions. I am forced to admit it. They run through the list of our social sins and tell me that in all of them the present generation goes to excess. It is not for me to whitewash these things.

But there is another side to it all. There is an irresistible attraction for men in God. They always turn back to Him. There are deep needs of the human soul that are not satisfied except through faith in Him. Anti-theistic philosophies never are secure; they are strewn along the beach like wrecked ships. There is at this time more deep and earnest questioning about religious realities than perhaps ever before. Youth may be adrift but it is scanning the horizon wistfully. There are signs that men are turning back to God, multitudes of signs convincing and conclusive to those who stand upon the watch-tower with experienced eyes.

You will say, then, "In what form will this revival come?" And I would answer, "That is not the first question. Revivals do not come by the devisings of men, they are not organised into existence, they are invasions of life by spiritual forces. They are in the hands of God."

The first great necessity is not that we should discern or decide upon the form in which the quickening of religious life should come, but rather that we should wait upon God. He will send it in His own time as He has always done. The coming of God's quickening is like the coming of spring; it is often upon us before we are aware of it; revealed to us and not achieved by us.

Great religious movements of a sweeping character have always brought with them something of excess. They have never been entirely unmixed blessings. There has always been reaction afterward, and a one-sided emphasis upon some things that were not profoundly true. If it were permitted for one to wish and to decide by one's wish what would be the manner of the next religious awakening, a wise man, I think, would not really desire that it should come with great noise and demonstration. Much better were it to come as the tides come, by a silent raising of the general level due to apparently remote attractive forces. Maybe it is coming even now in that way.

It is quite possible that generations subsequent to ours will look back upon this very period through which we are passing, and which mayhap seems to us very chaotic and disturbed, as one of the great epochs in history. These periods are judged only in a secondary way by their events; their distinguishing characteristic lies in the widening of the thoughts of men.

In our time, I honestly believe we are being guided to a clearer apprehension of the things that are true and real. We are feeling out after the permanent, we are throwing aside much that is useless and encumbering.

There are perils in religious revival as it is ordinarily conceived. It is doubtful if at this precise moment we are ready for it. One would not wish for a great religious awakening that would stereotype some of the present features of our religious life but against which our souls are in revolt.

If revival came to the forces which are obscurantist, it would confirm them in their obscurantism. If it came to the forces that are reckless in their modernism, it might destroy much that has been valuable in the past. If revival came in a form that blurred over and obscured great social anomalies, it would be a calamity. If revival came to the Church in a way that confirmed it in its bourgeois attitude to life and stripped it of the spirit of adventurous self-denial, we might check the wheels of progress. It will be for the good of the Church in the long run if she learns her lesson yet more deeply in the midst of failure. If we recapture the note of heroism which is the very key-note of Christianity, if we discern more clearly that it is the highest of all enterprises to attempt to follow in the footsteps of Jesus Christ, all the present disorganisation will have been well worth while.

Always those who bring religious quickening are those who are most conscious of God and who wait upon Him.

They who seem to do nought but pray are perhaps making a greater contribution than those who run before they are sent.

I want to stress this point, that the supreme duty of the time is to wait upon God; He will send the quickening when His time is come.

But you will say, "Have you no ideas at all to set forth concerning the characteristics of this revitalised religion you seem to visualise?" And in response to that demand I want now to state at least a few of the things (*Continued on page* 99)

12

Copyright, 1926, by the Rev. Dr. F. W. Norwood, in the U.S.A.

13

177 Double-page illustration to the Revd Dr F.W. Norwood's article 'The Religious Hunger of Youth' in *Good Housekeeping*, November 1926

Nations outside the Deputy Director's room. Harry had visited Geneva in April to see the various sites suggested for the window, and now set to prepare a draft scheme for the design. The commission was to be worth £450.[34] During the same month *Good Housekeeping* published another double-spread article illustrated in two vertical rectangular sections by Harry: The Revd Dr F.W. Norwood's 'The Religious Hunger of Youth — A stimulating and hopeful review of the present-day expression of the religious sense innate in every human being' (pp. 12-13; fig. 177). Unmistakably peopled with pious, menacing, haunted and fiendish Clarke archetypes, the familiar decorative and geometrical devices are set against a sheet of black.

Because of Harrap's dissatisfaction with his *Faust* illustrations, Harry felt he should employ an agent to act for him in dealing with publishers, and on 7 November he went to see John Austen's agents, Sharmid's in Jermyn Street, run by the Misses Sharman and Middleton, who arranged a meeting with Mr Willett of John Lane at the Bodley Head to discuss the possibility of his illustrating a book for them. From its foundation in the 1890s, the Bodley Head had been in the forefront of publishers of finely designed books. The firm had issued the *Salome* of Oscar Wilde with Beardsley's drawings, one of the finest illustrated books of its time, and had also published *The Yellow Book*, which from its first appearance in 1894 until it ceased publication, was the outlet for new and daring illustration and literature. Beardsley, Walter Crane, Selwyn Image, Charles Ricketts and Laurence Housman had all designed for Lane, and Basil Willett was the firm's expert on book production. Harry was desperately keen to be the illustrator for *The Playboy of the Western World*, which the executors of J.M. Synge had agreed that Allen and Unwin should publish, and early in December he informed Miss Middleton of Sharmid's that he had written to Sir Stanley Unwin offering to do this. He quoted Allen and Unwin's reply to her: 'Arrangements have already been made for an illustrated edition … by the executors of the late John Millington Synge for whom we act, but there is no harm in your writing to them if you choose'.[35]

Harry affirmed his anxiety to do the book and offered to make 'special terms' if he should get the commission. He had already done several drawings based on Synge's play, among them the drawing entitled *The Mad Mulrannies* which he gave to Bodkin in 1917 (and which had been reproduced in Bodkin's article in *The Studio* in 1919) and an earlier, unfinished pen and ink design which probably dates from 1915. In the event, however, he did not get the commission from Allen and Unwin, who produced their limited edition of *The Playboy of the Western World* with ten illustrations in colour from oil paintings by Seán Keating, RHA in September 1927.

In January 1927 a further meeting with Mr Willett of John Lane's resulted in a suggestion that Harry should illustrate a selection of Swinburne's poetry for an edition to appear in 1928. He wrote to Bodkin about this:

> I know only two of his poems that I want to do — 'Faustine' and 'Queens'. You are a Swinbournite [*sic*] and I wonder if you would help me, or lend me some of his books. Lane said if I would give him six poems that I wanted, he would base the selection on them.[36]

Harry himself was particularly keen on illustrating Baudelaire's *Fleurs du Mal*, while also considering Sir Richard Burton's *Arabian Nights*, *Dracula*, *Macbeth* and *The Turn of the Screw*. However, by the end of March agreement about the edition was reached and Harry informed his agents that he would illustrate his own selection of twenty-seven poems by Swinburne. A final decision was to be made on the number of colour plates and on the format and typography of the book.

On Harry's return to Dublin, his life was once more fully occupied by design and administrative work at the Studios. The three-light *Mother of Sorrows* window was finished and sent off to join its earlier companion, *The Coronation of the Virgin*, at Dowanhill convent in Glasgow, where it was dedicated as a memorial to Sr Superior Mary of St Wilfred, who had been responsible for the commission;[37] the Exton window was also installed;

and other projects included a dining room ceiling and glazing at Beaulieu in Co. Meath and a substantial range of decorative windows for the new premises of Bewley's Oriental Café in Grafton Street, Dublin. On 17 February, Harry was 'tremendously pleased and proud' to be given a firm formal commission to provide a window as Ireland's gift to Geneva which he would execute either in 'a technique which is I believe peculiarly my own' or, if they preferred, a 'more ordinary technical treatment . . . similar to that employed by the Germans in their window.'[38] He reckoned the window should take 'about four months to complete, as this is work I'd have to do entirely myself' but was too busy to start on it for another two or three months. His church commissions included a three-light window at Tullycross in Co. Galway, a two-light at Killaloe, a three-light ordered

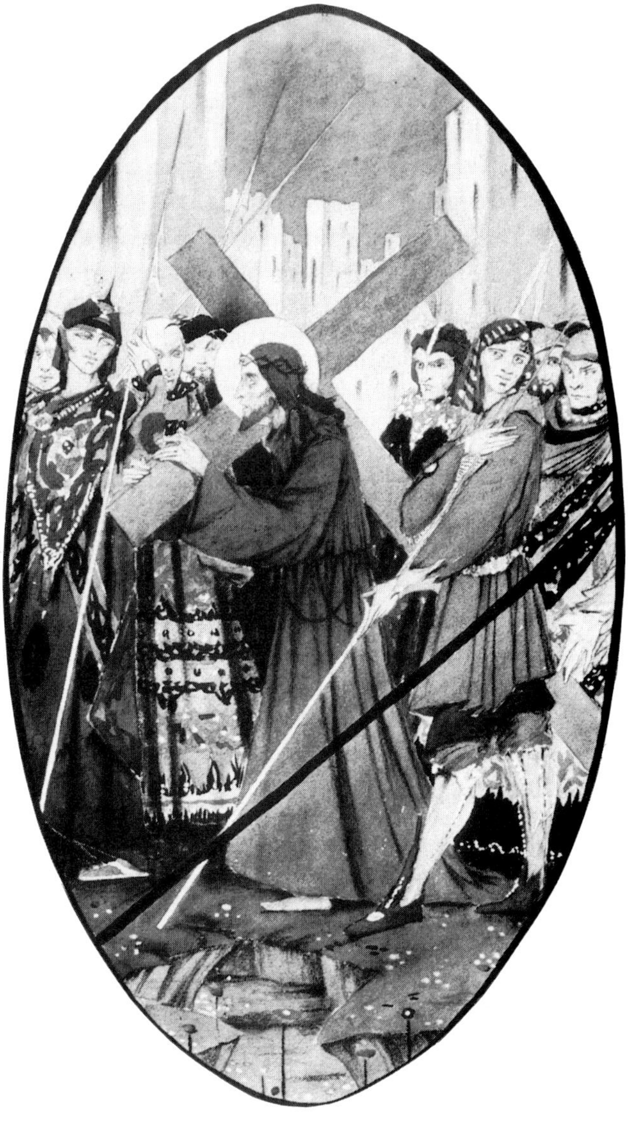

178 Full-scale design for a Station of the Cross inset panel, Lough Derg, pencil and watercolour, 1927

by the Colthursts for Blarney in Co. Cork, three windows for St Patrick's College, Thurles, further windows for Carrickmacross, and a series of *Stations of the Cross* conceived as small oval panels leaded into a scheme of fourteen windows depicting the Apostles, St Paul and our Lord for William Scott's new basilica at St Patrick's Purgatory, Lough Derg; he sent pencil designs and three exquisite full-scale colour studies of the inset panels in these (fig. 178) to his patron, Canon Keown, in February. Graphic work included a letterheading for Karl Parsons, which he designed on a Sunday, a badge for Fr O'Connor, late of Belcamp, and a cover design for Fr Matthew Bodkin's *Floodtide*. By the end of March he had taken on a scheme of windows for the Jesuit retreat chapel at Rathfarnham Castle, Dublin and a window for the Franciscan Church in Cork.

He was also working on the minutely detailed scale drawing in pencil and the colour scheme for the Newport *Last Judgment*, which he sent to Canon MacDonald for approval on 1 April, and later in the month was preparing a scheme for a two-light window for the Church of Ireland at Sandford Road, Ranelagh in Dublin, in which he suggested each ope should

> contain a single figure with subjects or incidents from his life at the base of the window; figures such as David, Solomon, Moses, Elijah, Joshua, Gideon would be suitable, or if you wish to take subjects from N.T., any two of the twelve Apostles.[39]

The subject chosen for the window was *Sts Peter and Paul* and the finished window, Harry's most Art Deco, was erected before the end of the year. Another window, in which he took a special interest at the time,was to commemorate Oliver St John Gogarty's parents-in-law at Tullycross, near Renvyle. The pencil design and colour scheme, depicting Sts Bernard and Barbara and the Sacred Heart in three lights, are particularly fine and display his current 'gadgett' of setting the principal figures against a deep blue sky threaded with gossamer and brightly coloured galactic phenomena. The window was installed in July. Its dramatic background device is repeated to even greater effect in the larger three-light window commissioned in May by Raymond Brooke for Castleknock Church of Ireland, Co. Dublin, to commemorate military, hunting and artistic members of his family.

At the Royal Hibernian Academy exhibition in April, at which he showed a *Faust* illustration and a stained glass design, to his delight his wife Margaret was elected an Academician.[40] By the end of the month the contract for the Swinburne had been agreed with John Lane. Harry was to receive back the originals on publication with the exception of any drawing he might present to Willett, and he would receive a fee of £127 10s., being £150 less the agent's fifteen per cent fee, for the twelve illustrations agreed upon. In May, he was represented by two *Faust* drawings at an exhibition of Irish art at The Fine Art Society in London organized to coincide with the publication of Crampton Walker's *Irish Life and Landscape*.[41] As Walter was away from the Studios for a long time being treated for 'neuritis', the pressure on Harry was extreme, because his own deadline for the Geneva window proposals and the Swinburne illustrations had to be met. Nevertheless, he set out proposals for windows at the Dominican Convent on the Falls Road, Belfast in competition with a German firm and travelled to Belfast to see the location in mid June. By the end of the month the Studios were given the order (their first in Ulster), which involved over a thousand feet of leaded glass, a rose window and a stained glass window in the chancel of *St Dominic receiving the Rosary*.[42] He also travelled to Glasgow in view of another window at Dowanhill and co-judged the annual Taylor Art Competition with the painters Paul Henry and Sarah Purser, the latter enraged at Bodkin's recent appointment as director of the National Gallery.

By the end of July he had submitted to the Government a preparatory pencil draft for the Geneva window. W.B. Yeats was 'wildly enthusiastic'[43] about Harry's plan to interpret excerpts from the work of fifteen Irish writers and helped with suggestions about the literary references. During the latter part of the year, which he spent mainly in London, Harry prepared the coloured designs for the panels, which were to be finished in the technique used for *The Eve of St Agnes*. He rented studio A and then studio D at the Glass House,[44] where he worked on two further windows for Dowanhill (both single lights), but found he had to make several journeys back to Dublin to see to things there. He made designs for the decoration of the third floor lounge of the new Metropole cinema in Dublin and for mural decorations at the Jesuit retreat house in Milltown near Dublin which he painted himself on canvas panels in December, advising his client, Fr Hannon, that they should not be fixed in position while the chapel walls were still damp. His second design for the Dublin Drama League programmes appeared in November,[45] a light-hearted piece showing a vampish lady manipulating a row of marionettes, one of which is a caricature of W.B. Yeats as a gangster shooting another of the puppet figures in the leg. About this time, for no accountable or recorded reason, his long friendship with Bodkin came to an end.[46]

Perhaps as an antidote to having to turn out all the drawings of saints for the Studios, Harry resumed his pen-and-ink drawing with great enthusiasm toward the end of the year. Allan Odle, who was at the time drawing illustrations to Rabelais, wrote before Christmas:

> seasonable salutation . . . how are you? I imagine you standing in the midst of a hierarchy of stained glass saints distributing haloes with a fine generosity or — cigarette in mouth — bending over a sheet of your inimitable Bruegelesque bogies, smiling — perhaps — as you balance the ultimate hair on a ulcer, or define the textures of a putrifying limb![47]

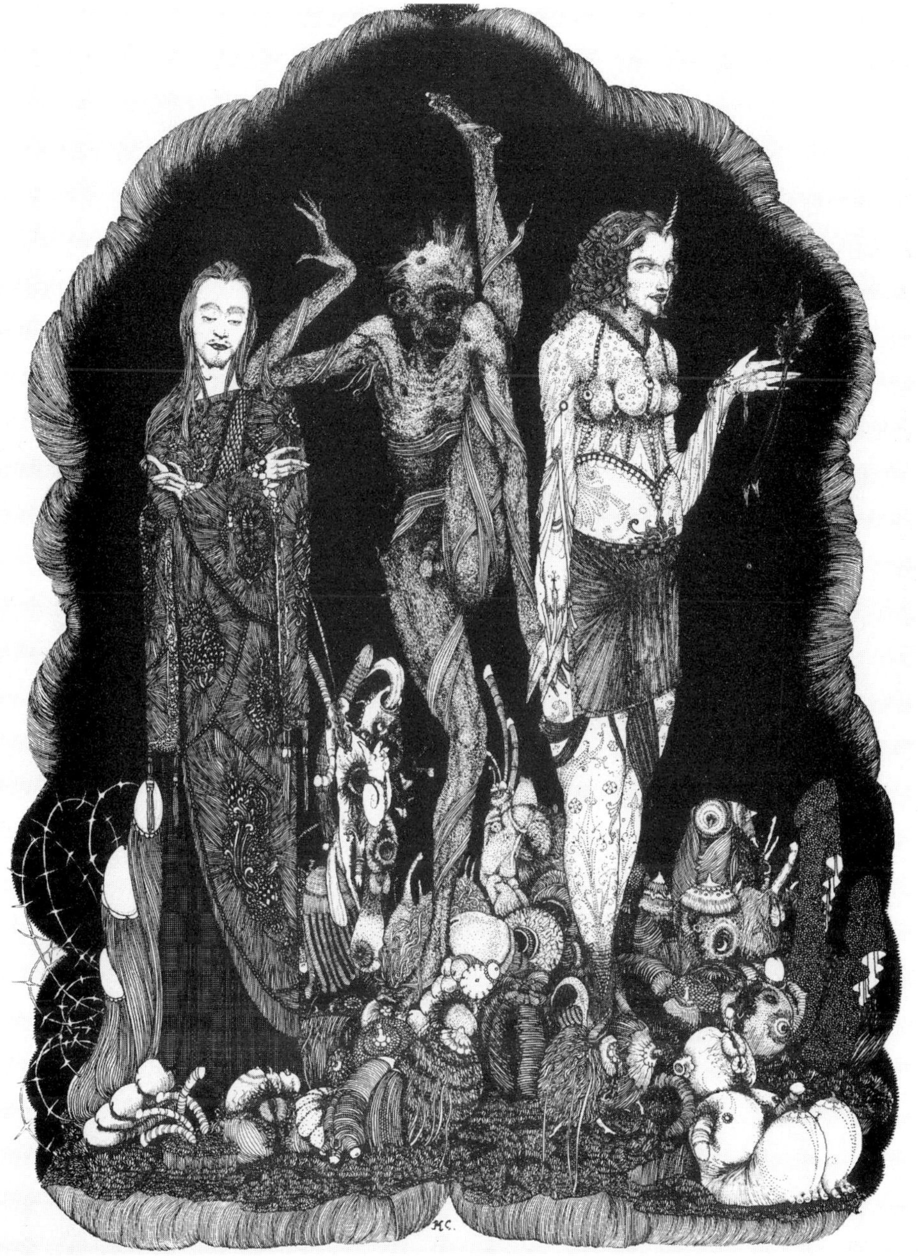

179 *Sts Vitus, Placidus and Hermaphroditus*, pen and ink, *c.* 1927; in the amended version Hermaphroditus' outsize phallus has been inked out and a shakily initialled signature added

In November Harry drew a number of studies of a skull he had acquired. He was working at the full-page and double-spread drawings for the Swinburne illustrations and, perhaps as a cathartic release from his morbid imaginings and the endless run of saints, produced a very detailed pen and ink study entitled *Sts Vitus, Placidus and Hermaphroditus* which seems to parody the many saints he had drawn over the years (fig. 179). The three ill-matched figures, poised within an almost surgically dissected vulva, are

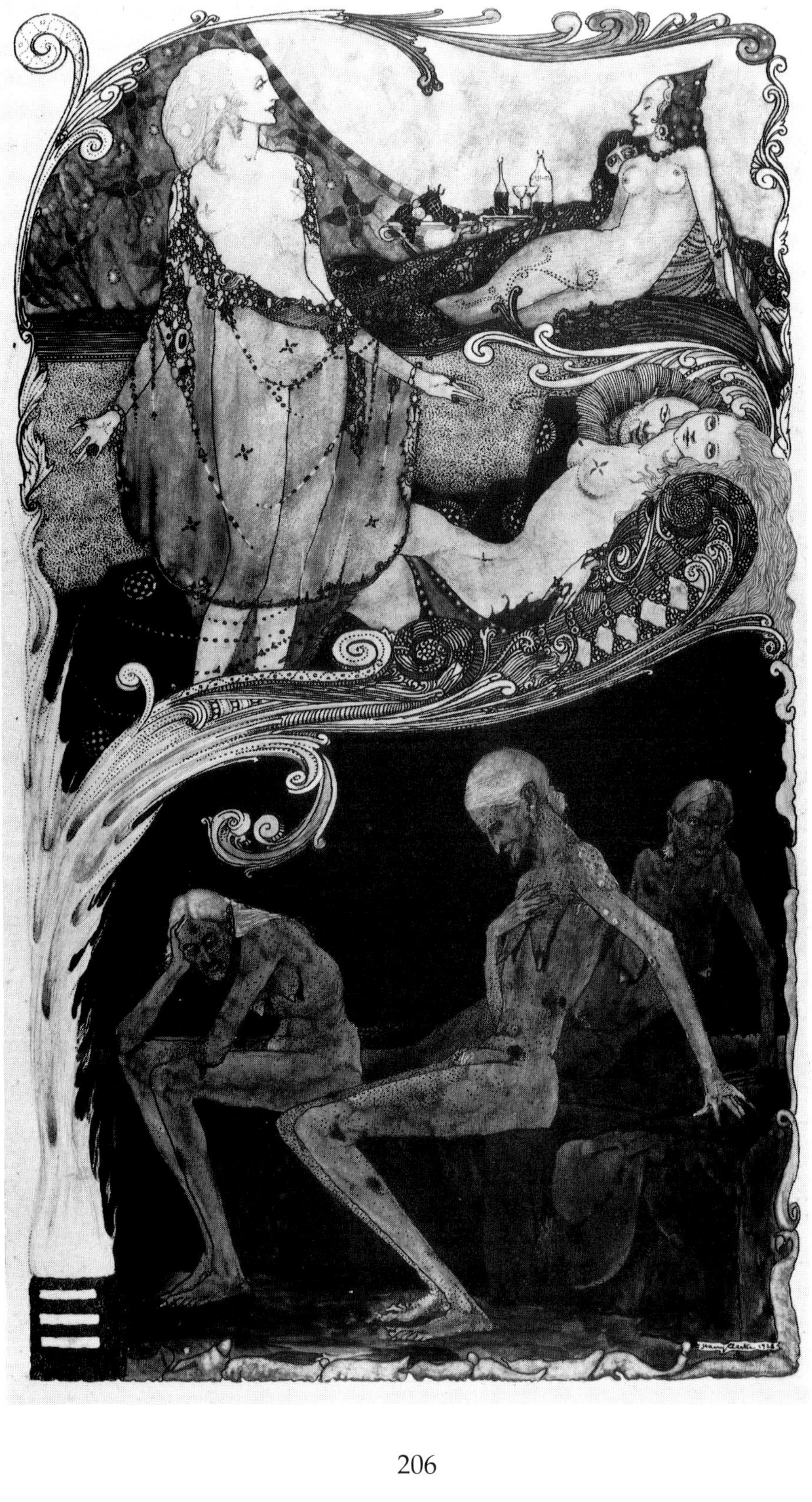

180 Illustration to Villon's 'Complaint of the Fair Armouress', photogravure plate from *Selected Poems of Charles Algernon Swinburne* (1928)

surrounded by monsters and genitalia in a bizarre composition.[48] The skull figures as a detail in the drawing.

Early in January 1928 the first group of the Swinburne illustrations had been sent to Willett at John Lane for approval — *Aholibah,* the double-spread *Queens* in conte and wash, and Villon's *Complaint of the Fair Armouress* (fig. 180), which was on vellum. A profile of Harry in the *Irish Times* of 7 January described a visit to the Studios where work was proceeding on the Geneva window, the Lough Derg panels, the large *Last Judgment* for Newport, and the first of six decorative windows for the rear of Bewley's Café:

> Another delightful window of a different type almost completed is destined to remain in Dublin in a business house, where Dublin's citizens will have frequent opportunities of seeing it. It consists of minute decorations of country life, butterflies of vivid blue, red birds, pale shells and flowers [fig. 181].

Harry took great trouble over the Bewley's windows, particularly the four showing the Orders of Architecture in which Doric, Ionic, Corinthian and Composite columns are adorned and topped by vases full of flowers. The black leafy tendrils disguising the leads — a device already seen in the decorative lunettes above *The Eve of St Agnes* window — are interspersed with exotic birds, butterflies, flowers and submarine creatures acided against a lightly painted clear background, as though suspended in a parchment solution. The black lacy borders punctuated with small beads of colour are echoed in the two other windows of the scheme overlooking Swan Alley. Their simple, abstract treatment is particularly effective in its restraint.[49]

His health was deteriorating badly. 'I am in a bad way with neuralgia and can not get speeded up',[50] he wrote to Fr Hannon of Milltown to explain delays in finishing his angel pictures. Tuberculosis was advancing rapidly and he found it increasingly difficult to keep up with his work: he had to see his doctor almost daily. Despite this, he continued to take most of the responsibility for running the Studios and keeping up the increasingly voluminous correspondence. He was therefore greatly relieved when Leonard Potter arrived in February from London to help him. By 8 February he had made the amendments requested by Willett to the first group of *Swinburne* illustrations, and apologized for the delay in returning them. He was glad that the Curwen Press was to print the book, and approved the specimen of text setting which was sent to him. But he could not meet the deadline of March for the remainder of the illustrations and had to ask Willett for more time.

At the Studios his work on the Geneva window also fell behind as he tried to deal with copious enquiries, management and stock problems, and the new work coming in, which he would design and detail with minute instructions so that his staff could carry out the schemes. They were using Raines' photographic services to such an extent they had opened an account with them in January. He had to write to the Government that the Geneva window would not be ready by 30 May, the agreed delivery date. The Franciscans in Cork ordered two further windows, a *Sacred Heart* with attendant Irish saints and an *Immaculate Conception*, both two-lights. All Saints Church in Penarth wanted a successor to their *Simeon* baptistery design and colour scheme. The rector of the Vincentian Church at Bayonne in New Jersey had come to Dublin and placed an order which, as it was the first American order for work from the Studios, Harry was anxious to design and oversee personally.[51] At Easter he sent his scheme to the

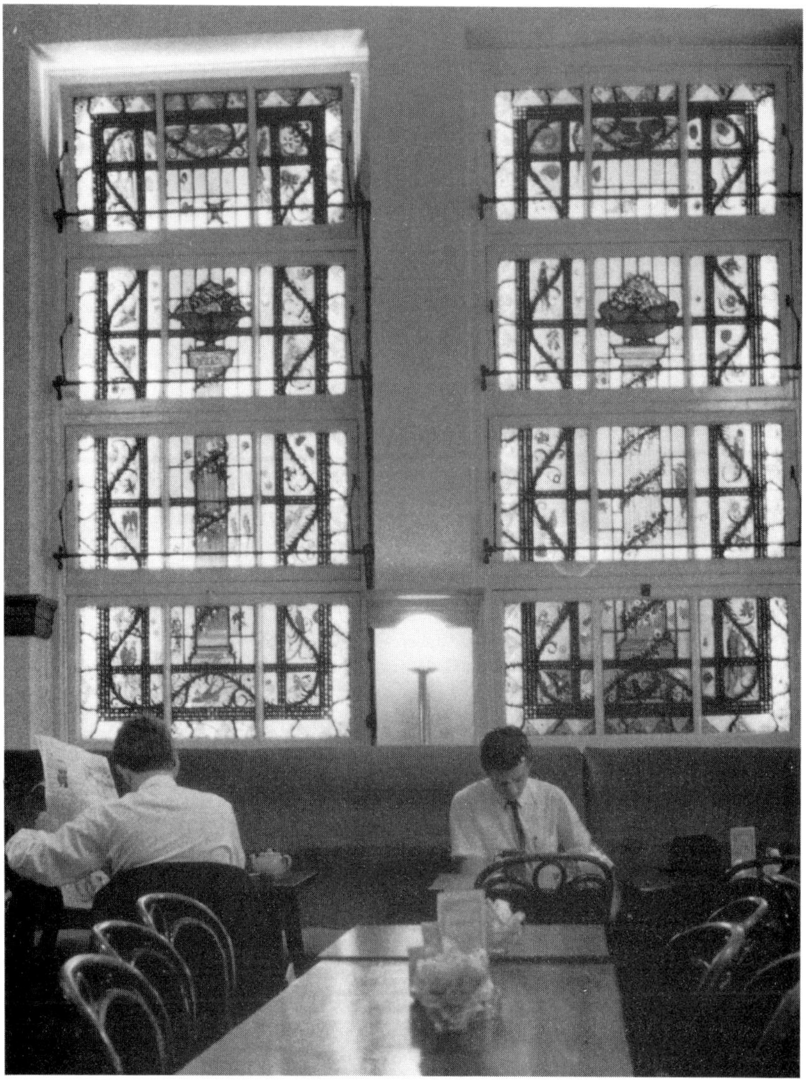

181 Clarke's windows, 1927-8, in Bewley's Oriental Cafe, Grafton Street, Dublin, photographed in 1988

architects for nine chancel windows with angels bearing the symbols of the Mass (fig. 182), a 'decorative wheel window of richly ornamented glasses of varied quality and tones', fourteen two-light clerestory windows with emblems of the Passion and ten two-light aisle windows with single figures representing one of the three types of sacrifice in the Old Law, each with a base medallion of types of sacrifice in the New Law.

On 7 May he wrote to Willett sending eight tailpieces and a drawing for the endpapers in the *Swinburne*, and asked his opinion on one of the endpaper devices and the tailpiece for 'Sapphic' which he had considered altering but refrained because Willett had thought his alterations to the double-page 'Masque of Queens' drawing too drastic. Three days later he sent the remaining ten tailpieces and asked Miss Sharman to return the 'Sapphic' tailpiece as Willett did feel he should draw an alternative. The full-page illustrations still were not finished, for he had altered the scale at

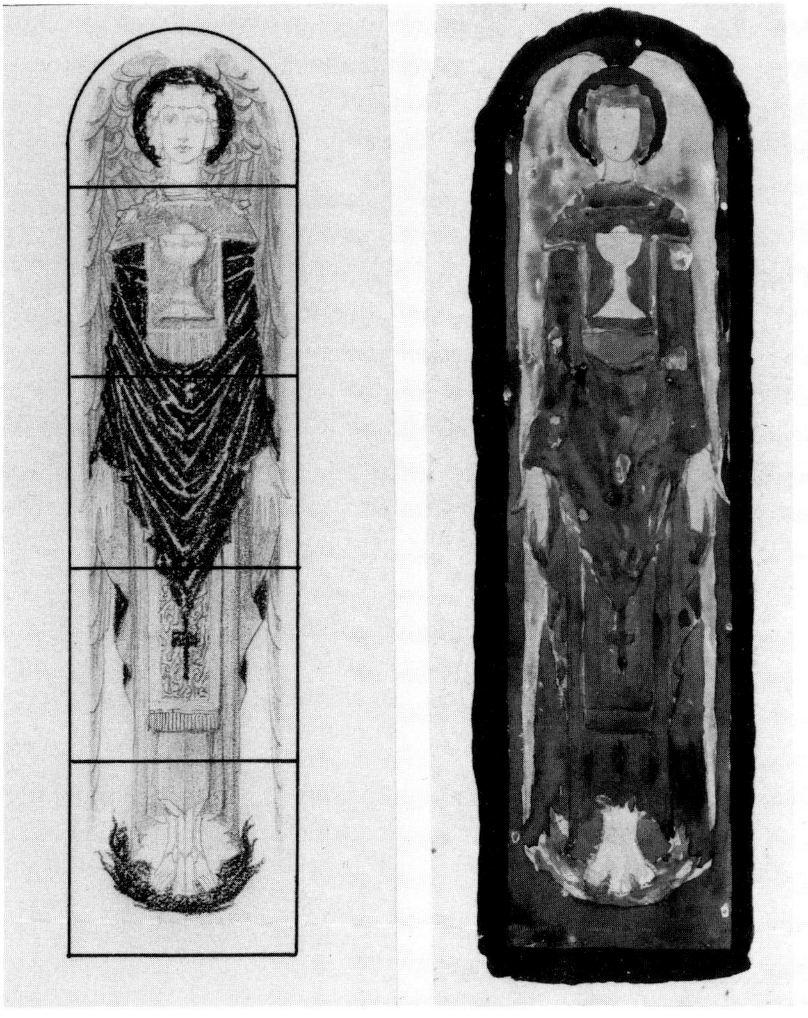

182 Pencil design and colour scheme for a chancel window depicting an *Angel bearing a Symbol of the Mass*, Bayonne, New Jersey, 1928

which he was working because the degree of reduction which had to be adopted in his first drawings was too great to retain the fine detail. His next two illustrations, *Faustine* and *The Weary Wedding*, sent at the end of May, were drawn to a scale much closer to the printed reproductions. Pressure to finish the job was extreme and he eventually managed to send the final drawings on 29 June.

On 14 May he wrote to George Roberts, the Irish publisher, formerly the partner of Joseph Maunsell Hone in Maunsel and Roberts, and now based in London, about a proposed book:

> I remember our discussing an illustrated translation of an old Irish story and had at that time reckoned to be in London this month. . . . Re my illustrating this book, I am in rather a difficulty, being very busy here with my glass, and if my present venture with John Lane is a success, I have no doubt he'll want me for 1929 — and even should he not do so, I have a provisional arrangement with Messrs Harrap for that year. If the question of the illustrations can be postponed till Autumn and my time were available, I'd with pleasure discuss the matter with you, but at the moment I don't want to undertake a commission I may find later I can't fulfil.[52]

He hoped he might be able to reduce the burden of work for the *Swinburne* and wrote to Miss Sharman:

> As you know, I originally stipulated for twelve full pages and there was a verbal agreement mentioned to me by Mr Willett re lessening the number of full pages and thus write off the cost of the additional drawings [in] tail pieces. . . . At the moment I'm terribly weary and hope you can arrange that I shall finish with the next four drawings.[53]

He hoped Willett would settle for ten full-page drawings but this proposal was not acceptable and Harry wrote to amend things, saying how very anxious he was to make the book a success and that he would fulfil the agreement

> as soon as consistent with doing drawings up to the standard we want . . . the smaller line drawings I'll do . . .on completion of the full-sized pages and shall do an additional one instead of the one for which you sent me the Block Maker's proof today.[54]

Four further proofs arrived on 22 June. Harry was pleased with *Faustine* but did not like the line reproductions. He had almost finished the full-page drawings and despatched the final four, with two small drawings Willet had requested, by the end of June. He also agreed that the captions to the full-page plates should be printed on tissues overlaid on the plates rather than under the pictures. The strain was evident to Lennox Robinson, who wrote in his autobiography that Harry

> finished up his day by sitting at his great desk till the early hours of the morning, working under a blazingly bright electric light . . . with febrile intensity. . . . But such intense work those days that began early and stretched deep into the night could not continue . . .[55]

and asked, in his obituary notice[56] whether Harry instinctively felt that he must crush as much work as possible into his remaining days.

By 2 August Harry had seen and passed the page proofs of the *Swinburne*, but there was no relaxation except, perhaps, for a whimsical certificate drawn for Robinson's Abbey Theatre School of Acting that summer.[57] Walter was still unwell and spent very little time at the Studios and Harry had to take on the considerable problems of administration and all the correspondence as well as planning the new work. An enquiry from Fr O'Meara of St Oswald's in Ashton-in-Makerfield resulted in all the glass in the church being supplied by the Studios, a contract which extended well after Harry's death. The two windows at Penarth, the latter commemorating his admirer, the late Revd A.W. Flux Dundas, were at last confirmed, and a domestic order was received from Janet Cunningham at St Pauls Girls' School in London for a *St Patrick* window.[58] The prospect of a large order at St Eunan's Cathedral in Letterkenny, Co. Donegal, meant a visit there which so exhausted him that he had to spend several days recovering. And the commission was confirmed for the windows at Bayonne, New Jersey so that he had to commence the sketches and colour schemes. The final two tailpieces for *Swinburne* were sent to Sharmid's on 17 July. Immediately afterwards the rough designs for ten two-light clerestory windows for Letterkenny were sent to the Bishop of Raphoe with an explanatory letter:

> In my design and in the glass I shall endeavour to get a general effect of warm colour such as shown in the three colour reproductions of stained glass at S. Ouen, Rouen, which we both saw yesterday in your office. I haven't designed or suggested any figurative work for these windows, as I am convinced at such a height they wouldn't be properly seen and be misapplied.[59]

On 3 August he was given the commission.

His departure to London in the last week of July seems to have been a despairing attempt to distance himself from the day to day preoccupations of his Dublin life so as to get ahead with his own work. He had sadly confided to Mr Salmond of Hetley's that 'plans with my great friend [Karl Parsons]' at Fulham 'will now I fear never materialize'. On 2 August he closed his London bank account.[60] His chief concern was the Geneva window, about which he had to write again to Gordon Campbell, later Lord Glenavy, the Minister responsible, that he now hoped to have the window finished by March at the latest but would arrange a special showing for the

Minister early in January 1929. By early October he had completed designs and colour schemes for the nine chancel windows at Bayonne, a three-light *Ascension* for Lady Dillon at Skryne, the Flux Dundas *Sts Michael and Gabriel* and a two light *Music and Literature* for Ballycumber, Co. Westmeath, but he was desperately far behind with most of his work and had to work on designs on Saturdays and Sundays. 'I cannot get more out of myself than I am getting',[61] he wrote. He got a Cardiff firm to erect the Payne memorial window, *Simeon*, in All Saints, Penarth on 1 November, the same day that two advance copies of his illustrated *Swinburne* arrived.

Selected Poems of Algernon Charles Swinburne, introduced by Humbert Wolfe, has eleven full-page illustrations by Harry, one of them a double spread. Nine of the full-page plates are in photogravure and the others are

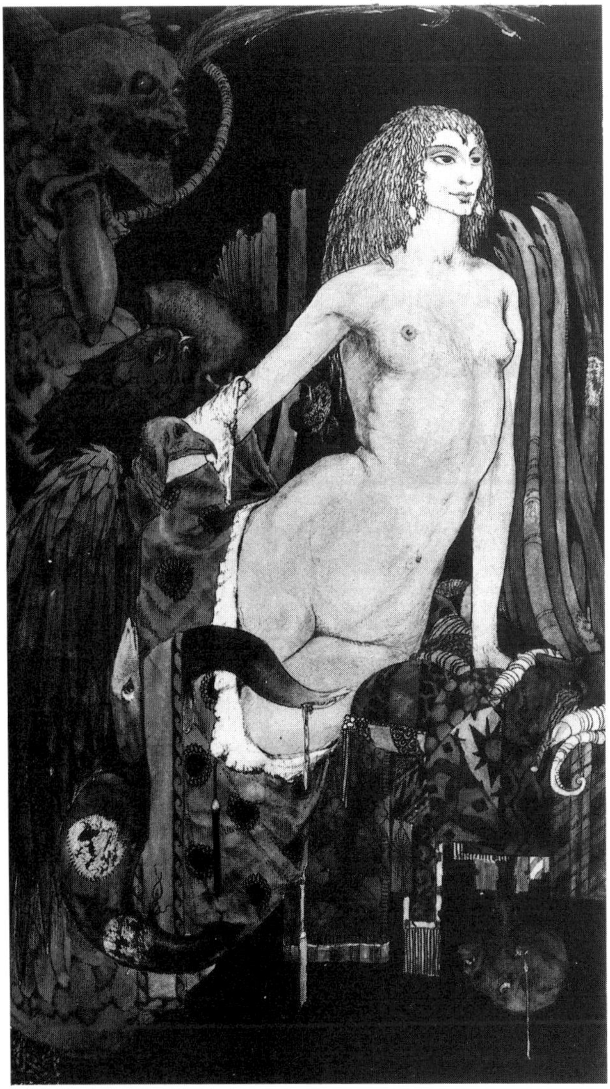

183 'Faustine', illustration in pen and ink and wash for Swinburne's *Selected Poems* (1928)

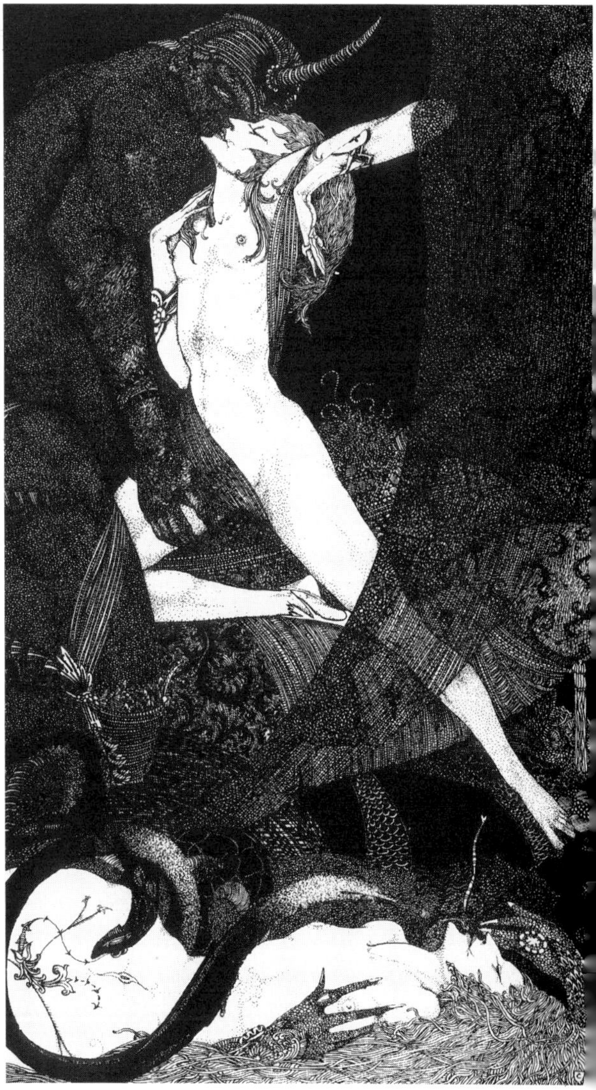

184 'Aholibah', photogravure plate intended for Swinburne's *Selected Poems* but omitted from the publication

in line, as are the text decorations. The magenta cloth case is gold blocked and the endpapers are printed in a magenta design over a buff paper. The binding style and the black jacket with a green device are uniform in style with the publisher's edition of *Madame Bovary*, which had illustrations by John Austen. Issued in London by John Lane at 25/-, the *Swinburne* was published in New York by Dodd Mead and Company. Although he was generally pleased with the book, Harry was disappointed that one of his full-page illustrations was omitted:

> in all I did twelve drawings. Eleven are actually reproduced. The one which is left out, 'Aholibah', was perhaps the best drawing I did in the series [fig. 184] and I am greatly disappointed it should have been left out without my having being consulted.[62]

He wrote to Willett, 'I like the way the book has been done very much and the Curwen Press have as usual done their job splendidly'.[63]

He asked Miss Sharman to have his originals collected, and had one framed as a gift to Willett. Despite all the care lavished on the production, the book did not receive a great deal of attention. In his introduction Humbert Wolfe disassociated himself from Harry's interpretations of Swinburne's themes,[64] and even Æ, writing in the *Irish Statesman*, felt that the decadence associated with Swinburne had not 'the character of gloom with which Clarke invests his creations', even though the drawings were 'remarkable'.[65]

Harry's illustrations to Swinburne show a development of the microscopically fine pen and ink and wash technique he had first used for *Faust* and for illustrations like *Ophelia* and *Prelude at the Theatre* in 1925,[66] and a new sensual, usually naked, devouress inscrutably dominating the narrow rectangular picture frame, a beguiling, provocative ideal of female beauty,[67] versed in 'The shameless nameless love that makes' Hell's iron gin shut on you like a trap that breaks', born of the 'sterile growths of sexless root'. Where Swinburne (in *Dolores*) wrote of our Lady of Pain, 'In a twilight where virtues are vices, / In thy chapels, unknown of the sun', Harry's imagination is in harmony with the poet's.

Although the illustrations present what amounts to a review of his entire repertoire in both glass and graphics, a new, sharply geometric element heightens the dramatic impact of the compositions in which familiar motifs and idiosyncracies are subordinate to the central design. As in *Faust* his own doomed, disturbed self-portrait recurs (fig. 185).

Back at the Studios, the pace was unrelenting. Work was in progress on the panels for the Geneva window. The *Presentation* window for Killaloe in Co. Clare was finished and despatched on 20 November, a richly coloured design in its gold, turquoise, emerald and blue hues, its design reminiscent of the Ashdown Park *Presentation* made some three years earlier. A week later the first group of windows for Lough Derg was despatched. He sent five illustrations to the first exhibition of contemporary Irish art in New York, organized by Patrick Tuohy at his old friends, the Byrne Hacketts', gallery.[68] Daily visits to the doctor became necessary as his health deteriorated further, aggravated by the great pressure of his own work and responsibility for the Studios, only relieved by weekly evenings at the Arts Club or the Moira Hotel with a small dining club to which he belonged with his friends Lennox Robinson, Walter Starkie, Bryan Cooper and others. That year there was no time to design an advertising inset for the Studios, nor to make a Christmas card. Soon after Christmas he managed to complete the Geneva window with the help of the Studios' staff, but had to get Government approval before showing it.[69] Late in January he made a trip to Northern England to check the prospects of some new commissions, but returned after a week, ill and utterly exhausted. His health continued to worsen and he was very ill by March, when he submitted two of the *Swinburne* drawings for the Royal Hibernian Academy exhibition. On 18 March 1929 he had to leave for a sanatorium at Davos in Switzerland in an attempt to arrest the advance of the tuberculosis which was affecting both his lungs.

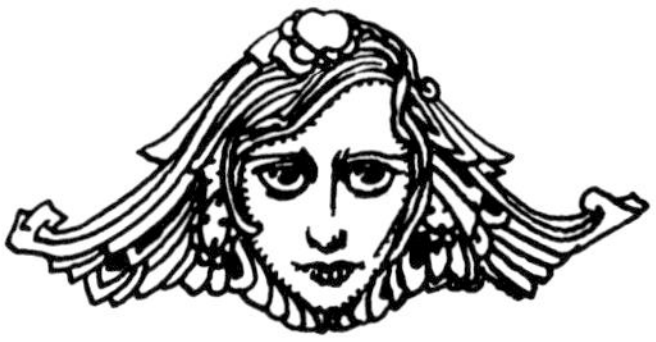

185 Self-portrait, endpiece from *Swinburne*, 1928

10

Final attempts to honour his many commitments from a Swiss sanatorium — Last visit home before death overtakes him in Switzerland early in 1931, aged 41

Lennox Robinson felt very guilty that he had not accompanied Harry out to Switzerland. After two days of travelling, via Euston and Basle, Harry arrived at the Victoria Sanatorium at Davos-Platz. An article on 'The Cure'[1] describes the town with more than its normal share of sophisticated amenities for its winter sports visitors but even more for the invalids who frequented its sixteen sanatoria and over forty pensions. For the benefit of the hundred or so patients who arrived each winter from Ireland, the article advised that the 'Davos cure is founded on rest' as well as 'the dry windless cold' and sun:

> New arrivals should not worry their doctor with requests to be allowed to walk, for strict rest at the beginning often works miracles and always shortens the cure. It is no great hardship to lie for a time in the warm sunshine on a Davos balcony, looking at the pastel-blue snow-fields dotted with skiers and the dark pine-woods in the solemn, yet hope-inspiring silence that is characteristic of the Davos Valley, apart from the bustle of the Promenade.

It warned 'Cures at Davos are not automatic; only those who use their will and intelligence get well. And the cure requires time; light cases up to six months, severe cases longer, sometimes very much longer.'

Harry was there for one year and nearly two months. Helplessly, he noted down in his diary every week and month that passed. He hated having to be confined to bed when he arrived. Lennox Robinson wrote, bucking up his flagging spirits:

> I know life is beastly and hell for you but what is there for us to say except grin and bear it? Do what you're told and don't worry. I don't see that one can, life gets you by the throat or pours gold and happiness into your pocket for no reason and there's no controlling the bally jade.

Robinson fed him with gossip, scandal, news, *The Observer* and the *Sunday Times* and books to read. He was fond of Harry's wife and sent him reassuring news about her and the children.

Most people in Ireland had no idea how ill Harry was. On the night after the opening of the RHA exhibition, Robinson wrote to Harry:

> I want particularly to tell you this; I met old Sally [Sarah Purser] at the Hibernian Academy opening, she said something about my going to Spain with Margaret and I said it was a bit uncertain owing to your illness. She hadn't heard about it and jumped a foot when I told her, was really concerned. She said again and again, 'I am so sorry' and then said, 'He has done more work than all the people in the Tower of Glass put together'. Maybe you'll laugh cynically at this but really she was quite sincere in her reaction.

The next time he met her, she specially asked after Harry. Robinson reported that Bodkin had professed to know nothing of Harry's illness and had expressed concern and promised to write.[2] Robinson was trying to assist the Clarkes' precarious financial situation, considerably affected by doctors' fees and Harry's upkeep at Davos, getting painting commissions for Margaret (fig. 186), having the children to stay in Dalkey and getting the Studios to paint Sorrento Cottage. He also chose one of the two *Swinburne* illustrations representing Harry in the current Royal Hibernian Academy show for Lady Lavery to buy; she wrote: 'The lovely Harry Clarke picture arrived safely, thank you so much, I *do* hope he is better, he is such a great artist.'

On 25 April, Alan and Belinda Duncan arrived in Davos to visit Harry and found him bored but cheerful. His doctor, Dr Hudson, wrote to his younger sister Dolly on 6 July:

> Your brother . . . certainly is improving, but I am afraid it will be a long job in his case as both his lungs are considerably affected. He is very cheerful and well in himself. He is on his balcony all day long and he has now begun to do a little drawing. He is having treatment by injections with gold which I think are doing him good.[3]

Harry had hoped to be allowed home for a week in September and even that he, his wife and Lennox Robinson might manage a trip to Spain. But as his health made little improvement he had to content himself with reading (for example, *The Diary of a Nobody* and *All Quiet on the Western Front*), writing letters adorned with little drawings and caricatures, and his wife came out to see him there instead. She reported that he looked 'ten years younger' and very sun-tanned. On her visit she painted an oil portrait of him sitting on his balcony in a royal blue dressing gown.[4] Shortly after her visit, Lennox Robinson planned,

> weather permitting, overdraft in a healthy state etc. to pop out to see

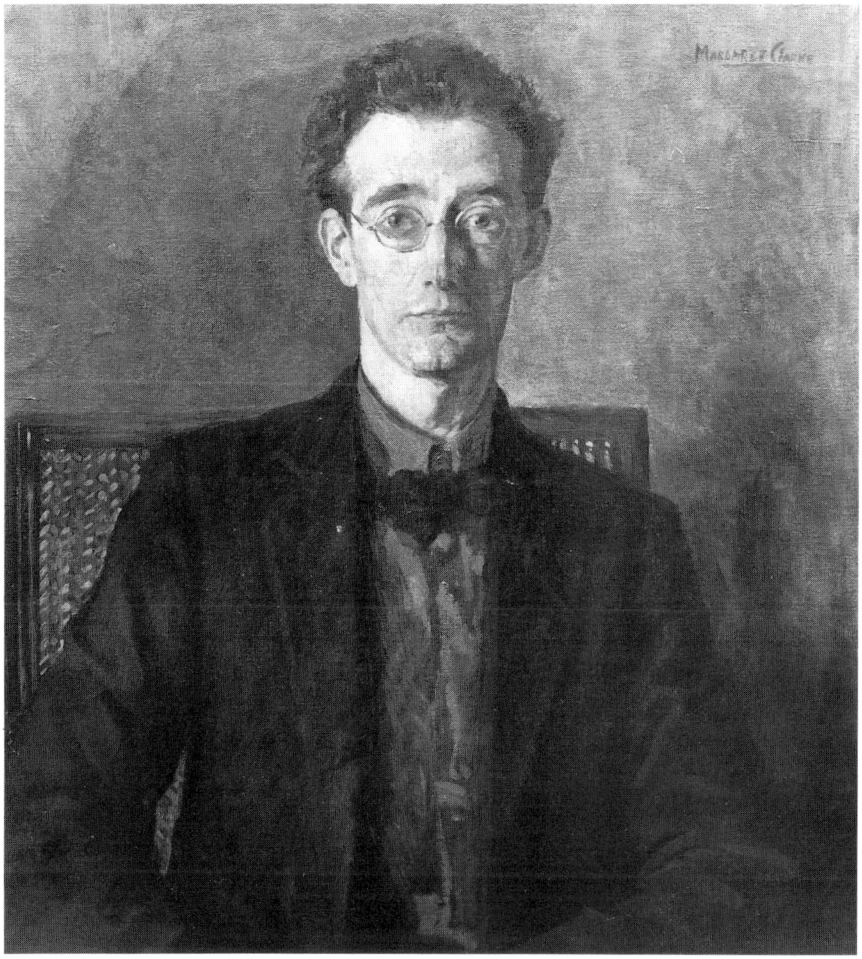

186 Margaret Clarke, *Portrait of Lennox Robinson*, probably commissioned by Robinson to ease the financial difficulties of his friend's family

> you in October and I don't care a damn whether you want to see me or not, I'm going for my own pleasure, not yours.[5] Grand to hear you are working on the ballet, go ahead — tho' of course you know that 'the Abbey is finished' — that is the correct thing to say now and that the Gate Theatre is the only thing worth going to in Dublin (meantime we are playing to capacity).

Perhaps this was the ballet evoked by the poignant spectacle of the consumptives gazing at the young, athletic skaters and skiers at Davos, for which Harry 'might have designed the costumes and decor.'[6]

Lennox Robinson arrived in Davos on 20 October for a week. He described the scene:

> The larches were still golden, the pines green-black, there was just enough snow here and there to make a startling contrast. Harry lay in bed all day holding court. Davos, to Ireland's shame, was crowded

> with Irishmen and women — and the Irish (and the English too) visited Harry's room all day long in twos and threes. He talked so well, he was so amusing, so Irish (this last from the English). The visitors would walk home to their pensions or hospitals to rest on the verandahs for their prescribed hours and their places at Harry's bedside would be taken by others. I bore this situation for a few days and then took the doctor aside. From that time on there were at least three hours a day when the card forbidding entrance was hung on his door.[7]

His parting gift to Harry was a blue gramophone, which 'cheered him up tremendously'.[8] Blue had always been his favourite colour. In Davos, they discussed what he, Margaret Clarke and his solicitor George Meares had long been considering — the future prospects of the Studios, and what appeared to be the only solution: to divide the dwindling decorating business from the thriving stained glass, which would become a limited company. Harry asked Lennox Robinson to take power of attorney on his behalf and to ensure that Meares finalize proceedings as speedily as possible.

The Studios were being run by Walter and Florence (Dolly) Clarke; Deegan had been admitted into Grangegorman Mental Asylum with manic depression; Michael Dunne, Reuben Matthews, William Dowling, Richard King, George Walsh and fifteen others remained. Although several clients knew where Harry was, it was in the Studios' interest to prevent this being generally known. By the end of September (1929), Harry was once more being consulted about Studio business. The Lough Derg windows had been consecrated in June, to great acclaim. Alice Curtayne refers to the windows:[9]

> In St Patrick's Basilica on Station Island, Lough Derg, the Stations of the Cross are set up in a very distinctive manner. The pilgrim will find them depicted in fourteen stained glass windows. . . . Each window holds the figure of one of the Twelve Apostles, but Judas is, of course, missing and his place is taken by Matthias. St Paul is added to the twelve, and Our Blessed Lady is also brought into the scheme to complete the number fourteen [fig. 187]. Otherwise, the Apostles are ranged in that order given in the tenth chapter of St Matthew's Gospel. Each of these fourteen . . . holds up a Station, which is shown on an inset plaque of lighter glass, more delicately coloured, so that it stands out in bold relief from the window. In this way it is the Station chiefly which holds the attention, while the attendant Apostle seems to hover attentively in the background.

While deeming Harry 'perhaps the greatest master of modern times . . . in the artistry of line, colour and use of symbol', she vividly describes how 'the colours in these windows are . . .used to express the emotions most prominently associated with each subject'.

Perhaps the most interesting aspect of these windows, apart from their iconography and colour symbolism, is the inventive way in which the background of each window is treated, so that the robes of each entranced saint are complemented by a relevant abstract decorative backdrop, whose patterns give the impression of dramatic activity. Similar backgrounds, jagged, whirling and wheeling, are used behind the chancel windows for Ashton-in-Makerfield and Bayonne.

The nine lancet windows for the latter, depicting *Angels bearing Symbols of the Mass*, in deep glowing colours, were dispatched to New Jersey on 3 October, having been shown in the Studios beforehand. Accompanied by fourteen plain two-light clerestory windows, they were acclaimed when the church was dedicated in November 1930.[10]

There were a number of American enquiries at this time, including one for Harry's coloured stained glass designs from Mrs Helen Byrne Hackett, as a result of the show in her gallery earlier that year. Walter felt he could not send her the design she had particularly admired — the Knowles memorial at Nantwich — without Harry's permission, and feared there were no other similar designs to hand. She was also interested in securing work for the Studios, on commission.

Other commissions had been confirmed — Lady Dillon's two for the Isle of Wight, some small panels after Dürer, Botticelli and Hans Baldung for Fr Meagher of St Cuthbert's, Old Elvet, near Durham, whose brother was in Davos with Harry, seven chancel windows for Ashton-in-Makerfield, in the same vein as those for Lusk and Bayonne, begun for Fr O'Meara. The clerestory windows and decoration for St Eunan's, Letterkenny, had been completed; and ten windows for the sister convent of Ashdown Park, at Leeds, were underway.

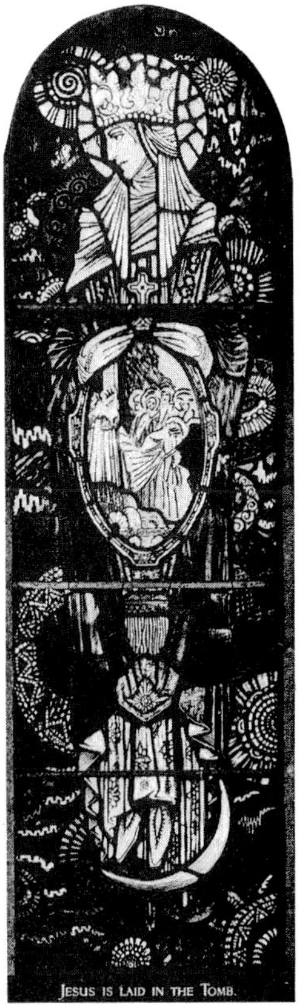

187 *Our Lady*, holding an inset panel depicting the Fourteenth Station of the Cross, Lough Derg, 1927; this series of windows was made by the Clarke Studios.

On 28 November, Lennox Robinson wrote to MacGreevy: 'Alan [Duncan] is in his element getting up a show of Harry's drawings. I've got him the Governor General for the opening day and *he* will buy something'.[11] This was to be Harry's last show during his lifetime, held in the Mill's Hall in Dublin, from 12 to 19 December, to try and raise some money and remind people he was still alive. Governor General McNeill's 'young and elegant'[12] wife (whose portrait had been recently painted by Margaret Clarke) bought *The Masque of Queen Bersabe* from Swinburne, and a number of the other sixty-five items were sold. Lennox Robinson bought *Ophelia* (fig. 160)[13] for his sister for Christmas and Rutherford Mayne bought *Mesmerism* for Robinson. Æ wrote a long and full review of the show, which he published in the *Irish Statesman*:[14]

> The Irish, in their own country, are perhaps in the mass the most orthodox of any, adhering, ninety-nine per cent of them, to cultural or

social orthodoxies. But from the one per cent come the most original and unorthodox characters and imaginations, the James Joyces, Dunsanys, O'Flahertys, Synges, . . . indeed almost the whole tribe of writers are in psychic opposition to the conventions established in their country.

In art this personal character runs riot in Jack Yeats, and in Harry Clarke . . . for those who like feeding in imagination on the worm and the wormy grave, and their sinister and spectral emanations, would have been satiated. Harry Clarke seems in these drawings as unearthly as Lord Dunsany in his Pegana Tales. He might have incarnated here from the dark side of the moon. His imaginations are all of a piece. He preserves the character of the strange psychic populace which inhabit his brain, and we feel that though they might have lived on earth they are now psychic larvae and nothing remains of the world they once lived in but the passions which cast them into that nightmare existence in Purgatory, is it, or Hell. There is a kind of dark beauty in the work which reminds us that there never was a sin of man which could not whisper duskily to us of the heaven from which it fell. Sometimes these creatures of Clarke's imagination seem like the fabulous incubi and succubi of mediaeval wizardry living beyond the grave with the dark passions persisting, but with forms too frail for bodily enjoyment of any desire. We look at these fingers thin as the limbs of spiders, these attenuated limbs, and shudder, as at creatures who must endlessly be the prey of desire and yet never enjoy. . . .

I am sorry there were not more watercolours, for when he uses colour, his great gift, he seems to be more completely himself, and in the stained glass the glory of colour overcomes the sinister character which occasionally we find in the design, and flushes the figures with a heavenly lustre, as in the windows in the University in Cork. When he uses colour, too, we are no more reminded of Beardsley, whose decorative use of black and white seems to have influenced Clarke in his early work, though I think it was never imitation, but was in its way as vital as Beardsley, and the black and white now has become more personal to Clarke and has recognisably a character of its own. These drawings are certainly things for the collector to possess. I am certain they will rise in value. There are always people who are on the prowl for the work of strange genius, and Harry Clarke is one of the strangest geniuses of his time.

On 6 January, Lennox Robinson wrote to Harry that there seemed hope that the 'North Frederick Street business' was at last moving, delayed because Walter had been ill since Christmas. The considerable responsibility of having to run the Studios was left to Dolly Clarke. It was decided to form a trust and Robinson had to explain to Walter what they had in mind. On 17 January, a meeting was attended by Meares, Fraser (Harry's accountant), Robinson, Walter and Dolly Clarke. Lennox Robinson reported it to Harry:

> The business is to be divided, the date of the division March 1st (I don't think things could be satisfactorily settled earlier); Walter takes the decoration, and the value of the stuff he takes is subtracted from the money he has in the business and he is gradually and as quickly as possible bought out by payment on March 1st of £200 and then in quarterly instalments of £100 or £150. The premises — 6 and 7 — are made a Trust with a capital redemption policy of £1000, payable in 20 years (unless the premium is too high, if it is, payable in 30 years, this is a matter which has to be enquired into). All this is agreed to by Walter 'without prejudice' and he will have to consult his solicitor, he was very amiable but I don't trust him a yard. I note that you want to continue in the business; in that case do you intend to leave all your capital in it? I am inclined to think that you should withdraw a certain amount spread over, say, two or three years. It is bound to be some time before you are able to work hard again and every year the children will be more expensive. I don't know what drain the business can stand — Walter *must* be paid off. . . . You will have to write your views about this.[15]

On 30 January he wrote again:

> Dolly has already discussed your idea of pensioning Walter with Meares and they seem against it, it certainly does seem dreadful if that drag has to be put on the business. . . . I discussed with Dolly and with Margaret the question of manager and both from their completely different angles say that the manager should be man and artist enough to meet the men on their own technical ground — even if not a creative artist himself. Dolly says she and Miss [O'] Sullivan can manage the clerical side all right, what is wanted is someone to deal firmly with the workmen as well as interview clients. I must find out from Fraser what salary the business can afford to pay such a man, perhaps it cannot afford to get the kind of all round man I think it needs.

On 7 February Lennox Robinson wrote again, more conclusively:

> I had a long talk with Fraser a few days ago and got a lot of details settled subject to your approval. He proposes that the new company's capital shall be £1,200; 600 shares held by you and 300 by each of your sisters. This will leave about £1,600 or £1,700 of your cash loose in the business and you could draw on this as you wanted it and as the

business could let you have it. Then we have to arrange what salary you are to draw even when you are doing no work for the firm. I submit that your name is worth £300 a year to the firm, and Fraser agrees; you would besides of course get half profits and, I take it, 5% interest on your loose money; we didn't go into the question of what you would get when you are working. We discussed the question of Walter and all agree against a pension.

Harry was working on several sketch designs in Davos: and had done a pencil design and colour scheme for the two-light Flux Dundas memorial window at Penarth. This depicts *St Michael* as a Wagnerian hero, conquering (as Harry wrote on the drawing) 'the great dragon that deceived the world', and *St Gabriel*, mantled as a prince and Angel of Judgment. The window was installed by 19 February.

A number of Harry's earlier designs seem to have gone astray at this period, as Dolly Clarke frequently sent Harry's original work to prospective clients, who did not always bother to return them. In February, Harry sent his sister designs for two Leeds Notre Dame Convent rose windows and pencil designs and colour schemes for several windows of *Saints devoted to the Eucharist*. Attached to them was his note: 'As some of the figures must be in neutral (or black) habits, I arranged a neutral figure and rich background beside a richly coloured figure and a neutral ground, getting variety and harmony.'

Soon after doing these, he had a relapse. He was dreadfully frustrated to hear of the work which could have been his, had he been there to pursue it, while instead the Studios he had done so much to build up were floundering and desperately writing to him for advice. He was also very homesick. At the end of February, Alan Duncan wrote from Paris:

I am entirely in favour of Harry's getting away from Davos — for the present at any rate. I think he is so fed up with the place, and that a change will improve him more rapidly.[16]

Dr Hudson had tended to agree with him when they discussed the matter in Davos. Duncan continued,

I should meet him at Basel and we would both go down to Pau with him, if Pau is decided upon. I think, therefore, that you need not worry at all about him. He will not, I think, be home in April, but might manage June-September, or part of that time at any rate. A good deal will depend on how he stands journeys.

As Duncan's wife, Belinda, also tended to be consumptive,the South of France would benefit both her and Harry. Dr Hudson wrote that Harry had 'come to a standstill',[17] was no longer improving, having had enough of the mountains, and that the change to Pau could do nothing but good, mentally and physically. A few days later Harry left Davos.

On 1 March, the legal division of the Studios took place. A few days later, on the recommendation of Karl Parsons and William Rothenstein, twenty-six-year old Charles Simmonds arrived from London to be interviewed for the job of managing the Studios. Lennox Robinson was favourably impressed, thinking him 'solid and steady' and

> old for his years. . . . Parsons wrote to me very warmly about him but he didn't know him as a student, he was sent to him by Rothenstein. I like his work and hope you will agree to give him a trial. . . .

On his forty-first birthday, his last, Harry sent his sister a wire, sanctioning Charles Simmonds' appointment for a year as from 1 April 1930. Harry seemed to take on a new lease of life once he knew that Simmonds was due and that he would be allowed home early in the summer. He greatly preferred Pau to Davos and was happy to see a number of Irish friends, such as the Laverys.

Lennox Robinson left for the United States at the beginning of April. On 5 April, the first letter was issued from 6 North Frederick Street under the new title of Harry Clarke Stained Glass (rather than Joshua Clarke & Sons Ltd). This meant that letters could avail of the printed letters 'HARRY CLARKE' with the initialled signature of Simmonds or of Dolly Clarke. Harry's name carried such weight that this was important. It also accounts for the number of people who mistakenly thought they were getting Harry's own work. Certainly, a number of letters seem to have been deliberately misleading, using the first person singular, with the words 'Harry Clarke' firmly printed at the end of the letter.

By the end of April, Harry was on his way home and on 16 May was back in the Studios writing letters. He had even hoped to call in on Ashton-in-Makerfield on the way back, but did not feel up to it. As Lennox Robinson later wrote, he literally 'proceeded to work himself to death'[18] until the first week in October, when he had to return to Davos, this time accompanied by Robinson, never to return to Ireland again.

These four and a half months were the saving of the Studios, although Harry himself produced no work of any value during the period. His first letter was to W.G. Lockett, the British consul at Davos, who would later write of him:

> Clarke was a great reader of books as well as illustrator of them. He was a lover of poetry, and a friend of poets, such as his compatriot W.B. Yeats. Last winter he was one of a small group of Davosers who tried to promote a memorial at Davos to the poet James Elroy Flecker, without, frankly, the least local public encouragement or support, then

or hereafter. . . . If only the memorial scheme had succeeded it is just possible that we might have had one of Clarke's wonderful windows in the English Church at Davos.[19]

In fact, the only extant art work from Switzerland, apart from a few sketches for windows and doodles, were two Shakespearean studies. One is a loosely washed watercolour of *Falstaff*, in burnished tones inscribed 'Arabesque with unsuited limbs and appointments'; the other, a pencil study of *Prince Prospero*, dressed like Porphyro in the *Eve of St Agnes*. He also drew a simple cover device for *The Torque*, the first annual journal published in April 1930 by the Davos Irish Circle, of which he was a founder member. As he had been elected the Circle's first president (for the 1929/30 season) at their first general meeting held in November 1929, his caricature appeared in this issue.

Harry was not strong enough to go into the Studios every day and was only available to interview clients from 3.00 to 4.00 p.m. by special appointment. He had to reassure Canon McDonald, who was wondering if he would ever get his window, commissioned nearly four years earlier —

I am at the moment . . . clearing the decks for action to enable me to take up your big Newport commission. This clearance of commissions I expect will take about a fortnight, so a month from now I should have a portion at least of your window.[20]

Similar letters were sent to scores of clients, a few from Harry but mostly from Simmonds on his behalf. His old college, Belvedere, was anxious to have some of his glass in their chapel. Harry suggested five windows depicting Jesuit saints, to be shown in 'the costumes of Nobles of their various countries and periods',[21] as habits were monotonous and accorded ill with the light. He was delighted by a eulogy printed in the *Irish Independent* on 26 May 1930 by Beatrice Toal Coogan on Professor Scott's octagonal church on Lough Derg, floating on a hundred and twenty-seven pillars of reinforced concrete, whose windows she had found a complete revelation, particularly at sunset 'when the Western glow suffuses the white marble with prismatic tints and the whole church is filled with coloured rays streaming from off the sun like seraph's wings'.

Early in June, he had to impress upon the Prior of Warrington that

all my work executed here is either my own personal work or is under my personal supervision, and other than this no work is permitted to leave the Studios. My manager, Mr Simmonds, is in all ways in sympathy with my work and I assure you any influence he may have on your windows will be perfectly consistent with my own traditions.[22]

In Davos, Harry had done a rough draft for a two-light window for Old Elvet, when Fr Meagher came out to see his sick brother; he now sent him a pencil design and colour scheme of *St Cuthbert, William Bede, Thomas Plumtree and the Blessed Thomas Percy*. There was an enormous backlog of administrative work to be done in the Studios, partly because of the new constitution but also because during his long absence papers, files and drawings had been muddled up, bills had not been paid nor fees collected, letters and orders misplaced, glass stocks allowed to run down and the muddles in the decorating side of the business had not been untangled, despite the valiant efforts of Miss O'Sullivan, Dolly Clarke and the high standard of work maintained by the Studio craftsmen under the competent Simmonds. However, Harry was finding that, although happy to be back, his constitution was not as strong as he had hoped, and he frequently felt too ill to go into the Studios. He had to ask the despairing Canon McDonald if he could have until the third week in July to show him 'quite a portion of the L.H. ope of the *Last Judgment*'.[23]

On Sunday, 20 July, Walter Clarke died in a nursing home. Harry wrote to Fr Meagher that

> it was exceedingly sudden and unexpected and came as a heart-breaking shock to us all. . . . I can only be thankful that the end was merciful in its absence of suffering. Further than this I cannot hope to express myself.[24]

With Walter's death, the decorating business came to an end.

On 6 August, the first meeting took place of the three directors of Harry Clarke Stained Glass Ltd, that is, Harry as managing director and his two sisters. At the end of August, he took on a new painter/draughtsman, George Altendorf. Tempting job proposals began to appear once it was known that Harry himself was back. He was consulted about a new single-light for St Patrick's Cathedral in Dublin, and Sharmid's wrote asking him to illustrate a book to which his art was ideally suited — J.K. Huysmans' *Against the Grain* (A Rebours). He wrote to Miss Sharman on 6 September, explaining what a thin time the bad weather had been giving him:

> I regret it seems after all I cannot definitely promise to have the drawings for the Argus Press finished by January 1931, and therefore think it'd be better we should call the commission off. I could endeavour to reopen the matter at some future date.

Although he did not

> want to interfere with the selection of another artist for this book, I

think I know who could do it superbly. I may have spoken of him to you as 'the finest black and white artist in the world'. This is not an exaggeration.

He therefore asked her to forward his copy of *Against the Grain* to his old friend Allan Odle, which she did and tried to get him the commission, but on 18 November, she wrote:

> We are very disappointed we did not get the commission for Mr Odle. We tried our hardest with letters and cables but in vain. They gave the work to Alastair.[25]

As it turned out, the Chicago-based Argus Press, which had previously published two of John Austen's books, did not publish the book with Alastair's illustrations because of the Great Depression.[26] It is perhaps one of the great losses to history of book illustration that Harry was already too ill to depict the neurotic Duc Jean Floressas des Esseintes on his fevered quest through the pages of this Symbolist text, rich with lengthy purple descriptions of arcane intellectual, sensual and aesthetic adventures, in what Arthur Symons described as the 'Breviary of the Decadence'.[27]

Early in September, on one of her visits to the Studios, Evie Hone expressed interest in buying Harry's long, thin cartoon for the Lusk *St Maculind* before she left for M. Gleizes' studio in France. The Studios just managed to install the sanctuary windows in Ashton-in-Makerfield in time for the dedication of the new church of St Oswald on 14 September. By 15 September, Harry knew he would have to return for the winter either to Davos or Pau. He was in favour of the latter because it would be much cheaper, but presumably his doctor felt he would receive better treatment at Davos. He was expected to be abroad for the whole of 1931.

This time Lennox Robinson would not let him travel alone:

> He had admitted to me how much he had suffered on his first long lonely journey across England and France with a high temperature and insufficient French and I was determined that this time he must not travel alone, besides he was a sicker man than he had been . . . before.[28]

They arranged to travel out at the end of the first week in October.

> Of necessity it was a slow journey. A night at Holyhead, a night at Euston, at Paris, at Bâle. In Paris we arranged to dine with the Bethel Jacobses. Mrs Jacobs — Sophie Solomons as she used to be — was an old friend of mine but she and Harry had never met. He delighted in her and we dined well and went on for coffee to some little place shaped like the bar of a ship. There was dancing upstairs, we sat below

> and there was good talk. I knew that I should get Harry to bed by nine o'clock for we had a long journey before us next day. But he was so enjoying himself, talking too much, smoking too many cigarettes and drinking too many cognacs and I thought — 'What the hell! All's bound to be over soon. Let him have one last good night.' We didn't get to our hotel till one. Sophie sent him an armful of flowers next morning and I just managed to get him dressed in time to catch a mid-day train at the Gare d'Est. I met thirteen dwarfs on the platform and I hate dwarfs, I think them unlucky. The journey was dreadful. Next day from Bâle we reached Davos, I left the next evening and did not see him again until I saw him in a Swiss mortuary chapel four months later.[29]

From Davos, Harry kept in touch with the Studios all the time. He was worried about the as yet unglazed *Geneva* window and the Newport *Last Judgment*. On October, Simmonds wrote to Canon McDonald that the left hand light was complete, the right hand opening nearly complete and the glass for the centre light cut. The dramatic design shows Christ surrounded by angels in the centre light, flanked by the Virgin and Apostles with the Blessed assembled beneath her and St Patrick with Apostles and the Damned beneath him. Among the amorphous mass of the damned, Harry's anguished self-portrait is discernible. The base of the three lights is spanned by a huge globe from which tiny figures float up into the earth's dark outer atmosphere. Here is evidence of Harry's delight in 'the utterly beautiful and the macabre . . . a mediaeval delight in monstrosities, in abortions, in devils',[30] juxtaposed and contrasted with the sublimely ecstatic and ethereally beatific; however only the left opening was completed under Harry's supervision and although Simmonds assured Fr McDonald that the two remaining lights would be in harmony with this, the latter was apprehensive. The window was erected at the end of February 1931, but Canon McDonald was not happy with it. He had waited patiently so as to be sure of having Harry's own personal work and nothing would console him that he was too late for that.

Harry died in his sleep during the night of Monday, 6 January 1931, at Coire, a small Swiss village. He was only forty-one (fig. 188). He must have known he was dying, as he had left Davos with Alan Duncan bound for Dublin, even though it was the middle of the winter. By his own wish, he was buried at Coire,[31] although, sadly, because he was not a Swiss national, the simple grave erected by his wife only survived fifteen years in the church graveyard.

The first of a number of obituaries in Ireland, England, America was Lennox Robinson's appreciation printed in the *Irish Times* on 7 January:

> In the death of Harry Clarke Ireland has lost her greatest designer in

188 Margaret Clarke, *Posthumous portrait of Harry Clarke, c.* 1931; based on one she did while visiting him in Davos and on a studio photograph taken by Lafayette's of Dublin

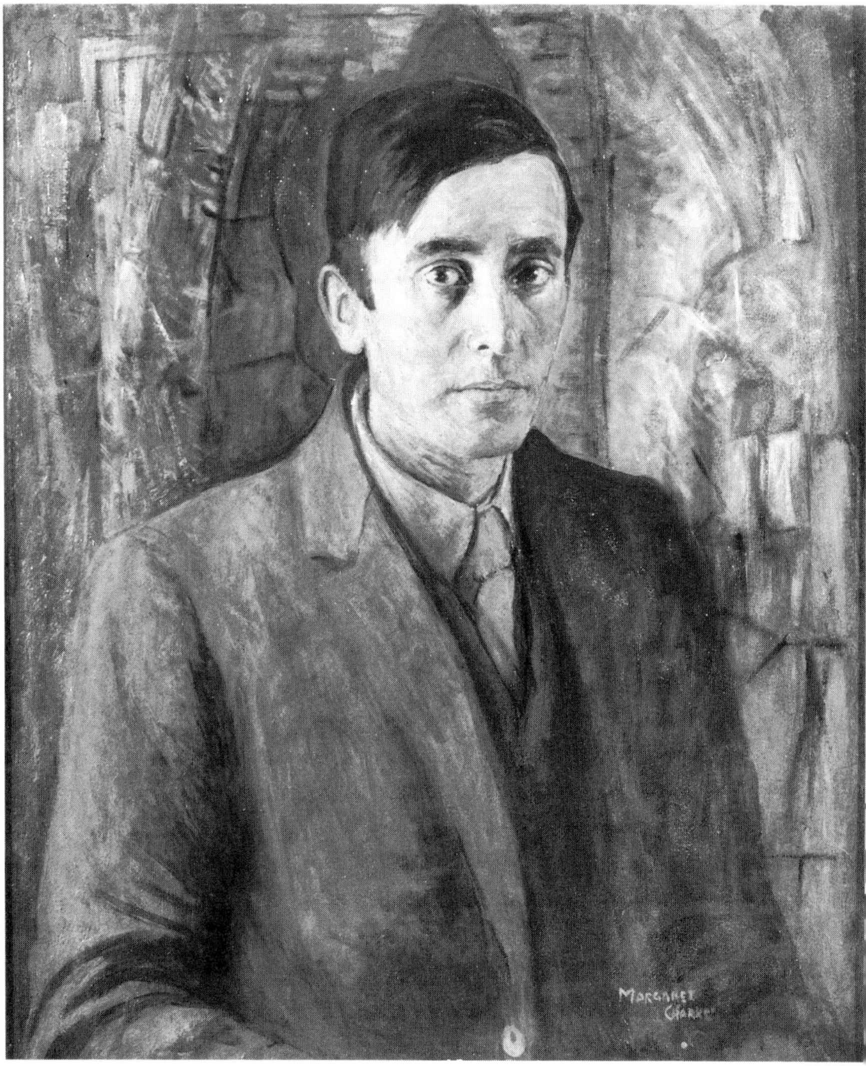

stained glass, and her greatest black-and-white artist. It is tragic that in a little country like this, where, as a matter of numerical proportion, artists must be few, we should lose such an artist at an early age. He died a martyr to his art. Had he been more casual, more 'Irish' in the easy conception of the word, he might have had many more years of work ahead of him, but he was never easy, and always worked with a febrile intensity.

At any rate, they are there, for our generation, and for generations to come: those windows. . . . They will shine and glow, those blues and reds — how he loved blue! — an inspiration to the faithful, these conceptions of a Dublin man who loved Dublin before everything, loved its slums and its north side, and all the O'Casey side of Dublin

There were two sides to his imagination: the religious side, which found its expression in stained glass, and another side which expressed itself in black and white, in designs which had about them something of the macabre. . . . Both these sides came together in his last great work, his window for the Labour Building in Geneva. . . . In that window Harry Clarke has fully expressed a side of himself. There are beauty and mysticism and humour and character, St Brigid and Joxer, the Playboy and Robert Emmet.

Only a few years later Lennox Robinson would write:

The subject of the [Geneva] window was modern Irish literature expressed in a series of panels each containing figures and a quotation [plate 46]. Thus, the two panels at the top were Bernard Shaw's *Saint Joan* and Lady Gregory's *Saint Brigid* . . .; lower down was Synge's Playboy and Pegeen Mike, an illustration from Seumas O'Kelly's *Weaver's Grave*, George Fitzmaurice's *Magic Glasses*, Robert Emmet from my *Dreamers*, Joxer and Mr Gilhooley. In the Joxer panel an essential object was a bottle of Guinness — I imagine the first appearance this useful object had made in stained glass.

But the Irish Government discovered that the window might conceivably give foreigners a false conception of the Island of Saints. The bottle of Guinness was not seriously objected to but did not the Playboy's tight breeches show him a little too virile, was not the female's clothing in the Gilhooley panel slightly too diaphanous? The window was erected in Government buildings in Merrion Street and could be sniffed over. After many, many months of evasions and half-truths Harry's widow was allowed to buy it back for the price the Government had paid for it.[32]

Only a month before he died, Harry had written from Switzerland to President Cosgrave that he was anxiously awaiting a decision over his window. Three weeks after his death, a cheque for £450 (his fee for the window) arrived at the Studios and a letter to the effect that the window was to be erected 'in a suitable frame' in Government Buildings in Merrion Street; its fate thereafter was not mentioned, despite frequent letters from Simmonds asking what the situation was. The Government's attitude was almost as equivocal as that of the *Catholic Bulletin*, which specialized in cheaply abusing art, poetry, literature and anything not to their narrow taste.[33] One Dublin paper drew its readers' attention to the window which

it is understood . . . is worthy to rank amongst his foremost achievements. . . . Less pleasing is the rumour which is unconfirmed that the Cabinet, some members of which are stated to have inspected the work, is not disposed to accept it for the original purpose for which it was commissioned. The suggestion is that some of the allegorical [*sic*] figures represented in the window were considered to mar the spirit of the artist's design.[34]

Less euphemistic is Tony Gray's novel *Starting from Tomorrow* (London 1965),[35] which describes the unveiling of a long-lost 'work of art' known as Lindsey's Lecherous Window:

> . . . a masterpiece, rumour has it, based on Irish Mythology and depicting naked ladies of Eunania with, it is whispered, a wealth of detail unusual both in the stained glass medium and the Island of Saints and Sinners. . . .
>
> [If you're] a writer or an artist you've got to shake the dust of Dublin off of your feet and turn to face to foreign shores or you'll never doe anything — only talk. . . . Unless you're prepared to kowtow and toe the line and soak up to all the priests and politicians, you're not wanted in Dublin. That's the long and short of it.

The window was for some years on loan to the Hugh Lane Municipal Gallery of Modern Art in Dublin from the artist's family, but after several years unseen in storage, it was exhibited in London at The Fine Art Society in May 1988 and has now been acquired by the Wolfsonian Foundation for its premises in Miami, Florida where it will be displayed in the near future. The window illustrates Harry's own selection of fifteen excerpts from Irish literature, worked from a series of evocative watercolour studies (plate 45).[36] Each is is minutely inscribed:

Patrick Pearse's *The Wayfarer* —

> The beauty of the world hath made me sad
> This beauty will pass,
> Sometimes my heart hath shaken with great joy.

A decorative inset of flowers, painted on gold-pink and on black around the text.

Lady Gregory's *The Story brought by Brigid* —

> They bruised His brow with their crown of briars
> They mocked Him with every ugly thing
> He that could shrivel them all with fire
> He held His silence and He a king.

The elegant little figure, holding her abbey church, is poised in a moonlit sky over the hills of her native Kildare as she points to the Crucifixion in a golden vesica.[37]

George Bernard Shaw's *St Joan* —

O God, that made this beautiful earth
when will it be ready to receive the Saints;
How long, O Lord, how long?

The androgynous figure of Joan, dressed for battle, hovers above a similarly moonlit hilly landscape. Both she and St Brigid are framed by wreaths of flowers, cypress trees and leafy tendrils which conceal the sinuous leadlines and some of the cockatoos, moths, birds and butterflies already seen at the head of the *Eve of St Agnes* and in the Bewleys' *Orders of Architecture* windows.

John Millington Synge's *Playboy of the Western World* —

Well, the heart's a wonder;
and I'm thinking there
won't be our like in Mayo
for gallant lovers from this hour today.

The coy young lovers radiate against the dark blue of the night sky, flowers glowing richly at their feet; he in a fanciful version of the (much- patched) clothes Harry had seen on the men of the West of Ireland, she in a dress and slippers of incandescent ruby.

Seumas O'Sullivan's *The Others* (plate 47) —

And now they pause
in their dancing and
look with troubled eyes,
Earth's straying children
with sudden memory wise.

A companion pair of lovers but painted on gold-pink plated with blue; she dreams, enchanted, in her dress of swirling pink and blue while he, clad only in a bolero and ruched leggings, seems half-goblin as he takes her hand in their dance over the crescent moon. Barely visible behind them are the tiny prancing green figures of elves.

James Stephens' *The Demi-Gods* —

The dark curtain of night moved noiselessly,
and the
three angels stepped nobly in the firelight.

The three radiant hierophants summoned miraculously from the flames are particularly striking because of their small scale; their lavishly decorated robes, wings and headdresses contrast with the tattered suit of the aghast beholder.

Sean O'Casey's *Juno and the Paycock* —

> Joxer's song, Joxer's song
> give us wan of your shut-eyed ones.

This portrait of the actor F.J. McCormick was copied from a photograph; the details of the set around him were adapted from the Abbey Theatre's performances of the play, which Harry had enjoyed on so many occasions.

Lennox Robinson's *The Dreamers* —

> If I were to die tomorrow all I would ask
> from the world would be the charity of its silence.

Harry's interpretation of Robert Emmet, taken from a portrait, shows the proud young patriot uniformed, standing before the Irish flag and the gallows on a flowery verge, as he utters the words from his famous last speech.

W.B.Yeats' *The Countess Cathleen* —

> I have heard a sound of wailing in unnumbered
> Hovels, and I must go down, down, I know not where.

One of Harry's most beautiful female creations in glass, Countess Cathleen, dressed in a sumptuously brocaded robe bound tightly up to her chin and an ornate Russian Ballet headdress, prepares to descend into a cave in a rocky landscape.

Liam O'Flaherty's *Mr Gilhooley* —

> She came towards him dancing, moving
> The folds of the veil so that they
> Unfolded slowly as she danced.

The wart-faced Gilhooley, cigar smouldering in one hand, champagne glass bubbling in the other, his fat body slumped in an armchair, ogles at the siren's naked form visible beneath her ruched veil. With her disdainful profile and tightly heaped curls, she is a sister of *Felise* (the Swinburne frontispiece illustration), with which she is contemporary.[38]

Æ's *Deirdre* —

> I know the great gift we will give to the
> Gael will be a memory to pity and sigh
> Over: and I shall be the Priestess of Tears.

The androgynous Deirdre with cropped blond hair, naked but for a diaphanous negligée, reclines on one elbow gazing into the distance, adored by a medievalized, mantled swain.

Padraic Colum's *A Cradle Song* —

Mavoureen is going
from me and from you
Where Mary will fold him in Mantle of Blue.

The mournful, cloaked woman with her baby is echoed by the tiny effigy of the Madonna and Child above her, set in lotus petals of rich blue, olive and russet-pink.

George Fitzmaurice's *The Magic Glasses* —

It's the pleasure and diversion of the world
You'll hear and see in them magic glasses.

Three ominous figures, one with a green face, warn the befuddled boy in his country boots, baggy trousers and waistcoat of the temptations of three red wineglasses, nearly as big as he is, in which tiny naked sirens with flowing hair play seductively; a serpentine throng of minuscule figures like the one issuing from the World to hear the *Last Judgment* at Newport can be seen approaching him, like Dante's lovers in the Circle of the Lustful, as depicted by Blake.[39]

Seumas O'Kelly's *The Weaver's Grave* —

The widow thought that the world was strange,
The sky extraordinary,
The man's head against the sky a wonder, a poem.

The beautiful young widow, ornately dressed in crimson velvet and lace, muses in the graveyard, attended by a youth in a pseudo-military uniform and spade; the minute silhouettes of two gravediggers are set against the golden orb of a setting sun in a streaked red and black sky.

James Joyce's *On Music* —

There's music along the river
For love wanders there
Pale flowers on his Mantle
Dark leaves on his hair.

An Aryan vision of male youth, in golden boots, mauve cloak, tabard and breeches, embroidered with golden flowers, strums on his mandolin, poised beside the silver water overhung with dripping fronds. The window is composed of eight square panels and measures 6′ 3″ x 3′ 5″.

In his *Times* obituary Thomas Bodkin referred to the Geneva window as 'the last work he completed'[40] and concluded his piece with a description of Harry:

In appearance [he] was singularly prepossessing — tall, graceful, dark and wide-eyed. His beautiful manners won him a host of devoted and admiring friends. Though reserved to the point of shyness, he was, in the company of his intimates a talker of charm and brilliancy, observant, witty and incisive. He was modest, though not unconscious of his own worth, and prompt to recognize, praise and help talent in whatever sphere he might find it.

W.G. Lockett emphasized similar characteristics in his appreciation:

He was one of those magnetic men, to whom, if you had once talked with him, you were always afterwards drawn. There was a quiet charm about him that would not let you go. . . . He was one of those men whose devotion to the national hearth and home, left him wide-minded and broad-hearted, open-eyed for all that is good and beautiful in man and woman and in nature everywhere, ever true to the kindred points of Heaven and Home. When I first went to see him, in the autumn of 1929, I was full of interest in him and his work, and wanted to make him talk about himself; but as I came away I realised with a kind of shock that we had been talking mostly about myself. He had a way of turning it back on you like that. It was part of his charm, the natural modesty of a man who knows his own worth. But from his own words — and he dearly loved a talk — you would never have realised that you were speaking with Ireland's greatest artist. ...

He has left in many a heart an ache of emptiness. He was one of those genial givers of the greatest things, who enrich our lives with spiritual wealth. We may be thankful to have had him.[41]

Walter Starkie wrote:

Harry Clarke was one of the most lovable personalities I have ever met in Dublin; he had a wistful, imaginative gaiety that haunted me and I still find myself evoking his ghost like a wonderful lost soul from the Limbo of Memory. I remember him with his wife and I always wondered what happened to her: she, too, was part of my dream of Fair Women that shed their radiance on our *tertulias* of art and music and literature in those far-off days when Dublin in 1921-1923 for an immortal instant recalled the Athens of Pericles. . . . Harry loved music and he was always asking me to play special motives and melodies for him on my fiddle. . . . He was unique as an artist in stained glass, for he had his own imagination, style and genius that was unlike the work of any other artist.[42]

Lennox Robinson was consoled that:

People who write books and plays and poems have their work put away on shelves where it may lie for years, unopened and unread.

Harry Clarke in the east end or transept of many a church in Ireland and elsewhere comes to life with every dawn and will have his daily resurrection — until the bomb drops. He thought his best work was his earliest — for instance, the windows he did for the Honan Chapel in University College, Cork. . . . What is the use of railing? Yet the things one sees in bus and tram and drawing room — graveyards in Switzerland might be filled with them and the world be no jot the poorer.[43]

Fr Thomas Ryan, SJ, who had known Harry since his Belvedere days, wrote an appreciative and perceptive obituary in *The Belvederian*:[44]

There are not many of whom it can be said that their death is a national calamity. It is not, however, an exaggeration to say this of Harry Clarke. In any country he would have been reckoned an artist of outstanding merit, but he was more than that to Ireland for as the greatest stained glass artist that our country ever produced and one who in many spheres of art had won fame far beyond his native shores, he has enriched Ireland with treasures that are already regarded as a national asset, while his fame abroad did much to enhance our national prestige. It is sad to have to record his early death that cut short at the age of little more than forty, a career so full of achievement and so rich in promise.

He described Harry's career and development from

a reserved and rather sensitive boy, a little aloof from the rough and tumble of school life. . . . Always a keen student, he was for many years exploring and experimenting, working towards that highly individual style which he finally developed and causing something near despair to those who wanted to direct his genius along conventional lines.

He pointed out how Harry could easily have left Ireland instead of joining his father's Studios:

critics were not wanting who prophesied failure for him. His stained glass was something altogether new, and the taste of the public, accustomed to German windows of inferior design, was low. The outlook was not bright.

He recalled how a fellow Belvederian, the Revd Sir John O'Connell, had given him his first great chance in the Honan Chapel —

and chapel and artist have ever since been famous. The years that followed, fifteen of them remained, were years of bewildering activity.

> Orders poured in for windows, book illustrations, schemes of decoration, fabric designs, and many other things, so that his services were booked ahead for several years. His output was enormous. He worked with a nervous intensity that would have taxed the strength of a more robust constitution than his and he spared no pains to ensure that everything he did was up to the high standard which he set for himself. All his windows are distinguished by brilliance of colouring and delicacy of draftsmanship, while the reverent treatment of every sacred subject and the wealth of symbolism in the decoration reveal the deep spirituality of the artist.

After citing examples of both ecclesiastical and secular glass, Fr Ryan described his black and white work:

> His drawings were conspicuous for delicacy of line and variety of ornamental pattern. As an illustrator he had the faculty of being able to reach such a degree of sympathy with his subject that matter and manner were in perfect harmony. This was especially the case in dealing with the macabre. . . . In his coloured illustrations he displayed that unerring sense of colour which found its proper medium in stained glass, but his work was too subtle to be satisfactorily reproduced by any printing process, and in the published books his black and white drawings have greater distinction. . . .

He concluded with a description of Harry himself:

> The abiding memory of Harry which will remain with those who had the privilege of his friendship is of a man of extraordinary sincerity. He disliked sham of all kind, whether material or human, and sometimes created enmities by saying so. He could never utter praise if he did not feel that it was deserved but when he found merit of any kind he proclaimed it enthusiastically. To young artists without number he gave delighted encouragement, he never forgot something good done by one whose ordinary level of achievement was poor, he never tired of speaking of the loyalty of his own staff or workers. All his other qualities seemed to be rooted in this sincerity. It made him devoted to his family and true to his friends, honourable in all his dealings and scornful of the suggestion that he should sink the artist in the business man and take the rapid road to wealth that was open to him; it made him impose a hard discipline of work on his own life, even when he felt that his strength was growing less; it reached its finest flowering when he faced illness with resignation and grew more light-hearted and joyous as he saw the end approaching. It came as something of a surprise to those who knew him intimately to hear him spoken of, after

his death, as shy and often silent. He was in reality a delightful talker, revealing in a hundred different ways that universal appreciation of beauty which he seemed to possess, and which enabled him to find as much pleasure in a line of beautiful prose as in some work of art within his own particular sphere.

Fr Ryan rued the fact that now his old school chapel would never have the five chancel windows they had commissioned from him and which 'his second last letter from Davos dealt with'.

The *Irish Builder*[45] described his death as 'an incalculable loss to art in Ireland . . . his passing leaves a great blank in the art of the country. . . . Real artists in the constructive or applied branches are so very rare. . . .' They praised his

> fertile imagination, which he expressed in the richest and most brilliant colouring in his glass, in masterly grouping and in the handling of the material with all its limitations. He sought and achieved a brilliant jewel-like effect; beauty, mystery and character are all expressed.

In the spring of 1931, the 102nd exhibition of the RHA featured a special *In Memoriam* section[46] devoted to Harry, who had been an Academician for five years; Patrick Tuohy was also commemorated. The twenty-two exhibits, none of which was for sale, included illustrations for Poe, Swinburne, Perrault and *Faust* and designs for stained glass.

Harry had made his last will on 29 September 1930, a few days before his final departure for Switzerland. His treasured painting by W.J. Leech, *La Bouvette Verte*, he left to Lennox Robinson; his effects (valued at £3,765 15s 6d) to his widow. These included 'a Ming vase, drawings for illustration in black and white and coloured drawings having a literary connection and furniture at the office and Studios of my company at 6/7 North Frederick Street'. He wished her to give a drawing or personal belonging to his solicitor, the Studios' accountants, his English doctor, Johnny Doran his old piper friend, Alan and Belinda Duncan, Dermod O'Brien, and his two sisters. His house in the North Circular Road he left to his widow and then to his daughter. He made special provision should any of his three children enter the Studios after the age of twenty-five.

In 1935, Charles Simmonds returned to England, married to an Irish girl, and was succeeded by Richard King as Studio manager. He was succeeded in 1940 by William J. Dowling,[47] who continued as Studio manager until the closure in 1973. The Harry Clarke style with all its idiosyncratic 'gadgets' was faithfully continued by the Studios to the end; during Harry's lifetime by Philip Deegan, Leo Cartwright and others like Kathleen Quigley and Millicent Girling for shorter periods; by Reuben Matthews (there from 1919 until 1973), his elder brother Henry (who left for America *c.* 1927), James McNamara (*c.* 1922-73), Richard King (until he started experimenting on his own and left the Studios), Harry's nephew Terence, who showed a promising talent before his tragically early death, William Dowling and others who came and went off on their own. Among these were George Walsh (*c.* 1926-42), Stan Tomlin (*c.* 1933-41), Patrick Heaney (1934-40) Christopher Campbell (*c.* 1953-62) and George Nolan (*c.* 1954-65). Miss O'Sullivan retired only when she was eighty-three and the deceptively frail-looking Dolly Clarke, with her sister Lally, controlled the Studios' employees and funds even more strictly than their father Joshua had in his time. Margaret Clarke painted from a studio in the top of the house and kept an eye on the proceedings until her death in 1961. Ann and David Clarke each took an active interest in the Studios.

It did not come as a surprise to hear from several sources that the ghost of Harry Clarke is still reputed to haunt the Studios. Right up to the time of their closure, one felt his presence everywhere in the two old houses, as his craftsman perpetuated his memory, and his work covered every wall. Felix Topolski, in one of his evocative spidery sketches of the Studios for the *Irish Press*[48] in the Patrician year of 1961, evoked their spirit; so has Lucy O'Brien, Dermod O'Brien's sister, who went to work there as an apprentice in 1935:

> Up a short flight of steps with railings, one entered the hall from which stairs went up and down. On the left the office and elderly permanent typist, the only other female who worked there besides myself [Miss O'Sullivan], kind soul — she gave out the weekly pay envelopes. Across the hall was the glassroom, not entered much by me but early on I was shown over the very large stocks there of plain, flashed streaky and some small expensive slab glass and told care had to be taken over economy. There was a cloakroom on this floor (and racks of bicycles) and another room, I think, a Margaret Clarke private room. She was friendly and encouraging the few times that I met her. . . . She must have been worried as the undercurrent was always of tension between getting enough orders and making them pay to keep the place going and profit to maintain herself and family — and keeping up the Artistic Reputation of H.C. This in glass was established by achieving a jewel-like twinkle and depth of colour by using many small pieces, and deep, mainly red and blue colours in the best traditions of the craft. But larger and larger pieces of many cheaper colours, more and more painted and stained for yellows and etched with acid were used to economise in leading and time, reducing the standard considerably while I was there.
>
> One went upstairs to a big sitting room, reception studio, sofah and chairs, marble mantlepiece and with v. large original H.C. cartoons on

the walls 20 ft high 8 ft wide — and I think books and drawings were kept there too. Clients were interviewed there, clerics and donors, directors meetings — Tug o'war one heard — only the manager of the staff attending. . . . Besides the main reception room there were two main working studios where, in the back one, glass easels were set up with the cut pieces of glass waxed on for painting and staining yellow with silver stain, for details of faces, hands and feet, drapery, emblems, border-patterns and inscriptions. In the front studio, sketches small to scale and coloured of Saints and scholars, Crucifixions, many subjects and full-sized cartoons were prepared. . . . We worked hard from 9 to 6, one hour off for lunch and half a day off per week and overtime. ... We all used push-bikes . . . except the manager. . . . There were six men, the manager, sub-manager and myself on that floor and then down from the hall to the basement where the kiln and leading benches were, the main hard-work of putting windows together went on with two . . . more men and a couple of upstairs men helping. Down there also was a small wettish pantry-like room where turns were take taken to do the aciding — white areas etched out of flashed glass by dabbing on hydrofluoric acid, the coloured areas being protected by wax — nobody liked that job.[49]

Such was the strength of this acid that the metal door fittings in this room had been virtually corroded away.

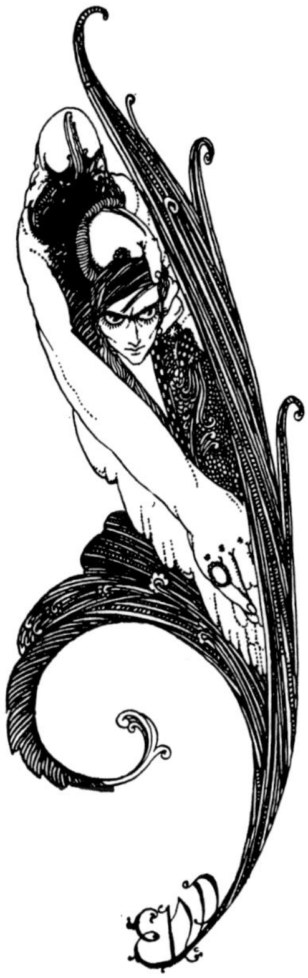

189 Self-portrait, final tailpiece from *Faust* (1925)

Harry Clarke.
Saint's hall-mark.
Eyes, dark, placid.
Broken glass.
Pan of acid.
Pan on box.
Box on form.
Glass bits changing.
Liquid smoking.
Brush-stroking.
Slight arranging.

(Musical strains.)
Intonation.
Action on stains.
Concentration.
Colour shifting.
Skilful lifting.
("Primrose" burning.)
Laid in cool.
Cold water pool.
More bits turning.*

*This poem was found among Clarke's drawings, typed and signed by an unidentified hand.

APPENDIX 1

Some Notes on Stained Glass*

The possibilities of glass are unbounded and if it were taken up by architects and others for domestic purposes Artists would not be hampered by tradition as they are in dealing with ecclesiastical stained glass.

The main support of the craft is obtained from the Church, but in all Church work there is some tradition or preconceived notion as to the appearance of each Saint or other object which is to be incorporated in the design required. This would not be the case in Domestic subjects where the artist would be absolutely at liberty to exercise his own ideas and skill in the arrangement of his decoration and the treatment of his surfaces. Knowing of such liberty the craft would attract greater men than it has up to the present, which would doubtless be for the advancement of the craft in decorative arrangement and technique.

It will be interesting to trace back a little the history of stained glass, which in point of antiquity goes back for many centuries.

Stained glass, as we know it, first occurred in France. Coloured glass probably came originally from the East. The art of the maker of coloured glass found its way from Ancient Egypt to Phoenicia and so on to Greece, Rome, Byzantium, Venice and so to France. The finest Stained Glass Windows extant are at Chartres, situated in the Department of the Eure-et-Loire, some 55 miles south-west of Paris — its Cathedral, containing the windows, having been founded by Bishop Fulbert in the eleventh century. The actual windows are mostly thirteenth century work. There are some beautiful examples of the twelfth century work in some of the other Cathedrals in Northern France. As far as England is concerned York has very fine glass as also has Fairford, a village in Gloucestershire, lying at the foot of the Cotswold Hills. The stained glass windows of the little church are attributed to Flemish workmanship. Although they are of a later date than those of York, many interesting and romantic stories are related about their origin.

The tendency from the thirteenth to the fifteenth century was rather towards the improvement of the technique, while from the sixteenth century the craft became more or less decadent. The revival of this art may

*An article based on information supplied by Harry Clarke; first published in the *Illustrated Country Review* (London), vol. V, no. 8, November 1925, pp. 290-3.

be attributed to John Westlake, and occurred in the seventies or eighties of the last century, while a little later a real stride was made through the knowledge and energy of Christopher Whall and his band of brilliant assistants.

It may be authoritatively stated that practically no advance in technique has been made since the fifteenth century, with the exception of the more skilled application and manipulation of the medieval craft.

Stained Glass means pieces of glass of different colours held together by strips of leads: it is not as so many people believe, a subject or picture painted on a large sheet of glass with pigment or enamel. For instance, one could make a tiny coloured panel from pieces of bottles; for your blues you could take poison bottles, reds and oranges could be obtained from various wine bottles, white from soda water bottles and black from the common beer bottle. The raw material used in making bottles is exactly the same as that used in the making of the raw material for stained glass.

So little is known by the general public as to the various processes employed to produce the final beautiful windows and panels that are so admired, that we think that it will be interesting to go into these various steps thoroughly. The first thing that is necessary is the production of a scale drawing of the subject to be contained in the panel or window; after this a full sized drawing is made; after this a tracing of the lead lines is made from the full sized drawing. This last is known as the 'Cutline'.

The next step is the selecting and cutting of the glass. After cutting the different small pieces of glass, each is assembled in its correct position on a sheet of plate glass under which is placed the Cutline. Each small piece is fixed in its proper place by means of a hot beeswax [. . . skilfully . . . piece.] The methods of painting and the means of drawing the lines, modelling flesh and drapery with pigments on the glass vary according to the technique of individual artists. After the painting is finished, the whole is fired in a gas kiln. The glass is laid in iron trays on which has been placed a fairly deep bed of plaster of paris. To get the best results, it is essential that the firing should be slow. What is required is a quiet soaking heat, until the glass is cherry red. It is then taken out and allowed to cool gradually.

The pigment will be found to have fired away a little, so it is second painted after cooling, to prevent it looking thin and washy when finished. After this has been done, it is again put into the kiln and the second painting is fired in. The glass is then laid on the 'Cutline' and leaded up. Finally cement is rubbed in between the glass and the leads to make it watertight, and then you have the finished article ready for erection.

From the above brief description it will be seen what care and skill is required to obtain the results that one has casually admired in the churches of Great Britain and Ireland and the Continent.

Mr Harry Clarke, RHA, to whose courtesy we owe the information contained in this article, and who recently showed some of his productions in London, supervises the entire work of the Studios. They employ altogether some 24/30 workers, artists, assistants, glaziers and tradesmen. Mr Harry Clarke supervises all these personally and is responsible for the entire production; he also does all the designing of windows and schemes of decoration.

In addition to this work, Mr Clarke has illustrated many books for Messrs George Harrap and Company, amongst others, Hans Anders[e]n's Stories and two editions of Poe's Tales of Mystery, while in the Autumn, Messrs Harrap and Co. are bringing out a limited edition of Faust containing over a hundred of his drawings. Reverting to his activities in stained glass, Mr Clarke has sent windows to Nantwich and Sturminister, and in October will have completed a series of 17 subjects in Stained Glass for the Convent of Notre Dame, Ashdown, Sussex. In addition to this he has executed many orders for both England and Ireland, and there are commissions in progress for Australia and New Zealand.

It has been impossible in this article to do more than touch on the fringe of his activities and of the great artistic skill which is required to turn out the works of art that he turns out, but from their beauty we feel certain that there will be a large and growing demand for his work.

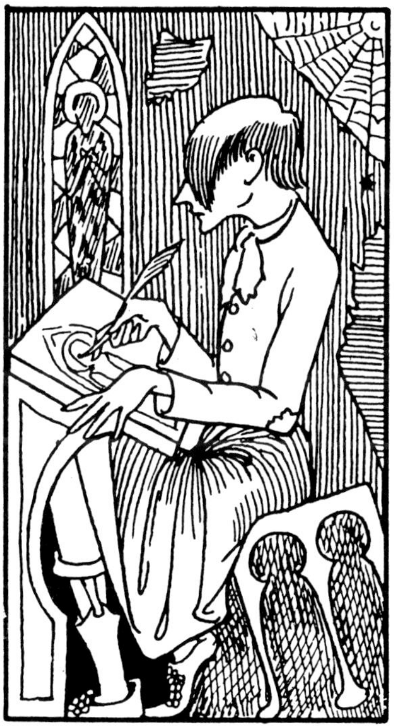

190 Caricature self-portrait in a medieval garret

APPENDIX 2

List of Stained Glass Windows by Harry Clarke

The information given in this appendix is taken, with permission, from Bowe, Caron, Wynne, *Gazetteer of Irish Stained Glass* (Irish Academic Press, Dublin, 1988).

Where no abbreviation appears after the name of the work, this means that Clarke was entirely responsible for its design and execution.

Where (A) follows the title of the window, this means that Clarke was actively involved in part of the window's execution, the rest being executed under his supervision in his Studio. Where (B) follows the title, this means that it was initially conceived and designed by him but executed by his Studio under his close supervision.

All windows are single-light unless otherwise mentioned.

C of E	Church of England (Anglican)
C of I	Church of Ireland (Anglican)
C of S	Church of Scotland (Presbyterian)
CC	Catholic Church

AUSTRALIA

Brisbane, Queensland: CC (St Stephen's Cathedral)
The Ascension (B) 1923 (3 lights)

ENGLAND

Cheshire: C of E (St Mary's), Nantwich
The Virgin and Child with St Cecilia and Richard Coeur de Lion 1920 (3 lights)

Dorset: C of E (St Mary's), Sturminster Newton
Madonna and Child with St Elizabeth of Hungary and St Barbara 1921 (3 lights)

Durham: C of E (St Cuthbert's), Old Elvet
Sts Cuthbert, William Bede, Thomas Plumtree and Blessed Thomas Percy (A) 1930-1 (2 lights)

Hertfordshire: The Chapel Studio, Kings Langley
St Wilfred and St John Berchmans, and the Presentation of our Lady in the Temple 1927 (made for the Lady Chapel, Convent of Notre Dame, Dowanhill, Glasgow)

Hertfordshire: C of E (St Michael and All Angels), Waterford, nr Welwyn Water
St Cecilia and a listening angel (designed by Clarke in 1921, executed freely from Clarke's two cartoons by Karl Parsons in 1929)

Lancashire: CC (Basilica of St Oswald and St Edmund), Ashton-in-Makerfield
Seven windows depicting saints devoted to the Eucharist: (A) 1930
St John the Evangelist
St Clare
St Ita
St Juliana Falconieri
St Paschal Baylon
St Catherine of Siena
St Tarcisius

Rutland: CC (Chapel of the Noel family, Exton Park), Exton
The Blessed Oliver Plunkett and the Blessed Thomas More (A) 1926 (2 lights)

Sussex: Barclay's Bank Training Centre (formerly Chapel of Our Lady, Convent of Notre Dame), Ashdown Park, Wych Cross, East Grinstead
The Immaculate Conception with St Anne (A) 1925 (3 lights; in the memorial chapel tower)
Scenes from the life of our Lady with base panels depicting emblems of her litany: (A) 1925:
The Immaculate Conception (Emblem: The Queen of Virgins) *and the Visitation of Our Lady and St Anne* (Emblem: Morning star) (2 lights)
Our Lady's Presentation (Emblem: Mystical rose) *and the Annunciation* (Emblem: Ivory tower) (2 lights)
The Visitation (Emblem: Mother of Good Counsel), *and The Espousal* (2 lights)
Our Lady of the Angels (Emblem: Queen of Angels) (2 lights)
The Family of our Lady and the Presentation of our Lord (Emblem: Queen of Martyrs) (2 lights)
The Adoration of the Magi and the Descent of the Holy Ghost (Emblem: Seat of Wisdom) (2 lights)
The Assumption (Emblem: Gate of heaven) *and the Coronation* (Emblem: Queen of all Saints) (2 lights)

Warwickshire: C of E, Bedworth, nr Nuneaton
Sts Peter, Paul, Luke and John (B) 1929 (4 lights)

IRELAND

CO. ANTRIM

Belfast, Falls Road: Dominican Convent Chapel
Rose window (A) 1927

CO. CLARE

Killaloe: CC
The Presentation of our Lord, with the Annunciation and Flight into Egypt (B) 1927 (2 lights)

CO. CORK

Castletownshend: C of I (St Barrahane's)
The Nativity with the Adoration of the Kings and the Shepherds, with Sts Brigid, Bearcan and Fachtna (tracery lights) 1918 (3 lights)
Sts Louis IX, King of France, and Martin of Tours 1921 (2 lights)
St Luke attended by Sts Cecilia, Barrahane and Fidelio 1926 (A)

Cork City, Emmet Place: Crawford Municipal Art Gallery
The Consecration of St Mel by St Patrick 1910 (panel)
The Godhead Enthroned 1911 (panel)
The Meeting of St Brendan with the unhappy Judas 1911 (panel)

Cork City, Western Road: The Honan Chapel of St Finbarr, University College
Sts Patrick, Brigid and Columcille 1915 (3 lights)
St Finbarr 1916
St Ita 1916
St Albert 1916
St Gobnait 1916
St Brendan 1916
St Declan 1916
St Joseph 1917
Our Lady of Sorrows 1917

CO. DONEGAL

Letterkenny: Catholic Cathedral (St Eunan's)
Ten decorative clerestory windows (B) 1929 (each 2 lights)

Lough Derg, Pettigo: Basilica of St Patrick's Purgatory
Fourteen single lights incorporating the Stations of the Cross in vesica-shaped panels held by each figure: (B) 1929

CO. DUBLIN

Dublin Central, Grafton Street: Bewley's Oriental Cafe
Two decorative windows (A) 1928
Four decorative windows depicting the Corinthian, Doric, Ionic and composite orders of architecture (A) 1928

Dublin Central, Parnell Square: Hugh Lane Municipal Gallery of Modern Art
The Eve of St Agnes 1924 (22 panels in one window)

Dublin Central, Thomas Street: National College of Art and Design
The Baptism of St Patrick 1912 (panel)

Dublin north, Balbriggan: CC
The Widow's Son 1924 (2 lights)
The Visitation 1924 (2 lights)

Dublin north, Castleknock: C of I
Sts Hubert, Luke and George (A) 1928 (3 lights)

Dublin north, Clontarf: Presbyterian Church
Pietà and Ascension: war memorial (B) 1919 (4 lights)

Dublin north, Donabate: CC
'Suffer little children' (B) 1926 (2 lights)

Dublin north, Lusk: CC (St Maculind's)
St Maculind (A) 1924
Nine decorative chancel windows with floral ornament (A) 1924

Dublin north, Phibsborough: CC (Vincentian Fathers' Church of St Peter)
The Sacred Heart, St Margaret Mary and St John Eudes 1919 (the tracery lights were destroyed in 1972).
Four ornamental windows with amber quarry slabs and symbols of the Passion 1924 (mortuary chapel, each 2 lights)

Dublin north, Raheny: Chapel of the Novitiate of the Oblate Fathers of St Mary Immaculate, Belcamp Hall
Blessed Oliver Plunkett and St Patrick (A)
The two princesses, Eithne and Fidelma, and St Gobnait (A)
Sts Laurence O'Toole and Kevin (A)
Sts Dymphna and Brigid (A)
Sts Doulough and Columcille (A)
Sts Malachy and Brendan (A) (all 1925, 2 lights; borders altered in the late 1950s)

Dublin south, Donnybrook: CC (Church of the Sacred Heart)
Sts Rita and Bernard (B) 1924 (the outer two of 3 lights; the central one is by William McBride)

Dublin south, Killiney: C of I (Holy Trinity)
The Angel of Hope and Peace 1919

Dublin south, Ranelagh: C of I, Sandford Road
Sts Peter and Paul (A) 1927 (2 lights)

Dublin south, Rathfarnham: see under Co. Offaly: Tullamore: CC for details of windows formerly at the Jesuit Retreat House, Rathfarnham Castle

Dublin south, Terenure: CC (St Joseph's)
The Crucifixion and the Adoration of the Cross by Irish saints 1920 (3 lights)
The Annunciation 1922 and *The Coronation of the Virgin in Glory* 1923 (2 lights; lady chapel)

CO. GALWAY

Ballinasloe: CC (St Michael's)
Sts Patrick and Rose of Lima (B) 1925 (2 lights)

Tullycross, Renvyle: CC
Sts Bernard and Barbara with Christ revealing the Sacred Heart (A) 1927 (3 lights)

CO. KERRY

Dingle: Presentation Convent Chapel

The Nativity (B) 1924 (2 lights)
The Baptism (B) 1924 (2 lights)
The Sermon on the Mount (B) 1924 (2 lights)
Suffer little children (B) 1924 (2 lights)
The Apparition of Jesus to Mary Magdalen (B) 1924 (2 lights)
The Garden of Gethsemane (B) 1924 (2 lights)

CO. KILDARE

Carnalway, Harristown, nr Kilcullen: C of I (St Patrick's)

St Hubert 1921

CO. MAYO

Ballinrobe: CC (St Mary's)

The Baptism in Jordan and the Ascension (B) 1925 (2 lights)
Ecce Homo, and Magdalen in the Garden (B) 1925 (2 lights)
The Assumption and the Coronation (B) 1925 (2 lights)
The Purification (Presentation in the Temple) and *The Immaculate Conception* (B) 1925 (2 lights)
Sts Fursey and Fechin (B) 1925 (2 lights)
Sts Colman and Brendan 1925 (2 lights)
Sts Gormgail and Kieran (B) 1925 (2 lights)
Sts Enda and Jarlath (B) 1925 (2 lights)

Hollymount: CC

The Ascension (B) 1926 (7 lights)

Kilmaine: CC

The Nativity 1926 (3 lights)

Newport: CC

The Last Judgment (B) 1930 (3 lights; only the left-hand opening completed under Clarke's supervision)

CO. MEATH

Skryne: C of I

The Ascension 1929 (3 lights)

Trim: C of I (in storage)

Ascension (B) 1929 (3 lights)

CO. MONAGHAN

Carrickmacross: CC (St Joseph's)

Of ten two-light windows in the nave and mortuary chapel:
St Ceara (A) 1926 (2 lights)
Sts Macartan and Tigernach (B) 1928 (2 lights)
Sts Fachnea and Enda (B) 1928 (2 lights)
St Dymphna (B) 1928 (2 lights)
The rest in the extensive series are by the Studios.

St Peter (Jesus is condemned to death)
St Paul (Jesus is made to bear his Cross)
St Andrew (Jesus falls the first time)
St James Major (Jesus meets his afflicted Mother)
St John the Evangelist (Simon the Cyrenaean assists Jesus to carry his Cross)
St Philip the Wayfarer (Veronica wipes the face of Jesus)
St Bartholomew (Jesus falls the second time)
St Thomas (Jesus consoles the women of Jerusalem)
St Matthew (Jesus falls the third time)
St James Minor (Jesus is stripped of his garments)
St Thaddeus (Jesus is nailed to the Cross)
St Simon (Jesus dies on the Cross)
St Matthias (Jesus is taken down from the Cross)
Our Lady (Jesus is laid in the tomb)

CO. OFFALY

Ballycumber: C of I
Music and Literature (B) 1929 (2 lights)

Tullamore: CC (windows formerly at Rathfarnham Castle, South Dublin)
Decorative window with Christ's Wounds (B) 1927
Sts Peter and Paul (B) 1928 (2 lights)
St Brendan (B) 1928
Sts Patrick and Benignus (A) 1928
St Ignatius (B) 1928
The Sacred Heart, St Joseph and our Lady (B) *c.* 1928 (3 lights)

CO. TIPPERARY

Ballylooby, nr Cahir: CC
The Beheading of John the Baptist (B) 1925 (2 lights)
The Vision of Bernadette at Lourdes (B) 1925 (2 lights)

Cloughjordan: CC
The Ascension with five Irish saints and Sts Michael and James (B) 1924 (5 lights)

CO. WEXFORD

Gorey: C of I
St Stephen 1922
St Luke and St Martin of Tours (A) 1923 (2 lights)

Wexford Town: CC (Church of the Assumption, Bride Street)
Our Lady and Child adored by St Aidan of Ferns and St Adrian 1919 (2 lights)

CO. WICKLOW

Eneriley and Kilbride, nr Arklow: C of I
The Resurrection 1924 (3 lights)
Abstract window with slab glass 1924 (in the north transept over a door)

SCOTLAND

Glasgow: Notre Dame College of Education, Bearsden: moved from Dowanhill, Glasgow in 1979

The Coronation of the Blessed Virgin 1923 (3 lights) (made for the lady chapel)

The Mother of Sorrows 1926 (3 lights) (made for the Sacred Heart chapel)

The Blessed Julie with two children and *The Visitation of our Lady to St Elisabeth* 1927 (made for the Sacred Heart chapel)

USA

New Jersey: CC (Basilica of St Vincent de Paul), Bayonne

Nine chancel windows depicting angels bearing symbols of the Mass: (B) 1929

The stole
The cross
The thurible
The wine and the water
The chasuble
The maniple
The candle
The ciborium
The book

WALES

Wales, Cardiff: C of E (All Saints), Penarth

The aged Simeon holding the Infant Christ (B) 1928 (in the baptistery)

St Michael and the Giving of the Laws to Moses, with St Gabriel and the Annunciation (B) 1930 (2 lights)

Notes

INTRODUCTION

1. 'Sailing to Byzantium' from *The Tower* (1929), *Collected Poems* (London 1933).
2. Mario Praz, *The Romantic Agony* (1933): chapter on 'Byzantium'.
3. Edmund Wilson, in his essay on W.B. Yeats as Symbolist, in *Axel's Castle* (1931).
4. Brian Fallon, 'The Irish Symbolist', *Irish Times*, 10 December 1983.
5. Brian Fallon, 'Harry Clarke Exhibition', *Irish Times*, 8 March 1982.
6. Fallon, 'The Irish Symbolist', *art. cit.*
7. *Irish Statesman*, 21 December 1929.
8. *A Portrait of the Artist as a Young Man* (1916).
9. James Huneker in *Overtones* (1904), a book Clarke recorded in his diary, described George Moore as the Irish Huysmans, importing French decadent notions and 'the noble, morbid, disquieting and fascinating art of Gustave Moreau' into these islands.
10. See Sotheby's catalogue, *Victorian Watercolours and Drawings*, 10 October 1985, no. 129; the watercolour is inscribed 'Dublin 24th April 1913'.
11. See Delevoy, *Symbolists* (1978).
12. John Russell Taylor, 'Clarke's Subtle Taste' (1980).
13. *Ibid.*
14. Quoted by Havelock Ellis in *Affirmations* (1898), a book which Clarke knew.
15. See Stephen Tschudi Madsen, section on the Celtic Revival in *Sources of Art Nouveau* (Oslo 1956) and Peter Selz (ed.), section on Graphic Design in *Art Nouveau* (New York 1975).
16. For the latter see Elizabeth S. Cumming, *Arts and Crafts in Edinburgh, 1880-1930* published in tandem with *The Arts and Crafts in Dublin 1886-1930* (Edinburgh 1985); also John Christian (ed.), *The Last Romantics* (1989). I am currently preparing material for publication on the wider implications of the Irish movement, in 'Design and Nationalism: the Arts and Crafts Movement in Ireland 1886-1925'. J. Herbert MacNair's *Tamlainc* (1905) and Frances MacDonald MacNair's *The Birth of the Rose* were presented to the Dublin Municipal Art Gallery by the artists in 1908.
17. 'Illuminated Manuscripts' (1968).
18. See Bowe, Caron, Wynne, *Gazetteer* (1988).
19. *The Picture of Dorian Gray* (London 1891).
20. For Mossa, see *Gustav Adolf Mossa (1883-1971) et les Symboles* (Nice 1978); his *Pierrot s'en Va* (1906), *Christus* and *L'Aveugle* (1907) resemble condemned portraits of Clarke, while his *Les Parques* (1905) are angelic travesties.

    There are remarkable analogies with Mikhail Vrubel's painting, 'like the sparkle of precious stones' (A. Rylov, quoted in Kaplanova, *Vrubel* (1975), particularly his ghostly moonlit *Swan Tsarevna* (1900) and tormented demonic visions.

    Clarke collected magazines reproducing Bakst's designs for the Russian Ballet as early as 1914. Bakst's sumptuously bejewelled and exotically coloured and patterned costumes set against a rich variety of dramatic backdrops are obvious sources for Clarke's Julian, Porphyro, Mad Prince, Bluebeard, Merman and Countess Cathleen.

    Forty-Three Drawings by Alastair (introduced by Robert Ross) were published by John Lane in 1914. There are obvious similarities between the two artists' insubstantial feverishly emaciated decadent drawings. Austin Spare featured illustrations by both in his *Golden Hind* (1922-4), both illustrated Poe (Alastair in 1928), and in 1928 John Lane published Alastair's *Manon Lescaut* and Clarke's Swinburne anthology. That year the plans of each artist to illustrate *Peer Gynt* fell through. The Chicago-based Richards Press asked Alastair to illustrate Huysmans' *Against the Grain* when Clarke was too ill (see Victor Arwas, *Alastair, Illustrator of Decadence*, London 1979).

    The Javanese-born Dutch Toorop's wide-eyed marionettes encased in symbolic lines bear obvious affinities with some of Clarke's early figures.
21. Werner Hoffman, *Gustav Klimt* (1979), p. 33.
22. Werner Hoffman, *Gustav Klimt* (London 1972), p. 36.
23. For Lechter (1865-1937) see Suzanne Beeh-Lustenberger (ed.), *Das Bild in Glas* (1979), no. 58.

    For Róth, Nagy and their contemporaries, see Katalin Gellér, 'Hungarian Stained Glass of the

Early 20th Century', *Journal of Stained Glass*, vol. XVIII, no. 2, 1986-7. The Vienna Secessionist Koloman Moser (1868-1918) might also be included here.

24. See Bowe, 'Wilhelmina Geddes' (1988) and 'Wilhelmina Geddes 1887-1955, Her Life and Work — A Reappraisal', *Journal of Stained Glass*, vol. XVIII, no. 3 (1988).
25. See Weiss, *Kandinsky in Munich* (1979) and Mathieu, *Moreau* (1977).
26. Sullivan, 'Jugendstil' in *Kindergarten Notes* (1901); also see Hoffmann (1972 and 1979), *op. cit.*
27. *Op. cit.*, pp. 158-211.
28. In 1907 Dulac, a frequent visitor to Ireland and close friend of W.B. Yeats, exhibited his *Arabian Nights* illustrations in London. In 1914 his enormously popular *Stories from Hans Andersen* was published, two years before Clarke's, which they undoubtedly influenced.

    Nielsen and Clarke were not only remarkably physically alike; the influence of Nielsen's Pierrot illustrations to *The Book of Death* (1912), to Hans Andersen's *Fairy Tales* (1912), to *In Powder and Crinoline* (1913) and *East of the Sun, West of the Moon* (1914), all exhibited in London after publication, bear many similarities stylistically and iconographically to Clarke's Hans Andersen illustrations.

    For Hoppé, see Pepper, *Hoppé* (1978) and Hillier, *Art Deco* (1968). For Sheringham, see *George Sheringham*, exhibition catalogue (Nottingham 1980). See also Nahum (ed.), *Jessie M. King and E.A. Taylor* (1977).
29. See Mircea Eliade, chapter on 'Androgyny and Wholeness' in her *Myths, Dreams and Mysteries* (London 1968).
30. Ezra Pound, 'Yeux Glauques', *Personae*, with reference to Burne-Jones cartoons, quoted in Jullian, *Dreamers of Decadence* (1971), p. 201.
31. Letter to the author.
32. Quoted in Amory, *Dunsany* (London 1972). See also Heneage and Ford, *Sidney Sime* (1980).
33. Hugh Salmond, 'Aunt Mabel Asks the Questions', *Journal of the British Society of Master Glass Painters*, vol. XV, no. 1, 1972-3.
34. Manning Robertson, 'The Craft Revival in Dublin', *Architecture*, February 1926.
35. Y.O. (pseudonym), 'The Work of Harry Clarke', *Irish Statesman*, 8 August 1925.

CHAPTER ONE

1. In Elliott, *Art and Ireland*, chap. IX.
2. 'Light in Dark Places', *The Living Torch*, ed. Gibbon (1937), p. 195.
3. Gwynn, *Edward Martyn* (1930); see also Sheehy, *Rediscovery* (1980).
4. Winston, *Ancient Glass Paintings*, 2 vols (1847); *Art of Glass Painting* (1865). In his earlier book Winston published excerpts from the monkish Theophilus' famous *Treatise* (*c.* 1120) on stained glass. These volumes were partly based on his careful analysis of the structure of fragments of medieval glass, which lead him to try to recreate the secret magic of 'antique' pot metals at Powell's Whitefriars Glass Works. See also Warrington, *History of Stained Glass* (1848), and Harrison, 'Victorian Stained Glass' (1973), pp. 251-4 and *Victorian Stained Glass* (1980).
5. Cormack, *Christopher Whall* (1980).
6. *Ibid.*, n.p.
7. Whall, *Stained Glass Work* (1905). In his book he wrote of the deep, brilliant colours, small pieces of glass used, rich backgrounds characteristic of mid thirteenth century glazing, which Harry Clarke would try to emulate. He preached Ruskin's *Aratra Pentelici* (1872) and, in turn, his book became the gospel of Child and his students at the Art School. The quotation in the text is taken from Peter Cormack's introduction to his valuable catalogue, *Christopher Whall*, the first critical account and assessment of Whall and his school. I am indebted to Peter Cormack for a number of discussions on the relationship between the English and Irish Revivals in stained glass and for his generous information.
8. I am grateful to the late Vic Drury, for a number of interviews and for allowing me to visit the Glass House and go through their ledgers. Harry Clarke was introduced to the Glass House by Karl Parsons, one of Whall's most talented pupils, who also taught at the RCA and the Central School of Art; Wilhelmina Geddes rented a studio there for a number of years, and it was there that she taught the craft to Evie Hone.
9. See Bowe, 'Early Twentieth-Century Irish Stained Glass in context' in Bowe, Caron and Wynne, *Gazetteer* (1988). Charles Williams, a half-brother of Mr Drury and a master glazier, was also sent over with Child from Whall's studio to assist at the Tower of Glass. This link between London and Dublin continued to be of great importance until the end of the 1930s.
10. Dublin 1928, p. 9.
11. Letter, 21 December 1922, quoted by kind permission of Christopher T. Whall.
12. The Department's *Annual Report and List of Prizewinners* quotes a speech made by the Lord Lieutenant, Lord Cadogan, on 10 January 1901 in which he said that 'the first of the technical courses

for the practice of stained glass painting and the study of design in connection therewith has been commenced within the last few weeks'. By February 1903, it reported that 'a small class has been established' (*Report* for 1903/4 session). See also *Ireland Industrial and Agricultural* published by the Department (1902); also John Turpin, 'The South Kensington System . . .' (1983).

13. Several artist/craftsmen and women who worked in stained glass or opus sectile among other media availed of the cooperative's facilities when commissions arose — for example, Kathleen Quigley, Harry's assistant for a number of years. See Bowe, Caron, Wynne, *Gazetteer*, for biographies of these artists.
14. Manuscript letter from Harry Clarke to W.B. Yeats, 4 April 1924: Letterbook no. 5995, Clarke MSS, Trinity College Dublin. From now on, all letters, unless otherwise stated, are extracted from the 69 volumes of Letterbooks (nos. 5970-6038), each comprising a minimum of 1000 carbon copies of letters sent out from the Studios, in the archives of the Harry Clarke Stained Glass Studios deposited in the Manuscript Room of TCD in July 1973. The archival material also includes wage books, ledgers, cash books, private ledgers, estimates, sales lists of designs sent out, invoice books, assorted papers (MSS 6086-6167), some press cuttings, two visitors' books (6083/4) and three books of stained glass orders (6058-60); of these 6059 and 6060 proved to be of considerable help. Unfortunately the Letterbooks for 1913, February 1922-January 1924 and November 1928-September 1929 are missing, as are a number of clients' letters, estimates and press cuttings.

    I am most grateful to William O'Sullivan, former Keeper of Manuscripts, TCD and his staff for their unstinted cooperation, advice and encouragement during the period in which I was studying this material.
15. Thomas J. Ryan, obituary, *The Belvederian*, January 1931, pp. 47-51.
16. Letter from Joshua Clarke to J.B. Payne, 8 December 1903.
17. See 'An Appreciation of Thomas F. McNamara (1867-1947)', *Irish Builder*, 11 January 1947, p. 10.
18. For a stained glass window, *St Patrick and the Two Princesses* (6′ 6″ x 2′).
19. Listed in the catalogue as *St Cecilia* (after Raphael). At the 2nd Exhibition held at Earlsfort Terrace, Dublin in 1899, Joshua had only felt confident enough to exhibit a scheme of church decoration, painted by himself and H. Morran, exhibited by the Scottish paint manufacturers of Duresco, J. Duthie & Co., Glasgow.
20. Letter from Joshua to Orr, November 1904. Joshua Clarke's own words are quoted directly as recorded in the Letterbooks, where they were usually written down as dictated to Miss O'Sullivan.
21. Letter from Joshua to Orr, 12 January 1906.
22. It seems almost certain that Christopher Whall would have been the Master of Stained Glass during Harry's period at the RCA.
23. Letter from Joshua, 19 April 1906.
24. Letter from Joshua 23 May 1906.
25. See Hugh P. Lane, 'A Prefatory Notice' to the *Catalogue of the Municipal Gallery of Modern Art in Dublin* (Dublin 1907), pp. vii-ix; A. Gregory, *Hugh Lane's Life and Achievement* (London 1921); Thomas Bodkin, *Hugh Lane and his Pictures* (1956).
26. The introduction in 1906 of the Irish Trades Act, which gave protection to the users of the Irish Trade Mark, had led to an increased awareness of native products.
27. The same window exhibited at the 3rd Arts and Crafts Exhibition in 1904.
28. Letter, 4 May 1908.
29. Among whom were Joshua Clarke and Sarah Purser. The following quotation is taken from the illustrated *Souvenir* (Dublin 1909) in which the Stained Glass Lady is illustrated on p. 36.
30. I am indebted to Hugh Salmond of Hetley's for his advice, and information concerning the Clarke Studios' materials.

    Prior's 'early English' slab glass had been invented in 1889. Peter Cormack writes (*op. cit.*), n.p. that this invention 'at the very beginning of Whall's career as an independent artist was an important factor in the development of the new school of stained glass designers. Like Winston's "antique" glass, it provided a stimulus for artists to experiment in glass, and its deliberately uneven texture and properties of intensifying light and colour emphasized the importance of materials as the basis for style. Prior's glass was also an illustration of an interest among architects in the decorative arts; this was one of the ideals of the Art Workers' Guild (founded by [Edward] Prior and others in 1884) and was enthusiastically endorsed by Whall, who writes of "a little Byzantium" of master craftsmen who would provide for the architect "the bright tools of the accessory crafts".' Harry Clarke was to favour this glass more and more, as he worked out the most effective way to lead up the often very thick slabs.

    It is interesting to note Guimard's use of similar 'heavy double-curved glass panels of alternating shapes' in the back staircase wall in his Castel

Béranger block of flats in Paris (1897-8): see Pevsner, *The Sources of Modern Architecture* (1968), ill. 102, later echoed in Bruno Taut's Glass House (1914) at the Cologne Werkbund Exhibition (*ibid.*, ill. 180).

31. Letter, 23 July 1909.
32. These were for the *Irish Cyclist* and *Motor News*; his first illustration for the former appeared in the 3 August 1910 trade supplement, the next on 26 October 1910. Signed and dated, they are standard caricatures of well-known men in 'Dublin Bicycle Trade Circles'. Pencil studies for the *Motor News* illustrations in a 1910 sketch book give an impressive sensation of speed. Other sketches include several coats of arms for religious orders, copies of Delft tiles and a sensitive pencil study of the group of kneeling Swiss Guards and priests from Raphael's *Mass of Bolsena* fresco in the Vatican Stanza della Segnatura.
33. Joshua to Arthur Orr, 25 January 1910.
34. He received 7/6d for two of these on 23 June.
35. Letter, 6 August 1910.
36. Patrick Tuohy (1894-1930) was born at 15 North Frederick Street and, encouraged by William Pearse, the sculptor brother of Patrick, at St Enda's School, had enrolled for night classes at the School of Art, where he became one of Orpen's best pupils.
37. Joshua to Mr Salmond, 29 September 1910.
38. It was at this time that R. M. Butler got him to do an illustration for the *Irish Builder* to help his financial situation; see *Irish Builder*, 30 September 1916, p. 469.
39. I discovered this panel in a storeroom in the Crawford Municipal Art Gallery, Cork in 1975; it is the earliest extant piece of stained glass made by Harry and already shows an adept handling of the craft — sensitive, skilled and detailed painting, rich, golden tones obtained with silver nitrate stain, accurate and effective aciding (such as the Queen of Heaven lozenge behind the group, and St Mel's clasp), rich, deep colouring in his choice of glass and an imaginative use of the leadlines. The men's faces are particularly expressive. This panel shows the Whall influence via Child in its use of quarries of silvery white glass and in its monumental treatment. The panel was a section worked from a full-length cartoon.
40. Letter from Joshua Clarke, 24 March 1911.
41. Letter from Harry Clarke, 6 June 1911.
42. *List of Successful Competitors and Reports*, Board of Education National Competition 1911 (London 1912), p. 63.
43. This three-light design, full of swirling movement and expressive features, was reproduced in the *Judges' Report*, plate XX, and its stained glass section as Plate XXI. The latter plate enabled me to identify the panel when I discovered it in the Crawford Municipal Gallery at the same time as the *St Mel* and *St Brendan with Judas* panels.
44. Orpen wrote of these days: 'For 5 or 6 years before the war, I used to go to Dublin and teach in the School for a fortnight twice a term. . . . The school was really turning out good work and there was a lot of promising youth — James Sl[e]ator, John Keating, Miss Crilly, Fox, Miss O'Kelly and young Whelan and Tuohy, all with talent, and all (or mostly all) working like blacks; it was rather like a happy working family': *Stories* (1924), p.78.
45. Given the distinction of being reproduced in colour as the frontispiece to the *Examiner's Report* (London 1913). This motif of a cascade of water had been used by Karl Parsons in his first window in the baptistery of St Alban's, Hindhead, Surrey (1908).
46. He had specially borrowed a Carmelite habit to make sure he got the drawing correct in this and a number of other illustrations at the time.

    This panel was discovered in a cupboard in the Art School by the former Head of the Stained Glass Department, John Murphy, when I was able to identify it from the cartoon illustrated in the *Judges' Report* (London 1913), plate XX, and the *Catalogue* of the Exhibition of Decorative Arts of Great Britain and Ireland (Paris and London, 1914), p. 35.
47. Only eleven gold medals were awarded throughout the whole of the rest of the competion. He was also awarded 9 gns. worth of book prizes and £5, an unknown record in the Dublin Art School. Joshua wrote proudly to Mr Salmond at Hetley's (5 February 1912) that it was the 'highest honour as any of them that got Gold Medals did not get the amount of prizes he got and it appears our School of Art ranks in same place as best school in London and in point of cash prizes a little advanced'. In March, Joshua had written to Orr that Harry was 'too busy with stained glass to finish any paintings. He started one, I know it really surprised me as he had very little experience of painting, it had the style of old painting. I do not know if he intends to finish it.' The full length cartoon was reproduced as plate XXI in the *Examiners' Reports* (London 1914).
48. Repr. no. 8 in Houvet's Chartres Cathedral portfolio, 1926.
49. Found in a locker by a student in the School of Art, *c.* 1935. Paganini seems the only correct subject of this illustration, although there is no MS reference to it. Harry may have read Heinrich Heine's

description of how the ill-fated virtuoso fiddler sold his soul to the devil.

CHAPTER TWO

1. A report on the exhibition in the *Proceedings of the RDS* (1913).
2. Card dated 28 August 1913, in the manuscript collection of Sir Robert's grandchildren; I am grateful to Dr E.M. Woods for drawing my attention to this.
3. In the collection of Wilhelmina Geddes's niece, Elizabeth Kerr, to whom I am most grateful for revealing its existence.
4. In the collections of Mrs E. Sheehy and Miss Lucy O'Brien respectively. There is also an autograph book, formerly belonging to the Clarke Studios' secretary, Miss O'Sullivan, now in the Dublin Municipal Art Gallery collection, which contains a further assortment of early work by Clarke between 1910 and 1912.
5. From *The Wind among the Reeds* (1899) and *Collected Poems* (1939); the poem begins, 'I went out to the hazel wood,/ because a fire was in my head,/ I will find out where she has gone,/ And walk among long dappled grass,/ And pluck till time and times are done/ The silver apples of the moon,/ The golden apples of the sun'.

   In the July 1913 issue of the *Irish Review* the drawing appears with the caption, extracted from Yeats' poem, inscribed beneath it.
6. Colum may have decided the illustration fitted the latter part of the last verse of Yeats' poem since both figures have fires in their heads, the man's hands are old and there are flickering, winging, moth-like creatures in the air around them. The female figure does bear glittering fruit and it is possible they are walking through 'long dappled grass', beneath suspended shining fruit which they could 'pluck till time and times are done'. Æ's poem, 'The City', begins: 'The air that I inhale/ Is like enchanted wine poured from the Holy Grail./ What was that glimmer then?/ Was it the flash of wings. . .'.
7. Vol. I, no. 1, April 1893.
8. Kenneth Clark has written — *The Best of Aubrey Beardsley* (1979), p. 66 — 'The elegantly knock-kneed Siegfried is comically unWagnerian, and if, as must be presumed, Beardsley had seen the heavyweights who normally interpret this character, there may have been an element of mischief in depicting him as this effete Dandy'; and (p. 20), quoting Whistler's description of Beardsley, 'He's all hairs and peacock plumes — hairs on his head, hairs on his finger ends, hairs in his ears, hairs on his toes.' Both apposite descriptions of Harry's Aengus.
9. He illustrated 'The Lake Isle of Inisfree' and 'The Fiddler of Dooney' in Lettice d'Oyly Walters (ed.), *The Year's at the Spring*, an illustrated anthology (1920) and *Countess Cathleen* in the Geneva Window (1927-8).
10. Letter from Joshua to R.M. Butler, 11 October 1913.
11. *The Belvederian*, vol. III, no. 1, 1912, p. 33.
12. *Irish Times*, 13 January 1924.
13. In a letter to me, 5 May 1974. I am indebted to the late Walter Starkie for several invaluable interviews in Dublin during May 1974.
14. Oliver St John Gogarty, *As I was going down Sackville Street* (1937) and Ulick O'Connor, *The Times I've Seen* (1963).
15. Starkie, *A Lady's Child* (1941). He features in an *Ode to my Friend*, The Rt Hon. Lorcan Galeran, A Great Householder, twenty-one anonymously composed verses: 'Magee no longer thinks alone/ Clarke talks and rouses silent Hone,/ While booming through the mist is heard/ Responsible, the clear-thoughted word' (verse 14), Bodkin MSS, TCD.
16. Copies of this are to be found in the private Waldron family MSS and in the Bodkin MSS, TCD (see Chapter 3, note 14).
17. Beardsley's *The Battle of the Beaux and the Belles* (the eight in his series) had been reproduced in Smithers' publication of *A Book of Fifty Drawings by Aubrey Beardsley* (1897), as had the 'cul-de-lampe', *The New Star*. See Brian Reade and Frank Dickinson's *Catalogue* of the Aubrey Beardsley Exhibition at the V. & A. (London 1966) for the various editions and formats in which Harry could have seen Beardsley's illustrated *Rape of the Lock*.
18. The scenes illustrated by both men are (Beardsley 1895-6 and Harry Clarke 1913): *The Dream, The Toilet, The Rape of the Lock, The Cave of Spleen, The Battle of the Beaux and the Belles, The New Star.* Clarke's are reproduced in Bowe, *Harry Clarke: His Graphic Art* (1983), pp. 108-111.
19. Kenneth Clark, *op. cit.*, p. 142.
20. From these illustrations one can see why, in later years, Harry became so defensive at the mention of Beardsley's influence. He is still labelled as belonging to the Beardsley School — for example, in Hillier, *Art Deco* (1968), p. 62.
21. Clarke's illustrations are featured in Bowe, *Harry Clarke: His Graphic Art, op. cit.*, pp.112-116.
22. These two latter illustrate verses chosen by Sir Robert Woods' two eldest children, who picked out the most frightening of the whole poem, so much so that when the illustrations were hanging

up the stairs of the Woods' house, the children dreaded having to pass them. I am grateful to Mrs Patricia Proctor and Dr E.M. Woods for their help in working out the provenance of these illustrations.

23. It is interesting to note Thomas Mackenzie's (1887-1944) borrowing of the haunted face and halo-like beret of the Mariner and even the device of a furtive foreground onlooker, emerging into the frame on the L.H., only his face and half of his cloak visible, in a pen and ink and watercolour illustration (dated 1915) of two men watching the combat of a snake and a cockerel; presumably he had seen the two reproductions of Harry's illustrations in the Autumn 1914 *Studio* special number. The Mariner's face is combined with elements of Beardsley and Sime in an earlier (undated) illustration by Mackenzie of Baudelaire's 'Eagles and insects, streams and woods/ Stand still to hear him chaunt his colorous moods'. Both these illustrations are reproduced (p. 181, plates 130-1) in Diana L. Johnson, *Fantastic Illustration and Design in Britain 1850-1930* Rhode Island 1979). Harry himself repeated this pale, bereted face in his Hans Andersen illustration, *The Garden of Paradise* (p. 282), and in his *Year's at the Spring* illustration to H.H. Abbot's 'Black and White' (p. 126), minus the beret.
24. Present whereabouts unknown; reproduced in Rheims, *The Age of Art Nouveau* (1966), p. 144, plate 211.
25. Letter, 14 November 1913.
26. *Some Memories* (1935).
27. Quarto cloth gilt: cover design and decorations, 28 colour plates; issued also in a de luxe limited edition of 750 copies bound in vellum, numbered and signed by Dulac, with specially designed endpapers. Issued also as a breakdown into a series of 8vo volumes, each with a coloured picture cover: i) *The Mermaid*, ii) *The Nightingale* (to which Harry's subsequent colour illustration is nearly identical); iii) *The Real Princess*; iv) *The Snow Queen* (2 vols); v) *The Wind's Tale*. See Colin White, *Edmund Dulac* (London 1976), p. 200.
28. Peppin, *Fantasy* (1975) p. 21. Harry may well have visited Nielsen's exhibition in London at the Leicester Galleries during the autumn.
29. Described henceforth as the unravelled knitting motif. The lantern was inherited by Sir Robert Woods when he bought Marino in 1924, after Waldron's death; it now belongs to the former's grandson.
30. See Charles J. Connick's descriptions of his European stained glass tours before the Second War in *Adventures in Light and Colour* (1937).
31. Houvet's superbly illustrated four volumes on the stained glass in Chartres Cathedral, written with l'Abbé Delaporte, were not published until 1926, although his six volumes on the cathedral were first published in 1920.
32. For example, the figure of King Solomon, with his transfixing eyes, in one of the lancets beneath the north transept rose window (thirteenth century).
33. Although technically called 'calmes', I have referred to the grooved strips of lead which surround each piece of glass as lead lines, since this seems to better express their intrinsic artistic function, which Harry understood so well.
34. In 1900, at the age of sixteen, Karl Parsons (1884-1934) had become one of Whall's pupils, and had succeeded Whall as principal stained glass teacher at the Central School by 1908. Peter Cormack (*op. cit.*) writes that his own style 'though firmly rooted in the Whall tradition owed much to mediaeval glass'. It is more than likely that it was he who subsequently advised Harry which glass to visit in France after the fiasco of his first attempted visit.
35. I am grateful to Charles Blakeman and Martin Harrison for putting me in touch with the late Joseph Nuttgens, who was of help in establishing when Parsons and Harry first met.
36. Such exact details of Harry's procedure in carrying out this commission are possible because of the careful notes he made in his diary. There is an unpublished but very fine colour illustration to this story, undated and in many respects superior to the one published, which shows the Emperor walking through the crowds in his drawers; a tiny effigy of the Madonna, similar to that of *La Belle Verrière* in Chartres Cathedral, embroidered on to a banner behind him is particularly delightful.
37. There is also a similarly fine but unpublished colour illustration to this story, dated 1914, and inscribed *The Little Mermaid*. From Harry's diary entries, it would seem to have been done in February 1914 but abandoned in favour of the oval (p. 212) showing the little Sea Maid 'dancing over the floor as no one yet had danced', probably done later. In the earlier, unpublished version the Japanese influence is transposed to the maiden's kimono and sash and the decorative curtain ties; an attenuated Salome-like figure with raven hair, she is also a subtly coloured echo of a Beardsley heroine; her reddened finger tips and toes, frozen as she dances for her life, may be derived from Harry's study of Indian miniatures in the V. & A Museum. Certainly the intricate and subtle treatment of colour and line in this and his other colour illustrations would suggest an

acquaintance with the miniature tradition. In the mirror, far back in the palace room, the reflection appears, a mere ½" high, of Harry's self portrait in blue and brown ink; derived from Velasquez' *Las Meninas,* where the small background figure of the artist is silhouetted in a doorway behind the principal figures, Harry would repeat this device in subsequent illustrations and had already inserted a similar figure in his Poe *M. Valdémar.* There is another unpublished colour illustration to Hans Andersen in the Clarke family collection; untitled, it depicts a princely dandy being shown a vision of outsize fantastic flowers, moths and butterflies by a traditional Japanese actor, watched by two peacocks and three damsels all in glowing colours. There is also a fine, unused illustration to *The Swinehead* of this period. In a letter to Arthur Howell (25 June 1925, Clarke MSS), Harry wrote that Brentano's, Harraps' publishing partners in New York, 'took all my originals for Hans Andersen . . . and they were shown in their bookshop in 5th Avenue'. A number were sold to Mr Byrne Hackett of the Brick Row Bookshop in New York; some Harry gave to George Harrap but these are reputed to have been destroyed in the Blitz. Judging from the high quality of Harry's colour illustrations of this period, it is very sad that not a single full-page published illustration for Hans Andersen has yet come to light.

38. Letter, 31 March 1914.
39. These two periodicals are specifically noted in Harry's diary; both were published in Darmstadt, the first in 1869, the second in 1889 onwards. The various other international periodicals of the same nature which Harry would have been drawn to include *Innen-dekoration* (founded 1890), *L'Art Decoratif, Art et Décoration* (both 1897), *Dekorative Kunst* (1897), *The Yellow Book* (1894), and, above all *The Studio* and *The Studio Yearbooks* and *Special Numbers,* whose importance cannot be over-emphasized. In England there were also *The Artist* (published by the Society of Designers), *The Connoisseur, Artwork* and a sporadic publication, *The Imprint,* copies of which are still in the Dublin Art School library.
40. Joan Hughson records that 'stained glass [had] occupied much of Taylor's energies from 1900-1914' in her essay, 'E.A. Taylor' (1874-1951), pp. i-v. in Nahum (ed.), *Jessie M. King and E.A. Taylor* (1977). Beatrice Parsons, Karl Parson's elder sister, was an able flower and garden water-colourist who in March 1899 (in *The Artist,* no. 231, p. 140f) is referred to as learning stained glass under Christopher Whall, and who may have been responsible for the introduction.
41. The catalogue section of 'Books from the Collection of Jessie M. King and Ernest A. Taylor' (pp. 18-23) sold by Sotheby Parke Bernet & Co. in Glasgow on 21 June 1977 is particularly interesting. Among these were Beardsley's illustrated *Le Morte d'Arthur* (1893-4); issues of *The Bookman* between 1913 and 1934; a presentation copy of *Charles Conder, His Life and Work* 'To that rare Artist Jessie M. King, from her first publisher, John Lane' (1914); Lady Gregory, *A Book of Saints and Wonders* (1907); James Stephens, *Songs from the Clay* (1915); Katharine Tynan, *Collected Poems* (1930); Padraic Colum, *Old Pastures* (New York 1930); Frank Harris, *Unpath'd Waters* (1913); Seán O'Casey, *The Flying Wasp* (1937), Æ, *Homeward Songs, by the Way* (1901), *The Divine Vision and Other Poems* (1904), *The Mask of Apollo, Imaginations and Reveries* (1915), *The Candle of Vision* (1918), *Vale and Other Poems* (1931), and *Song and Its Fountains* (1932); five of S.H. Sime's illustrated books to Lord Dunsany's *The Gods of Pegana* (1905), *Time and the Gods* (1906), *The Sword of Welleran* (1908), *The Book of Wonder* (1912) and *A Dreamer's Tale* (1911); and W.B. Yeats, *The Celtic Twilight* (1893), *The Secret Rose* (1892), *The Shadowy Waters* (1900), *Ideas Good and Evil,* (1903) *Discoveries* (1907), *The Wind among the Reeds* (1899), *Poems* (1901), *Per Amica Silentia Lunae* (1918), *The Hour Glass, Cathleen Ni Houlihan, The Pot of Broth* (1904), *The King's Threshold and the Old Baile's Stand* (1904), and *Deirdre* (1907). Harry would later add to their collection the 1919 edition of his illustrated Poe's *Tales of Mystery and Imagination,* an inscribed copy of *The Year's at the Spring,* which bears a number of (perhaps unconscious) tributes to Jessie King's work, 'To Mrs Taylor (Jessie M.King) from her friend Harry Clarke' and his illustrated *Perrault* in 1922 with a Christmas card he had designed himself.
42. Joan Hughson, *art. cit.,* p. v.
43. These two *Ancient Mariner* illustrations (nos. 3 and 5 in the series) were well reproduced on pp. 56 and 57; Jessie King's were reproduced on pp. 89-91.
44. Connick, *op.cit.,* p.289. The connection was 'especially rich in examples of early work followed by those of succeeding periods so you can easily trace, in eloquent details against clear light, the decline and fall of the craft'. Some of the examples, still in their original leads at the time, are illustrated. In the autumn of 1935 extensive alterations and 'ruthless dismantling' led to the erection of the new Palace of the Trocadero, prospective marvel of the 1937 Paris Exposition: *ibid.,* p. 410.

45. *Ibid.*, p. 289.
46. *Ibid.*, p. 410. For further observations on the relevance of the theories of Theophilus and Viollet-le-Duc's theories to Clarke's work, see Bowe, 'The Life and Work of Harry Clarke', unpublished PhD thesis, U. of Dublin, 1982, I, pp. 88-92, where the considerable number of books on the craft history and theory of stained glass published between those of Charles Winston (*op. cit.)* are listed alphabetically. Harry was particularly attached to Laurence Saint's *Stained Glass of the Middle Ages in England and France* (1913).
47. A full survey of the cathedral's glass had been made by Jean Lafond in 1911.
48. He would incorporate a similar autographical invocation at the foot of his Honan Chapel *St Patrick* window in 1915, and in 1910 he would illustrate Flaubert's interpretation of the *St Julian* window in a miniature panel.
49. In the spring of 1979, when I visited the abbey, the whole building was in the process of being restored and there was no information available on the glass, which was severely damaged in the Second World War.
50. Letter, 16 June 1914.
51. Noted by Thomas Bodkin on a *Catalogue* of an Exhibition of Irish Artists from the Municipal Gallery, Dublin in London in 1948; Bodkin MSS, TCD (see Chapter 3, note 14).
52. Reproduced in *The Belvederian*, vol. IV, no. 3, 1917, p. 36 and Bowe, *Harry Clarke: His Graphic Art*, *op. cit.*, p. 121.
53. Reproduced *British Book Illustrators Yesterday and Today* (Studio special number, 1923), p. 171; Thomas Bodkin, 'The Art of Mr Harry Clarke', *The Studio*, November 1919, p. 49; also see Bowe, *Harry Clarke* catalogue (1979), no. 30 (the catalogue to the Douglas Hyde Gallery exhibition: see n. 55 below).
54. Waldron is recorded as being a frequent visitor to University College, Cork and went on a protracted visit there in 1914, shortly before Harry received his first commission. Windle usually stayed with Waldron on his Dublin visits. See Sr Monica Taylor, *Sir Bertram Windle* (1932), pp. 228-9. For further context and the roles of O'Connell and Windle in the erection of this Celtic Revival see Bowe, 'The Life and Work . . .', op. cit., 99-102. Sr Monica Taylor wrote the preface for her book from Notre Dame, Dowanhill in Glasgow, for whose convent chapel Harry later designed and made four windows. Sir Bertram used to visit the convent often to see the daughter of an old friend of his and became very friendly with Sr Mary of St Wilfrid, the superioress of the convent and principal of the training college (who gave Harry the first two of his commissions and recommended him for the subsequent very large commission at their sister convent of Ashdown Park and other sister convents). Sir Bertram would also introduce Harry to his cousin, Edith OE Somerville, who gave him his first public commission after the Honan Chapel series.
55. This picture was catalogued by the Fine Art Society in London in June 1971 (*British Drawings and Watercolours of the 20th Century*) as *Queen Mab* (no. 24), provenance unknown, although the Lady bears no resemblance to Keats' heroine and was never referred to by Harry as such. *The Lady of Decoration* was Harry's own name for her, although when she was (excellently) reproduced by John Duthie she was untitled. The picture was exhibited at the Harry Clarke exhibition in 1979 (no. 25) and featured on the cover of Sotheby's catalogue when it was again sold on 3 June 1988 in London (no. 399).

    It is not recorded whether Harry had visited the Musée des Arts Decoratifs while he was in Paris and seen Bakst's designs for *Schéhérazade* (1910) with their 'rich flowing colours — canary yellow, bright blue, jade, cerise, cyclamen and concentric patterns and richly textured fabrics, wigs and turbans, blues and greens, purples and reds' (Spencer, *Leon Bakst*, 1973, p. 186); the delicate pale blue arabesques on a white background on parts of the Lady's costume are reminiscent of fine painting on china or delft.
56. In treatment, design and style, this illustration is very similar to the small-scale Honan Chapel designs Harry was preparing concurrently. It was featured in the 1979 *Harry Clarke* exhibition catalogue no. 26A.
57. Inscribed 'Reduce to proportion of 10½" x 15½" outside writing to edge of . . . [illegible]'. The illustration is still in the collection of the Cruise family, who have no evidence or recollection of it having been reproduced. Unfortunately the present Hibernian Insurance Company has no records dating back further than the last decade. It was exhibited in the 1979 *Harry Clarke* catalogue (no. 26B).
58. These panels bear a marked resemblance to Oscar Paterson's rectangular glass door panels (1900) in the entrance hall of 12 University Gardens, Glasgow, as reproduced fig. 26 in Larner, *The Glasgow Style* (1979). Cullet panels were a feature of many arts and crafts stained glass artists' work at the time.
59. Around this time, he illustrated the Lovers' flight from Keats' *Eve of St Agnes* which he would later

incorporate into a stained glass window. His notes indicate he was contemplating 'La Belle Dame' as a stained glass panel for the Woods.

CHAPTER THREE

1. This brought the cost of the window to £41. 5*s*. There are substantial differences between most of the designs and exquisitely finished cartoons for this first major commission. The cartoons amount to monochrome paper versions of the windows whose detailed treatment made the real cost of the windows considerably more than the price of their materials indicates.
2. Letter, 14 April 1915; for an account of stained glass manufacture in Britain during the First World War, see H.J. Powell (of Whitefriars), *Glass Making in England* (1923).
3. Where he was much entertained by their British army officer neighbour's drilling of lady recruits next door, on his front lawn.
4. Letter to Arthur Orr, 7 June 1915.
5. Another explanation may be that Joshua was by now wavering between a predilection for a Westlake (*History of Design in Painted Glass*, 1879-94) style and a Hardman of Birmingham style and Orr's work did not sufficiently tally with either of these. As it was, he usually got MacBride to 'fill in' ornament on Orr's designs.
6. Letter, 10 July 1915. Joshua Clarke arranged a meeting between Edward Martyn and his son in July, to vindicate Martyn's earlier, fully justified despair at finding an Irish artist versed in stained glass.
7. Documented in the MSS of Maunsel & Co. (formerly Maunsel and Roberts) in the collection of George Allen & Unwin. I am grateful to Frances-Jane French for obtaining this material in the course of research for a J.M. Synge bibliography.
8. Which was still causing him problems in April 1916. He had some trouble with the arrangement of this window, changing around the various symbols of Ita's royalty and faith and completely altering the base panel, as well as her face. The main difference between the small coloured drawing and the cartoon is that in the former her face is young, innocent, doe-like and the colours pale and neutral, whereas in the cartoon and window it is ascetic, wise, even zealous and the colours around her unusually deep and rich.
9. Letter, 17 December 1915, He was also trying to persuade his father to buy a cutting desk from Heaton's in Cumberland Market, in London.
10. Letter, 4 January 1916.
11. Denis Gwynn, *op. cit.*
12. Letter, 17 February 1916.
13. Letter, 5 April 1916, Clarke MSS.
14. Letter, 6 April 1916, Bodkin MSS, coll. Ann Bourke. All the letters from Harry Clarke to Thomas Bodkin are quoted from the originals — until her recent death in the collection of Harry's daughter, Ann Bourke (now inherited by her daughter) and given to her by Bodkin's widow, Mrs Aileen Bodkin. Mrs Bodkin also presented typed copies of these letters with other Clarke/Bodkin material to the Manuscript Room, TCD as part of the extensive Bodkin MSS. Some of this additional Clarke material, as well as letters from L.A. Waldron *et al.* to Bodkin were not in the late Mrs Bourke's possession; when this is the case, the TCD Bodkin MSS sources are quoted. In this context, I am most grateful to the late Mrs Aileen Bodkin, to Alan Denson and his Bodkin *Bibliography* (1966), to William O'Sullivan, former Keeper of Manuscripts and his staff, TCD and to the late Mrs Ann Bourke for her generosity in making her father's letters so freely available to me, as well as other related material.
15. Leo Cartwright, 'Harry Clarke: Artist and Craftsman', *Stained Glass*, Spring 1933, p. 31.
16. The late Victor Wood remembered Harry always describing his peculiar idiosyncracies as 'gadgetts'.
17. For example, in the *Queens* and *The Song of the Mad Prince* panels as well as the 1917 *Angel of Peace* Christmas card.
18. Letter, 8 May 1916.
19. The second illustration in the series, one of the later two commissioned by Sir Robert Woods, was later reproduced in *Drawings in Pen and Pencil from Dürer's Day to Ours*, with notes and appreciations by George Sheringham, *The Studio*, special number, 1922, p. 151. The third and fifth had already been reproduced in *The Studio* Autumn special number of 1914 (M.C. Salama, *Modern Book Illustrators and their Work*, pp. 56, 67). I am again grateful to Frances-Jane French for supplying me with these compensation figures from the Maunsel MSS.
20. Quoted by Hilary Pyle, in her catalogue to ROSC, *An Exhibition of Irish Art 1900-1950*, p.12. Bodkin's stern review was published in the *Irish Review*, April 1913, p. 84.
21. Letter, 4 July 1916, Bodkin MSS, coll. Ann Bourke.
22. Monica Taylor, *op. cit..*, p. 254.
23. J. White and M. Wynne, *Irish Stained Glass* (Dublin 1963), p. 13.

24. *The Bookman*, Christmas Supplement, no. 50, p. 84. See Bowe, *Harry Clarke: His Graphic Art*, *op. cit.*, fig. 24 for Harrap's prospectus.
25. *Irish Builder and Engineer*, 30 September 1916. I can find no trace of such.
26. *The Studio*, vol. 69, p. 105.
27. *Studies* (Dublin), June 1917, p. 299.
28. *Irish Builder and Engineer*, 5 December 1914, 28 October 1916, 31 March 1917. The unprecedentedly high standard of the all Irish stained glass was praised in the *Irish Builder*, 11 March 1916. For a more detailed account of all the stained glass in the chapel with a full background account of the stained glass revival, see 28 April 1917 issue.
29. Thomas Bodkin, 'The Art of Mr Harry Clarke', *The Studio*, November 1919, p. 46.
30. P. Oswald Reeves, 'Irish Arts and Crafts' (1917), pp. 21 and 22.
31. John Ruskin, *The Stones of Venice*, II, Appendix 12 (1898: 3rd ed).
32. Reeves, *art. cit.*, p. 21.
33. The lower R.H. angel is clearly adapted from Ambrogio Preda's profiled *Portrait of a Lady* in the National Gallery, London.
34. Among the many books, apart from those specifically related to stained glass, which dwell on this element, one might cite Kandinsky, *The Art of Spiritual Harmony* (1914), Sidney Heath, *The Romance of Symbolism* (London 1909) and Ellen Conroy, *The Symbolism of Colour* (London 1921).
35. London 1905, *op. cit.*
36. Kandinsky, *op. cit.*, pp. 43f.
37. Harry's use of very thick glass led to considerable strain on the leads, so that, ten years later, much of the glass had to be releaded and in the 1960s, all the windows were entirely reglazed.
38. 'The Work of Harry Clarke', *Irish Statesman*, 8 August 1925, p. 692.
39. On 26 July 1919, Harry sent Bodkin a letter in which he noted down his curriculum vitae, details of the iconography of the Ita, Finbarr, Columcille and Brigid windows and notes on the colour symbolism of each of his eleven windows in the chapel; this was for Bodkin to work from when compiling the November 1919 *Studio* article.

    Sir John O'Connell, *The Collegiate Chapel, Cork* (1916), pp. 41-57, is another valuable source for the iconographical details of these windows.
40. *Op. cit.* (1968), p. 323; quoted in the Introduction above.
41. Lennox Robinson, 'An Appreciation', *Irish Times*, 7 January 1931; 'Those windows . . . will shine and glow, those blues and reds — how he loved blue!'.
42. Kandinsky, *op.cit.*, p.38; he elaborates in n. 19: 'The halos are golden for emperors and prophets (i.e. for mortals), and sky-blue for symbolic figures (i.e. spiritual beings); Kondakoff, *Histoire de l'Art Byzantine considerée principalement dans les miniatures*, II, p. 382, Paris 1886-91'. The colours of the haloes of Harry's figures are always most carefully chosen but whether these are decorative or symbolic is not recorded.
43. Jean Lorrain's description of a *fin-de-siècle* heroine (quoted by Jullian, *French Symbolist Painters*, 1972, p. 9) is apposite here: 'The disquieting pallor of the Host, the emaciated oval of a face bearing an expression of both spirituality and suffering, the wide-staring eyes, ultramarine turning to black, circles under her eyes tinged with blue, bruised and flecked with mother of pearl; remote and fragile, she personified the psychic beauty of the 20th century. Where else have I seen this delicate nose with the vibrant nostrils, and where else the panting of that flat breast?'
44. For a discussion of Clarke's use of symbolism and his place in the Symbolist aspects of the Celtic Revival in Ireland, see Bowe, 'The Life and Work . . .', *op. cit.*, pp. 165-9 and 'Symbolism in Turn of the Century Irish Art', *GPA Irish Arts Review Yearbook 1989*. The nostalgia for Yeats' lost Byzantium seems to be particularly powerfully evoked in these windows.
45. It may be mere coincidence that Bakst designed a cloak of large lustrous blue honeycombed lozenges in 1911 for Ida Rubinstein to wear in the second act of d'Annunzio's ballet, *St Sébastien*, where they are juxtaposed with emerald green.
46. An ivory complexion and red-gold hair constituted an ideal feminine aesthetic, first for the Pre-Raphaelites and later for the Symbolists.

    Hair, which Harry uses to such effect in his work (for example, even as early as the *Ancient Mariner* illustration of Life-in-Death) was a well known Symbolist obsession: see Goldwater, *Symbolism* (1979), pp. 60-9. The profiled outline of her face is identical with A. Baldovinetti's *Portrait of a Lady in Yellow*, which Harry would have seen in the National Gallery in London.
47. *Op. cit.*, p. 330.
48. This profiled head, of which Harry was particularly fond and which he frequently adapted throughout his work in whatever medium from this point on so that it became one of his ideal archetypes, seems to be derived from the small gilt terracotta relief of the *Virgin and Child* by Donatello which he would have been able to see at the V. & A. (where it had been since 1867). Donatello's bronze roundel, known as the *Chellini Madonna*, bears an even closer resemblance to Harry's roundel, but he could only have known

this from reproductions as it was not presented to the V. & A. until 1976.

The convention of the bust of a Madonna and Child set in a small decorative roundel was also used as early as *c.* 1260 by the great English school of illumination at St Albans (see W. Gaunt, *A Concise History of English Painting*, London 1964, plate 1).

49. Mysteriously, a letter exists, dated 17 December 1918, from Waldron to Bodkin (Bodkin MSS) in which Waldron writes that Harry had sent him a beautiful little drawing of 'S. Gobianette (? spelt on your and other principles I fear) a beautiful thing with gold bees which I am anxious to show you'. There is no other record of this; because of its date, medium and the absence of bees on the roundel, it could not refer to the *Madonna* roundel. There is a vague memory in the Waldron family of another stained glass roundel by Harry, similar to the *Madonna*, hitherto untraced, for which the *Gobianette* drawing might have been a study. There is a surreal painting by Seán (then John) Keating, *Thinking Out Gobnet*, dedicated by the artist to Harry Clarke on 29 August 1917.
50. This small scene would seem to be based on the small cartoon for domestic glass reproduced in C. Whall, *op. cit.*, p. 348, fig. VI by Miss M.J. Newill. The background of the same cartoon was similarly adapted in the base panels of the *Laurence O'Toole* and *Malachy* windows in Belcamp (1925).
51. These seem to be derived from the Vienna Secessionist poster, *Kunstschau Wien*, 1908 by Berthold Löffler, and are among several Viennese Secession influences apparent in these windows.
52. The names of most of the tiny subsidiary figures in these windows are inscribed around their haloes, a habit Harry repeated in subsequent windows — once more a medieval legacy.
53. The stippled treatment of the ravaged flesh is particularly reminiscent of that on the faces of some of the little horned devils in the Fairford fifteenth century *Last Judgment* window, also the twelfth and thirteenth century medallion windows in Canterbury Cathedral, naturally pitted with age.
54. 'St Brandan' published in his *Poetical Works* (London 1890).
55. Silver nitrate, gum and gamboge, painted on to the back of the glass in solution fuses into the glass by molecular action when fired, giving a wide variety of shades ranging from pale lemon to deep gold and orange-red; this was only used as from the fourteenth century (the Middle Gothic/ Decorated period of stained glass). See A.C. Sewter, 'William Morris's Designs for Stained Glass', *Architectural Review*, March 1960 for Morris' rediscovery of the possibilities of yellow stain: 'In time the Morris workshop attained an unrivalled mastery in the use of this stain, and was able to produce a range of tints and tones of gold from the palest yellow to the most intense reddish bronze. It was only when experience with this technique had been acquired that some of the glories of the firm's output . . . could be produced.' See also Sewter, *The Stained Glass of William Morris*, I (Newhaven, Conn. 1974), especially Chapters I, V and Glossary.

Hydrofluoric acid was not discovered until the late nineteenth century after the secret of flashing glass had been rediscovered: even diamond cutters were not used until the seventeenth century.
56. O'Connell, *op. cit.*, p. 42.
57. For example, *The Annunciation*, Terenure (1921), *The Virgin and Child with Sts Aidan and Adrian*, Wexford (1919) and *The Visitation* and *The Widow's Son*, Balbriggan (1923-4).
58. Similar to a number drawn by Burne-Jones, who adapted them from Japanese seals and from the grisaille roundels illustrating Dante's *Divina Commedia* by Signorelli in Orvieto Cathedral, although they were more likely to be a direct borrowing from the six small roundels set in quarries ($4\frac{1}{2}''$ x 4") illustrated in C. Whall, *op. cit.*, p. 352, fig. VIII by pupils of H.A. Payne at Birmingham School of Art. It is interesting to compare these with Kandinsky's studies for Signets for the Neue Künstler Vereinigung München, 1908-9 (coll. Lenbachhaus, Munich).
59. By Elizabeth Suscenko after a lecture given by the writer at the Victoria and Albert Museum in August 1978.
60. Quoted by Piper, *Stained Glass — Art or Anti-Art?* (1968).

CHAPTER FOUR

1. For a list of Harry Clarke's illustrated books, see Bowe, *Harry Clarke: His Graphic Art, op. cit.*, Appendix A.
2. *The Belvederian*, vol. IV, no. 3, pp. 36-38.
3. It would seem to be contemporary with the Hans Andersen illustrations. It is now in the private collection of a direct heir of Waldron's.
4. In the same collection. C. Whall, *op. cit.*, pp. 77-8, wrote, 'The real test in glass is being able to produce in glass a real facsimile of a head by Botticelli or Holbein, and when you can do that satis-

factorily you can do anything in glass-painting.'

5. See Bowe, 'The Arts and Crafts Society of Ireland' (1985), also Bowe, 'The Life and Work . . .', *op. cit.*, pp. 224-31.
6. Vol. 72, no. 295, 15 October 1917, pp. 15-22.
7. Harry often mentioned how much he liked Synge's *Playboy of the Western World* (first performed in 1907) and he also had a particular fondness for depicting little queens; his book illustrations, stained glass and graphic work abound with them, often in the guise of Queens of Heaven or lady saints. He later took great pleasure in illustrating Swinburne's *Masque of Queens; c.* 1915 he had drawn an unpublished illustration of *The Playboy* (repr. p. 122, Bowe, *Harry Clarke: His Graphic Art, op. cit.*) and would depict him in glass in the Geneva window (1927), ten years after his *Mad Mulrannies* illustration for Bodkin.
8. Eventually, he used a piece of gold-pink from the Studios' own stock and rubies from a local hardware merchant in Dublin.
9. See C. Whall, pp. 72-82.
10. The panels have been reproduced with Synge's text in a Dolmen Press volume with a commentary by N. Gordon Bowe and Liam Miller intended for publication prior to the publication of this book.
11. In *Amours and the Odes, The Penguin Book of French Verse* (Harmondsworth 1958), p. 53.
12. *The Complete Poems of François Villon* (London 1968). The Ballad is taken from Le Téstament.
13. Now in the Mellon collection in the National Gallery of Washington, DC; then, as Bodkin subsequently noted in his November 1919 *Studio* article, in the Petrograd Hermitage.
14. In the National Gallery, London, whose features Harry had previously adapted in the Honan Chapel *St Brigid* window. Bodkin refers to the fact (November 1919, *Studio*, p. 50) that the sitter was at that time believed to be Lucrezia Crivelli.
15. Bodkin, *art. cit.*, recalls a Judith 'in similar form' by Mantegna; although there has been a small grey monochrome *Judith and Holofernes* panel in tempera on linen in the National Gallery, Dublin since 1896, there is virtually no resemblance between Harry's and any of Mantegna's four extant treatments of the subject. The dramatic décolletage of Judith and several of the other ladies in these panels would suggest Harry had been studying Stuart portraits. Judith's facial features and the treatment of the decapitated head of Holofernes bear more of a resemblance to Gustav Klimt's *Judith II* (1909), the painting now in the Galleria d'Arte Moderna, Venice.
16. Antwerp 1581; see Strong, *The Elizabethan Image* (1969), no. 153. In the portrait by Gheerhaerts, the mood of the queen is reflected in the words inscribed on the cartouche beside her. Bodkin (*op. cit.*) draws attention to the former attribution of the painting to Zucchero and mentions it was then hanging at Hampton Court.
17. Gaunt, *op. cit.*, p. 25, where he describes the 'almost Byzantine formality' of portraits seen 'as abstract symbols of majesty and with a tremendous lavishness of detail' with reference to the *Ditchley* portrait of Elizabeth I.
18. Wilhelmina Geddes maintained that men working in stained glass tended to produce work of a feminine character while women frequently produced the reverse. This is certainly borne out in Clarke's and Geddes' own work.
19. 'Mr Harry Clarke's Glass', *Dublin Evening Mail*, July (? date unclear) 1918; taken from Jeffrey Jenkins' press cuttings, for which I am grateful.
20. 'The Art of Mr Harry Clarke', (1919), pp. 45-51.
21. *Ibid.*, p. 50. See also the *Dublin Evening Mail* article referred to above. Harry had provided the technical notes for this article in a letter to Mrs Bodkin, dated 2 November 1918, in which he tried to 'explain the technical advance in this and further miniature glass panels' he had made. He explained how aciding and plating (doubling two pieces of different coloured glass) were usually resorted to when it would be impossible to lead up the colours wanted, and were particularly common in heraldic work (e.g. 'a dragon in red with a blue tongue and a green eye kind of thing'). Plating was also used to tone or change a colour when a window was already completed, or to give extra depth of colour. He then described the development of the above methods as used in making the Bodkins' panel: 'A piece of blue glass was acided five times and gave me four blue tones and white, on which I could get three stains varying from pale lemon or orange. A piece of ruby acided five times gave me four ruby tones and white for three stains. The two glasses doubled and acided in a way to leave some parts of the ruby clear, where the blues show and the blue clear where the rubies show — gave eight colours; then came the colours got by leaving colour on each glass — pale blue and pale ruby — ruby tinged with blue — deep ruby backed with the orange stain on both glasses — greens — pale whites — warm whites (like around the lady's head). There is no limit to the quality of colour one can get — the panels could be acided to give ten tones each — if one had a glass with a good body of colour to start on. Purple is the only colour which goes a little "inky", but that only happens when the wrong quantities of either the ruby or

blue are left. Panels could be done with "gold-pink" and blue — if ever I do another I will use these two glasses. [He subsequently used this combination on four of the panels in the *Eve of St Agnes* window (1923-4) and the *Mr Gilhooley* and *Deirdre of the Sorrows* panels in his Geneva window (*c.* 1927).] There are lots of things I had to do to get my coloured lines clean and in your panel and Miss Jane French's a good deal of the stopping out was penned with a hot nib in hot wax. I also penned with the pigment and the face of the Mad Prince — the outline is firm and far from "rotten" — was done in this manner. It could not have been done with a brush without niggling at it afterwards with a needle. I could keep on at this for a long time but I think the foregoing may explain things and should you need a demonstration I will show you whenever you like, how I worked on your own panel. I will believe Louis Davis did similar panels himself when I see them. [Louis Davis (1861-1941) was a close friend of Whall's from the 1890s onwards; his stained glass can be seen in the Law Memorial in St Patrick's Cathedral, Dublin. Neither Peter Cormack nor Hugh Salmond can see any grounds for comparison.] These panels are unique. With the exception of the two stained panels of Mr Waldron's *Queens* the remaining seven are unique in as much as the craft employed has not I think hitherto been used for doing minute figure subjects.'

22. Acquired by the National Gallery of Ireland in 1988. See the gallery's *Acquisitions 1986-1988* catalogue (Dublin 1988), pp. 147-8.
23. Inserted after Bodkin's article 'The Arts and Crafts Society of Ireland' (1921), p. 263.
24. Unfortunately, there is no trace of the preparatory pencil and watercolour studies which must have preceded both the *Queens* panels and *The Song of the Mad Prince.*
25. Poems selected from Heinrich Heine by Kate F. Kroeker, *Ballads* (Romanzen) 1839-1842, (London n.d.), p. 219; *A Meeting* (Begegnung) translated by Sir Theodore Martin. It is worth noting that Heine had written lines on the evocative figure of Paganini who sold his soul to the devil. Many of his poems would have appealed to Harry (see Praz, *The Romantic Agony*, p. 306).
26. Praz, *op.cit*, p. 306. 35n. refers to Heine's fascination with women already dead and cites one such creature: 'She was so slim so young and lovely — this lily born of the tomb, this daughter of death, this ghost with the face of an angel and the body of a bayadère'. This concept of the 'synthetic Fatal Woman' is recognizable in Harry's work and an integral part of the decadent Symbolist vision of a female archetype inevitably deathly pale and gaunt with glazed eyes.
27. The angel alone was later reproduced without the surrounding landscape and Nativity scene opposite the acknowledgements page in *The Year's at the Spring* (1920). Harry gave the original drawing *c.* 1920 to his friend, the English graphic artist John Austen. The tiny galleon in the sea seems to be a direct borrowing from the *Ditchley* Elizabeth I.

CHAPTER FIVE

1. In the St Barrahane Guidebook, April 1970.
2. Letter to the author from Professor Nevill Coghill, 16 February 1978.
3. The cottage depicted is Waldron's in the Dublin mountains. The illustration is one of Harry's most comparable with those of Sidney Sime.
4. This cartoon is drawn surprisingly loosely and sketchily in charcoal and conté in comparison with those for the Honan Chapel; there is no trace of the initial coloured design.
5. It was always his practice to keep several jobs running concurrently.
6. Jeffrey Jenkins cutting, dated simply 'July 1918'.
7. 30 July 1918.
8. Peter Cormack, 1979, *op. cit.* 'The value of light, and the notion of stained glass as a form of illumination are exemplified in Whall's use of white glass: this had, for technical as well as stylistic reasons, been replaced in many Victorian firms by tinted greenish or yellowish whites, which, having a rather dingy appearance, were in compensation excessively decorated with silver-stain and matting. Whall re-introduced relatively large areas of pure white glass, both in quarry glazing and figures, and so greatly enriched his windows, giving them a silvery quality'. Whall, Piper, Robert Elliott, and Edward Martyn all expressed a preference for clear leaded glass rather than what G.B. Shaw described as 'dirty linoleum'.
9. See Martin Battersby, *The Decorative Twenties* (London 1971), p. 22, and p. 181. The vogue for stylized floral motifs surrounded by tiny spirals, swags, ribbons, dotted lines, decorative geometrical forms and variations on lizard skin reached a climax in Europe with the 1925 Arts Décoratifs exhibition in Paris. The Symbolists had favoured proto-Art Nouveau swirling arabesques and curving curlicues, magnified microcosms revealed under the microscopes of Renan and

Zola: the rose, the iris, the violet and the lily to enhance their synthetic visions. By the end of World War I, decoration had tightened and formalized. Harry's decorative taste, while eclectic, was none the less avant-garde, certainly compared with the work to which he had direct access, and was in keeping with the European movement.

10. The kneeling king is a direct precursor of the aged *St Aidan* (Wexford, 1919) both in apparel and facial features, while the kneeling shepherd has the same features as *St John* (Phibsborough, 1918/19).
11. Werner Hofmann, *Gustav Klimt, op. cit.* (1972), p. 36; Klimt's work was regularly featured in decorative and applied art magazines; the work of both Clarke and Klimt was exhibited in the 1912 Dresden Exhibition of Arts and Crafts; from 1908 to 1914, 60 heliogravure facsimile art prints (10 of which were in colour and gold) were published in Vienna in instalments — *Das Werk Gustav Klimts* — as well as in later editions. The first English edition was not until 1921, accompanied by Max Eisler's monograph (Vienna 1920).
12. See Martin Battersby, *op.cit.*, p. 75.
13. Late that year MacBride left the studio and formed the Irish Craftworkers Guild with Albert Power, the sculptor. His earliest window done on his own, the Seaver War Memorial in St John's, Malone Road, Belfast of that year, is eclectic.
14. Letter, 18 June 1918.
15. Letter, 20 June, 1918.
16. Letter, 4 June 1918.
17. Letter, 12 August 1918.
18. Letter, September 1918.
19. Letter, 28 September 1918.
20. *Ibid.*
21. Letter, 2 November 1918.
22. Letter, 11 November 1918.
23. At the height of 'the explosive atmosphere in Dublin in [August] 1913', when 'political and religious partisanship complicated the technical, financial and aesthetic imbroglio' of the projected Lutyens bridge gallery, 'that impetuous, testy dealer in dreams... removed his pictures and sent them on loan to the London National Gallery, to which he bequeathed them in that October, though he afterwards executed an unwitnessed codicil leaving them to Dublin' (Hussey, *The Life of Sir Edwin Lutyens*, 1950, p. 234).
24. Printed on each of their programme sheets.
25. In later years Harry would retreat to this little haven when ill or overworked; his wife and children would also spend bathing holidays there.
26. Interview with the author, 5 December 1975. Although MacLiammoir was reluctant to admit it, his graphic work was influenced by Harry's to a certain extent, despite the more predominant influences of Beardsley and Bakst.
27. Letter, 3 November 1918, Bodkin MSS, TCD.
28. Letter, 28 February 1917, Clarke MSS.
29. Letter, 12 May 1917.
30. Letter, 19 May 1917.
31. Letter, 9 January 1919.
32. From the point above the highest adoring Saint's head, he used the upper portion of the L.H. ope cartoon in reverse for the upper R.H. cartoon section; there is no trace of this preliminary small-scale coloured design.
33. The faces of the figures in the cartoons and windows are much more dramatically depicted than in the small-scale designs. This is particularly noticeable in *St John* (in the R.H. opening), as it was with the *St Ita* in the Honan Chapel.
34. The sub-committee met on 20 May 1919 to consider the 41 designs submitted anonymously, each being labelled with a letter of the alphabet. In June, the report by Thomas Bodkin and Richard Caulfield Orpen recorded a unanimous preference for 'J', described as a distinguished design set in a vesica, as both Harry's were. Three other letters, 'M', 'I' and 'Y' were mentioned. However after discussion, Oswald Reeves' circular design was appoved and sent to the Royal Mint in London (recorded in the NGI Minute Books at the time). Bodkin's widow subsequently presented one of Harry's designs to the NGI. Both are reproduced on p. 127 of Bowe, *Harry Clarke: His Graphic Art, op. cit.*
35. This is a particularly fine cartoon, virtually a monochrome translation of the window; sadly there is no trace of the small-scale coloured design.
36. Letter, 28 November 1918, Bodkin MSS, coll. Ann Bourke.
37. Letter, dated 'Sunday evening', from 36 Mount Merrion Avenue, Bodkin MSS, coll. Ann Bourke.
38. See Studios' visitors' book 1923-30, TCD MS 6083.
39. The name and address of W.B. Yeats' wife George (whom he married in October 1917) often featur in Clarke's diaries *c.* 1926-7 when he was in London.
40. *Catalogue*, The Fine Art Society London Exhibition, no. 520, 1916. In a book entitled *High Society* (1920), which was an illustrated monograph on Ann Fish and her work, we are told how her drawings first began to appear in 1914, when she was a 'tall, slender, young girl' of 22; for six years her work appeared in *The Tatler* and, i

America, in *Vanity Fair*, and since 1918 her work had been seen in British *Vogue* and *The Patrician* (the English edition of *Vanity Fair*).

41. It is unrecorded whether it was Fish or Sefton who made the initial contact with Harry; probably they had seen his Hans Andersen illustrations, which abound in novel decorative and ornamental details, admirably suited to textile designs. It is interesting that Mrs Sefton 'greatly admired' the work of Charles Rennie Mackintosh and his wife Margaret MacDonald and was instrumental in securing useful introductions for them when she was introduced to them through Chelsea friends. 'Between 1916 and 1919 the Mackintoshes directed their attention mainly to designing printed fabrics of one kind and another, and to watercolour painting' for Sefton and Foxton. Their experiments in this new field achieved some measure of success and during the year 1920 alone, the only period for which a reliable record exists, they received about £200 in fees from the two firms . . . Most of the designs are of highly conventionalized floral forms . . . and reveal [an] interest in two dimensional pattern and rich colour. (Howarth, *Charles Rennie Mackintosh*, 1952, p. 204). Jessie King's earliest fabric designs were for Liberty's in 1902, but she does not appear to have designed for either Sefton or Foxton.
42. It was later reproduced less clearly on p. 30, beneath the list of illustrations in *The Year's at the Spring* (1920) and painted on to the glass of the L.H. opening of the Wexford *Adoration* window (1919).
43. On 24 February: Letterbook no. 5992.
44. At Sefton's factory, which specialized in printed handkerchief and textile designs in Ormeau Avenue, Belfast; their premises has been burnt to the ground and all their records destroyed. I am grateful to Charles Brett for his help on this point.
45. The two sets can be dated by the signatures Harry has used on each. On the first set and their box, this is invariably 'HARRY CLARKE/Sefton Fabrics'; on the second set, and their box lid, there is nothing but a small 'c' device. Neither the handkerchiefs nor their box lids are dated.
46. For example, *Thumbelina, The Tinder Box, The Butterfly, What the Moon Saw* (black and white), *The Nightingale, The Marsh King's Daughter, The Tinder Box, New Clothes for the Emperor and Thumbelina* (colour).
47. Later described by Æ in his *Irish Statesman* review of the large exhibition Harry held in North Frederick Street *(The Work of Harry Clarke*, August 1925), where it was curiously entitled *Tom Allalone*.
48. This magazine provides an important context for the decorative element in Harry's work; it would also have been a magazine which Harry would have enjoyed, as it contains work by, or references to Karl Parsons' sister, Beatrice, John Austen, Allan Odle's wife Dorothy Richardson, Edith Somerville and others he already knew or who would subsequently become friends, as well as frequent material on ballet, the arts and music. Allusions to Ireland occur quite frequently in its pages.
49. *Eve*, vol. I, no. 1, p. 20.
50. *Eve*, vol. I, no. 2, p. 56.
51. Here are tight, spiralling 'Gloire de Dijon' rosebuds, ribbons, beads, mermaids, ladies in Greek nymph costumes poised beside waterfalls, stylized Japanese screens and costumes, the new unisex trend contrasting images such as a Bacchanalian photographic study of the daughter-in-law of the Rural Dean of Brighton baring her breast and swooning in ecstasy at an upheld bunch of grapes; ladies everywhere in exotic costumes, dancing Eurythmics in the back garden or being worshipped by adoring Adams. FOs abound and show that Harry's decorative motifs were strongly related to fashionable current trends. Popular colour combinations varied from orange/scarlet/gold/purple and black to navy/pink/cream and violet/lilac/ yellow/jade and ultramarine.
52. *Eve*, vol. I, no. 3, p. 92 and vol. I, no 5, p. 164.
53. It was probably through Fish that Harry met John Austen,whom Kenneth Grant reckons he met at the end of the war (see *Images and Oracles of Austin Osman Spare*, London 1975).
54. Vol. I, no. 9, p. 363.
55. It reproduced in black and white on pp. 116 and 117 two handkerchiefs by Harry and two by Sheringham and, on neighbouring pages, cretonne designs by Hoppé and more 'Fauve' designs printed by W. Foxton in their 'Decorative and Applied Art' section (pp. 59-120); their comment: 'In spite of the difficult conditions prevailing during the last year, many new and excellent designs in fabrics have been put upon the market. Admirable are the printed silks by Messrs Sefton'.
56. Twenty eight of these photographs were exhibited and published in London in 1913. These were accessible in libraries in Ireland and England and show close-up details of the costumes worn by the dancers, the spangled, pearl-strung helmets and rich brocades that Harry loved to adapt.
57. First published in the *Illustrated London News* in 1910.

58. Reproduced fig. 5, Pepper, *Hoppé* (National Portrait Gallery, London,1978). Lady Lavery, Clifford and Arnold Bax, Sheringham and Mackintosh served on the committee of Hoppé's theatrical group, *The Plough,* and Hoppé visited Ireland in 1925.
59. Siegfried Wichmann, *Japonisme* (London 1981), 201. There were several sets of *katagami* stencils in the Dublin School of Art at this period. For a detailed discussion of this, see the author's 'Life and Work . . .', *op. cit.*, pp. 292-3.
60. The only volume to copiously illustrate marine flora and fauna was Philip Henry Gosse's *The British Sea Anemones and Corals* (1860), part of the writer's extensive *Actinologia Britannica.* Gustave Moreau certainly copied some of Gosse's coloured illustrations for use in his paintings, for example, *Galatea* (1880).
61. It would be interesting to know whether Harry based this illustration on a photograph of St Patrick's Well at Orvieto; certain views of the latter are identical with Harry's powerful picture.
62. Harry loved visiting the NGL and NPG when in London; the *Ditchley* portrait has been exhibited in the NPG since 1896,so he would have been well acquainted with it. He used the map device in his Wexford (1919) window, in the Terenure *Crucifixion* (1920), etc.
63. For a detailed discussion on Symbolist analogies and texts for Clarke's *Angel*, see Bowe, 'Life and Work . . .', *op. cit.*, pp. 297-99.
64. The galleon in full sail and ornamental cartouche refer, once more, to the *Ditchley* portrait, as does the coastline map. Apart from the young man's initials (WOK), the various chalices, sometimes set in flaming aureoles, symbolize his sacrifice after suffering; the symbolism of the triangle set with an eye (already seen in the Honan Chapel *Ita* window) and another being struck by lightning, is more obscure. The third eye reappears set within the helmet of St Adrian. The symbolism of the exquisitely detailed tiny Crucifixion and Ascension scenes is obvious, as applied to the young man's life.
65. This helmet is an adaption of that worn by Perseus in Burne-Jones' painting *The Doom Fulfilled* (1884-8) (see fig. 117), although its form is reminiscent of a chrysalis.
66. It was to have been printed in June, but, due to a printers' strike in Dublin, did not appear until 30 August 1919 in vol LXI, no. 13.
67. As the base panel is signed 'H.C.', this is undoubtedly Harry's own work. Harry was always generous to his students, giving them ample opportunities for credit; he probably felt Quigley's part in the execution of the lantern, notably the Zodiac panels, warranted her being credited.
68. It is interesting how close is the best work of the enamellists at this period to a Symbolist mode of expression, when they steer an inspired course between Byzantium and the Celtic Revival; this is notable not only in the work of Reeves and a number of his students, like Dora Allen, Kathleen Fox, Ernest Corr and Daisy O'Keefe, but also in the work of his older Dublin-born contemporary, Phoebe Traquair. Certain pieces of early sculpture by Beatrice Elvery, Oliver Sheppard and Albert Power could be described as Symbolist. See Bowe 'Symbolism in Early 20th Century Irish Art' (1989).
69. According to Harry's sister, Dolly Robinson and Aileen Bodkin attended as the latter carefully kept the programmes (Bodkin MSS, TCD) 31 May, 2 June, and 3 June.
70. George Painter, *Marcel Proust,* II (London 1965).
71. Interview with the author, December 1975. Harry's interest in Russian art and design was such that he subscribed to *Jar-Ptitza,* the illustrated review published in Berlin by Alexander Kogan, when it first appeared in 1921.
72. Letter, 27 May, 1919.
73. Letter, 1 June 1919, Bodkin MSS, TCD.
74. Letter, 27 May 1919, Bodkin MSS, TCD. Bodkin would have met Lutyens through Sir Hugh Lane. Lane, in the unattested codicil to his last will, had written: 'I would like my friend Thomas Bodkin to be asked to help in the obtaining of this new gallery of modern art for Ireland' — so Bodkin had obviously been involved in Lane's scheme for Lutyens to design a bridge over the Liffey to house his collection (see Thomas Bodkin, *Hugh Lane and his Pictures,* Dublin 1956). The plan had been scotched mostly because the Mayor of Dublin objected to Lutyens being the architect on the grounds of his being foreign. Many sorely regretted the punctuation of such a romantic idea and it was Bodkin who commissioned the *Homage to Hugh Lane* group portrait from Keating later that year (1919). The only obvious connection with Harcourt-Smith was that the latter, had served on the Delhi advisory committee, set up in 1917. On the receipt of £2,000 per annum, the committee was, over a period of five years (i.e. until 1922), to purchase articles of historic interest or artistic merit for Government House. At one time they proposed to hold an exhibition of Indian arts and crafts either in Delhi or in London.
75. Gustave Flaubert, *Les Trois Contes* (1877), final page.

76. Once again, Donatello's gilt terracotta relief of the *Virgin and Child* (acq. V. & A 1867) seems an obvious source, where the Virgin's profiled features are close to the androgynous Julian's — noble, sharply pointed and sensitive.
77. G. Flaubert, 'The Legend of S. Julien the Hospitalier', from *Les Trois Contes*, published in a dual French/English edition by Harrap (1946). The colour notation on the preparatory design for the panel shows that Harry had originally intended Julian to be 'vêtu de pourpre' (which Flaubert specifically says he was when he married the Emperor of Occitania's daughter); in the design, purple far outweighs the blue and red which are so effective in the panel. There are other minor differences between the coloured design and the panel: in the former, Julian's right foot is visible, a Crucifix appears behind him, he wears an oriental turban rather than the exotic balaclava of the panel, he looks much holier and the stiff-fold drapes of his robe fall around him, rather than diagonally across the frame. The initial pencil sketch shows Julian as a skeletal hermit after his conversion, holding a Crucifix, with rabbits, which he would certainly have killed in his earlier bloodthirsty days, frisking at his feet; the ominous stag in the story is given considerable importance. For a full discussion of this panel, see Bowe, 'Life and Work . . .', *op. cit.*, pp. 321-7.
78. In October 1919, Lutyens sailed for India, having been tied up with the Cenotaph designs for Lloyd George since the end of July. Margaret Richardson, deputy curator of the RIBA library writes (1 March 1979): 'We do have Lutyens's letters to his wife, Lady Emily in the RIBA Library, including those for the year 1919. All the letters have been carefully catalogued and indexed, with the names of all clients, friends and schemes abstracted. I have been through this index several times looking for all the names you mention in your letter, i.e. Clarke, Flaubert, St Julian, Bodkin, Dublin but can find nothing relating to them'.
79. Letter, Victoria Lupton to Bodkin, 9 January 1943, Bodkin MSS, TCD; only the effective ebonized wood frame Harry made remains now. That February, at Bodkin's instigation, Keating was painting the beautiful Victoria Lupton, Edmond's wife and a professional violinist. It was she who wanted to (and eventually did) sell the panel *c.* 1943, holding out for Bodkin's advised price of £75, to Arthur Cox, the solicitor, in whose stepdaughter's collection it now is. It is odd that Bodkin showed no interest in buying it, even though he wrote in February 1943, 'It is an extraordinarily beautiful thing and there are very few of the kind in existence' and approached Harcourt-Smith to see if he would buy it.
80. A note in his diary reads — 'Julian — 19 pages — black and white'.
81. Although thus identified to me by the Father Superior of the Order, she could equally well be Mary Magdalen who, with St John, stood in vigil at the foot of the Cross; the casket of spikenard is usually her emblem. There is no record in Harry's hand as to the precise iconography of the two outer lights. Points in favour of St Margaret Mary are that she particularly venerated the Sacred Heart and the Eucharist and was canonized in 1920. In the Studios, she was known as Mary Magdalen, but that may simply be because she is better known. Although I was informed by the Father Superior of the Order that St John Eudes was depicted, the figure does conform in every way to a depiction of St John the Apostle: traditionally seen as a young man, distinguishable from the other Apostles by having no beard, by his usual emblem of a cup with a snake or dragon emerging from within, relating to the incident when a priest of Artemis challenged him to drink poison and John blessed the cup with the sign of the cross, rendering it harmless. The eagle at his feet is shown (standing on his Gospel) because he soared aloft to contemplate Christ's divine nature.
82. Scribbled in his diary, 29-31 August 1919.
83. *Journals* (1932), II (1911-21), p. 256.
84. *Ibid.*
85. Letter, 29 September 1919, Bodkin MSS, coll. Ann Bourke.
86. Letter, 21 November 1919, Bodkin MSS, coll. Ann Bourke.
87. Pp. 45-51.
88. *The Studio* critic (December 1919, p.130) felt Clarke's 'predilection for weaving . . . an intricate almost lace-like fabric of lines' was sometimes 'carried to the extent of obscuring the meaning of the drawings'; the *Irish Times* (November 1925 p. 3) felt his genius had found its ideal theme: 'wild imaginings with which the unbridled fancy could play, dark and jewelled magnificence, terror and wonder — all cast in a tone of delicate and gloomy beauty'. Bodkin agreed that the book allowed him to 'give full reign to his talent for the macabre, the fantastic and the terrible' (*Irish Statesman*, 13 December 1919, pp. 606-7).
89. Despite further correspondence between Bodkin and Harrap plans for a volume in which the colour illustrations would be from Harry's miniature glass panels did not materialize.

CHAPTER SIX

1. It is not clear which of the two *Richard* cartoons this was; probably the second, revised after a meeting with Mr Knowles at Nantwich at the end of the previous year.
2. For example, the busts from Balfe and Shakespeare that the Studios were executing in stained glass for the entrance to the new La Scala Theatre in Dublin.
3. Entry in Harry's personal diary, coll. artist's daughter.
4. The selection committee had rejected his Poe illustrations, *The Goldbug* and *The Maelstrom*. Harry particularly admired the Festus Kellys, 'two dandy still lifes by Kathleen Fox' and Keating's *Homage to Hugh Lane* commissioned by Bodkin; this features Bodkin, W.B. Yeats, Æ, Sir William Hutcheson Poë, Dermod O'Brien, R.C. Orpen and Alderman T. Kelly. Relatively unenthusiastic reviews of the exhibition appeared in 'Notes from Ireland', *The Athenaeum,* April 1920, and *The Sphere,* 17 April 1920.
5. Several of his Hans Andersen fairy tales e.g. *The Storks* (p. 102) had employed Japonnist compositional devices.
6. There were a number of these in the School of Art library, as well as pattern books by Christopher Dresser, who had taught at South Kensington and written *The Art of Decorative Design* (1862), the many from Japan (frequently illustrated in *The Studio,* whose editor, Charles Holme was the vice-president of the Japanese Society of the Order of the Rising Sun), as well as the many Japanese-influenced illustrators, like Beardsley and Dulac.
7. It has now lost a great deal of its imposing effect by having been relegated to the east end of a long nave extension where its surface is interfered with by light shed from a series of plain leaded windows in pastel shades.
8. *Stained Glass Memorial Window, St Joseph's Terenure* (1920).
9. 'A Wonderful Window', pp. 27-30. Alan Denson writes in his Bodkin *Bibliography* (1966) that Bodkin wrote an article about Harry's windows for St Joseph's in May 1920 at the request of Fr Healy. The acting editor of the *Evening Telegraph* in Dublin had promised to print it on 22 May 1920, but did not. The editor of the parent paper, the *Freeman's Journal,* then undertook to publish any article on the theme by Bodkin. Eventually he admitted that the original article had been too highly laudatory and had been thrown into the *Evening Telegraph's* waste paper basket. At Fr Healy's urgent request Bodkin agreed to write another article to be included in the commemorative booklet.
10. 'One Thing Beautiful', pp. 31-3, reprinted from the *Irish Statesman,* 12 June 1920.
11. 'A Notable Addition to Our Dublin Art Treasures — Irish Artist's Fine Work', pp. 34-37, printed by the *Daily Express* and the *Irish Daily Mail* on the eve of the dedication and written from Sir John's home in Killiney the same night after he had returned 'from seeing one of the most beautiful things which has been set up in Dublin for many a long day'.
12. 'The Art of Stained Glass — An Appreciation', pp. 38 and 39.
13. *The Athenaeum,* 12 June 1920.
14. It is interesting to remember that when Léon Bakst had painted Christ's mother as a Russian Jewish peasant woman less than twenty years earlier in St Petersburg, he had been expelled from the Art School there, whereas Clarke's idiosyncratic portrait of the Mother of Christ as an Irish peasant woman intrigued pilgrims to the church,imbued with a new nationalistic pride.
15. *A Penny in the Clouds* (1960), p. 191.
16. Dublin, pp. 64-70.
17. Letter, 5 June 1920, Bodkin MSS, coll. Ann Bourke.
18. Harry later gave this illustration as a present to Tilly Fleischmann,the pianist. The self-portrait is apparently based on his own appearance while awaiting the tram into Dublin on Mount Merrion Avenue, outside his home.
19. In July 1923 Harry held an exhibition in the Studios, at which he exhibited this illustration with several others for his books. Thomas MacGreevy concluded his long review in the *Irish Daily Independent* (24 July 1923): 'Some will think the procession of S. Augustine and his monks to Canterbury the most perfect of all Mr Clarke's drawings'. Harry promptly gave the illustration to MacGreevy, who replied, 'My dear generous Harry, it really is good of you to give me St Augustine and his men. I have been looking at him all day and I am very glad to have him. I find more reasons and more for liking the whole thing. . . . The monk with veiled face is . . . oh, I don't know, "right" is the only word. . . . I squeeze your hand.'
20. Recorded in his personal Diary, as are all these references.
21. *A Guide to the Church of St Mary, Nantwich, Cheshire* (Warrington, n.d.), p.3. For a detailed description of the window see the author's 'Life and Work ....', *op. cit.*, pp. 402-6.
22. The first (much finer) cartoon drawn by Harry is very close to the coloured design, but it was

abandoned. The second (adopted) version drawn on the back of the first would seem to have been executed at the request of Mr Knowles; its charcoal treatment is very loose and comparatively uninspired.

23. Vol. XLIV, 1920, p. 112: 'Studio Talk', p. 113: 'We illustrate [a window] recently designed . . . by Mr Harry Clarke of Dublin whose work . . . is becoming more and more appreciated elsewhere than in Ireland.'
24. He was irritated to find his ill-fated Phibsborough window obscured by drapery, compounding his depression about 'ART in Ireland . . . ridiculous shows and judges . . . and the Yeats family spend eleven months a year sitting for their portraits. ... If the rotten Arts and Crafts was worth a damn, we might do something but it is not': Letter, 11 July 1920, Bodkin MSS., coll. Ann Bourke.
25. Coincidentally, the same house the Studios would buy less than five years later when No. 33 became too cramped.
26. Letter to the author, 15 February 1978.
27. There is no trace of the initial small-scale coloured drawing for the window by virtue of which Harry had been given the commission.
28. The cartoons for all three lights were reproduced in *The Studio*, vol. 82, no. 345, 15 December 1921, p. 265.
29. Vol. LVIII, December 1920, p. 38.
30. *Ibid.*, p. 79.
31. Vol. 81, no. 338, 13 May 1921, p. 82.
32. Vol. III, February 1921, pp. 546-8.
33. Letter from Harrap to Bodkin, 8 November 1920, Bodkin MSS coll. Ann Bourke. In the case of *The Year's at the Spring*, the small popular unillustrated version of the book, which had to pay for the expenses incurred in obtaining copyright permissions, used a reduction of Harry's illustration, *April*, as a frontispiece and was first published in April 1920 and later that September.
34. Letter, 23 November 1920, Bodkin MSS, coll. Ann Bourke.
35. His illustration to Chesterton's 'The Donkey' had just been published in *The Year's at the Spring*.
36. Letter, 1 January 1921, Bodkin MSS, coll. Ann Bourke.
37. Clarke's device of allowing various details to pierce the border at irregular intervals and also that of placing the figures at different, complementary heights within their respective narrow openings, already seen in the Wexford *Adoration*, may well be derived from Japanese pillar prints; a similar treatment is to be seen in Harry's Terenure *Annunciation* (1923) and Balbriggan *Visitation* (1923).
38. Lennox Robinson later wrote (*Curtain Up*, 1942, pp. 211-2): 'He was a sharply contrasted two-sided man. Dublin, gutty Dublin, North side Dublin, Sean O'Casey Dublin on one side — I mean that he delighted in everything that was Joxerish and Paycockish, everything that smelt of the slums or of the shabby genteel; on his other side there was the most lovely sensitive artist.'
39. Letter from Walter Clarke, 3 May 1921.
40. So that by the end of May, he was six and a half weeks behind on the Clontarf *Pietà* letter, 9 May 1921.
41. Morshead, *The Parish Church of St Mary . . .* (1971), p. 23.
42. Harry noted in his diary, November 1920 (coll. Ann Bourke): 'South — 5 feet from ground — borrowed light from transept and porch, but clear when facing. 'Front light. Don't paint heavy. Will stand delicate treatment. Trees.'
43. Letter, 6 June 1921, Bodkin MSS, coll. Ann Bourke.
44. Their head glazier, who had come from London twenty five years ago, had just died.
45. Letter, 3 August 1921.
46. She worked in the Studios from 7 October 1921 until 4 January 1924. At the end of August Harry hoped she could start on a 'nice job' as soon as possible; this may well have been the Lea Wilson Gorey window. He also hoped to import a good glass painter from London.
47. Letter, 12 September 1921
48. Letter, 16 September 1921. In 1924, their friend Albert Power the sculptor, completed a sculpted cross expressing 'what the poor old governor really would have liked — simplicity and chasteness'.
49. Letter, 19 September 1921.
50. Letter, 4 April 1924.

CHAPTER SEVEN

1. This story was told to the author in 1976 by Victor Wood (Great Claus in Clarke's Hans Andersen illustration), whose father, Albert, subsequently bought the picture at Harry's London exhibition in May 1925. He did not think Harry had thought of calling the picture anything in particular before espying the barge.
2. *The Studio*, December 1921, pp. 257-263.
3. Harry may first have been given the idea of depicting the dramatic moment of St Hubert's evocative conversation by the fifteenth century

painting depicting the event in the NGL (acq. 1854), where the background is evoked in shades of blue, whereas the composition of this panel is based on the exquisite copperplate engraving by Albrecht Dürer (*c.* 1500) which depicts St Eustace's similar conversation; the kneeling pose of the graceful, attenuated young hunter is almost identical, the stag is in a similar position and the snoozing hound is closer to Dürer's than that of the anonymous German master. Dürer's engraving was well known and reproduction easily accessible at the time. His subtle treatment of tones of blue is surely derived from the Limoges enamels he would have seen in the Victoria and Albert Museum.

4. Aléxandre, *The Decorative Art of Léon Bakst* (1913), pp. 40-41. Cocteau even described the glowing embers at her feet as a 'magic carpet fashioned of the miraculous lilies in the blue arcades beyond', analogous with the backdrop to Harry's *Hubert*. Harry had already alluded to Rubinstein in his Cork *St Gobnait* (1916), whose blue cloak resembles Bakst's costume for *St Sebastien*, and earlier in his depiction of *Salome* drawn in 1913, the year after her production of Wilde's play of the same name.
5. A reminder that the saint is the protector against hydrophobia, which is emphasized in the predella panel by the watery brook illuminated in the moonlit forest.
6. This figure of a dancing maid poised on a bridge in a garden is to be found traditionally as *Ludmilla in Chernomov's Garden* on Soviet miniature lacquered box lids, in a composition very like Harry's, also in Ivan Bilibin's (1896-1942) depiction of an *Oriental Woman* reproduced in the Russian art periodical (to which Harry subscribed) *Jar-Ptitza*, no. 12, p. 32.
7. Letter, 18 October 1921.
8. This was probably the baptistery window at Cong, Co. Mayo, exhibited in the Studios in February 1922. Harry's own part in this window was minimal. He had stressed to Deegan that 'nearly all the assistants here are young people . . . all work is done now under my own supervision' but 'for the first 3-4 months you would be working here I cannot definitely state you would be working from my own actual cartoons but rather from those drawn by another draftsman in the Studios' (letter, 24 September 1921).
9. Letter, 20 October 1921. Nagle's irregular behaviour had led to an increased need for set timekeeping.
10. Letter, 1 November 1921.
11. Letter, 9 October 1921.
12. Letter, 25 October 1921.
13. A keen supporter of the Irish Arts and Crafts movement and a neighbour of Waldron and Sir John O'Connell in Killiney.
14. The affair is recorded in a letter (21 November 1921) from Clarke to Maurice Drake, hon. sec. of the diocesan advisory committee and author of *A History of English Glass Painting* (London 1912), in his opinion the best contemporary book on stained glass with Laurence Saint's *Stained Glass of the Middle Ages in England and France*.
15. Verified by his daughter, Margaret Parsons. The window is described as being 'executed by Karl Parsons of Dublin in 1929', in *St Michael and All Angels* (Waterford, n.d.), p. 6, although the window was not made in Dublin. I am most grateful to Mr A.S. Cox, the Clerk of the Worshipful Company of Grocers for going through the Company's records, which make no mention of Harry, only recording that the window was erected by Colonel and Mrs Prentice in memory of their daughter Rachel. Clarke's two cartoons, for which Mrs Prentice paid £30 in 1921 but held no copyright, have not survived.
16. Letter, 10 November 1921, Bodkin MSS, coll. Ann Bourke.
17. Letter to Bodkin, 22 December 1921, Bodkin MSS, coll. Ann Bourke.
18. See Mathieu, *Gustave Moreau* (1977) and Weiss, *Kandinsky in Munich* (1979).
19. It is interesting to remember that the mysterious Cottingley photographs featuring tiny fairies not dissimilar from these were currently being given some publicity and support by Sir Arthur Conan Doyle (see *Strand Magazine*, December 1920).
20. Letter, 21 December 1921.
21. The same Aléxandre as had written an appreciation in *The Decorative Art of Leon Bakst*, *op. cit.*
22. The substantial house, still standing, is one in a terrace close to the zoo entrance to the Phoenix Park and only ten minutes walk from the Studios in North Frederick Street.
23. Adapted from photographs in the *Irish Soldier* first published on 1 September 1918. The pavilions are illustrated in Hussey, *The Lutyens Memorial* (London 1950), plate 109; the same source gives the history of Lutyens' part in the memorial.
24. Sheehy (*Rediscovery*, *op. cit.*, p. 7, fig. 3) has pointed out how the sunrise became a symbol of the Fianna; it was also one of the most popular Art Deco motifs of the 1920s.
25. *The Studio*, vol. 86, July-December 1923, p. 215.
26. The Judges' Report, 17 October 1916, quoted in

the Minutes of the Civics Institute of Ireland, 1916, for the consultation of which I am grateful to Mrs Taylor of the Civics Institute, Dublin. It should be noted that Sir Bertram Windle was one of the Institute's four vice-presidents and Sir John O'Connell was a very active member of its council and executive committee.

27. This figure would seem to be ultimately derived from the Romanesque tiptoeing figure of Isaiah on the stone abutment of the doorway now inside the church at Souillac, *c.* 1120 (Beckwith, *Early Mediaeval Art*, 1968, fig. 199).
28. Leo Cartwright, *op. cit.*, p. 30.
29. Letter, 22 May 1924; see below, p. 171.
30. Harraps' prospectus, *The Art of Mr Harry Clarke*, which describes *The Fairy Tales of Charles Perrault*, *The Year's at the Spring* and *Hans Andersen's Fairy Tales* and reproduces in colour *Cinderella* (Perrault) and Harold Monro's *Overheard on a Saltmarsh* (from *The Year's at the Spring*).
31. *The Bookman Christmas Supplement*, no. LXIII, p. 136; Harry's photograph (taken by Lafayette of Dublin) is inset after p. 154; Robert Louis Stevenson's photograph appears opposite. John Austen's Perrault illustrations (*Tales of Passed Times*), published by Selwyn and Blount (London 1922) were reviewed in the same issue.
32. Vol. 84, no. 357, 14 December 1922, pp. 352f.
33. M.C. Salaman, *British Book Illustrators Yesterday and Today*, *op. cit.*, p. 171.
34. Quoted *ibid.* I have been unable to find this review in contemporary issues of either the Saturday or weekly *Westminster Gazette*.
35. Vol. XXXV, December 1922, p. 572.
36. The new 'gadgett' [*sic*] which Harry was intending to use would seem to refer to the treatment of the many quarries in the upper part of the window, randomly stained in the traditional grisaille manner, but set intermittently with thick, jewel-like slabs of richly coloured glass.
37. Letter, 2 March 1923, Bodkin MSS, coll. Ann Bourke.
38. Quoted from a letter to the author from the Administrator, St Stephen's Cathedral, Brisbane, 25 February 1975. I am indebted to the late Mrs James Little for all her help in researching this commission.
39. Dated Sunday 10 June 1923, coll. Ann Bourke.
40. Harry wanted to do 'something . . . out of the usual run of domestic stained glass' while giving him 'absolute freedom to use any methods I know on the whole surface'. Jacob had suggested somehow incorporating 'the ideas of night and morning, summer and winter' (letters, 30 April and 3 May 1923, coll. Jeffrey Jenkins, to whom I am most grateful).
41. 'Mr Harry Clarke's New Windows', *Irish Times*, 24 July 1923.
42. *Freeman's Journal*, 23 July 1923.
43. 'Irish Achievement in Stained Glass', *Irish Daily Independent*, 24 July 1923.
44. Also referred to as *The Coronation*, *The Immaculate Conception* and *The Assumption*.
45. The detailed, intricate and grotesque graphic work of Klee at the very beginning of this century bears a number of similarities to Harry's in the early 1920s, both as regards technique and choice of subject. We know Harry enjoyed German art magazines and there were several publications available featuring Klee's early work, e.g. Hans Bloesch, 'Ein Moderner Grafiker, Paul Klee', *Die Alpen*, vol. 6, no. 5, January 1912, Wilhelm Michael, *Das Teuflische und Groteske in der Kunst* (Munich 1911), as well as various articles on theatrical art in *The Mask*, which mentioned his work.
46. *Judith* 10:21 in *Apocryphal* (Oxford, n.d.).
47. Cutting dated 29 July 1923, coll Ann Bourke.
48. Clarke MSS, no. 6085.
49. In one letter (Seumas O'Sullivan MSS, TCD, Correspondence, MS no. 543), he referred Starkey to the white cover of Hilaire Belloc's *The Illustrated Review*. This design is reproduced in *Harry Clarke: His Graphic Art*, *op. cit.*, p. 131.
50. The concept of the artist as magician is also seen in Austin O. Spare's self-portrait (1907) in 'the death posture. . . . Where the fancy and the imagination . . . have full play . . . and the astral figures that surround the artist, creatures of the unconscious or personae worn for only a brief time are fully alive, vivified by the energies of which the body has been starved: see King, *Magic* (1975), fig. 66.
51. *Christmas Book Supplement*, no. 64.
52. My earlier conjecture that the jacket used for the 1923 edition is that drawn by Harry for the 1919 edition (*Catalogue* to the 1979 Douglas Hyde Gallery exhibition referenced earlier, no. 46) is not altogether satisfactory, since the design incorporates several features which one would not expect to find in his work as early as January 1919 (e.g., the many-breasted rat with wings and long hands and the little jock-strapped creature slumped in the bottom R.H. corner, as well as the fact that the design is depicted on a curtain, hung on a heavy pole, adorned by tassels, a feature not commonly used until the Perrault illustrations). However, the tiny background figure and the misshapen embryos embroidered on segmented

discs are to be found in the Poe *M. Valdémar* illustration of 1918. The publishers, wary as to its grotesque nature in 1919, when Harry was comparatively unknown, probably realized by 1923 that its very gruesomeness was what the public would enjoy.

53. In the footnote to Monos' philosophical speculation (p. 239) to Una, in praise of music for the soul, Plato is quoted *(Republic,* Book 3): 'For this reason is a musical education most essential, since it causes Rhythm and Harmony to penetrate most intimately into the soul, taking the strongest hold upon it, filling it with beauty and making the man beautiful-minded. He will praise and admire the beautiful; will receive it, and assimilate his own condition with it' — a fitting description for this ethereal couple, unearthly and spiritually beautiful, who have forsaken the world to describe the welcome release of Death and the elusive 'deep-toned' happiness of ages long since past.
54. Coll. Prof. Aloys Fleischmann.
55. Letter, Clarke MSS, April 1923, quoted by Harry the following summer, when there was some quibbling over the payment of the bill, following Canon Byrne's death.
56. *Irish Times,* 13 January 1924.
57. The small Cross used as the *Irish Memorial Records'* endpiece was printed on the verso of the handmade paper cards.

CHAPTER EIGHT

1. Letter, 22 January 1924.
2. London 1874; Mrs Jameson also wrote *Legends of the Monastic Orders, Legends of the Saints and Martyrs, Sacred and Legendary Art* (2 vols) and *A History of Our Lord* (in conjunction with Lady Eastlake).
3. Letter, 8 February 1924.
4. Held at the great British Empire Exhibition at Olympia.
5. Letter, 1 March 1924.
6. In a letter to the author, 15 March 1974; i.e. the son of the Lord Wicklow for whom Harry worked.
7. Letter, 19 March 1924.
8. Cormack *op. cit.*, n.p. Harry's total trust in Michael Dunne, his head glazier, to take command over all matters of glazing enabled him to design such a window.
9. Letter, 19 March 1924.
10. Bodkin MSS, coll. Ann Bourke.
11. Bland, *A History of Book Illustration* (1961), p. 374: 'Austen always avowed that he was more interested in decoration than character'.
12. By Dorothy M. Richardson, Allan Odle's wife, in *John Austen and the Inseparables* (1930), n.p.g.
13. Catalogued as 'E.159-1948, attr. Harry Clarke, *Judith slaying Holofernes'*. There is no evidence to support this attribution, not even a signature.
14. It is surely more than coincidence that the composition of Harry's picture is so similar to *Le Monstre* (fig. 143), a Symbolist gouache illumination by Marcel Lenoir, translated into a lithograph, pub. Arnould after being exhibited at the final Rose et Croix exhibition of 1897; also repr. R. Bouyer, 'L'Estampe murale' in *Art et Décoration* (1898), II, p. 188. As the Dublin School of Art subscribed to this magazine, Harry would doubtless have seen it there.
15. See Margaret Plant, *Paul Klee — Figures and Faces* (London 1978), figs. 1 to 10.
16. Including a minute self-portrait head peeping out.
17. John Keats, *The Eve of St Agnes,* 1819, published London 1820. The arrangement of the window, in its divisional compartments as well as some of its figurative and architectural details, orchestrated in tones of blue, was surely inspired by the Limoges painted enamels Harry knew from the V. and A. collection (e.g. the Master of the Louis XII Triptych, *c.* 1500, acq. 1877).
18. *Irish Times,* 7 August 1924. Other notable details include the tiny background figure at an open door (in panel 5) derived from the Velasquez's *Las Meninas.*
19. 'Dublin Notes', vol. 89, January-June 1925, p. 164, where the bottom R.H. section is reproduced well in black and white.
20. Reported in *Irish Times,* 4 April 1924.
21. Letter, 4 April 1924.
22. Letter, 7 April 1924.
23. Letter, 22 May 1924.
24. His self-portrait is featured among the sick, blind and dumb awaiting the saint's healing. Evie Hone bought the cartoon for this window when she saw it hanging in the Studios in the summer of 1930, four years before her first work in glass.
25. Letter, 26 May 1924.
26. In December 1968 the sexton of the church found seven rolled up canvases which had been ripped off the walls of the side chapels and stuffed into a tip outside. He had the presence of mind to take them to the NGI, which bought them from him for £100. Restoration work began on them in 1975 and was completed *c.* five years later. I am most grateful to Mairead McParland, who restored them, for her cooperation.
27. The design was copied on to canvas under Frank

MacGonigal's supervision; as the arch is over 20′ at the top, each figure had to be over 9′ high. The canvas was applied to the wall with varnish and white lead; it was in situ by 18 August. The design, drawing and painting, materials and travel brought the total bill to £150. Thomas MacGreevy was reminded of Puvis de Chavannes' murals in the Sorbonne when he visited the church. In the NGI, a similar colour scheme for the Loreto Convent, Killiney is inscribed on the verso by Frank MacGonigal: 'Harry was a master touch — see washes you can't see outside. Now he is dead and so untimely.'

28. Letter, 14 June 1924.
29. Letter, 21 June 1924.
30. Letter, 5 July 1924.
31. Letter to Madeleine Hurndall, 28 July 1924, private coll.
32. Letter, 2 September 1924.
33. Letter, 23 August 1924. The volume did eventually reproduce his *Bluebeard's Wife* panel on p. 156 of their miscellaneous British section.
34. Arranged through the help of Haldane MacFall, the writer and graphic artist, a good friend of John Austen.
35. Letter, 7 October 1924, Bodkin MSS, coll. Ann Bourke. The efficiency of the recently converted, spacious studios was a key factor in permitting such an extended absence.
36. These illustrations are ecstatically described in Dom E.A. Roulin, *Nos Églises* (Paris 1938), p. 455.
37. E.M. O'Rorke Dickey (1894-1977) was born in Belfast, educated in England and had studied and worked as a painter in London (and lived in Antrim) before taking up teaching; he was an original member of the Society of Wood Engravers.
38. Plans to open studios in London with John Austen on the strength of the Ashdown Park windows had to be abandoned when Austen's health necessitated his departure for the Sussex coast. Harry was convinced the 'public for really high class glass' was in England.
39. Letter, 16 December 1924.
40. In 1921 Joseph Albers had been experimenting with similar 'glas-assemblage' designs, repr. plates 31-33, Gomringer, *Josef Albers* (1971). Shortly after this job Harry ordered Hetley's entire stock of deep blue pressed slabs (a hundred in all) in one order.
41. This progression in concept is analogous with Kandinsky's increasing detachment 'from the details of the subject in hand': See Weiss, *Kandinsky in Munich*, *op. cit.*, p. 29.
42. Letter, 29 December 1924, coll. Jeffrey Jenkins.
43. Havinden (1903-73) became a well-known graphic and texile designer in the 1930s. By 1925 he was working with W.S. Crawford, the advertising agency, and for the Curwen Press. Harry probably met him through Karl Parsons, who taught night classes at the Central School of Arts and Crafts in London, where Havinden had studied.
44. Letter, 14 January 1925.
45. Letter, 2 February 1925 Bodkin MSS, coll. Ann Bourke.
46. Letter, 24 February 1925.
47. Letter, 8 March 1925.
48. *Irish Statesman*, 18 April 1925.
49. *Bookman's Journal*, vol. XII, no. 45, June 1925, p. 113.
50. *The Studio*, June 1925, p. 261.
51. Letter, 23 May 1925, Bodkin MSS, coll. Ann Bourke.
52. Letter, 7 May 1925, Bodkin MSS, coll. Ann Bourke.
53. Letter, 15 June 1925.
54. Harry had met her through Odle whom she married in 1917 although he was fifteen years her junior. Her thirteen-volume *Pilgrimage* (1915-17), and 'slow motion' novels have been described as anticipating the experiments of Joyce (Austin Clarke, *op. cit.*, p. 187); when Clarke met them, they 'lived sparsely in a shack in Cornwall, rented it in summer and came to Bloomsbury where they smoked innumerable cigarettes.' See also, Anthony Burgess, 'A Fictional Mistresspiece', *The Observer*, 13 January 1980, and Martin Steenson, 'Alan Odle' *Antiquarian* (1979). She was an obvious reviewer of *Faust* because she knew Harry's work and accepted Goethe's programme for fiction (Burgess, *op. cit.*). She was renowned for her extravagant, ready-made headwear (birds' nests etc.).
55. Letter, 13 June 1925.
56. Letter, 2 July 1925.
57. Letter, 13 July 1925.
58. Letter, 14 July 1925.
59. Letter, 16 July 1925.
60. Letter, 7 September 1925.
61. 'Dublin Stained Glass Work', *Irish Times*, 4 August 1925.
62. 'The Work of Harry Clarke', *Irish Statesman*, 8 August 1925.
63. Letter, 25 June 1925.
64. Letter, 5 October 1925.

CHAPTER NINE

1. Undated letter, Bodkin MSS, coll. Ann Bourke.

2. A number of these were embellished with gold and/or silver ink which was not reproduced. The one for 'Night — Open Plain' is interesting for its adaptation from a titlepiece on p. 53 of an un-numbered early issue of *Jar-Ptitza*.
3. 14 November 1925, pp. 310-12.
4. 20 November 1925. The review is unsigned and, as Alan Denson has remarked in his Bodkin *Bibliography* (Kendal 1966), the tone is one of such repulsed distaste that it can surely not have been written by Bodkin: 'Delicate ugliness, indeed, is an epithet which seems to sum up Mr Clarke's latest work.... Here is a very cornucopia of almost bestial creation. . . . Every creature depicted is diseased and indescribable abortions people the dim backgrounds of the scenes. . . . The clash of pinks and greens in the very colour scheme seems to symbolize the mood of the whole. Every picture shocks, but shocks only as might some horror of the operating theatre or some untold abnormal thing of a surgeon's museum.' The reviewer concluded: 'We think that no artist of the Beardsley School could hope to capture the rugged, Gothic strength of Goethe's imagery.... Goethe's Margaret never resembled the consumptive creature with black-ringed eyes and languid hoopy figure which seems to be the only kind of woman that artists of the Beardsley School can draw.'
5. *Artwork*, vol. II, no. 6, January/March 1926, p. 103.
6. London 1975, pp. 21-2.
7. Interview with the author, August 1978.
8. Undated latter, Bodkin MSS, coll. Ann Bourke.
9. Letter, 2 November 1925, Bodkin MSS, coll. Ann Bourke.
10. See *Harry Clarke*, catalogue no. 89 and *Harry Clarke: His Graphic Art*, *op. cit.*, plate XLV.
11. Described in the *Harry Clarke Catalogue* (no. 119): 'A fat and ugly belted harlot, with Punch nose, brolly and tiny feet, who stands, arms akimbo, between two beautifully coiffed ladies with decorated breasts. On her right is a little Mephistophelean scowling person, gloved, capped and antenna'd, who defies description as he postures in G string on crutch-like stilts, his fat body tapering to tiny cloven feet, his catsuit slit to just above his navel, out of which a placental cord leads downwards, to become the tail of a deranged clown, whose torso, in turn, is that of a deformed sausage dog, crawling towards us and whose hat culminates in the torso of an amorphous embryo.'
12. Cartwright had been doing this for the past three months but was now given increased responsibilities and remuneration to try to ensure that the pace and standing of the Studio work did not slacken in his absence.
13. Letter, 28 December 1925, Clarke MSS. There is much use of thick, textured slab glass, especially blue and deep greens, indigos, greys and olives offset with gold and rubies.
14. Letter, 8 January 1926, Clarke MSS. On 8 March after a series of disputes over cost, style, iconography and delays caused by Harry's illness, he reluctantly felt obliged to point out: 'I don't think that I could completely efface myself nor would I like to do a window in which my style and general ideas of treatment are completely absent.' This was particularly disappointing for Harry as the commission had come through Gerald Heard, author of *Narcissus — an Anatomy of Clothes* (London and New York 1924), subsequently (in 1929) literary editor of *The Realist* and Somerset Maugham's secretary.
15. Bernard Rackham's request was for a series of three articles, 'Glass Painting as an Art for Today', for *Artwork*. Part I, 'Antecedents', had appeared in vol. II, no. 5 (October/December 1925) in an issue which also featured a woodcut by E.M. O'Rorke Dickey, entitled 'Lamplight Flirtation', and a lengthy piece, 'Symbology in Aesthetics in Relation to the Art of Austin O. Spare'. Part II, 'The Modern Revival', appeared in the January/March 1926 issue (vol. II, no. 6) and featured Christopher Whall's and J. Thorn Prikker's work. The final part appeared in the Summer 1926 issue (vol. II, no. 7) and on p. 184 reproduced the bottom R.H. section of *The Eve of St Agnes*, which Walter sent him as the best photograph they had in the Studios. This had already been featured in *The Studio* and the *Illustrated Country Review* — unfortunately, as surely Harry would have sent a new photograph if he had been compos mentis.
16. Letter, Seumas O'Sullivan MSS, TCD, MSS 4632-3/ no. 686.
17. Letter, 4 March 1926, MacGreevy MSS, TCD.
18. Warre B. Wells notes in his 'Notes from Ireland' in *The Athenaeum*, 18 June 1920, that Lennox Robinson had fled to Spain: 'Thither have betaken themselves, by the way, quite a number of our men of letters and painters. What the lure of Spain may be I do not know unless it be that there also in a semi-revolutionary country, they look to find something of the same intellectual environment as here, with the added attraction of being *au dessus de la mêlée*.'
19. Letter, 4 March 1926, MacGreevy MSS, TCD.
20. These included Helen Byrne Hackett at the Brick Row Bookshop on New York's East 47th Street

for whom he hoped he would have enough material to exhibit by 1927, and Oundle, who still had his *Moses* window proposal. He was pleased with the effect of the screen he had designed and Hicks had made for the *Queens* panels on exhibition at the Municipal Gallery, and delighted to be consulted about the Army's flag designs.

21. Lennox Robinson wrote in *Curtain Up*, *op. cit.*, p. 212: 'His first sketch for, let us say, an immense East window would be drawn to the scale of an inch to a foot. Enlarged, photographically, twelve times the cartoons would need little working over, every smallest line appeared accurate and perfect, and ornamentation almost too small to see in the original stood out firm and clear.' This practice was employed by Burne-Jones for cartoons to be used for both stained glass and tapestry.
22. Letter, 25 March 1926, Bodkin MSS, coll. Ann Bourke.
23. Letter, 27 March 1926, MacGreevy MSS, TCD.
24. *Curtain Up*, *op. cit.*, p. 212.
25. The coloured cartoon was reproduced in colour in the Studios' church directories advertising insets in 1928 and 1929.
26. In the manner of Odilon Redon, the French Symbolist painter, e.g. the charcoal drawings, *Profil de femme avec fleurs* (*c.* 1890-5) or *Songe* (*c.* 1895), or the earlier charcoal drawing, *Profil de lumière* (*c.* 1875).
27. Reminiscent of those painted by Burne-Jones for e.g. Perseus in *The Birth of Pegasus and Chrysaor* (*c.* 1877) or the fallen angelic army in *The Fall of Lucifer* (1894).
28. Pp. 522-4. Hunter, a graduate of the RCA and TCD as well as the Dublin Metropolitan School had worked with Harry at the same period (1916-18) before becoming a Government art inspector in N. Ireland in 1923. Unfortunately, after endless quibbling with the original client, Fr O'Connor's difficult successor, the borders to these windows were removed and replaced by clear glass, so that too much light now floods in around the principal figures in their decorative settings, lessening the effect of both the coloured glass and the lines and tones.
29. Letter, 18 July 1926, MacGreevy MSS, TCD.
30. Walter assured clients insisting on Harry's own work that he would only be away for 'a few days'.
31. The impecunious Odles came to London in the summer when rents at home in Cornwall were at their preclusive holiday-rate highest. There they would entertain Charlie Chaplin, Paul Robeson and Ford Maddox Ford among their wide circle of friends.
32. In an interview with the author shortly before his death, 4 February 1974.
33. *A Penny in the Clouds* (1960).
34. See Michael Laurence Clarke, 'The Geneva Window' (1988).
35. Letter, 15 December 1926, Clarke MSS.
36. Letter, 17 January 1927, Bodkin MSS, coll. Ann Bourke.
37. Harry exhibited the window at the Glass House on 12 and 13 January, where it was seen by about fifty visitors. See *Dowanhill Training College Magazine* (Glasgow 1927), pp. 3-4. I am indebted to Aileen Vaughan (a grand-daughter of Thomas Bodkin), to Sr Ellen Henry, SND and to Alfred Fisher, FMGP for their generous help and information re the Dowanhill windows. This window has recently been re-erected and artificially lit in a new position.
38. Letter, 28 February 1927, Clarke MSS.
39. Letter, 13 April 1927, Clarke MSS. As had become the norm by now, Harry took on this commission because of the lively interest and enthusiasm of the Rector, the enlightened Canon Harvey.
40. In his copy of the catalogue, now in the library of the National Gallery of Ireland, Orpen ringed her name and noted the date of her election. He had written in *Stories of Old Ireland and Myself* (1924), p. 80: 'Miss Crilly is married and has children — half a dozen or so . . . we are all spread about in a strange way.'
41. Dublin and Cork, 1927; Harry's *Mad Mulrannies* illustration to *The Playboy of the Western World* was reproduced on p. 84.
42. It is not certain that this latter window was eventually erected, although Sr M. Barbara OP, who is in charge of the convent's records, remembers there was an earlier figured stained glass window depicting a similar subject removed in favour of M. Gabriel Loire's fine semi-abstract windows, which were erected on 19 July 1962.
43. Letter, 8 August 1927, Bodkin MSS, coll. Ann Bourke.
44. Harry shared Studio D with his assistant Leonard Potter and Karl Parsons. His friendship with Parsons led to his introducing W.B. Yeats to the Parsons' precocious daughter Jacynth's drawings. Yeats later wrote a preface to her illustrations for Blake's *Songs of Innocence* (published in September 1927 by Medici) and both he and Clarke lent work to her exhibition in London and Birmingham. It was reviewed in the *Illustrated London News*, 12 November 1927. I am grateful to Jacynth's late sister, Margaret, for sending me this cutting and to John Gilmartin for photocopying the Birmingham exhibition list.

45. He was closely involved with the Abbey Theatre at this period: 'I never tire of the Abbey, we go week after week and their work seems always fresh and spontaneous' (letter, 12 December 1927, coll. Prof. Aloys Fleischmann). Dame Ninette de Valois, ballet mistress at the Abbey for a short time, remembers (letter to the author, 9 July 1974) what good company he was and how he gave her a signed copy of one of his books.
46. Despite this break, Bodkin did write Harry's *Times* obituary and referred, in *A Report on the Arts in Ireland* (1949), p. 25, to his being one of the 'outstanding talents of his time'.
47. Letter, 29 December 1927, coll. Ann Bourke.
48. A photograph taken by Harry of the original state of this drawing in which Hermaphroditus is endowed with an outsize phallus (subsequently inked out along with other outlandish details) is now in the collection of his grand-daughter.
49. Harry's original scheme was for all six windows to be treated similarly. His first coloured drawings were destroyed by fire in 1978. Two later pencil designs are now on display in the Cafe's Museum in Grafton Street.
50. Letter, 27 January 1928, Clarke MSS.
51. Charles Connick, one of the central figures in the American East Coast Arts and Crafts stained glass revival, writes (*Adventures in Light and Colour*, 1937, p. 334) that this commission and 'the one given to The Tower of Glass for the Chapel of the Sacred Heart School, Newton, Mass. were from the office of Maginnis and Walsh, Boston architects, to whom the Irish Craftsmen were recommended by an appreciative American glassman' (i.e. himself). Charles Maginnis wrote the foreword to Connick's book; a sketch by Connick of Leo Cartwright, by then working in Connick's well-known stained glass studio in Boston, appears in it on p. 226.
52. Letter, 14 May 1928, Clarke MSS.
53. Letter, 1 June 1929, Clarke MSS.
54. Letter, 7 June 1928, Clarke MSS.
55. *Curtain Up*, *op. cit.*, pp. 212f.
56. *Irish Times* 7 January 1931.
57. Reproduced *Harry Clarke: His Graphic Art*, *op. cit.*, plate XLIX.
58. That is, the price would suggest a window of some size. The late Lionel Perry, a frequent visitor to Bute House until it was destroyed in the Blitz, vaguely remembered a picturesque stained glass window on the landing (as well as the little head of *St Patrick* from Glasgow which Miss Cunningham had commissioned in 1923). There is now no trace of the house and the High Mistress of St Paul's Girls' School has been unable to find any record of the window; investigations in Donegal, where Miss Cunningham retired, have been equally unproductive.
59. Letter, 9 October 1928, Clarke MSS.
60. Letter, 29 May 1928, Clarke MSS.
61. Letter, 29 October 1928, Clarke MSS.
62. Letter, 1 November 1928, Clarke MSS. He had this plate specially bound into two copies of the book at p. 52, one for himself, the other for Lennox Robinson.
63. Letter, 13 November 1928, Clarke MSS.
64. 'I had written this Preface before I had seen Mr Clarke's illustrations. . . . It will be noticed that Mr Clarke presents an interpretation of Swinburne completely opposed to mine; with what I should conceive students of drawings would admit was distinguished ability, he develops in more than one picture that side of the poet which I have suggested was only boyish delight in something rich and strange.'

    Another critic (unspecified in press cuttings, coll. Ann Bourke) disagreed: Swinburne 'wrote with the strange ignorant gravity of a child of a Hermaphroditus — of Sappho, of all that glittered and darkened in the wildest legend of Greece and Rome. Those things . . . had, indeed, exactly that quality of meditative passion which Mr Clarke has so beautifully translated into form in his illustrations.'
65. Y.O., 'Harry Clarke's Drawings', *Irish Statesmen*, 21 December 1929, pp. 320-1.
66. It is interesting to note that Harry and Beardsley, in the last stages of consumption, should both have turned in their final years to 'a new phrase. [Beardsley] produced six illustrations to Gautier's *Mademoiselle de Maupin*, consisting of a frontispiece in watercolour, and five other drawings in indian ink and wash, including *The Lady at the Dressing Table* . . . and *The Lady with the Monkey*. These careful, polished designs in a full scale of tones were published in photogravure by Smithers after Beardsley's death in 1898' (Reade, *Aubrey Beardsley*, 1966, p. 10). 'The composition [in these drawings] . . . is something new in Beardsley's art. . . . Beardsley has returned to the use of greys as in the early *Studio* drawings, leaving clear black for the mirror and the chevelure. The lady herself shows a great change in [his] sense of feminine beauty. Instead of the impudent 'modern' faces, with their short lips and tip-tilted noses, he has depicted her as a type of classic sensuality' (Clark, *The Best of Beardsley* 1979, p. 162).

    The shimmering tones instead of forthright lines and the sensual nature of the last drawings of both illustrators surely stem from advancing tuberculosis and are all the more tragic for their evanescent skill.

67. Harry's preparatory pencil sketch for the imperious beauty 'Faustine' demonstrates how he worked up each illustration (always keeping three or four going at the same time): beside the deadly siren's body are noted the key words he wanted to evoke —
    From drained-out pores dripped thick red sweat . . .
    Small serpents with soft stretching throats . . .
    Splendid hair . . .
    Bright heavy brows . . .
    Carvéd lips . . .
    Man's laughter heard in hell
    Far down
    Hard bright chin . . . Shameful scornful lips . . .'.
68. The exhibition proceeded to Grace Horne's gallery outside Boston, where it opened on 1 May 1929.
69. 'If the [panels] are too sensual they must go straight to Geneva, otherwise the President and Co. will throw at least nine fits' (undated letter from Lennox Robinson to Harry Clarke, coll. Ann Bourke).

CHAPTER TEN

All the letters dating from this final period are now in the collection of Sara Bourke. They will only be annotated in this chapter if the date is given or they are from another collection.

1. *The Torque* (Davos), 30 April 1930, pp. 36-43 (published expressly for the Irish community).
2. Robinson doubted Bodkin would find time as he was too busy 'strutting around like a paycock' since being appointed the NGI's new director.
3. Letter, formerly coll. Miss Florence Clarke.
4. Coll. David Clarke.
5. Margaret Clarke had not been sure if Harry really wanted her to come out.
6. *Curtain Up*, *op. cit.*, p. 214.
7. *Ibid.*, pp. 213-14.
8. Letter, 1 November 1929 to his children from Davos.
9. *Lough Derg* (1944), pp. 156f and *The Fourteen Stations of the Cross in St Patrick's Basilica, Lough Derg* (Sligo n.d.).
10. See *The Spirit of St Vincent's*, Diamond Jubilee publication (Bayonne, NJ, 1969). The Clarke Studios continued to fill the windows with stained glass until well into the 1940s.
11. Letter, MacGreevy MSS, TCD.
12. Mark Bence-Jones, *Twilight of the Ascendancy* (London 1987), p. 249.
13. This drawing was one of the series of microscopically detailed pen and wash on vellum illustrations of 1925, exhibited in the St George's Gallery show (as *Lobster*) and subsequently in Dublin, which anticipate in their feverish intensity and ghostly half-tones the *Swinburne* series (see *Harry Clarke*, catalogue no. 118 and *Harry Clarke: His Graphic Art*, *op. cit.*, plate XLIII). It would appear to be derived from a much more explicit Japanese 'shunga', or erotic print, by Hokusai illustrating *The Amorous Octopus — A Female Fantasy.*
14. 21 December 1929, pp. 320f.
15. The Studios were supporting not only their employees and Harry's family, but also the two Clarke sisters and Walter, his wife and six children.
16. Letter, 23 February 1920, coll. Ann Bourke.
17. Letter, 17 February 1930, formerly coll. Miss Florence Clarke.
18. *Curtain Up*, *op. cit.*, p. 214.
19. *Davos Courier*, 16 January 1931.
20. Letter, 20 May 1930, Clarke MSS (Letterbook 6001). The letterbook references resume on Harry's return to Dublin.
21. Letter, 23 May 1930, Clarke MSS.
22. Letter, 6 June 1930, Clarke MSS.
23. Letter, 26 June 1930, Clarke MSS.
24. Letter, 25 July 1930, Clarke MSS.
25. Letter, coll. Ann Bourke.
26. Instead they published a limited edition in 1931, based on their illustrated edition of 1926. I am grateful to Martin Steenson for this information.
27. Quoted by Robert Baldick in his introduction to his translation of the book (London 1959), p. 13. In *Affirmations* (1898), a book Harry knew, Havelock Ellis (pp. 158-211) refers to the Symbolist writer's face 'with the sensitive, luminous eyes' like a resigned and benevolent Mephistopheles who has discovered the absurdity of the divine order but has no wish to make any improper use of his discovery. He quotes des Esseintes' heart-rending words at the realization of 'l'éternelle bêtise de l'humanité': 'Take pity, O Lord, on the Christian who doubts, on the sceptic who desires to believe, on the convict of life who embarks alone in the night beneath a sky no longer lit by the consoling beacons of ancient faith.' From all one hears from those who knew Harry well and from what one reads (e.g. in his private diaries), these words seem to eloquently express what Harry felt by the end

of his life, and make it doubly tragic that he never illustrated the vicissitudes of Huysmans' des Esseintes.

28. *Curtain Up*, *op. cit.*, p. 214.
29. *Ibid.*, pp. 214f.
30. *Ibid.*, p. 213.
31. A Mass was said for him on Friday 16 January in St Francis Xavier's Church in Dublin.
32. *Curtain Up*, *op. cit.*, pp. 215f.
33. The *Bulletin* was incensed that Walter Starkie and Thomas Bodkin, the only Catholic Fellows of Protestant Trinity College, should support the window, not to mention Æ, Lennox Robinson and W.B. Yeats, and that the *Sunday Times* of 11 January 1931 should be publicizing what they regarded as an obscenity: 'The Wonderful Window is to become the centre of worship in the Restored Shrine of the Russell Religion, which is to be set up on the Teapot Dome Site, Merrion Square. . . . The Plotter and Planner of the Genevan Window, that wonder of Gaeldom, will parade them in Plunkett House. To the soft strains of citherns and citoles, of sackbuts and shaums, the Shrine of the new Russell Religion on Merrion Square . . . will be inaugurated. The Mellifluous Mahatma will be enthroned amid the rosy radiance diffused from the Geneva Window' (*Catholic Bulletin*, March 1931, pp. 218-21); Æ's *Deirdre* is the target here.
34. Untitled cutting, coll. Ann Bourke.
35. Referred to by Alan Denson in his Bodkin *Bibliography*, *op. cit.*
36. Three of these have recently been rediscovered and were on show at the Fine Art Society in May 1988; *The Countess Cathleen* was exhibited in *The Last Romantics* exhibition in 1989 at the Barbican Art Gallery in London (no. 422).
37. This enchanted scene is a miniaturized version of the left-hand light of the Carrickmacross *St Ceara* window, although the profiled head of Brigid is reminiscent of that of the Honan Chapel *Gobnait*, an archetype favoured by Harry from 1915 onwards.
38. This figure is adapted from a photograph of a Russian Ballet dancer Harry had enlarged. The first attempts to fire her on gold-pink glass led to breakages before she was plated. She was therefore leaded up as an individual panel. She is now in a private collection, having been in the Clarke family's doctor's collection for many years.
39. The tiny figure tickling his ear recalls Beardsley's design for 'Bon Mots' for Dent in which tiny malevolent putti issue forth from an ear (*The Early Work of Aubrey Beardsley*, ed. H.C. Marillier, John Lane, The Bodley Head, 1920, plate 92). The tiny fairies emerging from wine glasses probably derive from an advertisement for 'Charlott Internationale Weinstuben' featured in *Jar-Ptitz* (1921), n.p.
40. 10 January 1931.
41. *Davos Courier*, 16 January 1931, coll. Ann Bourke
42. Letter to the author, 5 May 1974. Starkie was also a director of the Abbey Theatre, a frequent contributor to the *Irish Statesman*, as well as serving on countless academic, musical and literary boards in Dublin. During summer vacations he used to travel through Europe like a gypsy playing his fiddle (cf. his autobiography, *Scholars and Gypsies*, London 1963).
43. *Curtain Up*, *op. cit.*, p. 211.
44. January 1931, pp. 47-50.
45. 17 January 1931, p. 56.
46. I am grateful to Sean O'Criadain for showing me this Appendix to the RHA catalogue.
47. I am indebted to the late W.J. Dowling for his careful and helpful recollections of the exact periods during which the following were in the Studios; also to the late George Walsh and Jim McNamara for helpful interviews.
48. *The March of Life* (commissioned by the Irish Life Assurance Company), *Irish Press*, 20 October 1961
49. Letter to the author, 6 March 1974.

Bibliography

Detailed references to manuscript and periodical sources are given in the notes. Where a source contains a direct reference to Harry Clarke, the entry is followed by the symbol *.

*Adam Stephen, *Decorative Stained Glass* (London 1980).

Alexandre, Arsène, *The Decorative Art of Léon Bakst* (London 1913; reprinted Toronto and London 1972).

*___, *Exposition d'art irlandais*, catalogue of the Galleries Barbazanges exhibition, Paris 1922, introduction.

Amory, Mark, *A Biography of Lord Dunsany* (London 1972).

Andersen, Hans, *Stories from Hans Andersen*, illustrated by Edmund Dulac (London 1910).

*Aonach Tailteann, *Irish Art*, programmes etc. of the Dublin 1924 exhibition.

*___, catalogue of an exhibition of Irish Art at the Metropolitan School of Art, Dublin 1928.

*Armitage, E. Liddell, *Stained Glass — History, Technique and Practice* (London 1959)

Arnold Bruce, *Orpen, Mirror to an Age* (London 1981).

Arnold, Hugh, *Stained Glass of the Middle Ages in England and France* (London 1925).

Art et Décoration, monthly (Paris), occasional issues in the library of the National College of Art and Design, Dublin.

**Artist and the Child, The*, Exhibition of Children's Book and original illustrations from the John D. Merriam Collection, Boston Public Library (Boston 1980).

Arts and Crafts Society of Ireland, *First Journal* (Dublin 1896); *Second Journal* (Dublin 1898); *Third Journal* (Dublin 1901); *Fourth Journal* (Dublin 1906).

*___, catalogues of exhibitions (Dublin 1910, 1917, 1921, 1925).

**Arts Décoratifs de Grande Bretagne et d'Irlande, April-October 1914*, official report of the exhibition organised by the British Government in the Palais du Louvre (London and Paris 1914).

Arwas, Victor, *Alastair, Illustrator of Decadence* (London 1979).

Asbjörnsen, P.C. and J.I. Möe, *East of the Sun, West of the Moon*, illustrated by Kay Nielsen (London 1914).

Battersby, Martin, *The Decorative Twenties* (London 1969).

___, *Art Nouveau* (Feltham 1969).

___, *The Decorative Twenties* (London 1971).

Bax, Clifford, *Inland Far — A Book of Thoughts and Impressions* (London 1925).

*Beeh-Lustenberger, Suzanne (ed.), *Das Bild in Glas von der europaïschen Kabinettscheibe zum New Glass*, Hessisches Landesmuseum (Darmstadt 1979).

Bell, Quentin, *The Schools of Design* (London 1963).

Bénédite, Léonce, *Deux Idéalistes — G. Moreau et E. Burne-Jones* (Paris 1899).

*Bennett, Arnold, *The Journals of Arnold Bennett*, II: 1911-21 (London 1932).

Bland, David, *A History of Book Illustration* (London 1969).

Board of Education, *Annual Reports*, especially the 30th Report 1883, 'History of the Science and Art Department of the Committee of Council on Education since its creation' and 'The South Kensington Museum and Bethnal Green Branch Museum'.

*Board of Education (Department of Science and Art), Judges' Reports of the annual National Competition (London 1911-14).

*Bodkin, Thomas, 'The Art of Mr Harry Clarke', *The Studio*, vol. 79, no. 320 (November 1919).

*___, 'The Arts and Crafts Society of Ireland', *The Studio*, vol. 82, no. 345 (December 1921).

*___, 'Mr Harry Clarke's New Windows', *Irish Times*, 24 July 1923.

*___, Obituary, *The Times*, 10 January 1931.

*___, *The Importance of Art to Ireland*, text of a public lecture at Trinity College, Dublin (Dublin 1935).

*___, *A Report of the Arts in Ireland* (Dublin 1949).

*Bodkin Mss (uncatalogued when consulted), Trinity

College, Dublin, Manuscripts Library.

**Bodkin Irish Collection*, exhibition catalogue (Dublin 1962).

Bookplate, The (London), 8 vols (July 1919-September 1921).

Bouyer, R., 'L'estampe murale', *Art et Décoration*, II (Paris, 1898).

*Bowe, Nicola Gordon, 'A Masterpiece in Stained Glass', *Ireland of the Welcomes* (Dublin), vol. 26, no. 5 (September/October 1977).

*___, 'Harry Clarke, Ireland's Magical Stained Glass Artist', *Stained Glass* (Journal of the Stained Glass Association of America, St Louis, Missouri), vol. 73, no. 4 (Winter 1978/9).

*___, *Harry Clarke*, a monograph and catalogue published to coincide with the Douglas Hyde Gallery, Dublin, exhibition (Dublin 1979).

*___, *Harry Clarke: His Graphic Art* (Mountrath, Co. Laois, Ireland, and Los Angeles 1983).

*___, 'The Life and Work of Harry Clarke 1889-1931', unpublished PhD thesis, University of Dublin 1982.

*___, *Irish Stained Glass*, Recent Irish Art series, no. 3, The Arts Council in Ireland (Dublin 1983).

*___, 'Harry Clarke, Miniatur-Glasscheiben aus den Jahren 1917- 1927', *Weltkunst* (Munich), vol. 56, no. 2 (January 1986).

*___, 'The Arts and Crafts Society of Ireland (1894-1925) with particular reference to Harry Clarke', *Journal of the Decorative Arts Society 1850 — The Present*, 9 (Brighton 1985).

*___, 'The Miniature Stained Glass Panels of Harry Clarke', *Apollo* (London), vol. CXV, no. 240 (February 1982).

*___, *The Arts and Crafts Movement in Dublin 1885-1930*, catalogue of the Edinburgh 1985 exhibition.

*___, David Caron, Michael Wynne, *Gazetteer of Irish Stained Glass* (Dublin 1988), introductory essay and biography.

*___, 'Wilhelmina Geddes', *Irish Arts Review* (Belfast), vol. 4, no. 3 (Autumn 1987).

*___, 'Wilhelmina Geddes, Harry Clarke and their Part in the Arts and Crafts Movement in Ireland', *Journal of Decorative and Propaganda Arts* (Miami), 8 (Spring 1988).

*___, 'Wilhelmina Geddes 1887-1955: Her Life and Work — A Reappraisal', *The Journal of Stained Glass* (London), vol. XVIII, no. 3 (1988).

*___, 'Symbolism in Early Twentieth Century Irish Art', *GPA Irish Arts Review Yearbook* (Belfast 1989).

Breffny, Brian de, (ed.), *The Irish World* (London 1977)

___, and G. Mott, *The Churches and Abbeys of Ireland* (London 1978).

___, (ed.), *Ireland — A Cultural Encyclopaedia* (London 1983).

Burdett, Osbert, *The Beardsley Period — An Essay in Perspective* (London 1925).

*Cartwright, Leo, 'Harry Clarke: Artist and Craftsman', *Stained Glass* (Concord, N.H.). A quarterly devoted to the Craft of Painted and Stained Glas published by The Stained Glass Association of America, vol. 28, no. 1 (Spring 1933).

**Catholic Directory* (Dublin), advertising inserts of Joshua Clarke & Sons Ltd from 1914 to 1930.

Chadd, David and John Gage, *The Diaghilev Ballet in England* (Norwich 1979).

*Christian, John (ed.), *The Last Romantics — The Romantic Tradition in British Art*, published in association with the Barbican Art Gallery Exhibition (London 1989).

**Church of St Barrahane, The* (Castlehaven, Co. Cork 1970).

**Church of St Oswald and St Edmund, The* (Ashton-in-Makerfield n.d.).

*Clarke, Austin, *A Penny in the Clouds* (London 1960), ch. 24.

*Clarke, Harry, illustrator:

___, *Fairy Tales by Hans Christian Andersen* (London 1916).

___, *Tales of Mystery and Imagination by Edgar Allan Poe* (London 1919).

___, *The Year's at the Spring*, An Anthology of Recent Poetry selected by Lettice d'Oyly Walters (London 1920).

___, *The Fairy Tales of Perrault* with an introduction by Thomas Bodkin (London 1922).

___, *Ireland's War Memorial Records 1914-1918*, being the names of Irishmen who fell in the Great European War 1914-1918 (Dublin 1923).

___, *Tales of Mystery and Imagination by Edgar Allan Poe* (London 1923).

___, *The History of a Great House — Origin of John Jameson Whiskey* (Dublin 1924).

___, *Elixir of Life* (Uisge Beatha) — Being a slight Account of the Romantic Rise to Fame of a Great House, by Geoffrey Warren (Dublin 1925).

___, *Goethe's Faust*, translated by John Anster (London 1925).

___, *Selected Poems of Algernon Charles Swinburne* introduced by Humbert Wolfe (London and New York 1928).

___, 'Some Notes on Stained Glass', *Illustrated Country Review* (London), vol. V, no. 8 (November 1925) reproduced in this volume as Appendix 1.

Clark, Kenneth, *The Best of Aubrey Beardsley* (London 1979).

*Connick, Charles J., *Adventures in Light and Colour. An Introduction to the Stained Glass Craft* (London and New York 1937).

*Cormack, Peter, *Christopher Whall 1849-1924: Arts and Crafts Stained Glass Worker*, catalogue of the William Morris Gallery exhibition (London 1979).
*___, *Karl Parsons*, catalogue of the William Morris Gallery Exhibition (London 1988).
*Crookshank, Anne O. and the Knight of Glin, *The Painters of Ireland* (London 1978).
*___, *Irish Art from 1600 to the Present Day* (Dublin 1979).
*Curtayne, Alice, *The Fourteen Stations of the Cross in St Patrick's Basilica, Lough Derg* (Sligo n.d.).
*___, *Lough Derg* (London and Dublin 1944).
Day, Lewis F., *Stained Glass* (London 1897 and 1913).
Delevoy, Robert, *Symbolists and Symbolism* (London 1978).
*Denson, Alan, *A Bibliography of Thomas Bodkin*, (Kendal 1966).
Department of Agriculture and Technical Instruction for Ireland, *Ireland Industrial and Agricultural* (Dublin 1902).
Design — Modern Art Bibliographical Series (Oxford and Santa Barbara 1984).
Deutsche Kunst und Dekoration (Darmstadt), random issues in the library of the National College of Art and Design, Dublin.
Donnelly, Michael, *Glasgow Stained Glass*, A Preliminary Study (Glasgow 1981).
Dowanhill Training College Magazine (Glasgow), articles on 'The Memorial Window', in 1924 and 1927.
*Dowling, William J., 'Stained Glass', *Irish Art Handbook* (Dublin 1943).
*___, 'Harry Clarke, R.H.A., Dublin Stained Glass Artist', *Dublin Historical Record*, vol. 17, no. 2 (March 1962).
Drake, Maurice, *A History of English Glass Painting* (London 1912).
Dresser, Christopher, *Japan, its Architecture, Art and Art Manufacturers* (London 1882).
Dublin Civic Week, catalogue of an Exhibition of Ecclesiastical Art, Dublin, September 1929.
Dublin Magazine, ed. Seumas O'Sullivan, vols. I and II covering the period August 1923 - January 1925.
Dunsany, Lord, *The Chronicles of Don Rodriguez*, cover and frontispiece by Sidney Sime (London 1922).
Eliade, Mircea, *Myths, Dreams and Mysteries* (London 1960).
Elliott, Robert, *Art and Ireland*, with preface by Edward Martyn (Dublin [1906]; reprinted New York and London 1979).
Ellis, Havelock, *Affirmations* (London 1898).
Eve, a weekly magazine, vol. I, nos. 1-3, 5, 9 (London 1919-20).
Exhibition of Book Illustrations and Drawings by John Austen, Allan Odle, Harry Clarke and Austin Spare, catalogue of the St George's Gallery, London exhibition, 21 May - 10 June 1925.
Exhibition of Contemporary Irish Art, list of exhibitors at the exhibition held at the Helen Byrne Hachett Gallery, New York and Grace Horne's Galleries, Boston, Spring 1929.
Exposition des Arts Décoratifs et Industriels Modernes, 28 April - 26 October 1925 (Paris 1925), official catalogue and reports, 'Stained Glass', p. 145ff., 'Book Illustrations', p. 157ff.
Fairford Church (St Mary the Virgin) and its stained glass windows (Bath 1956).
Farmar, Tony, *The Legendary Lofty, Clattery Cafe. Bewley's of Ireland* (Dublin, 1988).
Fine Art Society, The (London):
___, *Eve pictures by A.H. Fish*, exhibition catalogue no. 520, July 1916.
___, *An Exhibition of Irish Artists*, catalogue no. 724, 1927.
*___, *The Stained Glass of Harry Clarke 1889-1931* (London 1988), incl. contributions by James White, Michael Laurence Clarke and Nicola Gordon Bowe.
Flaubert, Gustave, 'La Légende de S. Julien', *Les Trois Contes* (Paris 1877; bilingual edition, London 1946).
Form, a quarterly journal edited by A.O. Spare and F. Marsden (London), vols. I and II (1916-17); new series edited by A.O. Spare and W.H. Davies, vol. I, nos. 1-3 (1921).
Fortuny nella Belle Epoque, exhibition catalogue, Palazzo Strozzi (Florence 1984).
Fowl, *The Third Eve Book*, illustrated by Fish (London 1919).
Frazer, J.G., *The Golden Bough: A Study in Magic and Religion* (London 1922; new ed., London and Basingstoke 1957).
Gallatin, A.E., *Aubrey Beardsley's Drawings* (London 1983).
Gellér, Katalin, 'Hungarian Stained Glass of the Early 20th century', *Journal of Stained Glass* (London), vol. XVIII, no. 2, 1986-7.
*Gibbon, Monk (ed.), *The Living Torch* (London 1937).
*Gluck, Felix (ed.), *World Graphic Design — 50 Years of Advertising Art* (London 1968), section on direct mail brochures 1918-30.
*Gogarty, Oliver St. John, *As I was Going down Sackville Street: A Phantasy in Fact* (London 1937).
Golden Hind, The, A.O. Spare and C. Bax, eds. (London 1922-4). Clarke's work is featured only in the final issue.
Goldwater, Robert, *Symbolism* (London 1979).
Gosse, Philip Henry, *The British Sea Anemones and Corals: Actinologia Britannica* (London 1860).
Grant, Kenneth, *Images and Oracles of Austin Osman*

Spare (London and New York 1975).
*Gray, Tony, *Starting from Tomorrow* (London 1965).
Gray, Camilla, *The Russian Experiment in Art 1863-1922* (London 1970).
*Guptill, L., *Drawing with Pen and Ink and a Word concerning the Brush and Ink* (New York 1928).
Gwynn, Denis, *Edward Martyn and the Irish Revival* (London 1930).
*Halton, Ernest J., *Modern Book Illustrators and their Work*, Special Number of *The Studio* (London 1914).
*Harrap, George G., *Some Memories 1901-1935* (London 1935)
Harris, Frank, *Contemporary Portraits* (London 1924).
Harrison, Martin, 'Victorian Stained Glass', *Apollo* (London), April 1973.
*Harrison, Martin (compiler), *Glass/Light*, catalogue of an International Exhibition of Stained Glass at the Royal Exchange (London 1978).
*___, *Victorian Stained Glass* (London 1980).
**Harry Clarke Centennial 1889-1989*, Ballinrobe, 17 March 1989.
*Healy, Revd John (ed.), *Stained Glass Memorial Window, St Joseph's Terenure*, souvenir of dedication (Dublin 1920).
Henderson, Philip, *William Morris, his Life, Work and Friends* (London 1967).
Heneage, Simon and Henry Ford, *Sidney Sime, Master of the Mysterious* (London 1980).
*Hillier, Bevis, *Art Deco of the 20s and 30s* (London 1968).
Hoffmann, Werner, *Gustav Klimt* (London 1972).
___, *Gustav Klimt* (Salzburg and Greenwich, Conn. 1979).
Holliday, Henry, *Stained Glass as an Art* (London 1896).
Horton, W.T., *A Book of Images*, introduction by W.B. Yeats (London 1898).
*Houfe, Simon, *The Dictionary of British Book Illustrators and Caricaturists 1800-1914* (Woodbridge 1978).
Housman, Laurence (retold by), *Stories from the Arabian Nights*, illustrated by Edmund Dulac (London 1907).
Houvet, E. and l'Abbé Delaporte, *Les Vitraux de la Cathédrale de Chartres*, 4 vols (Chartres 1926).
Howarth, Thomas, *Charles Rennie Mackintosh and The Modern Movement* (London, Boston and Henley, 1952; 2nd ed. 1977).
Hunneker, James, *Overtones — A Book of Temperaments* (London 1904).
Hussey, Christopher, *The Lutyens Memorial*, 4 vols incorporating 'The Life of Sir Edwin Lutyens (London 1950).
Huysmans, J-K., *Against Nature* [*A Rebours*], translated by R. Baldrick (Harmondsworth 1959).
Imprint, The London, vol. I, January-June, 1913.
Irish Industries Pageant, illustrated souvenir, Dublin 1909.
Irish International Exhibition souvenir programme, Dublin 1907. Catalogue of The Palace of Fine Arts (British and Foreign Artists).
Irish Race Congress, *Proceedings*, Dublin, January 1922.
Irish Soldier, The, Dublin, vol. I, no. 1 (1 September 1918).
Jameson, Anna Brownell, *Legends of the Madonna as represented in the Fine Arts* (London n.d.; 2nd ed., 1874).
Jar-Ptitza [Fire-bird], *Revue Russe d'art et de littérature* (Berlin), fourteen parts in thirteen issues, 1921-25.
*Johnson, Diana L., *Fantastic Illustration and Design in Britain 1850-1930*, Museum of Art (Providence, Rhode Island 1979).
Joyce, James, *The Fairford Windows* (London 1872).
Jullian, Philippe, *Dreamers of Decadence* (London 1971).
___, *French Symbolist Painters* (London 1972).
___, *The Symbolists* (2nd ed., London 1977).
Kallir, Jane, *Viennese Design and the Wiener Werkstatte* (London 1986).
Kandinsky, Wassily, *The Art of Spiritual Harmony* (London 1914).
Kaplanova, S., *Vrubel* (Leningrad 1975).
Langlois, Eustache-Hyacinthe, *Mémoire sur la peinture sur verre et sur quelques vitraux remarquables des églises de Rouen* (Rouen 1823).
Larner, Gerald and Celia, *The Glasgow Style* (Edinburgh 1979).
Lassaigne, Jacques, *Kandinsky* (Geneva 1964).
Leacock, Stephen, *The Marionettes Calendar*, illustrated by A.H. Fish (London 1916).
Lewis, John, *The Twentieth Century Book* (London 1967).
___, 'The Fantasy World of Sidney Sime', *The Saturday Book*, no. 34 (London 1975).
Little, George A., *The Oratory of the Sacred Heart, St Mary's Dominican Convent* (Dun Laoghaire, n.d.).
Lucie-Smith, Edward, *Symbolist Art* (London 1972).
*Lupano, Natal Luigi, 'Un artista irlandese dell'arte vetraria sacra', *L'Osservatore romano*, 10 April 1969.
___, 'Harry Clarke, Profeta delle immagini', *Il Narciso* (Turin), vol. 2, no. 5 (May 1969).
MacFall, Haldane, 'The Genius of Sidney H. Sime', *Illustrated London News*, November 1922.
___, *Aubrey Beardsley — The Man and His Work* (London 1928).
McGrath, Raymond and A.C. Frost, *Glass in Architecture and Decoration* (London 1937).
*MacGreevy, Thomas, 'Picasso, Mainie Jellet and Dublin Criticism', *The Klaxon* (Dublin), vol. I, no. 1 (Winter 1923/4).
*___, 'Fifty Years of Irish Painting', *Capuchin Annual* (Dublin 1949).

*MacGreevy MSS (uncatalogued when consulted), Trinity College, Dublin, Manuscripts Library.
Madsden, Tschudi, *Sources of Art Nouveau*, Oslo 1956.
Mâle, Emil, *Religious Art in France in the 13th Century — A Study in Medieval Iconography and its Sources of Inspiration*, translated by Dora Nussey from the 3rd ed. (London and New York, 1913).
*Mankowitz, Wolf, *The Extraordinary Mr Poe: A Biography of Edgar Allan Poe* (London 1978).
Marillier, H.C., *The Early Work of Aubrey Beardsley* (London 1899, revised 1920).
Mathieu, Pierre-Louis, *Gustave Moreau* (London 1977).
May, Phil, *Gutter-Snipes, Fifty Original Sketches in Pen and Ink of Gutter children at their Games* (London 1896).
___, *Phil May's ABC, 52 Original Designs forming two humorous alphabets from A-Z* (London 1897).
*Metropolitan School of Art, Dublin, *Report of the Annual Distribution of Prizes, 1884-1915*, issued by the Department of Agriculture and Technical Instruction for Ireland, Dublin 1916.
Miller, Liam, *The Dun Emer Press, later the Cuala Press* (Dublin 1973).
*Mills Hall, Dublin, *Exhibition of Drawings by Harry Clarke*, 12-19 December 1929, list of exhibits.
*Morshead, Sir Owen, *The Story of the Parish Church of St Mary, Sturminster Newton* (Gloucester 1971).
*Nahum, Peter (ed.), *Jessie M. King and E.A. Taylor, Illustrator and Designer* (Glasgow and London 1977).
Nally, T.H., *Aonac Tailteann, origin, history and ancient associations* (Dublin 1922).
Naylor, Gillian, *The Arts and Crafts Movement, a study of its sources, ideals and influences on design theory* (London 1971).
Nelson, Philip, *Ancient Painted Glass in England* (London 1913).
Nicholson, Keith (introduction), *Kay Nielsen*, London 1975.
*O'Connell, Sir John Robert, *The Collegiate Chapel, Cork: Some Notes on its Building and the Ideals which inspired it* (Cork 1916).
O'Connor, Ulick, *The Times I've Seen: O. St. John Gogarty* (New York 1963).
Oliver, Cordelia, *Jessie M. King 1875-1949* (Edinburgh 1971).
Orpen, Sir William, *Stories of Old Ireland and Myself* (London 1924).
*O'Sullivan, Seumas, O'Sullivan MSS, Trinity College, Dublin, Manuscripts Library, Correspondence, specific letters from MSS 4632-3, nos. 499; 542-4; 552; 561; 567; 686; 826. See also under *Dublin Magazine*.
Paladilhe, Jean, *Gustave Moreau* (Paris 1971).
Pearce Donald R. (ed.), *The Senate Speeches of W.B. Yeats* (London 1960).
Pepper, Terence, *Camara Portraits by E.O. Hoppé 1878-1972* (London 1978).
*Peppin, Brigid, *Fantasy — Book Illustration 1860-1920* (London 1975).
*___, with Lucy Micklethwait, *Dictionary of British Book Illustrators — The Twentieth Century* (London 1983).
Pevsner, Nikolaus, *The Sources of Modern Architecture and Design* (London 1968).
Pilgrim's Guide to the Parish Church, Nantwich, Cheshire (Warrington, n.d., *c.* 1955)
Pinkham, Roger, *Limoges Painted Enamels*, Victoria and Albert Museum booklet (London 1974).
*Piper, John, *Stained Glass — Art or Anti-Art?* (London 1968)
Pope, Alexander, *The Rape of the Lock, An Heroi-Comical Poem in Five Cantos*, embroidered with nine drawings by Aubrey Beardsley (London 1896).
Powell, H.J., *Glass Making in England* (Cambridge 1923).
*Power, Revd Professor, *The Chapel of St Finnbarr, University College, Cork. Its History, Architecture, and Symbolism* (Cork n.d.).
Praz, Mario, *The Romantic Agony* (Oxford 1933; 2nd ed., London 1951).
Priestley, J.B. *The Edwardians* (London 1972).
Propert, W.A., *The Russian Ballet in Western Europe 1909- 1920*, 2 vols (London 1921).
Purser, Olive, *Women in Dublin University 1904-1954* (Dublin 1954).
Purser, Sarah, 'Introduction', *An Túr Gloine on its 25th Anniversary* (Dublin 1928).
*Pyle, Hilary, *Irish Art 1900-1950*, catalogue of ROSC exhibition (Cork 1975).
Quiller-Couch, Sir Arthur, *The Sleeping Beauty and Other Fairy Tales*, illustrated by Edmund Dulac (London 1910).
___, *In Powder and Crinoline, Old Fairy Tales*, illustrated by Kay Nielsen (London 1912).
*Rackham, Bernard, 'Glass Painting as an Art for Today', *Artwork*, (London), vol. 2, nos. 5-7 (1926).
___, *A Guide to the Collections of Stained Glass in the Victoria and Albert Museum* (London 1936).
Read, Herbert, *English Stained Glass* (London 1926).
Reade, Brian, *Aubrey Beardsley* (London 1966).
Reade, Brian and Frank Dickinson, catalogue of the Aubrey Beardsley Exhibition, Victoria and Albert Museum (London 1966).
*Reeves, P. Oswald, 'Irish Arts and Crafts', *The Studio*, vol. 72, no. 295 (October 1917).
Reyntiens, Patrick, *The Technique of Stained Glass* (London 1967).
Rheims, Maurice, *The Age of Art Nouveau* (London 1966); also published as *L'Art 1900* (Paris 1965).

*Richardson, Dorothy M., 'Mr Harry Clarke's Pictures for Faust', *The Studio*, vol. 90, no. 391 (Autumn 1925).
___, *John Austen and the Inseparables* (London 1930).
Ritter, Georges, *Les Vitraux de la Cathédrale de Rouen* (Paris 1926).
*Robinson, Lennox, 'An Appreciation', *Irish Times*, 7 January 1931.
___, *Curtain Up* (London 1942), 'Third Act'.
___, *Palette and Plough* (London 1948), ch. III.
Ross, Robert, *Aubrey Beardsley* (London 1909)
___, *Forty Three Drawings by Alastair with a note of Exclamation* (London 1914)
*Roulin, Dom Eugène A., *Nos Églises* (Paris 1938), chs. III and V.
*Rowan, Alistair, 'Harry Clarke at the Douglas Hyde Gallery, Trinity College, Dublin', *The Burlington Magazine*, vol. CXXII, no. 923, February 1980.
*Ruskin, John, *The Stones of Venice*, 3 vols. especially vol. II, Appendix 12, 'Modern Painting on Glass' (3rd ed., London 1898).
*Russell, George (Æ), pseudonym 'YO', *Irish Statesman*, issues of 8 August and 14 November 1925, and 21 December 1929.
*___, 'Light in Dark Places', *The Living Torch*, ed. Monk Gibbon (New York 1937).
*Ryan, Thomas J., obituary, *The Belvederian* (Dublin) 1931.
Saint, Laurence, *Stained Glass in the Middle Ages in England and France* (London 1913).
St Michael and All Angels, Waterford, church guide (n.d.).
*Salaman, M.C., *British Book Illustration, Yesterday and Today*, Special Number of *The Studio* (London 1923).
Sewter, A. Charles, *The Stained Glass of William Morris and his Circle*, 2 vols (New Haven, Conn. 1974-5).
*Sheehy, Jeanne and George Mott, *The Rediscovery of Ireland's Past: the Celtic Revival 1830-1930* (London 1980).
*Sheringham, George, *Drawings in Pen and Pencil from Dürer's Day to Ours*, Special Number of *The Studio* (London 1922).
Simms, George, 'Illuminated Manuscripts', *The Encyclopedia of Ireland* (Dublin 1968).
Smithers, Leonard, *A Book of Fifty Drawings* by Aubrey Beardsley (London 1897).
___, *A Second Book of Fifty Drawings* (London 1899).
*Society of Graphic Art (London), catalogues of exhibitions, January 1921 (first exhibition) to June 1925 (fifth exhibition) inclusive.
Spare, Austin Osman, *The Focus of Life, the Mutterings of Aaos*, introduction by Francis Marsen (London 1921).
Spencer, Charles, *Erté*, London 1970.
___, *Leon Bakst* (London 1973).
**Spirit of St Vincent's, The* (Bayonne, New Jersey 1969).
Starkie, Enid, *A Lady's Child* (London 1941).
*Steenson, Martin, 'The Book Illustrations of Harry Clarke', *Antiquarian Book Monthly Review*, vol. II, no. 6 (June 1975).
___, 'Allan Odle', *Antiquarian Book Monthly Review*, vol. VI, no. 10 (October 1979).
Strong, Roy, *The Elizabethan Image, Painting in England 1540-1620* (London 1969).
Studio, The (London), *Year Book of Decorative Art* from 1906 to 1932 inclusive; for *Clarke, see the 1920 Year Book, section on decorative and applied art.
Studio, The, Special Number, *Arts and Crafts — A Review of the Work executed by Students in the leading Art Schools of Great Britain and Ireland* (London 1916). For other Special Numbers, see under Halton; Salaman; Sheringham.
Sullivan, Louis, 'Jugendstil', *Kindergarten Notes* (New York 1901).
Summerfield, Henry, *That Myriad-Minded Man: A biography of George William Russell, Æ, 1867-1935* (Gerrards Cross 1975).
Symonds, John Addington, *In the Key of Blue and other prose essays* (London 1918).
*Synge, John Millington, *Queens*, with nine full-colour reproductions of stained glass by Harry Clarke and notes by Nicola Gordon Bowe (Mountrath, Co. Laois 1986).
*Taylor, John Russell, *The Art Nouveau Book in Britain* (London 1966).
___, 'Clarke's Subtle Taste for the Perfumed Sinner', *The Times*, 15 January 1980.
___, 'Magic Casements — A Report on the Harry Clarke Exhibition', *Art and Antiques Weekly*, vol. 39, no. 10 (9 February 1980).
*Taylor, Monica, SND, *Sir Bertram Windle, a Memoir* (London 1932).
Thirties, British Art and Design before the War, Hayward Gallery Exhibition catalogue (London 1979).
Titania's Palace, Christie's illustrated catalogue for the sale on 10 January 1978 (London 1978).
Turpin, John, The Metropolitan School of Art, 1900-1923' in two parts, *Dublin Historical Record*, vol. XXXVII, no. 2 (March 1984) and vol. XXXVIII, no. 2 (March 1985).
Twining, E.W., *The Art and Craft of Stained Glass* (London 1928).
*Walker, Crampton J., *Irish Life and Landscape* (Dublin and Cork 1926).
Ware, Mary Lee, A Letter to Professor Ames on 'How were the Blaschka Glass Flowers made?', Dresden, October 3rd 1928, *Botanical Museum leaflets*, Harvard University, Cambridge, Mass., vol. 19, no

6 (9 January 1961).
Warrington W., *The History of Stained Glass from the Earliest Period of the Art to the Present Time* (London 1848).
Waters, Bill and Martin Harrison, *Burne-Jones* (London 1973).
Weiss, Peg, *Kandinsky in Munich: the Formative Jugendstil Years* (Princeton 1979).
Westlake, N.H.J., *History of Design in Painted Glass*, 14 vols (London 1879-1894).
Whall, Christopher W., *Stained Glass Work: A Text Book for Students and Workers in Glass* with diagrams by two of his apprentices (London 1905).
White, Colin, *Edmund Dulac* (London 1976).
*White, James and Wynne, Michael, *Irish Stained Glass* (Dublin 1963).
Wilde, Oscar, 'De Profundis', *Complete Works of Oscar Wilde* (London and Glasgow 1966).
___, *Salome — A Tragedy in one act*, Pictures by A. Beardsley (London 1894).
Wilson, Edmund, *Axel's Castle — A Study in the Imaginative literature of 1870-1930* (Glasgow 1961).
Winston, Charles, *An Inquiry into the Differences of Style observable in Ancient Glass Paintings, especially in England, with Hints on Glass Painting*, 2 vols (Oxford 1847).
___, *Memoirs illustrative of the Art of Glass Painting* (London 1865).
Wissmann, Jurgen, *Melchior Lechter* (Recklinghausen 1966).
*Wynne, Michael, 'Stained Glass in Ireland: principally Irish Stained Glass 1760-1963', unpublished PhD series, University of Dublin 1975.
___, *Irish Stained Glass* (Dublin 1977).
Yeats, W.B., foreword to W. Blake's *Songs of Innocence*, illustrated by Jacynth Parsons (London 1927).

Photographic Credits

I am most grateful to all owners who have made their work by Harry Clarke available for photography.

A number of the illustrations have been photographed from primary material in the collection of the late Ann Bourke, and now her daughter Sara; others were recorded when in the collection of David Clarke during the selection and cataloguing for the 1979 Harry Clarke exhibition. I am particularly indebted to David Davison of Pieterse Davison International (PDI) and to Anthony Hobbs, Head of Photography, National College of Art and Design, for their generous co-operation in photographing primary, secondary and reference material. All copy work not specifically acknowledged is by Anthony Hobbs; other original photography is by the author.

Robert Allen fig. 175
Allied Irish Banks plc fig. 64
The Arts Council (Ireland) pl. 41
Bewley's Oriental Cafes fig. 181
The British Library fig. 152
David Caron pl. 42; figs. 132, 138
Peter Cormack *frontispiece*, fig. 176
The Crawford Municipal Art Gallery, Cork figs. 29, 146, 147, 148, 149, 186
David Davison (PDI) pls. 9 (courtesy of Julian Hartnoll), 19, 25, 26, 31, 30, 37, 38, 40; figs. 37, 40, 41, 61, 90, 95, 110, 113, 122, 137, 160, 170, 174, 179, 184
Donald Dean pl. 33
The Douglas Hyde Gallery pls. 29, 44
Mark Fiennes pls. 12 to 18; figs. 80, 81, 161
The Fine Art Society, London pls. 45, 46, 47; figs. 57, 154, 155, 156, 159, 182
Richard Haughton pls. 1, 4, 5, 6, 7, 8, 34; figs. 62, 63 65, 66, 67, 72, 73, 76, 78, 91, 92, 93, 94, 114, 116, 150, 173
Hessisches Landes-museum, Darmstadt pl. 20
The Hugh Lane Municipal Gallery, Dublin pl. 36; figs. 21, 35, 98, 135
The Isabella Stewart Gardner Museum, Boston fig. 65
Ciáran MacGonigal fig. 19
George Mott (courtesy of the *GPA Irish Arts Review*) pl. 24
The National Gallery of Art, Washington, DC fig. 82
The National Gallery of Ireland figs. 33, 38, 58, 87, 89, 151, 188
The National Gallery, London figs. 67, 83
The National Library of Ireland fig. 69
The National Portrait Gallery, London figs. 88, 102
Veronica Nicholson (PDI) figs. 60, 99, 100, 103, 117, 118, 124, 139, 140
The Cynthia O'Connor Gallery, Dublin fig. 24
John Piper pls. 27, 28
Susannah Pym fig. 18
Pym's Gallery, London fig. 34
Sotheby's (London) pls. 11; figs. 48, 55
Martin Steenson figs. 153, 177
The Victoria and Albert Museum, London fig. 68

Index

Works of art are by Harry Clarke (HC) unless otherwise stated; see entry *Clarke, Harry, work by.*